Family Maps
of
Vilas County, Wisconsin
Deluxe Edition

With Homesteads, Roads, Waterways, Towns, Cemeteries, Railroads, and More

by Gregory A. Boyd, J.D.

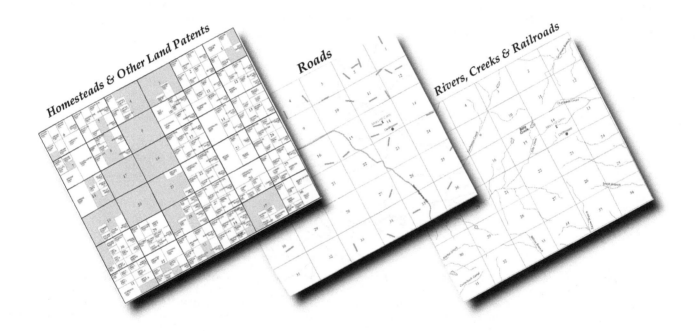

Featuring 3 *Maps Per Township…*

Arphax Publishing Co.
www.arphax.com

Family Maps of Vilas County, Wisconsin, Deluxe Edition: With Homesteads, Roads, Waterways, Towns, Cemeteries, Railroads, and More.
by Gregory A. Boyd, J.D.

ISBN 1-4203-1287-1

Printed in the United States of America

Published by Arphax Publishing Co., 2210 Research Park Blvd., Norman, Oklahoma, USA 73069
www.arphax.com

First Edition

ATTENTION HISTORICAL & GENEALOGICAL SOCIETIES, UNIVERSITIES, COLLEGES, CORPORATIONS, FAMILY REUNION COORDINATORS, AND PROFESSIONAL ORGANIZATIONS: Quantity discounts are available on bulk purchases of this book. For information, please contact Arphax Publishing Co., at the address listed above, or at (405) 366-6181, or visit our web-site at www.arphax.com and contact us through the "Bulk Sales" link.

—LEGAL—

The contents of this book rely on data published by the United States Government and its various agencies and departments, including but not limited to the General Land Office–Bureau of Land Management, the Department of the Interior, and the U.S. Census Bureau. The author has relied on said government agencies or re-sellers of its data, but makes no guarantee of the data's accuracy or of its representation herein, neither in its text nor maps. Said maps have been proportioned and scaled in a manner reflecting the author's primary goal—to make patentee names readable. This book will assist in the discovery of possible relationships between people, places, locales, rivers, streams, cemeteries, etc., but "proving" those relationships or exact geographic locations of any of the elements contained in the maps will require the use of other source material, which could include, but not be limited to: land patents, surveys, the patentees' applications, professionally drawn road-maps, etc.

Neither the author nor publisher makes any claim that the contents herein represent a complete or accurate record of the data it presents and disclaims any liability for reader's use of the book's contents. Many circumstances exist where human, computer, or data delivery errors could cause records to have been missed or to be inaccurately represented herein. Neither the author nor publisher shall assume any liability whatsoever for errors, inaccuracies, omissions or other inconsistencies herein.

This book is dedicated to my wonderful family:

Vicki, Jordan, & Amy Boyd

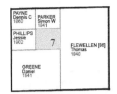

Contents

- Part I -

The Big Picture

- Part II -

Township Map Groups

(each Map Group contains a Patent Index, Patent Map, Road Map, & Historical Map)

Appendices

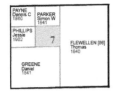

Preface

The quest for the discovery of my ancestors' origins, migrations, beliefs, and life-ways has brought me rewards that I could never have imagined. The *Family Maps* series of books is my first effort to share with historical and genealogical researchers, some of the tools that I have developed to achieve my research goals. I firmly believe that this effort will allow many people to reap the same sorts of treasures that I have.

Our Federal government's General Land Office of the Bureau of Land Management (the "GLO") has given genealogists and historians an incredible gift by virtue of its enormous database housed on its web-site at glorecords.blm.gov. Here, you can search for and find millions of parcels of land purchased by our ancestors in about thirty states.

This GLO web-site is one of the best FREE on-line tools available to family researchers. But, it is not for the faint of heart, nor is it for those unwilling or unable to to sift through and analyze the thousands of records that exist for most counties.

My immediate goal with this series is to spare you the hundreds of hours of work that it would take you to map the Land Patents for this county. Every Vilas County homestead or land patent that I have gleaned from public GLO databases is mapped here. Consequently, I can usually show you in an instant, where your ancestor's land is located, as well as the names of nearby land-owners.

Originally, that was my primary goal. But after speaking to other genealogists, it became clear that there was much more that they wanted. Taking their advice set me back almost a full year, but I think you will agree it was worth the wait. Because now, you can learn so much more.

Now, this book answers these sorts of questions:

- Are there any variant spellings for surnames that I have missed in searching GLO records?
- Where is my family's traditional home-place?
- What cemeteries are near Grandma's house?
- My Granddad used to swim in such-and-such-Creek—where is that?
- How close is this little community to that one?
- Are there any other people with the same surname who bought land in the county?
- How about cousins and in-laws—did they buy land in the area?

And these are just for starters!

The rules for using the *Family Maps* books are simple, but the strategies for success are many. Some techniques are apparent on first use, but many are gained with time and experience. Please take the time to notice the roads, cemeteries, creek-names, family names, and unique first-names throughout the whole county. You cannot imagine what YOU might be the first to discover.

I hope to learn that many of you have answered age-old research questions within these pages or that you have discovered relationships previously not even considered. When these sorts of things happen to you, will you please let me hear about it? I would like nothing better. My contact information can always be found at www.arphax.com.

One more thing: please read the "How To Use This Book" chapter; it starts on the next page. This will give you the very best chance to find the treasures that lie within these pages.

My family and I wish you the very best of luck, both in life, and in your research.   Greg Boyd

How to Use This Book - A Graphical Summary

Part I
"The Big Picture"

Map A ▸ *Counties in the State*
Map B ▸ *Surrounding Counties*
Map C ▸ *Congressional Townships (Map Groups) in the County*
Map D ▸ *Cities & Towns in the County*
Map E ▸ *Cemeteries in the County*
Surnames in the County ▸ *Number of Land-Parcels for Each Surname*
Surname/Township Index ▸ *Directs you to Township Map Groups in Part II*

The <u>*Surname/Township Index*</u> *can direct you to any number of* **Township Map Groups**

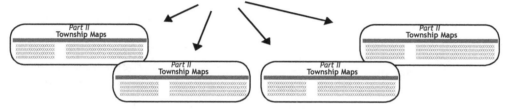

Part II
Township Map Groups
(1 for each Township in the County)

Each Township Map Group contains all four of of the following tools . . .

Land Patent Index ▸ *Every-name Index of Patents Mapped in this Township*
Land Patent Map ▸ *Map of Patents as listed in above Index*
Road Map ▸ *Map of Roads, City-centers, and Cemeteries in the Township*
Historical Map ▸ *Map of Railroads, Lakes, Rivers, Creeks, City-Centers, and Cemeteries*

Appendices

Appendix A ▸ *Congressional Authority enabling Patents within our Maps*
Appendix B ▸ *Section-Parts / Aliquot Parts (a comprehensive list)*
Appendix C ▸ *Multi-patentee Groups (Individuals within Buying Groups)*

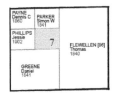

How to Use This Book

The two "Parts" of this *Family Maps* volume seek to answer two different types of questions. Part I deals with broad questions like: what counties surround Vilas County, are there any ASHCRAFTs in Vilas County, and if so, in which Townships or Maps can I find them? Ultimately, though, Part I should point you to a particular Township Map Group in Part II.

Part II concerns itself with details like: where exactly is this family's land, who else bought land in the area, and what roads and streams run through the land, or are located nearby. The Chart on the opposite page, and the remainder of this chapter attempt to convey to you the particulars of these two "parts", as well as how best to use them to achieve your research goals.

Part I
"The Big Picture"

Within Part I, you will find five "Big Picture" maps and two county-wide surname tools.

These include:

- Map A - Where Vilas County lies within the state
- Map B - Counties that surround Vilas County
- Map C - Congressional Townships of Vilas County (+ Map Group Numbers)
- Map D - Cities & Towns of Vilas County (with Index)
- Map E - Cemeteries of Vilas County (with Index)
- Surnames in Vilas County Patents (with Parcel-counts for each surname)
- Surname/Township Index (with Parcel-counts for each surname by Township)

The five "Big-Picture" Maps are fairly self-explanatory, yet should not be overlooked. This is particularly true of Maps "C", "D", and "E", all of which show Vilas County and its Congressional Townships (and their assigned Map Group Numbers).

Let me briefly explain this concept of Map Group Numbers. These are a device completely of our own invention. They were created to help you quickly locate maps without having to remember the full legal name of the various Congressional Townships. It is simply easier to remember "Map Group 1" than a legal name like: "Township 9-North Range 6-West, 5th Principal Meridian." But the fact is that the TRUE legal name for these Townships IS terribly important. These are the designations that others will be familiar with and you will need to accurately record them in your notes. This is why both Map Group numbers AND legal descriptions of Townships are almost always displayed together.

Map "C" will be your first intoduction to "Map Group Numbers", and that is all it contains: legal Township descriptions and their assigned Map Group Numbers. Once you get further into your research, and more immersed in the details, you will likely want to refer back to Map "C" from time to time, in order to regain your bearings on just where in the county you are researching.

Remember, township boundaries are a completely artificial device, created to standardize land descriptions. But do not let them become a boundary in your mind when choosing which townships to research. Your relative's in-laws, children, cousins, siblings, and mamas and papas, might just as easily have lived in the township next to the one your grandfather lived in—rather than in the one where he actually lived. So Map "C" can be your guide to which other Townships/Map Groups you likewise ought to analyze.

Of course, the same holds true for County lines; this is the purpose behind Map "B". It shows you surrounding counties that you may want to consider for further reserarch.

Map "D", the Cities and Towns map, is the first map with an index. Map "E" is the second (Cemeteries). Both, Maps "D" and "E" give you broad views of City (or Cemetery) locations in the County. But they go much further by pointing you toward pertinent Township Map Groups so you can locate the patents, roads, and waterways located near a particular city or cemetery.

Once you are familiar with these *Family Maps* volumes and the county you are researching, the "Surnames In Vilas County" chapter (or its sister chapter in other volumes) is where you'll likely start your future research sessions. Here, you can quickly scan its few pages and see if anyone in the county possesses the surnames you are researching. The "Surnames in Vilas County" list shows only two things: surnames and the number of parcels of land we have located for that surname in Vilas County. But whether or not you immediately locate the surnames you are researching, please do not go any further without taking a few moments to scan ALL the surnames in these very few pages.

You cannot imagine how many lost ancestors are waiting to be found by someone willing to take just a little longer to scan the "Surnames In Vilas County" list. Misspellings and typographical errors abound in most any index of this sort. Don't miss out on finding your Kinard that was written Rynard or Cox that was written Lox. If it looks funny or wrong, it very often is. And one of those little errors may well be your relative.

Now, armed with a surname and the knowledge that it has one or more entries in this book, you are ready for the "Surname/Township Index." Unlike the "Surnames In Vilas County", which has only one line per Surname, the "Surname/Township Index" contains one line-item for each Township Map Group in which each surname is found. In other words, each line represents a different Township Map Group that you will need to review.

Specifically, each line of the Surname/Township Index contains the following four columns of in-formation:

1. Surname
2. Township Map Group Number (these Map Groups are found in Part II)
3. Parcels of Land (number of them with the given Surname within the Township)
4. Meridian/Township/Range (the legal description for this Township Map Group)

The key column here is that of the Township Map Group Number. While you should definitely record the Meridian, Township, and Range, you can do that later. Right now, you need to dig a little deeper. That Map Group Number tells you where in Part II that you need to start digging.

But before you leave the "Surname/Township Index", do the same thing that you did with the "Surnames in Vilas County" list: take a moment to scan the pages of the Index and see if there are similarly spelled or misspelled surnames that deserve your attention. Here again, is an easy opportunity to discover grossly misspelled family names with very little effort. Now you are ready to turn to . . .

Part II
"Township Map Groups"

You will normally arrive here in Part II after being directed to do so by one or more "Map Group Numbers" in the Surname/Township Index of Part I.

Each Map Group represents a set of four tools dedicated to a single Congressional Township that is either wholly or partially within the county. If you are trying to learn all that you can about a particular family or their land, then these tools should usually be viewed in the order they are presented.

These four tools include:

1. a Land Patent Index
2. a Land Patent Map
3. a Road Map, and
4. an Historical Map

As I mentioned earlier, each grouping of this sort is assigned a Map Group Number. So, let's now move on to a discussion of the four tools that make up one of these Township Map Groups.

Land Patent Index

Each Township Map Group's Index begins with a title, something along these lines:

MAP GROUP 1: Index to Land Patents
Township 16-North Range 5-West (2nd PM)

The Index contains seven (7) columns. They are:

1. ID (a unique ID number for this Individual and a corresponding Parcel of land in this Township)
2. Individual in Patent (name)
3. Sec. (Section), and
4. Sec. Part (Section Part, or Aliquot Part)
5. Date Issued (Patent)
6. Other Counties (often means multiple counties were mentioned in GLO records, or the section lies within multiple counties).
7. For More Info . . . (points to other places within this index or elsewhere in the book where you can find more information)

While most of the seven columns are self-explanatory, I will take a few moments to explain the "Sec. Part." and "For More Info" columns.

The "Sec. Part" column refers to what surveryors and other land professionals refer to as an Aliquot Part. The origins and use of such a term mean little to a non-surveyor, and I have chosen to simply call these sub-sections of land what they are: a "Section Part". No matter what we call them, what we are referring to are things like a quarter-section or half-section or quarter-quarter-section. See Appendix "B" for most of the "Section Parts" you will come across (and many you will not) and what size land-parcel they represent.

The "For More Info" column of the Index may seem like a small appendage to each line, but please recognize quickly that this is not so. And to understand the various items you might find here, you need to become familiar with the Legend that appears at the top of each Land Patent Index.

Here is a sample of the Legend . . .

LEGEND

"For More Info . . . " column

A = Authority (Legislative Act, See Appendix "A")
B = Block or Lot (location in Section unknown)
C = Cancelled Patent
F = Fractional Section
G = Group (Multi-Patentee Patent, see Appendix "C")
V = Overlaps another Parcel
R = Re-Issued (Parcel patented more than once)

Most parcels of land will have only one or two of these items in their "For More Info" columns, but when that is not the case, there is often some valuable information to be gained from further investigation. Below, I will explain what each of these items means to you you as a researcher.

A = Authority
(Legislative Act, See Appendix "A")
All Federal Land Patents were issued because some branch of our government (usually the U.S. Congress) passed a law making such a transfer of title possible. And therefore every patent within these pages will have an "A" item next to it in the index. The number after the "A" indicates which item in Appendix "A" holds the citation to the particular law which authorized the transfer of land to the public. As it stands, most of the Public Land data compiled and released by our government, and which serves as the basis for the patents mapped here, concerns itself with "Cash Sale" homesteads. So in some Counties, the law which authorized cash sales will be the primary, if not the only, entry in the Appendix.

B = Block or Lot (location in Section unknown)
A "B" designation in the Index is a tip-off that the EXACT location of the patent within the map is not apparent from the legal description. This Patent will nonetheless be noted within the proper

Section along with any other Lots purchased in the Section. Given the scope of this project (many states and many Counties are being mapped), trying to locate all relevant plats for Lots (if they even exist) and accurately mapping them would have taken one person several lifetimes. But since our primary goal from the onset has been to establish relationships between neighbors and families, very little is lost to this goal since we can still observe who all lived in which Section.

C = Cancelled Patent

A Cancelled Patent is just that: cancelled. Whether the original Patentee forfeited his or her patent due to fraud, a technicality, non-payment, or whatever, the fact remains that it is significant to know who received patents for what parcels and when. A cancellation may be evidence that the Patentee never physically re-located to the land, but does not in itself prove that point. Further evidence would be required to prove that. *See also*, Re-issued Patents, *below*.

F = Fractional Section

A Fractional Section is one that contains less than 640 acres, almost always because of a body of water. The exact size and shape of land-parcels contained in such sections may not be ascertainable, but we map them nonetheless. Just keep in mind that we are not mapping an actual parcel to scale in such instances. Another point to consider is that we have located some fractional sections that are not so designated by the Bureau of Land Management in their data. This means that not all fractional sections have been so identified in our indexes.

G = Group
(Multi-Patentee Patent, see Appendix "C")

A "G" designation means that the Patent was issued to a GROUP of people (Multi-patentees). The "G" will always be followed by a number. Some such groups were quite large and it was impractical if not impossible to display each individual in our maps without unduly affecting readability. EACH person in the group is named in the Index, but they won't all be found on the Map. You will find the name of the first person in such a Group

on the map with the Group number next to it, enclosed in [square brackets].

To find all the members of the Group you can either scan the Index for all people with the same Group Number or you can simply refer to Appendix "C" where all members of the Group are listed next to their number.

O = Overlaps another Parcel

An Overlap is one where PART of a parcel of land gets issued on more than one patent. For genealogical purposes, both transfers of title are important and both Patentees are mapped. If the ENTIRE parcel of land is re-issued, that is what we call it, a Re-Issued Patent (*see below*). The number after the "O" indicates the ID for the overlapping Patent(s) contained within the same Index. Like Re-Issued and Cancelled Patents, Overlaps may cause a map-reader to be confused at first, but for genealogical purposes, all of these parties' relationships to the underlying land is important, and therefore, we map them.

R = Re-Issued (Parcel patented more than once)

The label, "Re-issued Patent" describes Patents which were issued more than once for land with the EXACT SAME LEGAL DESCRIPTION. Whether the original patent was cancelled or not, there were a good many parcels which were patented more than once. The number after the "R" indicates the ID for the other Patent contained within the same Index that was for the same land. A quick glance at the map itself within the relevant Section will be the quickest way to find the other Patentee to whom the Parcel was transferred. They should both be mapped in the same general area.

I have gone to some length describing all sorts of anomalies either in the underlying data or in their representation on the maps and indexes in this book. Most of this will bore the most ardent reseracher, but I do this with all due respect to those researchers who will inevitably (and rightfully) ask: *"Why isn't so-and-so's name on the exact spot that the index says it should be?"*

In most cases it will be due to the existence of a Multi-Patentee Patent, a Re-issued Patent, a Cancelled Patent, or Overlapping Parcels named in separate Patents. I don't pretend that this discussion will answer every question along these lines, but I hope it will at least convince you of the complexity of the subject.

Not to despair, this book's companion web-site will offer a way to further explain "odd-ball" or errant data. Each book (County) will have its own web-page or pages to discuss such situations. You can go to www.arphax.com to find the relevant web-page for Vilas County.

Land Patent Map

On the first two-page spread following each Township's Index to Land Patents, you'll find the corresponding Land Patent Map. And here lies the real heart of our work. For the first time anywhere, researchers will be able to observe and analyze, on a grand scale, most of the original land-owners for an area AND see them mapped in proximity to each one another.

We encourage you to make vigorous use of the accompanying Index described above, but then later, to abandon it, and just stare at these maps for a while. This is a great way to catch misspellings or to find collateral kin you'd not known were in the area.

Each Land Patent Map represents one Congressional Township containing approximately 36-square miles. Each of these square miles is labeled by an accompanying Section Number (1 through 36, in most cases). Keep in mind, that this book concerns itself solely with Vilas County's patents. Townships which creep into one or more other counties will not be shown in their entirety in any one book. You will need to consult other books, as they become available, in order to view other countys' patents, cities, cemeteries, etc.

But getting back to Vilas County: each Land Patent Map contains a Statistical Chart that looks like the following:

Township Statistics

Parcels Mapped	:	173
Number of Patents	:	163
Number of Individuals	:	152
Patentees Identified	:	151
Number of Surnames	:	137
Multi-Patentee Parcels	:	4
Oldest Patent Date	:	11/27/1820
Most Recent Patent	:	9/28/1917
Block/Lot Parcels	:	0
Parcels Re-Issued	:	3
Parcels that Overlap	:	8
Cities and Towns	:	6
Cemeteries	:	6

This information may be of more use to a social statistician or historian than a genealogist, but I think all three will find it interesting.

Most of the statistics are self-explanatory, and what is not, was described in the above discussion of the Index's Legend, but I do want to mention a few of them that may affect your understanding of the Land Patent Maps.

First of all, Patents often contain more than one Parcel of land, so it is common for there to be more Parcels than Patents. Also, the Number of Individuals will more often than not, not match the number of Patentees. A Patentee is literally the person or PERSONS named in a patent. So, a Patent may have a multi-person Patentee or a single-person patentee. Nonetheless, we account for all these individuals in our indexes.

On the lower-righthand side of the Patent Map is a Legend which describes various features in the map, including Section Boundaries, Patent (land) Boundaries, Lots (numbered), and Multi-Patentee Group Numbers. You'll also find a "Helpful Hints" Box that will assist you.

One important note: though the vast majority of Patents mapped in this series will prove to be reasonably accurate representations of their actual locations, we cannot claim this for patents lying along state and county lines, or waterways, or that have been platted (lots).

Shifting boundaries and sparse legal descriptions in the GLO data make this a reality that we have nonetheless tried to overcome by estimating these patents' locations the best that we can.

Road Map

On the two-page spread following each Patent Map you will find a Road Map covering the exact same area (the same Congressional Township).

For me, fully exploring the past means that every once in a while I must leave the library and travel to the actual locations where my ancestors once walked and worked the land. Our Township Road Maps are a great place to begin such a quest.

Keep in mind that the scaling and proportion of these maps was chosen in order to squeeze hundreds of people-names, road-names, and place-names into tinier spaces than you would traditionally see. These are not professional road-maps, and like any secondary genealogical source, should be looked upon as an entry-way to original sources—in this case, original patents and applications, professionally produced maps and surveys, etc.

Both our Road Maps and Historical Maps contain cemeteries and city-centers, along with a listing of these on the left-hand side of the map. I should note that I am showing you city center-points, rather than city-limit boundaries, because in many instances, this will represent a place where settlement began. This may be a good time to mention that many cemeteries are located on private property, Always check with a local historical or genealogical society to see if a particular cemetery is publicly accessible (if it is not obviously so). As a final point, look for your surnames among the road-names. You will often be surprised by what you find.

Historical Map

The third and final map in each Map Group is our attempt to display what each Township might have looked like before the advent of modern roads. In frontier times, people were usually more determined to settle near rivers and creeks than they were near roads, which were often few and

far between. As was the case with the Road Map, we've included the same cemeteries and city-centers. We've also included railroads, many of which came along before most roads.

While some may claim "Historical Map" to be a bit of a misnomer for this tool, we settled for this label simply because it was almost as accurate as saying "Railroads, Lakes, Rivers, Cities, and Cemeteries," and it is much easier to remember.

In Closing . . .

By way of example, here is *A Really Good Way to Use a Township Map Group.* First, find the person you are researching in the Township's Index to Land Patents, which will direct you to the proper Section and parcel on the Patent Map. But before leaving the Index, scan all the patents within it, looking for other names of interest. Now, turn to the Patent Map and locate your parcels of land. Pay special attention to the names of patent-holders who own land surrounding your person of interest. Next, turn the page and look at the same Section(s) on the Road Map. Note which roads are closest to your parcels and also the names of nearby towns and cemeteries. Using other resources, you may be able to learn of kin who have been buried here, plus, you may choose to visit these cemeteries the next time you are in the area.

Finally, turn to the Historical Map. Look once more at the same Sections where you found your research subject's land. Note the nearby streams, creeks, and other geographical features. You may be surprised to find family names were used to name them, or you may see a name you haven't heard mentioned in years and years—and a new research possibility is born.

Many more techniques for using these *Family Maps* volumes will no doubt be discovered. If from time to time, you will navigate to Vilas County's web-page at www.arphax.com (use the "Research" link), you can learn new tricks as they become known (or you can share ones you have employed). But for now, you are ready to get started. So, go, and good luck.

– Part I –

The Big Picture

Map A - Where Vilas County, Wisconsin Lies Within the State

--- Legend ---

━━━ State Boundary

─── County Boundaries

▨ Vilas County, Wisconsin

--- Helpful Hints ---

1 We start with Map "A" which simply shows us where within the State this county lies.

2 Map "B" zooms in further to help us more easily identify surrounding Counties.

3 Map "C" zooms in even further to reveal the Congressional Townships that either lie within or intersect Vilas County.

Map B - Vilas County, Wisconsin and Surrounding Counties

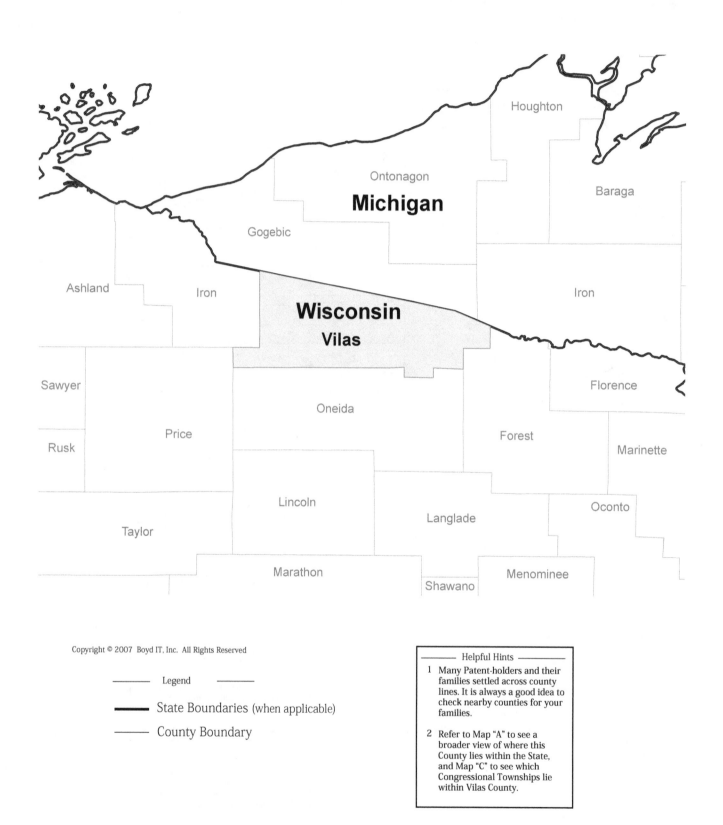

Legend

State Boundaries (when applicable)

County Boundary

---- Helpful Hints ----

1 Many Patent-holders and their families settled across county lines. It is always a good idea to check nearby counties for your families.

2 Refer to Map "A" to see a broader view of where this County lies within the State, and Map "C" to see which Congressional Townships lie within Vilas County.

Map C - Congressional Townships of Vilas County, Wisconsin

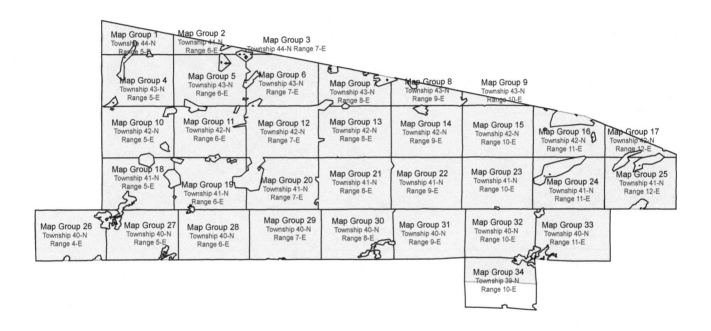

—— Legend ——

Vilas County, Wisconsin

Congressional Townships

—— Helpful Hints ——

1 Many Patent-holders and their families settled across county lines. It is always a good idea to check nearby counties for your families (See Map "B").

2 Refer to Map "A" to see a broader view of where this county lies within the State, and Map "B" for a view of the counties surrounding Vilas County.

Map D Index: Cities & Towns of Vilas County, Wisconsin

The following represents the Cities and Towns of Vilas County, along with the corresponding Map Group in which each is found. Cities and Towns are displayed in both the Road and Historical maps in the Group.

City/Town	Map Group No.
Arbor Vitae	29
Boulder Junction	12
Conover	23
Eagle River	32
Katinka Village	5
Lac du Flambeau	27
Land O' Lakes	9
Manitowish Waters	10
Marlands	27
Phelps	24
Presque Isle	2
Saint Germain	30
Sayner	21
Star Lake	21
Winchester	4

Map D - Cities & Towns of Vilas County, Wisconsin

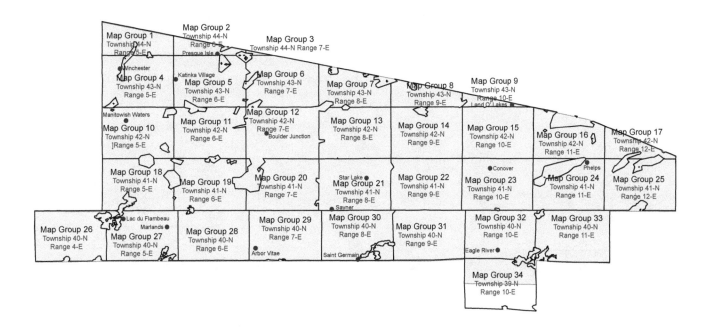

——— Helpful Hints ———

1 Cities and towns are marked only at their center-points as published by the USGS and/or NationalAtlas.gov. This often enables us to more closely approximate where these might have existed when first settled.

2 To see more specifically where these Cities & Towns are located within the county, refer to both the Road and Historical maps in the Map-Group referred to above. See also, the Map "D" Index on the opposite page.

Map E Index: Cemeteries of Vilas County, Wisconsin

The following represents many of the Cemeteries of Vilas County, along with the corresponding Township Map Group in which each is found. Cemeteries are displayed in both the Road and Historical maps in the Map Groups referred to below.

Cemetery	Map Group No.
Hildegard Cem.	23
Land O Lakes Cem.	9
Oak Hill Cem.	15
Pines Cem.	12
Presque Isle Cem.	2
Saint Germain Cem.	30
Winchester Memorial Cem.	1

Map E - Cemeteries of Vilas County, Wisconsin

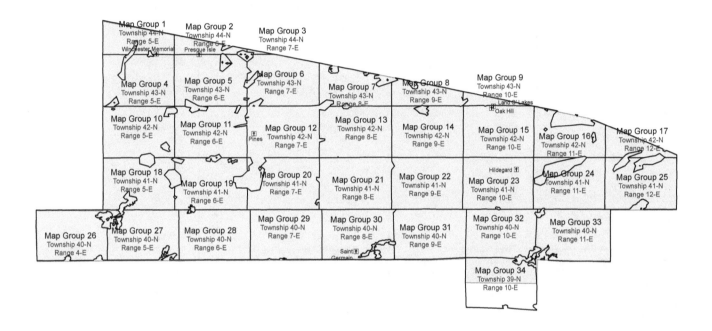

——— Helpful Hints ———

1 Cemeteries are marked at locations as published by the USGS and/or NationalAtlas.gov.

2 To see more specifically where these Cemeteries are located, refer to the Road & Historical maps in the Map-Group referred to above. See also, the Map "E" Index on the opposite page to make sure you don't miss any of the Cemeteries located within this Congressional township.

Surnames in Vilas County, Wisconsin Patents

The following list represents the surnames that we have located in Vilas County, Wisconsin Patents and the number of parcels that we have mapped for each one. Here is a quick way to determine the existence (or not) of Patents to be found in the subsequent indexes and maps of this volume.

Surname	# of Land Parcels	Surname	# of Land Parcels	Surname	# of Land Parcels	Surname	# of Land Parcels
ABBOTT	2	BOLGER	2	COOPER	3	EARLY	35
ADAMS	4	BOLLES	4	CORWITH	30	EBY	1
ALBAN	1	BOREMAN	2	COTTER	7	EDWARDS	5
ALEXANDER	4	BOROWITZ	1	COUSINS	6	ELDRIDGE	1
ALLEN	52	BOWEN	1	COVEY	1	ELIASON	2
ANDERSON	15	BOWMAN	1	COX	1	ELLIOTT	1
ANDREWS	9	BRADLEY	15	CROKER	4	ELLIS	4
ANSON	1	BRADY	9	CROSBY	6	ELSEN	1
ARNDT	2	BRASLEY	1	CROSS	2	EMERY	19
ARPIN	30	BRAUN	1	CUNNINGHAM	2	ENO	1
AUCUTT	1	BRAZIL	1	CURRAN	1	ERICKSON	1
AVERILL	9	BREHMER	3	CURTIS	1	ERVIN	2
AVERY	1	BRESNAN	3	CUSICK	1	EVANS	3
AYERS	4	BREWER	2	CUTTER	2	EWALD	2
BABCOCK	8	BREWSTER	17	CYR	2	EXTINE	1
BACKMAN	1	BROOKS	6	DALEY	6	FABIAN	1
BAILEY	6	BROWN	113	DANIELS	1	FARNHAM	7
BAIN	3	BRUSS	3	DANNEKER	1	FARWELL	18
BAKER	7	BRYDEN	4	DASKAM	3	FAY	3
BALCOM	1	BUCK	1	DAVIDSON	1	FELTON	4
BALDWIN	19	BUCKINGHAM	10	DAVIS	50	FETT	3
BALKE	1	BUCKSTAFF	55	DAVISON	3	FISH	4
BANGS	1	BUDDE	2	DAWLEY	9	FISK	1
BARNES	5	BURNS	2	DAY	5	FITCH	1
BARNETT	8	BURROWS	1	DE GROOT	3	FITZGERALD	3
BARROWS	139	CALLAGHAN	3	DECKERT	2	FLYNN	1
BARTLETT	1	CAMP	11	DELANEY	1	FOELKNER	1
BAUMAN	7	CAMPBELL	4	DELEGLISE	3	FORBES	39
BAUMANN	1	CARLEY	4	DENT	2	FORD	1
BAYER	2	CARPENTER	4	DENTON	4	FOREST	2
BEACH	2	CARR	4	DEREG	9	FORSMAN	35
BEAN	2	CARRIVEAU	1	DERN	1	FORSYTH	1
BEAU	9	CARROLL	1	DESROSIERS	4	FOSTER	6
BEAUDIEN	1	CARSKADDON	30	DEVINE	2	FOURNIER	1
BEAUME	2	CARTER	5	DEVLIN	9	FOX	1
BEGLE	2	CARVER	1	DEVOIN	3	FRANK	8
BEHLE	6	CASE	1	DIAMOND	24	FRANKFURTH	12
BELANGER	3	CASKEY	1	DICER	3	FREEMAN	5
BELISLE	1	CAVANEY	4	DICK	3	FRENCH	78
BELLIS	2	CAVNER	2	DICKENSON	1	FRIEND	17
BEMISS	4	CHAPMAN	1	DICKEY	2	FRITZ	1
BENJAMIN	2	CHASE	20	DICKINSON	2	FROEHLICH	2
BENNER	1	CHIDESTER	1	DISHAW	4	FROST	3
BENSON	4	CHOUSSE	3	DIXON	3	FULLER	5
BENT	6	CHRISTEN	1	DOCKERAY	3	GABRIELSON	1
BERG	1	CHRISTENSEN	1	DOCKEREY	2	GAEBLER	1
BERGER	1	CLARK	78	DONOHUE	5	GAFFNEY	2
BERGSTROM	2	CLASON	1	DOOLITTLE	2	GALLAGHER	3
BERON	3	CLEMENS	1	DORE	3	GARRETT	3
BETTIS	3	CLEMENTS	1	DORIOT	6	GATES	86
BEYER	20	CO	24	DOW	3	GEBHART	2
BINGHAM	1	COCHRAN	1	DOYLE	23	GELEFT	2
BIRD	3	COHN	42	DRAPER	4	GILBERT	6
BIRGE	1	COLBURN	44	DRAVES	1	GILBERTSON	1
BLACKWELL	1	COLE	7	DREGER	2	GILE	1
BLAISDELL	1	COLEMAN	9	DRINKER	18	GILKEY	7
BLAND	1	COLLINS	4	DUNBAR	16	GILLET	19
BLANDING	1	COLMAN	5	DUNFIELD	17	GILLETT	3
BLISH	1	COMPANY	62	DUSOLD	3	GILMORE	1
BLONG	2	CONANT	3	DUSSAULT	1	GLEASON	3
BLYTHE	1	COOK	8	DUTCHER	3	GOERLING	1
BOILEAU	1	COON	5	DWIGHT	103	GOODENOW	3

Surname	# of Land Parcels	Surname	# of Land Parcels	Surname	# of Land Parcels	Surname	# of Land Parcels
GOODRICH	2	JADISCHKE	3	MARCON	1	NELSON	5
GOODSPEED	1	JAHN	1	MARKEE	3	NEUMANN	2
GOODWILL	2	JARCHOW	1	MARKHAM	4	NEVILLE	2
GORMAN	9	JENNINGS	5	MARSHALL	1	NEWCOMB	3
GOULD	31	JOHNSON	20	MARTEN	2	NEWELL	1
GRAHAM	9	JOHNSTON	3	MARVIN	4	NEWMAN	9
GRAY	4	JONES	26	MASCHAUER	12	NIELSEN	10
GRAYSON	1	KAHN	1	MASHINO	1	NOEL	1
GRIFFITH	1	KAISER	3	MATHER	1	NORTON	115
GRISWOLD	4	KAO	3	MATHEWS	4	NORWAY	1
GROSS	1	KARGER	2	MATTKE	1	OBERG	2
GROUNDWATER	3	KAYZER	1	MAXON	77	OBERHOLTZER	1
GROVER	7	KEESLER	1	MAYO	6	OBERMANN	4
GUSE	3	KELLY	20	MCARTHUR	1	OBRAY	2
GUSTAFSON	2	KENEDY	1	MCBAIN	4	OCONNOR	2
HAGERMAN	64	KENNAN	1	MCCALL	2	OSTERBERG	1
HAGSTROM	2	KIKENDALL	8	MCCARTHY	2	OTTEROL	5
HAIGHT	34	KILROE	2	MCCLINTOCK	17	OTTO	4
HALL	66	KING	50	MCCORD	13	PAFF	4
HALLINAN	1	KINNEY	6	MCCORMICK	4	PALEN	2
HALMINIAK	1	KISSINGER	9	MCCROSSEN	3	PALMS	24
HAMILTON	76	KNAPP	11	MCCUAIG	1	PAQUETTE	3
HANSON	1	KNOX	4	MCCULLOUGH	2	PARSONS	23
HARPER	14	KOHL	5	MCDANIEL	1	PATRICK	79
HARRIGAN	14	KRAMER	3	MCDONALD	7	PATTEN	19
HARRINGTON	17	KREITE	2	MCFARLAND	1	PAULSON	1
HARTMAN	1	KREITZER	1	MCGRAW	105	PAULUS	1
HASELTINE	1	KUENZLI	1	MCGREGOR	1	PECK	1
HASTINGS	1	KULANDA	1	MCGUIRE	1	PERCIVAL	1
HAUPTMAN	4	LA CROSSE	2	MCILREE	1	PERKINS	1
HAYNNE	1	LABBE	1	MCKINNEY	3	PERRY	3
HAYWARD	1	LACAU	2	MCKNIGHT	1	PETERS	34
HEADFLYER	4	LAEV	13	MCMILLEN	3	PETERSON	1
HEATHER	3	LAFONTAISIE	1	MCPARTLIN	3	PETEY	4
HEAZLIT	20	LAIRD	115	MCSHERRY	1	PHELPS	6
HEIMER	1	LAMBORN	1	MEADE	18	PHILLIPS	5
HEINEMANN	8	LAMOTTE	6	MEIHACK	3	PIER	4
HEISMAN	3	LAMOUREUX	1	MEISNER	2	PIERCE	2
HENDRY	1	LANDERS	1	MELANG	3	PILLSBURY	412
HERMANSON	1	LANE	1	MERCER	19	PINKERTON	2
HEURICH	17	LANGILL	11	MERRICK	1	PINTO	1
HICKS	106	LARRABEE	5	MERRILL	2	POLAR	7
HIGGINS	1	LARZELERE	2	MERRYMAN	4	POND	1
HILLIS	2	LAWLER	7	MILES	13	POOR	3
HIRZEL	2	LEAVERTON	1	MILLAR	1	POPE	2
HIZEL	1	LEDURSE	1	MILLARD	1	PORTER	6
HJELMSTAD	1	LEE	1	MILLER	102	PRESCOTT	6
HOBART	4	LENTZ	35	MILLERD	1	PRESTON	27
HOGUE	1	LEONE	1	MILLS	1	PRICE	1
HOLDEN	6	LEVINGSTON	3	MINER	18	PROCTOR	1
HOLDSHIP	2	LEWIS	3	MITCHELL	2	PULLING	2
HOLLINDER	1	LIBBEY	4	MOFFAT	1	PUNCHES	6
HOLLISTER	6	LILJEQVEST	2	MONTGOMERY	1	PURCELL	1
HOLWAY	5	LINDSAY	14	MOON	1	PURTELL	8
HOWE	16	LINDSTEDT	1	MOONEY	6	PUTNAM	3
HOWES	6	LOGG	3	MOOR	2	QUAW	1
HOWLETT	6	LOMBARD	4	MOORE	1	RABLIN	16
HOXIE	5	LONG	4	MORAN	5	RACES	1
HUGHES	1	LOOMIS	1	MOREY	3	RADCLIFFE	2
HUNTER	4	LOUGHRIN	2	MORGAN	13	REAY	1
HUTCHISON	1	LOVEJOY	118	MORIN	3	REED	1
HYDE	2	LOVELESS	4	MORRIS	2	REEVE	9
HYLAND	136	LUCK	1	MORRISON	1	REGNER	1
IDE	5	LUETZER	3	MUCHLER	2	REHFELD	3
INGERSOLL	1	LUHN	1	MULHOLON	3	REMMERT	8
INGRAHAM	6	MACK	3	MULVANE	1	RETTLER	1
IRVIN	6	MAGEE	1	MURRAY	3	REYNOLDS	1
IRWIN	8	MALCOLM	1	MUTTER	1	RHINELANDER	7
JACKSON	24	MANSON	1	NAGEL	1	RIBENACK	2
JACOBS	1	MANUEL	3	NAST	2	RICHARDS	3

Surname	# of Land Parcels	Surname	# of Land Parcels	Surname	# of Land Parcels
RICHARDSON	1	ST LOUIS	1	WEST	2
RICHMOND	2	STAMP	3	WESTCOTT	3
RILEY	1	STANDISH	1	WESTON	7
RINGLE	10	STANTON	1	WHEELIHAN	2
RIPLEY	59	STARKS	4	WHITE	1
ROBERTS	2	STARR	2	WIEGAND	2
ROBISON	33	STEIN	4	WILBER	1
ROBSON	9	STEINBERG	8	WILCOX	14
ROCKWELL	3	STEINMETZ	4	WILD	1
ROE	18	STEVENS	3	WILEY	64
ROGERS	4	STEVENSON	6	WILHELM	7
ROIT	2	STEWART	3	WILLCOX	2
ROLLENHAGEN	2	STICKLES	4	WILLIAMS	4
ROSENBERRY	1	STOECKEL	4	WILSON	15
ROSS	16	STONE	1	WILTERDING	2
ROUNDS	4	STORM	1	WINSLOW	3
ROWELL	6	STRANDBERG	1	WINTON	22
ROWLEY	2	STREATOR	1	WIPPERMANN	1
ROY	3	STREETER	3	WISCONSIN	7
RUMSEY	11	STROUP	1	WISE	1
RUSSELL	126	STUBBINGS	7	WITTER	6
RUST	71	STURDEVANT	3	WOLFRAM	2
RYAN	3	SULLIVAN	3	WOODLOCK	1
SACKETT	1	SWIMM	3	WOOLWORTH	3
SAGE	26	TALMAGE	2	WRIGHT	2
SALZMAN	2	TAMBLING	4	WYLIE	57
SAMPSON	6	TAYLOR	1	YAWKEY	2
SANBORN	6	TELLEFSON	4	YOUNG	84
SANDERS	1	TELLER	1	ZAHNER	1
SANSTER	10	THAYER	2	ZIEMKE	3
SARGENT	5	THOMAS	1	ZIMPELMANN	2
SAYNER	2	THOMPSON	70		
SCHAETZLE	1	TILLOTSON	23		
SCHAUDER	2	TOBEY	3		
SCHERIBEL	2	TOBIN	2		
SCHMIDT	4	TOLMAN	24		
SCHOFIELD	1	TOOLEY	2		
SCHRIBER	36	TOWNSEND	25		
SCHWALM	1	TRASTEL	15		
SCOTT	146	TRIPP	2		
SECHRIST	1	TRUSSEL	4		
SEEGER	5	UPHAM	2		
SEIM	1	VAN BRUNT	43		
SELL	4	VAN OSTRAND	3		
SEMER	12	VENNER	2		
SEVERANCE	4	VINECORE	6		
SEWARD	2	WACHTER	2		
SEYER	1	WADE	1		
SHADICK	2	WAKEFIELD	3		
SHAFFER	16	WALLICH	6		
SHAPE	1	WALLING	1		
SHAW	3	WALSH	17		
SHEPARD	5	WALTER	4		
SHEPPARD	22	WALTERS	2		
SHERIDAN	1	WAMBOLD	1		
SHERMAN	4	WARNER	3		
SHERRY	12	WASHBURN	24		
SHEW	3	WASTE	8		
SIEGEL	3	WATERMAN	58		
SIEVWRIGHT	1	WATTERMAN	4		
SILVERSTONE	17	WATTERS	1		
SILVERTHORN	23	WEBSTER	6		
SIMPSON	2	WELCH	4		
SLATTERY	1	WELKER	2		
SLAUSON	41	WELLINGTON	21		
SLOCUM	140	WELLS	29		
SLONAKER	1	WENNBERG	1		
SMITH	13	WENTWORTH	2		
SOMERS	3	WERNICH	4		
SPAFFORD	1	WESCOTT	6		

Surname/Township Index

This Index allows you to determine which *Township Map Group(s)* contain individuals with the following surnames. Each *Map Group* has a corresponding full-name index of all individuals who obtained patents for land within its Congressional township's borders. After each index you will find the Patent Map to which it refers, and just thereafter, you can view the township's Road Map and Historical Map, with the latter map displaying streams, railroads, and more.

So, once you find your Surname here, proceed to the Index at the beginning of the **Map Group** indicated below.

Surname	Map Group	Parcels of Land	Meridian/Township/Range		
ABBOTT	**6**	2	4th PM - 1831 MN/WI	43-N	7-E
ADAMS	**32**	3	4th PM - 1831 MN/WI	40-N	10-E
" "	**23**	1	4th PM - 1831 MN/WI	41-N	10-E
ALBAN	**8**	1	4th PM - 1831 MN/WI	43-N	9-E
ALEXANDER	**31**	2	4th PM - 1831 MN/WI	40-N	9-E
" "	**15**	2	4th PM - 1831 MN/WI	42-N	10-E
ALLEN	**28**	20	4th PM - 1831 MN/WI	40-N	6-E
" "	**22**	13	4th PM - 1831 MN/WI	41-N	9-E
" "	**30**	6	4th PM - 1831 MN/WI	40-N	8-E
" "	**29**	5	4th PM - 1831 MN/WI	40-N	7-E
" "	**21**	4	4th PM - 1831 MN/WI	41-N	8-E
" "	**31**	2	4th PM - 1831 MN/WI	40-N	9-E
" "	**10**	1	4th PM - 1831 MN/WI	42-N	5-E
" "	**14**	1	4th PM - 1831 MN/WI	42-N	9-E
ANDERSON	**8**	7	4th PM - 1831 MN/WI	43-N	9-E
" "	**22**	4	4th PM - 1831 MN/WI	41-N	9-E
" "	**9**	3	4th PM - 1831 MN/WI	43-N	10-E
" "	**15**	1	4th PM - 1831 MN/WI	42-N	10-E
ANDREWS	**31**	9	4th PM - 1831 MN/WI	40-N	9-E
ANSON	**31**	1	4th PM - 1831 MN/WI	40-N	9-E
ARNDT	**31**	2	4th PM - 1831 MN/WI	40-N	9-E
ARPIN	**5**	14	4th PM - 1831 MN/WI	43-N	6-E
" "	**6**	8	4th PM - 1831 MN/WI	43-N	7-E
" "	**30**	3	4th PM - 1831 MN/WI	40-N	8-E
" "	**11**	2	4th PM - 1831 MN/WI	42-N	6-E
" "	**12**	2	4th PM - 1831 MN/WI	42-N	7-E
" "	**14**	1	4th PM - 1831 MN/WI	42-N	9-E
AUCUTT	**2**	1	4th PM - 1831 MN/WI	44-N	6-E
AVERILL	**21**	9	4th PM - 1831 MN/WI	41-N	8-E
AVERY	**32**	1	4th PM - 1831 MN/WI	40-N	10-E
AYERS	**16**	4	4th PM - 1831 MN/WI	42-N	11-E
BABCOCK	**5**	5	4th PM - 1831 MN/WI	43-N	6-E
" "	**6**	2	4th PM - 1831 MN/WI	43-N	7-E
" "	**7**	1	4th PM - 1831 MN/WI	43-N	8-E
BACKMAN	**15**	1	4th PM - 1831 MN/WI	42-N	10-E
BAILEY	**12**	6	4th PM - 1831 MN/WI	42-N	7-E
BAIN	**15**	3	4th PM - 1831 MN/WI	42-N	10-E
BAKER	**30**	3	4th PM - 1831 MN/WI	40-N	8-E
" "	**15**	2	4th PM - 1831 MN/WI	42-N	10-E
" "	**12**	2	4th PM - 1831 MN/WI	42-N	7-E
BALCOM	**7**	1	4th PM - 1831 MN/WI	43-N	8-E
BALDWIN	**17**	19	4th PM - 1831 MN/WI	42-N	12-E
BALKE	**16**	1	4th PM - 1831 MN/WI	42-N	11-E
BANGS	**30**	1	4th PM - 1831 MN/WI	40-N	8-E

Surname	Map Group	Parcels of Land	Meridian/Township/Range
BARNES	**25**	3	4th PM - 1831 MN/WI 41-N 12-E
" "	**29**	2	4th PM - 1831 MN/WI 40-N 7-E
BARNETT	**7**	3	4th PM - 1831 MN/WI 43-N 8-E
" "	**13**	2	4th PM - 1831 MN/WI 42-N 8-E
" "	**22**	1	4th PM - 1831 MN/WI 41-N 9-E
" "	**14**	1	4th PM - 1831 MN/WI 42-N 9-E
" "	**5**	1	4th PM - 1831 MN/WI 43-N 6-E
BARROWS	**11**	67	4th PM - 1831 MN/WI 42-N 6-E
" "	**12**	37	4th PM - 1831 MN/WI 42-N 7-E
" "	**10**	11	4th PM - 1831 MN/WI 42-N 5-E
" "	**19**	10	4th PM - 1831 MN/WI 41-N 6-E
" "	**4**	6	4th PM - 1831 MN/WI 43-N 5-E
" "	**5**	4	4th PM - 1831 MN/WI 43-N 6-E
" "	**6**	2	4th PM - 1831 MN/WI 43-N 7-E
" "	**20**	1	4th PM - 1831 MN/WI 41-N 7-E
" "	**7**	1	4th PM - 1831 MN/WI 43-N 8-E
BARTLETT	**23**	1	4th PM - 1831 MN/WI 41-N 10-E
BAUMAN	**5**	5	4th PM - 1831 MN/WI 43-N 6-E
" "	**6**	2	4th PM - 1831 MN/WI 43-N 7-E
BAUMANN	**23**	1	4th PM - 1831 MN/WI 41-N 10-E
BAYER	**28**	2	4th PM - 1831 MN/WI 40-N 6-E
BEACH	**15**	2	4th PM - 1831 MN/WI 42-N 10-E
BEAN	**10**	2	4th PM - 1831 MN/WI 42-N 5-E
BEAU	**11**	9	4th PM - 1831 MN/WI 42-N 6-E
BEAUDIEN	**28**	1	4th PM - 1831 MN/WI 40-N 6-E
BEAUME	**28**	2	4th PM - 1831 MN/WI 40-N 6-E
BEGLE	**31**	1	4th PM - 1831 MN/WI 40-N 9-E
" "	**22**	1	4th PM - 1831 MN/WI 41-N 9-E
BEHLE	**10**	3	4th PM - 1831 MN/WI 42-N 5-E
" "	**11**	3	4th PM - 1831 MN/WI 42-N 6-E
BELANGER	**14**	3	4th PM - 1831 MN/WI 42-N 9-E
BELISLE	**28**	1	4th PM - 1831 MN/WI 40-N 6-E
BELLIS	**28**	2	4th PM - 1831 MN/WI 40-N 6-E
BEMISS	**32**	4	4th PM - 1831 MN/WI 40-N 10-E
BENJAMIN	**30**	2	4th PM - 1831 MN/WI 40-N 8-E
BENNER	**21**	1	4th PM - 1831 MN/WI 41-N 8-E
BENSON	**10**	3	4th PM - 1831 MN/WI 42-N 5-E
" "	**32**	1	4th PM - 1831 MN/WI 40-N 10-E
BENT	**8**	6	4th PM - 1831 MN/WI 43-N 9-E
BERG	**15**	1	4th PM - 1831 MN/WI 42-N 10-E
BERGER	**10**	1	4th PM - 1831 MN/WI 42-N 5-E
BERGSTROM	**16**	2	4th PM - 1831 MN/WI 42-N 11-E
BERON	**33**	3	4th PM - 1831 MN/WI 40-N 11-E
BETTIS	**28**	3	4th PM - 1831 MN/WI 40-N 6-E
BEYER	**33**	8	4th PM - 1831 MN/WI 40-N 11-E
" "	**24**	5	4th PM - 1831 MN/WI 41-N 11-E
" "	**17**	5	4th PM - 1831 MN/WI 42-N 12-E
" "	**34**	2	4th PM - 1831 MN/WI 39-N 10-E
BINGHAM	**34**	1	4th PM - 1831 MN/WI 39-N 10-E
BIRD	**28**	1	4th PM - 1831 MN/WI 40-N 6-E
" "	**30**	1	4th PM - 1831 MN/WI 40-N 8-E
" "	**21**	1	4th PM - 1831 MN/WI 41-N 8-E
BIRGE	**34**	1	4th PM - 1831 MN/WI 39-N 10-E
BLACKWELL	**20**	1	4th PM - 1831 MN/WI 41-N 7-E
BLAISDELL	**19**	1	4th PM - 1831 MN/WI 41-N 6-E
BLAND	**10**	1	4th PM - 1831 MN/WI 42-N 5-E
BLANDING	**10**	1	4th PM - 1831 MN/WI 42-N 5-E
BLISH	**15**	1	4th PM - 1831 MN/WI 42-N 10-E
BLONG	**16**	2	4th PM - 1831 MN/WI 42-N 11-E
BLYTHE	**5**	1	4th PM - 1831 MN/WI 43-N 6-E

Surname	Map Group	Parcels of Land	Meridian/Township/Range
BOILEAU	**28**	1	4th PM - 1831 MN/WI 40-N 6-E
BOLGER	**10**	2	4th PM - 1831 MN/WI 42-N 5-E
BOLLES	**7**	2	4th PM - 1831 MN/WI 43-N 8-E
" "	**19**	1	4th PM - 1831 MN/WI 41-N 6-E
" "	**6**	1	4th PM - 1831 MN/WI 43-N 7-E
BOREMAN	**28**	2	4th PM - 1831 MN/WI 40-N 6-E
BOROWITZ	**5**	1	4th PM - 1831 MN/WI 43-N 6-E
BOWEN	**29**	1	4th PM - 1831 MN/WI 40-N 7-E
BOWMAN	**32**	1	4th PM - 1831 MN/WI 40-N 10-E
BRADLEY	**20**	9	4th PM - 1831 MN/WI 41-N 7-E
" "	**26**	3	4th PM - 1831 MN/WI 40-N 4-E
" "	**19**	2	4th PM - 1831 MN/WI 41-N 6-E
" "	**21**	1	4th PM - 1831 MN/WI 41-N 8-E
BRADY	**16**	9	4th PM - 1831 MN/WI 42-N 11-E
BRASLEY	**23**	1	4th PM - 1831 MN/WI 41-N 10-E
BRAUN	**10**	1	4th PM - 1831 MN/WI 42-N 5-E
BRAZIL	**19**	1	4th PM - 1831 MN/WI 41-N 6-E
BREHMER	**29**	3	4th PM - 1831 MN/WI 40-N 7-E
BRESNAN	**15**	2	4th PM - 1831 MN/WI 42-N 10-E
" "	**32**	1	4th PM - 1831 MN/WI 40-N 10-E
BREWER	**14**	2	4th PM - 1831 MN/WI 42-N 9-E
BREWSTER	**28**	10	4th PM - 1831 MN/WI 40-N 6-E
" "	**19**	7	4th PM - 1831 MN/WI 41-N 6-E
BROOKS	**14**	6	4th PM - 1831 MN/WI 42-N 9-E
BROWN	**31**	25	4th PM - 1831 MN/WI 40-N 9-E
" "	**32**	22	4th PM - 1831 MN/WI 40-N 10-E
" "	**15**	16	4th PM - 1831 MN/WI 42-N 10-E
" "	**23**	15	4th PM - 1831 MN/WI 41-N 10-E
" "	**34**	9	4th PM - 1831 MN/WI 39-N 10-E
" "	**33**	7	4th PM - 1831 MN/WI 40-N 11-E
" "	**24**	6	4th PM - 1831 MN/WI 41-N 11-E
" "	**30**	4	4th PM - 1831 MN/WI 40-N 8-E
" "	**21**	4	4th PM - 1831 MN/WI 41-N 8-E
" "	**22**	4	4th PM - 1831 MN/WI 41-N 9-E
" "	**29**	1	4th PM - 1831 MN/WI 40-N 7-E
BRUSS	**8**	3	4th PM - 1831 MN/WI 43-N 9-E
BRYDEN	**8**	4	4th PM - 1831 MN/WI 43-N 9-E
BUCK	**10**	1	4th PM - 1831 MN/WI 42-N 5-E
BUCKINGHAM	**29**	8	4th PM - 1831 MN/WI 40-N 7-E
" "	**30**	2	4th PM - 1831 MN/WI 40-N 8-E
BUCKSTAFF	**22**	21	4th PM - 1831 MN/WI 41-N 9-E
" "	**15**	14	4th PM - 1831 MN/WI 42-N 10-E
" "	**9**	7	4th PM - 1831 MN/WI 43-N 10-E
" "	**32**	4	4th PM - 1831 MN/WI 40-N 10-E
" "	**7**	4	4th PM - 1831 MN/WI 43-N 8-E
" "	**11**	3	4th PM - 1831 MN/WI 42-N 6-E
" "	**6**	2	4th PM - 1831 MN/WI 43-N 7-E
BUDDE	**23**	2	4th PM - 1831 MN/WI 41-N 10-E
BURNS	**33**	1	4th PM - 1831 MN/WI 40-N 11-E
" "	**16**	1	4th PM - 1831 MN/WI 42-N 11-E
BURROWS	**12**	1	4th PM - 1831 MN/WI 42-N 7-E
CALLAGHAN	**12**	3	4th PM - 1831 MN/WI 42-N 7-E
CAMP	**16**	11	4th PM - 1831 MN/WI 42-N 11-E
CAMPBELL	**11**	3	4th PM - 1831 MN/WI 42-N 6-E
" "	**31**	1	4th PM - 1831 MN/WI 40-N 9-E
CARLEY	**30**	4	4th PM - 1831 MN/WI 40-N 8-E
CARPENTER	**32**	3	4th PM - 1831 MN/WI 40-N 10-E
" "	**21**	1	4th PM - 1831 MN/WI 41-N 8-E
CARR	**28**	1	4th PM - 1831 MN/WI 40-N 6-E
" "	**29**	1	4th PM - 1831 MN/WI 40-N 7-E

Surname	Map Group	Parcels of Land	Meridian/Township/Range		
CARR (Cont'd)	**19**	1	4th PM - 1831 MN/WI	41-N	6-E
" "	**20**	1	4th PM - 1831 MN/WI	41-N	7-E
CARRIVEAU	**28**	1	4th PM - 1831 MN/WI	40-N	6-E
CARROLL	**11**	1	4th PM - 1831 MN/WI	42-N	6-E
CARSKADDON	**11**	30	4th PM - 1831 MN/WI	42-N	6-E
CARTER	**32**	3	4th PM - 1831 MN/WI	40-N	10-E
" "	**34**	2	4th PM - 1831 MN/WI	39-N	10-E
CARVER	**11**	1	4th PM - 1831 MN/WI	42-N	6-E
CASE	**33**	1	4th PM - 1831 MN/WI	40-N	11-E
CASKEY	**16**	1	4th PM - 1831 MN/WI	42-N	11-E
CAVANEY	**16**	4	4th PM - 1831 MN/WI	42-N	11-E
CAVNER	**10**	2	4th PM - 1831 MN/WI	42-N	5-E
CHAPMAN	**21**	1	4th PM - 1831 MN/WI	41-N	8-E
CHASE	**15**	10	4th PM - 1831 MN/WI	42-N	10-E
" "	**7**	4	4th PM - 1831 MN/WI	43-N	8-E
" "	**11**	3	4th PM - 1831 MN/WI	42-N	6-E
" "	**6**	2	4th PM - 1831 MN/WI	43-N	7-E
" "	**33**	1	4th PM - 1831 MN/WI	40-N	11-E
CHIDESTER	**14**	1	4th PM - 1831 MN/WI	42-N	9-E
CHOUSSE	**29**	2	4th PM - 1831 MN/WI	40-N	7-E
" "	**30**	1	4th PM - 1831 MN/WI	40-N	8-E
CHRISTEN	**29**	1	4th PM - 1831 MN/WI	40-N	7-E
CHRISTENSEN	**22**	1	4th PM - 1831 MN/WI	41-N	9-E
CLARK	**22**	25	4th PM - 1831 MN/WI	41-N	9-E
" "	**14**	23	4th PM - 1831 MN/WI	42-N	9-E
" "	**28**	8	4th PM - 1831 MN/WI	40-N	6-E
" "	**23**	7	4th PM - 1831 MN/WI	41-N	10-E
" "	**19**	3	4th PM - 1831 MN/WI	41-N	6-E
" "	**21**	3	4th PM - 1831 MN/WI	41-N	8-E
" "	**11**	3	4th PM - 1831 MN/WI	42-N	6-E
" "	**13**	3	4th PM - 1831 MN/WI	42-N	8-E
" "	**30**	2	4th PM - 1831 MN/WI	40-N	8-E
" "	**26**	1	4th PM - 1831 MN/WI	40-N	4-E
CLASON	**5**	1	4th PM - 1831 MN/WI	43-N	6-E
CLEMENS	**33**	1	4th PM - 1831 MN/WI	40-N	11-E
CLEMENTS	**33**	1	4th PM - 1831 MN/WI	40-N	11-E
CO	**15**	10	4th PM - 1831 MN/WI	42-N	10-E
" "	**8**	9	4th PM - 1831 MN/WI	43-N	9-E
" "	**31**	2	4th PM - 1831 MN/WI	40-N	9-E
" "	**14**	2	4th PM - 1831 MN/WI	42-N	9-E
" "	**32**	1	4th PM - 1831 MN/WI	40-N	10-E
COCHRAN	**22**	1	4th PM - 1831 MN/WI	41-N	9-E
COHN	**31**	42	4th PM - 1831 MN/WI	40-N	9-E
COLBURN	**6**	33	4th PM - 1831 MN/WI	43-N	7-E
" "	**5**	11	4th PM - 1831 MN/WI	43-N	6-E
COLE	**25**	3	4th PM - 1831 MN/WI	41-N	12-E
" "	**15**	2	4th PM - 1831 MN/WI	42-N	10-E
" "	**16**	2	4th PM - 1831 MN/WI	42-N	11-E
COLEMAN	**28**	9	4th PM - 1831 MN/WI	40-N	6-E
COLLINS	**5**	4	4th PM - 1831 MN/WI	43-N	6-E
COLMAN	**25**	3	4th PM - 1831 MN/WI	41-N	12-E
" "	**24**	1	4th PM - 1831 MN/WI	41-N	11-E
" "	**14**	1	4th PM - 1831 MN/WI	42-N	9-E
COMPANY	**29**	19	4th PM - 1831 MN/WI	40-N	7-E
" "	**12**	7	4th PM - 1831 MN/WI	42-N	7-E
" "	**11**	6	4th PM - 1831 MN/WI	42-N	6-E
" "	**30**	5	4th PM - 1831 MN/WI	40-N	8-E
" "	**23**	5	4th PM - 1831 MN/WI	41-N	10-E
" "	**21**	5	4th PM - 1831 MN/WI	41-N	8-E
" "	**20**	3	4th PM - 1831 MN/WI	41-N	7-E

Surname	Map Group	Parcels of Land	Meridian/Township/Range		
COMPANY (Cont'd)	**10**	3	4th PM - 1831 MN/WI	42-N	5-E
" "	**33**	2	4th PM - 1831 MN/WI	40-N	11-E
" "	**15**	2	4th PM - 1831 MN/WI	42-N	10-E
" "	**34**	1	4th PM - 1831 MN/WI	39-N	10-E
" "	**31**	1	4th PM - 1831 MN/WI	40-N	9-E
" "	**19**	1	4th PM - 1831 MN/WI	41-N	6-E
" "	**16**	1	4th PM - 1831 MN/WI	42-N	11-E
" "	**6**	1	4th PM - 1831 MN/WI	43-N	7-E
CONANT	**12**	3	4th PM - 1831 MN/WI	42-N	7-E
COOK	**14**	2	4th PM - 1831 MN/WI	42-N	9-E
" "	**28**	1	4th PM - 1831 MN/WI	40-N	6-E
" "	**29**	1	4th PM - 1831 MN/WI	40-N	7-E
" "	**31**	1	4th PM - 1831 MN/WI	40-N	9-E
" "	**23**	1	4th PM - 1831 MN/WI	41-N	10-E
" "	**20**	1	4th PM - 1831 MN/WI	41-N	7-E
" "	**21**	1	4th PM - 1831 MN/WI	41-N	8-E
COON	**30**	3	4th PM - 1831 MN/WI	40-N	8-E
" "	**19**	2	4th PM - 1831 MN/WI	41-N	6-E
COOPER	**24**	2	4th PM - 1831 MN/WI	41-N	11-E
" "	**5**	1	4th PM - 1831 MN/WI	43-N	6-E
CORWITH	**30**	19	4th PM - 1831 MN/WI	40-N	8-E
" "	**31**	4	4th PM - 1831 MN/WI	40-N	9-E
" "	**10**	4	4th PM - 1831 MN/WI	42-N	5-E
" "	**4**	3	4th PM - 1831 MN/WI	43-N	5-E
COTTER	**30**	6	4th PM - 1831 MN/WI	40-N	8-E
" "	**31**	1	4th PM - 1831 MN/WI	40-N	9-E
COUSINS	**12**	6	4th PM - 1831 MN/WI	42-N	7-E
COVEY	**16**	1	4th PM - 1831 MN/WI	42-N	11-E
COX	**19**	1	4th PM - 1831 MN/WI	41-N	6-E
CROKER	**32**	4	4th PM - 1831 MN/WI	40-N	10-E
CROSBY	**10**	2	4th PM - 1831 MN/WI	42-N	5-E
" "	**11**	2	4th PM - 1831 MN/WI	42-N	6-E
" "	**12**	2	4th PM - 1831 MN/WI	42-N	7-E
CROSS	**28**	1	4th PM - 1831 MN/WI	40-N	6-E
" "	**11**	1	4th PM - 1831 MN/WI	42-N	6-E
CUNNINGHAM	**34**	2	4th PM - 1831 MN/WI	39-N	10-E
CURRAN	**31**	1	4th PM - 1831 MN/WI	40-N	9-E
CURTIS	**23**	1	4th PM - 1831 MN/WI	41-N	10-E
CUSICK	**6**	1	4th PM - 1831 MN/WI	43-N	7-E
CUTTER	**19**	2	4th PM - 1831 MN/WI	41-N	6-E
CYR	**17**	2	4th PM - 1831 MN/WI	42-N	12-E
DALEY	**19**	2	4th PM - 1831 MN/WI	41-N	6-E
" "	**4**	2	4th PM - 1831 MN/WI	43-N	5-E
" "	**20**	1	4th PM - 1831 MN/WI	41-N	7-E
" "	**10**	1	4th PM - 1831 MN/WI	42-N	5-E
DANIELS	**1**	1	4th PM - 1831 MN/WI	44-N	5-E
DANNEKER	**8**	1	4th PM - 1831 MN/WI	43-N	9-E
DASKAM	**33**	3	4th PM - 1831 MN/WI	40-N	11-E
DAVIDSON	**28**	1	4th PM - 1831 MN/WI	40-N	6-E
DAVIS	**7**	14	4th PM - 1831 MN/WI	43-N	8-E
" "	**1**	12	4th PM - 1831 MN/WI	44-N	5-E
" "	**30**	9	4th PM - 1831 MN/WI	40-N	8-E
" "	**8**	7	4th PM - 1831 MN/WI	43-N	9-E
" "	**29**	4	4th PM - 1831 MN/WI	40-N	7-E
" "	**4**	4	4th PM - 1831 MN/WI	43-N	5-E
DAVISON	**23**	2	4th PM - 1831 MN/WI	41-N	10-E
" "	**22**	1	4th PM - 1831 MN/WI	41-N	9-E
DAWLEY	**30**	5	4th PM - 1831 MN/WI	40-N	8-E
" "	**31**	2	4th PM - 1831 MN/WI	40-N	9-E
" "	**15**	2	4th PM - 1831 MN/WI	42-N	10-E

Surname	Map Group	Parcels of Land	Meridian/Township/Range		
DAY	**11**	3	4th PM - 1831 MN/WI	42-N	6-E
" "	**30**	1	4th PM - 1831 MN/WI	40-N	8-E
" "	**31**	1	4th PM - 1831 MN/WI	40-N	9-E
DE GROOT	**25**	3	4th PM - 1831 MN/WI	41-N	12-E
DECKERT	**34**	1	4th PM - 1831 MN/WI	39-N	10-E
" "	**32**	1	4th PM - 1831 MN/WI	40-N	10-E
DELANEY	**13**	1	4th PM - 1831 MN/WI	42-N	8-E
DELEGLISE	**32**	3	4th PM - 1831 MN/WI	40-N	10-E
DENT	**33**	1	4th PM - 1831 MN/WI	40-N	11-E
" "	**23**	1	4th PM - 1831 MN/WI	41-N	10-E
DENTON	**33**	3	4th PM - 1831 MN/WI	40-N	11-E
" "	**34**	1	4th PM - 1831 MN/WI	39-N	10-E
DEREG	**21**	9	4th PM - 1831 MN/WI	41-N	8-E
DERN	**20**	1	4th PM - 1831 MN/WI	41-N	7-E
DESROSIERS	**28**	4	4th PM - 1831 MN/WI	40-N	6-E
DEVINE	**10**	2	4th PM - 1831 MN/WI	42-N	5-E
DEVLIN	**22**	9	4th PM - 1831 MN/WI	41-N	9-E
DEVOIN	**28**	3	4th PM - 1831 MN/WI	40-N	6-E
DIAMOND	**19**	12	4th PM - 1831 MN/WI	41-N	6-E
" "	**10**	11	4th PM - 1831 MN/WI	42-N	5-E
" "	**24**	1	4th PM - 1831 MN/WI	41-N	11-E
DICER	**23**	2	4th PM - 1831 MN/WI	41-N	10-E
" "	**22**	1	4th PM - 1831 MN/WI	41-N	9-E
DICK	**5**	3	4th PM - 1831 MN/WI	43-N	6-E
DICKENSON	**31**	1	4th PM - 1831 MN/WI	40-N	9-E
DICKEY	**34**	1	4th PM - 1831 MN/WI	39-N	10-E
" "	**32**	1	4th PM - 1831 MN/WI	40-N	10-E
DICKINSON	**29**	1	4th PM - 1831 MN/WI	40-N	7-E
" "	**21**	1	4th PM - 1831 MN/WI	41-N	8-E
DISHAW	**32**	3	4th PM - 1831 MN/WI	40-N	10-E
" "	**15**	1	4th PM - 1831 MN/WI	42-N	10-E
DIXON	**24**	2	4th PM - 1831 MN/WI	41-N	11-E
" "	**32**	1	4th PM - 1831 MN/WI	40-N	10-E
DOCKERAY	**32**	3	4th PM - 1831 MN/WI	40-N	10-E
DOCKEREY	**34**	2	4th PM - 1831 MN/WI	39-N	10-E
DONOHUE	**9**	3	4th PM - 1831 MN/WI	43-N	10-E
" "	**16**	2	4th PM - 1831 MN/WI	42-N	11-E
DOOLITTLE	**19**	1	4th PM - 1831 MN/WI	41-N	6-E
" "	**20**	1	4th PM - 1831 MN/WI	41-N	7-E
DORE	**32**	3	4th PM - 1831 MN/WI	40-N	10-E
DORIOT	**10**	3	4th PM - 1831 MN/WI	42-N	5-E
" "	**11**	3	4th PM - 1831 MN/WI	42-N	6-E
DOW	**4**	2	4th PM - 1831 MN/WI	43-N	5-E
" "	**16**	1	4th PM - 1831 MN/WI	42-N	11-E
DOYLE	**14**	12	4th PM - 1831 MN/WI	42-N	9-E
" "	**22**	6	4th PM - 1831 MN/WI	41-N	9-E
" "	**11**	2	4th PM - 1831 MN/WI	42-N	6-E
" "	**28**	1	4th PM - 1831 MN/WI	40-N	6-E
" "	**23**	1	4th PM - 1831 MN/WI	41-N	10-E
" "	**19**	1	4th PM - 1831 MN/WI	41-N	6-E
DRAPER	**16**	4	4th PM - 1831 MN/WI	42-N	11-E
DRAVES	**29**	1	4th PM - 1831 MN/WI	40-N	7-E
DREGER	**32**	2	4th PM - 1831 MN/WI	40-N	10-E
DRINKER	**21**	13	4th PM - 1831 MN/WI	41-N	8-E
" "	**20**	5	4th PM - 1831 MN/WI	41-N	7-E
DUNBAR	**31**	8	4th PM - 1831 MN/WI	40-N	9-E
" "	**16**	5	4th PM - 1831 MN/WI	42-N	11-E
" "	**15**	2	4th PM - 1831 MN/WI	42-N	10-E
" "	**23**	1	4th PM - 1831 MN/WI	41-N	10-E
DUNFIELD	**22**	13	4th PM - 1831 MN/WI	41-N	9-E

Surname	Map Group	Parcels of Land	Meridian/Township/Range
DUNFIELD (Cont'd)	**14**	2	4th PM - 1831 MN/WI 42-N 9-E
" "	**32**	1	4th PM - 1831 MN/WI 40-N 10-E
" "	**12**	1	4th PM - 1831 MN/WI 42-N 7-E
DUSOLD	**1**	3	4th PM - 1831 MN/WI 44-N 5-E
DUSSAULT	**15**	1	4th PM - 1831 MN/WI 42-N 10-E
DUTCHER	**34**	3	4th PM - 1831 MN/WI 39-N 10-E
DWIGHT	**12**	41	4th PM - 1831 MN/WI 42-N 7-E
" "	**11**	16	4th PM - 1831 MN/WI 42-N 6-E
" "	**10**	12	4th PM - 1831 MN/WI 42-N 5-E
" "	**6**	12	4th PM - 1831 MN/WI 43-N 7-E
" "	**20**	11	4th PM - 1831 MN/WI 41-N 7-E
" "	**19**	10	4th PM - 1831 MN/WI 41-N 6-E
" "	**21**	1	4th PM - 1831 MN/WI 41-N 8-E
EARLY	**12**	26	4th PM - 1831 MN/WI 42-N 7-E
" "	**19**	6	4th PM - 1831 MN/WI 41-N 6-E
" "	**11**	2	4th PM - 1831 MN/WI 42-N 6-E
" "	**20**	1	4th PM - 1831 MN/WI 41-N 7-E
EBY	**29**	1	4th PM - 1831 MN/WI 40-N 7-E
EDWARDS	**16**	4	4th PM - 1831 MN/WI 42-N 11-E
" "	**15**	1	4th PM - 1831 MN/WI 42-N 10-E
ELDRIDGE	**34**	1	4th PM - 1831 MN/WI 39-N 10-E
ELIASON	**30**	2	4th PM - 1831 MN/WI 40-N 8-E
ELLIOTT	**32**	1	4th PM - 1831 MN/WI 40-N 10-E
ELLIS	**28**	4	4th PM - 1831 MN/WI 40-N 6-E
ELSEN	**11**	1	4th PM - 1831 MN/WI 42-N 6-E
EMERY	**11**	19	4th PM - 1831 MN/WI 42-N 6-E
ENO	**28**	1	4th PM - 1831 MN/WI 40-N 6-E
ERICKSON	**16**	1	4th PM - 1831 MN/WI 42-N 11-E
ERVIN	**34**	2	4th PM - 1831 MN/WI 39-N 10-E
EVANS	**29**	2	4th PM - 1831 MN/WI 40-N 7-E
" "	**24**	1	4th PM - 1831 MN/WI 41-N 11-E
EWALD	**32**	2	4th PM - 1831 MN/WI 40-N 10-E
EXTINE	**21**	1	4th PM - 1831 MN/WI 41-N 8-E
FABIAN	**32**	1	4th PM - 1831 MN/WI 40-N 10-E
FARNHAM	**9**	5	4th PM - 1831 MN/WI 43-N 10-E
" "	**8**	2	4th PM - 1831 MN/WI 43-N 9-E
FARWELL	**14**	10	4th PM - 1831 MN/WI 42-N 9-E
" "	**13**	8	4th PM - 1831 MN/WI 42-N 8-E
FAY	**25**	2	4th PM - 1831 MN/WI 41-N 12-E
" "	**17**	1	4th PM - 1831 MN/WI 42-N 12-E
FELTON	**34**	2	4th PM - 1831 MN/WI 39-N 10-E
" "	**30**	2	4th PM - 1831 MN/WI 40-N 8-E
FETT	**34**	3	4th PM - 1831 MN/WI 39-N 10-E
FISH	**16**	4	4th PM - 1831 MN/WI 42-N 11-E
FISK	**10**	1	4th PM - 1831 MN/WI 42-N 5-E
FITCH	**22**	1	4th PM - 1831 MN/WI 41-N 9-E
FITZGERALD	**15**	3	4th PM - 1831 MN/WI 42-N 10-E
FLYNN	**21**	1	4th PM - 1831 MN/WI 41-N 8-E
FOELKNER	**28**	1	4th PM - 1831 MN/WI 40-N 6-E
FORBES	**14**	19	4th PM - 1831 MN/WI 42-N 9-E
" "	**22**	13	4th PM - 1831 MN/WI 41-N 9-E
" "	**23**	7	4th PM - 1831 MN/WI 41-N 10-E
FORD	**10**	1	4th PM - 1831 MN/WI 42-N 5-E
FOREST	**8**	2	4th PM - 1831 MN/WI 43-N 9-E
FORSMAN	**12**	26	4th PM - 1831 MN/WI 42-N 7-E
" "	**19**	6	4th PM - 1831 MN/WI 41-N 6-E
" "	**11**	2	4th PM - 1831 MN/WI 42-N 6-E
" "	**20**	1	4th PM - 1831 MN/WI 41-N 7-E
FORSYTH	**33**	1	4th PM - 1831 MN/WI 40-N 11-E
FOSTER	**32**	3	4th PM - 1831 MN/WI 40-N 10-E

Surname	Map Group	Parcels of Land	Meridian/Township/Range
FOSTER (Cont'd)	**24**	2	4th PM - 1831 MN/WI 41-N 11-E
" "	**14**	1	4th PM - 1831 MN/WI 42-N 9-E
FOURNIER	**5**	1	4th PM - 1831 MN/WI 43-N 6-E
FOX	**10**	1	4th PM - 1831 MN/WI 42-N 5-E
FRANK	**16**	4	4th PM - 1831 MN/WI 42-N 11-E
" "	**8**	3	4th PM - 1831 MN/WI 43-N 9-E
" "	**32**	1	4th PM - 1831 MN/WI 40-N 10-E
FRANKFURTH	**5**	12	4th PM - 1831 MN/WI 43-N 6-E
FREEMAN	**23**	4	4th PM - 1831 MN/WI 41-N 10-E
" "	**15**	1	4th PM - 1831 MN/WI 42-N 10-E
FRENCH	**1**	32	4th PM - 1831 MN/WI 44-N 5-E
" "	**4**	27	4th PM - 1831 MN/WI 43-N 5-E
" "	**8**	10	4th PM - 1831 MN/WI 43-N 9-E
" "	**7**	9	4th PM - 1831 MN/WI 43-N 8-E
FRIEND	**10**	6	4th PM - 1831 MN/WI 42-N 5-E
" "	**11**	5	4th PM - 1831 MN/WI 42-N 6-E
" "	**4**	2	4th PM - 1831 MN/WI 43-N 5-E
" "	**5**	2	4th PM - 1831 MN/WI 43-N 6-E
" "	**6**	2	4th PM - 1831 MN/WI 43-N 7-E
FRITZ	**11**	1	4th PM - 1831 MN/WI 42-N 6-E
FROEHLICH	**30**	2	4th PM - 1831 MN/WI 40-N 8-E
FROST	**8**	3	4th PM - 1831 MN/WI 43-N 9-E
FULLER	**32**	5	4th PM - 1831 MN/WI 40-N 10-E
GABRIELSON	**33**	1	4th PM - 1831 MN/WI 40-N 11-E
GAEBLER	**8**	1	4th PM - 1831 MN/WI 43-N 9-E
GAFFNEY	**30**	1	4th PM - 1831 MN/WI 40-N 8-E
" "	**9**	1	4th PM - 1831 MN/WI 43-N 10-E
GALLAGHER	**29**	2	4th PM - 1831 MN/WI 40-N 7-E
" "	**30**	1	4th PM - 1831 MN/WI 40-N 8-E
GARRETT	**11**	3	4th PM - 1831 MN/WI 42-N 6-E
GATES	**1**	42	4th PM - 1831 MN/WI 44-N 5-E
" "	**4**	31	4th PM - 1831 MN/WI 43-N 5-E
" "	**5**	7	4th PM - 1831 MN/WI 43-N 6-E
" "	**6**	6	4th PM - 1831 MN/WI 43-N 7-E
GEBHART	**28**	2	4th PM - 1831 MN/WI 40-N 6-E
GELEFT	**29**	2	4th PM - 1831 MN/WI 40-N 7-E
GILBERT	**5**	4	4th PM - 1831 MN/WI 43-N 6-E
" "	**34**	1	4th PM - 1831 MN/WI 39-N 10-E
" "	**20**	1	4th PM - 1831 MN/WI 41-N 7-E
GILBERTSON	**33**	1	4th PM - 1831 MN/WI 40-N 11-E
GILE	**32**	1	4th PM - 1831 MN/WI 40-N 10-E
GILKEY	**25**	5	4th PM - 1831 MN/WI 41-N 12-E
" "	**31**	1	4th PM - 1831 MN/WI 40-N 9-E
" "	**16**	1	4th PM - 1831 MN/WI 42-N 11-E
GILLET	**30**	13	4th PM - 1831 MN/WI 40-N 8-E
" "	**21**	6	4th PM - 1831 MN/WI 41-N 8-E
GILLETT	**31**	1	4th PM - 1831 MN/WI 40-N 9-E
" "	**23**	1	4th PM - 1831 MN/WI 41-N 10-E
" "	**15**	1	4th PM - 1831 MN/WI 42-N 10-E
GILMORE	**8**	1	4th PM - 1831 MN/WI 43-N 9-E
GLEASON	**28**	2	4th PM - 1831 MN/WI 40-N 6-E
" "	**19**	1	4th PM - 1831 MN/WI 41-N 6-E
GOERLING	**30**	1	4th PM - 1831 MN/WI 40-N 8-E
GOODENOW	**32**	3	4th PM - 1831 MN/WI 40-N 10-E
GOODRICH	**16**	2	4th PM - 1831 MN/WI 42-N 11-E
GOODSPEED	**21**	1	4th PM - 1831 MN/WI 41-N 8-E
GOODWILL	**15**	2	4th PM - 1831 MN/WI 42-N 10-E
GORMAN	**29**	9	4th PM - 1831 MN/WI 40-N 7-E
GOULD	**12**	12	4th PM - 1831 MN/WI 42-N 7-E
" "	**24**	9	4th PM - 1831 MN/WI 41-N 11-E

Surname	Map Group	Parcels of Land	Meridian/Township/Range		
GOULD (Cont'd)	**31**	4	4th PM - 1831 MN/WI	40-N	9-E
" "	**13**	4	4th PM - 1831 MN/WI	42-N	8-E
" "	**32**	1	4th PM - 1831 MN/WI	40-N	10-E
" "	**30**	1	4th PM - 1831 MN/WI	40-N	8-E
GRAHAM	**30**	5	4th PM - 1831 MN/WI	40-N	8-E
" "	**33**	2	4th PM - 1831 MN/WI	40-N	11-E
" "	**31**	2	4th PM - 1831 MN/WI	40-N	9-E
GRAY	**7**	4	4th PM - 1831 MN/WI	43-N	8-E
GRAYSON	**20**	1	4th PM - 1831 MN/WI	41-N	7-E
GRIFFITH	**22**	1	4th PM - 1831 MN/WI	41-N	9-E
GRISWOLD	**13**	3	4th PM - 1831 MN/WI	42-N	8-E
" "	**14**	1	4th PM - 1831 MN/WI	42-N	9-E
GROSS	**1**	1	4th PM - 1831 MN/WI	44-N	5-E
GROUNDWATER	**30**	3	4th PM - 1831 MN/WI	40-N	8-E
GROVER	**32**	7	4th PM - 1831 MN/WI	40-N	10-E
GUSE	**15**	3	4th PM - 1831 MN/WI	42-N	10-E
GUSTAFSON	**29**	2	4th PM - 1831 MN/WI	40-N	7-E
HAGERMAN	**25**	32	4th PM - 1831 MN/WI	41-N	12-E
" "	**17**	32	4th PM - 1831 MN/WI	42-N	12-E
HAGSTROM	**15**	2	4th PM - 1831 MN/WI	42-N	10-E
HAIGHT	**11**	18	4th PM - 1831 MN/WI	42-N	6-E
" "	**10**	4	4th PM - 1831 MN/WI	42-N	5-E
" "	**28**	3	4th PM - 1831 MN/WI	40-N	6-E
" "	**19**	2	4th PM - 1831 MN/WI	41-N	6-E
" "	**5**	2	4th PM - 1831 MN/WI	43-N	6-E
" "	**12**	1	4th PM - 1831 MN/WI	42-N	7-E
" "	**4**	1	4th PM - 1831 MN/WI	43-N	5-E
" "	**6**	1	4th PM - 1831 MN/WI	43-N	7-E
" "	**7**	1	4th PM - 1831 MN/WI	43-N	8-E
" "	**8**	1	4th PM - 1831 MN/WI	43-N	9-E
HALL	**14**	28	4th PM - 1831 MN/WI	42-N	9-E
" "	**13**	19	4th PM - 1831 MN/WI	42-N	8-E
" "	**15**	6	4th PM - 1831 MN/WI	42-N	10-E
" "	**9**	5	4th PM - 1831 MN/WI	43-N	10-E
" "	**8**	4	4th PM - 1831 MN/WI	43-N	9-E
" "	**7**	3	4th PM - 1831 MN/WI	43-N	8-E
" "	**16**	1	4th PM - 1831 MN/WI	42-N	11-E
HALLINAN	**5**	1	4th PM - 1831 MN/WI	43-N	6-E
HALMINIAK	**16**	1	4th PM - 1831 MN/WI	42-N	11-E
HAMILTON	**29**	13	4th PM - 1831 MN/WI	40-N	7-E
" "	**30**	12	4th PM - 1831 MN/WI	40-N	8-E
" "	**23**	9	4th PM - 1831 MN/WI	41-N	10-E
" "	**8**	8	4th PM - 1831 MN/WI	43-N	9-E
" "	**31**	7	4th PM - 1831 MN/WI	40-N	9-E
" "	**32**	6	4th PM - 1831 MN/WI	40-N	10-E
" "	**14**	6	4th PM - 1831 MN/WI	42-N	9-E
" "	**24**	4	4th PM - 1831 MN/WI	41-N	11-E
" "	**33**	3	4th PM - 1831 MN/WI	40-N	11-E
" "	**17**	3	4th PM - 1831 MN/WI	42-N	12-E
" "	**21**	2	4th PM - 1831 MN/WI	41-N	8-E
" "	**34**	1	4th PM - 1831 MN/WI	39-N	10-E
" "	**25**	1	4th PM - 1831 MN/WI	41-N	12-E
" "	**20**	1	4th PM - 1831 MN/WI	41-N	7-E
HANSON	**13**	1	4th PM - 1831 MN/WI	42-N	8-E
HARPER	**22**	6	4th PM - 1831 MN/WI	41-N	9-E
" "	**14**	6	4th PM - 1831 MN/WI	42-N	9-E
" "	**8**	2	4th PM - 1831 MN/WI	43-N	9-E
HARRIGAN	**10**	13	4th PM - 1831 MN/WI	42-N	5-E
" "	**11**	1	4th PM - 1831 MN/WI	42-N	6-E
HARRINGTON	**15**	6	4th PM - 1831 MN/WI	42-N	10-E

Surname	Map Group	Parcels of Land	Meridian/Township/Range
HARRINGTON (Cont'd)	**24**	2	4th PM - 1831 MN/WI 41-N 11-E
" "	**22**	2	4th PM - 1831 MN/WI 41-N 9-E
" "	**16**	2	4th PM - 1831 MN/WI 42-N 11-E
" "	**13**	2	4th PM - 1831 MN/WI 42-N 8-E
" "	**14**	2	4th PM - 1831 MN/WI 42-N 9-E
" "	**23**	1	4th PM - 1831 MN/WI 41-N 10-E
HARTMAN	**20**	1	4th PM - 1831 MN/WI 41-N 7-E
HASELTINE	**14**	1	4th PM - 1831 MN/WI 42-N 9-E
HASTINGS	**16**	1	4th PM - 1831 MN/WI 42-N 11-E
HAUPTMAN	**29**	4	4th PM - 1831 MN/WI 40-N 7-E
HAYNNE	**25**	1	4th PM - 1831 MN/WI 41-N 12-E
HAYWARD	**15**	1	4th PM - 1831 MN/WI 42-N 10-E
HEADFLYER	**11**	4	4th PM - 1831 MN/WI 42-N 6-E
HEATHER	**11**	3	4th PM - 1831 MN/WI 42-N 6-E
HEAZLIT	**31**	20	4th PM - 1831 MN/WI 40-N 9-E
HEIMER	**10**	1	4th PM - 1831 MN/WI 42-N 5-E
HEINEMANN	**28**	5	4th PM - 1831 MN/WI 40-N 6-E
" "	**29**	2	4th PM - 1831 MN/WI 40-N 7-E
" "	**15**	1	4th PM - 1831 MN/WI 42-N 10-E
HEISMAN	**6**	2	4th PM - 1831 MN/WI 43-N 7-E
" "	**12**	1	4th PM - 1831 MN/WI 42-N 7-E
HENDRY	**5**	1	4th PM - 1831 MN/WI 43-N 6-E
HERMANSON	**29**	1	4th PM - 1831 MN/WI 40-N 7-E
HEURICH	**4**	17	4th PM - 1831 MN/WI 43-N 5-E
HICKS	**6**	106	4th PM - 1831 MN/WI 43-N 7-E
HIGGINS	**25**	1	4th PM - 1831 MN/WI 41-N 12-E
HILLIS	**19**	2	4th PM - 1831 MN/WI 41-N 6-E
HIRZEL	**32**	1	4th PM - 1831 MN/WI 40-N 10-E
" "	**33**	1	4th PM - 1831 MN/WI 40-N 11-E
HIZEL	**33**	1	4th PM - 1831 MN/WI 40-N 11-E
HJELMSTAD	**29**	1	4th PM - 1831 MN/WI 40-N 7-E
HOBART	**14**	3	4th PM - 1831 MN/WI 42-N 9-E
" "	**15**	1	4th PM - 1831 MN/WI 42-N 10-E
HOGUE	**12**	1	4th PM - 1831 MN/WI 42-N 7-E
HOLDEN	**12**	6	4th PM - 1831 MN/WI 42-N 7-E
HOLDSHIP	**28**	2	4th PM - 1831 MN/WI 40-N 6-E
HOLLINDER	**30**	1	4th PM - 1831 MN/WI 40-N 8-E
HOLLISTER	**8**	4	4th PM - 1831 MN/WI 43-N 9-E
" "	**33**	1	4th PM - 1831 MN/WI 40-N 11-E
" "	**24**	1	4th PM - 1831 MN/WI 41-N 11-E
HOLWAY	**28**	5	4th PM - 1831 MN/WI 40-N 6-E
HOWE	**32**	14	4th PM - 1831 MN/WI 40-N 10-E
" "	**34**	1	4th PM - 1831 MN/WI 39-N 10-E
" "	**33**	1	4th PM - 1831 MN/WI 40-N 11-E
HOWES	**24**	6	4th PM - 1831 MN/WI 41-N 11-E
HOWLETT	**22**	3	4th PM - 1831 MN/WI 41-N 9-E
" "	**15**	3	4th PM - 1831 MN/WI 42-N 10-E
HOXIE	**21**	3	4th PM - 1831 MN/WI 41-N 8-E
" "	**13**	2	4th PM - 1831 MN/WI 42-N 8-E
HUGHES	**15**	1	4th PM - 1831 MN/WI 42-N 10-E
HUNTER	**30**	3	4th PM - 1831 MN/WI 40-N 8-E
" "	**34**	1	4th PM - 1831 MN/WI 39-N 10-E
HUTCHISON	**10**	1	4th PM - 1831 MN/WI 42-N 5-E
HYDE	**28**	1	4th PM - 1831 MN/WI 40-N 6-E
" "	**20**	1	4th PM - 1831 MN/WI 41-N 7-E
HYLAND	**20**	62	4th PM - 1831 MN/WI 41-N 7-E
" "	**13**	33	4th PM - 1831 MN/WI 42-N 8-E
" "	**21**	23	4th PM - 1831 MN/WI 41-N 8-E
" "	**12**	7	4th PM - 1831 MN/WI 42-N 7-E
" "	**19**	6	4th PM - 1831 MN/WI 41-N 6-E

Surname	Map Group	Parcels of Land	Meridian/Township/Range		
HYLAND (Cont'd)	**14**	5	4th PM - 1831 MN/WI	42-N	9-E
IDE	**28**	5	4th PM - 1831 MN/WI	40-N	6-E
INGERSOLL	**31**	1	4th PM - 1831 MN/WI	40-N	9-E
INGRAHAM	**19**	2	4th PM - 1831 MN/WI	41-N	6-E
" "	**4**	2	4th PM - 1831 MN/WI	43-N	5-E
" "	**20**	1	4th PM - 1831 MN/WI	41-N	7-E
" "	**10**	1	4th PM - 1831 MN/WI	42-N	5-E
IRVIN	**12**	6	4th PM - 1831 MN/WI	42-N	7-E
IRWIN	**28**	5	4th PM - 1831 MN/WI	40-N	6-E
" "	**29**	3	4th PM - 1831 MN/WI	40-N	7-E
JACKSON	**12**	10	4th PM - 1831 MN/WI	42-N	7-E
" "	**10**	6	4th PM - 1831 MN/WI	42-N	5-E
" "	**13**	4	4th PM - 1831 MN/WI	42-N	8-E
" "	**11**	2	4th PM - 1831 MN/WI	42-N	6-E
" "	**6**	1	4th PM - 1831 MN/WI	43-N	7-E
" "	**7**	1	4th PM - 1831 MN/WI	43-N	8-E
JACOBS	**32**	1	4th PM - 1831 MN/WI	40-N	10-E
JADISCHKE	**32**	3	4th PM - 1831 MN/WI	40-N	10-E
JAHN	**5**	1	4th PM - 1831 MN/WI	43-N	6-E
JARCHOW	**11**	1	4th PM - 1831 MN/WI	42-N	6-E
JENNINGS	**25**	5	4th PM - 1831 MN/WI	41-N	12-E
JOHNSON	**19**	10	4th PM - 1831 MN/WI	41-N	6-E
" "	**11**	6	4th PM - 1831 MN/WI	42-N	6-E
" "	**34**	1	4th PM - 1831 MN/WI	39-N	10-E
" "	**32**	1	4th PM - 1831 MN/WI	40-N	10-E
" "	**28**	1	4th PM - 1831 MN/WI	40-N	6-E
" "	**5**	1	4th PM - 1831 MN/WI	43-N	6-E
JOHNSTON	**15**	3	4th PM - 1831 MN/WI	42-N	10-E
JONES	**32**	10	4th PM - 1831 MN/WI	40-N	10-E
" "	**34**	5	4th PM - 1831 MN/WI	39-N	10-E
" "	**33**	4	4th PM - 1831 MN/WI	40-N	11-E
" "	**22**	2	4th PM - 1831 MN/WI	41-N	9-E
" "	**12**	2	4th PM - 1831 MN/WI	42-N	7-E
" "	**19**	1	4th PM - 1831 MN/WI	41-N	6-E
" "	**20**	1	4th PM - 1831 MN/WI	41-N	7-E
" "	**8**	1	4th PM - 1831 MN/WI	43-N	9-E
KAHN	**4**	1	4th PM - 1831 MN/WI	43-N	5-E
KAISER	**23**	3	4th PM - 1831 MN/WI	41-N	10-E
KAO	**29**	3	4th PM - 1831 MN/WI	40-N	7-E
KARGER	**31**	2	4th PM - 1831 MN/WI	40-N	9-E
KAYZER	**11**	1	4th PM - 1831 MN/WI	42-N	6-E
KEESLER	**16**	1	4th PM - 1831 MN/WI	42-N	11-E
KELLY	**30**	8	4th PM - 1831 MN/WI	40-N	8-E
" "	**29**	6	4th PM - 1831 MN/WI	40-N	7-E
" "	**20**	6	4th PM - 1831 MN/WI	41-N	7-E
KENEDY	**11**	1	4th PM - 1831 MN/WI	42-N	6-E
KENNAN	**20**	1	4th PM - 1831 MN/WI	41-N	7-E
KIKENDALL	**5**	5	4th PM - 1831 MN/WI	43-N	6-E
" "	**6**	2	4th PM - 1831 MN/WI	43-N	7-E
" "	**7**	1	4th PM - 1831 MN/WI	43-N	8-E
KILROE	**11**	2	4th PM - 1831 MN/WI	42-N	6-E
KING	**29**	27	4th PM - 1831 MN/WI	40-N	7-E
" "	**30**	23	4th PM - 1831 MN/WI	40-N	8-E
KINNEY	**32**	6	4th PM - 1831 MN/WI	40-N	10-E
KISSINGER	**4**	9	4th PM - 1831 MN/WI	43-N	5-E
KNAPP	**30**	9	4th PM - 1831 MN/WI	40-N	8-E
" "	**29**	2	4th PM - 1831 MN/WI	40-N	7-E
KNOX	**32**	4	4th PM - 1831 MN/WI	40-N	10-E
KOHL	**15**	3	4th PM - 1831 MN/WI	42-N	10-E
" "	**31**	1	4th PM - 1831 MN/WI	40-N	9-E

Surname	Map Group	Parcels of Land	Meridian/Township/Range		
KOHL (Cont'd)	**22**	1	4th PM - 1831 MN/WI	41-N	9-E
KRAMER	**34**	3	4th PM - 1831 MN/WI	39-N	10-E
KREITE	**4**	2	4th PM - 1831 MN/WI	43-N	5-E
KREITZER	**24**	1	4th PM - 1831 MN/WI	41-N	11-E
KUENZLI	**32**	1	4th PM - 1831 MN/WI	40-N	10-E
KULANDA	**5**	1	4th PM - 1831 MN/WI	43-N	6-E
LA CROSSE	**28**	2	4th PM - 1831 MN/WI	40-N	6-E
LABBE	**11**	1	4th PM - 1831 MN/WI	42-N	6-E
LACAU	**33**	2	4th PM - 1831 MN/WI	40-N	11-E
LAEV	**24**	9	4th PM - 1831 MN/WI	41-N	11-E
" "	**25**	3	4th PM - 1831 MN/WI	41-N	12-E
" "	**33**	1	4th PM - 1831 MN/WI	40-N	11-E
LAFONTAISIE	**20**	1	4th PM - 1831 MN/WI	41-N	7-E
LAIRD	**13**	72	4th PM - 1831 MN/WI	42-N	8-E
" "	**7**	27	4th PM - 1831 MN/WI	43-N	8-E
" "	**12**	9	4th PM - 1831 MN/WI	42-N	7-E
" "	**10**	4	4th PM - 1831 MN/WI	42-N	5-E
" "	**14**	3	4th PM - 1831 MN/WI	42-N	9-E
LAMBORN	**22**	1	4th PM - 1831 MN/WI	41-N	9-E
LAMOTTE	**10**	6	4th PM - 1831 MN/WI	42-N	5-E
LAMOUREUX	**28**	1	4th PM - 1831 MN/WI	40-N	6-E
LANDERS	**31**	1	4th PM - 1831 MN/WI	40-N	9-E
LANE	**7**	1	4th PM - 1831 MN/WI	43-N	8-E
LANGILL	**24**	8	4th PM - 1831 MN/WI	41-N	11-E
" "	**15**	3	4th PM - 1831 MN/WI	42-N	10-E
LARRABEE	**11**	4	4th PM - 1831 MN/WI	42-N	6-E
" "	**10**	1	4th PM - 1831 MN/WI	42-N	5-E
LARZELERE	**8**	2	4th PM - 1831 MN/WI	43-N	9-E
LAWLER	**22**	3	4th PM - 1831 MN/WI	41-N	9-E
" "	**16**	2	4th PM - 1831 MN/WI	42-N	11-E
" "	**32**	1	4th PM - 1831 MN/WI	40-N	10-E
" "	**31**	1	4th PM - 1831 MN/WI	40-N	9-E
LEAVERTON	**12**	1	4th PM - 1831 MN/WI	42-N	7-E
LEDURSE	**12**	1	4th PM - 1831 MN/WI	42-N	7-E
LEE	**21**	1	4th PM - 1831 MN/WI	41-N	8-E
LENTZ	**12**	26	4th PM - 1831 MN/WI	42-N	7-E
" "	**19**	6	4th PM - 1831 MN/WI	41-N	6-E
" "	**11**	2	4th PM - 1831 MN/WI	42-N	6-E
" "	**20**	1	4th PM - 1831 MN/WI	41-N	7-E
LEONE	**12**	1	4th PM - 1831 MN/WI	42-N	7-E
LEVINGSTON	**20**	3	4th PM - 1831 MN/WI	41-N	7-E
LEWIS	**32**	2	4th PM - 1831 MN/WI	40-N	10-E
" "	**4**	1	4th PM - 1831 MN/WI	43-N	5-E
LIBBEY	**15**	2	4th PM - 1831 MN/WI	42-N	10-E
" "	**14**	2	4th PM - 1831 MN/WI	42-N	9-E
LILJEQVEST	**29**	2	4th PM - 1831 MN/WI	40-N	7-E
LINDSAY	**8**	14	4th PM - 1831 MN/WI	43-N	9-E
LINDSTEDT	**5**	1	4th PM - 1831 MN/WI	43-N	6-E
LOGG	**32**	3	4th PM - 1831 MN/WI	40-N	10-E
LOMBARD	**28**	4	4th PM - 1831 MN/WI	40-N	6-E
LONG	**28**	4	4th PM - 1831 MN/WI	40-N	6-E
LOOMIS	**23**	1	4th PM - 1831 MN/WI	41-N	10-E
LOUGHRIN	**19**	2	4th PM - 1831 MN/WI	41-N	6-E
LOVEJOY	**22**	22	4th PM - 1831 MN/WI	41-N	9-E
" "	**15**	16	4th PM - 1831 MN/WI	42-N	10-E
" "	**24**	14	4th PM - 1831 MN/WI	41-N	11-E
" "	**21**	14	4th PM - 1831 MN/WI	41-N	8-E
" "	**23**	11	4th PM - 1831 MN/WI	41-N	10-E
" "	**14**	7	4th PM - 1831 MN/WI	42-N	9-E
" "	**16**	6	4th PM - 1831 MN/WI	42-N	11-E

Surname	Map Group	Parcels of Land	Meridian/Township/Range		
LOVEJOY (Cont'd)	**9**	6	4th PM - 1831 MN/WI	43-N	10-E
" "	**33**	4	4th PM - 1831 MN/WI	40-N	11-E
" "	**29**	4	4th PM - 1831 MN/WI	40-N	7-E
" "	**28**	3	4th PM - 1831 MN/WI	40-N	6-E
" "	**13**	3	4th PM - 1831 MN/WI	42-N	8-E
" "	**32**	2	4th PM - 1831 MN/WI	40-N	10-E
" "	**31**	2	4th PM - 1831 MN/WI	40-N	9-E
" "	**25**	2	4th PM - 1831 MN/WI	41-N	12-E
" "	**8**	2	4th PM - 1831 MN/WI	43-N	9-E
LOVELESS	**20**	2	4th PM - 1831 MN/WI	41-N	7-E
" "	**10**	2	4th PM - 1831 MN/WI	42-N	5-E
LUCK	**22**	1	4th PM - 1831 MN/WI	41-N	9-E
LUETZER	**23**	3	4th PM - 1831 MN/WI	41-N	10-E
LUHN	**30**	1	4th PM - 1831 MN/WI	40-N	8-E
MACK	**16**	3	4th PM - 1831 MN/WI	42-N	11-E
MAGEE	**32**	1	4th PM - 1831 MN/WI	40-N	10-E
MALCOLM	**14**	1	4th PM - 1831 MN/WI	42-N	9-E
MANSON	**20**	1	4th PM - 1831 MN/WI	41-N	7-E
MANUEL	**24**	3	4th PM - 1831 MN/WI	41-N	11-E
MARCON	**32**	1	4th PM - 1831 MN/WI	40-N	10-E
MARKEE	**28**	3	4th PM - 1831 MN/WI	40-N	6-E
MARKHAM	**16**	4	4th PM - 1831 MN/WI	42-N	11-E
MARSHALL	**12**	1	4th PM - 1831 MN/WI	42-N	7-E
MARTEN	**22**	2	4th PM - 1831 MN/WI	41-N	9-E
MARVIN	**10**	4	4th PM - 1831 MN/WI	42-N	5-E
MASCHAUER	**5**	12	4th PM - 1831 MN/WI	43-N	6-E
MASHINO	**5**	1	4th PM - 1831 MN/WI	43-N	6-E
MATHER	**15**	1	4th PM - 1831 MN/WI	42-N	10-E
MATHEWS	**17**	2	4th PM - 1831 MN/WI	42-N	12-E
" "	**20**	1	4th PM - 1831 MN/WI	41-N	7-E
" "	**22**	1	4th PM - 1831 MN/WI	41-N	9-E
MATTKE	**28**	1	4th PM - 1831 MN/WI	40-N	6-E
MAXON	**4**	36	4th PM - 1831 MN/WI	43-N	5-E
" "	**5**	22	4th PM - 1831 MN/WI	43-N	6-E
" "	**1**	19	4th PM - 1831 MN/WI	44-N	5-E
MAYO	**32**	4	4th PM - 1831 MN/WI	40-N	10-E
" "	**15**	1	4th PM - 1831 MN/WI	42-N	10-E
" "	**13**	1	4th PM - 1831 MN/WI	42-N	8-E
MCARTHUR	**19**	1	4th PM - 1831 MN/WI	41-N	6-E
MCBAIN	**28**	4	4th PM - 1831 MN/WI	40-N	6-E
MCCALL	**19**	2	4th PM - 1831 MN/WI	41-N	6-E
MCCARTHY	**16**	2	4th PM - 1831 MN/WI	42-N	11-E
MCCLINTOCK	**5**	17	4th PM - 1831 MN/WI	43-N	6-E
MCCORD	**31**	12	4th PM - 1831 MN/WI	40-N	9-E
" "	**12**	1	4th PM - 1831 MN/WI	42-N	7-E
MCCORMICK	**11**	4	4th PM - 1831 MN/WI	42-N	6-E
MCCROSSEN	**21**	3	4th PM - 1831 MN/WI	41-N	8-E
MCCUAIG	**33**	1	4th PM - 1831 MN/WI	40-N	11-E
MCCULLOUGH	**25**	2	4th PM - 1831 MN/WI	41-N	12-E
MCDANIEL	**10**	1	4th PM - 1831 MN/WI	42-N	5-E
MCDONALD	**20**	2	4th PM - 1831 MN/WI	41-N	7-E
" "	**32**	1	4th PM - 1831 MN/WI	40-N	10-E
" "	**29**	1	4th PM - 1831 MN/WI	40-N	7-E
" "	**30**	1	4th PM - 1831 MN/WI	40-N	8-E
" "	**19**	1	4th PM - 1831 MN/WI	41-N	6-E
" "	**12**	1	4th PM - 1831 MN/WI	42-N	7-E
MCFARLAND	**12**	1	4th PM - 1831 MN/WI	42-N	7-E
MCGRAW	**12**	41	4th PM - 1831 MN/WI	42-N	7-E
" "	**11**	16	4th PM - 1831 MN/WI	42-N	6-E
" "	**10**	12	4th PM - 1831 MN/WI	42-N	5-E

Surname	Map Group	Parcels of Land	Meridian/Township/Range
MCGRAW (Cont'd)	**6**	12	4th PM - 1831 MN/WI 43-N 7-E
" "	**20**	11	4th PM - 1831 MN/WI 41-N 7-E
" "	**19**	10	4th PM - 1831 MN/WI 41-N 6-E
" "	**26**	2	4th PM - 1831 MN/WI 40-N 4-E
" "	**21**	1	4th PM - 1831 MN/WI 41-N 8-E
MCGREGOR	**30**	1	4th PM - 1831 MN/WI 40-N 8-E
MCGUIRE	**10**	1	4th PM - 1831 MN/WI 42-N 5-E
MCILREE	**28**	1	4th PM - 1831 MN/WI 40-N 6-E
MCKINNEY	**10**	3	4th PM - 1831 MN/WI 42-N 5-E
MCKNIGHT	**32**	1	4th PM - 1831 MN/WI 40-N 10-E
MCMILLEN	**8**	3	4th PM - 1831 MN/WI 43-N 9-E
MCPARTLIN	**14**	3	4th PM - 1831 MN/WI 42-N 9-E
MCSHERRY	**32**	1	4th PM - 1831 MN/WI 40-N 10-E
MEADE	**33**	6	4th PM - 1831 MN/WI 40-N 11-E
" "	**24**	5	4th PM - 1831 MN/WI 41-N 11-E
" "	**16**	4	4th PM - 1831 MN/WI 42-N 11-E
" "	**32**	1	4th PM - 1831 MN/WI 40-N 10-E
" "	**23**	1	4th PM - 1831 MN/WI 41-N 10-E
" "	**15**	1	4th PM - 1831 MN/WI 42-N 10-E
MEIHACK	**22**	3	4th PM - 1831 MN/WI 41-N 9-E
MEISNER	**12**	2	4th PM - 1831 MN/WI 42-N 7-E
MELANG	**28**	3	4th PM - 1831 MN/WI 40-N 6-E
MERCER	**22**	13	4th PM - 1831 MN/WI 41-N 9-E
" "	**21**	3	4th PM - 1831 MN/WI 41-N 8-E
" "	**28**	2	4th PM - 1831 MN/WI 40-N 6-E
" "	**14**	1	4th PM - 1831 MN/WI 42-N 9-E
MERRICK	**31**	1	4th PM - 1831 MN/WI 40-N 9-E
MERRILL	**8**	2	4th PM - 1831 MN/WI 43-N 9-E
MERRYMAN	**17**	3	4th PM - 1831 MN/WI 42-N 12-E
" "	**25**	1	4th PM - 1831 MN/WI 41-N 12-E
MILES	**21**	6	4th PM - 1831 MN/WI 41-N 8-E
" "	**11**	4	4th PM - 1831 MN/WI 42-N 6-E
" "	**20**	2	4th PM - 1831 MN/WI 41-N 7-E
" "	**10**	1	4th PM - 1831 MN/WI 42-N 5-E
MILLAR	**30**	1	4th PM - 1831 MN/WI 40-N 8-E
MILLARD	**21**	1	4th PM - 1831 MN/WI 41-N 8-E
MILLER	**20**	30	4th PM - 1831 MN/WI 41-N 7-E
" "	**16**	17	4th PM - 1831 MN/WI 42-N 11-E
" "	**29**	15	4th PM - 1831 MN/WI 40-N 7-E
" "	**21**	11	4th PM - 1831 MN/WI 41-N 8-E
" "	**24**	6	4th PM - 1831 MN/WI 41-N 11-E
" "	**4**	6	4th PM - 1831 MN/WI 43-N 5-E
" "	**32**	4	4th PM - 1831 MN/WI 40-N 10-E
" "	**19**	3	4th PM - 1831 MN/WI 41-N 6-E
" "	**1**	3	4th PM - 1831 MN/WI 44-N 5-E
" "	**15**	2	4th PM - 1831 MN/WI 42-N 10-E
" "	**31**	1	4th PM - 1831 MN/WI 40-N 9-E
" "	**22**	1	4th PM - 1831 MN/WI 41-N 9-E
" "	**10**	1	4th PM - 1831 MN/WI 42-N 5-E
" "	**11**	1	4th PM - 1831 MN/WI 42-N 6-E
" "	**7**	1	4th PM - 1831 MN/WI 43-N 8-E
MILLERD	**20**	1	4th PM - 1831 MN/WI 41-N 7-E
MILLS	**10**	1	4th PM - 1831 MN/WI 42-N 5-E
MINER	**4**	17	4th PM - 1831 MN/WI 43-N 5-E
" "	**7**	1	4th PM - 1831 MN/WI 43-N 8-E
MITCHELL	**7**	2	4th PM - 1831 MN/WI 43-N 8-E
MOFFAT	**5**	1	4th PM - 1831 MN/WI 43-N 6-E
MONTGOMERY	**28**	1	4th PM - 1831 MN/WI 40-N 6-E
MOON	**30**	1	4th PM - 1831 MN/WI 40-N 8-E
MOONEY	**30**	6	4th PM - 1831 MN/WI 40-N 8-E

Surname	Map Group	Parcels of Land	Meridian/Township/Range		
MOOR	**34**	2	4th PM - 1831 MN/WI	39-N	10-E
MOORE	**10**	1	4th PM - 1831 MN/WI	42-N	5-E
MORAN	**30**	3	4th PM - 1831 MN/WI	40-N	8-E
" "	**23**	1	4th PM - 1831 MN/WI	41-N	10-E
" "	**15**	1	4th PM - 1831 MN/WI	42-N	10-E
MOREY	**32**	3	4th PM - 1831 MN/WI	40-N	10-E
MORGAN	**1**	7	4th PM - 1831 MN/WI	44-N	5-E
" "	**32**	6	4th PM - 1831 MN/WI	40-N	10-E
MORIN	**32**	3	4th PM - 1831 MN/WI	40-N	10-E
MORRIS	**10**	1	4th PM - 1831 MN/WI	42-N	5-E
" "	**6**	1	4th PM - 1831 MN/WI	43-N	7-E
MORRISON	**22**	1	4th PM - 1831 MN/WI	41-N	9-E
MUCHLER	**22**	2	4th PM - 1831 MN/WI	41-N	9-E
MULHOLON	**1**	3	4th PM - 1831 MN/WI	44-N	5-E
MULVANE	**5**	1	4th PM - 1831 MN/WI	43-N	6-E
MURRAY	**29**	1	4th PM - 1831 MN/WI	40-N	7-E
" "	**31**	1	4th PM - 1831 MN/WI	40-N	9-E
" "	**24**	1	4th PM - 1831 MN/WI	41-N	11-E
MUTTER	**30**	1	4th PM - 1831 MN/WI	40-N	8-E
NAGEL	**24**	1	4th PM - 1831 MN/WI	41-N	11-E
NAST	**31**	2	4th PM - 1831 MN/WI	40-N	9-E
NELSON	**16**	2	4th PM - 1831 MN/WI	42-N	11-E
" "	**28**	1	4th PM - 1831 MN/WI	40-N	6-E
" "	**21**	1	4th PM - 1831 MN/WI	41-N	8-E
" "	**5**	1	4th PM - 1831 MN/WI	43-N	6-E
NEUMANN	**4**	2	4th PM - 1831 MN/WI	43-N	5-E
NEVILLE	**34**	2	4th PM - 1831 MN/WI	39-N	10-E
NEWCOMB	**8**	3	4th PM - 1831 MN/WI	43-N	9-E
NEWELL	**6**	1	4th PM - 1831 MN/WI	43-N	7-E
NEWMAN	**28**	7	4th PM - 1831 MN/WI	40-N	6-E
" "	**19**	2	4th PM - 1831 MN/WI	41-N	6-E
NIELSEN	**29**	9	4th PM - 1831 MN/WI	40-N	7-E
" "	**20**	1	4th PM - 1831 MN/WI	41-N	7-E
NOEL	**20**	1	4th PM - 1831 MN/WI	41-N	7-E
NORTON	**13**	72	4th PM - 1831 MN/WI	42-N	8-E
" "	**7**	27	4th PM - 1831 MN/WI	43-N	8-E
" "	**12**	9	4th PM - 1831 MN/WI	42-N	7-E
" "	**10**	4	4th PM - 1831 MN/WI	42-N	5-E
" "	**14**	3	4th PM - 1831 MN/WI	42-N	9-E
NORWAY	**34**	1	4th PM - 1831 MN/WI	39-N	10-E
OBERG	**16**	2	4th PM - 1831 MN/WI	42-N	11-E
OBERHOLTZER	**31**	1	4th PM - 1831 MN/WI	40-N	9-E
OBERMANN	**4**	4	4th PM - 1831 MN/WI	43-N	5-E
OBRAY	**28**	2	4th PM - 1831 MN/WI	40-N	6-E
OCONNOR	**29**	1	4th PM - 1831 MN/WI	40-N	7-E
" "	**11**	1	4th PM - 1831 MN/WI	42-N	6-E
OSTERBERG	**15**	1	4th PM - 1831 MN/WI	42-N	10-E
OTTEROL	**5**	3	4th PM - 1831 MN/WI	43-N	6-E
" "	**11**	1	4th PM - 1831 MN/WI	42-N	6-E
" "	**6**	1	4th PM - 1831 MN/WI	43-N	7-E
OTTO	**15**	3	4th PM - 1831 MN/WI	42-N	10-E
" "	**8**	1	4th PM - 1831 MN/WI	43-N	9-E
PAFF	**32**	1	4th PM - 1831 MN/WI	40-N	10-E
" "	**30**	1	4th PM - 1831 MN/WI	40-N	8-E
" "	**10**	1	4th PM - 1831 MN/WI	42-N	5-E
" "	**7**	1	4th PM - 1831 MN/WI	43-N	8-E
PALEN	**8**	2	4th PM - 1831 MN/WI	43-N	9-E
PALMS	**23**	8	4th PM - 1831 MN/WI	41-N	10-E
" "	**32**	7	4th PM - 1831 MN/WI	40-N	10-E
" "	**33**	4	4th PM - 1831 MN/WI	40-N	11-E

Surname	Map Group	Parcels of Land	Meridian/Township/Range		
PALMS (Cont'd)	**34**	3	4th PM - 1831 MN/WI	39-N	10-E
" "	**16**	2	4th PM - 1831 MN/WI	42-N	11-E
PAQUETTE	**28**	2	4th PM - 1831 MN/WI	40-N	6-E
" "	**29**	1	4th PM - 1831 MN/WI	40-N	7-E
PARSONS	**4**	9	4th PM - 1831 MN/WI	43-N	5-E
" "	**20**	4	4th PM - 1831 MN/WI	41-N	7-E
" "	**11**	4	4th PM - 1831 MN/WI	42-N	6-E
" "	**5**	4	4th PM - 1831 MN/WI	43-N	6-E
" "	**10**	2	4th PM - 1831 MN/WI	42-N	5-E
PATRICK	**31**	28	4th PM - 1831 MN/WI	40-N	9-E
" "	**30**	23	4th PM - 1831 MN/WI	40-N	8-E
" "	**12**	13	4th PM - 1831 MN/WI	42-N	7-E
" "	**19**	8	4th PM - 1831 MN/WI	41-N	6-E
" "	**22**	3	4th PM - 1831 MN/WI	41-N	9-E
" "	**21**	2	4th PM - 1831 MN/WI	41-N	8-E
" "	**20**	1	4th PM - 1831 MN/WI	41-N	7-E
" "	**13**	1	4th PM - 1831 MN/WI	42-N	8-E
PATTEN	**22**	10	4th PM - 1831 MN/WI	41-N	9-E
" "	**14**	5	4th PM - 1831 MN/WI	42-N	9-E
" "	**23**	2	4th PM - 1831 MN/WI	41-N	10-E
" "	**24**	2	4th PM - 1831 MN/WI	41-N	11-E
PAULSON	**13**	1	4th PM - 1831 MN/WI	42-N	8-E
PAULUS	**16**	1	4th PM - 1831 MN/WI	42-N	11-E
PECK	**6**	1	4th PM - 1831 MN/WI	43-N	7-E
PERCIVAL	**32**	1	4th PM - 1831 MN/WI	40-N	10-E
PERKINS	**10**	1	4th PM - 1831 MN/WI	42-N	5-E
PERRY	**32**	3	4th PM - 1831 MN/WI	40-N	10-E
PETERS	**20**	15	4th PM - 1831 MN/WI	41-N	7-E
" "	**21**	11	4th PM - 1831 MN/WI	41-N	8-E
" "	**31**	8	4th PM - 1831 MN/WI	40-N	9-E
PETERSON	**34**	1	4th PM - 1831 MN/WI	39-N	10-E
PETEY	**32**	4	4th PM - 1831 MN/WI	40-N	10-E
PHELPS	**34**	2	4th PM - 1831 MN/WI	39-N	10-E
" "	**24**	2	4th PM - 1831 MN/WI	41-N	11-E
" "	**32**	1	4th PM - 1831 MN/WI	40-N	10-E
" "	**33**	1	4th PM - 1831 MN/WI	40-N	11-E
PHILLIPS	**24**	5	4th PM - 1831 MN/WI	41-N	11-E
PIER	**1**	4	4th PM - 1831 MN/WI	44-N	5-E
PIERCE	**28**	2	4th PM - 1831 MN/WI	40-N	6-E
PILLSBURY	**20**	79	4th PM - 1831 MN/WI	41-N	7-E
" "	**19**	53	4th PM - 1831 MN/WI	41-N	6-E
" "	**29**	48	4th PM - 1831 MN/WI	40-N	7-E
" "	**21**	48	4th PM - 1831 MN/WI	41-N	8-E
" "	**28**	26	4th PM - 1831 MN/WI	40-N	6-E
" "	**15**	22	4th PM - 1831 MN/WI	42-N	10-E
" "	**11**	22	4th PM - 1831 MN/WI	42-N	6-E
" "	**22**	21	4th PM - 1831 MN/WI	41-N	9-E
" "	**6**	21	4th PM - 1831 MN/WI	43-N	7-E
" "	**30**	15	4th PM - 1831 MN/WI	40-N	8-E
" "	**10**	13	4th PM - 1831 MN/WI	42-N	5-E
" "	**12**	12	4th PM - 1831 MN/WI	42-N	7-E
" "	**13**	9	4th PM - 1831 MN/WI	42-N	8-E
" "	**8**	7	4th PM - 1831 MN/WI	43-N	9-E
" "	**7**	5	4th PM - 1831 MN/WI	43-N	8-E
" "	**14**	3	4th PM - 1831 MN/WI	42-N	9-E
" "	**9**	3	4th PM - 1831 MN/WI	43-N	10-E
" "	**5**	2	4th PM - 1831 MN/WI	43-N	6-E
" "	**31**	1	4th PM - 1831 MN/WI	40-N	9-E
" "	**23**	1	4th PM - 1831 MN/WI	41-N	10-E
" "	**4**	1	4th PM - 1831 MN/WI	43-N	5-E

Surname	Map Group	Parcels of Land	Meridian/Township/Range
PINKERTON	**22**	2	4th PM - 1831 MN/WI 41-N 9-E
PINTO	**16**	1	4th PM - 1831 MN/WI 42-N 11-E
POLAR	**31**	6	4th PM - 1831 MN/WI 40-N 9-E
" "	**23**	1	4th PM - 1831 MN/WI 41-N 10-E
POND	**5**	1	4th PM - 1831 MN/WI 43-N 6-E
POOR	**34**	3	4th PM - 1831 MN/WI 39-N 10-E
POPE	**22**	2	4th PM - 1831 MN/WI 41-N 9-E
PORTER	**8**	4	4th PM - 1831 MN/WI 43-N 9-E
" "	**26**	2	4th PM - 1831 MN/WI 40-N 4-E
PRESCOTT	**1**	4	4th PM - 1831 MN/WI 44-N 5-E
" "	**4**	2	4th PM - 1831 MN/WI 43-N 5-E
PRESTON	**14**	16	4th PM - 1831 MN/WI 42-N 9-E
" "	**22**	6	4th PM - 1831 MN/WI 41-N 9-E
" "	**16**	3	4th PM - 1831 MN/WI 42-N 11-E
" "	**8**	2	4th PM - 1831 MN/WI 43-N 9-E
PRICE	**8**	1	4th PM - 1831 MN/WI 43-N 9-E
PROCTOR	**15**	1	4th PM - 1831 MN/WI 42-N 10-E
PULLING	**33**	1	4th PM - 1831 MN/WI 40-N 11-E
" "	**25**	1	4th PM - 1831 MN/WI 41-N 12-E
PUNCHES	**32**	6	4th PM - 1831 MN/WI 40-N 10-E
PURCELL	**30**	1	4th PM - 1831 MN/WI 40-N 8-E
PURTELL	**5**	5	4th PM - 1831 MN/WI 43-N 6-E
" "	**6**	2	4th PM - 1831 MN/WI 43-N 7-E
" "	**11**	1	4th PM - 1831 MN/WI 42-N 6-E
PUTNAM	**12**	2	4th PM - 1831 MN/WI 42-N 7-E
" "	**26**	1	4th PM - 1831 MN/WI 40-N 4-E
QUAW	**21**	1	4th PM - 1831 MN/WI 41-N 8-E
RABLIN	**32**	14	4th PM - 1831 MN/WI 40-N 10-E
" "	**34**	1	4th PM - 1831 MN/WI 39-N 10-E
" "	**33**	1	4th PM - 1831 MN/WI 40-N 11-E
RACES	**31**	1	4th PM - 1831 MN/WI 40-N 9-E
RADCLIFFE	**24**	2	4th PM - 1831 MN/WI 41-N 11-E
REAY	**16**	1	4th PM - 1831 MN/WI 42-N 11-E
REED	**23**	1	4th PM - 1831 MN/WI 41-N 10-E
REEVE	**22**	2	4th PM - 1831 MN/WI 41-N 9-E
" "	**15**	2	4th PM - 1831 MN/WI 42-N 10-E
" "	**13**	2	4th PM - 1831 MN/WI 42-N 8-E
" "	**14**	2	4th PM - 1831 MN/WI 42-N 9-E
" "	**23**	1	4th PM - 1831 MN/WI 41-N 10-E
REGNER	**10**	1	4th PM - 1831 MN/WI 42-N 5-E
REHFELD	**10**	2	4th PM - 1831 MN/WI 42-N 5-E
" "	**12**	1	4th PM - 1831 MN/WI 42-N 7-E
REMMERT	**28**	5	4th PM - 1831 MN/WI 40-N 6-E
" "	**29**	3	4th PM - 1831 MN/WI 40-N 7-E
RETTLER	**32**	1	4th PM - 1831 MN/WI 40-N 10-E
REYNOLDS	**8**	1	4th PM - 1831 MN/WI 43-N 9-E
RHINELANDER	**15**	7	4th PM - 1831 MN/WI 42-N 10-E
RIBENACK	**16**	2	4th PM - 1831 MN/WI 42-N 11-E
RICHARDS	**28**	3	4th PM - 1831 MN/WI 40-N 6-E
RICHARDSON	**10**	1	4th PM - 1831 MN/WI 42-N 5-E
RICHMOND	**22**	2	4th PM - 1831 MN/WI 41-N 9-E
RILEY	**28**	1	4th PM - 1831 MN/WI 40-N 6-E
RINGLE	**11**	10	4th PM - 1831 MN/WI 42-N 6-E
RIPLEY	**10**	15	4th PM - 1831 MN/WI 42-N 5-E
" "	**5**	8	4th PM - 1831 MN/WI 43-N 6-E
" "	**29**	7	4th PM - 1831 MN/WI 40-N 7-E
" "	**33**	6	4th PM - 1831 MN/WI 40-N 11-E
" "	**11**	6	4th PM - 1831 MN/WI 42-N 6-E
" "	**28**	5	4th PM - 1831 MN/WI 40-N 6-E
" "	**24**	5	4th PM - 1831 MN/WI 41-N 11-E

Surname	Map Group	Parcels of Land	Meridian/Township/Range
RIPLEY (Cont'd)	**16**	4	4th PM - 1831 MN/WI 42-N 11-E
" "	**32**	1	4th PM - 1831 MN/WI 40-N 10-E
" "	**23**	1	4th PM - 1831 MN/WI 41-N 10-E
" "	**15**	1	4th PM - 1831 MN/WI 42-N 10-E
ROBERTS	**7**	2	4th PM - 1831 MN/WI 43-N 8-E
ROBISON	**21**	20	4th PM - 1831 MN/WI 41-N 8-E
" "	**13**	6	4th PM - 1831 MN/WI 42-N 8-E
" "	**11**	4	4th PM - 1831 MN/WI 42-N 6-E
" "	**10**	3	4th PM - 1831 MN/WI 42-N 5-E
ROBSON	**13**	9	4th PM - 1831 MN/WI 42-N 8-E
ROCKWELL	**31**	3	4th PM - 1831 MN/WI 40-N 9-E
ROE	**15**	7	4th PM - 1831 MN/WI 42-N 10-E
" "	**24**	2	4th PM - 1831 MN/WI 41-N 11-E
" "	**22**	2	4th PM - 1831 MN/WI 41-N 9-E
" "	**16**	2	4th PM - 1831 MN/WI 42-N 11-E
" "	**13**	2	4th PM - 1831 MN/WI 42-N 8-E
" "	**14**	2	4th PM - 1831 MN/WI 42-N 9-E
" "	**23**	1	4th PM - 1831 MN/WI 41-N 10-E
ROGERS	**32**	3	4th PM - 1831 MN/WI 40-N 10-E
" "	**24**	1	4th PM - 1831 MN/WI 41-N 11-E
ROIT	**29**	2	4th PM - 1831 MN/WI 40-N 7-E
ROLLENHAGEN	**5**	2	4th PM - 1831 MN/WI 43-N 6-E
ROSENBERRY	**32**	1	4th PM - 1831 MN/WI 40-N 10-E
ROSS	**10**	10	4th PM - 1831 MN/WI 42-N 5-E
" "	**11**	5	4th PM - 1831 MN/WI 42-N 6-E
" "	**5**	1	4th PM - 1831 MN/WI 43-N 6-E
ROUNDS	**9**	3	4th PM - 1831 MN/WI 43-N 10-E
" "	**22**	1	4th PM - 1831 MN/WI 41-N 9-E
ROWELL	**8**	6	4th PM - 1831 MN/WI 43-N 9-E
ROWLEY	**12**	2	4th PM - 1831 MN/WI 42-N 7-E
ROY	**13**	3	4th PM - 1831 MN/WI 42-N 8-E
RUMSEY	**4**	5	4th PM - 1831 MN/WI 43-N 5-E
" "	**1**	3	4th PM - 1831 MN/WI 44-N 5-E
" "	**5**	2	4th PM - 1831 MN/WI 43-N 6-E
" "	**6**	1	4th PM - 1831 MN/WI 43-N 7-E
RUSSELL	**7**	85	4th PM - 1831 MN/WI 43-N 8-E
" "	**30**	22	4th PM - 1831 MN/WI 40-N 8-E
" "	**6**	6	4th PM - 1831 MN/WI 43-N 7-E
" "	**5**	5	4th PM - 1831 MN/WI 43-N 6-E
" "	**4**	4	4th PM - 1831 MN/WI 43-N 5-E
" "	**10**	3	4th PM - 1831 MN/WI 42-N 5-E
" "	**8**	1	4th PM - 1831 MN/WI 43-N 9-E
RUST	**29**	27	4th PM - 1831 MN/WI 40-N 7-E
" "	**30**	23	4th PM - 1831 MN/WI 40-N 8-E
" "	**34**	10	4th PM - 1831 MN/WI 39-N 10-E
" "	**14**	8	4th PM - 1831 MN/WI 42-N 9-E
" "	**22**	3	4th PM - 1831 MN/WI 41-N 9-E
RYAN	**30**	1	4th PM - 1831 MN/WI 40-N 8-E
" "	**15**	1	4th PM - 1831 MN/WI 42-N 10-E
" "	**14**	1	4th PM - 1831 MN/WI 42-N 9-E
SACKETT	**22**	1	4th PM - 1831 MN/WI 41-N 9-E
SAGE	**5**	12	4th PM - 1831 MN/WI 43-N 6-E
" "	**12**	8	4th PM - 1831 MN/WI 42-N 7-E
" "	**26**	4	4th PM - 1831 MN/WI 40-N 4-E
" "	**6**	2	4th PM - 1831 MN/WI 43-N 7-E
SALZMAN	**24**	2	4th PM - 1831 MN/WI 41-N 11-E
SAMPSON	**19**	2	4th PM - 1831 MN/WI 41-N 6-E
" "	**4**	2	4th PM - 1831 MN/WI 43-N 5-E
" "	**20**	1	4th PM - 1831 MN/WI 41-N 7-E
" "	**10**	1	4th PM - 1831 MN/WI 42-N 5-E

Surname	Map Group	Parcels of Land	Meridian/Township/Range
SANBORN	**23**	2	4th PM - 1831 MN/WI 41-N 10-E
" "	**32**	1	4th PM - 1831 MN/WI 40-N 10-E
" "	**33**	1	4th PM - 1831 MN/WI 40-N 11-E
" "	**24**	1	4th PM - 1831 MN/WI 41-N 11-E
" "	**17**	1	4th PM - 1831 MN/WI 42-N 12-E
SANDERS	**15**	1	4th PM - 1831 MN/WI 42-N 10-E
SANSTER	**4**	10	4th PM - 1831 MN/WI 43-N 5-E
SARGENT	**25**	3	4th PM - 1831 MN/WI 41-N 12-E
" "	**16**	2	4th PM - 1831 MN/WI 42-N 11-E
SAYNER	**30**	2	4th PM - 1831 MN/WI 40-N 8-E
SCHAETZLE	**5**	1	4th PM - 1831 MN/WI 43-N 6-E
SCHAUDER	**29**	2	4th PM - 1831 MN/WI 40-N 7-E
SCHERIBEL	**34**	1	4th PM - 1831 MN/WI 39-N 10-E
" "	**15**	1	4th PM - 1831 MN/WI 42-N 10-E
SCHMIDT	**33**	4	4th PM - 1831 MN/WI 40-N 11-E
SCHOFIELD	**5**	1	4th PM - 1831 MN/WI 43-N 6-E
SCHRIBER	**21**	21	4th PM - 1831 MN/WI 41-N 8-E
" "	**29**	8	4th PM - 1831 MN/WI 40-N 7-E
" "	**30**	5	4th PM - 1831 MN/WI 40-N 8-E
" "	**20**	2	4th PM - 1831 MN/WI 41-N 7-E
SCHWALM	**21**	1	4th PM - 1831 MN/WI 41-N 8-E
SCOTT	**22**	39	4th PM - 1831 MN/WI 41-N 9-E
" "	**21**	27	4th PM - 1831 MN/WI 41-N 8-E
" "	**15**	15	4th PM - 1831 MN/WI 42-N 10-E
" "	**13**	15	4th PM - 1831 MN/WI 42-N 8-E
" "	**24**	13	4th PM - 1831 MN/WI 41-N 11-E
" "	**34**	9	4th PM - 1831 MN/WI 39-N 10-E
" "	**31**	6	4th PM - 1831 MN/WI 40-N 9-E
" "	**16**	6	4th PM - 1831 MN/WI 42-N 11-E
" "	**20**	4	4th PM - 1831 MN/WI 41-N 7-E
" "	**32**	3	4th PM - 1831 MN/WI 40-N 10-E
" "	**29**	3	4th PM - 1831 MN/WI 40-N 7-E
" "	**30**	3	4th PM - 1831 MN/WI 40-N 8-E
" "	**33**	2	4th PM - 1831 MN/WI 40-N 11-E
" "	**14**	1	4th PM - 1831 MN/WI 42-N 9-E
SECHRIST	**5**	1	4th PM - 1831 MN/WI 43-N 6-E
SEEGER	**4**	5	4th PM - 1831 MN/WI 43-N 5-E
SEIM	**10**	1	4th PM - 1831 MN/WI 42-N 5-E
SELL	**1**	4	4th PM - 1831 MN/WI 44-N 5-E
SEMER	**17**	12	4th PM - 1831 MN/WI 42-N 12-E
SEVERANCE	**32**	1	4th PM - 1831 MN/WI 40-N 10-E
" "	**30**	1	4th PM - 1831 MN/WI 40-N 8-E
" "	**20**	1	4th PM - 1831 MN/WI 41-N 7-E
" "	**12**	1	4th PM - 1831 MN/WI 42-N 7-E
SEWARD	**33**	2	4th PM - 1831 MN/WI 40-N 11-E
SEYER	**11**	1	4th PM - 1831 MN/WI 42-N 6-E
SHADICK	**16**	2	4th PM - 1831 MN/WI 42-N 11-E
SHAFFER	**19**	10	4th PM - 1831 MN/WI 41-N 6-E
" "	**11**	6	4th PM - 1831 MN/WI 42-N 6-E
SHAPE	**21**	1	4th PM - 1831 MN/WI 41-N 8-E
SHAW	**28**	2	4th PM - 1831 MN/WI 40-N 6-E
" "	**23**	1	4th PM - 1831 MN/WI 41-N 10-E
SHEPARD	**13**	2	4th PM - 1831 MN/WI 42-N 8-E
" "	**29**	1	4th PM - 1831 MN/WI 40-N 7-E
" "	**31**	1	4th PM - 1831 MN/WI 40-N 9-E
" "	**21**	1	4th PM - 1831 MN/WI 41-N 8-E
SHEPPARD	**5**	9	4th PM - 1831 MN/WI 43-N 6-E
" "	**7**	6	4th PM - 1831 MN/WI 43-N 8-E
" "	**6**	3	4th PM - 1831 MN/WI 43-N 7-E
" "	**2**	3	4th PM - 1831 MN/WI 44-N 6-E

Surname	Map Group	Parcels of Land	Meridian/Township/Range		
SHEPPARD (Cont'd)	**8**	1	4th PM - 1831 MN/WI	43-N	9-E
SHERIDAN	**15**	1	4th PM - 1831 MN/WI	42-N	10-E
SHERMAN	**15**	2	4th PM - 1831 MN/WI	42-N	10-E
" "	**10**	2	4th PM - 1831 MN/WI	42-N	5-E
SHERRY	**21**	5	4th PM - 1831 MN/WI	41-N	8-E
" "	**34**	2	4th PM - 1831 MN/WI	39-N	10-E
" "	**29**	2	4th PM - 1831 MN/WI	40-N	7-E
" "	**31**	1	4th PM - 1831 MN/WI	40-N	9-E
" "	**23**	1	4th PM - 1831 MN/WI	41-N	10-E
" "	**13**	1	4th PM - 1831 MN/WI	42-N	8-E
SHEW	**28**	3	4th PM - 1831 MN/WI	40-N	6-E
SIEGEL	**30**	2	4th PM - 1831 MN/WI	40-N	8-E
" "	**29**	1	4th PM - 1831 MN/WI	40-N	7-E
SIEVWRIGHT	**30**	1	4th PM - 1831 MN/WI	40-N	8-E
SILVERSTONE	**11**	13	4th PM - 1831 MN/WI	42-N	6-E
" "	**10**	4	4th PM - 1831 MN/WI	42-N	5-E
SILVERTHORN	**19**	12	4th PM - 1831 MN/WI	41-N	6-E
" "	**28**	4	4th PM - 1831 MN/WI	40-N	6-E
" "	**29**	3	4th PM - 1831 MN/WI	40-N	7-E
" "	**13**	2	4th PM - 1831 MN/WI	42-N	8-E
" "	**23**	1	4th PM - 1831 MN/WI	41-N	10-E
" "	**14**	1	4th PM - 1831 MN/WI	42-N	9-E
SIMPSON	**14**	2	4th PM - 1831 MN/WI	42-N	9-E
SLATTERY	**22**	1	4th PM - 1831 MN/WI	41-N	9-E
SLAUSON	**12**	14	4th PM - 1831 MN/WI	42-N	7-E
" "	**11**	13	4th PM - 1831 MN/WI	42-N	6-E
" "	**10**	12	4th PM - 1831 MN/WI	42-N	5-E
" "	**13**	2	4th PM - 1831 MN/WI	42-N	8-E
SLOCUM	**5**	71	4th PM - 1831 MN/WI	43-N	6-E
" "	**2**	51	4th PM - 1831 MN/WI	44-N	6-E
" "	**6**	15	4th PM - 1831 MN/WI	43-N	7-E
" "	**1**	2	4th PM - 1831 MN/WI	44-N	5-E
" "	**3**	1	4th PM - 1831 MN/WI	44-N	7-E
SLONAKER	**12**	1	4th PM - 1831 MN/WI	42-N	7-E
SMITH	**31**	4	4th PM - 1831 MN/WI	40-N	9-E
" "	**32**	3	4th PM - 1831 MN/WI	40-N	10-E
" "	**28**	2	4th PM - 1831 MN/WI	40-N	6-E
" "	**8**	2	4th PM - 1831 MN/WI	43-N	9-E
" "	**30**	1	4th PM - 1831 MN/WI	40-N	8-E
" "	**15**	1	4th PM - 1831 MN/WI	42-N	10-E
SOMERS	**32**	3	4th PM - 1831 MN/WI	40-N	10-E
SPAFFORD	**26**	1	4th PM - 1831 MN/WI	40-N	4-E
ST LOUIS	**32**	1	4th PM - 1831 MN/WI	40-N	10-E
STAMP	**10**	3	4th PM - 1831 MN/WI	42-N	5-E
STANDISH	**29**	1	4th PM - 1831 MN/WI	40-N	7-E
STANTON	**4**	1	4th PM - 1831 MN/WI	43-N	5-E
STARKS	**29**	3	4th PM - 1831 MN/WI	40-N	7-E
" "	**20**	1	4th PM - 1831 MN/WI	41-N	7-E
STARR	**21**	1	4th PM - 1831 MN/WI	41-N	8-E
" "	**12**	1	4th PM - 1831 MN/WI	42-N	7-E
STEIN	**8**	3	4th PM - 1831 MN/WI	43-N	9-E
" "	**22**	1	4th PM - 1831 MN/WI	41-N	9-E
STEINBERG	**32**	4	4th PM - 1831 MN/WI	40-N	10-E
" "	**34**	1	4th PM - 1831 MN/WI	39-N	10-E
" "	**31**	1	4th PM - 1831 MN/WI	40-N	9-E
" "	**15**	1	4th PM - 1831 MN/WI	42-N	10-E
" "	**9**	1	4th PM - 1831 MN/WI	43-N	10-E
STEINMETZ	**33**	3	4th PM - 1831 MN/WI	40-N	11-E
" "	**15**	1	4th PM - 1831 MN/WI	42-N	10-E
STEVENS	**24**	2	4th PM - 1831 MN/WI	41-N	11-E

Surname	Map Group	Parcels of Land	Meridian/Township/Range		
STEVENS (Cont'd)	**19**	1	4th PM - 1831 MN/WI	41-N	6-E
STEVENSON	**20**	3	4th PM - 1831 MN/WI	41-N	7-E
" "	**14**	3	4th PM - 1831 MN/WI	42-N	9-E
STEWART	**24**	2	4th PM - 1831 MN/WI	41-N	11-E
" "	**16**	1	4th PM - 1831 MN/WI	42-N	11-E
STICKLES	**29**	3	4th PM - 1831 MN/WI	40-N	7-E
" "	**20**	1	4th PM - 1831 MN/WI	41-N	7-E
STOECKEL	**28**	2	4th PM - 1831 MN/WI	40-N	6-E
" "	**19**	2	4th PM - 1831 MN/WI	41-N	6-E
STONE	**32**	1	4th PM - 1831 MN/WI	40-N	10-E
STORM	**34**	1	4th PM - 1831 MN/WI	39-N	10-E
STRANDBERG	**10**	1	4th PM - 1831 MN/WI	42-N	5-E
STREATOR	**5**	1	4th PM - 1831 MN/WI	43-N	6-E
STREETER	**15**	3	4th PM - 1831 MN/WI	42-N	10-E
STROUP	**22**	1	4th PM - 1831 MN/WI	41-N	9-E
STUBBINGS	**14**	3	4th PM - 1831 MN/WI	42-N	9-E
" "	**8**	2	4th PM - 1831 MN/WI	43-N	9-E
" "	**34**	1	4th PM - 1831 MN/WI	39-N	10-E
" "	**29**	1	4th PM - 1831 MN/WI	40-N	7-E
STURDEVANT	**23**	3	4th PM - 1831 MN/WI	41-N	10-E
SULLIVAN	**34**	2	4th PM - 1831 MN/WI	39-N	10-E
" "	**21**	1	4th PM - 1831 MN/WI	41-N	8-E
SWIMM	**16**	3	4th PM - 1831 MN/WI	42-N	11-E
TALMAGE	**24**	2	4th PM - 1831 MN/WI	41-N	11-E
TAMBLING	**32**	2	4th PM - 1831 MN/WI	40-N	10-E
" "	**33**	2	4th PM - 1831 MN/WI	40-N	11-E
TAYLOR	**1**	1	4th PM - 1831 MN/WI	44-N	5-E
TELLEFSON	**22**	2	4th PM - 1831 MN/WI	41-N	9-E
" "	**31**	1	4th PM - 1831 MN/WI	40-N	9-E
" "	**23**	1	4th PM - 1831 MN/WI	41-N	10-E
TELLER	**31**	1	4th PM - 1831 MN/WI	40-N	9-E
THAYER	**15**	2	4th PM - 1831 MN/WI	42-N	10-E
THOMAS	**16**	1	4th PM - 1831 MN/WI	42-N	11-E
THOMPSON	**21**	24	4th PM - 1831 MN/WI	41-N	8-E
" "	**13**	17	4th PM - 1831 MN/WI	42-N	8-E
" "	**6**	12	4th PM - 1831 MN/WI	43-N	7-E
" "	**7**	6	4th PM - 1831 MN/WI	43-N	8-E
" "	**30**	3	4th PM - 1831 MN/WI	40-N	8-E
" "	**32**	2	4th PM - 1831 MN/WI	40-N	10-E
" "	**20**	2	4th PM - 1831 MN/WI	41-N	7-E
" "	**15**	2	4th PM - 1831 MN/WI	42-N	10-E
" "	**14**	2	4th PM - 1831 MN/WI	42-N	9-E
TILLOTSON	**4**	9	4th PM - 1831 MN/WI	43-N	5-E
" "	**20**	4	4th PM - 1831 MN/WI	41-N	7-E
" "	**11**	4	4th PM - 1831 MN/WI	42-N	6-E
" "	**5**	4	4th PM - 1831 MN/WI	43-N	6-E
" "	**10**	2	4th PM - 1831 MN/WI	42-N	5-E
TOBEY	**29**	3	4th PM - 1831 MN/WI	40-N	7-E
TOBIN	**11**	2	4th PM - 1831 MN/WI	42-N	6-E
TOLMAN	**22**	19	4th PM - 1831 MN/WI	41-N	9-E
" "	**32**	2	4th PM - 1831 MN/WI	40-N	10-E
" "	**23**	2	4th PM - 1831 MN/WI	41-N	10-E
" "	**15**	1	4th PM - 1831 MN/WI	42-N	10-E
TOOLEY	**20**	2	4th PM - 1831 MN/WI	41-N	7-E
TOWNSEND	**32**	12	4th PM - 1831 MN/WI	40-N	10-E
" "	**34**	5	4th PM - 1831 MN/WI	39-N	10-E
" "	**33**	4	4th PM - 1831 MN/WI	40-N	11-E
" "	**22**	2	4th PM - 1831 MN/WI	41-N	9-E
" "	**23**	1	4th PM - 1831 MN/WI	41-N	10-E
" "	**14**	1	4th PM - 1831 MN/WI	42-N	9-E

Surname	Map Group	Parcels of Land	Meridian/Township/Range		
TRASTEL	**1**	15	4th PM - 1831 MN/WI	44-N	5-E
TRIPP	**12**	2	4th PM - 1831 MN/WI	42-N	7-E
TRUSSEL	**28**	4	4th PM - 1831 MN/WI	40-N	6-E
UPHAM	**8**	2	4th PM - 1831 MN/WI	43-N	9-E
VAN BRUNT	**4**	21	4th PM - 1831 MN/WI	43-N	5-E
" "	**7**	14	4th PM - 1831 MN/WI	43-N	8-E
" "	**8**	7	4th PM - 1831 MN/WI	43-N	9-E
" "	**1**	1	4th PM - 1831 MN/WI	44-N	5-E
VAN OSTRAND	**31**	2	4th PM - 1831 MN/WI	40-N	9-E
" "	**32**	1	4th PM - 1831 MN/WI	40-N	10-E
VENNER	**29**	2	4th PM - 1831 MN/WI	40-N	7-E
VINECORE	**20**	6	4th PM - 1831 MN/WI	41-N	7-E
WACHTER	**19**	2	4th PM - 1831 MN/WI	41-N	6-E
WADE	**15**	1	4th PM - 1831 MN/WI	42-N	10-E
WAKEFIELD	**25**	3	4th PM - 1831 MN/WI	41-N	12-E
WALLICH	**25**	6	4th PM - 1831 MN/WI	41-N	12-E
WALLING	**12**	1	4th PM - 1831 MN/WI	42-N	7-E
WALSH	**24**	7	4th PM - 1831 MN/WI	41-N	11-E
" "	**32**	3	4th PM - 1831 MN/WI	40-N	10-E
" "	**33**	3	4th PM - 1831 MN/WI	40-N	11-E
" "	**11**	3	4th PM - 1831 MN/WI	42-N	6-E
" "	**19**	1	4th PM - 1831 MN/WI	41-N	6-E
WALTER	**5**	4	4th PM - 1831 MN/WI	43-N	6-E
WALTERS	**15**	2	4th PM - 1831 MN/WI	42-N	10-E
WAMBOLD	**7**	1	4th PM - 1831 MN/WI	43-N	8-E
WARNER	**12**	2	4th PM - 1831 MN/WI	42-N	7-E
" "	**21**	1	4th PM - 1831 MN/WI	41-N	8-E
WASHBURN	**13**	8	4th PM - 1831 MN/WI	42-N	8-E
" "	**14**	7	4th PM - 1831 MN/WI	42-N	9-E
" "	**15**	5	4th PM - 1831 MN/WI	42-N	10-E
" "	**12**	2	4th PM - 1831 MN/WI	42-N	7-E
" "	**6**	2	4th PM - 1831 MN/WI	43-N	7-E
WASTE	**30**	5	4th PM - 1831 MN/WI	40-N	8-E
" "	**31**	2	4th PM - 1831 MN/WI	40-N	9-E
" "	**21**	1	4th PM - 1831 MN/WI	41-N	8-E
WATERMAN	**14**	18	4th PM - 1831 MN/WI	42-N	9-E
" "	**13**	13	4th PM - 1831 MN/WI	42-N	8-E
" "	**5**	10	4th PM - 1831 MN/WI	43-N	6-E
" "	**7**	9	4th PM - 1831 MN/WI	43-N	8-E
" "	**11**	4	4th PM - 1831 MN/WI	42-N	6-E
" "	**12**	3	4th PM - 1831 MN/WI	42-N	7-E
" "	**6**	1	4th PM - 1831 MN/WI	43-N	7-E
WATTERMAN	**11**	4	4th PM - 1831 MN/WI	42-N	6-E
WATTERS	**14**	1	4th PM - 1831 MN/WI	42-N	9-E
WEBSTER	**28**	4	4th PM - 1831 MN/WI	40-N	6-E
" "	**16**	2	4th PM - 1831 MN/WI	42-N	11-E
WELCH	**7**	2	4th PM - 1831 MN/WI	43-N	8-E
" "	**31**	1	4th PM - 1831 MN/WI	40-N	9-E
" "	**21**	1	4th PM - 1831 MN/WI	41-N	8-E
WELKER	**20**	1	4th PM - 1831 MN/WI	41-N	7-E
" "	**12**	1	4th PM - 1831 MN/WI	42-N	7-E
WELLINGTON	**32**	10	4th PM - 1831 MN/WI	40-N	10-E
" "	**34**	5	4th PM - 1831 MN/WI	39-N	10-E
" "	**33**	4	4th PM - 1831 MN/WI	40-N	11-E
" "	**22**	2	4th PM - 1831 MN/WI	41-N	9-E
WELLS	**4**	9	4th PM - 1831 MN/WI	43-N	5-E
" "	**8**	6	4th PM - 1831 MN/WI	43-N	9-E
" "	**20**	4	4th PM - 1831 MN/WI	41-N	7-E
" "	**11**	4	4th PM - 1831 MN/WI	42-N	6-E
" "	**5**	4	4th PM - 1831 MN/WI	43-N	6-E

Surname	Map Group	Parcels of Land	Meridian/Township/Range
WELLS (Cont'd)	**10**	2	4th PM - 1831 MN/WI 42-N 5-E
WENNBERG	**28**	1	4th PM - 1831 MN/WI 40-N 6-E
WENTWORTH	**24**	2	4th PM - 1831 MN/WI 41-N 11-E
WERNICH	**11**	4	4th PM - 1831 MN/WI 42-N 6-E
WESCOTT	**8**	4	4th PM - 1831 MN/WI 43-N 9-E
" "	**33**	1	4th PM - 1831 MN/WI 40-N 11-E
" "	**24**	1	4th PM - 1831 MN/WI 41-N 11-E
WEST	**31**	2	4th PM - 1831 MN/WI 40-N 9-E
WESTCOTT	**24**	3	4th PM - 1831 MN/WI 41-N 11-E
WESTON	**10**	5	4th PM - 1831 MN/WI 42-N 5-E
" "	**4**	2	4th PM - 1831 MN/WI 43-N 5-E
WHEELIHAN	**21**	1	4th PM - 1831 MN/WI 41-N 8-E
" "	**13**	1	4th PM - 1831 MN/WI 42-N 8-E
WHITE	**12**	1	4th PM - 1831 MN/WI 42-N 7-E
WIEGAND	**15**	2	4th PM - 1831 MN/WI 42-N 10-E
WILBER	**9**	1	4th PM - 1831 MN/WI 43-N 10-E
WILCOX	**12**	7	4th PM - 1831 MN/WI 42-N 7-E
" "	**26**	3	4th PM - 1831 MN/WI 40-N 4-E
" "	**11**	2	4th PM - 1831 MN/WI 42-N 6-E
" "	**13**	2	4th PM - 1831 MN/WI 42-N 8-E
WILD	**22**	1	4th PM - 1831 MN/WI 41-N 9-E
WILEY	**14**	18	4th PM - 1831 MN/WI 42-N 9-E
" "	**13**	13	4th PM - 1831 MN/WI 42-N 8-E
" "	**5**	10	4th PM - 1831 MN/WI 43-N 6-E
" "	**7**	9	4th PM - 1831 MN/WI 43-N 8-E
" "	**11**	8	4th PM - 1831 MN/WI 42-N 6-E
" "	**12**	3	4th PM - 1831 MN/WI 42-N 7-E
" "	**23**	2	4th PM - 1831 MN/WI 41-N 10-E
" "	**6**	1	4th PM - 1831 MN/WI 43-N 7-E
WILHELM	**5**	7	4th PM - 1831 MN/WI 43-N 6-E
WILLCOX	**12**	2	4th PM - 1831 MN/WI 42-N 7-E
WILLIAMS	**15**	2	4th PM - 1831 MN/WI 42-N 10-E
" "	**16**	2	4th PM - 1831 MN/WI 42-N 11-E
WILSON	**25**	12	4th PM - 1831 MN/WI 41-N 12-E
" "	**5**	2	4th PM - 1831 MN/WI 43-N 6-E
" "	**14**	1	4th PM - 1831 MN/WI 42-N 9-E
WILTERDING	**34**	2	4th PM - 1831 MN/WI 39-N 10-E
WINSLOW	**28**	3	4th PM - 1831 MN/WI 40-N 6-E
WINTON	**21**	8	4th PM - 1831 MN/WI 41-N 8-E
" "	**20**	5	4th PM - 1831 MN/WI 41-N 7-E
" "	**30**	4	4th PM - 1831 MN/WI 40-N 8-E
" "	**31**	4	4th PM - 1831 MN/WI 40-N 9-E
" "	**15**	1	4th PM - 1831 MN/WI 42-N 10-E
WIPPERMANN	**16**	1	4th PM - 1831 MN/WI 42-N 11-E
WISCONSIN	**10**	3	4th PM - 1831 MN/WI 42-N 5-E
" "	**11**	2	4th PM - 1831 MN/WI 42-N 6-E
" "	**34**	1	4th PM - 1831 MN/WI 39-N 10-E
" "	**6**	1	4th PM - 1831 MN/WI 43-N 7-E
WISE	**32**	1	4th PM - 1831 MN/WI 40-N 10-E
WITTER	**19**	2	4th PM - 1831 MN/WI 41-N 6-E
" "	**4**	2	4th PM - 1831 MN/WI 43-N 5-E
" "	**20**	1	4th PM - 1831 MN/WI 41-N 7-E
" "	**10**	1	4th PM - 1831 MN/WI 42-N 5-E
WOLFRAM	**34**	2	4th PM - 1831 MN/WI 39-N 10-E
WOODLOCK	**31**	1	4th PM - 1831 MN/WI 40-N 9-E
WOOLWORTH	**24**	2	4th PM - 1831 MN/WI 41-N 11-E
" "	**16**	1	4th PM - 1831 MN/WI 42-N 11-E
WRIGHT	**30**	2	4th PM - 1831 MN/WI 40-N 8-E
WYLIE	**9**	16	4th PM - 1831 MN/WI 43-N 10-E
" "	**15**	15	4th PM - 1831 MN/WI 42-N 10-E

Surname	Map Group	Parcels of Land	Meridian/Township/Range
WYLIE (Cont'd)	**14**	13	4th PM - 1831 MN/WI 42-N 9-E
" "	**30**	9	4th PM - 1831 MN/WI 40-N 8-E
" "	**23**	1	4th PM - 1831 MN/WI 41-N 10-E
" "	**22**	1	4th PM - 1831 MN/WI 41-N 9-E
" "	**16**	1	4th PM - 1831 MN/WI 42-N 11-E
" "	**8**	1	4th PM - 1831 MN/WI 43-N 9-E
YAWKEY	**29**	2	4th PM - 1831 MN/WI 40-N 7-E
YOUNG	**5**	71	4th PM - 1831 MN/WI 43-N 6-E
" "	**6**	8	4th PM - 1831 MN/WI 43-N 7-E
" "	**32**	5	4th PM - 1831 MN/WI 40-N 10-E
ZAHNER	**5**	1	4th PM - 1831 MN/WI 43-N 6-E
ZIEMKE	**22**	3	4th PM - 1831 MN/WI 41-N 9-E
ZIMPELMANN	**10**	2	4th PM - 1831 MN/WI 42-N 5-E

– Part II –

Township Map Groups

Map Group 1: Index to Land Patents

Township 44-North Range 5-East (4th PM - 1831 MN/WI)

After you locate an individual in this Index, take note of the Section and Section Part then proceed to the Land Patent map on the pages immediately following. You should have no difficulty locating the corresponding parcel of land.

The "For More Info" Column will lead you to more information about the underlying Patents. See the *Legend* at right, and the "How to Use this Book" chapter, for more information.

```
                        LEGEND
              "For More Info . . . " column
A = Authority (Legislative Act, See Appendix "A")
B = Block or Lot (location in Section unknown)
C = Cancelled Patent
F = Fractional Section
G = Group  (Multi-Patentee Patent, see Appendix "C")
V = Overlaps another Parcel
R = Re-Issued (Parcel patented more than once)

(A & G items require you to look in the Appendixes referred
to above. All other Letter-designations followed by a number
require you to locate line-items in this index that possess
the ID number found after the letter).
```

ID	Individual in Patent	Sec.	Sec. Part	Date Issued	Other Counties	For More Info . . .
65	DANIELS, George B	22	SWSW	1918-04-17		A3 G65
93	DAVIS, Joseph B	22	1	1888-07-10		A1
94	" "	22	E½NW	1888-07-10		A1
95	" "	22	NWSW	1888-07-10		A1
96	" "	22	SWNE	1888-07-10		A1
97	" "	22	SWNW	1888-07-10		A1
98	" "	23	2	1888-07-10		A1
99	" "	23	3	1888-07-10		A1
100	" "	23	4	1888-07-10		A1
101	" "	23	5	1888-07-10		A1
102	" "	24	2	1888-07-10		A1
103	" "	24	3	1888-07-10		A1
104	" "	33	E½SE	1888-07-10		A1
23	DUSOLD, Christian	34	NWSE	1888-07-10		A1
24	" "	34	SW	1888-07-10		A1
25	" "	34	SWNE	1888-07-10		A1
26	FRENCH, D D	15	1	1886-03-01		A1
27	" "	22	2	1886-03-01		A1
28	" "	22	NWNW	1886-03-01		A1
29	" "	22	SENE	1886-03-01		A1
30	" "	23	1	1886-03-01		A1
31	" "	24	4	1886-03-01		A1
32	" "	25	1	1886-03-01		A1
33	" "	25	2	1886-03-01		A1
34	" "	25	N½SE	1886-03-01		A1
35	" "	25	NE	1886-03-01		A1
36	" "	25	S½NW	1886-03-01		A1
37	" "	26	4	1886-03-01		A1
38	" "	26	5	1886-03-01		A1
40	" "	28	1	1886-03-01		A1
41	" "	28	2	1886-03-01		A1
42	" "	28	3	1886-03-01		A1
43	" "	28	4	1886-03-01		A1
44	" "	28	N½NW	1886-03-01		A1
45	" "	28	NWNE	1886-03-01		A1
46	" "	28	SWNW	1886-03-01		A1
47	" "	28	W½SW	1886-03-01		A1
39	" "	26	6	1886-07-30		A1
48	" "	34	2	1886-07-30		A1
49	" "	34	E½NE	1886-07-30		A1
50	" "	35	1	1886-07-30		A1
51	" "	35	4	1886-07-30		A1
52	" "	35	5	1886-07-30		A1
53	" "	35	NESW	1886-07-30		A1
54	" "	35	SENW	1886-07-30		A1
55	" "	35	SESE	1886-07-30		A1

ID	Individual in Patent	Sec.	Sec. Part	Date Issued	Other Counties	For More Info . . .
56	FRENCH, D D (Cont'd)	35	W½NW	1886-07-30		A1
57	" "	35	W½SE	1886-07-30		A1
109	GATES, William	17	1	1886-07-30		A1
110	" "	17	2	1886-07-30		A1
111	" "	17	6	1886-07-30		A1
112	" "	17	W½SW	1886-07-30		A1
113	" "	18	2	1886-07-30		A1
114	" "	18	3	1886-07-30		A1
115	" "	18	4	1886-07-30		A1
116	" "	18	E½SW	1886-07-30		A1
117	" "	18	SE	1886-07-30		A1
118	" "	18	SENW	1886-07-30		A1
134	" "	29	2	1886-07-30		A1
135	" "	29	3	1886-07-30		A1
136	" "	29	4	1886-07-30		A1
137	" "	29	5	1886-07-30		A1
138	" "	29	6	1886-07-30		A1
139	" "	29	E½NW	1886-07-30		A1
140	" "	29	NESE	1886-07-30		A1
141	" "	29	W½NE	1886-07-30		A1
142	" "	29	W½SE	1886-07-30		A1
143	" "	30	10	1886-07-30		A1
144	" "	30	5	1886-07-30		A1
145	" "	30	6	1886-07-30		A1
146	" "	30	7	1886-07-30		A1
147	" "	30	9	1886-07-30		A1
148	" "	30	E½SW	1886-07-30		A1
149	" "	30	SWSW	1886-07-30		A1 F
150	" "	30	W½SE	1886-07-30		A1
151	" "	36	1	1886-07-30		A1
152	" "	36	E½NW	1886-07-30		A1
153	" "	36	E½SW	1886-07-30		A1
154	" "	36	SWNW	1886-07-30		A1
155	" "	36	SWSW	1886-07-30		A1
156	" "	36	W½NE	1886-07-30		A1
157	" "	36	W½SE	1886-07-30		A1
119	" "	19	2	1888-05-11		A1 C R120
121	" "	19	4	1888-05-11		A1 C R122
123	" "	19	5	1888-05-11		A1 C R124
125	" "	19	6	1888-05-11		A1 C R126
127	" "	19	7	1888-05-11		A1 C R128
130	" "	19	SENE	1888-05-11		A1 C R131
132	" "	19	W½NE	1888-05-11		A1 C R133
120	" "	19	2	1888-10-24		A1 R119
122	" "	19	4	1888-10-24		A1 R121
124	" "	19	5	1888-10-24		A1 R123
126	" "	19	6	1888-10-24		A1 R125
128	" "	19	7	1888-10-24		A1 R127
129	" "	19	NWSE	1888-10-24		A1
131	" "	19	SENE	1888-10-24		A1 R130
133	" "	19	W½NE	1888-10-24		A1 R132
58	GROSS, Edwin W	34	S½NW	1888-07-10		A1
74	MAXON, Glenway	23	7	1888-07-18		A1
75	" "	23	NESE	1888-07-18		A1
76	" "	24	SWSE	1888-07-18		A1
77	" "	25	NWNW	1888-07-18		A1
78	" "	26	2	1888-07-18		A1
79	" "	26	3	1888-07-18		A1
80	" "	27	NENE	1888-07-18		A1
81	" "	27	SWNW	1888-07-18		A1
82	" "	27	W½SW	1888-07-18		A1
83	" "	28	5	1888-07-18		A1
84	" "	28	6	1888-07-18		A1
85	" "	28	7	1888-07-18		A1
86	" "	28	NENE	1888-07-18		A1
87	" "	31	SWSW	1888-07-18		A1 F
88	" "	33	1	1888-07-18		A1
89	" "	33	2	1888-07-18		A1
90	" "	33	3	1888-07-18		A1
91	" "	33	6	1888-07-18		A1
92	" "	34	NWNW	1888-07-18		A1
106	MILLER, W H	19	E½SE	1886-07-30		A1 G147
107	" "	30	NENE	1886-07-30		A1 G147

ID	Individual in Patent	Sec.	Sec. Part	Date Issued	Other Counties	For More Info . . .
108	MILLER, W H (Cont'd)	36	NWSW	1886-07-30		A1 G147
1	MORGAN, A T	31	N½SW	1888-07-10		A1 G149
2	" "	31	NE	1888-07-10		A1 G149
3	" "	31	NW	1888-07-10		A1 G149
4	" "	31	SE	1888-07-10		A1 G149
5	" "	31	SESW	1888-07-10		A1 G149
6	" "	32		1888-07-10		A1 G149
7	" "	33	NW	1888-07-10		A1 G149
1	MORGAN, J E	31	N½SW	1888-07-10		A1 G149
2	" "	31	NE	1888-07-10		A1 G149
3	" "	31	NW	1888-07-10		A1 G149
4	" "	31	SE	1888-07-10		A1 G149
5	" "	31	SESW	1888-07-10		A1 G149
6	" "	32		1888-07-10		A1 G149
7	" "	33	NW	1888-07-10		A1 G149
158	MULHOLON, William S	35	2	1904-09-08		A1
159	" "	35	3	1904-09-08		A1
160	" "	35	NESE	1904-09-08		A1
66	PIER, George M	19	8	1911-01-16		A3 G155 C R67
68	" "	30	2	1911-01-16		A3 G155 C R69
70	" "	30	3	1911-01-16		A3 G155 C R71
72	" "	30	8	1911-01-16		A3 G155 C R73
67	" "	19	8	1911-03-01		A3 G155 R66
69	" "	30	2	1911-03-01		A3 G155 R68
71	" "	30	3	1911-03-01		A3 G155 R70
73	" "	30	8	1911-03-01		A3 G155 R72
66	PIER, Sedate	19	8	1911-01-16		A3 G155 C R67
68	" "	30	2	1911-01-16		A3 G155 C R69
70	" "	30	3	1911-01-16		A3 G155 C R71
72	" "	30	8	1911-01-16		A3 G155 C R73
67	" "	19	8	1911-03-01		A3 G155 R66
69	" "	30	2	1911-03-01		A3 G155 R68
71	" "	30	3	1911-03-01		A3 G155 R70
73	" "	30	8	1911-03-01		A3 G155 R72
61	PRESCOTT, Frederick M	29	SESE	1888-07-07		A1
62	" "	33	4	1888-07-07		A1
63	" "	33	5	1888-07-07		A1
64	" "	33	NWSW	1888-07-07		A1
106	RUMSEY, T H	19	E½SE	1886-07-30		A1 G147
107	" "	30	NENE	1886-07-30		A1 G147
108	" "	36	NWSW	1886-07-30		A1 G147
66	SELL, John L	19	8	1911-01-16		A3 G155 C R67
68	" "	30	2	1911-01-16		A3 G155 C R69
70	" "	30	3	1911-01-16		A3 G155 C R71
72	" "	30	8	1911-01-16		A3 G155 C R73
67	" "	19	8	1911-03-01		A3 G155 R66
69	" "	30	2	1911-03-01		A3 G155 R68
71	" "	30	3	1911-03-01		A3 G155 R70
73	" "	30	8	1911-03-01		A3 G155 R72
59	SLOCUM, Elliott T	36	E½NE	1884-06-20		A1 G162
60	" "	36	E½SE	1884-06-20		A1 G162
59	SLOCUM, Giles B	36	E½NE	1884-06-20		A1 G162
60	" "	36	E½SE	1884-06-20		A1 G162
65	TAYLOR, Miron B	22	SWSW	1918-04-17		A3 G65
8	TRASTEL, Albert	17	3	1886-07-30		A1
9	" "	17	4	1886-07-30		A1
10	" "	18	1	1886-07-30		A1
11	" "	18	SWNW	1886-07-30		A1 F
12	" "	18	W½SW	1886-07-30		A1 F
13	" "	19	1	1886-07-30		A1
14	" "	19	3	1886-07-30		A1
15	" "	21		1886-07-30		A1
16	" "	29	1	1886-07-30		A1
17	" "	29	E½NE	1886-07-30		A1
18	" "	29	NWNW	1886-07-30		A1
19	" "	30	1	1886-07-30		A1
20	" "	30	4	1886-07-30		A1
21	" "	30	NWSW	1886-07-30		A1 F
22	" "	30	W½NW	1886-07-30		A1 F
105	VAN BRUNT, W A	20		1886-03-01		A1 F

Patent Map

T44-N R5-E
4th PM - 1831 MN/WI

Map Group 1

Township Statistics

Parcels Mapped	:	160
Number of Patents	:	33
Number of Individuals	:	21
Patentees Identified	:	15
Number of Surnames	:	18
Multi-Patentee Parcels	:	21
Oldest Patent Date	:	6/20/1884
Most Recent Patent	:	4/17/1918
Block/Lot Parcels	:	81
Parcels Re - Issued	:	11
Parcels that Overlap	:	0
Cities and Towns	:	0
Cemeteries	:	1

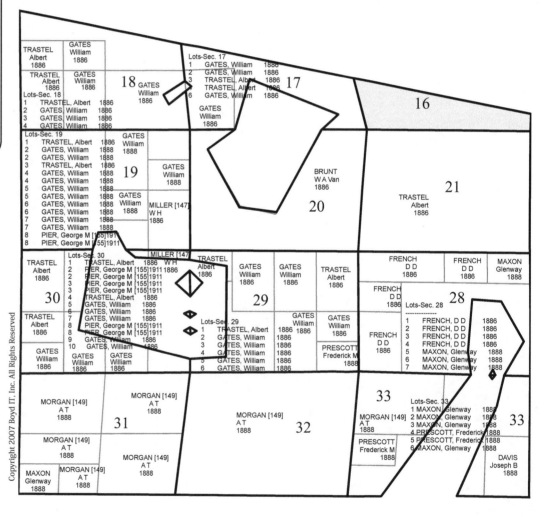

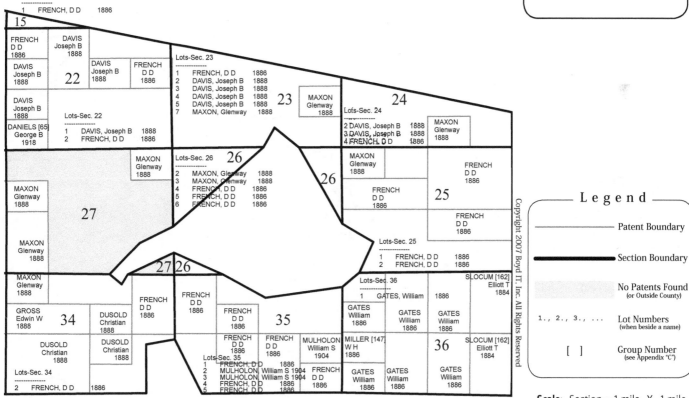

Helpful Hints

1. This Map's INDEX can be found on the preceding pages.

2. Refer to Map "C" to see where this Township lies within Vilas County, Wisconsin.

3. Numbers within square brackets [   ] denote a multi-patentee land parcel (multi-owner). Refer to Appendix "C" for a full list of members in this group.

4. Areas that look to be crowded with Patentees usually indicate multiple sales of the same parcel (Re-issues) or Overlapping parcels. See this Township's Index for an explanation of these and other circumstances that might explain "odd" groupings of Patentees on this map.

Legend

― Patent Boundary

━ Section Boundary

No Patents Found (or Outside County)

1., 2., 3., ... Lot Numbers (when beside a name)

[   ] Group Number (see Appendix "C")

Scale: Section = 1 mile X 1 mile (generally, with some exceptions)

Road Map

T44-N R5-E
4th PM - 1831 MN/WI

Map Group 1

Cities & Towns
None

Cemeteries
Winchester Memorial Cemetery

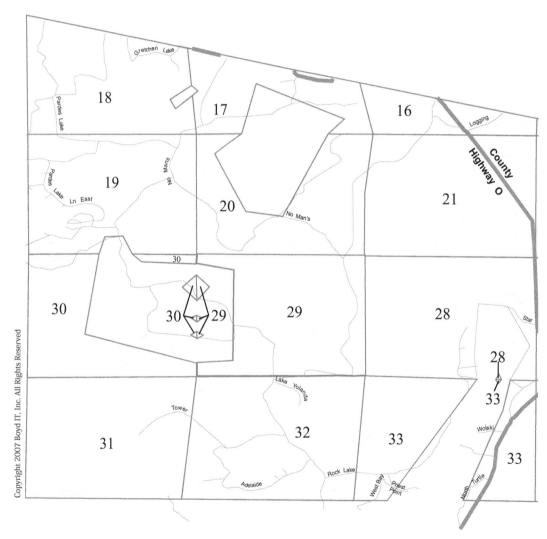

Helpful Hints

1. This road map has a number of uses, but primarily it is to help you: a) find the present location of land owned by your ancestors (at least the general area), b) find cemeteries and city-centers, and c) estimate the route/roads used by Census-takers & tax-assessors.

2. If you plan to travel to Vilas County to locate cemeteries or land parcels, please pick up a modern travel map for the area before you do. Mapping old land parcels on modern maps is not as exact a science as you might think. Just the slightest variations in public land survey coordinates, estimates of parcel boundaries, or road-map deviations can greatly alter a map's representation of how a road either does or doesn't cross a particular parcel of land.

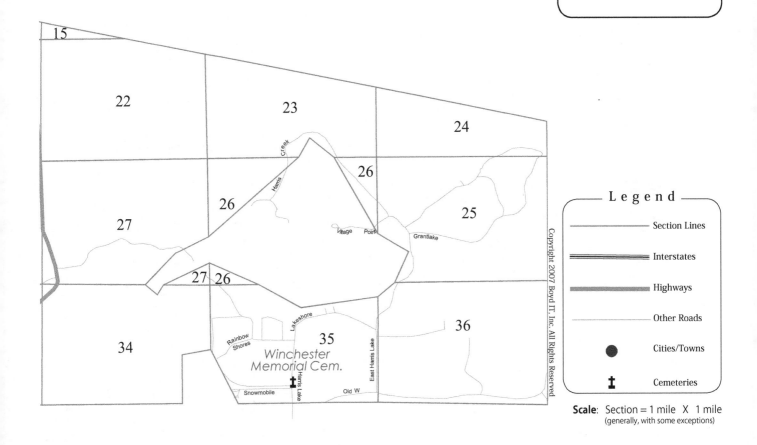

Legend

———	Section Lines
▬▬▬	Interstates
▬▬▬	Highways
———	Other Roads
●	Cities/Towns
✝	Cemeteries

Scale: Section = 1 mile X 1 mile
(generally, with some exceptions)

Historical Map

T44-N R5-E
4th PM - 1831 MN/WI

Map Group 1

Cities & Towns
None

Cemeteries
Winchester Memorial Cemetery

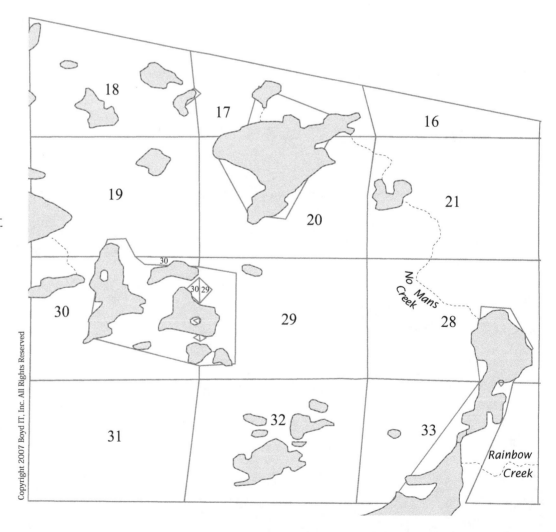

Helpful Hints

1. This Map takes a different look at the same Congressional Township displayed in the preceding two maps. It presents features that can help you better envision the historical development of the area: a) Water-bodies (lakes & ponds), b) Water-courses (rivers, streams, etc.), c) Railroads, d) City/town center-points (where they were oftentimes located when first settled), and e) Cemeteries.

2. Using this "Historical" map in tandem with this Township's Patent Map and Road Map, may lead you to some interesting discoveries. You will often find roads, towns, cemeteries, and waterways are named after nearby landowners: sometimes those names will be the ones you are researching. See how many of these research gems you can find here in Vilas County.

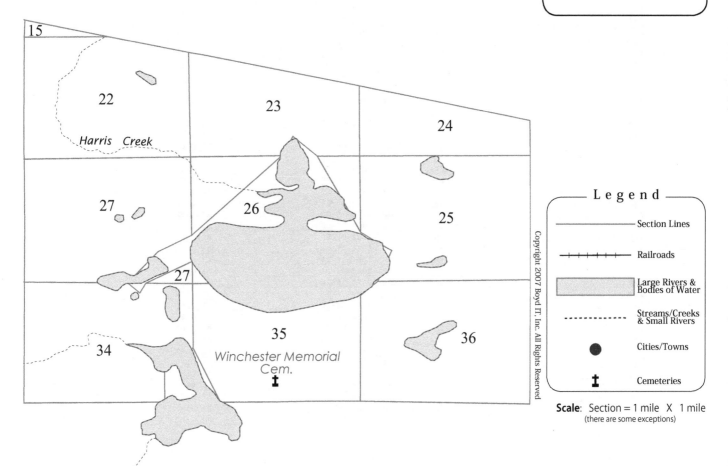

Legend

——————	Section Lines
—+——+——+—	Railroads
▭	Large Rivers & Bodies of Water
- - - - - -	Streams/Creeks & Small Rivers
●	Cities/Towns
✝	Cemeteries

Scale: Section = 1 mile X 1 mile
(there are some exceptions)

Map Group 2: Index to Land Patents

Township 44-North Range 6-East (4th PM - 1831 MN/WI)

After you locate an individual in this Index, take note of the Section and Section Part then proceed to the Land Patent map on the pages immediately following. You should have no difficulty locating the corresponding parcel of land.

The "For More Info" Column will lead you to more information about the underlying Patents. See the *Legend* at right, and the "How to Use this Book" chapter, for more information.

```
                          LEGEND
                "For More Info . . . " column
A = Authority (Legislative Act, See Appendix "A")
B = Block or Lot (location in Section unknown)
C = Cancelled Patent
F = Fractional Section
G = Group  (Multi-Patentee Patent, see Appendix "C")
V = Overlaps another Parcel
R = Re-Issued (Parcel patented more than once)

(A & G items require you to look in the Appendixes referred
to above. All other Letter-designations followed by a number
require you to locate line-items in this index that possess
the ID number found after the letter).
```

ID	Individual in Patent	Sec.	Sec. Part	Date Issued	Other Counties	For More Info . . .
212	AUCUTT, Harriet A	20	1	1884-06-20		A1
213	SHEPPARD, Robert L	36	12	1911-08-04		A2
214	" "	36	13	1911-08-04		A2
215	" "	36	14	1911-08-04		A2
161	SLOCUM, Elliott T	26	1	1883-09-15		A1
162	" "	26	2	1883-09-15		A1
163	" "	35	1	1883-09-15		A1
164	" "	35	2	1883-09-15		A1
165	" "	19	1	1884-06-20		A1 G162
166	" "	19	2	1884-06-20		A1 G162
167	" "	19	3	1884-06-20		A1 G162
168	" "	27	1	1884-06-20		A1 G162
169	" "	27	2	1884-06-20		A1 G162
170	" "	27	3	1884-06-20		A1 G162
171	" "	27	4	1884-06-20		A1 G162
172	" "	27	SWSW	1884-06-20		A1 G162
173	" "	28	1	1884-06-20		A1 G162
174	" "	28	2	1884-06-20		A1 G162
175	" "	28	3	1884-06-20		A1 G162
176	" "	28	4	1884-06-20		A1 G162
177	" "	28	N½SW	1884-06-20		A1 G162
178	" "	28	S½SE	1884-06-20		A1 G162
179	" "	28	SESW	1884-06-20		A1 G162
180	" "	29	1	1884-06-20		A1 G162
181	" "	29	2	1884-06-20		A1 G162
182	" "	29	3	1884-06-20		A1 G162
183	" "	29	4	1884-06-20		A1 G162
184	" "	29	S½NW	1884-06-20		A1 G162
185	" "	29	SE	1884-06-20		A1 G162
186	" "	29	SW	1884-06-20		A1 G162
187	" "	30	N½NE	1884-06-20		A1 G162
188	" "	30	NW	1884-06-20		A1 G162
189	" "	30	S½	1884-06-20		A1 G162
190	" "	30	SENE	1884-06-20		A1 G162
191	" "	30	SWNE	1884-06-20		A1 G162
192	" "	31	N½	1884-06-20		A1 G162
193	" "	31	N½SE	1884-06-20		A1 G162
194	" "	31	N½SW	1884-06-20		A1 G162
195	" "	31	S½SW	1884-06-20		A1 G162
196	" "	31	SESE	1884-06-20		A1 G162
197	" "	31	SWSE	1884-06-20		A1 G162
198	" "	32		1884-06-20		A1 G162
199	" "	33	NE	1884-06-20		A1 G162
200	" "	33	NENW	1884-06-20		A1 G162
201	" "	33	S½	1884-06-20		A1 G162
202	" "	33	S½NW	1884-06-20		A1 G162

ID	Individual in Patent	Sec.	Sec. Part	Date Issued	Other Counties	For More Info . . .
203	SLOCUM, Elliott T (Cont'd)	34		1884-06-20		A1 G162 F
204	" "	35	3	1884-06-20		A1 G162
205	" "	35	4	1884-06-20		A1 G162
209	" "	35	8	1884-06-20		A1 G162
206	" "	35	5	1884-06-30		A1 G162
207	" "	35	6	1884-06-30		A1 G162
208	" "	35	7	1884-06-30		A1 G162
210	" "	35	SE	1884-06-30		A1 G162
211	" "	36		1884-06-30		A1 G162 F
165	SLOCUM, Giles B	19	1	1884-06-20		A1 G162
166	" "	19	2	1884-06-20		A1 G162
167	" "	19	3	1884-06-20		A1 G162
168	" "	27	1	1884-06-20		A1 G162
169	" "	27	2	1884-06-20		A1 G162
170	" "	27	3	1884-06-20		A1 G162
171	" "	27	4	1884-06-20		A1 G162
172	" "	27	SWSW	1884-06-20		A1 G162
173	" "	28	1	1884-06-20		A1 G162
174	" "	28	2	1884-06-20		A1 G162
175	" "	28	3	1884-06-20		A1 G162
176	" "	28	4	1884-06-20		A1 G162
177	" "	28	N½SW	1884-06-20		A1 G162
178	" "	28	S½SE	1884-06-20		A1 G162
179	" "	28	SESW	1884-06-20		A1 G162
180	" "	29	1	1884-06-20		A1 G162
181	" "	29	2	1884-06-20		A1 G162
182	" "	29	3	1884-06-20		A1 G162
183	" "	29	4	1884-06-20		A1 G162
184	" "	29	S½NW	1884-06-20		A1 G162
185	" "	29	SE	1884-06-20		A1 G162
186	" "	29	SW	1884-06-20		A1 G162
187	" "	30	N½NE	1884-06-20		A1 G162
188	" "	30	NW	1884-06-20		A1 G162
189	" "	30	S½	1884-06-20		A1 G162
190	" "	30	SENE	1884-06-20		A1 G162
191	" "	30	SWNE	1884-06-20		A1 G162
192	" "	31	N½	1884-06-20		A1 G162
193	" "	31	N½SE	1884-06-20		A1 G162
194	" "	31	N½SW	1884-06-20		A1 G162
195	" "	31	S½SW	1884-06-20		A1 G162
196	" "	31	SESE	1884-06-20		A1 G162
197	" "	31	SWSE	1884-06-20		A1 G162
198	" "	32		1884-06-20		A1 G162
199	" "	33	NE	1884-06-20		A1 G162
200	" "	33	NENW	1884-06-20		A1 G162
201	" "	33	S½	1884-06-20		A1 G162
202	" "	33	S½NW	1884-06-20		A1 G162
203	" "	34		1884-06-20		A1 G162 F
204	" "	35	3	1884-06-20		A1 G162
205	" "	35	4	1884-06-20		A1 G162
209	" "	35	8	1884-06-20		A1 G162
206	" "	35	5	1884-06-30		A1 G162
207	" "	35	6	1884-06-30		A1 G162
208	" "	35	7	1884-06-30		A1 G162
210	" "	35	SE	1884-06-30		A1 G162
211	" "	36		1884-06-30		A1 G162 F

Patent Map

T44-N R6-E
4th PM - 1831 MN/WI

Map Group 2

Township Statistics

Parcels Mapped	:	55
Number of Patents	:	17
Number of Individuals	:	4
Patentees Identified	:	4
Number of Surnames	:	3
Multi-Patentee Parcels	:	47
Oldest Patent Date	:	9/15/1883
Most Recent Patent	:	8/4/1911
Block/Lot Parcels	:	29
Parcels Re - Issued	:	0
Parcels that Overlap	:	0
Cities and Towns	:	1
Cemeteries	:	1

Note: the area contained in this map amounts to far less than a full Township. Therefore, its contents are completely on this single page (instead of a "normal" 2-page spread).

Legend

——— Patent Boundary

▬▬▬ Section Boundary

No Patents Found
(or Outside County)

1., 2., 3., ... Lot Numbers
(when beside a name)

[ ] Group Number
(see Appendix "C")

Scale: Section = 1 mile X 1 mile
(generally, with some exceptions)

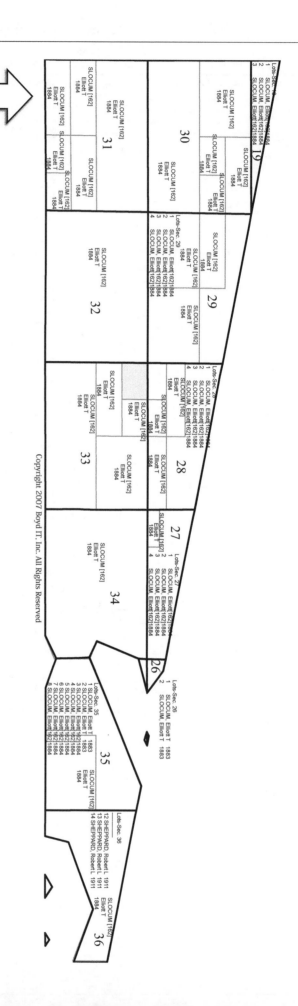

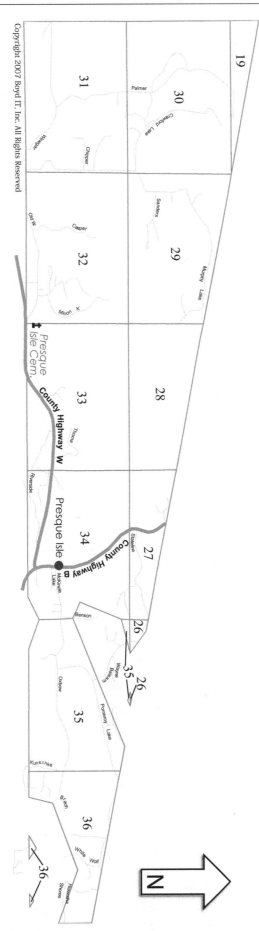

Section	
31	30
	19
32	29
33	28
34	27
35	26
36	

Palmer
Crawford Lake
Winegar
Chipper
Old W
Casper
Sanders
Minon K
Murphy Lake
Presque Isle Cem.
County Highway W
Thoma
Riverside
Presque Isle
Statake
County Highway B
McKinzie Lake
Benson
Wayne Baker
Oxbow
Pomeroy Lake
Kunschke
B'ach
White Wolf
Hiawatha Shores
35
26
36

N

Road Map

T44-N R6-E
4th PM - 1831 MN/WI

Map Group 2

Note: the area contained in this map amounts to far less than a full Township. Therefore, its contents are completely on this single page (instead of a "normal" 2-page spread).

Cities & Towns
Presque Isle

Cemeteries
Presque Isle Cemetery

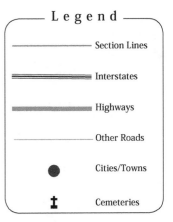

Legend

— Section Lines

═ Interstates

▬ Highways

— Other Roads

● Cities/Towns

☦ Cemeteries

Scale: Section = 1 mile X 1 mile
(generally, with some exceptions)

61

Historical Map

T44-N R6-E
4th PM - 1831 MN/WI

Map Group 2

Note: the area contained in this map amounts to far less than a full Township. Therefore, its contents are completely on this single page (instead of a "normal" 2-page spread).

Cities & Towns
Presque Isle

Cemeteries
Presque Isle Cemetery

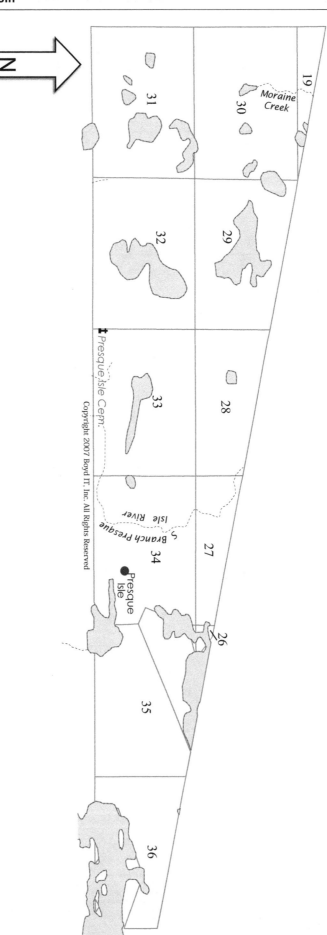

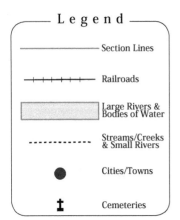

Legend

Section Lines

Railroads

Large Rivers & Bodies of Water

Streams/Creeks & Small Rivers

Cities/Towns

Cemeteries

Scale: Section = 1 mile X 1 mile
(there are some exceptions)

Map Group 3: Index to Land Patents

Township 44-North Range 7-East (4th PM - 1831 MN/WI)

After you locate an individual in this Index, take note of the Section and Section Part then proceed to the Land Patent map on the pages immediately following. You should have no difficulty locating the corresponding parcel of land.

The "For More Info" Column will lead you to more information about the underlying Patents. See the *Legend* at right, and the "How to Use this Book" chapter, for more information.

```
                          LEGEND
              "For More Info . . . " column
A = Authority (Legislative Act, See Appendix "A")
B = Block or Lot (location in Section unknown)
C = Cancelled Patent
F = Fractional Section
G = Group  (Multi-Patentee Patent, see Appendix "C")
V = Overlaps another Parcel
R = Re-Issued (Parcel patented more than once)

(A & G items require you to look in the Appendixes referred
to above. All other Letter-designations followed by a number
require you to locate line-items in this index that possess
the ID number found after the letter).
```

ID	Individual in Patent	Sec.	Sec. Part	Date Issued	Other Counties	For More Info . . .
216	SLOCUM, Elliott T			1884-06-30		A1 F

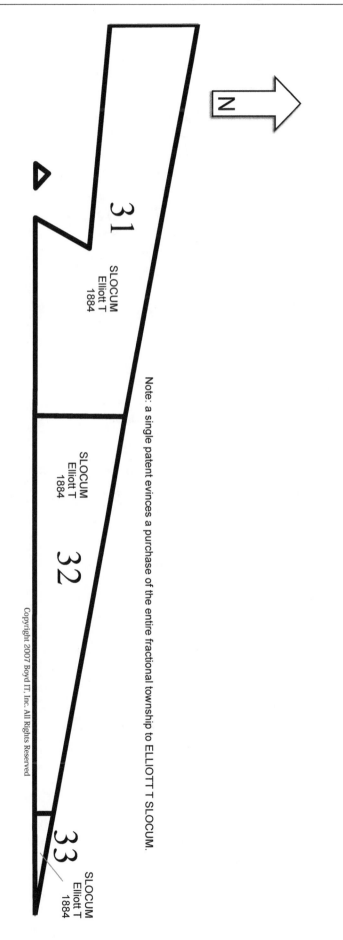

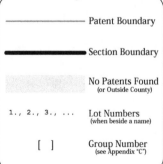

Patent Map

T44-N R7-E
4th PM - 1831 MN/WI

Map Group 3

Township Statistics

Parcels Mapped	:	1
Number of Patents	:	1
Number of Individuals	:	1
Patentees Identified	:	1
Number of Surnames	:	1
Multi-Patentee Parcels	:	0
Oldest Patent Date	:	6/30/1884
Most Recent Patent	:	6/30/1884
Block/Lot Parcels	:	0
Parcels Re - Issued	:	0
Parcels that Overlap	:	0
Cities and Towns	:	0
Cemeteries	:	0

Note: the area contained in this map amounts to far less than a full Township. Therefore, its contents are completely on this single page (instead of a "normal" 2-page spread).

Legend

——— Patent Boundary

━━━ Section Boundary

No Patents Found
(or Outside County)

1., 2., 3., ... Lot Numbers
(when beside a name)

[ ] Group Number
(see Appendix "C")

Scale: Section = 1 mile X 1 mile
(generally, with some exceptions)

31

SLOCUM
Elliott T
1884

SLOCUM
Elliott T
1884

32

SLOCUM
Elliott T
1884

33

Note: a single patent evinces a purchase of the entire fractional township to ELLIOTT T SLOCUM.

Road Map

T44-N R7-E
4th PM - 1831 MN/WI

Map Group 3

Note: the area contained in this map amounts to far less than a full Township. Therefore, its contents are completely on this single page (instead of a "normal" 2-page spread).

Cities & Towns
None

Cemeteries
None

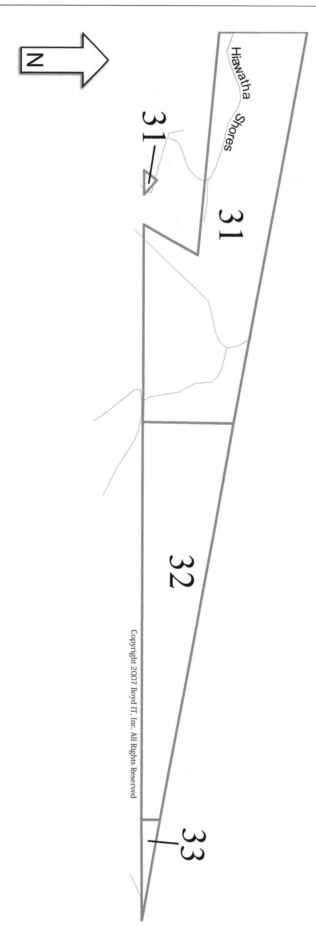

Legend

—— Section Lines

══ Interstates

—— Highways

—— Other Roads

● Cities/Towns

✝ Cemeteries

Scale: Section = 1 mile X 1 mile
(generally, with some exceptions)

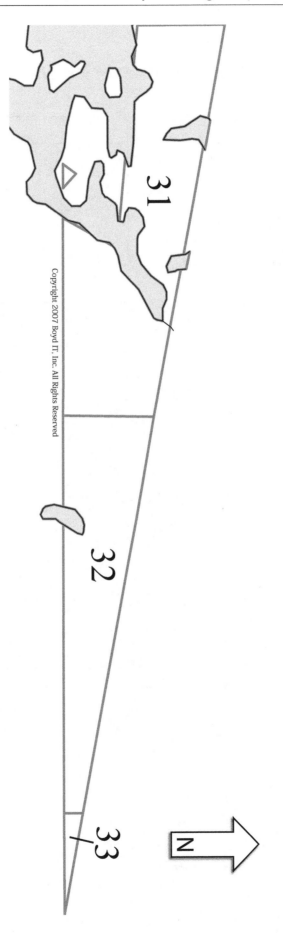

Historical Map

T44-N R7-E
4th PM - 1831 MN/WI

Map Group 3

Note: the area contained in this map amounts to far less than a full Township. Therefore, its contents are completely on this single page (instead of a "normal" 2-page spread).

Cities & Towns
None

Cemeteries
None

Legend

———————	Section Lines
┼┼┼┼┼┼┼	Railroads
▨	Large Rivers & Bodies of Water
- - - - - - -	Streams/Creeks & Small Rivers
●	Cities/Towns
✝	Cemeteries

Scale: Section = 1 mile X 1 mile
(there are some exceptions)

Map Group 4: Index to Land Patents

Township 43-North Range 5-East (4th PM - 1831 MN/WI)

After you locate an individual in this Index, take note of the Section and Section Part then proceed to the Land Patent map on the pages immediately following. You should have no difficulty locating the corresponding parcel of land.

The "For More Info" Column will lead you to more information about the underlying Patents. See the *Legend* at right, and the "How to Use this Book" chapter, for more information.

```
LEGEND
        "For More Info . . . " column
A = Authority (Legislative Act, See Appendix "A")
B = Block or Lot (location in Section unknown)
C = Cancelled Patent
F = Fractional Section
G = Group  (Multi-Patentee Patent, see Appendix "C")
V = Overlaps another Parcel
R = Re-Issued (Parcel patented more than once)

(A & G items require you to look in the Appendixes referred
to above. All other Letter-designations followed by a number
require you to locate line-items in this index that possess
the ID number found after the letter).
```

ID	Individual in Patent	Sec.	Sec. Part	Date Issued	Other Counties	For More Info . . .
218	BARROWS, Augustus R	15	S½SW	1873-05-01		A1
219	" "	22	N½NW	1873-05-01		A1
220	" "	22	SENW	1873-05-01		A1
221	" "	22	SWNE	1873-05-01		A1
222	" "	27	N½SW	1873-05-01		A1
223	" "	28	NW	1873-05-01		A1
369	CORWITH, Nathan	27	S½SW	1872-11-01		A1
370	" "	28	E½SE	1872-11-01		A1
371	" "	33	NESE	1872-11-01		A1
357	DALEY, John	21	SWSW	1884-06-20		A1 G64
358	" "	8	1	1884-06-20		A1 G64
379	DAVIS, S E	1	NWSW	1886-07-30		A1
380	" "	1	S½SW	1886-07-30		A1
381	" "	1	SWNW	1886-07-30		A1
382	" "	8	4	1888-07-28		A1
333	DOW, H T	28	NESW	1884-06-30		A1 G76
334	" "	28	NWSE	1884-06-30		A1 G76
244	FRENCH, D D	17	1	1886-03-01		A1
245	" "	17	2	1886-03-01		A1
246	" "	17	3	1886-03-01		A1
255	" "	20	1	1886-03-01		A1
256	" "	20	NESE	1886-03-01		A1
257	" "	20	SENE	1886-03-01		A1
258	" "	21	NWSW	1886-03-01		A1
259	" "	21	W½NW	1886-03-01		A1
260	" "	4	7	1886-03-01		A1
261	" "	4	8	1886-03-01		A1
262	" "	5	2	1886-03-01		A1
263	" "	5	3	1886-03-01		A1
264	" "	5	5	1886-03-01		A1
265	" "	5	6	1886-03-01		A1
266	" "	5	7	1886-03-01		A1
267	" "	5	8	1886-03-01		A1
268	" "	5	SWNE	1886-03-01		A1
269	" "	5	SWNW	1886-03-01		A1
243	" "	11	2	1886-07-30		A1
247	" "	2	1	1886-07-30		A1
248	" "	2	2	1886-07-30		A1
249	" "	2	E½NW	1886-07-30		A1 F
250	" "	2	N½SW	1886-07-30		A1
251	" "	2	SE	1886-07-30		A1
252	" "	2	SESW	1886-07-30		A1
253	" "	2	SWNW	1886-07-30		A1
254	" "	2	W½NE	1886-07-30		A1 F
272	FRIEND, Elias	23	SWNE	1885-11-25		A1
273	" "	36	SWSE	1885-11-25		A1

ID	Individual in Patent	Sec.	Sec. Part	Date Issued	Other Counties	For More Info . . .
413	GATES, William	1	N½NE	1886-07-30		A1 F
414	" "	1	N½NW	1886-07-30		A1 F
415	" "	1	SENW	1886-07-30		A1
416	" "	13	S½SE	1886-07-30		A1
422	" "	23	NWNE	1886-07-30		A1
423	" "	23	W½	1886-07-30		A1
424	" "	24	2	1886-07-30		A1
425	" "	24	3	1886-07-30		A1
426	" "	24	4	1886-07-30		A1
427	" "	24	N½NE	1886-07-30		A1
428	" "	24	N½SW	1886-07-30		A1
429	" "	24	NENW	1886-07-30		A1
430	" "	24	S½NW	1886-07-30		A1
431	" "	24	SWSE	1886-07-30		A1
432	" "	25	1	1886-07-30		A1
433	" "	25	3	1886-07-30		A1
434	" "	25	4	1886-07-30		A1
435	" "	25	5	1886-07-30		A1
436	" "	25	6	1886-07-30		A1
437	" "	25	SW	1886-07-30		A1
438	" "	26	E½SE	1886-07-30		A1
439	" "	26	W½	1886-07-30		A1
440	" "	26	W½NE	1886-07-30		A1
417	" "	15	NESW	1888-05-11		A1
418	" "	15	SE	1888-05-11		A1
419	" "	21	E½SW	1888-05-11		A1
420	" "	22	E½NE	1888-05-11		A1
421	" "	22	E½SE	1888-05-11		A1
441	" "	27	N½SE	1888-05-11		A1
442	" "	27	NENW	1888-05-11		A1
443	" "	28	NE	1888-05-11		A1
217	HAIGHT, Augustus	34	S½SE	1872-11-01		A1
225	HEURICH, C	1	NESW	1888-07-10		A1
226	" "	1	SE	1888-07-10		A1
227	" "	1	SWNE	1888-07-10		A1
228	" "	11	4	1888-07-10		A1
229	" "	11	5	1888-07-10		A1
230	" "	11	6	1888-07-10		A1
231	" "	12	E½	1888-07-10		A1
232	" "	12	N½SW	1888-07-10		A1
233	" "	12	NENW	1888-07-10		A1
234	" "	12	S½NW	1888-07-10		A1
235	" "	13	N½SW	1888-07-10		A1
236	" "	13	NENE	1888-07-10		A1
237	" "	13	S½NW	1888-07-10		A1
238	" "	14	1	1888-07-10		A1
239	" "	14	2	1888-07-10		A1
240	" "	14	3	1888-07-10		A1
241	" "	14	E½NE	1888-07-10		A1
357	INGRAHAM, James E	21	SWSW	1884-06-20		A1 G64
358	" "	8	1	1884-06-20		A1 G64
373	KAHN, Otto P	31	4	1920-04-08		A3
344	KISSINGER, J P	20	NWNW	1889-03-28		A1
345	" "	20	NWSE	1889-03-28		A1
346	" "	22	NWNE	1889-03-28		A1
347	" "	22	SWNW	1889-03-28		A1
348	" "	23	E½NE	1889-03-28		A1
349	" "	23	SE	1889-03-28		A1
350	" "	24	NWNW	1889-03-28		A1
351	" "	26	E½NE	1889-03-28		A1
352	" "	26	W½SE	1889-03-28		A1
270	KREITE, Edward N	10	3	1888-07-10		A1
271	" "	10	NWSE	1888-07-10		A1
224	LEWIS, C E	5	4	1888-07-10		A1 G132
299	MAXON, Glenway	17	4	1888-07-07		A1
300	" "	17	5	1888-07-07		A1
301	" "	17	6	1888-07-07		A1
302	" "	17	7	1888-07-07		A1
303	" "	17	8	1888-07-07		A1
304	" "	17	SWSW	1888-07-07		A1
306	" "	18	N½	1888-07-07		A1 F
309	" "	19	NW	1888-07-07		A1 F
310	" "	19	NWNE	1888-07-07		A1

ID	Individual in Patent	Sec.	Sec. Part	Date Issued	Other Counties	For More Info . . .
311	MAXON, Glenway (Cont'd)	19	S½NE	1888-07-07		A1
317	" "	3	2	1888-07-07		A1
318	" "	3	3	1888-07-07		A1
319	" "	3	N½NW	1888-07-07		A1 F
320	" "	3	NWSW	1888-07-07		A1
321	" "	4	1	1888-07-07		A1
322	" "	5	N½NE	1888-07-07		A1 F
323	" "	5	N½NW	1888-07-07		A1 F
324	" "	5	SENW	1888-07-07		A1
325	" "	6	N½NE	1888-07-07		A1 F
326	" "	6	N½SW	1888-07-07		A1 F
327	" "	6	NW	1888-07-07		A1 F
328	" "	7	S½SW	1888-07-07		A1 F
329	" "	7	SE	1888-07-07		A1 F
330	" "	9	NE	1888-07-07		A1 F
331	" "	9	NWSE	1888-07-07		A1
332	" "	9	S½SE	1888-07-07		A1
297	" "	11	1	1889-03-28		A1
298	" "	15	2	1889-03-28		A1
305	" "	18	E½SW	1889-03-28		A1
307	" "	18	N½SE	1889-03-28		A1
308	" "	18	SWSE	1889-03-28		A1
312	" "	20	2	1889-03-28		A1
313	" "	20	SWNW	1889-03-28		A1
314	" "	24	5	1889-03-28		A1
315	" "	24	6	1889-03-28		A1
316	" "	25	7	1889-03-28		A1
412	MILLER, W H	2	NENE	1886-07-30		A1 G147
407	" "	10	4	1888-07-18		A1
408	" "	10	SWSE	1888-07-18		A1
409	" "	11	7	1888-07-18		A1
410	" "	15	1	1888-07-18		A1
411	" "	15	NENW	1888-07-18		A1
280	MINER, G B	10	10	1889-03-28		A1
281	" "	10	8	1889-03-28		A1
282	" "	10	9	1889-03-28		A1
283	" "	10	SWNW	1889-03-28		A1
284	" "	13	N½SE	1889-03-28		A1
285	" "	13	S½SW	1889-03-28		A1
286	" "	15	NWSW	1889-03-28		A1
287	" "	15	SENW	1889-03-28		A1
288	" "	15	SWNE	1889-03-28		A1
289	" "	15	W½NW	1889-03-28		A1
290	" "	18	SESE	1889-03-28		A1
291	" "	18	W½SW	1889-03-28		A1
292	" "	19	E½SE	1889-03-28		A1
293	" "	19	NESW	1889-03-28		A1
294	" "	19	NWSE	1889-03-28		A1
295	" "	19	W½SW	1889-03-28		A1 F
296	" "	6	SWNE	1889-03-28		A1
333	NEUMANN, George W	28	NESW	1884-06-30		A1 G76
334	" "	28	NWSE	1884-06-30		A1 G76
274	OBERMANN, Frederick L	10	5	1888-07-10		A1
275	" "	10	6	1888-07-10		A1
276	" "	10	7	1888-07-10		A1
277	" "	9	1	1888-07-10		A1
335	PARSONS, Isaac	27	S½SE	1884-06-30		A1 G153
336	" "	28	SWSE	1884-06-30		A1 G153
337	" "	33	N½NW	1884-06-30		A1 G153
338	" "	33	NWNE	1884-06-30		A1 G153
339	" "	35	NE	1884-06-30		A1 G153
340	" "	35	NWNW	1884-06-30		A1 G153
341	" "	36	N½NW	1884-06-30		A1 G153
342	" "	36	NENE	1884-06-30		A1 G153
343	" "	36	NWSE	1884-06-30		A1 G153
372	PILLSBURY, Oliver P	7	NENW	1885-01-15		A1
278	PRESCOTT, Frederick M	3	S½NW	1888-07-07		A1
279	" "	4	2	1888-07-07		A1
412	RUMSEY, T H	2	NENE	1886-07-30		A1 G147
224	" "	5	4	1888-07-10		A1 G132
383	RUMSEY, Tunis H	11	3	1886-07-30		A1
384	" "	12	NWNW	1886-07-30		A1
385	" "	2	SENE	1886-07-30		A1

ID	Individual in Patent	Sec.	Sec. Part	Date Issued	Other Counties	For More Info . . .
355	RUSSELL, Jesse M	25	SWSE	1885-05-20		A1
356	" "	36	NWNE	1885-05-20		A1
353	" "	20	E½NW	1888-07-07		A1
354	" "	20	SWNE	1888-07-07		A1
357	SAMPSON, Henry	21	SWSW	1884-06-20		A1 G64
358	" "	8	1	1884-06-20		A1 G64
359	SANSTER, Merritt	33	E½NE	1873-05-01		A1
360	" "	34	N½	1873-05-01		A1
361	" "	34	NESE	1873-05-01		A1
362	" "	34	NESW	1873-05-01		A1
363	" "	34	W½SW	1873-05-01		A1
364	" "	35	NENW	1873-05-01		A1
365	" "	35	S½	1873-05-01		A1
366	" "	35	S½NW	1873-05-01		A1
367	" "	36	NWSW	1873-05-01		A1
368	" "	36	SWNW	1873-05-01		A1
374	SEEGER, Paul A	10	1	1888-07-10		A1 F
375	" "	10	2	1888-07-10		A1 F
376	" "	10	SWNE	1888-07-10		A1 F
377	" "	11	8	1888-07-10		A1 F
378	" "	3	E½	1888-07-10		A1 F
242	STANTON, Celestia C	25	2	1888-05-11		A1
335	TILLOTSON, Levy	27	S½SE	1884-06-30		A1 G153
336	" "	28	SWSE	1884-06-30		A1 G153
337	" "	33	N½NW	1884-06-30		A1 G153
338	" "	33	NWNE	1884-06-30		A1 G153
339	" "	35	NE	1884-06-30		A1 G153
340	" "	35	NWNW	1884-06-30		A1 G153
341	" "	36	N½NW	1884-06-30		A1 G153
342	" "	36	NENE	1884-06-30		A1 G153
343	" "	36	NWSE	1884-06-30		A1 G153
395	VAN BRUNT, W A	6	SE	1886-03-01		A1
396	" "	6	SENE	1886-03-01		A1
397	" "	6	SESW	1886-03-01		A1
398	" "	7	E½NE	1886-03-01		A1
399	" "	7	W½NW	1886-03-01		A1 F
402	" "	8	7	1886-03-01		A1
403	" "	8	8	1886-03-01		A1
404	" "	8	9	1886-03-01		A1
405	" "	8	NWNW	1886-03-01		A1
386	" "	14	SWSE	1886-07-30		A1
387	" "	21	E½	1886-07-30		A1
388	" "	21	E½NW	1886-07-30		A1
389	" "	22	SW	1886-07-30		A1
390	" "	22	W½SE	1886-07-30		A1
391	" "	4	3	1886-07-30		A1
392	" "	4	4	1886-07-30		A1
393	" "	4	5	1886-07-30		A1
394	" "	4	6	1886-07-30		A1
400	" "	8	2	1886-07-30		A1
401	" "	8	3	1886-07-30		A1
406	" "	9	W½	1886-07-30		A1
335	WELLS, Charles W	27	S½SE	1884-06-30		A1 G153
336	" "	28	SWSE	1884-06-30		A1 G153
337	" "	33	N½NW	1884-06-30		A1 G153
338	" "	33	NWNE	1884-06-30		A1 G153
339	" "	35	NE	1884-06-30		A1 G153
340	" "	35	NWNW	1884-06-30		A1 G153
341	" "	36	N½NW	1884-06-30		A1 G153
342	" "	36	NENE	1884-06-30		A1 G153
343	" "	36	NWSE	1884-06-30		A1 G153
444	WESTON, William	31	5	1872-07-01		A1
445	" "	32	4	1872-07-01		A1
357	WITTER, Jere D	21	SWSW	1884-06-20		A1 G64
358	" "	8	1	1884-06-20		A1 G64

Patent Map

T43-N R5-E
4th PM - 1831 MN/WI

Map Group 4

Township Statistics

Parcels Mapped	:	229
Number of Patents	:	54
Number of Individuals	:	35
Patentees Identified	:	29
Number of Surnames	:	34
Multi-Patentee Parcels	:	15
Oldest Patent Date	:	7/1/1872
Most Recent Patent	:	4/8/1920
Block/Lot Parcels	:	75
Parcels Re - Issued	:	0
Parcels that Overlap	:	0
Cities and Towns	:	1
Cemeteries	:	0

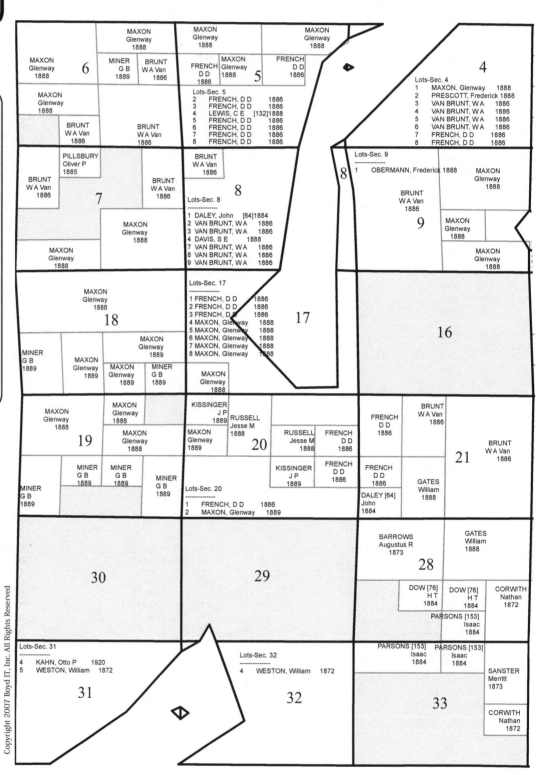

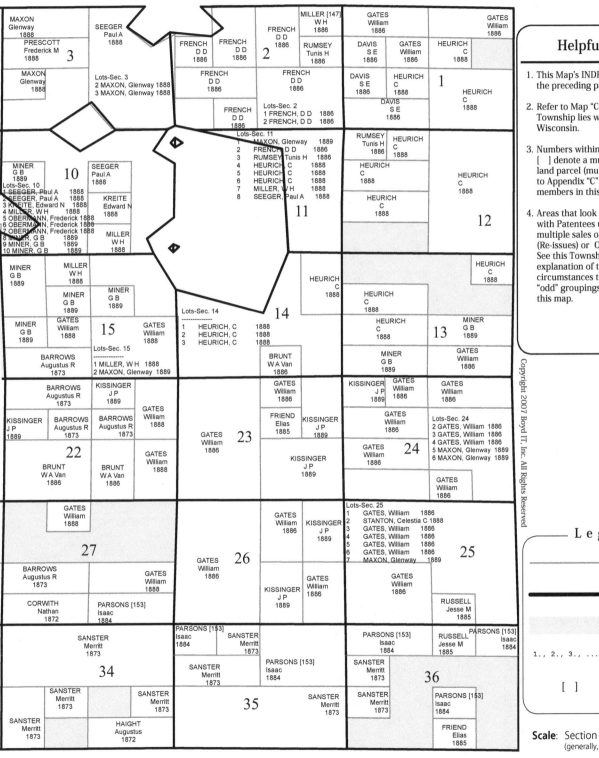

Helpful Hints

1. This Map's INDEX can be found on the preceding pages.

2. Refer to Map "C" to see where this Township lies within Vilas County, Wisconsin.

3. Numbers within square brackets [ ] denote a multi-patentee land parcel (multi-owner). Refer to Appendix "C" for a full list of members in this group.

4. Areas that look to be crowded with Patentees usually indicate multiple sales of the same parcel (Re-issues) or Overlapping parcels. See this Township's Index for an explanation of these and other circumstances that might explain "odd" groupings of Patentees on this map.

Legend

— Patent Boundary

━ Section Boundary

No Patents Found (or Outside County)

1., 2., 3., ... Lot Numbers (when beside a name)

[ ] Group Number (see Appendix "C")

Scale: Section = 1 mile X 1 mile (generally, with some exceptions)

Road Map

T43-N R5-E
4th PM - 1831 MN/WI

Map Group 4

Cities & Towns
Winchester

Cemeteries
None

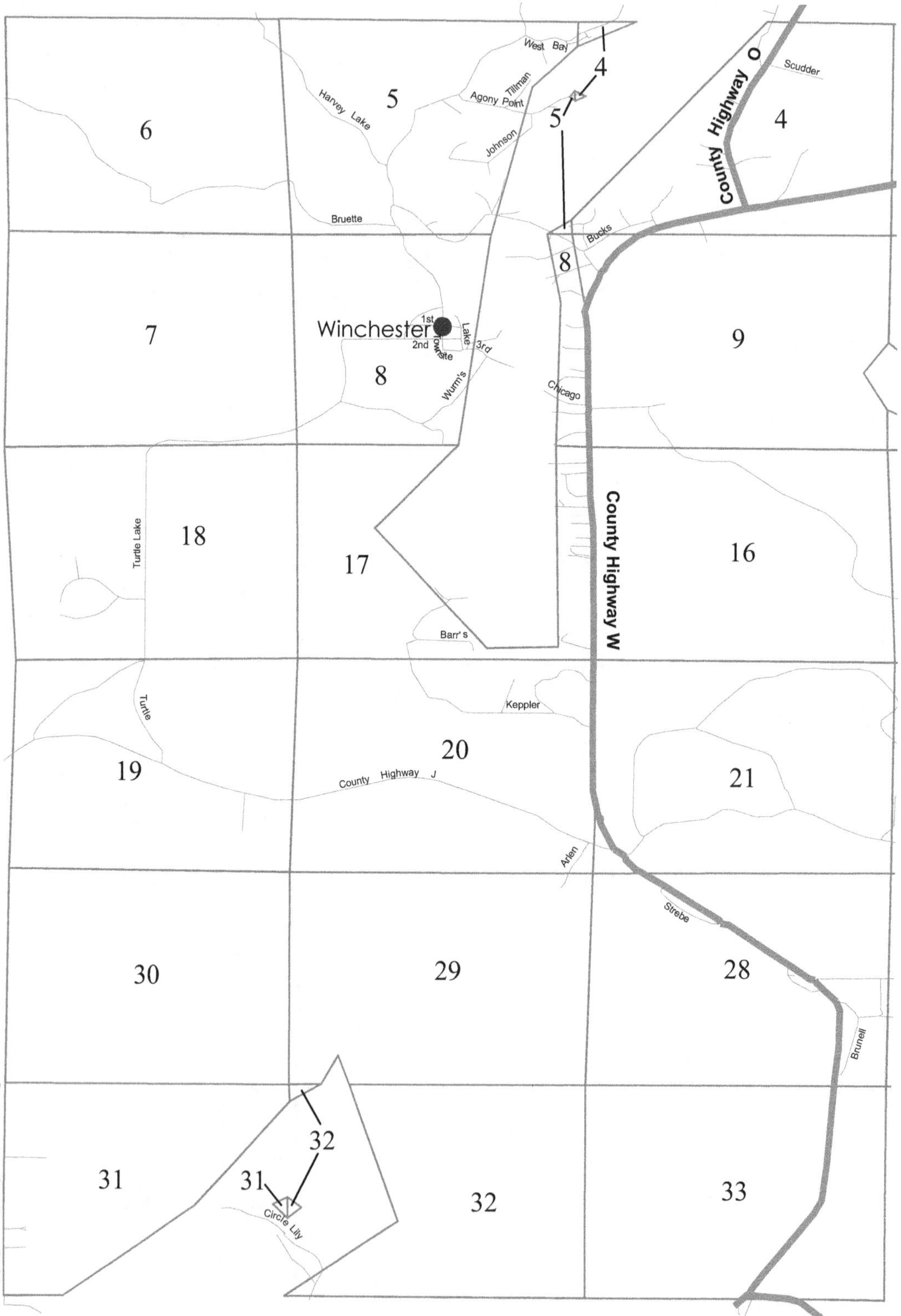

West Bay

Tillman

4

Agony Point

5

Harvey Lake

5

Johnson

Scudder

County Highway O

4

6

Bucks

8

Bruette

Winchester

1st

Townsite

Lake

3rd

2nd

8

Wurm's

Chicago

9

Turtle Lake

18

17

16

County Highway W

Barr's

Keppler

Turtle

20

County Highway J

19

21

Arlen

Strebe

30

29

28

Brunell

32

31

31

32

Circle Lily

33

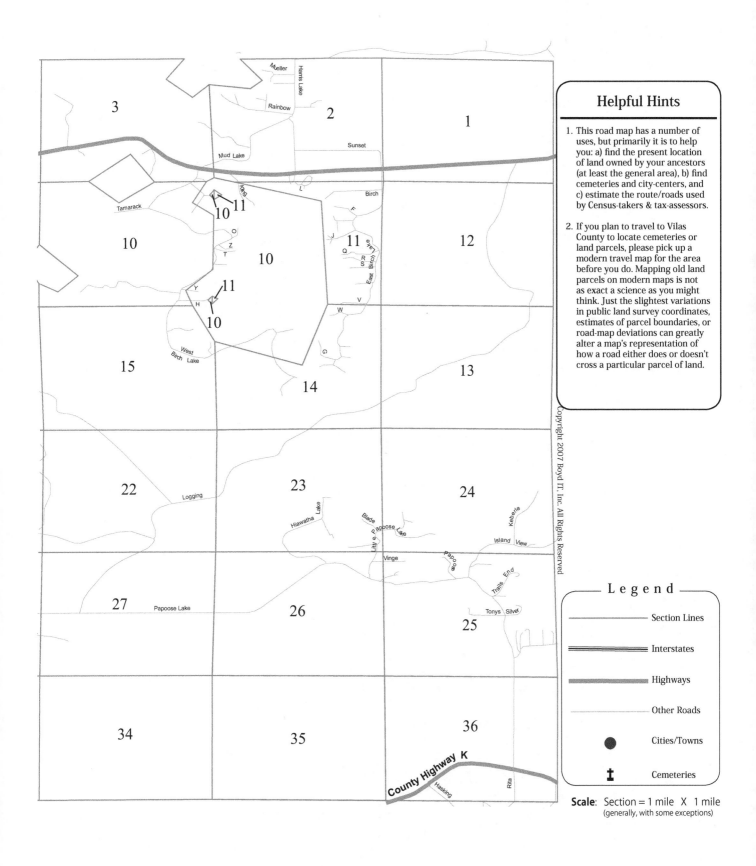

Helpful Hints

1. This road map has a number of uses, but primarily it is to help you: a) find the present location of land owned by your ancestors (at least the general area), b) find cemeteries and city-centers, and c) estimate the route/roads used by Census-takers & tax-assessors.

2. If you plan to travel to Vilas County to locate cemeteries or land parcels, please pick up a modern travel map for the area before you do. Mapping old land parcels on modern maps is not as exact a science as you might think. Just the slightest variations in public land survey coordinates, estimates of parcel boundaries, or road-map deviations can greatly alter a map's representation of how a road either does or doesn't cross a particular parcel of land.

Legend

——————	Section Lines
≡≡≡≡≡≡	Interstates
━━━━━	Highways
——————	Other Roads
●	Cities/Towns
☩	Cemeteries

Scale: Section = 1 mile X 1 mile
(generally, with some exceptions)

Historical Map

T43-N R5-E
4th PM - 1831 MN/WI

Map Group 4

Cities & Towns
Winchester

Cemeteries
None

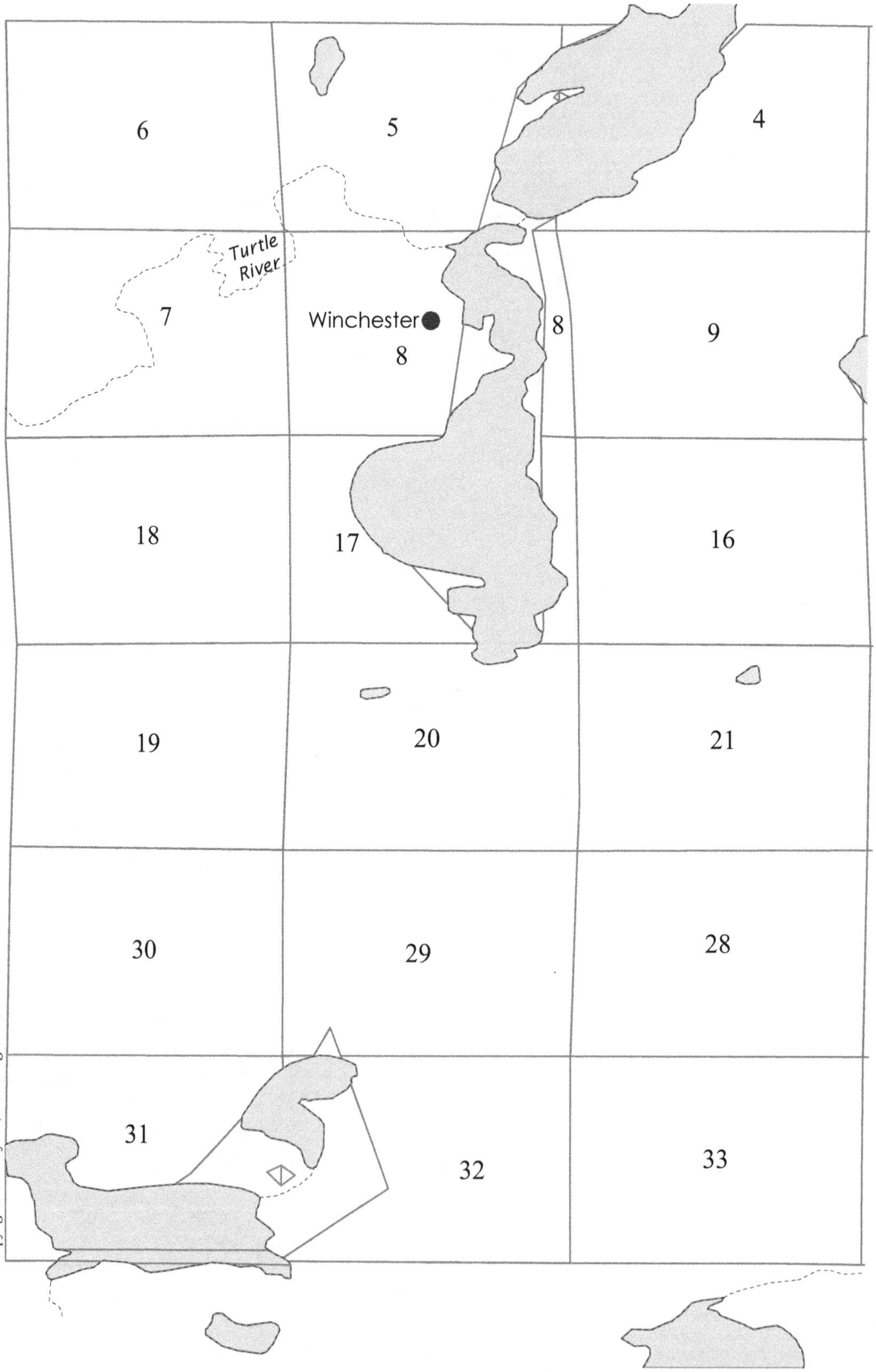

6	5	4
7	Winchester ● 8	8	9
18	17	16
19	20	21
30	29	28
31	32	33

Turtle River

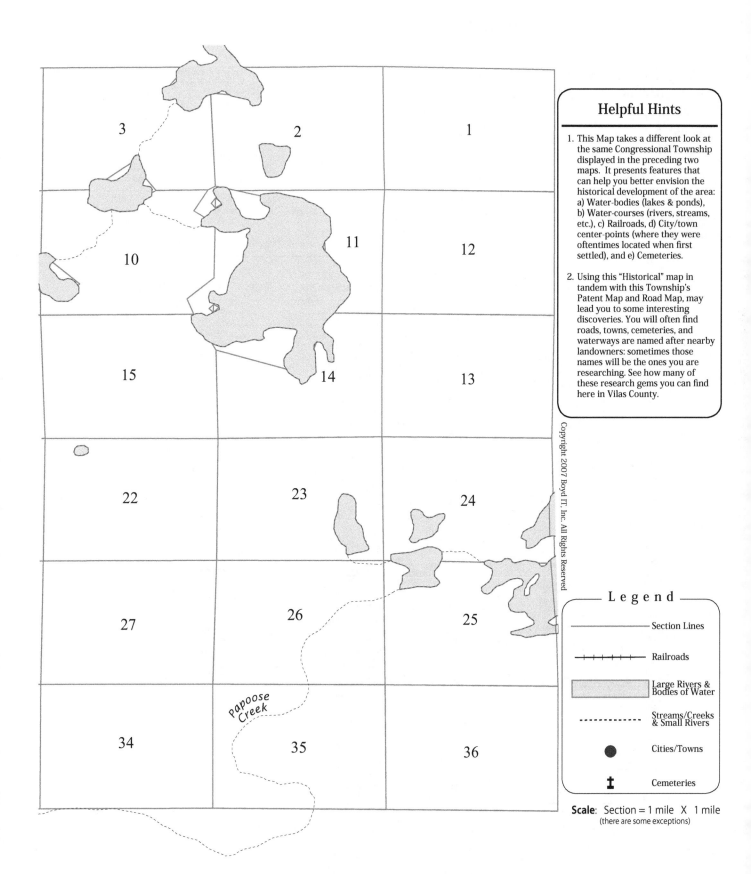

Helpful Hints

1. This Map takes a different look at the same Congressional Township displayed in the preceding two maps. It presents features that can help you better envision the historical development of the area: a) Water-bodies (lakes & ponds), b) Water-courses (rivers, streams, etc.), c) Railroads, d) City/town center-points (where they were oftentimes located when first settled), and e) Cemeteries.

2. Using this "Historical" map in tandem with this Township's Patent Map and Road Map, may lead you to some interesting discoveries. You will often find roads, towns, cemeteries, and waterways are named after nearby landowners: sometimes those names will be the ones you are researching. See how many of these research gems you can find here in Vilas County.

Papoose Creek

Legend

———	Section Lines
+++++	Railroads
�block	Large Rivers & Bodies of Water
- - - - -	Streams/Creeks & Small Rivers
●	Cities/Towns
✝	Cemeteries

Scale: Section = 1 mile X 1 mile
(there are some exceptions)

Map Group 5: Index to Land Patents

Township 43-North Range 6-East (4th PM - 1831 MN/WI)

After you locate an individual in this Index, take note of the Section and Section Part then proceed to the Land Patent map on the pages immediately following. You should have no difficulty locating the corresponding parcel of land.

The "For More Info" Column will lead you to more information about the underlying Patents. See the *Legend* at right, and the "How to Use this Book" chapter, for more information.

```
                          LEGEND
              "For More Info . . . " column
A = Authority (Legislative Act, See Appendix "A")
B = Block or Lot (location in Section unknown)
C = Cancelled Patent
F = Fractional Section
G = Group  (Multi-Patentee Patent, see Appendix "C")
V = Overlaps another Parcel
R = Re-Issued (Parcel patented more than once)

(A & G items require you to look in the Appendixes referred
to above. All other Letter-designations followed by a number
require you to locate line-items in this index that possess
the ID number found after the letter).
```

ID	Individual in Patent	Sec.	Sec. Part	Date Issued	Other Counties	For More Info . . .
542	ARPIN, Daniel	10	SENW	1888-07-18		A1 G9 R461
543	" "	25	3	1888-07-18		A1 G9
544	" "	25	4	1888-07-18		A1 G9
545	" "	25	SESE	1888-07-18		A1 G9
546	" "	25	SESW	1888-07-18		A1 G9
547	" "	26	6	1888-07-18		A1 G9
548	" "	26	7	1888-07-18		A1 G9
549	" "	26	8	1888-07-18		A1 G9
550	" "	26	9	1888-07-18		A1 G9
551	" "	26	NWSW	1888-07-18		A1 G9
552	" "	26	SESW	1888-07-18		A1 G9
553	" "	36	1	1888-07-18		A1 G9
554	" "	36	2	1888-07-18		A1 G9
555	" "	36	E½SE	1888-07-18		A1 G9
542	ARPIN, John	10	SENW	1888-07-18		A1 G9 R461
543	" "	25	3	1888-07-18		A1 G9
544	" "	25	4	1888-07-18		A1 G9
545	" "	25	SESE	1888-07-18		A1 G9
546	" "	25	SESW	1888-07-18		A1 G9
547	" "	26	6	1888-07-18		A1 G9
548	" "	26	7	1888-07-18		A1 G9
549	" "	26	8	1888-07-18		A1 G9
550	" "	26	9	1888-07-18		A1 G9
551	" "	26	NWSW	1888-07-18		A1 G9
552	" "	26	SESW	1888-07-18		A1 G9
553	" "	36	1	1888-07-18		A1 G9
554	" "	36	2	1888-07-18		A1 G9
555	" "	36	E½SE	1888-07-18		A1 G9
446	BABCOCK, Adelbert A	1	9	1910-12-01		A3 G12
447	" "	14	10	1910-12-01		A3 G12
448	" "	22	15	1910-12-01		A3 G12
449	" "	22	9	1910-12-01		A3 G12
450	" "	23	10	1910-12-01		A3 G12
556	BARNETT, E D	33	2	1884-06-30		A1 G14
556	BARNETT, Joel D	33	2	1884-06-30		A1 G14
454	BARROWS, Augustus R	29	2	1873-05-01		A1
455	" "	29	4	1873-05-01		A1
456	" "	29	NWSE	1873-05-01		A1
457	" "	29	SESE	1873-05-01		A1
659	BAUMAN, George M	13	8	1912-01-25		A3 G18
660	" "	21	10	1912-01-25		A3 G18
661	" "	21	11	1912-01-25		A3 G18
662	" "	22	16	1912-01-25		A3 G18
663	" "	23	12	1912-01-25		A3 G18
659	BAUMAN, Martha	13	8	1912-01-25		A3 G18
660	" "	21	10	1912-01-25		A3 G18

ID	Individual in Patent	Sec.	Sec. Part	Date Issued	Other Counties	For More Info . . .
661	BAUMAN, Martha (Cont'd)	21	11	1912-01-25		A3 G18
662	" "	22	16	1912-01-25		A3 G18
663	" "	23	12	1912-01-25		A3 G18
713	BLYTHE, John	14	13	1911-11-20		A3 G26
664	BOROWITZ, George W	13	7	1921-04-07		A1
532	CLASON, Charles L	23	5	1889-03-28		A1
770	COLBURN, Winfield S	13	2	1889-03-28		A1
771	" "	13	3	1889-03-28		A1
772	" "	13	SENW	1889-03-28		A1
773	" "	29	E½SW	1889-03-28		A1
774	" "	29	SWSE	1889-03-28		A1
775	" "	29	SWSW	1889-03-28		A1
776	" "	4	NW	1889-03-28		A1 F
777	" "	4	W½NE	1889-03-28		A1 F
778	" "	4	W½SE	1889-03-28		A1
779	" "	9	N½SE	1889-03-28		A1
780	" "	9	SWSE	1889-03-28		A1
738	COLLINS, Samuel O	18	NWSE	1889-03-28		A1
739	" "	18	SW	1889-03-28		A1 F
740	" "	19	1	1889-03-28		A1
741	" "	9	5	1889-03-28		A1
714	COOPER, John H	22	12	1910-10-10		A3 G58
701	DICK, Herman E	23	8	1911-04-24		A3 G72
713	" "	14	13	1911-11-20		A3 G26
714	DICK, Kenneth W	22	12	1910-10-10		A3 G58
531	FOURNIER, Charles D	22	10	1910-11-09		A3 G88
750	FRANKFURTH, William	15	7	1885-12-10		A1 G89
751	" "	21	3	1885-12-10		A1 G89
752	" "	21	4	1885-12-10		A1 G89
753	" "	21	5	1885-12-10		A1 G89
754	" "	21	6	1885-12-10		A1 G89
755	" "	21	E½NE	1885-12-10		A1 G89
756	" "	21	E½SE	1885-12-10		A1 G89
757	" "	22	1	1885-12-10		A1 G89
758	" "	22	2	1885-12-10		A1 G89
759	" "	22	3	1885-12-10		A1 G89
760	" "	22	4	1885-12-10		A1 G89
761	" "	22	SWSW	1885-12-10		A1 G89
557	FRIEND, Elias	22	5	1885-11-25		A1
558	" "	35	1	1885-11-25		A1
762	GATES, William	27	N½NW	1885-12-10		A1
763	" "	28	N½NE	1885-12-10		A1
764	" "	28	SENE	1885-12-10		A1
765	" "	28	SENW	1885-12-10		A1
766	" "	28	SW	1885-12-10		A1
767	" "	28	W½NW	1885-12-10		A1
768	" "	28	W½SE	1885-12-10		A1
533	GILBERT, Charles S	22	13	1913-12-23		A3 G90
534	" "	22	8	1913-12-23		A3 G90
744	GILBERT, W C	22	6	1888-07-18		A1
745	" "	22	7	1888-07-18		A1
452	HAIGHT, Augustus	29	NESE	1872-11-01		A1
453	" "	33	4	1873-05-01		A1
707	HALLINAN, James	15	SWSW	1886-07-30		A1
769	HENDRY, William	15	5	1888-07-07		A1
702	JAHN, Herman F	23	11	1910-06-27		A3 G117
701	JOHNSON, Emeline	23	8	1911-04-24		A3 G72
701	JOHNSON, Ezra	23	8	1911-04-24		A3 G72
446	KIKENDALL, John S	1	9	1910-12-01		A3 G12
447	" "	14	10	1910-12-01		A3 G12
448	" "	22	15	1910-12-01		A3 G12
449	" "	22	9	1910-12-01		A3 G12
450	" "	23	10	1910-12-01		A3 G12
715	KULANDA, John	19	7	1903-06-20		A3 G125 F
715	KULANDA, Mary	19	7	1903-06-20		A3 G125 F
715	LINDSTEDT, Julius	19	7	1903-06-20		A3 G125 F
750	MASCHAUER, Lorenz	15	7	1885-12-10		A1 G89
751	" "	21	3	1885-12-10		A1 G89
752	" "	21	4	1885-12-10		A1 G89
753	" "	21	5	1885-12-10		A1 G89
754	" "	21	6	1885-12-10		A1 G89
755	" "	21	E½NE	1885-12-10		A1 G89
756	" "	21	E½SE	1885-12-10		A1 G89

ID	Individual in Patent	Sec.	Sec. Part	Date Issued	Other Counties	For More Info . . .
757	MASCHAUER, Lorenz (Cont'd)	22	1	1885-12-10		A1 G89
758	" "	22	2	1885-12-10		A1 G89
759	" "	22	3	1885-12-10		A1 G89
760	" "	22	4	1885-12-10		A1 G89
761	" "	22	SWSW	1885-12-10		A1 G89
728	MASHINO, Nicholas	14	11	1911-01-16		A3 G135
665	MAXON, Glenway	10	1	1889-03-28		A1
666	" "	10	2	1889-03-28		A1
667	" "	10	3	1889-03-28		A1
668	" "	10	SWSE	1889-03-28		A1
669	" "	11	5	1889-03-28		A1
670	" "	11	E½SE	1889-03-28		A1
671	" "	13	1	1889-03-28		A1
672	" "	14	8	1889-03-28		A1
673	" "	15	1	1889-03-28		A1
674	" "	15	N½NE	1889-03-28		A1
675	" "	30	1	1889-03-28		A1
676	" "	30	10	1889-03-28		A1
677	" "	30	3	1889-03-28		A1
678	" "	30	4	1889-03-28		A1
679	" "	32	1	1889-03-28		A1
680	" "	32	2	1889-03-28		A1
681	" "	32	4	1889-03-28		A1
682	" "	32	5	1889-03-28		A1
683	" "	32	6	1889-03-28		A1
684	" "	32	7	1889-03-28		A1
685	" "	32	NENW	1889-03-28		A1
686	" "	32	NESE	1889-03-28		A1
639	MCCLINTOCK, Emory	21	7	1889-03-28		A1
640	" "	23	3	1889-03-28		A1
641	" "	23	6	1889-03-28		A1
642	" "	26	3	1889-03-28		A1
643	" "	27	W½SW	1889-03-28		A1
644	" "	28	NENW	1889-03-28		A1
645	" "	28	SESE	1889-03-28		A1
646	" "	28	SWNE	1889-03-28		A1
647	" "	31	SESW	1889-03-28		A1
648	" "	33	3	1889-03-28		A1
649	" "	34	E½NW	1889-03-28		A1
650	" "	34	N½NE	1889-03-28		A1
651	" "	36	3	1889-03-28		A1
652	" "	36	4	1889-03-28		A1
653	" "	36	7	1889-03-28		A1
654	" "	36	9	1889-03-28		A1
655	" "	36	NWNW	1889-03-28		A1
737	MOFFAT, Roger	23	9	1910-11-09		A3 G148
728	MULVANE, Joab	14	11	1911-01-16		A3 G135
737	NELSON, Edward D	23	9	1910-11-09		A3 G148
656	OTTEROL, Evelyn	25	SWSE	1885-07-13		A1
657	" "	35	4	1885-07-13		A1
658	" "	35	SWNW	1885-07-13		A1
703	PARSONS, Isaac	31	1	1884-06-30		A1 G153
704	" "	31	N½SW	1884-06-30		A1 G153
705	" "	31	NWNE	1884-06-30		A1 G153
706	" "	31	NWNW	1884-06-30		A1 G153
687	PILLSBURY, Harry M	14	2	1889-03-28		A1
688	" "	24	NWNE	1889-03-28		A1
630	POND, Ellis	14	12	1911-02-23		A3 G156
729	PURTELL, P W	10	NWSW	1885-06-12		A1
730	" "	35	2	1885-06-12		A1
731	" "	35	3	1885-06-12		A1
732	" "	35	SESW	1885-06-12		A1
733	" "	36	6	1885-06-12		A1
631	RIPLEY, Emma A	27	SENW	1871-04-01		A1
632	" "	30	6	1871-04-01		A1
633	" "	31	2	1871-04-01		A1
634	" "	31	3	1871-04-01		A1
635	" "	31	SWNW	1871-04-01		A1 F
636	" "	31	SWSW	1871-04-01		A1
637	" "	33	1	1871-04-01		A1
638	" "	33	NESE	1871-04-01		A1
533	ROLLENHAGEN, August	22	13	1913-12-23		A3 G90
534	" "	22	8	1913-12-23		A3 G90

ID	Individual in Patent	Sec.	Sec. Part	Date Issued	Other Counties	For More Info . . .
716	ROSS, John	30	7	1874-08-01		A1
742	RUMSEY, Tunis H	14	6	1885-11-25		A1
743	" "	20	7	1885-11-25		A1
708	RUSSELL, Jesse M	14	4	1885-05-20		A1
709	" "	23	4	1885-05-20		A1
710	" "	26	4	1885-05-20		A1
711	" "	31	4	1885-05-20		A1
712	" "	31	E½NW	1885-05-20		A1
700	SAGE, Henry W	26	SWNW	1883-04-20		A1
690	" "	14	3	1883-09-10		A1
691	" "	14	5	1883-09-10		A1
689	" "	13	SWSW	1883-09-15		A1
692	" "	24	2	1883-09-15		A1
693	" "	24	3	1883-09-15		A1
694	" "	24	SWNE	1883-09-15		A1
695	" "	24	W½SE	1883-09-15		A1
696	" "	25	5	1883-09-15		A1
697	" "	25	SWSW	1883-09-15		A1
698	" "	26	5	1883-09-15		A1
699	" "	26	NESE	1883-09-15		A1
727	SCHAETZLE, Max	9	6	1911-01-23		A1
702	SCHOFIELD, Hiram	23	11	1910-06-27		A3 G117
531	SECHRIST, John W	22	10	1910-11-09		A3 G88
451	SHEPPARD, Amos C	21	9	1911-02-23		A3 G160
734	SHEPPARD, Robert L	1	8	1911-08-04		A2
735	" "	10	5	1911-08-04		A2
736	" "	11	7	1911-08-04		A2
659	" "	13	8	1912-01-25		A3 G18
660	" "	21	10	1912-01-25		A3 G18
661	" "	21	11	1912-01-25		A3 G18
662	" "	22	16	1912-01-25		A3 G18
663	" "	23	12	1912-01-25		A3 G18
451	SHEPPARD, Sarah L	21	9	1911-02-23		A3 G160
559	SLOCUM, Elliot T	8	2	1884-06-30		A1 G161
560	" "	8	3	1884-06-30		A1 G161
561	" "	8	4	1884-06-30		A1 G161
562	" "	8	5	1884-06-30		A1 G161
563	" "	8	6	1884-06-30		A1 G161
564	" "	8	7	1884-06-30		A1 G161
565	" "	9	2	1884-06-30		A1 G161
566	" "	9	3	1884-06-30		A1 G161
578	SLOCUM, Elliott T	1		1884-06-20		A1 G162 F
579	" "	12	1	1884-06-20		A1 G162
580	" "	12	2	1884-06-20		A1 G162
581	" "	12	3	1884-06-20		A1 G162
582	" "	12	N½NE	1884-06-20		A1 G162
583	" "	12	NESW	1884-06-20		A1 G162
584	" "	12	NW	1884-06-20		A1 G162
585	" "	12	SWNE	1884-06-20		A1 G162
586	" "	12	W½SW	1884-06-20		A1 G162
587	" "	2	1	1884-06-20		A1 G162
588	" "	2	2	1884-06-20		A1 G162
589	" "	2	3	1884-06-20		A1 G162
590	" "	2	4	1884-06-20		A1 G162
591	" "	2	5	1884-06-20		A1 G162
592	" "	2	6	1884-06-20		A1 G162
593	" "	2	7	1884-06-20		A1 G162
594	" "	2	N½NE	1884-06-20		A1 G162
595	" "	2	SENE	1884-06-20		A1 G162
596	" "	3	1	1884-06-20		A1 G162
597	" "	3	2	1884-06-20		A1 G162
598	" "	3	3	1884-06-20		A1 G162
599	" "	3	4	1884-06-20		A1 G162
600	" "	3	5	1884-06-20		A1 G162
601	" "	3	6	1884-06-20		A1 G162
602	" "	3	7	1884-06-20		A1 G162
603	" "	3	N½NW	1884-06-20		A1 G162
604	" "	3	SWNW	1884-06-20		A1 G162
605	" "	3	W½SW	1884-06-20		A1 G162
608	" "	5	1	1884-06-20		A1 G162
609	" "	5	2	1884-06-20		A1 G162
610	" "	5	3	1884-06-20		A1 G162
611	" "	5	4	1884-06-20		A1 G162

ID	Individual in Patent	Sec.	Sec. Part	Date Issued	Other Counties	For More Info . . .
612	SLOCUM, Elliott T (Cont'd)	5	E½SE	1884-06-20		A1 G162
613	" "	5	NE	1884-06-20		A1 G162
614	" "	5	NENW	1884-06-20		A1 G162
615	" "	6	1	1884-06-20		A1 G162
616	" "	6	2	1884-06-20		A1 G162
617	" "	6	3	1884-06-20		A1 G162
618	" "	6	N½NE	1884-06-20		A1 G162
619	" "	6	NESW	1884-06-20		A1 G162
620	" "	6	NW	1884-06-20		A1 G162
621	" "	6	NWSW	1884-06-20		A1 G162
622	" "	6	SWSW	1884-06-20		A1 G162
623	" "	7	1	1884-06-20		A1 G162
624	" "	7	2	1884-06-20		A1 G162
625	" "	7	3	1884-06-20		A1 G162
626	" "	7	4	1884-06-20		A1 G162
567	" "	17	1	1884-06-30		A1
568	" "	17	2	1884-06-30		A1
569	" "	17	3	1884-06-30		A1
570	" "	17	4	1884-06-30		A1
571	" "	17	S½NW	1884-06-30		A1
572	" "	18	1	1884-06-30		A1
573	" "	18	2	1884-06-30		A1
574	" "	18	3	1884-06-30		A1
575	" "	18	4	1884-06-30		A1
576	" "	18	S½NE	1884-06-30		A1
577	" "	18	S½NW	1884-06-30		A1
606	" "	4	E½NE	1884-06-30		A1 G162
607	" "	4	E½SE	1884-06-30		A1 G162
627	" "	7	5	1884-06-30		A1 G162
628	" "	9	1	1884-06-30		A1 G162
629	" "	9	4	1884-06-30		A1 G162
578	SLOCUM, Giles B	1		1884-06-20		A1 G162 F
579	" "	12	1	1884-06-20		A1 G162
580	" "	12	2	1884-06-20		A1 G162
581	" "	12	3	1884-06-20		A1 G162
582	" "	12	N½NE	1884-06-20		A1 G162
583	" "	12	NESW	1884-06-20		A1 G162
584	" "	12	NW	1884-06-20		A1 G162
585	" "	12	SWNE	1884-06-20		A1 G162
586	" "	12	W½SW	1884-06-20		A1 G162
587	" "	2	1	1884-06-20		A1 G162
588	" "	2	2	1884-06-20		A1 G162
589	" "	2	3	1884-06-20		A1 G162
590	" "	2	4	1884-06-20		A1 G162
591	" "	2	5	1884-06-20		A1 G162
592	" "	2	6	1884-06-20		A1 G162
593	" "	2	7	1884-06-20		A1 G162
594	" "	2	N½NE	1884-06-20		A1 G162
595	" "	2	SENE	1884-06-20		A1 G162
596	" "	3	1	1884-06-20		A1 G162
597	" "	3	2	1884-06-20		A1 G162
598	" "	3	3	1884-06-20		A1 G162
599	" "	3	4	1884-06-20		A1 G162
600	" "	3	5	1884-06-20		A1 G162
601	" "	3	6	1884-06-20		A1 G162
602	" "	3	7	1884-06-20		A1 G162
603	" "	3	N½NW	1884-06-20		A1 G162
604	" "	3	SWNW	1884-06-20		A1 G162
605	" "	3	W½SW	1884-06-20		A1 G162
608	" "	5	1	1884-06-20		A1 G162
609	" "	5	2	1884-06-20		A1 G162
610	" "	5	3	1884-06-20		A1 G162
611	" "	5	4	1884-06-20		A1 G162
612	" "	5	E½SE	1884-06-20		A1 G162
613	" "	5	NE	1884-06-20		A1 G162
614	" "	5	NENW	1884-06-20		A1 G162
615	" "	6	1	1884-06-20		A1 G162
616	" "	6	2	1884-06-20		A1 G162
617	" "	6	3	1884-06-20		A1 G162
618	" "	6	N½NE	1884-06-20		A1 G162
619	" "	6	NESW	1884-06-20		A1 G162
620	" "	6	NW	1884-06-20		A1 G162
621	" "	6	NWSW	1884-06-20		A1 G162

ID	Individual in Patent	Sec.	Sec. Part	Date Issued	Other Counties	For More Info . . .
622	SLOCUM, Giles B (Cont'd)	6	SWSW	1884-06-20		A1 G162
623	" "	7	1	1884-06-20		A1 G162
624	" "	7	2	1884-06-20		A1 G162
625	" "	7	3	1884-06-20		A1 G162
626	" "	7	4	1884-06-20		A1 G162
606	" "	4	E½NE	1884-06-30		A1 G162
607	" "	4	E½SE	1884-06-30		A1 G162
627	" "	7	5	1884-06-30		A1 G162
559	" "	8	2	1884-06-30		A1 G161
560	" "	8	3	1884-06-30		A1 G161
561	" "	8	4	1884-06-30		A1 G161
562	" "	8	5	1884-06-30		A1 G161
563	" "	8	6	1884-06-30		A1 G161
564	" "	8	7	1884-06-30		A1 G161
628	" "	9	1	1884-06-30		A1 G162
565	" "	9	2	1884-06-30		A1 G161
566	" "	9	3	1884-06-30		A1 G161
629	" "	9	4	1884-06-30		A1 G162
451	STREATOR, Victor	21	9	1911-02-23		A3 G160
703	TILLOTSON, Levy	31	1	1884-06-30		A1 G153
704	" "	31	N½SW	1884-06-30		A1 G153
705	" "	31	NWNE	1884-06-30		A1 G153
706	" "	31	NWNW	1884-06-30		A1 G153
746	WALTER, Will P	12	4	1911-08-04		A2
747	" "	12	5	1911-08-04		A2
748	" "	12	6	1911-08-04		A2
749	" "	22	14	1911-08-04		A2
717	WATERMAN, Leslie J	25	SENE	1884-06-30		A1 G168
718	" "	32	3	1884-06-30		A1 G168
719	" "	32	N½NE	1884-06-30		A1 G168
720	" "	32	SENE	1884-06-30		A1 G168
721	" "	32	SWNE	1884-06-30		A1 G168
722	" "	33	5	1884-06-30		A1 G168
723	" "	33	N½NW	1884-06-30		A1 G168
724	" "	33	NWNE	1884-06-30		A1 G168
725	" "	33	SWNW	1884-06-30		A1 G168
726	" "	8	1	1884-06-30		A1 G168
703	WELLS, Charles W	31	1	1884-06-30		A1 G153
704	" "	31	N½SW	1884-06-30		A1 G153
705	" "	31	NWNE	1884-06-30		A1 G153
706	" "	31	NWNW	1884-06-30		A1 G153
717	WILEY, Charles L	25	SENE	1884-06-30		A1 G168
718	" "	32	3	1884-06-30		A1 G168
719	" "	32	N½NE	1884-06-30		A1 G168
720	" "	32	SENE	1884-06-30		A1 G168
721	" "	32	SWNE	1884-06-30		A1 G168
722	" "	33	5	1884-06-30		A1 G168
723	" "	33	N½NW	1884-06-30		A1 G168
724	" "	33	NWNE	1884-06-30		A1 G168
725	" "	33	SWNW	1884-06-30		A1 G168
726	" "	8	1	1884-06-30		A1 G168
535	WILHELM, Charles	17	10	1885-12-10		A1
536	" "	17	5	1885-12-10		A1
537	" "	17	6	1885-12-10		A1
538	" "	17	7	1885-12-10		A1
539	" "	17	8	1885-12-10		A1
540	" "	17	9	1885-12-10		A1
541	" "	18	S½SE	1885-12-10		A1 V484
529	WILSON, Charles A	14	14	1913-02-20		A1
530	" "	15	8	1913-02-20		A1
458	YOUNG, Benjamin	10	4	1885-12-10		A1
459	" "	10	E½SW	1885-12-10		A1
460	" "	10	N½NW	1885-12-10		A1
461	" "	10	SENW	1885-12-10		A1 R542
462	" "	10	SWSW	1885-12-10		A1
463	" "	11	1	1885-12-10		A1
464	" "	11	2	1885-12-10		A1
465	" "	11	3	1885-12-10		A1
466	" "	11	4	1885-12-10		A1
467	" "	11	6	1885-12-10		A1
468	" "	11	SENE	1885-12-10		A1
469	" "	11	W½SE	1885-12-10		A1
470	" "	13	4	1885-12-10		A1

ID	Individual in Patent	Sec.	Sec. Part	Date Issued	Other Counties	For More Info . . .
471	YOUNG, Benjamin (Cont'd)	13	5	1885-12-10		A1
472	" "	13	6	1885-12-10		A1
473	" "	13	N½NW	1885-12-10		A1
474	" "	13	NESE	1885-12-10		A1
475	" "	14	1	1885-12-10		A1
476	" "	14	7	1885-12-10		A1
477	" "	14	9	1885-12-10		A1
478	" "	15	2	1885-12-10		A1
479	" "	15	3	1885-12-10		A1
480	" "	15	4	1885-12-10		A1
481	" "	15	6	1885-12-10		A1
482	" "	15	NW	1885-12-10		A1
483	" "	15	NWSW	1885-12-10		A1
484	" "	18	SWSE	1885-12-10		A1 V541
485	" "	19	2	1885-12-10		A1
486	" "	19	3	1885-12-10		A1
487	" "	19	4	1885-12-10		A1
488	" "	19	5	1885-12-10		A1
489	" "	19	6	1885-12-10		A1
490	" "	19	E½SE	1885-12-10		A1
491	" "	19	W½NE	1885-12-10		A1
492	" "	20	1	1885-12-10		A1
493	" "	20	2	1885-12-10		A1
494	" "	20	3	1885-12-10		A1
495	" "	20	4	1885-12-10		A1
496	" "	20	5	1885-12-10		A1
497	" "	20	6	1885-12-10		A1
498	" "	20	NENE	1885-12-10		A1
499	" "	20	NWSE	1885-12-10		A1
500	" "	20	SW	1885-12-10		A1
501	" "	20	SWNE	1885-12-10		A1
502	" "	21	1	1885-12-10		A1
503	" "	21	2	1885-12-10		A1
504	" "	21	8	1885-12-10		A1
505	" "	23	1	1885-12-10		A1
506	" "	23	2	1885-12-10		A1
507	" "	24	1	1885-12-10		A1
508	" "	24	10	1885-12-10		A1
509	" "	24	4	1885-12-10		A1
510	" "	24	5	1885-12-10		A1
511	" "	24	6	1885-12-10		A1
512	" "	24	7	1885-12-10		A1
513	" "	24	8	1885-12-10		A1
514	" "	24	9	1885-12-10		A1
515	" "	25	1	1885-12-10		A1
516	" "	25	2	1885-12-10		A1
517	" "	25	6	1885-12-10		A1
518	" "	25	7	1885-12-10		A1
519	" "	25	NENE	1885-12-10		A1
520	" "	29	1	1885-12-10		A1
521	" "	29	3	1885-12-10		A1
522	" "	29	NW	1885-12-10		A1
523	" "	30	2	1885-12-10		A1
524	" "	4	SW	1885-12-10		A1
525	" "	9	E½NW	1885-12-10		A1
526	" "	9	NE	1885-12-10		A1
527	" "	9	NWNW	1885-12-10		A1
528	" "	9	SESE	1885-12-10		A1
630	ZAHNER, Augustus	14	12	1911-02-23		A3 G156

Patent Map

T43-N R6-E
4th PM - 1831 MN/WI

Map Group 5

Township Statistics

Parcels Mapped	:	335
Number of Patents	:	84
Number of Individuals	:	69
Patentees Identified	:	48
Number of Surnames	:	58
Multi-Patentee Parcels	:	123
Oldest Patent Date	:	4/1/1871
Most Recent Patent	:	4/7/1921
Block/Lot Parcels	:	216
Parcels Re - Issued	:	1
Parcels that Overlap	:	2
Cities and Towns	:	1
Cemeteries	:	0

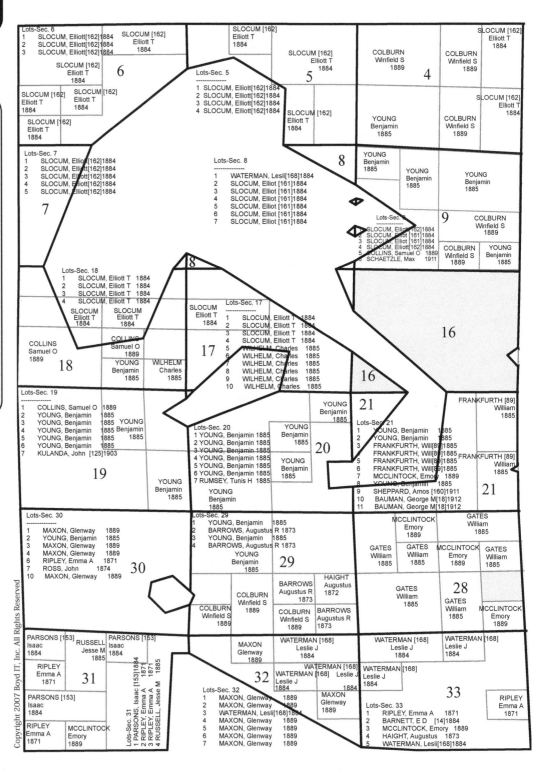

Copyright 2007 Boyd IT, Inc. All Rights Reserved

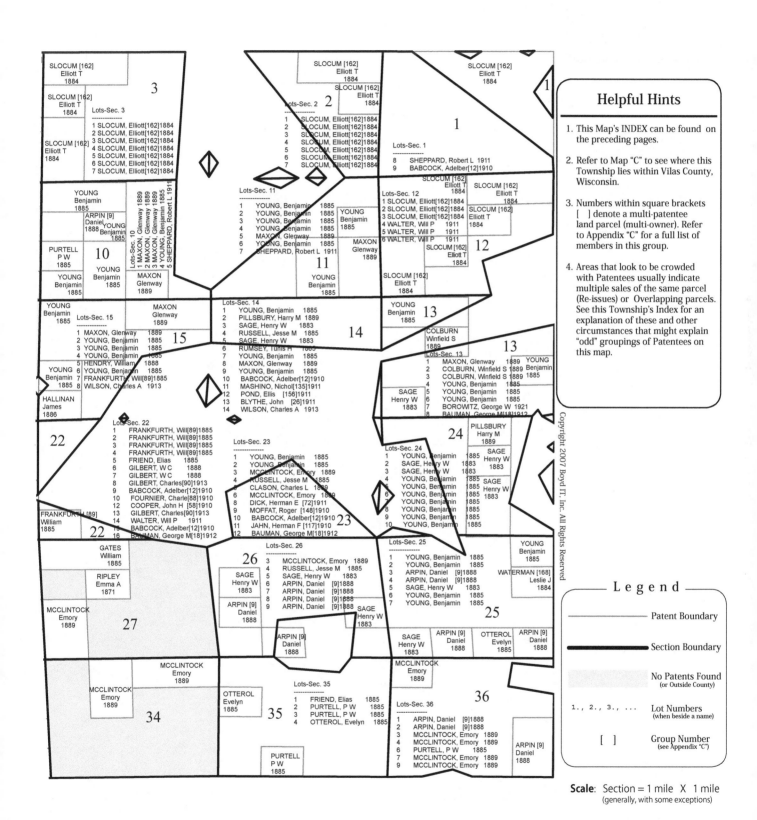

Helpful Hints

1. This Map's INDEX can be found on the preceding pages.

2. Refer to Map "C" to see where this Township lies within Vilas County, Wisconsin.

3. Numbers within square brackets [ ] denote a multi-patentee land parcel (multi-owner). Refer to Appendix "C" for a full list of members in this group.

4. Areas that look to be crowded with Patentees usually indicate multiple sales of the same parcel (Re-issues) or Overlapping parcels. See this Township's Index for an explanation of these and other circumstances that might explain "odd" groupings of Patentees on this map.

Legend

———————	Patent Boundary
▬▬▬▬▬▬	Section Boundary
(shaded)	No Patents Found (or Outside County)
1., 2., 3., ...	Lot Numbers (when beside a name)
[ ]	Group Number (see Appendix "C")

Scale: Section = 1 mile X 1 mile (generally, with some exceptions)

87

Road Map

T43-N R6-E
4th PM - 1831 MN/WI

Map Group 5

<u>Cities & Towns</u>
Katinka Village

<u>Cemeteries</u>
None

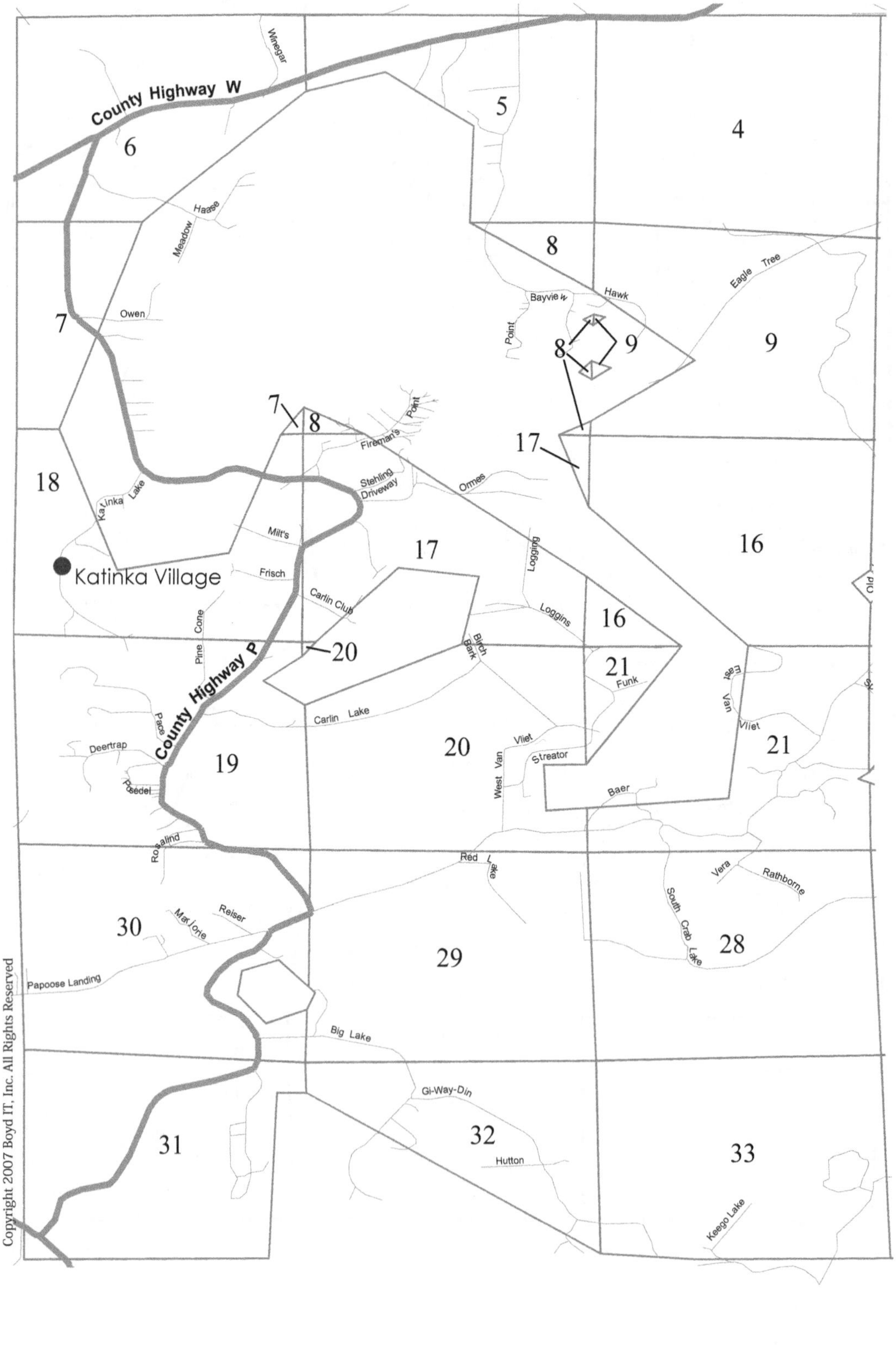

County Highway W

6

5

4

Waeegar

Haase

Meadow

8

Owen

7

Bayview   Hawk

Eagle Tree

Point

8   9

9

7   8

Firemant's

Point

Stehling
Driveway

Ormes

17

18

Katinka Lake

Milt's

Frisch

17

16

16

Logging

PIO

Katinka Village

Carlin Club

Loggins

Pine Cone

20

Birch
Bark

21

Funk

Isem Van

Paca

Carlin Lake

19

Deertrap

20

Vliet

Streator

Vliet

21

Poedel

West Van

Baer

Rosalind

Red Lake

Vera   Rathborne

30

Marione

Reiser

29

South Crab Lake

28

Papoose Landing

Big Lake

Gi-Way-Din

31

32

Hutton

33

Keego Lake

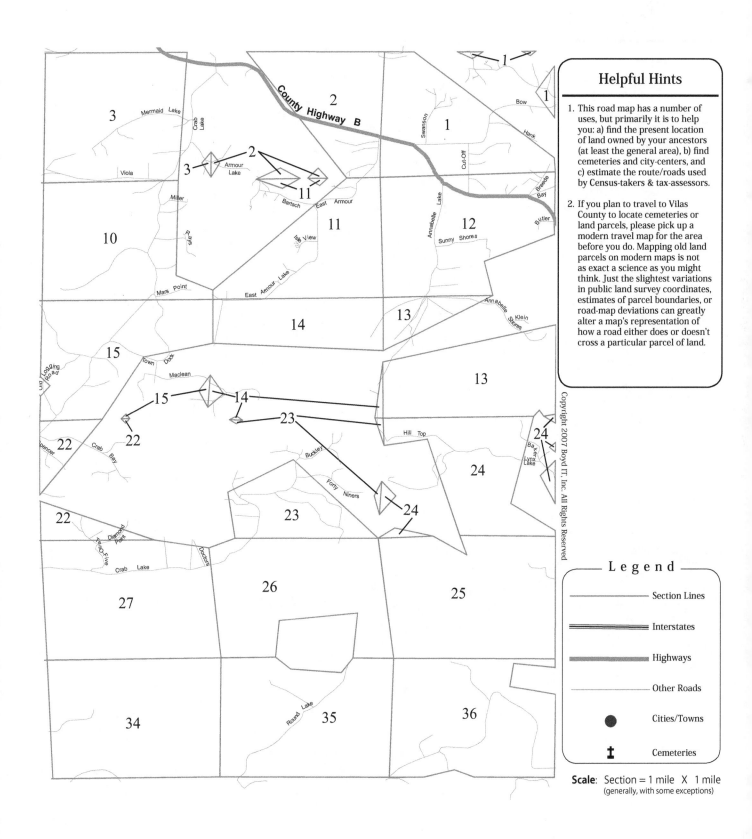

Helpful Hints

1. This road map has a number of uses, but primarily it is to help you: a) find the present location of land owned by your ancestors (at least the general area), b) find cemeteries and city-centers, and c) estimate the route/roads used by Census-takers & tax-assessors.

2. If you plan to travel to Vilas County to locate cemeteries or land parcels, please pick up a modern travel map for the area before you do. Mapping old land parcels on modern maps is not as exact a science as you might think. Just the slightest variations in public land survey coordinates, estimates of parcel boundaries, or road-map deviations can greatly alter a map's representation of how a road either does or doesn't cross a particular parcel of land.

L e g e n d

————————	Section Lines
═══════════	Interstates
━━━━━━━━━━	Highways
————————	Other Roads
●	Cities/Towns
⚥	Cemeteries

Scale: Section = 1 mile X 1 mile
(generally, with some exceptions)

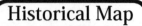

Historical Map

T43-N R6-E
4th PM - 1831 MN/WI

Map Group 5

Cities & Towns
Katinka Village

Cemeteries
None

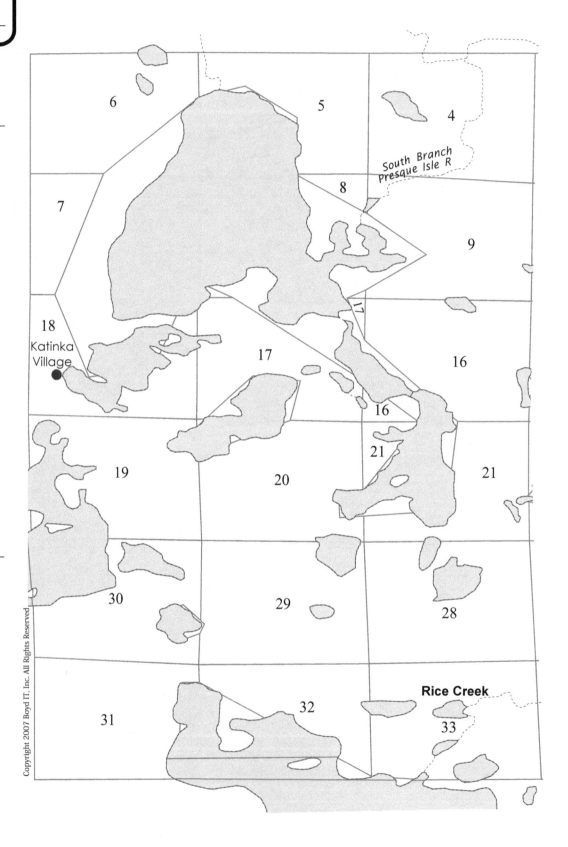

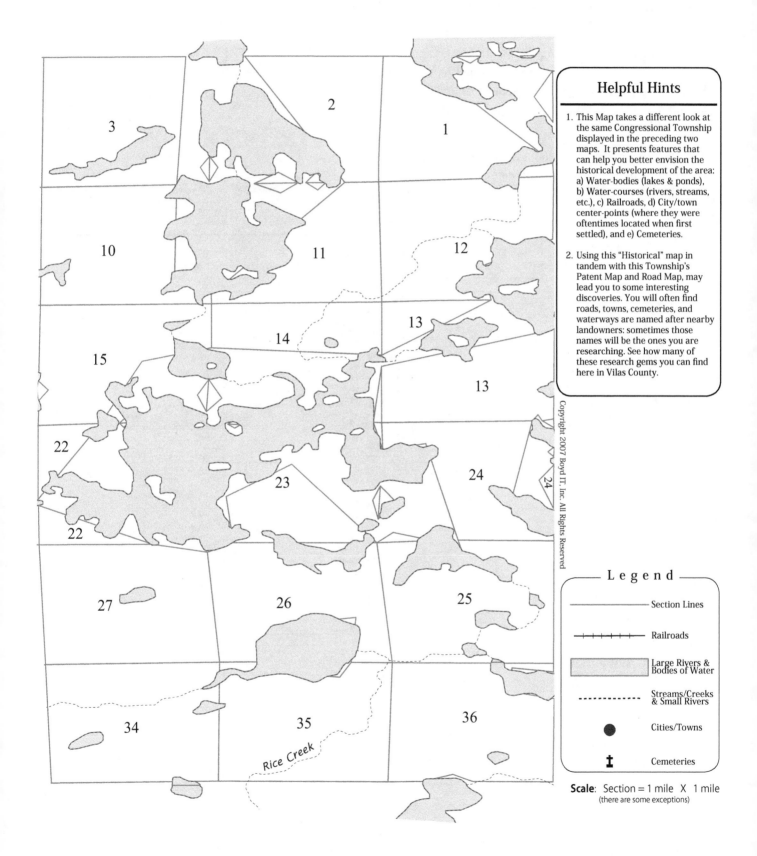

Helpful Hints

1. This Map takes a different look at the same Congressional Township displayed in the preceding two maps. It presents features that can help you better envision the historical development of the area: a) Water-bodies (lakes & ponds), b) Water-courses (rivers, streams, etc.), c) Railroads, d) City/town center-points (where they were oftentimes located when first settled), and e) Cemeteries.

2. Using this "Historical" map in tandem with this Township's Patent Map and Road Map, may lead you to some interesting discoveries. You will often find roads, towns, cemeteries, and waterways are named after nearby landowners: sometimes those names will be the ones you are researching. See how many of these research gems you can find here in Vilas County.

Rice Creek

Legend

———— Section Lines

++++++ Railroads

Large Rivers & Bodies of Water

----------- Streams/Creeks & Small Rivers

● Cities/Towns

✝ Cemeteries

Scale: Section = 1 mile X 1 mile
(there are some exceptions)

Map Group 6: Index to Land Patents

Township 43-North Range 7-East (4th PM - 1831 MN/WI)

After you locate an individual in this Index, take note of the Section and Section Part then proceed to the Land Patent map on the pages immediately following. You should have no difficulty locating the corresponding parcel of land.

The "For More Info" Column will lead you to more information about the underlying Patents. See the *Legend* at right, and the "How to Use this Book" chapter, for more information.

```
                              LEGEND
                    "For More Info . . . " column
A = Authority (Legislative Act, See Appendix "A")
B = Block or Lot (location in Section unknown)
C = Cancelled Patent
F = Fractional Section
G = Group  (Multi-Patentee Patent, see Appendix "C")
V = Overlaps another Parcel
R = Re-Issued (Parcel patented more than once)

(A & G items require you to look in the Appendixes referred
to above. All other Letter-designations followed by a number
require you to locate line-items in this index that possess
the ID number found after the letter).
```

ID	Individual in Patent	Sec.	Sec. Part	Date Issued	Other Counties	For More Info . . .
981	ABBOTT, Miron	6	7	1884-06-30		A1 G1
982	" "	7	W½NW	1884-06-30		A1 G1
797	ARPIN, Daniel	31	3	1888-07-18		A1 G9 C R798
799	" "	31	4	1888-07-18		A1 G9 C R800
801	" "	31	5	1888-07-18		A1 G9 C R802
803	" "	31	6	1888-07-18		A1 G9 C R804
805	" "	31	7	1888-07-18		A1 G9 C R806
807	" "	31	9	1888-07-18		A1 G9 C
798	" "	31	3	1916-12-02		A1 G9 R797
800	" "	31	4	1916-12-02		A1 G9 R799
802	" "	31	5	1916-12-02		A1 G9 R801
804	" "	31	6	1916-12-02		A1 G9 R803
806	" "	31	7	1916-12-02		A1 G9 R805
808	" "	31	NENW	1916-12-02		A1 G9
809	ARPIN, E P	31	8	1889-04-04		A1
797	ARPIN, John	31	3	1888-07-18		A1 G9 C R798
799	" "	31	4	1888-07-18		A1 G9 C R800
801	" "	31	5	1888-07-18		A1 G9 C R802
803	" "	31	6	1888-07-18		A1 G9 C R804
805	" "	31	7	1888-07-18		A1 G9 C R806
807	" "	31	9	1888-07-18		A1 G9 C
798	" "	31	3	1916-12-02		A1 G9 R797
800	" "	31	4	1916-12-02		A1 G9 R799
802	" "	31	5	1916-12-02		A1 G9 R801
804	" "	31	6	1916-12-02		A1 G9 R803
806	" "	31	7	1916-12-02		A1 G9 R805
808	" "	31	NENW	1916-12-02		A1 G9
781	BABCOCK, Adelbert A	6	11	1910-12-01		A3 G12
782	" "	6	12	1910-12-01		A3 G12
786	BARROWS, Augustus R	36	NESE	1873-05-01		A1
787	" "	36	SENE	1873-05-01		A1
934	BAUMAN, George M	19	10	1912-01-25		A3 G18
935	" "	19	11	1912-01-25		A3 G18
934	BAUMAN, Martha	19	10	1912-01-25		A3 G18
935	" "	19	11	1912-01-25		A3 G18
796	BOLLES, Charles	13	2	1873-11-15		A1
978	BUCKSTAFF, John	18	2	1885-01-20		A1 G35
979	" "	7	3	1885-01-20		A1 G35
978	CHASE, James	18	2	1885-01-20		A1 G35
979	" "	7	3	1885-01-20		A1 G35
1009	COLBURN, Winfield S	1		1889-03-28		A1 F
1010	" "	10	4	1889-03-28		A1
1011	" "	10	W½NW	1889-03-28		A1
1012	" "	11	1	1889-03-28		A1
1013	" "	2		1889-03-28		A1 F
1014	" "	3		1889-03-28		A1 F

ID	Individual in Patent	Sec.	Sec. Part	Date Issued	Other Counties	For More Info . . .
1015	COLBURN, Winfield S (Cont'd)	31	1	1889-03-28		A1
1016	" "	31	2	1889-03-28		A1
1017	" "	32	1	1889-03-28		A1
1018	" "	32	N½NW	1889-03-28		A1
1019	" "	32	W½NE	1889-03-28		A1
1020	" "	34	1	1889-03-28		A1
1021	" "	34	N½NE	1889-03-28		A1
1022	" "	34	SENE	1889-03-28		A1
1023	" "	36	NWNE	1889-03-28		A1
1024	" "	4	2	1889-03-28		A1
1025	" "	4	3	1889-03-28		A1
1026	" "	4	N½SE	1889-03-28		A1
1027	" "	4	SW	1889-03-28		A1
1028	" "	4	SWNE	1889-03-28		A1
1029	" "	4	SWSE	1889-03-28		A1
1030	" "	5	5	1889-03-28		A1
1031	" "	6	9	1889-03-28		A1
1032	" "	7	NE	1889-03-28		A1
1033	" "	7	NESE	1889-03-28		A1
1034	" "	8	3	1889-03-28		A1
1035	" "	8	4	1889-03-28		A1
1036	" "	8	6	1889-03-28		A1
1037	" "	8	7	1889-03-28		A1
1038	" "	9	1	1889-03-28		A1
1039	" "	9	2	1889-03-28		A1
1040	" "	9	E½NW	1889-03-28		A1
1041	" "	9	NE	1889-03-28		A1
1042	COMPANY, Wisconsin River Land	36	3	1889-05-31		A1
977	CUSICK, John B	19	9	1914-01-16		A3 G62
958	DWIGHT, Jeremiah W	33	NESE	1872-11-01		A1 G79
959	" "	33	S½SE	1872-11-01		A1 G79
960	" "	33	SENE	1872-11-01		A1 G79
961	" "	34	N½SE	1872-11-01		A1 G79
962	" "	34	NESW	1872-11-01		A1 G79
963	" "	34	SENW	1872-11-01		A1 G79
964	" "	34	W½NW	1872-11-01		A1 G79
965	" "	34	W½SW	1872-11-01		A1 G79
966	" "	35	NW	1872-11-01		A1 G79
967	" "	35	SESE	1872-11-01		A1 G79
968	" "	35	SWSE	1872-11-01		A1 G79
969	" "	35	W½NE	1872-11-01		A1 G79
810	FRIEND, Elias	19	1	1885-11-25		A1
811	" "	7	NENW	1885-11-25		A1
1003	GATES, William	14	S½SW	1885-12-10		A1
1004	" "	15	SESE	1885-12-10		A1
1005	" "	22	E½NE	1885-12-10		A1
1006	" "	23	1	1885-12-10		A1
1007	" "	23	8	1885-12-10		A1
1008	" "	23	NWNW	1885-12-10		A1
785	HAIGHT, Augustus	34	SESW	1873-05-01		A1
956	HEISMAN, Herman	10	NESE	1900-10-04		A1
957	" "	32	S½SW	1900-10-04		A1
923	HICKS, Emmett R	30	1	1881-03-28		A1
924	" "	30	2	1881-03-28		A1
925	" "	30	3	1881-03-28		A1
926	" "	30	E½SW	1881-03-28		A1
927	" "	30	NW	1881-03-28		A1 F
928	" "	30	SESE	1881-03-28		A1
929	" "	30	SWSW	1881-03-28		A1 F
930	" "	30	W½SE	1881-03-28		A1
825	" "	10	1	1889-03-28		A1
826	" "	10	2	1889-03-28		A1
827	" "	10	3	1889-03-28		A1
828	" "	10	5	1889-03-28		A1
829	" "	10	6	1889-03-28		A1
830	" "	10	E½NW	1889-03-28		A1
831	" "	10	NWNE	1889-03-28		A1
832	" "	10	SESE	1889-03-28		A1
833	" "	10	W½SE	1889-03-28		A1
834	" "	11	2	1889-03-28		A1
835	" "	11	3	1889-03-28		A1
836	" "	11	4	1889-03-28		A1
837	" "	11	6	1889-03-28		A1

ID	Individual in Patent	Sec.	Sec. Part	Date Issued	Other Counties	For More Info . . .
838	HICKS, Emmett R (Cont'd)	11	E½NE	1889-03-28		A1
839	" "	11	NESE	1889-03-28		A1
840	" "	12	N½SE	1889-03-28		A1
841	" "	12	N½SW	1889-03-28		A1
842	" "	12	NW	1889-03-28		A1
843	" "	12	SESE	1889-03-28		A1
844	" "	13	3	1889-03-28		A1
845	" "	13	4	1889-03-28		A1
846	" "	13	5	1889-03-28		A1
847	" "	13	6	1889-03-28		A1
848	" "	13	7	1889-03-28		A1
849	" "	13	NENE	1889-03-28		A1
850	" "	13	SWNW	1889-03-28		A1
851	" "	14	1	1889-03-28		A1
852	" "	14	N½SE	1889-03-28		A1
853	" "	14	N½SW	1889-03-28		A1
854	" "	14	SENE	1889-03-28		A1
855	" "	14	SENW	1889-03-28		A1
856	" "	14	SWSE	1889-03-28		A1
857	" "	15	1	1889-03-28		A1
858	" "	15	2	1889-03-28		A1
859	" "	15	3	1889-03-28		A1
860	" "	15	4	1889-03-28		A1
861	" "	15	N½SE	1889-03-28		A1
862	" "	15	NE	1889-03-28		A1
863	" "	15	SESW	1889-03-28		A1
864	" "	15	SWSE	1889-03-28		A1
865	" "	17	2	1889-03-28		A1
866	" "	17	3	1889-03-28		A1
867	" "	17	NENW	1889-03-28		A1
868	" "	17	NESW	1889-03-28		A1
869	" "	17	SESE	1889-03-28		A1
870	" "	17	W½SE	1889-03-28		A1
871	" "	18	1	1889-03-28		A1
872	" "	18	10	1889-03-28		A1
873	" "	18	8	1889-03-28		A1
874	" "	18	9	1889-03-28		A1
875	" "	19	2	1889-03-28		A1
876	" "	19	3	1889-03-28		A1
877	" "	19	4	1889-03-28		A1
878	" "	19	5	1889-03-28		A1
879	" "	19	6	1889-03-28		A1
880	" "	19	7	1889-03-28		A1
881	" "	19	8	1889-03-28		A1
882	" "	19	E½NE	1889-03-28		A1
883	" "	19	N½SE	1889-03-28		A1
884	" "	19	SESW	1889-03-28		A1
885	" "	19	SWSE	1889-03-28		A1
886	" "	20		1889-03-28		A1 F
887	" "	21		1889-03-28		A1
888	" "	22	E½NW	1889-03-28		A1
889	" "	22	N½SW	1889-03-28		A1
890	" "	22	NWNE	1889-03-28		A1
891	" "	22	SESE	1889-03-28		A1
892	" "	22	SWNW	1889-03-28		A1
893	" "	22	W½SE	1889-03-28		A1
894	" "	23	2	1889-03-28		A1
895	" "	23	3	1889-03-28		A1
896	" "	23	4	1889-03-28		A1
897	" "	23	5	1889-03-28		A1
898	" "	23	6	1889-03-28		A1
899	" "	23	7	1889-03-28		A1
900	" "	24	1	1889-03-28		A1
901	" "	24	2	1889-03-28		A1
902	" "	24	3	1889-03-28		A1
903	" "	24	6	1889-03-28		A1
904	" "	25	SE	1889-03-28		A1
905	" "	25	SENE	1889-03-28		A1
906	" "	25	W½	1889-03-28		A1
907	" "	25	W½NE	1889-03-28		A1
908	" "	26	1	1889-03-28		A1
909	" "	26	E½NE	1889-03-28		A1
910	" "	26	NW	1889-03-28		A1

ID	Individual in Patent	Sec.	Sec. Part	Date Issued	Other Counties	For More Info . . .
911	HICKS, Emmett R (Cont'd) (Cont'd)	26	SE	1889-03-28		A1
912	" "	26	SESW	1889-03-28		A1
913	" "	26	W½SW	1889-03-28		A1
914	" "	27	1	1889-03-28		A1
915	" "	27	2	1889-03-28		A1
916	" "	27	3	1889-03-28		A1
917	" "	27	4	1889-03-28		A1
918	" "	27	E½NW	1889-03-28		A1
919	" "	27	NE	1889-03-28		A1
920	" "	27	NWNW	1889-03-28		A1
921	" "	28		1889-03-28		A1 F
922	" "	29		1889-03-28		A1 F
784	JACKSON, Andrew B	35	N½SE	1911-11-16		A1 G114
784	JACKSON, E Gilbert	35	N½SE	1911-11-16		A1 G114
781	KIKENDALL, John S	6	11	1910-12-01		A3 G12
782	" "	6	12	1910-12-01		A3 G12
958	MCGRAW, John	33	NESE	1872-11-01		A1 G79
959	" "	33	S½SE	1872-11-01		A1 G79
960	" "	33	SENE	1872-11-01		A1 G79
961	" "	34	N½SE	1872-11-01		A1 G79
962	" "	34	NESW	1872-11-01		A1 G79
963	" "	34	SENW	1872-11-01		A1 G79
964	" "	34	W½NW	1872-11-01		A1 G79
965	" "	34	W½SW	1872-11-01		A1 G79
966	" "	35	NW	1872-11-01		A1 G79
967	" "	35	SESE	1872-11-01		A1 G79
968	" "	35	SWSE	1872-11-01		A1 G79
969	" "	35	W½NE	1872-11-01		A1 G79
976	MORRIS, Jessie	31	10	1885-07-13		A1
977	NEWELL, Edward W	19	9	1914-01-16		A3 G62
931	OTTEROL, Evelyn	7	SENW	1885-07-13		A1
783	PECK, Adelbert H	5	2	1916-01-05		A1
936	PILLSBURY, Harry M	17	4	1889-03-28		A1
937	" "	17	NE	1889-03-28		A1
938	" "	17	NESE	1889-03-28		A1
939	" "	17	S½SW	1889-03-28		A1
940	" "	18	3	1889-03-28		A1
941	" "	18	5	1889-03-28		A1
942	" "	18	6	1889-03-28		A1
943	" "	18	7	1889-03-28		A1
944	" "	6	6	1889-03-28		A1
945	" "	6	8	1889-03-28		A1
946	" "	6	SESW	1889-03-28		A1
947	" "	7	1	1889-03-28		A1
948	" "	7	2	1889-03-28		A1
949	" "	7	W½SE	1889-03-28		A1
950	" "	9	3	1889-03-28		A1
951	" "	9	N½SW	1889-03-28		A1
952	" "	9	SWSW	1889-03-28		A1
953	" "	9	W½NW	1889-03-28		A1
996	PILLSBURY, Oliver P	33	SENW	1885-01-15		A1
995	" "	33	NWSE	1885-01-20		A1
997	" "	33	SWNE	1885-01-20		A1
998	PURTELL, P W	18	4	1885-06-12		A1
999	" "	18	SESE	1885-06-12		A1
1002	RUMSEY, Tunis H	4	SESE	1885-11-25		A1
970	RUSSELL, Jesse M	11	5	1885-05-20		A1
971	" "	22	NESE	1885-05-20		A1
972	" "	22	SWNE	1885-05-20		A1
973	" "	26	NESW	1885-05-20		A1
974	" "	27	E½SE	1885-05-20		A1
975	" "	33	NENW	1885-05-20		A1
954	SAGE, Henry W	33	1	1883-09-15		A1
955	" "	33	NESW	1883-09-15		A1
1000	SHEPPARD, Robert L	6	10	1911-08-04		A2
934	" "	19	10	1912-01-25		A3 G18
935	" "	19	11	1912-01-25		A3 G18
819	SLOCUM, Elliott T	6	1	1884-06-30		A1
820	" "	6	2	1884-06-30		A1
981	" "	6	7	1884-06-30		A1 G1
982	" "	7	W½NW	1884-06-30		A1 G1
812	" "	4	1	1885-01-15		A1
813	" "	4	NWNW	1885-01-15		A1

ID	Individual in Patent	Sec.	Sec. Part	Date Issued	Other Counties	For More Info . . .
814	SLOCUM, Elliott T (Cont'd)	4	S½NW	1885-01-15		A1
815	" "	5	3	1885-01-15		A1
816	" "	5	N½NW	1885-01-15		A1
817	" "	5	NE	1885-01-15		A1
818	" "	5	NESE	1885-01-15		A1
821	" "	6	3	1885-01-15		A1
822	" "	6	4	1885-01-15		A1
823	" "	6	5	1885-01-15		A1
824	" "	6	NENE	1885-01-15		A1
981	SLOCUM, Giles B	6	7	1884-06-30		A1 G1
982	" "	7	W½NW	1884-06-30		A1 G1
983	THOMPSON, Neil A	11	S½SE	1873-11-15		A1
984	" "	11	SESW	1873-11-15		A1
985	" "	12	1	1873-11-15		A1
986	" "	13	8	1873-11-15		A1
987	" "	14	N½NE	1873-11-15		A1
988	" "	14	NENW	1873-11-15		A1
989	" "	24	SESE	1873-11-15		A1
990	" "	25	NENE	1874-08-01		A1
991	" "	36	NESW	1874-08-01		A1
992	" "	36	NW	1874-08-01		A1
993	" "	36	NWSE	1874-08-01		A1
994	" "	36	SWNE	1874-08-01		A1
932	WASHBURN, Ganem W	36	NENE	1872-11-01		A1
933	" "	36	W½SW	1872-11-01		A1
980	WATERMAN, Leslie J	17	1	1884-06-30		A1 G168
980	WILEY, Charles L	17	1	1884-06-30		A1 G168
1001	WISCONSIN, State Of	24	5	1911-05-08		A4
788	YOUNG, Benjamin	5	4	1885-12-10		A1
789	" "	5	SESE	1885-12-10		A1
790	" "	8	1	1885-12-10		A1
791	" "	8	2	1885-12-10		A1
792	" "	8	5	1885-12-10		A1
793	" "	8	N½NE	1885-12-10		A1
794	" "	8	NESE	1885-12-10		A1
795	" "	8	SENE	1885-12-10		A1

Patent Map

T43-N   R7-E
4th PM - 1831 MN/WI

Map Group 6

Township Statistics

Parcels Mapped	:	262
Number of Patents	:	62
Number of Individuals	:	43
Patentees Identified	:	34
Number of Surnames	:	37
Multi-Patentee Parcels	:	35
Oldest Patent Date	:	11/1/1872
Most Recent Patent	:	12/2/1916
Block/Lot Parcels	:	122
Parcels Re - Issued	:	5
Parcels that Overlap	:	0
Cities and Towns	:	0
Cemeteries	:	0

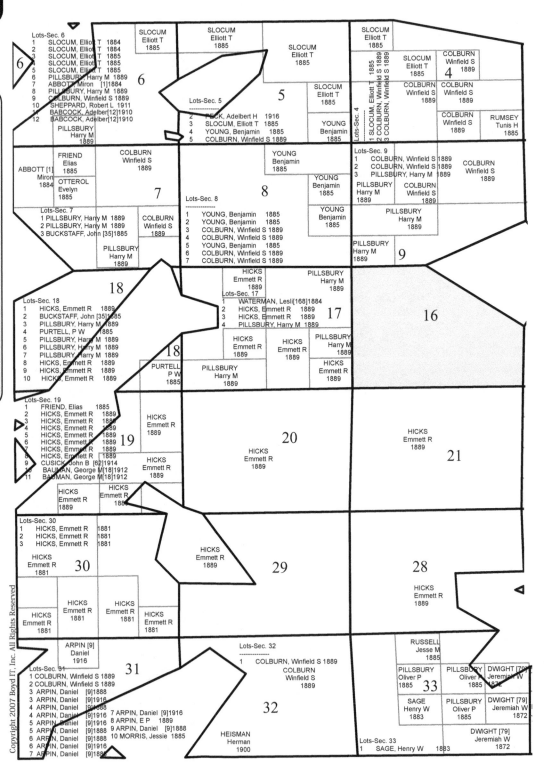

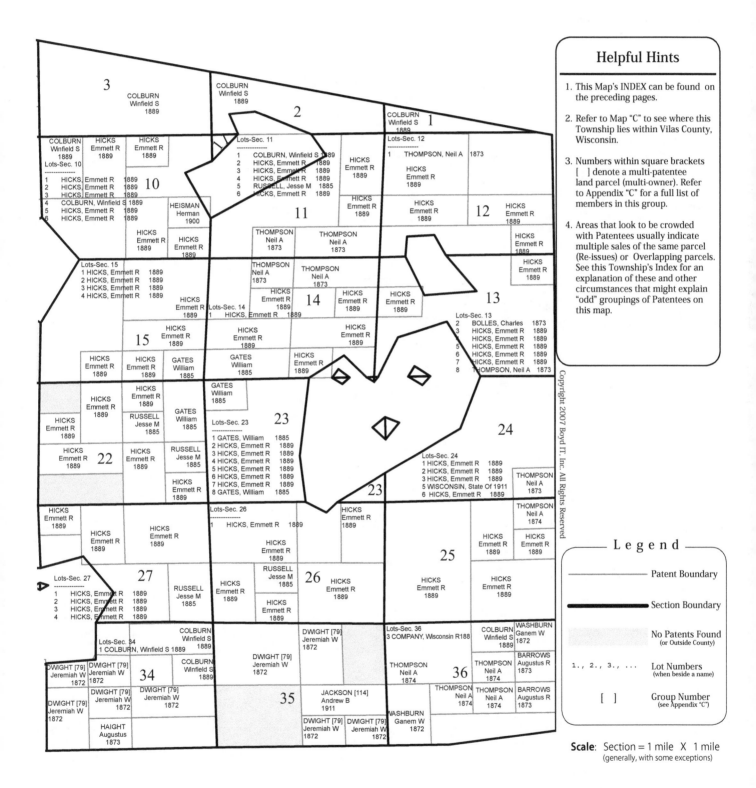

Helpful Hints

1. This Map's INDEX can be found on the preceding pages.

2. Refer to Map "C" to see where this Township lies within Vilas County, Wisconsin.

3. Numbers within square brackets [ ] denote a multi-patentee land parcel (multi-owner). Refer to Appendix "C" for a full list of members in this group.

4. Areas that look to be crowded with Patentees usually indicate multiple sales of the same parcel (Re-issues) or Overlapping parcels. See this Township's Index for an explanation of these and other circumstances that might explain "odd" groupings of Patentees on this map.

Legend

——— Patent Boundary

▬▬▬ Section Boundary

No Patents Found (or Outside County)

1., 2., 3., ... Lot Numbers (when beside a name)

[ ] Group Number (see Appendix "C")

Scale: Section = 1 mile X 1 mile (generally, with some exceptions)

Road Map

T43-N R7-E
4th PM - 1831 MN/WI

Map Group 6

Cities & Towns
None

Cemeteries
None

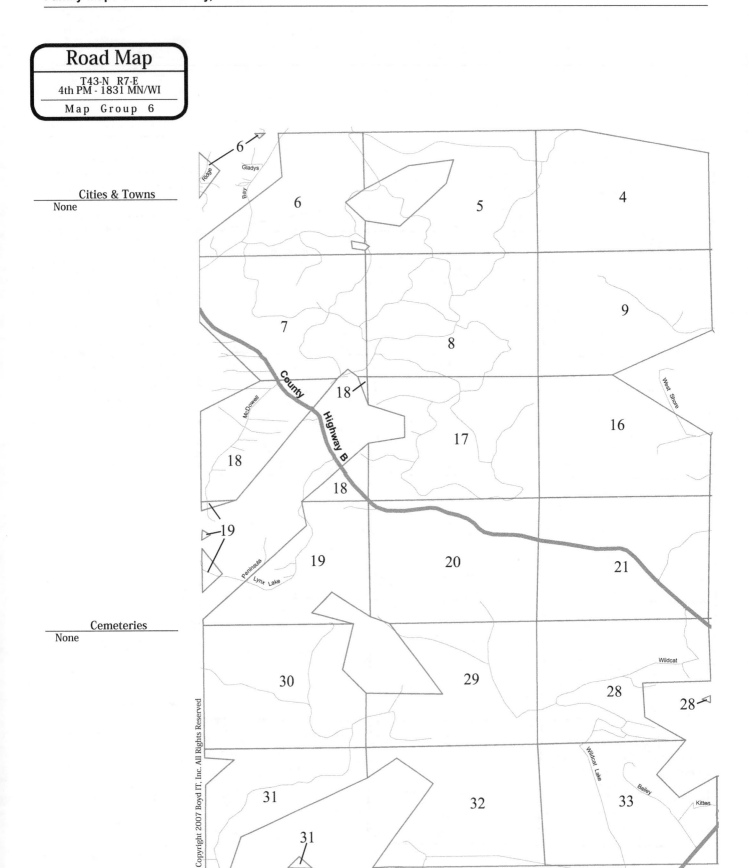

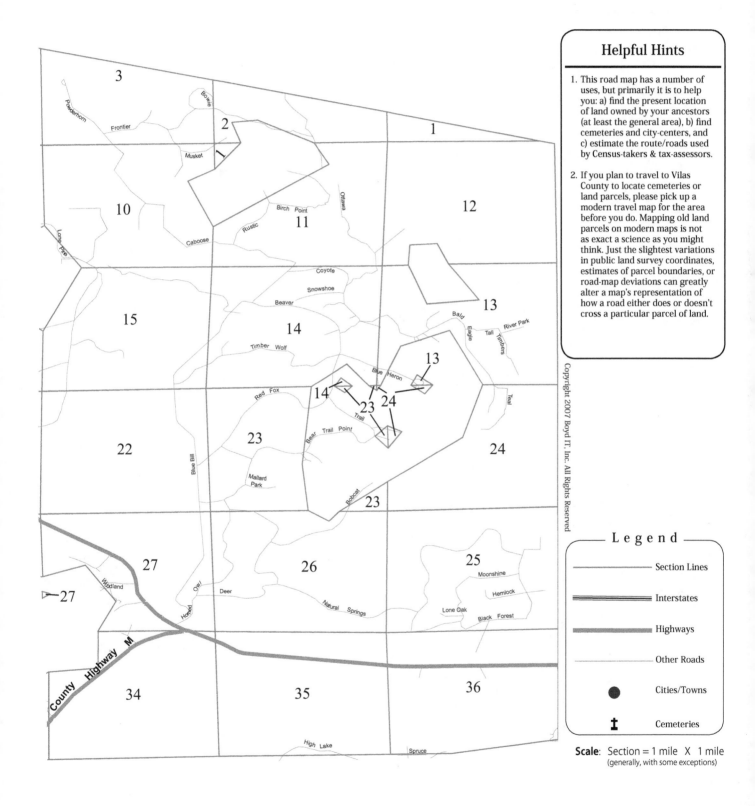

Helpful Hints

1. This road map has a number of uses, but primarily it is to help you: a) find the present location of land owned by your ancestors (at least the general area), b) find cemeteries and city-centers, and c) estimate the route/roads used by Census-takers & tax-assessors.

2. If you plan to travel to Vilas County to locate cemeteries or land parcels, please pick up a modern travel map for the area before you do. Mapping old land parcels on modern maps is not as exact a science as you might think. Just the slightest variations in public land survey coordinates, estimates of parcel boundaries, or road-map deviations can greatly alter a map's representation of how a road either does or doesn't cross a particular parcel of land.

L e g e n d

	Section Lines
	Interstates
	Highways
	Other Roads
●	Cities/Towns
✝	Cemeteries

Scale: Section = 1 mile X 1 mile
(generally, with some exceptions)

Historical Map

T43-N R7-E
4th PM - 1831 MN/WI

Map Group 6

Cities & Towns

None

Cemeteries

None

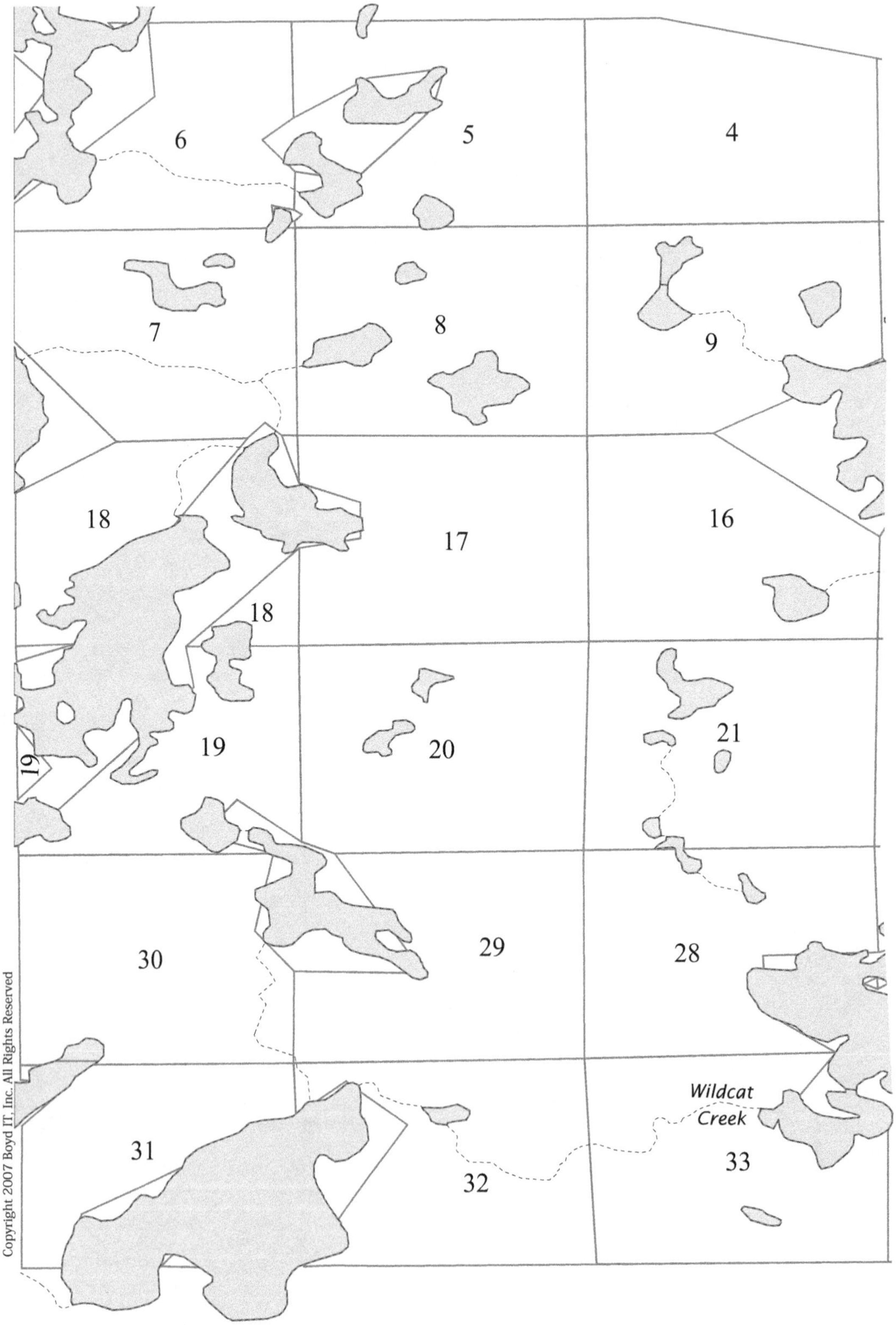

6

5

4

7

8

9

18

17

16

18

19

19

20

21

30

29

28

31

32

33

Wildcat
Creek

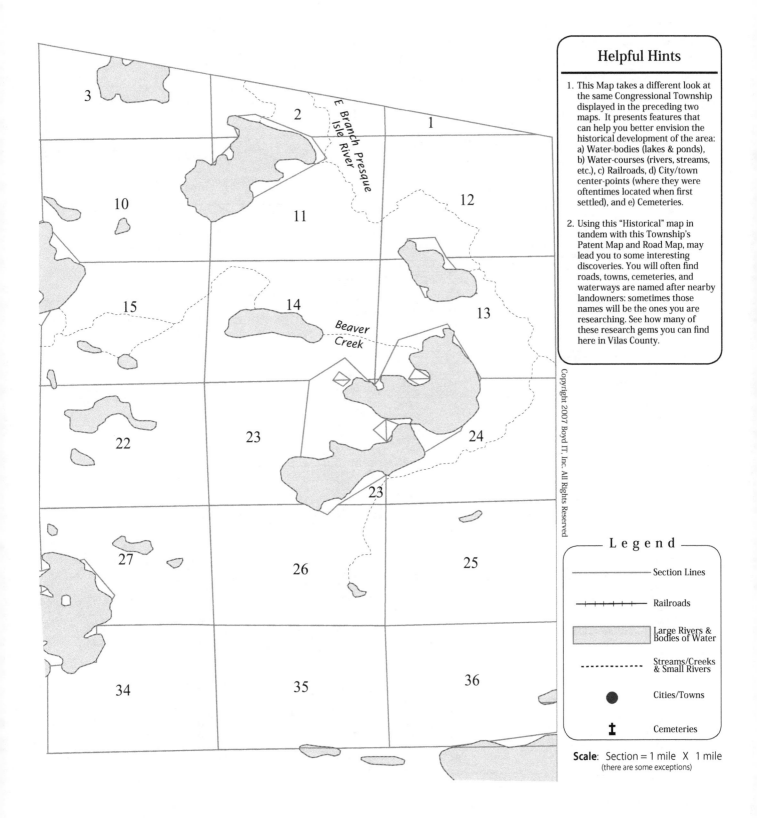

Helpful Hints

1. This Map takes a different look at the same Congressional Township displayed in the preceding two maps. It presents features that can help you better envision the historical development of the area: a) Water-bodies (lakes & ponds), b) Water-courses (rivers, streams, etc.), c) Railroads, d) City/town center-points (where they were oftentimes located when first settled), and e) Cemeteries.

2. Using this "Historical" map in tandem with this Township's Patent Map and Road Map, may lead you to some interesting discoveries. You will often find roads, towns, cemeteries, and waterways are named after nearby landowners: sometimes those names will be the ones you are researching. See how many of these research gems you can find here in Vilas County.

--- Legend ---

———— Section Lines

+—+—+—+ Railroads

▭ Large Rivers & Bodies of Water

- - - - - - - Streams/Creeks & Small Rivers

● Cities/Towns

† Cemeteries

Scale: Section = 1 mile X 1 mile
(there are some exceptions)

E Branch Presque Isle River

Beaver Creek

Map Group 7: Index to Land Patents

Township 43-North Range 8-East (4th PM - 1831 MN/WI)

After you locate an individual in this Index, take note of the Section and Section Part then proceed to the Land Patent map on the pages immediately following. You should have no difficulty locating the corresponding parcel of land.

The "For More Info" Column will lead you to more information about the underlying Patents. See the *Legend* at right, and the "How to Use this Book" chapter, for more information.

ID	Individual in Patent	Sec.	Sec. Part	Date Issued	Other Counties	For More Info . . .
1043	BABCOCK, Adelbert A	24	7	1910-12-01		A3 G12
1200	BALCOM, Samuel F	7	1	1873-11-15		A1
1062	BARNETT, E D	33	NWSE	1884-06-30		A1 G14
1063	" "	34	SESW	1884-06-30		A1 G14
1064	" "	36	NWSE	1884-06-30		A1 G14
1062	BARNETT, Joel D	33	NWSE	1884-06-30		A1 G14
1063	" "	34	SESW	1884-06-30		A1 G14
1064	" "	36	NWSE	1884-06-30		A1 G14
1048	BARROWS, Augustus R	31	W½NW	1873-05-01		A1
1049	BOLLES, Charles	7	5	1873-11-15		A1
1050	" "	7	6	1873-11-15		A1
1155	BUCKSTAFF, John	23	SWSE	1885-01-20		A1 G35
1156	" "	26	E½NE	1885-01-20		A1 G35 V1133
1157	" "	26	NENW	1885-01-20		A1 G35
1158	" "	26	NWNE	1885-01-20		A1 G35
1155	CHASE, James	23	SWSE	1885-01-20		A1 G35
1156	" "	26	E½NE	1885-01-20		A1 G35 V1133
1157	" "	26	NENW	1885-01-20		A1 G35
1158	" "	26	NWNE	1885-01-20		A1 G35
1169	DAVIS, Melson J	19	1	1885-11-25		A1 G67 F
1170	" "	19	2	1885-11-25		A1 G67 F
1171	" "	19	NWSW	1885-11-25		A1 G67 F
1172	" "	21	2	1885-11-25		A1 G67 F
1173	" "	21	3	1885-11-25		A1 G67 F
1174	" "	21	4	1885-11-25		A1 G67 F
1175	" "	22	NWSE	1885-11-25		A1 G67
1176	" "	22	S½SE	1885-11-25		A1 G67
1177	" "	22	W½	1885-11-25		A1 G67
1178	" "	25	E½SE	1885-11-25		A1 G67
1179	" "	25	SENE	1885-11-25		A1 G67
1180	" "	27	E½NW	1885-11-25		A1 G67
1181	" "	27	NE	1885-11-25		A1 G67
1182	" "	36	NENE	1885-11-25		A1 G67
1169	DAVIS, William H	19	1	1885-11-25		A1 G67 F
1170	" "	19	2	1885-11-25		A1 G67 F
1171	" "	19	NWSW	1885-11-25		A1 G67 F
1172	" "	21	2	1885-11-25		A1 G67 F
1173	" "	21	3	1885-11-25		A1 G67 F
1174	" "	21	4	1885-11-25		A1 G67 F
1175	" "	22	NWSE	1885-11-25		A1 G67
1176	" "	22	S½SE	1885-11-25		A1 G67
1177	" "	22	W½	1885-11-25		A1 G67
1178	" "	25	E½SE	1885-11-25		A1 G67
1179	" "	25	SENE	1885-11-25		A1 G67
1180	" "	27	E½NW	1885-11-25		A1 G67
1181	" "	27	NE	1885-11-25		A1 G67

ID	Individual in Patent	Sec.	Sec. Part	Date Issued	Other Counties	For More Info . . .
1182	DAVIS, William H (Cont'd)	36	NENE	1885-11-25		A1 G67
1053	FRENCH, D D	24	2	1885-07-13		A1
1054	" "	24	3	1885-07-13		A1
1055	" "	24	4	1885-07-13		A1
1056	" "	24	5	1885-07-13		A1
1057	" "	24	SWSE	1885-07-13		A1
1058	" "	28	SWSW	1885-07-13		A1
1059	" "	33	NWNW	1885-07-13		A1
1051	" "	15	1	1885-09-10		A1
1052	" "	15	2	1885-09-10		A1
1218	GRAY, William D	29	W½SE	1885-11-25		A1
1219	" "	32	N½NW	1885-11-25		A1
1220	" "	32	SENW	1885-11-25		A1
1221	" "	33	SWNW	1885-11-25		A1
1047	HAIGHT, Augustus	35	SESE	1872-11-01		A1
1065	HALL, Frederick	35	SWSE	1883-09-15		A1
1066	" "	36	S½SW	1883-09-15		A1
1067	" "	36	SWSE	1883-09-15		A1
1046	JACKSON, Andrew B	31	5	1872-07-01		A1 G113
1046	JACKSON, E G	31	5	1872-07-01		A1 G113
1043	KIKENDALL, John S	24	7	1910-12-01		A3 G12
1222	LAIRD, William H	18	1	1884-06-30		A1 G127
1223	" "	18	2	1884-06-30		A1 G127
1224	" "	18	3	1884-06-30		A1 G127
1225	" "	26	NESE	1884-06-30		A1 G127 V1132
1226	" "	31	1	1884-06-30		A1 G127
1227	" "	32	1	1884-06-30		A1 G127
1228	" "	32	4	1884-06-30		A1 G127
1229	" "	32	NWSE	1884-06-30		A1 G127
1230	" "	32	S½NE	1884-06-30		A1 G127
1231	" "	33	2	1884-06-30		A1 G127
1232	" "	33	3	1884-06-30		A1 G127
1233	" "	33	NESE	1884-06-30		A1 G127
1234	" "	33	SENW	1884-06-30		A1 G127
1235	" "	33	SWNE	1884-06-30		A1 G127
1236	" "	34	N½SE	1884-06-30		A1 G127
1237	" "	34	N½SW	1884-06-30		A1 G127
1238	" "	34	SWNE	1884-06-30		A1 G127
1239	" "	34	SWSW	1884-06-30		A1 G127
1240	" "	35	N½SE	1884-06-30		A1 G127
1241	" "	35	NESW	1884-06-30		A1 G127
1242	" "	35	S½SW	1884-06-30		A1 G127
1243	" "	35	SWNE	1884-06-30		A1 G127
1244	" "	36	N½SW	1884-06-30		A1 G127
1245	" "	36	SESE	1884-06-30		A1 G127
1246	" "	36	W½NW	1884-06-30		A1 G127
1247	" "	7	3	1884-06-30		A1 G127
1248	" "	7	4	1884-06-30		A1 G127
1168	LANE, Mary E	14	4	1905-07-13		A3 G128
1168	LANE, Smith	14	4	1905-07-13		A3 G128
1045	MILLER, Amanda H B	8	7	1911-03-23		A3
1168	MINER, Willis H	14	4	1905-07-13		A3 G128
1201	MITCHELL, Stanislaus	29	SESE	1885-11-25		A1
1202	" "	32	N½NE	1885-11-25		A1
1222	NORTON, James L	18	1	1884-06-30		A1 G127
1223	" "	18	2	1884-06-30		A1 G127
1224	" "	18	3	1884-06-30		A1 G127
1225	" "	26	NESE	1884-06-30		A1 G127 V1132
1226	" "	31	1	1884-06-30		A1 G127
1227	" "	32	1	1884-06-30		A1 G127
1228	" "	32	4	1884-06-30		A1 G127
1229	" "	32	NWSE	1884-06-30		A1 G127
1230	" "	32	S½NE	1884-06-30		A1 G127
1231	" "	33	2	1884-06-30		A1 G127
1232	" "	33	3	1884-06-30		A1 G127
1233	" "	33	NESE	1884-06-30		A1 G127
1234	" "	33	SENW	1884-06-30		A1 G127
1235	" "	33	SWNE	1884-06-30		A1 G127
1236	" "	34	N½SE	1884-06-30		A1 G127
1237	" "	34	N½SW	1884-06-30		A1 G127
1238	" "	34	SWNE	1884-06-30		A1 G127
1239	" "	34	SWSW	1884-06-30		A1 G127
1240	" "	35	N½SE	1884-06-30		A1 G127

ID	Individual in Patent	Sec.	Sec. Part	Date Issued	Other Counties	For More Info . . .
1241	NORTON, James L (Cont'd)	35	NESW	1884-06-30		A1 G127
1242	" "	35	S½SW	1884-06-30		A1 G127
1243	" "	35	SWNE	1884-06-30		A1 G127
1244	" "	36	N½SW	1884-06-30		A1 G127
1245	" "	36	SESE	1884-06-30		A1 G127
1246	" "	36	W½NW	1884-06-30		A1 G127
1247	" "	7	3	1884-06-30		A1 G127
1248	" "	7	4	1884-06-30		A1 G127
1222	NORTON, Matthew G	18	1	1884-06-30		A1 G127
1223	" "	18	2	1884-06-30		A1 G127
1224	" "	18	3	1884-06-30		A1 G127
1225	" "	26	NESE	1884-06-30		A1 G127 V1132
1226	" "	31	1	1884-06-30		A1 G127
1227	" "	32	1	1884-06-30		A1 G127
1228	" "	32	4	1884-06-30		A1 G127
1229	" "	32	NWSE	1884-06-30		A1 G127
1230	" "	32	S½NE	1884-06-30		A1 G127
1231	" "	33	2	1884-06-30		A1 G127
1232	" "	33	3	1884-06-30		A1 G127
1233	" "	33	NESE	1884-06-30		A1 G127
1234	" "	33	SENW	1884-06-30		A1 G127
1235	" "	33	SWNE	1884-06-30		A1 G127
1236	" "	34	N½SE	1884-06-30		A1 G127
1237	" "	34	N½SW	1884-06-30		A1 G127
1238	" "	34	SWNE	1884-06-30		A1 G127
1239	" "	34	SWSW	1884-06-30		A1 G127
1240	" "	35	N½SE	1884-06-30		A1 G127
1241	" "	35	NESW	1884-06-30		A1 G127
1242	" "	35	S½SW	1884-06-30		A1 G127
1243	" "	35	SWNE	1884-06-30		A1 G127
1244	" "	36	N½SW	1884-06-30		A1 G127
1245	" "	36	SESE	1884-06-30		A1 G127
1246	" "	36	W½NW	1884-06-30		A1 G127
1247	" "	7	3	1884-06-30		A1 G127
1248	" "	7	4	1884-06-30		A1 G127
1044	PAFF, Albert R	8	4	1889-05-31		A1
1189	PILLSBURY, Oliver P	24	6	1884-06-30		A1
1190	" "	25	NWNW	1884-06-30		A1
1191	" "	32	2	1884-06-30		A1
1192	" "	32	SESW	1884-06-30		A1
1193	" "	34	SWNW	1884-06-30		A1
1060	ROBERTS, David M	30	SE	1885-11-25		A1
1061	" "	31	N½NE	1885-11-25		A1
1068	RUSSELL, J M	13	1	1889-04-04		A1
1069	" "	13	2	1889-04-04		A1
1070	" "	13	3	1889-04-04		A1
1071	" "	13	4	1889-04-04		A1
1072	" "	13	5	1889-04-04		A1
1073	" "	14	6	1889-04-04		A1
1074	" "	17	1	1889-04-04		A1
1075	" "	17	5	1889-04-04		A1
1076	" "	17	6	1889-04-04		A1
1077	" "	17	7	1889-04-04		A1
1078	" "	17	8	1889-04-04		A1
1079	" "	17	9	1889-04-04		A1
1080	" "	18	4	1889-04-04		A1
1081	" "	18	5	1889-04-04		A1
1082	" "	18	8	1889-04-04		A1
1083	" "	18	N½NW	1889-04-04		A1 F
1084	" "	18	NESE	1889-04-04		A1
1085	" "	18	SWNW	1889-04-04		A1 F
1086	" "	19	3	1889-04-04		A1
1087	" "	19	4	1889-04-04		A1
1088	" "	19	5	1889-04-04		A1
1089	" "	19	SE	1889-04-04		A1
1090	" "	19	SENE	1889-04-04		A1
1091	" "	19	SESW	1889-04-04		A1
1092	" "	20	2	1889-04-04		A1
1093	" "	20	3	1889-04-04		A1
1094	" "	20	4	1889-04-04		A1
1095	" "	20	5	1889-04-04		A1
1096	" "	20	6	1889-04-04		A1
1097	" "	20	7	1889-04-04		A1

ID	Individual in Patent	Sec.	Sec. Part	Date Issued	Other Counties	For More Info . . .
1098	RUSSELL, J M (Cont'd)	20	8	1889-04-04		A1
1099	" "	20	9	1889-04-04		A1
1100	" "	20	NWNE	1889-04-04		A1
1101	" "	20	SWSW	1889-04-04		A1
1102	" "	23	3	1889-04-04		A1
1103	" "	24	1	1889-04-04		A1
1104	" "	25	E½SW	1889-04-04		A1
1105	" "	25	NWSE	1889-04-04		A1
1106	" "	25	SWSW	1889-04-04		A1
1107	" "	25	W½NE	1889-04-04		A1
1108	" "	27	NWSW	1889-04-04		A1
1109	" "	27	W½NW	1889-04-04		A1
1110	" "	29	2	1889-04-04		A1
1111	" "	29	3	1889-04-04		A1
1112	" "	29	NW	1889-04-04		A1
1113	" "	30	E½NW	1889-04-04		A1
1114	" "	30	NE	1889-04-04		A1
1115	" "	30	SW	1889-04-04		A1 F
1116	" "	30	SWNW	1889-04-04		A1 F
1117	" "	31	2	1889-04-04		A1
1118	" "	31	3	1889-04-04		A1
1119	" "	31	E½NW	1889-04-04		A1
1120	" "	31	SWNE	1889-04-04		A1
1121	" "	32	3	1889-04-04		A1
1122	" "	32	NESW	1889-04-04		A1
1123	" "	34	SENW	1889-04-04		A1
1124	" "	36	SENE	1889-04-04		A1
1125	" "	36	SENW	1889-04-04		A1
1126	" "	36	W½NE	1889-04-04		A1
1127	" "	7	8	1889-04-04		A1
1128	" "	8	2	1889-04-04		A1
1129	" "	8	3	1889-04-04		A1
1130	" "	9	4	1889-04-04		A1
1131	" "	9	SWSW	1889-04-04		A1
1149	RUSSELL, Jesse M	28	NWSW	1885-05-09		A1
1150	" "	29	NESE	1885-05-09		A1
1151	" "	33	1	1885-05-09		A1
1134	" "	14	1	1885-05-20		A1
1135	" "	14	2	1885-05-20		A1
1136	" "	14	3	1885-05-20		A1
1137	" "	14	7	1885-05-20		A1
1138	" "	15	8	1885-05-20		A1
1139	" "	22	NESE	1885-05-20		A1
1140	" "	23	4	1885-05-20		A1
1141	" "	23	NESW	1885-05-20		A1
1142	" "	23	NWSE	1885-05-20		A1
1143	" "	23	SESE	1885-05-20		A1
1144	" "	25	NENW	1885-05-20		A1
1145	" "	25	NWSW	1885-05-20		A1
1146	" "	25	S½NW	1885-05-20		A1
1147	" "	25	SWSE	1885-05-20		A1
1148	" "	26	SWNE	1885-05-20		A1 V1133
1152	" "	34	SWSE	1885-05-20		A1
1153	" "	35	NWNE	1885-05-20		A1
1154	" "	35	S½NW	1885-05-20		A1
1194	SHEPPARD, Robert L	17	10	1911-08-04		A2
1195	" "	23	5	1911-08-04		A2
1196	" "	24	8	1911-08-04		A2
1197	" "	24	9	1911-08-04		A2
1198	" "	8	5	1911-08-04		A2
1199	" "	8	6	1911-08-04		A2
1183	THOMPSON, Neil A	19	SWSW	1873-11-15		A1
1184	" "	30	NWNW	1873-11-15		A1
1185	" "	31	4	1873-11-15		A1
1186	" "	9	1	1873-11-15		A1
1187	" "	9	2	1873-11-15		A1
1188	" "	9	3	1873-11-15		A1
1204	VAN BRUNT, W A	14	5	1885-09-10		A1
1205	" "	14	SESW	1885-09-10		A1
1206	" "	14	W½SW	1885-09-10		A1
1207	" "	15	5	1885-09-10		A1
1208	" "	15	6	1885-09-10		A1
1209	" "	15	7	1885-09-10		A1

ID	Individual in Patent	Sec.	Sec. Part	Date Issued	Other Counties	For More Info . . .
1210	VAN BRUNT, W A (Cont'd)	15	SESE	1885-09-10		A1
1211	" "	15	W½SE	1885-09-10		A1
1212	" "	22	NE	1885-09-10		A1
1213	" "	23	SENW	1885-09-10		A1
1214	" "	23	SESW	1885-09-10		A1
1215	" "	23	W½NW	1885-09-10		A1
1216	" "	23	W½SW	1885-09-10		A1
1217	" "	26	NWNW	1885-09-10		A1
1203	WAMBOLD, Theodore F	29	SW	1885-11-25		A1
1159	WATERMAN, Leslie J	32	NESE	1884-06-30		A1 G168
1160	" "	32	SWSE	1884-06-30		A1 G168
1161	" "	33	SENE	1884-06-30		A1 G168
1162	" "	33	SESE	1884-06-30		A1 G168
1163	" "	34	SENE	1884-06-30		A1 G168
1164	" "	34	SESE	1884-06-30		A1 G168
1165	" "	35	E½NE	1884-06-30		A1 G168
1166	" "	35	NWSW	1884-06-30		A1 G168
1167	WATERMAN, Leslie W	29	1	1884-06-30		A1 G169
1132	WELCH, James	26	E½SE	1903-10-01		A3 V1225
1133	" "	26	S½NE	1903-10-01		A3 V1156, 1148
1167	WILEY, Charles L	29	1	1884-06-30		A1 G169
1159	" "	32	NESE	1884-06-30		A1 G168
1160	" "	32	SWSE	1884-06-30		A1 G168
1161	" "	33	SENE	1884-06-30		A1 G168
1162	" "	33	SESE	1884-06-30		A1 G168
1163	" "	34	SENE	1884-06-30		A1 G168
1164	" "	34	SESE	1884-06-30		A1 G168
1165	" "	35	E½NE	1884-06-30		A1 G168
1166	" "	35	NWSW	1884-06-30		A1 G168

Patent Map

T43-N R8-E
4th PM - 1831 MN/WI

Map Group 7

Township Statistics

Parcels Mapped	:	206
Number of Patents	:	50
Number of Individuals	:	38
Patentees Identified	:	28
Number of Surnames	:	31
Multi-Patentee Parcels	:	60
Oldest Patent Date	:	7/1/1872
Most Recent Patent	:	8/4/1911
Block/Lot Parcels	:	90
Parcels Re - Issued	:	0
Parcels that Overlap	:	5
Cities and Towns	:	0
Cemeteries	:	0

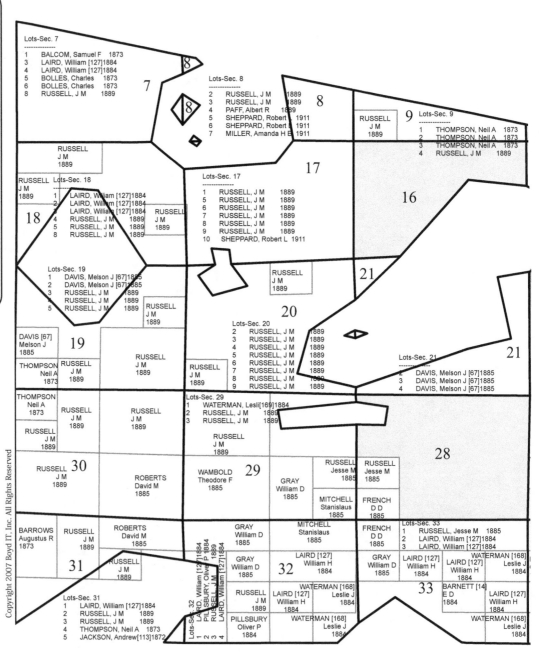

Lots-Sec. 7
----
1 BALCOM, Samuel F 1873
3 LAIRD, William [127]1884
4 LAIRD, William [127]1884
5 BOLLES, Charles 1873
6 BOLLES, Charles 1873
8 RUSSELL, J M 1889

Lots-Sec. 8
----
2 RUSSELL, J M 1889
3 RUSSELL, J M 1889
4 PAFF, Albert R 1889
5 SHEPPARD, Robert L 1911
6 SHEPPARD, Robert L 1911
7 MILLER, Amanda H B 1911

Lots-Sec. 9
----
1 THOMPSON, Neil A 1873
2 THOMPSON, Neil A 1873
3 THOMPSON, Neil A 1873
4 RUSSELL, J M 1889

Lots-Sec. 18
----
1 LAIRD, William [127]1884
2 LAIRD, William [127]1884
3 LAIRD, William [127]1884
4 RUSSELL, J M 1889
5 RUSSELL, J M 1889
8 RUSSELL, J M 1889

Lots-Sec. 17
----
1 RUSSELL, J M 1889
5 RUSSELL, J M 1889
6 RUSSELL, J M 1889
7 RUSSELL, J M 1889
8 RUSSELL, J M 1889
9 RUSSELL, J M 1889
10 SHEPPARD, Robert L 1911

Lots-Sec. 19
----
1 DAVIS, Melson J [67]1885
2 DAVIS, Melson J [67]1885
3 RUSSELL, J M 1889
4 RUSSELL, J M 1889
5 RUSSELL, J M 1889

Lots-Sec. 20
----
2 RUSSELL, J M 1889
3 RUSSELL, J M 1889
4 RUSSELL, J M 1889
5 RUSSELL, J M 1889
6 RUSSELL, J M 1889
7 RUSSELL, J M 1889
8 RUSSELL, J M 1889
9 RUSSELL, J M 1889

Lots-Sec. 21
----
2 DAVIS, Melson J [67]1885
3 DAVIS, Melson J [67]1885
4 DAVIS, Melson J [67]1885

Lots-Sec. 29
----
1 WATERMAN, Lesli[169]1884
2 RUSSELL, J M 1889
3 RUSSELL, J M 1889

Lots-Sec. 33
----
1 RUSSELL, Jesse M 1885
2 LAIRD, William [127]1884
3 LAIRD, William [127]1884

Lots-Sec. 31
----
1 LAIRD, William [127]1884
2 RUSSELL, J M 1889
3 RUSSELL, J M 1889
4 THOMPSON, Neil A 1873
5 JACKSON, Andrew[113]1872

Lots-Sec. 32
----
1 LAIRD, William [127]1884
2 PILLSBURY, Olive P 1884
3 RUSSELL, J M 1889
4 LAIRD, William [127]1884

Helpful Hints

1. This Map's INDEX can be found on the preceding pages.

2. Refer to Map "C" to see where this Township lies within Vilas County, Wisconsin.

3. Numbers within square brackets [ ] denote a multi-patentee land parcel (multi-owner). Refer to Appendix "C" for a full list of members in this group.

4. Areas that look to be crowded with Patentees usually indicate multiple sales of the same parcel (Re-issues) or Overlapping parcels. See this Township's Index for an explanation of these and other circumstances that might explain "odd" groupings of Patentees on this map.

Lots-Sec. 15

1	FRENCH, D D	1885
2	FRENCH, D D	1885
5	VAN BRUNT, W A	1885
6	VAN BRUNT, W A	1885
7	VAN BRUNT, W A	1885
8	RUSSELL, Jesse M	1885

Lots-Sec. 14

1	RUSSELL, Jesse M	1885
2	RUSSELL, Jesse M	1885
3	RUSSELL, Jesse M	1885
4	LANE, Mary E [128] 1905
5	VAN BRUNT, W A	1885
6	RUSSELL, J M	1889
7	RUSSELL, Jesse M	1885

Lots-Sec. 13

1	RUSSELL, J M	1889
2	RUSSELL, J M	1889
3	RUSSELL, J M	1889
4	RUSSELL, J M	1889
5	RUSSELL, J M	1889

Lots-Sec. 23

3	RUSSELL, J M	1889
4	RUSSELL, Jesse M	1885
5	SHEPPARD, Robert L	1911

Lots-Sec. 24

1	RUSSELL, J M	1889
2	FRENCH, D D	1885
3	FRENCH, D D	1885
4	FRENCH, D D	1885
5	FRENCH, D D	1885
6	PILLSBURY, Oliver P	1884
7	BABCOCK, Adelber [12] 1910
8	SHEPPARD, Robert L	1911
9	SHEPPARD, Robert L	1911

Legend

— Patent Boundary

━━ Section Boundary

No Patents Found (or Outside County)

1., 2., 3., ... Lot Numbers (when beside a name)

[ ] Group Number (see Appendix "C")

Scale: Section = 1 mile X 1 mile (generally, with some exceptions)

Road Map

T43-N R8-E
4th PM - 1831 MN/WI

Map Group 7

Cities & Towns

None

Cemeteries

None

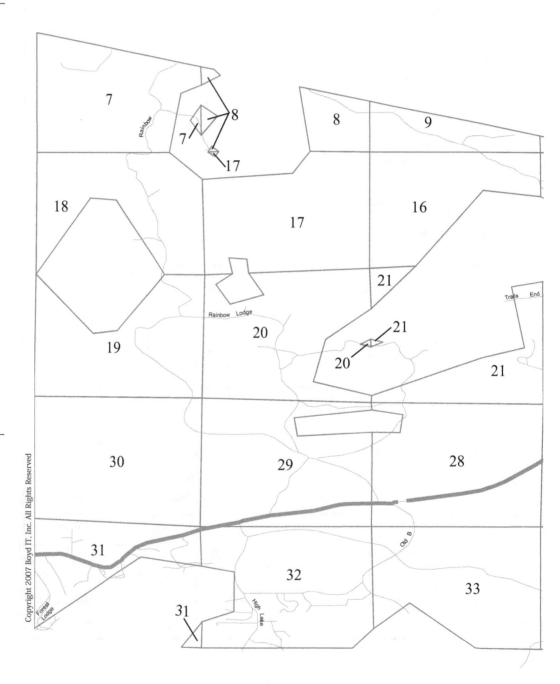

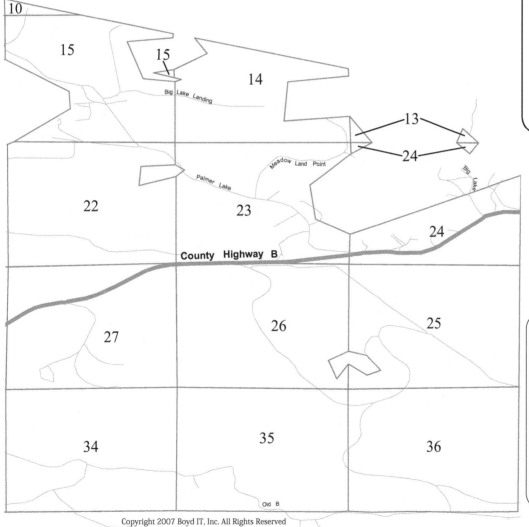

Legend

———	Section Lines
▬▬▬	Interstates
▬▬▬	Highways
———	Other Roads
●	Cities/Towns
⊥	Cemeteries

Scale: Section = 1 mile X 1 mile
(generally, with some exceptions)

Historical Map

T43-N R8-E
4th PM - 1831 MN/WI

Map Group 7

Cities & Towns
None

Cemeteries
None

Helpful Hints

1. This Map takes a different look at the same Congressional Township displayed in the preceding two maps. It presents features that can help you better envision the historical development of the area: a) Water-bodies (lakes & ponds), b) Water-courses (rivers, streams, etc.), c) Railroads, d) City/town center-points (where they were oftentimes located when first settled), and e) Cemeteries.

2. Using this "Historical" map in tandem with this Township's Patent Map and Road Map, may lead you to some interesting discoveries. You will often find roads, towns, cemeteries, and waterways are named after nearby landowners: sometimes those names will be the ones you are researching. See how many of these research gems you can find here in Vilas County.

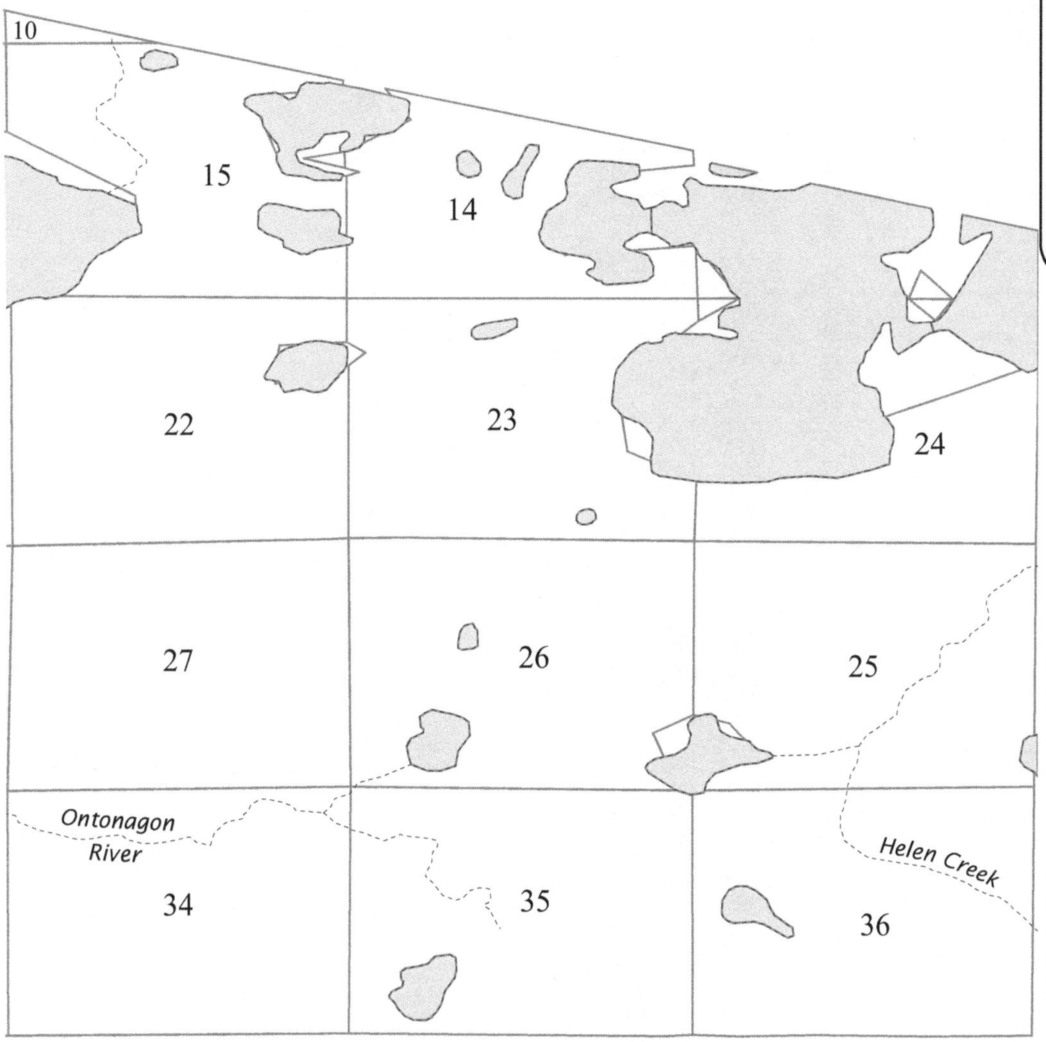
10
15
14
22
23
24
27
26
25
Ontonagon River
Helen Creek
34
35
36

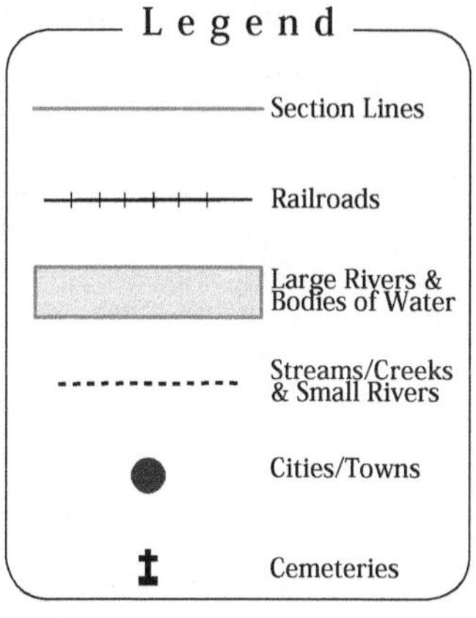
Legend
Section Lines
Railroads
Large Rivers & Bodies of Water
Streams/Creeks & Small Rivers
Cities/Towns
Cemeteries

Scale: Section = 1 mile X 1 mile
(there are some exceptions)

Map Group 8: Index to Land Patents

Township 43-North Range 9-East (4th PM - 1831 MN/WI)

After you locate an individual in this Index, take note of the Section and Section Part then proceed to the Land Patent map on the pages immediately following. You should have no difficulty locating the corresponding parcel of land.

The "For More Info" Column will lead you to more information about the underlying Patents. See the *Legend* at right, and the "How to Use this Book" chapter, for more information.

```
                        LEGEND
              "For More Info . . . " column
A = Authority (Legislative Act, See Appendix "A")
B = Block or Lot (location in Section unknown)
C = Cancelled Patent
F = Fractional Section
G = Group (Multi-Patentee Patent, see Appendix "C")
V = Overlaps another Parcel
R = Re-Issued (Parcel patented more than once)

(A & G items require you to look in the Appendixes referred
to above. All other Letter-designations followed by a number
require you to locate line-items in this index that possess
the ID number found after the letter).
```

ID	Individual in Patent	Sec.	Sec. Part	Date Issued	Other Counties	For More Info . . .
1356	ALBAN, S H	36	7	1885-06-12		A1
1289	ANDERSON, Edmund S	25	6	1891-04-23		A3
1290	" "	25	7	1891-04-23		A3
1291	" "	25	NESE	1891-04-23		A3
1292	ANDERSON, Erwin W	26	3	1891-04-23		A3
1293	" "	26	SWNW	1891-04-23		A3
1294	" "	27	NESE	1891-04-23		A3
1295	" "	27	SENE	1891-04-23		A3
1251	BENT, Amanda H	20	1	1906-05-23		A3 G23
1252	" "	20	2	1906-05-23		A3 G23
1253	" "	20	3	1906-05-23		A3 G23
1254	" "	20	SWNW	1906-05-23		A3 G23
1263	BENT, Charles A	20	5	1908-09-21		A1
1264	" "	20	SESW	1908-09-21		A1
1251	BENT, Horace W	20	1	1906-05-23		A3 G23
1252	" "	20	2	1906-05-23		A3 G23
1253	" "	20	3	1906-05-23		A3 G23
1254	" "	20	SWNW	1906-05-23		A3 G23
1255	BRUSS, August W	30	NESW	1908-11-05		A3
1256	" "	30	NWNW	1908-11-05		A3
1257	" "	30	S½NW	1908-11-05		A3
1324	BRYDEN, James W	21	E½SE	1885-11-25		A1 G33
1325	" "	22		1885-11-25		A1 G33
1326	" "	27	NW	1885-11-25		A1 G33
1327	" "	27	NWNE	1885-11-25		A1 G33
1267	CO, Cutler And Savidge Lumber	34	1	1885-01-15		A1
1268	" "	34	N½SE	1885-01-15		A1
1269	" "	34	SENE	1885-01-15		A1
1270	" "	34	SESE	1885-01-15		A1
1271	" "	34	W½NE	1885-01-15		A1
1272	" "	35	4	1885-01-15		A1
1273	" "	35	5	1885-01-15		A1
1274	" "	35	SWSW	1885-01-15		A1
1275	" "	36	8	1885-01-15		A1
1329	DANNEKER, John	32	N½SW	1885-11-25		A1
1260	DAVIS, C W	20	4	1884-06-30		A1 G66
1261	" "	30	NENW	1884-06-30		A1 G66
1262	" "	30	NWNE	1884-06-30		A1 G66
1352	DAVIS, S E	29	3	1885-09-10		A1
1353	" "	29	4	1885-09-10		A1
1354	" "	29	E½SW	1885-09-10		A1
1355	" "	30	4	1885-09-10		A1
1338	FARNHAM, Mary J	33	2	1889-05-09		A1
1339	" "	33	3	1889-05-09		A1
1265	FOREST, Charles	32	E½NE	1873-11-15		A1 G86
1266	" "	33	W½NW	1873-11-15		A1 G86

ID	Individual in Patent	Sec.	Sec. Part	Date Issued	Other Counties	For More Info . . .
1330	FRANK, John H	19	2	1909-10-14		A3
1331	" "	19	3	1909-10-14		A3
1332	" "	19	SENW	1909-10-14		A3
1282	FRENCH, D D	21	5	1885-07-13		A1
1283	" "	21	6	1885-07-13		A1
1276	" "	18	1	1885-09-10		A1
1277	" "	18	2	1885-09-10		A1
1278	" "	20	6	1885-09-10		A1
1279	" "	21	2	1885-09-10		A1
1280	" "	21	3	1885-09-10		A1
1281	" "	21	4	1885-09-10		A1
1284	" "	21	SWSE	1885-09-10		A1
1285	" "	29	SWNW	1885-09-10		A1
1313	FROST, Hiram E	36	1	1891-10-08		A1
1314	" "	36	2	1891-10-08		A1
1315	" "	36	3	1891-10-08		A1
1335	GAEBLER, M H	30	1	1890-07-15		A1
1360	GILMORE, W W	32	SESW	1884-06-30		A1
1258	HAIGHT, Augustus	35	SESE	1872-11-01		A1
1301	HALL, Frederick	32	SWSW	1883-09-15		A1
1302	" "	34	SWSE	1883-09-15		A1
1303	" "	35	2	1883-09-15		A1
1304	" "	35	8	1883-09-15		A1
1316	HAMILTON, Irenus K	25	2	1872-07-01		A1 G97
1317	" "	25	3	1872-07-01		A1 G97
1318	" "	25	4	1872-07-01		A1 G97
1319	" "	25	5	1872-07-01		A1 G97
1320	" "	25	NWSW	1872-07-01		A1 G97
1321	" "	25	SWNW	1872-07-01		A1 G97
1322	" "	26	1	1872-07-01		A1 G97
1323	" "	26	SENE	1872-07-01		A1 G97
1316	HAMILTON, Woodman C	25	2	1872-07-01		A1 G97
1317	" "	25	3	1872-07-01		A1 G97
1318	" "	25	4	1872-07-01		A1 G97
1319	" "	25	5	1872-07-01		A1 G97
1320	" "	25	NWSW	1872-07-01		A1 G97
1321	" "	25	SWNW	1872-07-01		A1 G97
1322	" "	26	1	1872-07-01		A1 G97
1323	" "	26	SENE	1872-07-01		A1 G97
1333	HARPER, John L	34	SESW	1874-08-01		A1 G98
1334	" "	34	SWSW	1874-08-01		A1 G98
1260	HOLLISTER, S W	20	4	1884-06-30		A1 G66
1261	" "	30	NENW	1884-06-30		A1 G66
1262	" "	30	NWNE	1884-06-30		A1 G66
1357	HOLLISTER, Seymour W	26	SWNE	1883-09-15		A1 G108
1259	JONES, Benjamin F	27	NWSW	1904-11-30		A1
1265	LARZELERE, Charles	32	E½NE	1873-11-15		A1 G86
1266	" "	33	W½NW	1873-11-15		A1 G86
1287	LINDSAY, E J	29	E½NW	1885-11-25		A1
1361	LINDSAY, Walter E	29	1	1885-11-25		A1
1362	" "	29	2	1885-11-25		A1
1363	" "	29	S½NE	1885-11-25		A1
1376	LINDSAY, William	29	N½SE	1885-11-25		A1
1377	" "	30	3	1885-11-25		A1
1378	" "	31	1	1885-11-25		A1
1379	" "	31	2	1885-11-25		A1
1380	" "	31	3	1885-11-25		A1
1381	" "	31	4	1885-11-25		A1
1382	" "	31	NWNW	1885-11-25		A1
1383	" "	31	SE	1885-11-25		A1
1384	" "	31	SENE	1885-11-25		A1
1385	" "	31	SW	1885-11-25		A1
1249	LOVEJOY, Allen P	36	5	1872-05-10		A1
1250	" "	36	6	1872-05-10		A1
1260	MCMILLEN, Robert	20	4	1884-06-30		A1 G66
1261	" "	30	NENW	1884-06-30		A1 G66
1262	" "	30	NWNE	1884-06-30		A1 G66
1336	MERRILL, Maggie J	34	E½NW	1892-10-15		A3
1337	" "	34	N½SW	1892-10-15		A3
1296	NEWCOMB, Frank B	26	N½SE	1890-07-15		A1
1297	" "	26	NESW	1890-07-15		A1
1298	" "	26	SENW	1890-07-15		A1
1351	OTTO, Rudolph	25	1	1888-07-18		A1

ID	Individual in Patent	Sec.	Sec. Part	Date Issued	Other Counties	For More Info . . .
1299	PALEN, Frank L	19	SESW	1910-01-13		A3
1300	" "	19	SWSE	1910-01-13		A3
1340	PILLSBURY, Oliver P	30	NWSW	1884-06-30		A1
1341	" "	30	SWSW	1884-06-30		A1
1342	" "	33	1	1884-06-30		A1
1343	" "	33	4	1884-06-30		A1
1344	" "	35	6	1884-06-30		A1
1345	" "	35	7	1884-06-30		A1
1346	" "	35	SESW	1884-06-30		A1
1324	PORTER, Rolland L	21	E½SE	1885-11-25		A1 G33
1325	" "	22		1885-11-25		A1 G33
1326	" "	27	NW	1885-11-25		A1 G33
1327	" "	27	NWNE	1885-11-25		A1 G33
1333	PRESTON, David	34	SESW	1874-08-01		A1 G98
1334	" "	34	SWSW	1874-08-01		A1 G98
1364	PRICE, Washington I	32	NW	1885-11-25		A1
1288	REYNOLDS, E M	29	S½SE	1885-11-25		A1
1305	ROWELL, Harvey	26	2	1892-05-31		A1
1306	" "	26	N½NW	1892-05-31		A1
1308	" "	27	NENE	1892-05-31		A1
1307	" "	27	1	1901-05-08		A3
1309	" "	27	SESW	1901-05-08		A3
1310	" "	27	W½SE	1901-05-08		A3
1328	RUSSELL, Jesse M	35	3	1885-05-09		A1
1350	SHEPPARD, Robert L	20	7	1911-08-04		A2
1265	SMITH, Amasa	32	E½NE	1873-11-15		A1 G86
1266	" "	33	W½NW	1873-11-15		A1 G86
1347	STEIN, Peter	33	E½NE	1893-03-21		A3
1348	" "	33	NESE	1893-03-21		A3
1349	" "	34	SWNW	1893-03-21		A3
1358	STUBBINGS, W H	30	2	1889-06-28		A1
1359	" "	30	S½NE	1889-06-28		A1
1265	UPHAM, Charles M	32	E½NE	1873-11-15		A1 G86
1266	" "	33	W½NW	1873-11-15		A1 G86
1365	VAN BRUNT, WILLARD A	28	1	1885-07-13		A1
1366	" "	28	E½NW	1885-07-13		A1
1367	" "	28	N½SE	1885-07-13		A1
1368	" "	28	NE	1885-07-13		A1
1369	" "	28	SW	1885-07-13		A1
1370	" "	28	SWNW	1885-07-13		A1
1371	" "	28	SWSE	1885-07-13		A1
1311	WELLS, Henry D	35	1	1885-05-20		A1
1312	" "	36	4	1885-05-20		A1
1372	WELLS, William H	25	SWSW	1890-04-16		A3
1373	" "	26	4	1890-04-16		A3
1374	" "	26	5	1890-04-16		A3
1375	" "	26	6	1890-04-16		A3
1357	WESCOTT, Marion	26	SWNE	1883-09-15		A1 G108
1260	WESCOTT, S P	20	4	1884-06-30		A1 G66
1261	" "	30	NENW	1884-06-30		A1 G66
1262	" "	30	NWNE	1884-06-30		A1 G66
1357	WESCOTT, Sheldon P	26	SWNE	1883-09-15		A1 G108
1286	WYLIE, Daniel B	35	SWSE	1883-09-15		A1 G172
1286	WYLIE, Winfred	35	SWSE	1883-09-15		A1 G172

Patent Map

T43-N R9-E
4th PM - 1831 MN/WI

Map Group 8

Township Statistics

Parcels Mapped	:	137
Number of Patents	:	54
Number of Individuals	:	57
Patentees Identified	:	44
Number of Surnames	:	45
Multi-Patentee Parcels	:	25
Oldest Patent Date	:	5/10/1872
Most Recent Patent	:	8/4/1911
Block/Lot Parcels	:	64
Parcels Re - Issued	:	0
Parcels that Overlap	:	0
Cities and Towns	:	0
Cemeteries	:	0

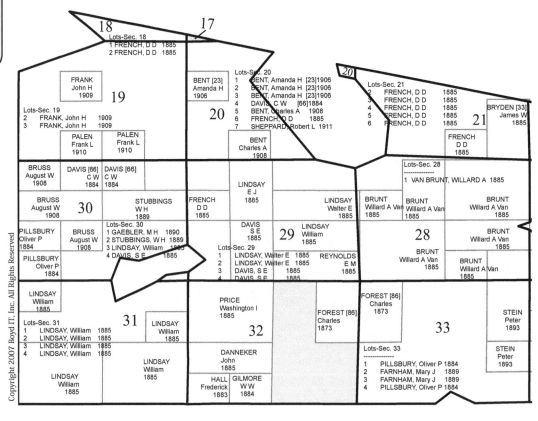

Helpful Hints

1. This Map's INDEX can be found on the preceding pages.

2. Refer to Map "C" to see where this Township lies within Vilas County, Wisconsin.

3. Numbers within square brackets [ ] denote a multi-patentee land parcel (multi-owner). Refer to Appendix "C" for a full list of members in this group.

4. Areas that look to be crowded with Patentees usually indicate multiple sales of the same parcel (Re-issues) or Overlapping parcels. See this Township's Index for an explanation of these and other circumstances that might explain "odd" groupings of Patentees on this map.

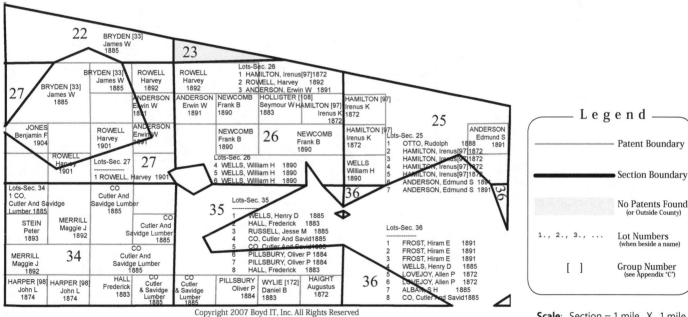

Legend

— Patent Boundary

— Section Boundary

No Patents Found (or Outside County)

1., 2., 3., ... Lot Numbers (when beside a name)

[ ] Group Number (see Appendix "C")

Scale: Section = 1 mile X 1 mile
(generally, with some exceptions)

Road Map

T43-N R9-E
4th PM - 1831 MN/WI

Map Group 8

Cities & Towns

None

Cemeteries

None

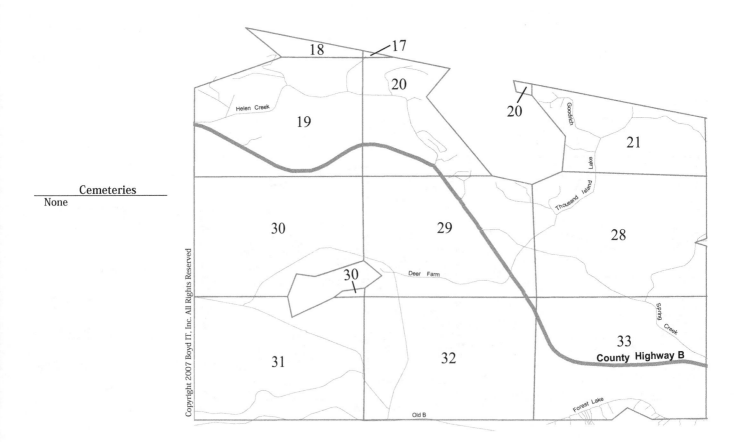

Helpful Hints

1. This road map has a number of uses, but primarily it is to help you: a) find the present location of land owned by your ancestors (at least the general area), b) find cemeteries and city-centers, and c) estimate the route/roads used by Census-takers & tax-assessors.

2. If you plan to travel to Vilas County to locate cemeteries or land parcels, please pick up a modern travel map for the area before you do. Mapping old land parcels on modern maps is not as exact a science as you might think. Just the slightest variations in public land survey coordinates, estimates of parcel boundaries, or road-map deviations can greatly alter a map's representation of how a road either does or doesn't cross a particular parcel of land.

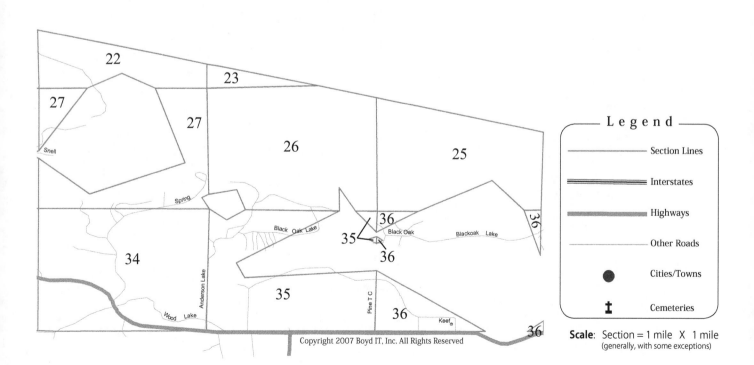

Legend

— Section Lines

≡ Interstates

━ Highways

— Other Roads

● Cities/Towns

✝ Cemeteries

Scale: Section = 1 mile X 1 mile
(generally, with some exceptions)

Historical Map

T43-N R9-E
4th PM - 1831 MN/WI

Map Group 8

Cities & Towns
None

Cemeteries
None

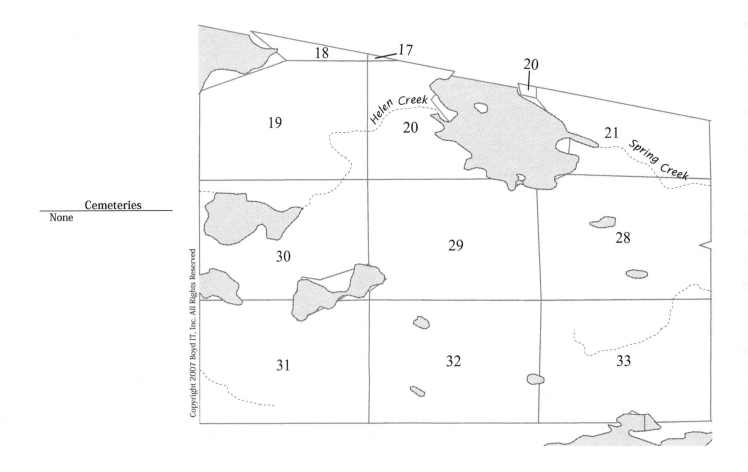

Helpful Hints

1. This Map takes a different look at the same Congressional Township displayed in the preceding two maps. It presents features that can help you better envision the historical development of the area: a) Water-bodies (lakes & ponds), b) Water-courses (rivers, streams, etc.), c) Railroads, d) City/town center-points (where they were oftentimes located when first settled), and e) Cemeteries.

2. Using this "Historical" map in tandem with this Township's Patent Map and Road Map, may lead you to some interesting discoveries. You will often find roads, towns, cemeteries, and waterways are named after nearby landowners: sometimes those names will be the ones you are researching. See how many of these research gems you can find here in Vilas County.

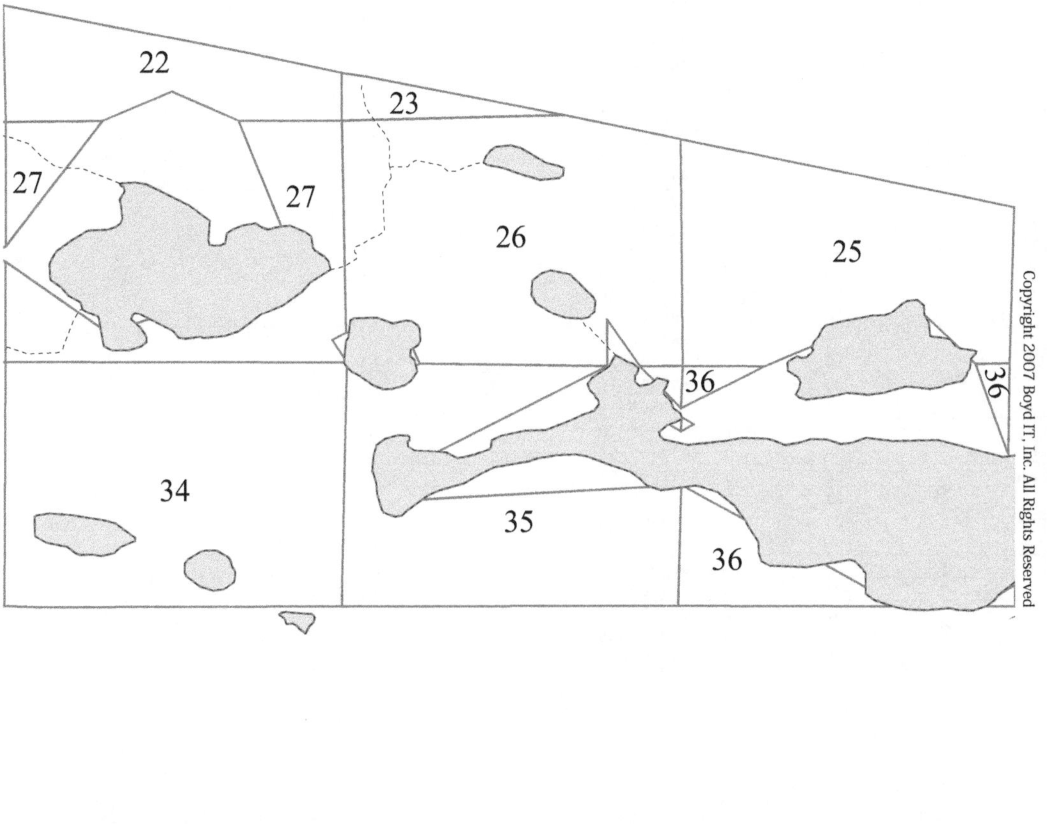

22
23
27
27
26
25
36
36
34
35
36
Copyright 2007 Boyd IT, Inc. All Rights Reserved

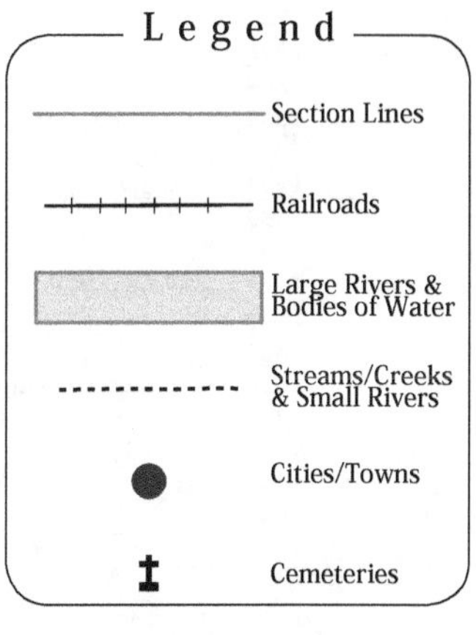

Legend
Section Lines
Railroads
Large Rivers & Bodies of Water
Streams/Creeks & Small Rivers
Cities/Towns
Cemeteries

Scale: Section = 1 mile X 1 mile
(there are some exceptions)

Map Group 9: Index to Land Patents

Township 43-North Range 10-East (4th PM - 1831 MN/WI)

After you locate an individual in this Index, take note of the Section and Section Part then proceed to the Land Patent map on the pages immediately following. You should have no difficulty locating the corresponding parcel of land.

The "For More Info" Column will lead you to more information about the underlying Patents. See the *Legend* at right, and the "How to Use this Book" chapter, for more information.

```
                      LEGEND
            "For More Info . . . " column
A = Authority (Legislative Act, See Appendix "A")
B = Block or Lot (location in Section unknown)
C = Cancelled Patent
F = Fractional Section
G = Group  (Multi-Patentee Patent, see Appendix "C")
V = Overlaps another Parcel
R = Re-Issued (Parcel patented more than once)

(A & G items require you to look in the Appendixes referred
to above. All other Letter-designations followed by a number
require you to locate line-items in this index that possess
the ID number found after the letter).
```

ID	Individual in Patent	Sec.	Sec. Part	Date Issued	Other Counties	For More Info . . .
1408	ANDERSON, Edmund S	30	SWSW	1891-04-23		A3
1425	ANDERSON, Joseph	30	NWSW	1885-11-25		A1
1426	ANDERSON, Mary J	33	5	1885-01-15		A1
1418	BUCKSTAFF, John	33	1	1873-11-15		A1
1419	" "	33	2	1873-11-15		A1
1420	" "	33	8	1873-11-15		A1
1421	" "	34	2	1873-11-15		A1
1422	" "	34	4	1873-11-15		A1
1423	" "	34	NESW	1873-11-15		A1
1424	" "	34	SWSE	1873-11-15		A1
1415	DONOHUE, Jerry	31	4	1885-05-20		A1
1416	" "	31	5	1885-05-20		A1
1417	" "	31	6	1885-05-20		A1
1427	FARNHAM, Mary J	30	1	1888-07-07		A1
1428	" "	30	2	1888-07-07		A1
1429	" "	30	3	1888-07-07		A1
1430	" "	30	4	1888-07-07		A1
1431	" "	30	6	1888-07-07		A1
1435	GAFFNEY, Patrick J	32	SESW	1904-01-11		A1
1409	HALL, Frederick	32	3	1883-09-15		A1
1410	" "	32	4	1883-09-15		A1
1411	" "	33	10	1883-09-15		A1
1412	" "	33	6	1883-09-15		A1
1413	" "	33	9	1883-09-15		A1
1386	LOVEJOY, Allen P	34	1	1872-05-10		A1
1387	" "	34	SESE	1872-05-10		A1
1388	" "	35	2	1872-05-10		A1
1389	" "	35	3	1872-05-10		A1
1390	" "	35	4	1872-05-10		A1
1391	" "	35	S½SW	1872-05-10		A1
1432	PILLSBURY, Oliver P	34	SESW	1884-06-30		A1
1433	" "	36	1	1884-06-30		A1
1434	" "	36	2	1884-06-30		A1
1437	ROUNDS, W P	31	7	1872-05-10		A1
1438	" "	31	8	1872-05-10		A1
1439	" "	31	E½SW	1872-05-10		A1
1414	STEINBERG, Henry	35	1	1872-07-01		A1 G167
1414	STEINBERG, Herman	35	1	1872-07-01		A1 G167
1436	WILBER, W E	33	11	1888-07-07		A1
1392	WYLIE, Daniel B	29	2	1883-09-15		A1 G172
1393	" "	29	3	1883-09-15		A1 G172
1394	" "	29	4	1883-09-15		A1 G172
1395	" "	31	1	1883-09-15		A1 G172
1396	" "	31	2	1883-09-15		A1 G172
1397	" "	31	3	1883-09-15		A1 G172
1398	" "	31	NESE	1883-09-15		A1 G172

ID	Individual in Patent	Sec.	Sec. Part	Date Issued	Other Counties	For More Info . . .
1399	WYLIE, Daniel B (Cont'd)	31	S½SE	1883-09-15		A1 G172
1400	" "	32	2	1883-09-15		A1 G172
1401	" "	32	NW	1883-09-15		A1 G172
1402	" "	32	NWNE	1883-09-15		A1 G172
1403	" "	32	W½SW	1883-09-15		A1 G172
1404	" "	33	3	1883-09-15		A1 G172
1405	" "	34	3	1883-09-15		A1 G172
1406	" "	34	W½SW	1883-09-15		A1 G172
1407	" "	36	3	1883-09-15		A1 G172
1392	WYLIE, Winfred	29	2	1883-09-15		A1 G172
1393	" "	29	3	1883-09-15		A1 G172
1394	" "	29	4	1883-09-15		A1 G172
1395	" "	31	1	1883-09-15		A1 G172
1396	" "	31	2	1883-09-15		A1 G172
1397	" "	31	3	1883-09-15		A1 G172
1398	" "	31	NESE	1883-09-15		A1 G172
1399	" "	31	S½SE	1883-09-15		A1 G172
1400	" "	32	2	1883-09-15		A1 G172
1401	" "	32	NW	1883-09-15		A1 G172
1402	" "	32	NWNE	1883-09-15		A1 G172
1403	" "	32	W½SW	1883-09-15		A1 G172
1404	" "	33	3	1883-09-15		A1 G172
1405	" "	34	3	1883-09-15		A1 G172
1406	" "	34	W½SW	1883-09-15		A1 G172
1407	" "	36	3	1883-09-15		A1 G172

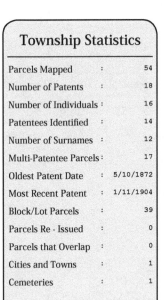

Patent Map

T43-N R10-E
4th PM - 1831 MN/WI

Map Group 9

Township Statistics

Parcels Mapped	:	54
Number of Patents	:	18
Number of Individuals	:	16
Patentees Identified	:	14
Number of Surnames	:	12
Multi-Patentee Parcels	:	17
Oldest Patent Date	:	5/10/1872
Most Recent Patent	:	1/11/1904
Block/Lot Parcels	:	39
Parcels Re - Issued	:	0
Parcels that Overlap	:	0
Cities and Towns	:	1
Cemeteries	:	1

Note: the area contained in this map amounts to far less than a full Township. Therefore, its contents are completely on this single page (instead of a "normal" 2-page spread).

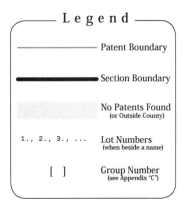

Legend

—————— Patent Boundary

——————— Section Boundary

No Patents Found
(or Outside County)

1., 2., 3., ...   Lot Numbers
(when beside a name)

[ ]   Group Number
(see Appendix "C")

Scale: Section = 1 mile X 1 mile
(generally, with some exceptions)

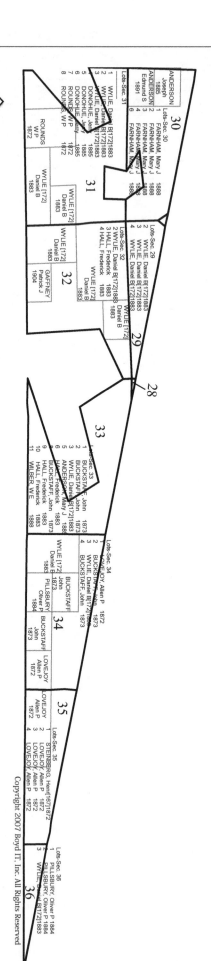

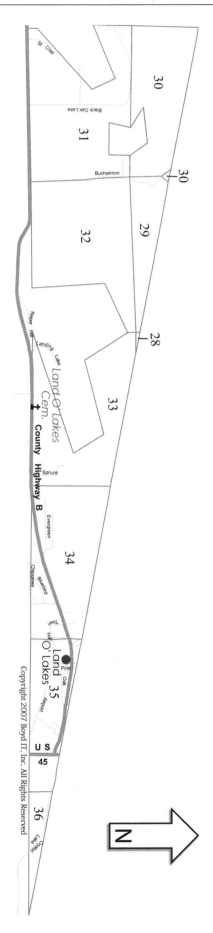

St. Clair

30

Black Oak Lake

31

Buchannon

30

32

29

28

Naper Hill

Landing Lake

Land O' Lakes

33

Cem.

Spruce

County Highway B

Evergreen

34

Chippewa

Bluebird

Town

Town Hall

Pine

Oak

Land O' Lakes

35

Airport

U S

45

36

Crystal Lake

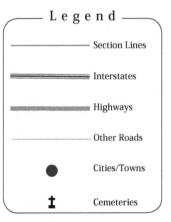

N

Road Map
T43-N R10-E
4th PM - 1831 MN/WI

M a p   G r o u p   9

Note: the area contained in this map amounts to far less than a full Township. Therefore, its contents are completely on this single page (instead of a "normal" 2-page spread).

_____

Cities & Towns
Land O' Lakes
_____

Cemeteries
Land O Lakes Cemetery
_____

L e g e n d

——————— Section Lines

═══════ Interstates

━━━━━━━ Highways

——————— Other Roads

● Cities/Towns

✝ Cemeteries

Scale: Section = 1 mile X 1 mile
(generally, with some exceptions)

129

Historical Map

T43-N R10-E
4th PM - 1831 MN/WI

Map Group 9

Note: the area contained in this map amounts to far less than a full Township. Therefore, its contents are completely on this single page (instead of a "normal" 2-page spread).

Cities & Towns
Land O' Lakes

Cemeteries
Land O Lakes Cemetery

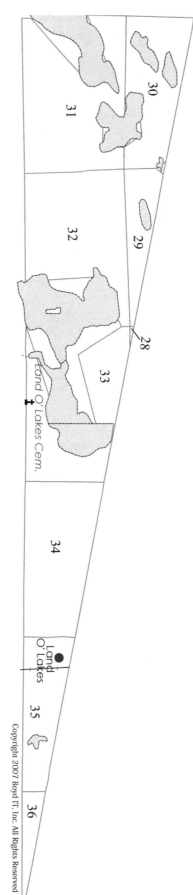

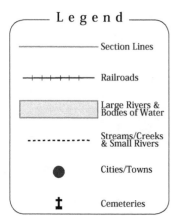

Legend

———————— Section Lines

++++++++++ Railroads

� Large Rivers & Bodies of Water

- - - - - - Streams/Creeks & Small Rivers

● Cities/Towns

♱ Cemeteries

Scale: Section = 1 mile X 1 mile
(there are some exceptions)

Map Group 10: Index to Land Patents

Township 42-North Range 5-East (4th PM - 1831 MN/WI)

After you locate an individual in this Index, take note of the Section and Section Part then proceed to the Land Patent map on the pages immediately following. You should have no difficulty locating the corresponding parcel of land.

The "For More Info" Column will lead you to more information about the underlying Patents. See the *Legend* at right, and the "How to Use this Book" chapter, for more information.

ID	Individual in Patent	Sec.	Sec. Part	Date Issued	Other Counties	For More Info . . .
1476	ALLEN, Earl A	3	NWSE	1905-05-09		A3 G3
1455	BARROWS, Augustus R	12	3	1873-05-01		A1
1456	" "	12	4	1873-05-01		A1
1457	" "	12	5	1873-05-01		A1
1458	" "	12	6	1873-05-01		A1
1459	" "	12	E½SE	1873-05-01		A1
1460	" "	12	NESW	1873-05-01		A1
1461	" "	13	5	1873-05-01		A1
1462	" "	2	NENE	1873-05-01		A1
1463	" "	24	N½NE	1873-05-01		A1
1464	" "	36	N½SE	1873-05-01		A1
1465	" "	36	SESW	1873-05-01		A1
1500	BEAN, Frank	26	2	1892-05-04		A1
1501	" "	26	3	1892-05-04		A1
1442	BEHLE, Albert	10	2	1894-06-15		A1
1443	" "	10	3	1894-06-15		A1
1444	" "	9	8	1894-06-15		A1
1599	BENSON, Peter	17	1	1899-10-23		A3
1600	" "	17	2	1899-10-23		A3
1601	" "	17	N½NW	1899-10-23		A3
1477	BERGER, Edward A	24	NW	1893-07-25		A1
1575	BLAND, Josiah	24	SESW	1902-09-26		A3 G25
1631	BLANDING, William M	26	E½NW	1884-06-20		A1
1450	BOLGER, Andrew J	30	SWNE	1915-09-08		A3 G27
1610	BOLGER, Thomas M	30	NWNE	1913-10-08		A3 G28
1508	BRAUN, George	36	NE	1893-12-22		A1
1510	BUCK, George W	14	9	1900-07-30		A1
1531	CAVNER, James	29	SWSW	1914-11-27		A3
1532	" "	30	SESE	1914-11-27		A3
1471	COMPANY, Chippewa Logging	2	NENW	1889-05-09		A1 F
1472	" "	2	SWNW	1889-05-09		A1
1473	" "	3	SENE	1889-05-09		A1
1582	CORWITH, Nathan	8	4	1872-11-01		A1
1583	" "	8	6	1872-11-01		A1
1584	" "	9	3	1872-11-01		A1
1585	" "	9	5	1872-11-01		A1
1505	CROSBY, Frederick W	4	8	1871-04-01		A1
1506	" "	9	2	1871-04-01		A1
1554	DALEY, John	18	NENE	1884-06-20		A1 G64
1474	DEVINE, Daniel	1	1	1904-03-01		A3 G70
1475	" "	1	2	1904-03-01		A3 G70
1474	DEVINE, Kate	1	1	1904-03-01		A3 G70
1475	" "	1	2	1904-03-01		A3 G70
1619	DIAMOND, William	18	5	1889-04-04		A1
1620	" "	20	6	1889-04-04		A1
1621	" "	21	3	1889-04-04		A1

ID	Individual in Patent	Sec.	Sec. Part	Date Issued	Other Counties	For More Info . . .
1622	DIAMOND, William (Cont'd)	21	4	1889-04-04		A1
1623	" "	21	7	1889-04-04		A1
1624	" "	21	8	1889-04-04		A1
1625	" "	21	SENW	1889-04-04		A1
1626	" "	21	SWSE	1889-04-04		A1
1627	" "	26	E½SW	1889-04-04		A1
1628	" "	26	W½SE	1889-04-04		A1
1629	" "	35	NENW	1889-04-04		A1
1466	DORIOT, Calvin H	21	NESE	1899-11-20		A1
1467	" "	22	NWSW	1899-11-20		A1
1576	DORIOT, Loen	13	6	1903-04-20		A1
1543	DWIGHT, Jeremiah W	36	3	1872-11-01		A1 G79
1544	" "	36	SWSE	1872-11-01		A1 G79
1537	" "	13	1	1873-05-01		A1 G79
1538	" "	13	10	1873-05-01		A1 G79
1539	" "	13	2	1873-05-01		A1 G79
1540	" "	13	3	1873-05-01		A1 G79
1541	" "	13	4	1873-05-01		A1 G79
1542	" "	13	9	1873-05-01		A1 G79
1545	" "	6	SESW	1873-05-01		A1 G79
1546	" "	7	N½NE	1873-05-01		A1 G79
1547	" "	8	3	1873-05-01		A1 G79
1548	" "	8	5	1873-05-01		A1 G79
1533	FISK, James E	3	NESE	1907-06-03		A1
1549	FORD, Jesse M	7	SESW	1905-05-23		A3 G85
1528	FOX, Horace E	9	1	1903-11-11		A1
1479	FRIEND, Elias	2	N½SE	1885-11-25		A1
1480	" "	2	NESW	1885-11-25		A1
1481	" "	2	SENW	1885-11-25		A1
1482	" "	26	NWNW	1885-11-25		A1
1483	" "	7	N½NW	1885-11-25		A1 F
1484	" "	7	SENW	1885-11-25		A1
1451	HAIGHT, Augustus	10	SENE	1872-11-01		A1
1452	" "	11	SWNW	1872-11-01		A1
1453	" "	2	SESW	1872-11-01		A1
1454	" "	3	NENE	1872-11-01		A1
1468	HARRIGAN, Charles E	17	S½NE	1902-01-25		A1
1509	HARRIGAN, George H	12	SWSE	1899-06-22		A1
1523	HARRIGAN, Helen G	15	5	1903-12-17		A3 G99
1565	HARRIGAN, John T	17	NESE	1900-07-30		A1
1566	" "	36	1	1901-11-22		A1
1567	" "	36	2	1901-11-22		A1
1568	" "	36	NESW	1901-11-22		A1
1569	" "	36	SWNW	1901-11-22		A1
1614	HARRIGAN, William D	17	N½NE	1900-06-11		A1
1615	" "	8	SESW	1900-06-11		A1
1616	" "	8	SWSE	1900-06-11		A1
1618	" "	27	NENE	1903-10-16		A3 G101
1617	" "	4	NWNW	1903-12-17		A3 G102 F
1618	HEIMER, Matthias C	27	NENE	1903-10-16		A3 G101
1617	HUTCHISON, James M	4	NWNW	1903-12-17		A3 G102 F
1554	INGRAHAM, James E	18	NENE	1884-06-20		A1 G64
1440	JACKSON, A B	15	4	1872-11-01		A1
1441	" "	15	N½NW	1872-11-01		A1
1446	JACKSON, Andrew B	30	SWSW	1872-07-01		A1 G113
1447	" "	8	2	1872-07-01		A1 G113
1448	" "	9	4	1872-07-01		A1 G113
1449	" "	9	7	1872-07-01		A1 G113
1446	JACKSON, E G	30	SWSW	1872-07-01		A1 G113
1447	" "	8	2	1872-07-01		A1 G113
1448	" "	9	4	1872-07-01		A1 G113
1449	" "	9	7	1872-07-01		A1 G113
1611	LAIRD, W H	10	NWNE	1883-09-15		A1 G126
1612	" "	20	7	1883-09-15		A1 G126
1613	" "	21	SWNW	1883-09-15		A1 G126
1630	LAIRD, William H	3	NWNE	1884-06-30		A1 G127
1575	LAMOTTE, Joseph A	24	SESW	1902-09-26		A3 G25
1570	" "	14	10	1903-01-20		A1
1571	" "	23	2	1903-01-20		A1
1572	" "	23	3	1903-01-20		A1
1573	" "	23	4	1903-01-20		A1
1574	" "	24	N½SW	1903-01-20		A1
1581	LARRABEE, Mellen P	26	SWNE	1889-03-29		A1 G129

ID	Individual in Patent	Sec.	Sec. Part	Date Issued	Other Counties	For More Info . . .
1602	LOVELESS, Robert F	25	3	1910-05-09		A3
1603	" "	25	4	1910-05-09		A3
1524	MARVIN, Henry P	22	2	1892-04-29		A1
1525	" "	22	3	1892-04-29		A1
1526	" "	22	4	1892-04-29		A1
1527	" "	22	5	1892-04-29		A1
1632	MCDANIEL, William	14	2	1906-10-24		A3 G140
1543	MCGRAW, John	36	3	1872-11-01		A1 G79
1544	" "	36	SWSE	1872-11-01		A1 G79
1537	" "	13	1	1873-05-01		A1 G79
1538	" "	13	10	1873-05-01		A1 G79
1539	" "	13	2	1873-05-01		A1 G79
1540	" "	13	3	1873-05-01		A1 G79
1541	" "	13	4	1873-05-01		A1 G79
1542	" "	13	9	1873-05-01		A1 G79
1545	" "	6	SESW	1873-05-01		A1 G79
1546	" "	7	N½NE	1873-05-01		A1 G79
1547	" "	8	3	1873-05-01		A1 G79
1548	" "	8	5	1873-05-01		A1 G79
1478	MCGUIRE, Edward	14	1	1904-02-25		A1
1534	MCKINNEY, James	8	7	1911-03-23		A3
1535	" "	8	E½SE	1911-03-23		A3
1536	" "	9	SWSW	1911-03-23		A3
1581	MILES, Eusebius M	26	SWNE	1889-03-29		A1 G129
1553	MILLER, John A	12	E½NE	1900-06-11		A3
1450	MILLS, James M	30	SWNE	1915-09-08		A3 G27
1507	MOORE, Frederick W	4	1	1910-06-09		A3
1523	MORRIS, James A	15	5	1903-12-17		A3 G99
1611	NORTON, J L	10	NWNE	1883-09-15		A1 G126
1612	" "	20	7	1883-09-15		A1 G126
1613	" "	21	SWNW	1883-09-15		A1 G126
1630	NORTON, James L	3	NWNE	1884-06-30		A1 G127
1611	NORTON, M G	10	NWNE	1883-09-15		A1 G126
1612	" "	20	7	1883-09-15		A1 G126
1613	" "	21	SWNW	1883-09-15		A1 G126
1630	NORTON, Matthew G	3	NWNE	1884-06-30		A1 G127
1445	PAFF, Albert R	6	1	1889-05-31		A1
1529	PARSONS, Isaac	7	NESE	1884-06-30		A1 G152
1530	" "	7	SWNE	1884-06-30		A1 G152
1610	PERKINS, Francillo	30	NWNE	1913-10-08		A3 G28
1586	PILLSBURY, Oliver P	11	SENW	1885-01-15		A1
1587	" "	18	1	1885-01-15		A1
1588	" "	18	2	1885-01-15		A1
1589	" "	18	NWNE	1885-01-15		A1
1590	" "	20	1	1885-01-15		A1
1591	" "	21	5	1885-01-15		A1
1592	" "	21	6	1885-01-15		A1
1593	" "	21	NENW	1885-01-15		A1
1594	" "	21	NWNW	1885-01-15		A1
1595	" "	26	NWNE	1885-01-15		A1
1596	" "	7	S½SE	1885-01-15		A1
1597	" "	7	SENE	1885-01-15		A1
1598	" "	8	W½SW	1885-01-15		A1
1504	REGNER, Frank P	14	3	1905-03-30		A3 G157
1476	REHFELD, William	3	NWSE	1905-05-09		A3 G3
1549	" "	7	SESW	1905-05-23		A3 G85
1504	RICHARDSON, William H	14	3	1905-03-30		A3 G157
1485	RIPLEY, Emma A	1	3	1871-04-01		A1
1486	" "	1	NWNW	1871-04-01		A1 F
1494	" "	4	2	1871-04-01		A1
1495	" "	4	3	1871-04-01		A1
1496	" "	4	6	1871-04-01		A1
1497	" "	4	7	1871-04-01		A1
1498	" "	4	NENE	1871-04-01		A1 F
1488	" "	23	5	1872-11-01		A1
1489	" "	25	1	1872-11-01		A1
1490	" "	26	1	1872-11-01		A1
1491	" "	29	1	1872-11-01		A1
1492	" "	29	4	1872-11-01		A1
1493	" "	29	NENE	1872-11-01		A1
1499	" "	8	1	1872-11-01		A1
1487	" "	12	2	1873-05-01		A1
1634	ROBISON, William	7	NESW	1906-02-05		A1

ID	Individual in Patent	Sec.	Sec. Part	Date Issued	Other Counties	For More Info . . .
1635	ROBISON, William (Cont'd)	7	SWNW	1906-02-05		A1
1636	" "	7	W½SW	1906-02-05		A1
1555	ROSS, John	1	7	1874-08-01		A1
1556	" "	14	8	1874-08-01		A1
1557	" "	15	2	1874-08-01		A1
1558	" "	15	3	1874-08-01		A1
1559	" "	21	1	1874-08-01		A1
1560	" "	21	2	1874-08-01		A1
1561	" "	22	1	1874-08-01		A1
1562	" "	22	6	1874-08-01		A1
1563	" "	22	7	1874-08-01		A1
1564	" "	22	SWSE	1874-08-01		A1
1550	RUSSELL, Jesse M	10	NESW	1885-05-20		A1
1551	" "	10	SENW	1885-05-20		A1
1552	" "	10	SWNE	1885-05-20		A1
1554	SAMPSON, Henry	18	NENE	1884-06-20		A1 G64
1632	SEIM, Henry J	14	2	1906-10-24		A3 G140
1502	SHERMAN, Frank G	30	SESW	1918-03-05		A3
1503	" "	30	W½SE	1918-03-05		A3
1577	SILVERSTONE, Louis	24	S½NE	1889-05-09		A1
1578	" "	24	SE	1889-05-09		A1
1579	" "	25	E½SE	1889-05-09		A1
1580	" "	25	NE	1889-05-09		A1
1511	SLAUSON, George W	11	2	1875-02-20		A1
1512	" "	11	4	1875-02-20		A1
1513	" "	11	5	1875-02-20		A1
1514	" "	11	6	1875-02-20		A1
1515	" "	13	7	1875-02-20		A1
1516	" "	13	8	1875-02-20		A1
1517	" "	14	4	1875-02-20		A1
1518	" "	14	6	1875-02-20		A1
1519	" "	25	2	1875-02-20		A1
1520	" "	25	5	1875-02-20		A1
1521	" "	3	SENW	1875-02-20		A1
1522	" "	3	SWSE	1875-02-20		A1
1604	STAMP, Robert	23	6	1896-11-24		A1
1605	" "	23	7	1896-11-24		A1
1606	" "	23	8	1896-11-24		A1
1633	STRANDBERG, William O	15	6	1913-02-18		A3
1529	TILLOTSON, Levi	7	NESE	1884-06-30		A1 G152
1530	" "	7	SWNE	1884-06-30		A1 G152
1529	WELLS, Charles W	7	NESE	1884-06-30		A1 G152
1530	" "	7	SWNE	1884-06-30		A1 G152
1637	WESTON, William	2	S½NE	1872-07-01		A1
1638	" "	6	5	1872-07-01		A1
1639	" "	6	S½SE	1872-07-01		A1
1640	" "	6	SWNW	1872-07-01		A1
1641	" "	6	W½SW	1872-07-01		A1
1607	WISCONSIN, State Of	15	7	1911-05-08		A4
1608	" "	3	SWNE	1911-05-08		A4
1609	" "	30	NENE	1911-05-08		A4
1554	WITTER, Jere D	18	NENE	1884-06-20		A1 G64
1469	ZIMPELMANN, Charles	10	E½SE	1902-01-25		A1
1470	" "	10	NWSE	1902-01-25		A1

Patent Map

T42-N R5-E
4th PM - 1831 MN/WI

Map Group 10

Township Statistics

Parcels Mapped	:	202
Number of Patents	:	74
Number of Individuals	:	82
Patentees Identified	:	63
Number of Surnames	:	69
Multi-Patentee Parcels	:	36
Oldest Patent Date	:	4/1/1871
Most Recent Patent	:	3/5/1918
Block/Lot Parcels	:	104
Parcels Re - Issued	:	0
Parcels that Overlap	:	0
Cities and Towns	:	1
Cemeteries	:	0

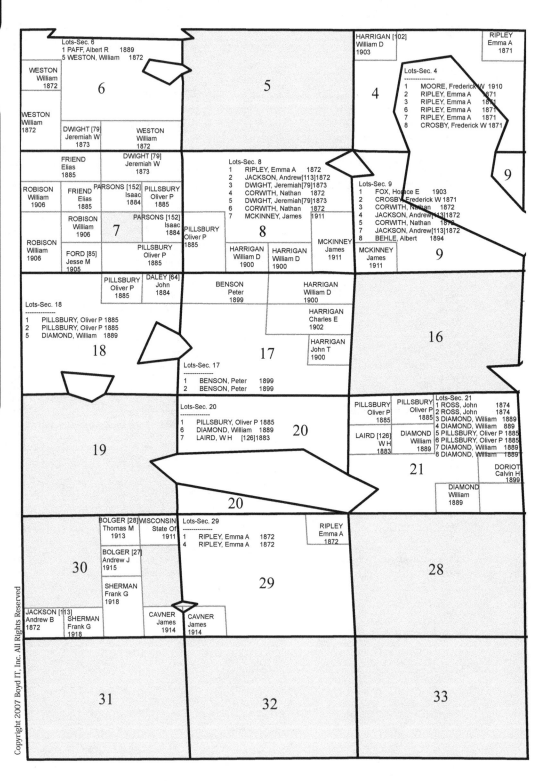

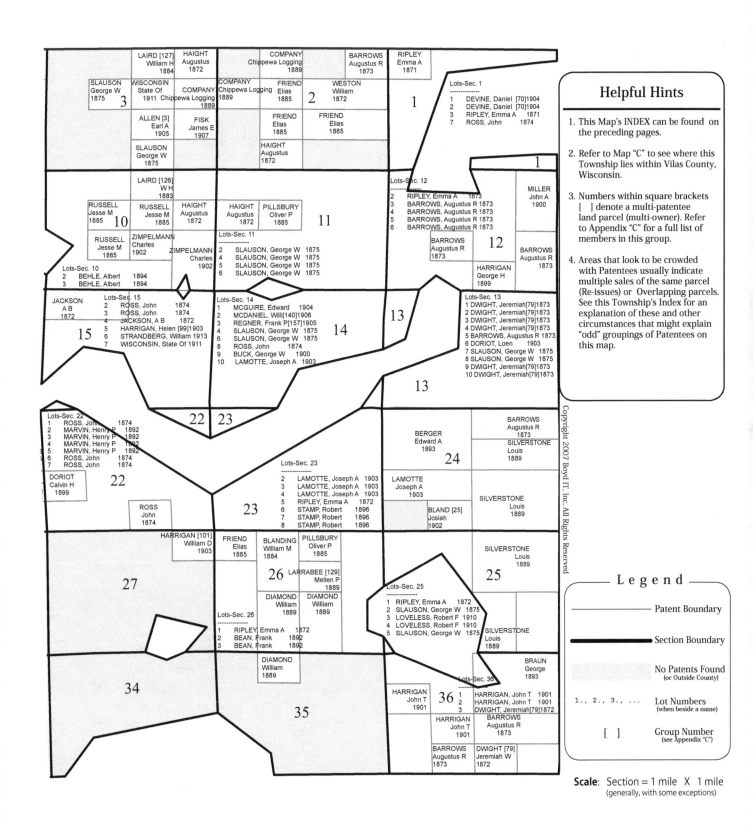

Helpful Hints

1. This Map's INDEX can be found on the preceding pages.

2. Refer to Map "C" to see where this Township lies within Vilas County, Wisconsin.

3. Numbers within square brackets [ ] denote a multi-patentee land parcel (multi-owner). Refer to Appendix "C" for a full list of members in this group.

4. Areas that look to be crowded with Patentees usually indicate multiple sales of the same parcel (Re-issues) or Overlapping parcels. See this Township's Index for an explanation of these and other circumstances that might explain "odd" groupings of Patentees on this map.

Section 3

LAIRD [127] William H 1884
HAIGHT Augustus 1872
SLAUSON George W 1875
WISCONSIN State Of 1911
COMPANY Chippewa Logging 1889
ALLEN [3] Earl A 1905
FISK James E 1907
SLAUSON George W 1875

Section 2

COMPANY Chippewa Logging 1889
COMPANY Chippewa Logging 1889
FRIEND Elias 1885
FRIEND Elias 1885
FRIEND Elias 1885
HAIGHT Augustus 1872
BARROWS Augustus R 1873
WESTON William 1872

Section 1

RIPLEY Emma A 1871

Lots-Sec. 1
1 DEVINE, Daniel [70] 1904
2 DEVINE, Daniel [70] 1904
3 RIPLEY, Emma A 1871
7 ROSS, John 1874

Section 10

LAIRD [126] W H 1883
RUSSELL Jesse M 1885
RUSSELL Jesse M 1885
HAIGHT Augustus 1872
RUSSELL Jesse M 1885
ZIMPELMANN Charles 1902
ZIMPELMANN Charles 1902

Lots-Sec. 10
2 BEHLE, Albert 1894
3 BEHLE, Albert 1894

Section 11

HAIGHT Augustus 1872
PILLSBURY Oliver P 1885

Lots-Sec. 11
2 SLAUSON, George W 1875
4 SLAUSON, George W 1875
5 SLAUSON, George W 1875
6 SLAUSON, George W 1875

Section 12

MILLER John A 1900

Lots-Sec. 12
2 RIPLEY, Emma A 1873
3 BARROWS, Augustus R 1873
4 BARROWS, Augustus R 1873
5 BARROWS, Augustus R 1873
6 BARROWS, Augustus R 1873

BARROWS Augustus R 1873
BARROWS Augustus R 1873
HARRIGAN George H

Section 15

JACKSON A B 1872

Lots-Sec. 15
2 ROSS, John 1874
3 ROSS, John 1874
4 JACKSON, A B 1872
5 HARRIGAN, Helen [99] 1903
6 STRANDBERG, William 1913
7 WISCONSIN, State Of 1911

Section 14

Lots-Sec. 14
1 MCGUIRE, Edward 1904
2 MCDANIEL, Willi [140] 1906
3 REGNER, Frank P [157] 1905
4 SLAUSON, George W 1875
5 SLAUSON, George W 1875
8 ROSS, John 1874
9 BUCK, George W 1900
10 LAMOTTE, Joseph A 1903

Section 13

Lots-Sec. 13
1 DWIGHT, Jeremiah [79] 1873
2 DWIGHT, Jeremiah [79] 1873
3 DWIGHT, Jeremiah [79] 1873
4 DWIGHT, Jeremiah [79] 1873
5 BARROWS, Augustus R 1873
6 DORIOT, Loen 1903
7 SLAUSON, George W 1875
8 SLAUSON, George W 1875
9 DWIGHT, Jeremiah [79] 1873
10 DWIGHT, Jeremiah [79] 1873

Section 22

Lots-Sec. 22
1 ROSS, John 1874
2 MARVIN, Henry P 1892
3 MARVIN, Henry P 1892
4 MARVIN, Henry P 1892
5 MARVIN, Henry P 1892
6 ROSS, John 1874
7 ROSS, John 1874

DORIOT Calvin H 1899
ROSS John 1874

Section 23

Lots-Sec. 23
2 LAMOTTE, Joseph A 1903
3 LAMOTTE, Joseph A 1903
4 LAMOTTE, Joseph A 1903
5 RIPLEY, Emma A 1872
6 STAMP, Robert 1896
7 STAMP, Robert 1896
8 STAMP, Robert 1896

Section 24

BERGER Edward A 1893
BARROWS Augustus R 1873
SILVERSTONE Louis 1889
LAMOTTE Joseph A 1903
SILVERSTONE Louis 1889
BLAND [25] Josiah 1902

Section 27

HARRIGAN [101] William D 1903

Section 26

FRIEND Elias 1885
BLANDING William M 1884
PILLSBURY Oliver P 1885
LARRABEE [129] Mellen P 1889
DIAMOND William 1889
DIAMOND William 1889

Lots-Sec. 26
1 RIPLEY, Emma A 1872
2 BEAN, Frank 1892
3 BEAN, Frank 1892

Section 25

SILVERSTONE Louis 1889
SILVERSTONE Louis 1889

Lots-Sec. 25
1 RIPLEY, Emma A 1872
2 SLAUSON, George W 1875
3 LOVELESS, Robert F 1910
4 LOVELESS, Robert F 1910
5 SLAUSON, George W 1875

Section 34

Section 35

DIAMOND William 1889

Section 36

HARRIGAN John T 1901
HARRIGAN John T 1901
BRAUN George 1893

Lots-Sec. 36
1 HARRIGAN, John T 1901
2 HARRIGAN, John T 1901
3 DWIGHT, Jeremiah [79] 1872

BARROWS Augustus R 1873
BARROWS Augustus R 1873
DWIGHT [79] Jeremiah W 1872

Legend

———— Patent Boundary

▬▬▬▬ Section Boundary

No Patents Found (or Outside County)

1., 2., 3., ... Lot Numbers (when beside a name)

[ ] Group Number (see Appendix "C")

Scale: Section = 1 mile X 1 mile (generally, with some exceptions)

Road Map

T42-N R5-E
4th PM - 1831 MN/WI

Map Group 10

Cities & Towns
Manitowish Waters

Circle Lilly

6

5

Transfer Station

County Highway W

Eight O'Clock

4

Tower   Wahoo

9

Dog Lake

Maitowish   River   Access

Forestry

8

Ilg

● Manitowish Waters

7

Benson Lake

30X30

9

Rest Lake

Airport   Mitchel

Hello

Marathon

18

17

16

Dead Pike

Stepping Stone

19

20

21

20

Petri

Cemeteries
None

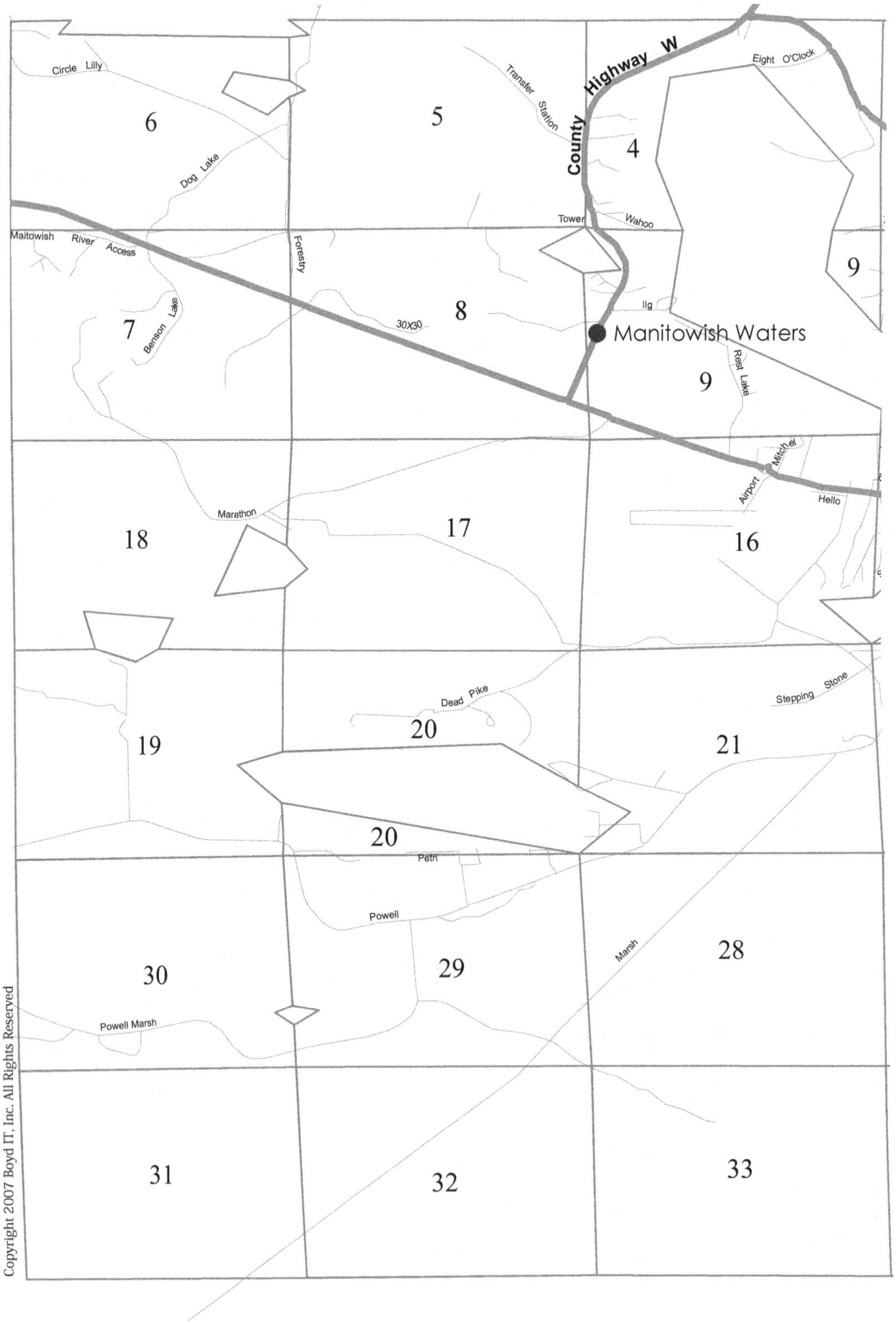

Powell

Marsh

30

29

28

Powell Marsh

31

32

33

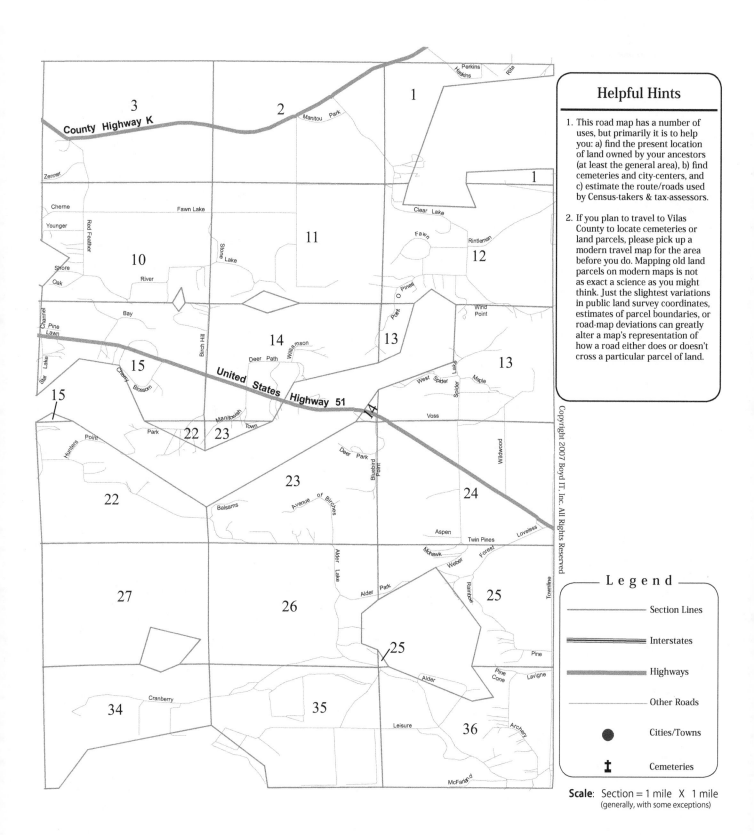

Helpful Hints

1. This road map has a number of uses, but primarily it is to help you: a) find the present location of land owned by your ancestors (at least the general area), b) find cemeteries and city-centers, and c) estimate the route/roads used by Census-takers & tax-assessors.

2. If you plan to travel to Vilas County to locate cemeteries or land parcels, please pick up a modern travel map for the area before you do. Mapping old land parcels on modern maps is not as exact a science as you might think. Just the slightest variations in public land survey coordinates, estimates of parcel boundaries, or road-map deviations can greatly alter a map's representation of how a road either does or doesn't cross a particular parcel of land.

Legend

———	Section Lines
═══	Interstates
━━━	Highways
———	Other Roads
●	Cities/Towns
✝	Cemeteries

Scale: Section = 1 mile X 1 mile
(generally, with some exceptions)

Historical Map

T42-N R5-E
4th PM - 1831 MN/WI

Map Group 10

Cities & Towns
Manitowish Waters

Cemeteries
None

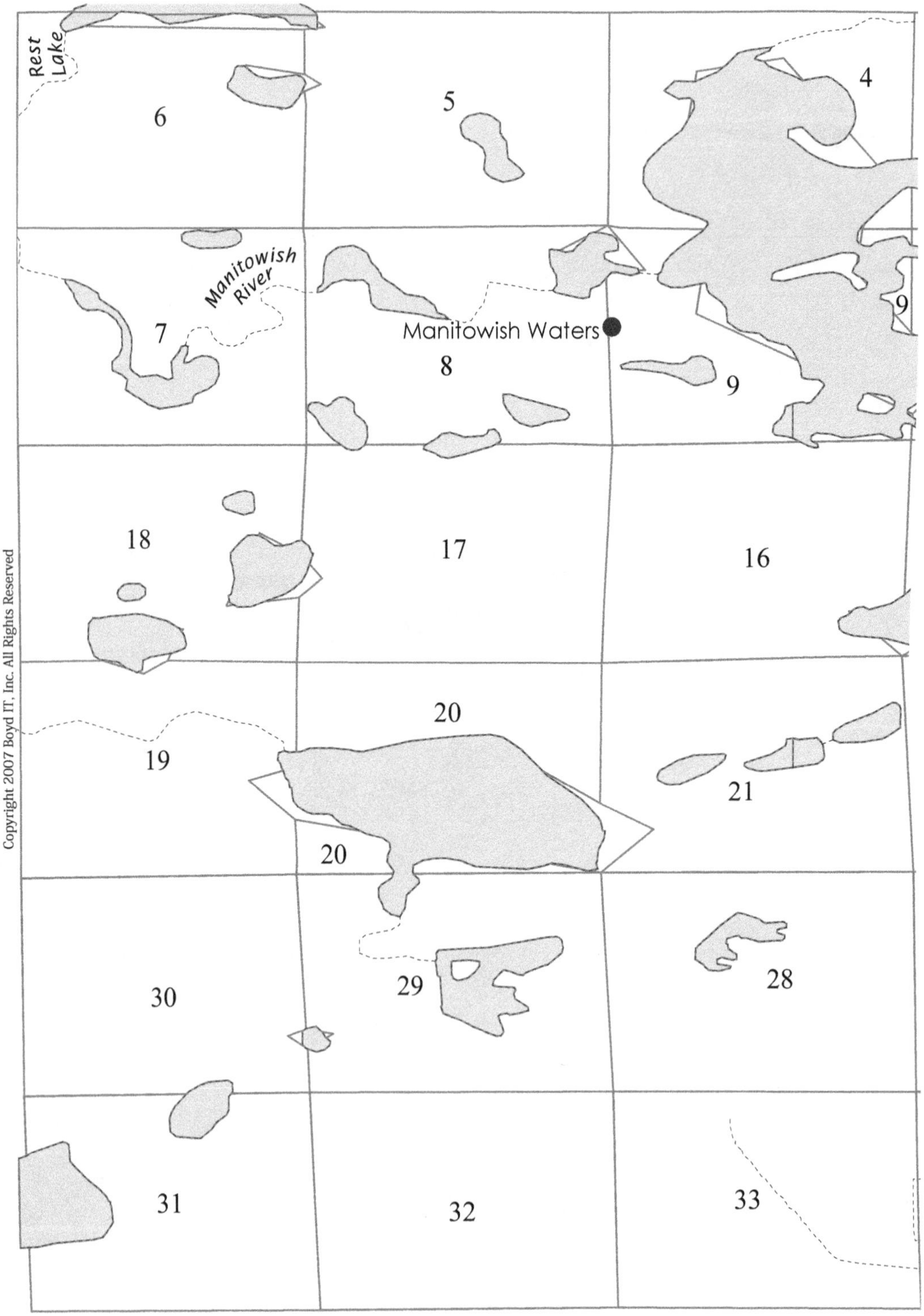

Rest Lake

6

5

4

Manitowish River

7

8

Manitowish Waters

9

9

18

17

16

19

20

20

21

30

29

28

31

32

33

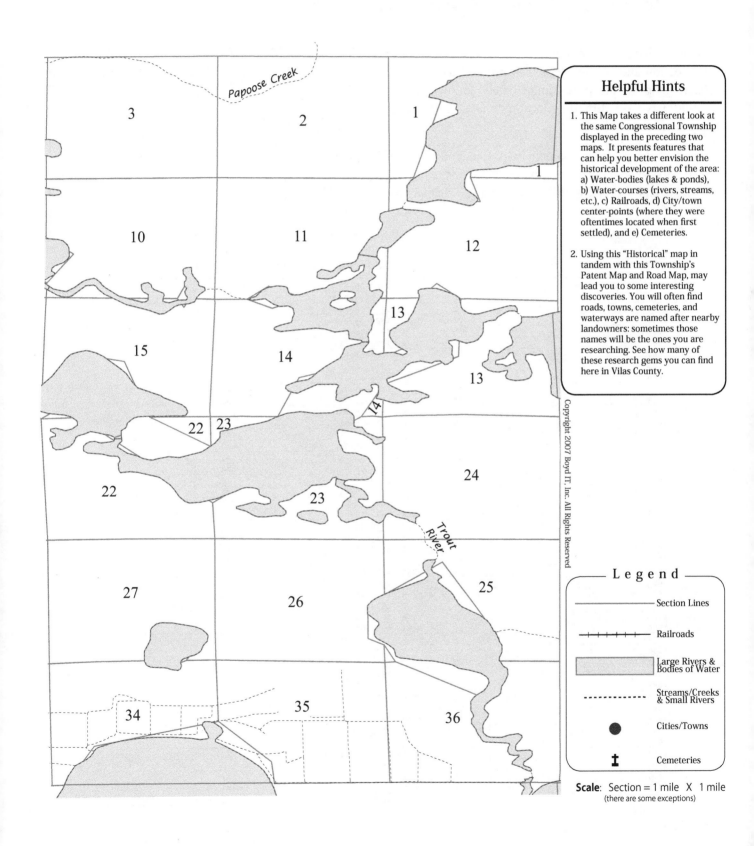

Papoose Creek

3

2

1

1

10

11

12

13

15

14

13

22 23

14

22

23

24

Trout River

27

26

25

34

35

36

Helpful Hints

1. This Map takes a different look at the same Congressional Township displayed in the preceding two maps. It presents features that can help you better envision the historical development of the area: a) Water-bodies (lakes & ponds), b) Water-courses (rivers, streams, etc.), c) Railroads, d) City/town center-points (where they were oftentimes located when first settled), and e) Cemeteries.

2. Using this "Historical" map in tandem with this Township's Patent Map and Road Map, may lead you to some interesting discoveries. You will often find roads, towns, cemeteries, and waterways are named after nearby landowners: sometimes those names will be the ones you are researching. See how many of these research gems you can find here in Vilas County.

Legend

———— Section Lines

++++++ Railroads

▭ Large Rivers & Bodies of Water

------ Streams/Creeks & Small Rivers

● Cities/Towns

✝ Cemeteries

Scale: Section = 1 mile X 1 mile
(there are some exceptions)

Map Group 11: Index to Land Patents

Township 42-North Range 6-East (4th PM - 1831 MN/WI)

After you locate an individual in this Index, take note of the Section and Section Part then proceed to the Land Patent map on the pages immediately following. You should have no difficulty locating the corresponding parcel of land.

The "For More Info" Column will lead you to more information about the underlying Patents. See the *Legend* at right, and the "How to Use this Book" chapter, for more information.

```
                        LEGEND
              "For More Info . . . " column
A = Authority (Legislative Act, See Appendix "A")
B = Block or Lot (location in Section unknown)
C = Cancelled Patent
F = Fractional Section
G = Group  (Multi-Patentee Patent, see Appendix "C")
V = Overlaps another Parcel
R = Re-Issued (Parcel patented more than once)

(A & G items require you to look in the Appendixes referred
to above. All other Letter-designations followed by a number
require you to locate line-items in this index that possess
the ID number found after the letter).
```

ID	Individual in Patent	Sec.	Sec. Part	Date Issued	Other Counties	For More Info . . .
1740	ARPIN, Daniel	1	4	1888-08-29		A1 G9 F
1741	"	1	NENE	1888-08-29		A1 G9 F
1740	ARPIN, John	1	4	1888-08-29		A1 G9 F
1741	"	1	NENE	1888-08-29		A1 G9 F
1662	BARROWS, Augustus R	1	5	1873-05-01		A1
1663	"	1	6	1873-05-01		A1
1664	"	1	7	1873-05-01		A1
1665	"	10	NENE	1873-05-01		A1
1666	"	10	NW	1873-05-01		A1
1667	"	10	SE	1873-05-01		A1
1668	"	10	SENE	1873-05-01		A1
1669	"	10	W½NE	1873-05-01		A1
1670	"	10	W½SW	1873-05-01		A1
1671	"	11	NE	1873-05-01		A1
1672	"	11	NWNW	1873-05-01		A1
1673	"	11	NWSW	1873-05-01		A1
1674	"	11	SE	1873-05-01		A1
1675	"	11	SWNW	1873-05-01		A1
1676	"	12	3	1873-05-01		A1
1677	"	12	4	1873-05-01		A1
1678	"	12	NWSW	1873-05-01		A1
1679	"	12	SWSE	1873-05-01		A1
1680	"	12	W½NW	1873-05-01		A1
1681	"	13	1	1873-05-01		A1
1682	"	14	1	1873-05-01		A1
1683	"	14	NENE	1873-05-01		A1
1684	"	14	NWNW	1873-05-01		A1
1685	"	14	SENW	1873-05-01		A1
1686	"	14	W½NE	1873-05-01		A1
1687	"	15	N½NE	1873-05-01		A1
1688	"	15	N½NW	1873-05-01		A1
1689	"	2	2	1873-05-01		A1
1690	"	2	3	1873-05-01		A1
1727	"	2	NESW	1873-05-01		A1 G16
1691	"	2	SESW	1873-05-01		A1
1692	"	23	1	1873-05-01		A1
1693	"	23	NENE	1873-05-01		A1
1694	"	23	NESE	1873-05-01		A1
1695	"	23	S½NE	1873-05-01		A1
1696	"	23	S½SW	1873-05-01		A1
1697	"	23	SWSE	1873-05-01		A1
1698	"	24	1	1873-05-01		A1
1699	"	24	SWNW	1873-05-01		A1
1700	"	25	1	1873-05-01		A1
1701	"	25	NESW	1873-05-01		A1
1702	"	25	S½NW	1873-05-01		A1

ID	Individual in Patent	Sec.	Sec. Part	Date Issued	Other Counties	For More Info . . .
1703	BARROWS, Augustus R (Cont'd)	26	1	1873-05-01		A1
1704	" "	26	2	1873-05-01		A1
1705	" "	26	3	1873-05-01		A1
1706	" "	26	4	1873-05-01		A1
1707	" "	26	6	1873-05-01		A1
1708	" "	26	8	1873-05-01		A1
1709	" "	26	N½NW	1873-05-01		A1
1710	" "	27	2	1873-05-01		A1
1711	" "	27	NENE	1873-05-01		A1
1712	" "	27	W½SW	1873-05-01		A1
1713	" "	28	NENE	1873-05-01		A1
1714	" "	28	NENW	1873-05-01		A1
1715	" "	28	W½SE	1873-05-01		A1
1716	" "	3	E½SW	1873-05-01		A1
1728	" "	3	NESE	1873-05-01		A1 G16
1717	" "	3	SESE	1873-05-01		A1
1718	" "	3	W½SE	1873-05-01		A1
1719	" "	33	E½NE	1873-05-01		A1
1720	" "	33	NWNW	1873-05-01		A1
1721	" "	34	NWNW	1873-05-01		A1
1722	" "	35	2	1873-05-01		A1
1723	" "	7	SW	1873-05-01		A1
1724	" "	9	E½NE	1873-05-01		A1
1725	" "	9	E½SE	1873-05-01		A1
1726	" "	9	SWNE	1873-05-01		A1
1764	BEAU, Frank	17	NENE	1893-07-25		A1
1765	" "	8	SESE	1893-07-25		A1
1766	" "	9	W½SW	1893-07-25		A1
1836	BEAU, Leo K	21	SWSE	1895-06-04		A1
1837	" "	28	NWNE	1895-06-04		A1
1838	" "	28	S½NE	1895-06-04		A1
1889	BEAU, Otto J	19	1	1893-07-25		A1
1890	" "	19	2	1893-07-25		A1
1891	" "	19	3	1893-07-25		A1
1886	BEHLE, Otto	17	NWNE	1894-07-02		A1
1887	" "	8	SESW	1894-07-02		A1
1888	" "	8	W½SE	1894-07-02		A1
1816	BUCKSTAFF, John	21	E½SE	1885-01-20		A1 G35
1817	" "	21	S½NE	1885-01-20		A1 G35
1818	" "	22	W½SW	1885-01-20		A1 G35
1743	CAMPBELL, Duncan M	7	E½SE	1916-08-07		A3 G37
1744	" "	7	SENE	1916-08-07		A3 G37
1745	" "	8	SWSW	1916-08-07		A3 G37
1743	CAMPBELL, Hannah M	7	E½SE	1916-08-07		A3 G37
1744	" "	7	SENE	1916-08-07		A3 G37
1745	" "	8	SWSW	1916-08-07		A3 G37
1775	CARROLL, George A	30	E½	1889-03-29		A1 G38
1928	CARSKADDON, William B	18	6	1873-05-01		A1 G39
1929	" "	19	W½NW	1873-05-01		A1 G39
1930	" "	21	E½SW	1873-05-01		A1 G39
1931	" "	21	NENE	1873-05-01		A1 G39
1932	" "	22	E½SW	1873-05-01		A1 G39
1933	" "	22	NWNE	1873-05-01		A1 G39
1934	" "	22	NWNW	1873-05-01		A1 G39
1935	" "	22	NWSE	1873-05-01		A1 G39
1936	" "	22	SENE	1873-05-01		A1 G39
1937	" "	25	S½SE	1873-05-01		A1 G39
1938	" "	25	SWSW	1873-05-01		A1 G39
1917	" "	27	1	1873-05-01		A1
1939	" "	27	3	1873-05-01		A1 G39
1940	" "	27	E½SW	1873-05-01		A1 G39
1941	" "	27	N½NW	1873-05-01		A1 G39
1942	" "	27	NWNE	1873-05-01		A1 G39
1943	" "	28	NWNW	1873-05-01		A1 G39
1944	" "	34	4	1873-05-01		A1 G39
1918	" "	34	5	1873-05-01		A1
1919	" "	34	6	1873-05-01		A1
1945	" "	34	NENE	1873-05-01		A1 G39
1946	" "	34	NESE	1873-05-01		A1 G39
1920	" "	35	1	1873-05-01		A1
1921	" "	35	3	1873-05-01		A1
1922	" "	35	4	1873-05-01		A1
1923	" "	35	SW	1873-05-01		A1

ID	Individual in Patent	Sec.	Sec. Part	Date Issued	Other Counties	For More Info . . .
1924	CARSKADDON, William B (Cont'd)	35	SWNE	1873-05-01		A1
1925	" "	36	NENE	1873-05-01		A1
1926	" "	36	S½SE	1873-05-01		A1
1927	" "	36	SWNW	1873-05-01		A1
1776	CARVER, George	27	SWNE	1902-10-11		A3 G40
1776	CARVER, Winifred	27	SWNE	1902-10-11		A3 G40
1816	CHASE, James	21	E½SE	1885-01-20		A1 G35
1817	" "	21	S½NE	1885-01-20		A1 G35
1818	" "	22	W½SW	1885-01-20		A1 G35
1749	CLARK, Eli C	15	SWNE	1873-05-01		A1 G44
1750	" "	22	E½SE	1873-05-01		A1 G44
1751	" "	30	SWSW	1873-05-01		A1 G44
1749	CLARK, Eli E	15	SWNE	1873-05-01		A1 G44
1750	" "	22	E½SE	1873-05-01		A1 G44
1751	" "	30	SWSW	1873-05-01		A1 G44
1895	COMPANY, Pioneers Lumber	4	S½SW	1883-09-10		A1
1896	" "	5	5	1883-09-10		A1
1897	" "	5	6	1883-09-10		A1
1898	" "	5	SESE	1883-09-10		A1
1899	" "	6	NWSE	1883-09-10		A1
1900	" "	8	N½NE	1883-09-10		A1
1773	CROSBY, Frederick W	13	2	1871-04-01		A1
1774	" "	25	SENE	1871-04-01		A1
1947	CROSS, William W	24	SWNE	1902-03-07		A3 G60
1904	DAY, Thomas	20	SESE	1892-05-04		A1
1905	" "	21	W½SW	1892-05-04		A1
1906	" "	29	NENE	1892-05-04		A1
1729	DORIOT, Calvin H	4	S½SE	1894-04-27		A1
1730	" "	9	NENW	1894-04-27		A1
1731	" "	9	NWNE	1894-04-27		A1
1947	DOYLE, Mike F	24	SWNE	1902-03-07		A3 G60
1776	" "	27	SWNE	1902-10-11		A3 G40
1799	DWIGHT, Jeremiah W	25	SESW	1872-11-01		A1 G79
1800	" "	31	NWSW	1872-11-01		A1 G79
1801	" "	31	SWNE	1872-11-01		A1 G79
1802	" "	33	1	1872-11-01		A1 G79
1803	" "	34	3	1872-11-01		A1 G79
1804	" "	35	E½SE	1872-11-01		A1 G79
1805	" "	35	NENE	1872-11-01		A1 G79
1808	" "	35	SWSE	1872-11-01		A1 G79
1809	" "	36	N½NW	1872-11-01		A1 G79
1810	" "	36	N½SE	1872-11-01		A1 G79
1811	" "	36	SENE	1872-11-01		A1 G79
1812	" "	36	SENW	1872-11-01		A1 G79
1813	" "	36	SW	1872-11-01		A1 G79
1814	" "	36	W½NE	1872-11-01		A1 G79
1806	" "	35	NWSE	1873-05-01		A1 G79
1807	" "	35	SENE	1873-05-01		A1 G79
1727	EARLY, Henry W	2	NESW	1873-05-01		A1 G16
1728	" "	3	NESE	1873-05-01		A1 G16
1819	ELSEN, John	15	6	1911-03-27		A3 G82
1928	EMERY, O H	18	6	1873-05-01		A1 G39
1929	" "	19	W½NW	1873-05-01		A1 G39
1930	" "	21	E½SW	1873-05-01		A1 G39
1931	" "	21	NENE	1873-05-01		A1 G39
1932	" "	22	E½SW	1873-05-01		A1 G39
1933	" "	22	NWNE	1873-05-01		A1 G39
1934	" "	22	NWNW	1873-05-01		A1 G39
1935	" "	22	NWSE	1873-05-01		A1 G39
1936	" "	22	SENE	1873-05-01		A1 G39
1937	" "	25	S½SE	1873-05-01		A1 G39
1938	" "	25	SWSW	1873-05-01		A1 G39
1939	" "	27	3	1873-05-01		A1 G39
1940	" "	27	E½SW	1873-05-01		A1 G39
1941	" "	27	N½NW	1873-05-01		A1 G39
1942	" "	27	NWNE	1873-05-01		A1 G39
1943	" "	28	NWNW	1873-05-01		A1 G39
1944	" "	34	4	1873-05-01		A1 G39
1945	" "	34	NENE	1873-05-01		A1 G39
1946	" "	34	NESE	1873-05-01		A1 G39
1727	FORSMAN, Robert M	2	NESW	1873-05-01		A1 G16
1728	" "	3	NESE	1873-05-01		A1 G16
1752	FRIEND, Elias	19	E½SE	1885-11-25		A1

ID	Individual in Patent	Sec.	Sec. Part	Date Issued	Other Counties	For More Info . . .
1753	FRIEND, Elias (Cont'd)	20	SWSW	1885-11-25		A1
1754	" "	29	SWSE	1885-11-25		A1
1755	" "	32	2	1885-11-25		A1
1756	" "	32	NWNE	1885-11-25		A1
1794	FRITZ, Henry	21	E½NW	1893-07-25		A1
1914	GARRETT, Willard	17	1	1903-04-20		A1
1915	" "	18	5	1903-04-20		A1
1916	" "	20	1	1903-04-20		A1
1644	HAIGHT, Augustus	11	E½NW	1872-11-01		A1
1645	" "	11	E½SW	1872-11-01		A1
1646	" "	12	1	1872-11-01		A1
1647	" "	12	2	1872-11-01		A1
1648	" "	12	E½NW	1872-11-01		A1
1649	" "	12	NESW	1872-11-01		A1
1650	" "	14	NENW	1872-11-01		A1
1651	" "	28	E½SE	1872-11-01		A1
1652	" "	28	SWSW	1872-11-01		A1
1653	" "	31	W½NW	1872-11-01		A1
1654	" "	33	N½SW	1872-11-01		A1
1655	" "	33	SESW	1872-11-01		A1
1656	" "	33	SWNW	1872-11-01		A1
1657	" "	33	SWSE	1872-11-01		A1
1660	" "	34	NENW	1872-11-01		A1
1661	" "	34	S½NW	1872-11-01		A1
1658	" "	34	1	1873-05-01		A1
1659	" "	34	2	1873-05-01		A1
1835	HARRIGAN, John T	20	SESW	1903-07-14		A3 G100
1732	HEADFLYER, Charles H	31	1	1898-01-12		A1
1733	" "	31	2	1898-01-12		A1
1734	" "	31	3	1898-01-12		A1
1735	" "	31	SESE	1898-01-12		A1
1749	HEATHER, Edmund	15	SWNE	1873-05-01		A1 G44
1750	" "	22	E½SE	1873-05-01		A1 G44
1751	" "	30	SWSW	1873-05-01		A1 G44
1642	JACKSON, Andrew B	13	3	1872-07-01		A1 G115
1643	" "	13	NWSE	1872-07-01		A1 G115
1819	JARCHOW, Frederick	15	6	1911-03-27		A3 G82
1767	JOHNSON, Frederick S	14	SWSW	1873-05-01		A1 G118
1768	" "	15	1	1873-05-01		A1 G118
1769	" "	17	NWSW	1873-05-01		A1 G118
1770	" "	17	SE	1873-05-01		A1 G118
1771	" "	17	SWNE	1873-05-01		A1 G118
1772	" "	9	SWSE	1873-05-01		A1 G118
1767	JOHNSON, Thew	14	SWSW	1873-05-01		A1 G118
1768	" "	15	1	1873-05-01		A1 G118
1769	" "	17	NWSW	1873-05-01		A1 G118
1770	" "	17	SE	1873-05-01		A1 G118
1771	" "	17	SWNE	1873-05-01		A1 G118
1772	" "	9	SWSE	1873-05-01		A1 G118
1901	KAYZER, Samuel	4	1	1897-02-17		A1
1775	KENEDY, Philip D	30	E½	1889-03-29		A1 G38
1907	KILROE, Thomas	20	N½SW	1892-05-16		A1
1908	" "	20	W½SE	1892-05-16		A1
1742	LABBE, Delia	9	E½SW	1904-08-23		A1
1860	LARRABEE, Mellen P	22	SWSE	1889-03-29		A1 G129
1861	" "	27	SENW	1889-03-29		A1 G129
1862	" "	32	1	1889-03-29		A1 G129
1863	" "	32	N½SE	1889-03-29		A1 G129
1727	LENTZ, George W	2	NESW	1873-05-01		A1 G16
1728	" "	3	NESE	1873-05-01		A1 G16
1736	MCCORMICK, Charles	6	6	1892-05-16		A1
1737	" "	6	7	1892-05-16		A1
1738	" "	6	8	1892-05-16		A1
1739	" "	6	9	1892-05-16		A1
1799	MCGRAW, John	25	SESW	1872-11-01		A1 G79
1800	" "	31	NWSW	1872-11-01		A1 G79
1801	" "	31	SWNE	1872-11-01		A1 G79
1802	" "	33	1	1872-11-01		A1 G79
1803	" "	34	3	1872-11-01		A1 G79
1804	" "	35	E½SE	1872-11-01		A1 G79
1805	" "	35	NENE	1872-11-01		A1 G79
1808	" "	35	SWSE	1872-11-01		A1 G79
1809	" "	36	N½NW	1872-11-01		A1 G79

ID	Individual in Patent	Sec.	Sec. Part	Date Issued	Other Counties	For More Info . . .
1810	MCGRAW, John (Cont'd)	36	N½SE	1872-11-01		A1 G79
1811	" "	36	SENE	1872-11-01		A1 G79
1812	" "	36	SENW	1872-11-01		A1 G79
1813	" "	36	SW	1872-11-01		A1 G79
1814	" "	36	W½NE	1872-11-01		A1 G79
1806	" "	35	NWSE	1873-05-01		A1 G79
1807	" "	35	SENE	1873-05-01		A1 G79
1860	MILES, Eusebius M	22	SWSE	1889-03-29		A1 G129
1861	" "	27	SENW	1889-03-29		A1 G129
1862	" "	32	1	1889-03-29		A1 G129
1863	" "	32	N½SE	1889-03-29		A1 G129
1815	MILLER, John A	7	NWNW	1900-06-11		A3 F
1909	OCONNOR, Timothy	3	N½NE	1900-06-11		A1
1763	OTTEROL, Evelyn	1	1	1885-07-13		A1
1795	PARSONS, Isaac	4	2	1884-06-30		A1 G153
1796	" "	4	3	1884-06-30		A1 G153
1797	" "	4	4	1884-06-30		A1 G153
1798	" "	5	7	1884-06-30		A1 G153
1879	PILLSBURY, Oliver P	7	NENE	1885-01-15		A1
1881	" "	8	NESW	1885-01-15		A1
1882	" "	8	NWNW	1885-01-15		A1
1864	" "	17	NESW	1885-01-20		A1
1865	" "	17	S½NW	1885-01-20		A1
1866	" "	17	SENE	1885-01-20		A1
1867	" "	21	NWNE	1885-01-20		A1
1868	" "	21	NWSE	1885-01-20		A1
1869	" "	21	W½NW	1885-01-20		A1
1870	" "	22	NENW	1885-01-20		A1
1871	" "	22	S½NW	1885-01-20		A1
1872	" "	27	SWNW	1885-01-20		A1
1873	" "	3	NWSW	1885-01-20		A1
1874	" "	4	5	1885-01-20		A1
1875	" "	4	6	1885-01-20		A1
1876	" "	4	7	1885-01-20		A1
1877	" "	4	N½SW	1885-01-20		A1
1878	" "	4	NESE	1885-01-20		A1
1880	" "	8	E½NW	1885-01-20		A1
1883	" "	8	SWNE	1885-01-20		A1
1884	" "	9	NWNW	1885-01-20		A1
1885	" "	9	NWSE	1885-01-20		A1
1892	PURTELL, P W	1	2	1885-06-12		A1
1820	RINGLE, John	19	SENW	1889-03-29		A1
1821	" "	19	SW	1889-03-29		A1
1822	" "	19	W½SE	1889-03-29		A1
1823	" "	28	N½SW	1889-03-29		A1
1824	" "	28	SESW	1889-03-29		A1
1825	" "	30	E½SW	1889-03-29		A1
1826	" "	30	NW	1889-03-29		A1
1827	" "	31	E½NW	1889-03-29		A1
1828	" "	31	N½NE	1889-03-29		A1
1829	" "	33	NENW	1889-03-29		A1
1757	RIPLEY, Emma A	10	E½SW	1873-05-01		A1
1758	" "	33	N½SE	1873-05-01		A1
1759	" "	33	SENW	1873-05-01		A1
1760	" "	33	SWNE	1873-05-01		A1
1761	" "	33	SWSW	1873-05-01		A1
1762	" "	5	1	1873-05-01		A1
1910	ROBISON, W	17	N½NW	1897-02-17		A3
1911	" "	18	1	1897-02-17		A3
1912	" "	18	2	1897-02-17		A3
1913	" "	18	3	1897-02-17		A3
1830	ROSS, John	6	1	1874-08-01		A1
1831	" "	7	SENW	1874-08-01		A1
1832	" "	7	W½SE	1874-08-01		A1
1833	" "	8	NWSW	1874-08-01		A1
1834	" "	8	SWNW	1874-08-01		A1
1835	SEYER, Jacob B	20	SESW	1903-07-14		A3 G100
1767	SHAFFER, Isaac	14	SWSW	1873-05-01		A1 G118
1768	" "	15	1	1873-05-01		A1 G118
1769	" "	17	NWSW	1873-05-01		A1 G118
1770	" "	17	SE	1873-05-01		A1 G118
1771	" "	17	SWNE	1873-05-01		A1 G118
1772	" "	9	SWSE	1873-05-01		A1 G118

ID	Individual in Patent	Sec.	Sec. Part	Date Issued	Other Counties	For More Info . . .
1847	SILVERSTONE, Louis	28	S½NW	1889-05-09		A1
1848	" "	29	E½SW	1889-05-09		A1
1849	" "	29	N½SE	1889-05-09		A1
1850	" "	29	SENE	1889-05-09		A1
1851	" "	29	SESE	1889-05-09		A1
1852	" "	29	SWSW	1889-05-09		A1
1853	" "	30	NWSW	1889-05-09		A1 F
1854	" "	31	N½SE	1889-05-09		A1
1855	" "	31	NESW	1889-05-09		A1
1856	" "	31	SENE	1889-05-09		A1
1857	" "	32	E½NE	1889-05-09		A1
1858	" "	32	SWNE	1889-05-09		A1
1859	" "	32	W½	1889-05-09		A1
1777	SLAUSON, George W	13	S½SE	1875-02-20		A1
1778	" "	14	N½SW	1875-02-20		A1
1779	" "	14	SESW	1875-02-20		A1
1780	" "	14	SWNW	1875-02-20		A1
1781	" "	14	W½SE	1875-02-20		A1
1782	" "	15	E½SE	1875-02-20		A1
1783	" "	15	SENE	1875-02-20		A1
1784	" "	22	NENE	1875-02-20		A1
1785	" "	22	SWNE	1875-02-20		A1
1786	" "	23	N½NW	1875-02-20		A1
1787	" "	23	NWNE	1875-02-20		A1
1788	" "	23	SWNW	1875-02-20		A1
1789	" "	24	NENE	1875-02-20		A1
1795	TILLOTSON, Levy	4	2	1884-06-30		A1 G153
1796	" "	4	3	1884-06-30		A1 G153
1797	" "	4	4	1884-06-30		A1 G153
1798	" "	5	7	1884-06-30		A1 G153
1893	TOBIN, Patrick	8	NESE	1905-12-30		A1
1894	" "	8	SENE	1905-12-30		A1
1746	WALSH, Eddie	20	2	1900-06-28		A3
1747	" "	20	E½NW	1900-06-28		A3
1748	" "	20	SWNE	1900-06-28		A3
1839	WATERMAN, Leslie J	17	SESW	1884-06-30		A1 G168
1840	" "	20	NESE	1884-06-30		A1 G168
1841	" "	20	NWNE	1884-06-30		A1 G168
1842	" "	20	SENE	1884-06-30		A1 G168
1843	WATTERMAN, Leslie J	11	SWSW	1884-06-30		A1 G170
1844	" "	15	2	1884-06-30		A1 G170
1845	" "	15	3	1884-06-30		A1 G170
1846	" "	15	4	1884-06-30		A1 G170
1795	WELLS, Charles W	4	2	1884-06-30		A1 G153
1796	" "	4	3	1884-06-30		A1 G153
1797	" "	4	4	1884-06-30		A1 G153
1798	" "	5	7	1884-06-30		A1 G153
1790	WERNICH, George	26	10	1889-03-29		A1
1791	" "	29	NW	1889-03-29		A1
1792	" "	29	NWSW	1889-03-29		A1
1793	" "	29	W½NE	1889-03-29		A1
1642	WILCOX, George G	13	3	1872-07-01		A1 G115
1643	" "	13	NWSE	1872-07-01		A1 G115
1843	WILEY, Charles L	11	SWSW	1884-06-30		A1 G170
1844	" "	15	2	1884-06-30		A1 G170
1845	" "	15	3	1884-06-30		A1 G170
1846	" "	15	4	1884-06-30		A1 G170
1839	" "	17	SESW	1884-06-30		A1 G168
1840	" "	20	NESE	1884-06-30		A1 G168
1841	" "	20	NWNE	1884-06-30		A1 G168
1842	" "	20	SENE	1884-06-30		A1 G168
1902	WISCONSIN, State Of	27	4	1911-05-08		A4
1903	" "	9	SENW	1911-05-08		A4

Patent Map

T42-N R6-E
4th PM - 1831 MN/WI

Map Group 11

Township Statistics

Parcels Mapped	:	306
Number of Patents	:	78
Number of Individuals	:	72
Patentees Identified	:	52
Number of Surnames	:	65
Multi-Patentee Parcels	:	77
Oldest Patent Date	:	4/1/1871
Most Recent Patent	:	8/7/1916
Block/Lot Parcels	:	78
Parcels Re - Issued	:	0
Parcels that Overlap	:	0
Cities and Towns	:	0
Cemeteries	:	0

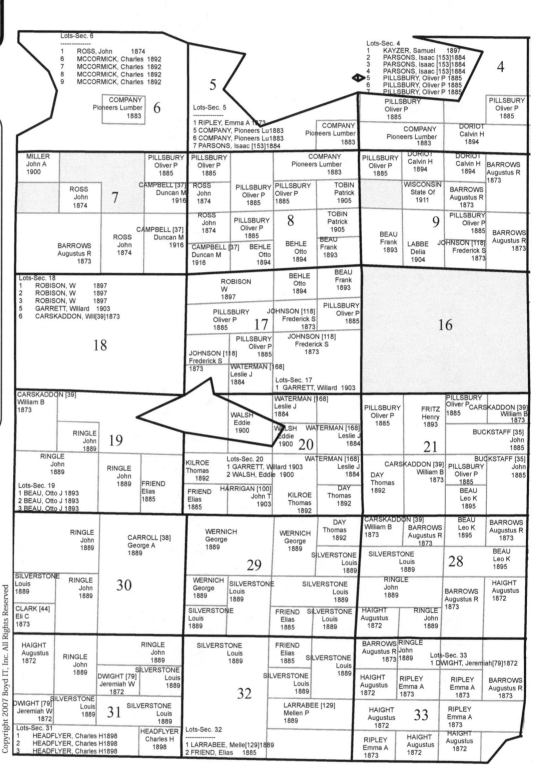

Lots-Sec. 6
----
1 ROSS, John 1874
6 MCCORMICK, Charles 1892
7 MCCORMICK, Charles 1892
8 MCCORMICK, Charles 1892
9 MCCORMICK, Charles 1892

Lots-Sec. 4
----
1 KAYZER, Samuel 1897
2 PARSONS, Isaac [153]1884
3 PARSONS, Isaac [153]1884
4 PARSONS, Isaac [153]1884
5 PILLSBURY, Oliver P 1885
6 PILLSBURY, Oliver P 1885
7 PILLSBURY, Oliver P 1885

Lots-Sec. 5
----
1 RIPLEY, Emma A 1873
5 COMPANY, Pioneers Lu1883
6 COMPANY, Pioneers Lu1883
7 PARSONS, Isaac [153]1884

Lots-Sec. 18
----
1 ROBISON, W 1897
2 ROBISON, W 1897
3 ROBISON, W 1897
5 GARRETT, Willard 1903
6 CARSKADDON, Will[39]1873

Lots-Sec. 19
----
1 BEAU, Otto J 1893
2 BEAU, Otto J 1893
3 BEAU, Otto J 1893

Lots-Sec. 17
----
1 GARRETT, Willard 1903

Lots-Sec. 20
----
1 GARRETT, Willard 1903
2 WALSH, Eddie 1900

Lots-Sec. 33
----
1 DWIGHT, Jeremiah[79]1872

Lots-Sec. 31
----
1 HEADFLYER, Charles H1898
2 HEADFLYER, Charles H1898
3 HEADFLYER, Charles H1898

Lots-Sec. 32
----
1 LARRABEE, Melle[129]1889
2 FRIEND, Elias 1885

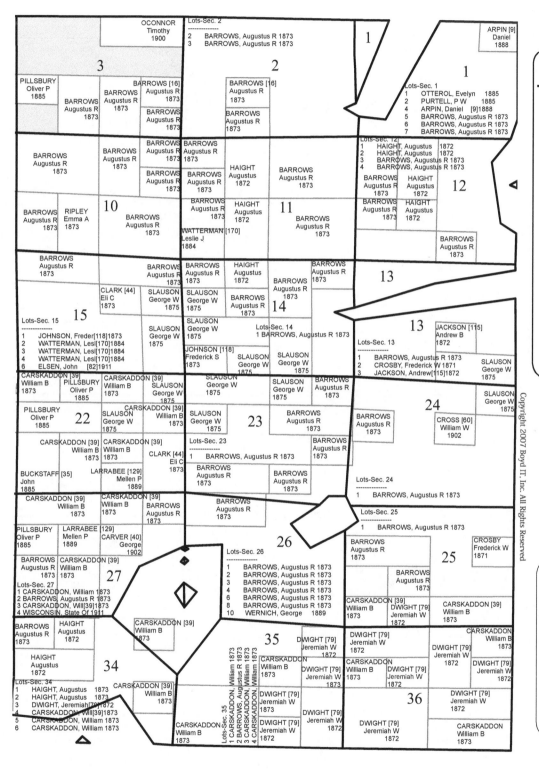

Helpful Hints

1. This Map's INDEX can be found on the preceding pages.

2. Refer to Map "C" to see where this Township lies within Vilas County, Wisconsin.

3. Numbers within square brackets [ ] denote a multi-patentee land parcel (multi-owner). Refer to Appendix "C" for a full list of members in this group.

4. Areas that look to be crowded with Patentees usually indicate multiple sales of the same parcel (Re-issues) or Overlapping parcels. See this Township's Index for an explanation of these and other circumstances that might explain "odd" groupings of Patentees on this map.

Legend

	Patent Boundary
	Section Boundary
	No Patents Found (or Outside County)
1., 2., 3., ...	Lot Numbers (when beside a name)
[ ]	Group Number (see Appendix "C")

Scale: Section = 1 mile X 1 mile
(generally, with some exceptions)

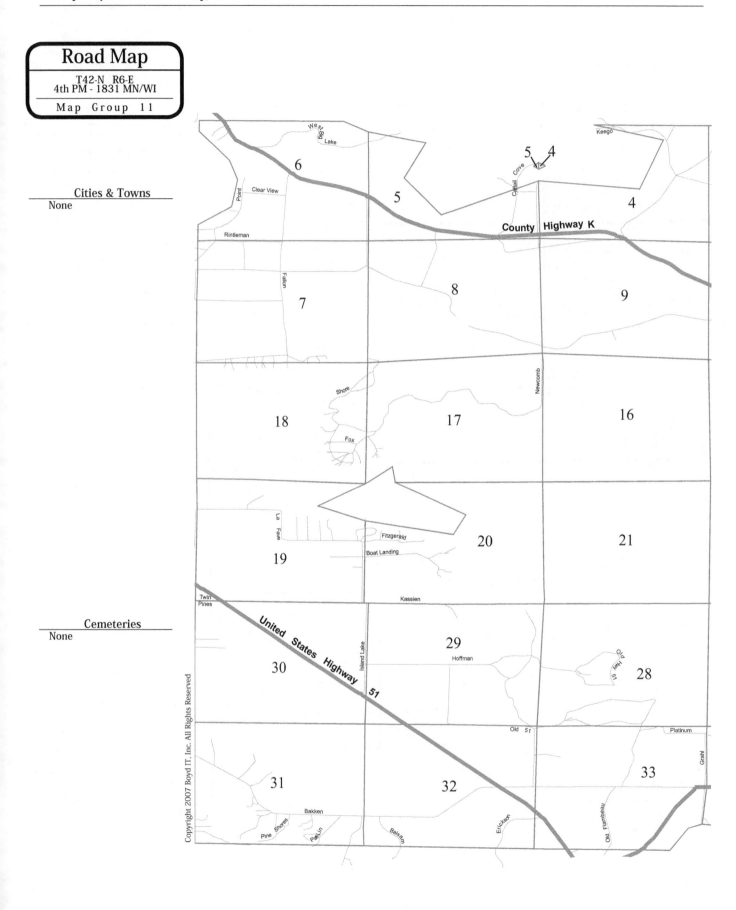

Road Map

T42-N R6-E
4th PM - 1831 MN/WI

Map Group 11

Cities & Towns
None

Cemeteries
None

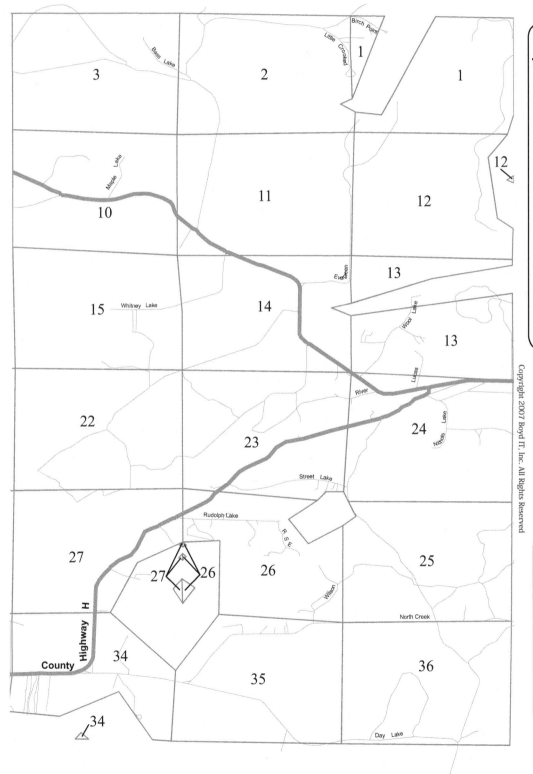

Birch Point

Little Crooked

Bass Lake

3

2

1

1

Maple Lake

10

11

12

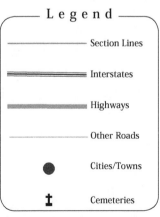

12

Evergreen

13

Whitney Lake

15

14

Wool Lake

13

Lucas

River

22

23

24

Nixon Lake

Street Lake

Rudolph Lake

R S W

27

27 26

26

25

Wilson

North Creek

Highway H

County

34

35

36

34

Day Lake

Helpful Hints

1. This road map has a number of uses, but primarily it is to help you: a) find the present location of land owned by your ancestors (at least the general area), b) find cemeteries and city-centers, and c) estimate the route/roads used by Census-takers & tax-assessors.

2. If you plan to travel to Vilas County to locate cemeteries or land parcels, please pick up a modern travel map for the area before you do. Mapping old land parcels on modern maps is not as exact a science as you might think. Just the slightest variations in public land survey coordinates, estimates of parcel boundaries, or road-map deviations can greatly alter a map's representation of how a road either does or doesn't cross a particular parcel of land.

L e g e n d

——— Section Lines

═══ Interstates

▬▬▬ Highways

——— Other Roads

● Cities/Towns

✝ Cemeteries

Scale: Section = 1 mile X 1 mile
(generally, with some exceptions)

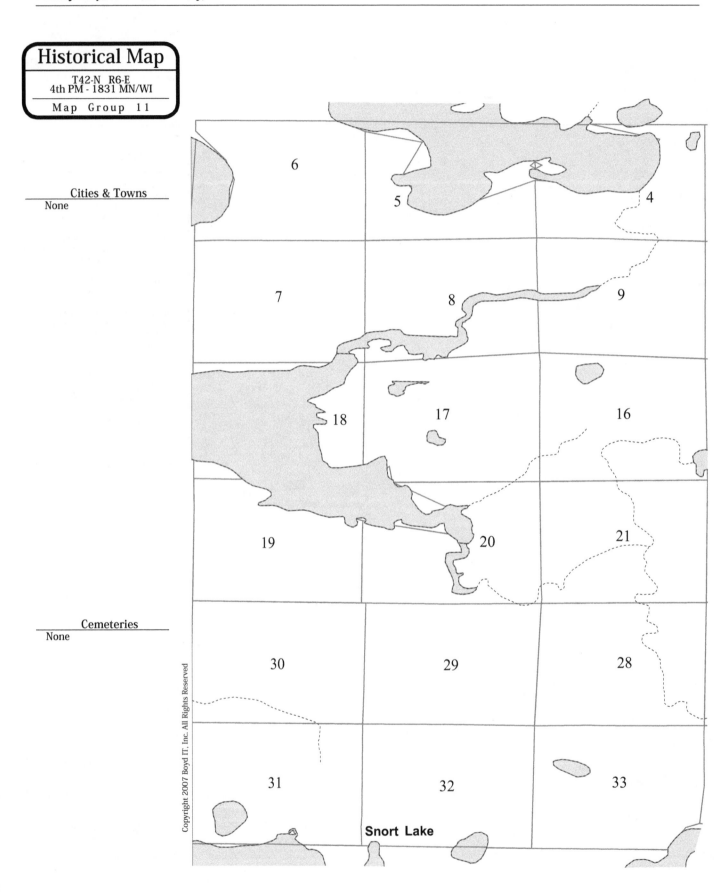

Historical Map

T42-N R6-E
4th PM - 1831 MN/WI

Map Group 11

Cities & Towns
None

Cemeteries
None

6

5

4

7

8

9

18

17

16

19

20

21

30

29

28

31

32

33

Snort Lake

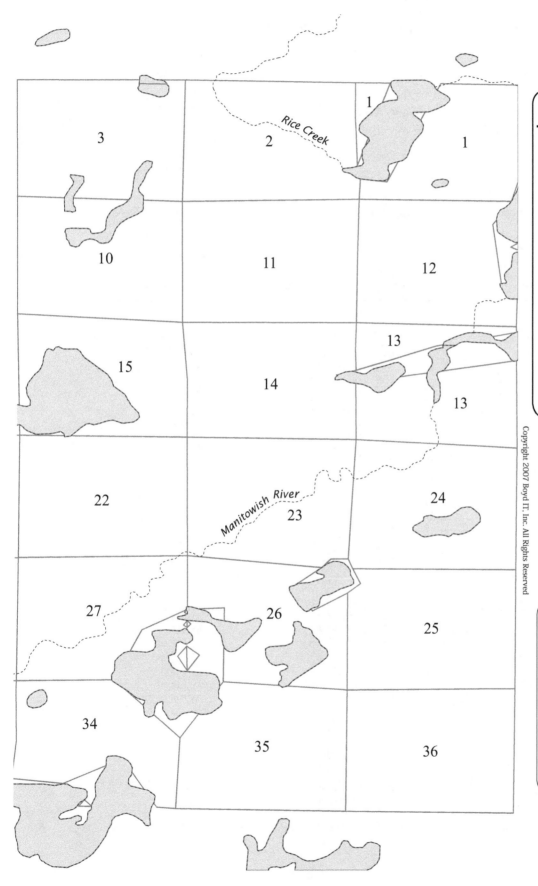

Helpful Hints

1. This Map takes a different look at the same Congressional Township displayed in the preceding two maps. It presents features that can help you better envision the historical development of the area: a) Water-bodies (lakes & ponds), b) Water-courses (rivers, streams, etc.), c) Railroads, d) City/town center-points (where they were oftentimes located when first settled), and e) Cemeteries.

2. Using this "Historical" map in tandem with this Township's Patent Map and Road Map, may lead you to some interesting discoveries. You will often find roads, towns, cemeteries, and waterways are named after nearby landowners: sometimes those names will be the ones you are researching. See how many of these research gems you can find here in Vilas County.

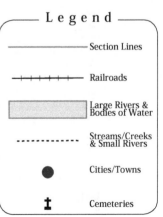

L e g e n d

————————	Section Lines
+–+–+–+–+–+	Railroads
▬▬▬▬	Large Rivers & Bodies of Water
- - - - - - - -	Streams/Creeks & Small Rivers
●	Cities/Towns
☦	Cemeteries

Scale: Section = 1 mile X 1 mile
(there are some exceptions)

Map Group 12: Index to Land Patents

Township 42-North Range 7-East (4th PM - 1831 MN/WI)

After you locate an individual in this Index, take note of the Section and Section Part then proceed to the Land Patent map on the pages immediately following. You should have no difficulty locating the corresponding parcel of land.

The "For More Info" Column will lead you to more information about the underlying Patents. See the *Legend* at right, and the "How to Use this Book" chapter, for more information.

```
                    LEGEND
          "For More Info . . . " column
A = Authority (Legislative Act, See Appendix "A")
B = Block or Lot (location in Section unknown)
C = Cancelled Patent
F = Fractional Section
G = Group  (Multi-Patentee Patent, see Appendix "C")
V = Overlaps another Parcel
R = Re-Issued (Parcel patented more than once)

(A & G items require you to look in the Appendixes referred
to above. All other Letter-designations followed by a number
require you to locate line-items in this index that possess
the ID number found after the letter).
```

ID	Individual in Patent	Sec.	Sec. Part	Date Issued	Other Counties	For More Info . . .
2002	ARPIN, D J	8	2	1889-03-28		A1
2003	" "	8	3	1889-03-28		A1
2118	BAILEY, Moses	29	N½SW	1873-11-15		A1 G13
2119	" "	29	NE	1873-11-15		A1 G13
2120	" "	29	NENW	1873-11-15		A1 G13
2121	" "	29	SE	1873-11-15		A1 G13
2122	" "	29	SESW	1873-11-15		A1 G13
2123	" "	29	SWNW	1873-11-15		A1 G13
2137	BAKER, Peter	3	5	1906-06-30		A1
2138	" "	3	6	1906-06-30		A1
1972	BARROWS, Augustus R	10	E½SW	1873-05-01		A1 G16
1973	" "	10	S½NE	1873-05-01		A1 G16
1974	" "	10	S½NW	1873-05-01		A1 G16
1975	" "	10	W½SE	1873-05-01		A1 G16
1976	" "	11	5	1873-05-01		A1 G16
1977	" "	11	6	1873-05-01		A1 G16
1960	" "	12	NWNE	1873-05-01		A1
1978	" "	14	NWNE	1873-05-01		A1 G16
1979	" "	14	SENW	1873-05-01		A1 G16
1980	" "	15	E½NW	1873-05-01		A1 G16
1981	" "	15	E½SW	1873-05-01		A1 G16
1982	" "	15	N½NE	1873-05-01		A1 G16
1983	" "	15	N½SE	1873-05-01		A1 G16
1961	" "	17	1	1873-05-01		A1
1962	" "	17	3	1873-05-01		A1
1963	" "	18	1	1873-05-01		A1
1984	" "	29	SWSW	1873-05-01		A1 G16
1985	" "	32	NWNW	1873-05-01		A1 G16
1986	" "	4	2	1873-05-01		A1 G16
1987	" "	4	N½SW	1873-05-01		A1 G16
1988	" "	4	SENW	1873-05-01		A1 G16
1989	" "	4	SWNE	1873-05-01		A1 G16
1990	" "	5	1	1873-05-01		A1 G16
1991	" "	5	E½SE	1873-05-01		A1 G16
1992	" "	5	NWSE	1873-05-01		A1 G16
1964	" "	7	1	1873-05-01		A1
1965	" "	7	3	1873-05-01		A1
1966	" "	7	4	1873-05-01		A1
1967	" "	7	5	1873-05-01		A1
1968	" "	7	6	1873-05-01		A1
1969	" "	7	7	1873-05-01		A1
1993	" "	8	1	1873-05-01		A1 G16
1970	" "	8	SESE	1873-05-01		A1
1994	" "	8	SWNW	1873-05-01		A1 G16
1995	" "	9	SESW	1873-05-01		A1 G16
1996	" "	9	SWSE	1873-05-01		A1 G16

ID	Individual in Patent	Sec.	Sec. Part	Date Issued	Other Counties	For More Info . . .
1971	BARROWS, Augustus R (Cont'd)	9	SWSW	1873-05-01		A1
1997	BURROWS, Augustus R	11	SWSW	1873-05-01		A1 G36
2115	CALLAGHAN, Michael	4	4	1911-11-01		A3
2116	" "	9	E½NE	1911-11-01		A3
2117	" "	9	NESE	1911-11-01		A3
2112	COMPANY, Menasha Wooden Ware	12	NWSE	1888-07-10		A1
2113	" "	12	SWNE	1888-07-10		A1
2114	" "	23	NENE	1888-07-10		A1
2139	COMPANY, Pioneers Lumber	21	NESW	1883-09-10		A1
2140	" "	33	NW	1883-09-10		A1
2141	" "	33	W½SW	1883-09-10		A1 R2000
2142	" "	5	SWNE	1883-09-10		A1
1998	CONANT, Benjamin F	24	4	1885-01-20		A1
1999	" "	24	NESW	1885-01-20		A1
2000	" "	33	W½SW	1885-01-20		A1 R2141
2035	COUSINS, Henry	8	N½NE	1873-11-15		A1
2036	" "	8	N½SE	1873-11-15		A1
2037	" "	8	SENE	1873-11-15		A1
2038	" "	9	NWNW	1873-11-15		A1
2039	" "	9	NWSE	1873-11-15		A1
2040	" "	9	SWNE	1873-11-15		A1
2006	CROSBY, Frederick W	19	SWSW	1871-04-01		A1
2007	" "	30	NWNW	1871-04-01		A1
2053	DUNFIELD, Hiram	27	7	1897-07-27		A1
2066	DWIGHT, Jeremiah W	22	N½SW	1872-11-01		A1 G79
2067	" "	22	S½NW	1872-11-01		A1 G79
2068	" "	22	SESW	1872-11-01		A1 G79
2069	" "	22	SWSE	1872-11-01		A1 G79
2070	" "	25	SESE	1872-11-01		A1 G79
2071	" "	25	SW	1872-11-01		A1 G79
2072	" "	25	W½NW	1872-11-01		A1 G79
2073	" "	26	3	1872-11-01		A1 G79
2074	" "	26	4	1872-11-01		A1 G79
2075	" "	26	5	1872-11-01		A1 G79
2076	" "	26	6	1872-11-01		A1 G79
2077	" "	26	7	1872-11-01		A1 G79
2079	" "	27	5	1872-11-01		A1 G79
2080	" "	27	6	1872-11-01		A1 G79
2081	" "	27	NENW	1872-11-01		A1 G79
2082	" "	29	SENW	1872-11-01		A1 G79
2083	" "	30	S½SE	1872-11-01		A1 G79
2084	" "	31	2	1872-11-01		A1 G79
2085	" "	31	3	1872-11-01		A1 G79
2087	" "	31	NENW	1872-11-01		A1 G79
2088	" "	31	SWNW	1872-11-01		A1 G79
2089	" "	33	E½NE	1872-11-01		A1 G79
2090	" "	33	NESE	1872-11-01		A1 G79
2093	" "	33	S½SE	1872-11-01		A1 G79
2095	" "	34	3	1872-11-01		A1 G79
2096	" "	34	6	1872-11-01		A1 G79
2097	" "	34	NENW	1872-11-01		A1 G79
2098	" "	34	NESW	1872-11-01		A1 G79
2099	" "	34	W½NW	1872-11-01		A1 G79
2100	" "	34	W½SW	1872-11-01		A1 G79
2101	" "	35	10	1872-11-01		A1 G79
2103	" "	35	5	1872-11-01		A1 G79
2105	" "	36	N½NW	1872-11-01		A1 G79
2106	" "	36	NWNE	1872-11-01		A1 G79
2078	" "	27	3	1873-05-01		A1 G79
2086	" "	31	4	1873-05-01		A1 G79
2091	" "	33	NESW	1873-05-01		A1 G79
2092	" "	33	NWSE	1873-05-01		A1 G79
2094	" "	33	SWNE	1873-05-01		A1 G79
2102	" "	35	2	1873-05-01		A1 G79
2104	" "	35	SENE	1873-05-01		A1 G79
1972	EARLY, Henry W	10	E½SW	1873-05-01		A1 G16
1973	" "	10	S½NE	1873-05-01		A1 G16
1974	" "	10	S½NW	1873-05-01		A1 G16
1975	" "	10	W½SE	1873-05-01		A1 G16
1976	" "	11	5	1873-05-01		A1 G16
1977	" "	11	6	1873-05-01		A1 G16
1997	" "	11	SWSW	1873-05-01		A1 G36
1978	" "	14	NWNE	1873-05-01		A1 G16

ID	Individual in Patent	Sec.	Sec. Part	Date Issued	Other Counties	For More Info . . .
1979	EARLY, Henry W (Cont'd)	14	SENW	1873-05-01		A1 G16
1980	" "	15	E½NW	1873-05-01		A1 G16
1981	" "	15	E½SW	1873-05-01		A1 G16
1982	" "	15	N½NE	1873-05-01		A1 G16
1983	" "	15	N½SE	1873-05-01		A1 G16
1984	" "	29	SWSW	1873-05-01		A1 G16
1985	" "	32	NWNW	1873-05-01		A1 G16
1986	" "	4	2	1873-05-01		A1 G16
1987	" "	4	N½SW	1873-05-01		A3 G16
1988	" "	4	SENW	1873-05-01		A1 G16
1989	" "	4	SWNE	1873-05-01		A1 G16
1990	" "	5	1	1873-05-01		A1 G16
1991	" "	5	E½SE	1873-05-01		A1 G16
1992	" "	5	NWSE	1873-05-01		A1 G16
1993	" "	8	1	1873-05-01		A1 G16
1994	" "	8	SWNW	1873-05-01		A1 G16
1995	" "	9	SESW	1873-05-01		A1 G16
1996	" "	9	SWSE	1873-05-01		A1 G16
1972	FORSMAN, Robert M	10	E½SW	1873-05-01		A1 G16
1973	" "	10	S½NE	1873-05-01		A1 G16
1974	" "	10	S½NW	1873-05-01		A1 G16
1975	" "	10	W½SE	1873-05-01		A1 G16
1976	" "	11	5	1873-05-01		A1 G16
1977	" "	11	6	1873-05-01		A1 G16
1997	" "	11	SWSW	1873-05-01		A1 G36
1978	" "	14	NWNE	1873-05-01		A1 G16
1979	" "	14	SENW	1873-05-01		A1 G16
1980	" "	15	E½NW	1873-05-01		A1 G16
1981	" "	15	E½SW	1873-05-01		A1 G16
1982	" "	15	N½NE	1873-05-01		A1 G16
1983	" "	15	N½SE	1873-05-01		A1 G16
1984	" "	29	SWSW	1873-05-01		A1 G16
1985	" "	32	NWNW	1873-05-01		A1 G16
1986	" "	4	2	1873-05-01		A1 G16
1987	" "	4	N½SW	1873-05-01		A1 G16
1988	" "	4	SENW	1873-05-01		A1 G16
1989	" "	4	SWNE	1873-05-01		A1 G16
1990	" "	5	1	1873-05-01		A1 G16
1991	" "	5	E½SE	1873-05-01		A1 G16
1992	" "	5	NWSE	1873-05-01		A1 G16
1993	" "	8	1	1873-05-01		A1 G16
1994	" "	8	SWNW	1873-05-01		A1 G16
1995	" "	9	SESW	1873-05-01		A1 G16
1996	" "	9	SWSE	1873-05-01		A1 G16
2054	GOULD, James P	25	SWSE	1872-11-01		A1
2055	" "	34	1	1872-11-01		A1
2056	" "	35	1	1872-11-01		A1
2057	" "	35	3	1872-11-01		A1
2058	" "	35	4	1872-11-01		A1
2059	" "	35	NENE	1872-11-01		A1
2060	" "	35	SWNE	1872-11-01		A1
2062	" "	36	NESW	1872-11-01		A1
2061	" "	36	NENE	1873-05-01		A1
2063	" "	36	NWSW	1873-05-01		A1
2064	" "	36	SENW	1873-05-01		A1
2065	" "	36	SWNE	1873-05-01		A1
1959	HAIGHT, Augustus	8	SWNE	1872-11-01		A1
2051	HEISMAN, Herman	12	NESE	1900-10-04		A1
2158	HOGUE, William J	23	NWNE	1904-12-20		A3 G107
2118	HOLDEN, Ralph A	29	N½SW	1873-11-15		A1 G13
2119	" "	29	NE	1873-11-15		A1 G13
2120	" "	29	NENW	1873-11-15		A1 G13
2121	" "	29	SE	1873-11-15		A1 G13
2122	" "	29	SESW	1873-11-15		A1 G13
2123	" "	29	SWNW	1873-11-15		A1 G13
2010	HYLAND, George	25	2	1883-09-15		A1 G111
2011	" "	25	3	1883-09-15		A1 G111
2012	" "	25	N½SE	1883-09-15		A1 G111
2013	" "	25	SENW	1883-09-15		A1 G111
2014	" "	32	E½NE	1883-09-15		A1 G111
2015	" "	36	SENE	1883-09-15		A1 G111
2016	" "	36	SWNW	1883-09-15		A1 G111
2010	HYLAND, John	25	2	1883-09-15		A1 G111

ID	Individual in Patent	Sec.	Sec. Part	Date Issued	Other Counties	For More Info . . .
2011	HYLAND, John (Cont'd)	25	3	1883-09-15		A1 G111
2012	" "	25	N½SE	1883-09-15		A1 G111
2013	" "	25	SENW	1883-09-15		A1 G111
2014	" "	32	E½NE	1883-09-15		A1 G111
2015	" "	36	SENE	1883-09-15		A1 G111
2016	" "	36	SWNW	1883-09-15		A1 G111
2118	IRVIN, James A	29	N½SW	1873-11-15		A1 G13
2119	" "	29	NE	1873-11-15		A1 G13
2120	" "	29	NENW	1873-11-15		A1 G13
2121	" "	29	SE	1873-11-15		A1 G13
2122	" "	29	SESW	1873-11-15		A1 G13
2123	" "	29	SWNW	1873-11-15		A1 G13
1952	JACKSON, Andrew B	12	1	1872-07-01		A1 G115
1953	" "	14	S½NE	1872-07-01		A1 G115
1954	" "	17	2	1872-07-01		A1 G115
1955	" "	17	5	1872-07-01		A1 G115
1956	" "	17	7	1872-07-01		A1 G115
1957	" "	17	NENE	1872-07-01		A1 G115
1948	" "	3	8	1872-07-01		A1 G113
1949	" "	3	9	1872-07-01		A1 G113
1950	" "	3	SESE	1872-07-01		A1 G113
1951	" "	7	2	1872-07-01		A1 G113
1948	JACKSON, E G	3	8	1872-07-01		A1 G113
1949	" "	3	9	1872-07-01		A1 G113
1950	" "	3	SESE	1872-07-01		A1 G113
1951	" "	7	2	1872-07-01		A1 G113
2031	JONES, Granville D	3	1	1902-03-07		A3 G120
2032	" "	18	2	1903-11-10		A3 G121
2149	LAIRD, William H	28	NESE	1884-06-20		A1 G127
2150	" "	28	SENE	1884-06-20		A1 G127
2151	" "	28	SWNW	1884-06-20		A1 G127
2152	" "	35	6	1884-06-20		A1 G127
2153	" "	35	7	1884-06-20		A1 G127
2154	" "	35	8	1884-06-20		A1 G127
2155	" "	6	3	1884-06-30		A1 G127
2156	" "	6	4	1884-06-30		A1 G127
2157	" "	6	8	1884-06-30		A1 G127
2159	LEAVERTON, William J	21	SWNW	1905-05-23		A3 G130
2136	LEDURSE, Paul	18	6	1903-11-10		A3
1972	LENTZ, George W	10	E½SW	1873-05-01		A1 G16
1973	" "	10	S½NE	1873-05-01		A1 G16
1974	" "	10	S½NW	1873-05-01		A1 G16
1975	" "	10	W½SE	1873-05-01		A1 G16
1976	" "	11	5	1873-05-01		A1 G16
1977	" "	11	6	1873-05-01		A1 G16
1997	" "	11	SWSW	1873-05-01		A1 G36
1978	" "	14	NWNE	1873-05-01		A1 G16
1979	" "	14	SENW	1873-05-01		A1 G16
1980	" "	15	E½NW	1873-05-01		A1 G16
1981	" "	15	E½SW	1873-05-01		A1 G16
1982	" "	15	N½NE	1873-05-01		A1 G16
1983	" "	15	N½SE	1873-05-01		A1 G16
1984	" "	29	SWSW	1873-05-01		A1 G16
1985	" "	32	NWNW	1873-05-01		A1 G16
1986	" "	4	2	1873-05-01		A1 G16
1987	" "	4	N½SW	1873-05-01		A1 G16
1988	" "	4	SENW	1873-05-01		A1 G16
1989	" "	4	SWNE	1873-05-01		A1 G16
1990	" "	5	1	1873-05-01		A1 G16
1991	" "	5	E½SE	1873-05-01		A1 G16
1992	" "	5	NWSE	1873-05-01		A1 G16
1993	" "	8	1	1873-05-01		A1 G16
1994	" "	8	SWNW	1873-05-01		A1 G16
1995	" "	9	SESW	1873-05-01		A1 G16
1996	" "	9	SWSE	1873-05-01		A1 G16
2031	LEONE, Charles B	3	1	1902-03-07		A3 G120
2143	MARSHALL, R D	8	NESW	1889-05-09		A1 G134
2143	MCCORD, W E	8	NESW	1889-05-09		A1 G134
1958	MCDONALD, Angus P	36	N½SE	1890-07-15		A1
2001	MCFARLAND, Charles W	36	SWSW	1890-07-15		A1
2066	MCGRAW, John	22	N½SW	1872-11-01		A1 G79
2067	" "	22	S½NW	1872-11-01		A1 G79
2068	" "	22	SESW	1872-11-01		A1 G79

ID	Individual in Patent	Sec.	Sec. Part	Date Issued	Other Counties	For More Info . . .
2069	MCGRAW, John (Cont'd)	22	SWSE	1872-11-01		A1 G79
2070	" "	25	SESE	1872-11-01		A1 G79
2071	" "	25	SW	1872-11-01		A1 G79
2072	" "	25	W½NW	1872-11-01		A1 G79
2073	" "	26	3	1872-11-01		A1 G79
2074	" "	26	4	1872-11-01		A1 G79
2075	" "	26	5	1872-11-01		A1 G79
2076	" "	26	6	1872-11-01		A1 G79
2077	" "	26	7	1872-11-01		A1 G79
2079	" "	27	5	1872-11-01		A1 G79
2080	" "	27	6	1872-11-01		A1 G79
2081	" "	27	NENW	1872-11-01		A1 G79
2082	" "	29	SENW	1872-11-01		A1 G79
2083	" "	30	S½SE	1872-11-01		A1 G79
2084	" "	31	2	1872-11-01		A1 G79
2085	" "	31	3	1872-11-01		A1 G79
2087	" "	31	NENW	1872-11-01		A1 G79
2088	" "	31	SWNW	1872-11-01		A1 G79
2089	" "	33	E½NE	1872-11-01		A1 G79
2090	" "	33	NESE	1872-11-01		A1 G79
2093	" "	33	S½SE	1872-11-01		A1 G79
2095	" "	34	3	1872-11-01		A1 G79
2096	" "	34	6	1872-11-01		A1 G79
2097	" "	34	NENW	1872-11-01		A1 G79
2098	" "	34	NESW	1872-11-01		A1 G79
2099	" "	34	W½NW	1872-11-01		A1 G79
2100	" "	34	W½SW	1872-11-01		A1 G79
2101	" "	35	10	1872-11-01		A1 G79
2103	" "	35	5	1872-11-01		A1 G79
2105	" "	36	N½NW	1872-11-01		A1 G79
2106	" "	36	NWNE	1872-11-01		A1 G79
2078	" "	27	3	1873-05-01		A1 G79
2086	" "	31	4	1873-05-01		A1 G79
2091	" "	33	NESW	1873-05-01		A1 G79
2092	" "	33	NWSE	1873-05-01		A1 G79
2094	" "	33	SWNE	1873-05-01		A1 G79
2102	" "	35	2	1873-05-01		A1 G79
2104	" "	35	SENE	1873-05-01		A1 G79
2052	MEISNER, Herman	14	NENE	1899-12-21		A1
2158	" "	23	NWNE	1904-12-20		A3 G107
2149	NORTON, James L	28	NESE	1884-06-20		A1 G127
2150	" "	28	SENE	1884-06-20		A1 G127
2151	" "	28	SWNW	1884-06-20		A1 G127
2152	" "	35	6	1884-06-20		A1 G127
2153	" "	35	7	1884-06-20		A1 G127
2154	" "	35	8	1884-06-20		A1 G127
2155	" "	6	3	1884-06-30		A1 G127
2156	" "	6	4	1884-06-30		A1 G127
2157	" "	6	8	1884-06-30		A1 G127
2149	NORTON, Matthew G	28	NESE	1884-06-20		A1 G127
2150	" "	28	SENE	1884-06-20		A1 G127
2151	" "	28	SWNW	1884-06-20		A1 G127
2152	" "	35	6	1884-06-20		A1 G127
2153	" "	35	7	1884-06-20		A1 G127
2154	" "	35	8	1884-06-20		A1 G127
2155	" "	6	3	1884-06-30		A1 G127
2156	" "	6	4	1884-06-30		A1 G127
2157	" "	6	8	1884-06-30		A1 G127
2160	PATRICK, William S	19	N½SW	1872-11-01		A1
2161	" "	19	S½SE	1872-11-01		A1
2162	" "	19	SENW	1872-11-01		A1
2163	" "	19	SESW	1872-11-01		A1
2164	" "	19	SWNW	1872-11-01		A1
2165	" "	20	NWSW	1872-11-01		A1
2166	" "	20	S½NW	1872-11-01		A1
2167	" "	20	SWSE	1872-11-01		A1
2168	" "	20	SWSW	1872-11-01		A1
2169	" "	29	NWNW	1872-11-01		A1
2170	" "	30	E½NW	1872-11-01		A1
2171	" "	30	NENE	1872-11-01		A1
2172	" "	30	W½NE	1872-11-01		A1
2124	PILLSBURY, Oliver P	12	2	1884-06-30		A1
2125	" "	12	SESE	1884-06-30		A1

ID	Individual in Patent	Sec.	Sec. Part	Date Issued	Other Counties	For More Info . . .
2131	PILLSBURY, Oliver P (Cont'd)	30	SESW	1885-01-15		A1
2126	" "	20	N½SE	1885-01-20		A1
2127	" "	20	SESE	1885-01-20		A1
2128	" "	21	NWSW	1885-01-20		A1
2129	" "	21	SENW	1885-01-20		A1
2130	" "	28	SENW	1885-01-20		A1
2132	" "	32	E½NW	1885-01-20		A1
2133	" "	32	NESE	1885-01-20		A1
2134	" "	4	NWNE	1885-01-20		A1
2135	" "	8	E½NW	1885-01-20		A1
2033	PUTNAM, Henry C	27	1	1873-05-01		A1
2034	" "	35	NESE	1873-05-01		A1
2159	REHFELD, William	21	SWNW	1905-05-23		A3 G130
2144	ROWLEY, Ralph E	12	SWSE	1903-11-11		A1
2145	" "	13	NWNE	1903-11-11		A1
2041	SAGE, Henry W	21	SENE	1883-09-10		A1
2042	" "	27	4	1883-09-10		A1
2044	" "	33	SESW	1883-09-10		A1
2045	" "	34	2	1883-09-10		A1
2047	" "	4	NENE	1883-09-10		A1
2048	" "	4	NENW	1883-09-10		A1
2043	" "	28	SESE	1883-09-15		A1
2046	" "	4	1	1883-09-15		A1
2108	SEVERANCE, Joseph	1	9	1903-11-10		A3 G158
2019	SLAUSON, George W	17	4	1875-02-20		A1
2020	" "	17	6	1875-02-20		A1
2021	" "	18	7	1875-02-20		A1
2022	" "	18	8	1875-02-20		A1
2023	" "	19	N½NE	1875-02-20		A1
2024	" "	19	NENW	1875-02-20		A1
2025	" "	20	1	1875-02-20		A1
2026	" "	20	NENW	1875-02-20		A1
2029	" "	28	E½SW	1875-02-20		A1
2030	" "	28	W½SE	1875-02-20		A1
2017	" "	1	SWNW	1875-04-20		A1
2018	" "	14	NENW	1875-04-20		A1
2027	" "	21	NWSE	1875-04-20		A1
2028	" "	22	SESE	1875-04-20		A1
2107	SLONAKER, John Wilson	2	9	1910-09-12		A3 G163
2173	STARR, William	28	NWNE	1874-08-01		A1
2004	TRIPP, F R	31	5	1889-05-09		A1
2005	" "	31	6	1889-05-09		A1
2032	WALLING, James P	18	2	1903-11-10		A3 G121
2049	WARNER, Herbert	10	W½SW	1902-01-25		A1
2050	" "	9	SESE	1902-01-25		A1
2008	WASHBURN, Ganem W	15	W½SW	1872-11-01		A1
2009	" "	27	2	1872-11-01		A1
2109	WATERMAN, Leslie J	6	5	1884-06-30		A1 G168
2110	" "	6	6	1884-06-30		A1 G168
2111	" "	6	7	1884-06-30		A1 G168
2108	WELKER, George W	1	9	1903-11-10		A3 G158
2107	WHITE, Herford	2	9	1910-09-12		A3 G163
1952	WILCOX, George G	12	1	1872-07-01		A1 G115
1953	" "	14	S½NE	1872-07-01		A1 G115
1954	" "	17	2	1872-07-01		A1 G115
1955	" "	17	5	1872-07-01		A1 G115
1956	" "	17	7	1872-07-01		A1 G115
1957	" "	17	NENE	1872-07-01		A1 G115
2146	WILCOX, Theodore B	5	NWNE	1883-09-15		A1
2109	WILEY, Charles L	6	5	1884-06-30		A1 G168
2110	" "	6	6	1884-06-30		A1 G168
2111	" "	6	7	1884-06-30		A1 G168
2147	WILLCOX, Theodore B	5	E½NW	1883-09-15		A1
2148	" "	5	NESW	1883-09-15		A1

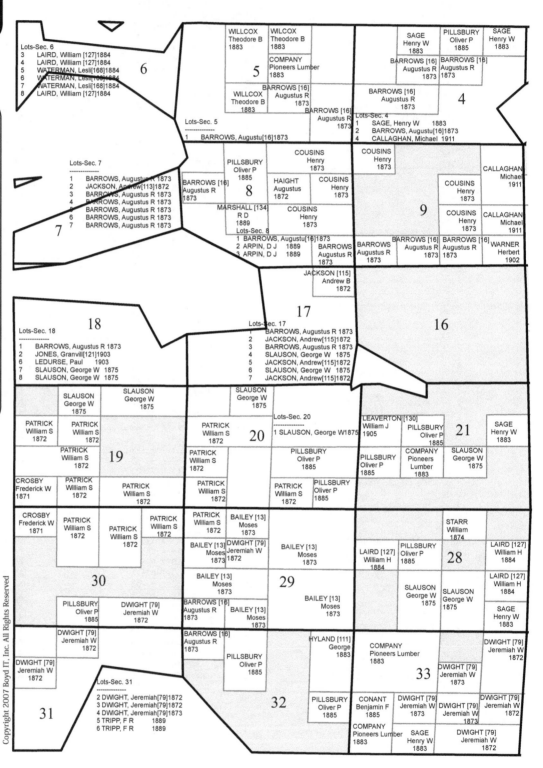

Patent Map

T42-N R7-E
4th PM - 1831 MN/WI

Map Group 12

Township Statistics

Parcels Mapped	:	226
Number of Patents	:	67
Number of Individuals	:	60
Patentees Identified	:	45
Number of Surnames	:	55
Multi-Patentee Parcels	:	109
Oldest Patent Date	:	4/1/1871
Most Recent Patent	:	11/1/1911
Block/Lot Parcels	:	77
Parcels Re - Issued	:	1
Parcels that Overlap	:	0
Cities and Towns	:	1
Cemeteries	:	1

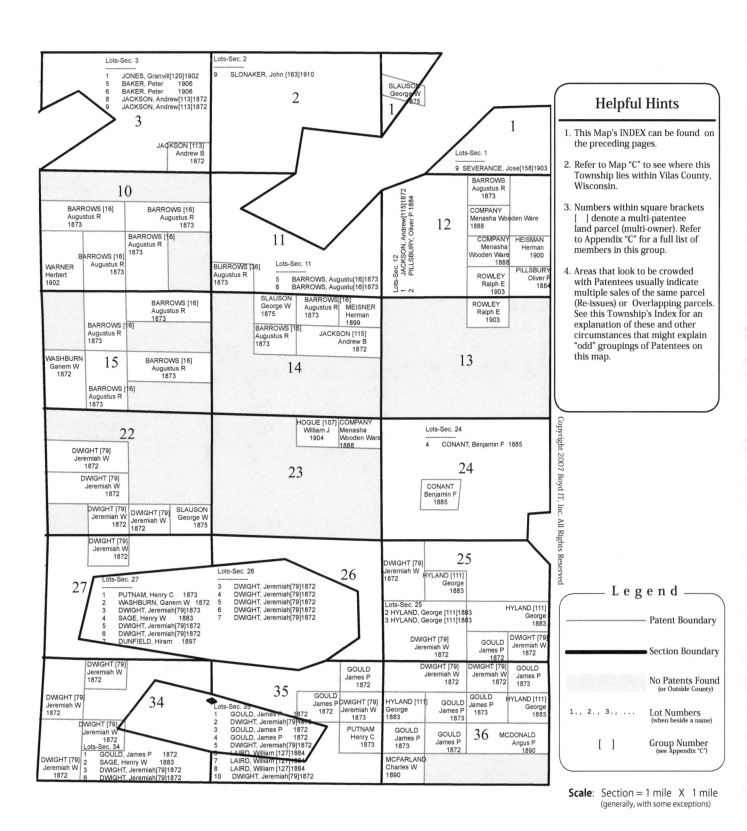

Lots-Sec. 3
----
1 JONES, Granvill[120]1902
5 BAKER, Peter   1906
6 BAKER, Peter   1906
8 JACKSON, Andrew[113]1872
9 JACKSON, Andrew[113]1872

3

JACKSON [113]
Andrew B
1872

Lots-Sec. 2
----
9 SLONAKER, John [163]1910

2

SLAUSON
George W
1875

1

1

Lots-Sec. 1
----
9 SEVERANCE, Jose[158]1903

10

BARROWS [16]
Augustus R
1873

BARROWS [16]
Augustus R
1873

BARROWS [16]
Augustus R
1873

WARNER
Herbert
1902

BARROWS [16]
Augustus R
1873

11

BURROWS [36]
Augustus R
1873

Lots-Sec. 11
----
5 BARROWS, Augustu[16]1873
6 BARROWS, Augustu[16]1873

JACKSON, Andrew[115]1872
PILLSBURY, Oliver P 1884

Lots-Sec. 12
1 JACKSON, Andrew[115]1872
2 PILLSBURY, Oliver P 1884

12

BARROWS
Augustus R
1873

COMPANY
Menasha Wooden Ware
1888

COMPANY
Menasha
Wooden Ware
1888

HEISMAN
Herman
1900

ROWLEY
Ralph E
1903

PILLSBURY
Oliver P
1884

15

WASHBURN
Ganem W
1872

BARROWS [16]
Augustus R
1873

BARROWS [16]
Augustus R
1873

BARROWS [16]
Augustus R
1873

BARROWS [16]
Augustus R
1873

SLAUSON
George W
1875

BARROWS [16]
Augustus R
1873

BARROWS [16]
Augustus R
1873

MEISNER
Herman
1899

JACKSON [115]
Andrew B
1872

14

13

ROWLEY
Ralph E
1903

22

DWIGHT [79]
Jeremiah W
1872

DWIGHT [79]
Jeremiah W
1872

DWIGHT [79]
Jeremiah W
1872

DWIGHT [79]
Jeremiah W
1872

SLAUSON
George W
1875

HOGUE [107]
William J
1904

COMPANY
Menasha
Wooden Ware
1888

23

Lots-Sec. 24
----
4 CONANT, Benjamin F 1885

24

CONANT
Benjamin F
1885

DWIGHT [79]
Jeremiah W
1872

27

Lots-Sec. 27
----
1 PUTNAM, Henry C   1873
2 WASHBURN, Ganem W 1872
3 DWIGHT, Jeremiah[79]1873
4 SAGE, Henry W   1883
5 DWIGHT, Jeremiah[79]1872
6 DWIGHT, Jeremiah[79]1872
7 DUNFIELD, Hiram   1897

Lots-Sec. 26
----
3 DWIGHT, Jeremiah[79]1872
4 DWIGHT, Jeremiah[79]1872
5 DWIGHT, Jeremiah[79]1872
6 DWIGHT, Jeremiah[79]1872
7 DWIGHT, Jeremiah[79]1872

26

DWIGHT [79]
Jeremiah W
1872

25

HYLAND [111]
George
1883

Lots-Sec. 25
2 HYLAND, George [111]1883
3 HYLAND, George [111]1883

HYLAND [111]
George
1883

DWIGHT [79]
Jeremiah W
1872

GOULD
James P
1872

DWIGHT [79]
Jeremiah W
1872

DWIGHT [79]
Jeremiah W
1872

34

DWIGHT [79]
Jeremiah W
1872

DWIGHT [79]
Jeremiah W
1872

DWIGHT [79]
Jeremiah W
1872

Lots-Sec. 34
1 GOULD, James P   1872
2 SAGE, Henry W   1883
3 DWIGHT, Jeremiah[79]1872
6 DWIGHT, Jeremiah[79]1872

35

Lots-Sec. 35
1 GOULD, James P   1872
2 DWIGHT, Jeremiah[79]1872
3 GOULD, James P   1872
4 GOULD, James P   1872
5 DWIGHT, Jeremiah[79]1872
7 LAIRD, William [127]1884
8 LAIRD, William [127]1884
10 DWIGHT, Jeremiah[79]1872

GOULD
James P
1872

GOULD
James P
1872

DWIGHT [79]
Jeremiah W
1873

HYLAND [111]
George
1883

PUTNAM
Henry C
1873

GOULD
James P
1872

DWIGHT [79]
Jeremiah W
1872

DWIGHT [79]
Jeremiah W
1872

HYLAND [111]
George
1883

GOULD
James P
1873

GOULD
James P
1872

GOULD
James P
1873

GOULD
James P
1872

DWIGHT [79]
Jeremiah W
1872

GOULD
James P
1873

HYLAND [111]
George
1883

36

MCDONALD
Angus P
1890

MCFARLAND
Charles W
1890

Helpful Hints

1. This Map's INDEX can be found on the preceding pages.

2. Refer to Map "C" to see where this Township lies within Vilas County, Wisconsin.

3. Numbers within square brackets [ ] denote a multi-patentee land parcel (multi-owner). Refer to Appendix "C" for a full list of members in this group.

4. Areas that look to be crowded with Patentees usually indicate multiple sales of the same parcel (Re-issues) or Overlapping parcels. See this Township's Index for an explanation of these and other circumstances that might explain "odd" groupings of Patentees on this map.

Legend

—————— Patent Boundary

━━━━━━ Section Boundary

No Patents Found
(or Outside County)

1., 2., 3., ... Lot Numbers
(when beside a name)

[ ] Group Number
(see Appendix "C")

Scale: Section = 1 mile X 1 mile
(generally, with some exceptions)

Road Map

T42-N R7-E
4th PM - 1831 MN/WI

Map Group 12

<u>Cities & Towns</u>
Boulder Junction

<u>Cemeteries</u>
Pines Cemetery

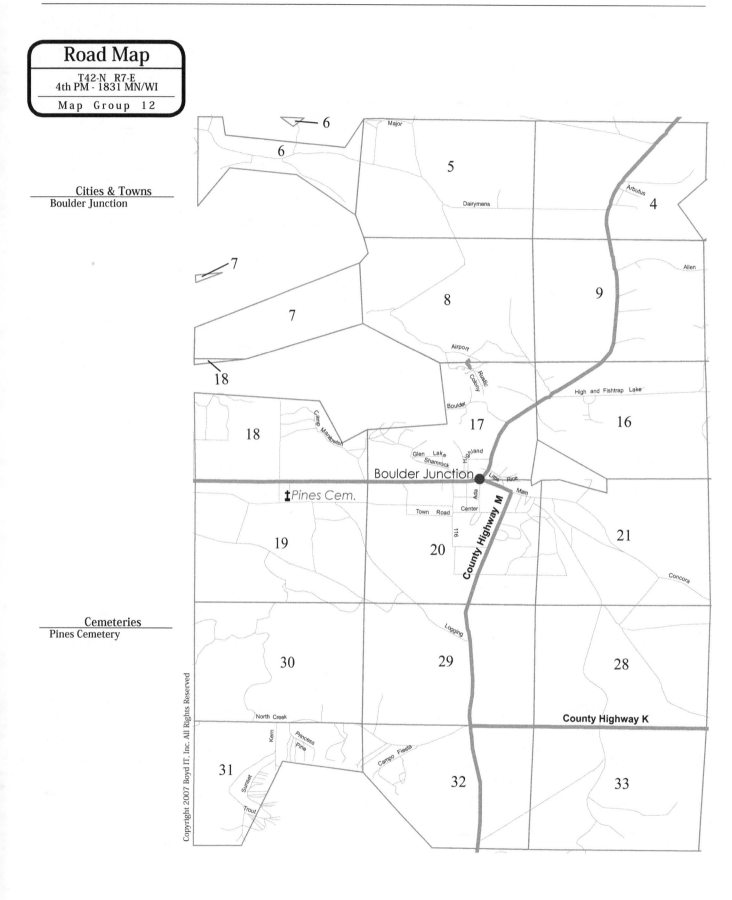

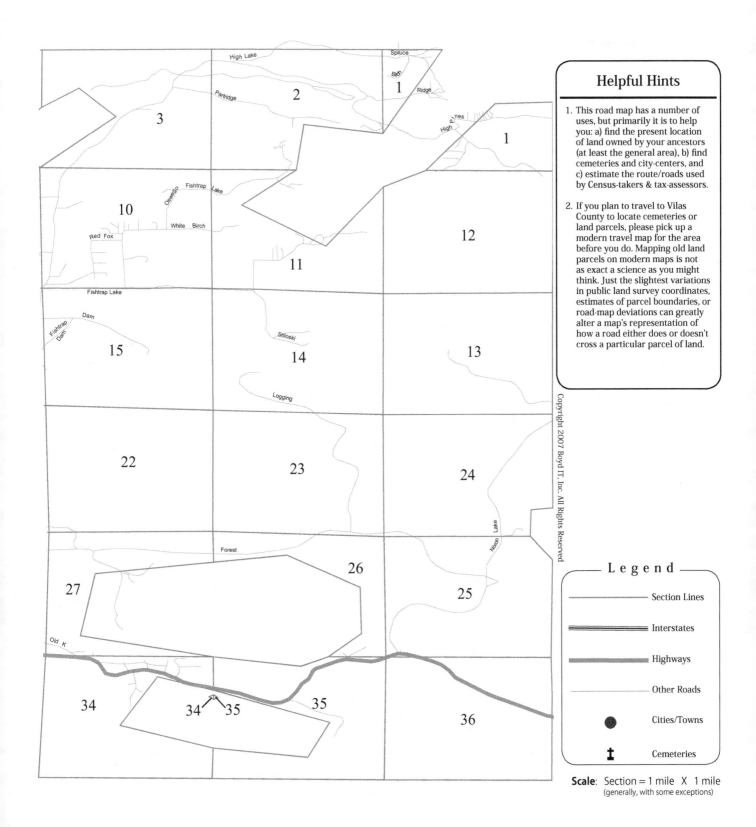

Helpful Hints

1. This road map has a number of uses, but primarily it is to help you: a) find the present location of land owned by your ancestors (at least the general area), b) find cemeteries and city-centers, and c) estimate the route/roads used by Census-takers & tax-assessors.

2. If you plan to travel to Vilas County to locate cemeteries or land parcels, please pick up a modern travel map for the area before you do. Mapping old land parcels on modern maps is not as exact a science as you might think. Just the slightest variations in public land survey coordinates, estimates of parcel boundaries, or road-map deviations can greatly alter a map's representation of how a road either does or doesn't cross a particular parcel of land.

Legend

————	Section Lines
═══	Interstates
━━━	Highways
————	Other Roads
●	Cities/Towns
✝	Cemeteries

Scale: Section = 1 mile X 1 mile
(generally, with some exceptions)

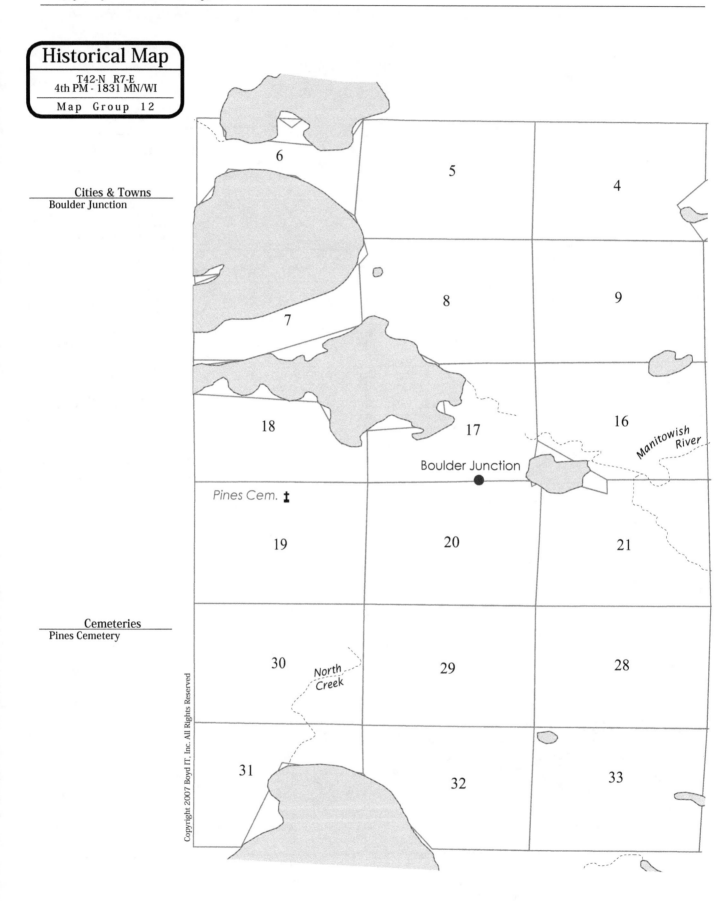

Historical Map

T42-N R7-E
4th PM - 1831 MN/WI

Map Group 12

Cities & Towns
Boulder Junction

Cemeteries
Pines Cemetery

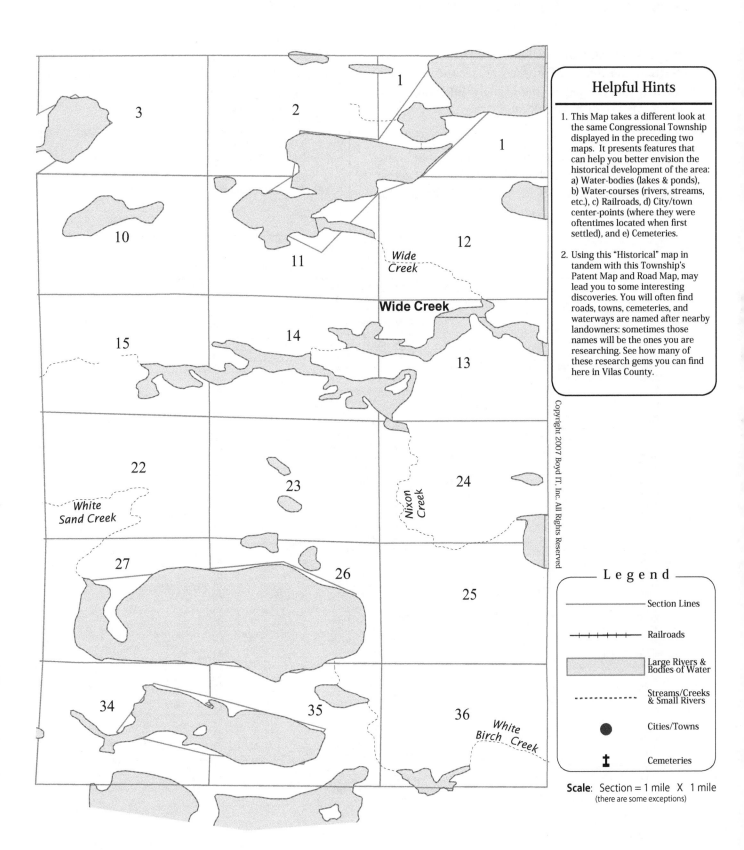

Helpful Hints

1. This Map takes a different look at the same Congressional Township displayed in the preceding two maps. It presents features that can help you better envision the historical development of the area: a) Water-bodies (lakes & ponds), b) Water-courses (rivers, streams, etc.), c) Railroads, d) City/town center-points (where they were oftentimes located when first settled), and e) Cemeteries.

2. Using this "Historical" map in tandem with this Township's Patent Map and Road Map, may lead you to some interesting discoveries. You will often find roads, towns, cemeteries, and waterways are named after nearby landowners: sometimes those names will be the ones you are researching. See how many of these research gems you can find here in Vilas County.

Legend

————————	Section Lines
+++++++	Railroads
�▭	Large Rivers & Bodies of Water
- - - - - - -	Streams/Creeks & Small Rivers
●	Cities/Towns
☩	Cemeteries

Scale: Section = 1 mile X 1 mile
(there are some exceptions)

Map Group 13: Index to Land Patents

Township 42-North Range 8-East (4th PM - 1831 MN/WI)

After you locate an individual in this Index, take note of the Section and Section Part then proceed to the Land Patent map on the pages immediately following. You should have no difficulty locating the corresponding parcel of land.

The "For More Info" Column will lead you to more information about the underlying Patents. See the *Legend* at right, and the "How to Use this Book" chapter, for more information.

```
                        LEGEND
               "For More Info . . . " column
A = Authority (Legislative Act, See Appendix "A")
B = Block or Lot (location in Section unknown)
C = Cancelled Patent
F = Fractional Section
G = Group  (Multi-Patentee Patent, see Appendix "C")
V = Overlaps another Parcel
R = Re-Issued (Parcel patented more than once)

(A & G items require you to look in the Appendixes referred
to above. All other Letter-designations followed by a number
require you to locate line-items in this index that possess
the ID number found after the letter).
```

ID	Individual in Patent	Sec.	Sec. Part	Date Issued	Other Counties	For More Info . . .
2192	BARNETT, E D	18	SWSW	1884-06-30		A1 G14
2193	" "	27	E½NW	1884-06-30		A1 G14
2192	BARNETT, Joel D	18	SWSW	1884-06-30		A1 G14
2193	" "	27	E½NW	1884-06-30		A1 G14
2194	CLARK, Eli C	17	SESE	1873-11-15		A1
2195	" "	20	NENE	1873-11-15		A1
2196	" "	25	SWSE	1873-11-15		A1
2322	DELANEY, Patrick	17	N½SE	1889-05-31		A1
2183	FARWELL, Charles B	12	S½SE	1883-03-30		A1
2184	" "	12	SENE	1883-03-30		A1
2185	" "	13	NENE	1883-03-30		A1
2186	" "	13	NESW	1883-03-30		A1
2187	" "	13	S½NE	1883-03-30		A1
2188	" "	13	SE	1883-03-30		A1
2189	" "	24	NE	1883-03-30		A1
2190	" "	24	NENW	1883-03-30		A1
2267	GOULD, James P	26	SESW	1872-11-01		A1
2268	" "	26	SWSE	1872-11-01		A1
2269	" "	30	W½SW	1872-11-01		A1
2270	" "	35	NWNE	1872-11-01		A1
2262	GRISWOLD, Harrison	2	SWNE	1889-05-31		A1
2263	" "	3	NWNW	1889-05-31		A1
2264	" "	35	NWSW	1889-05-31		A1
2198	HALL, Frederick	1	N½NE	1883-09-10		A1
2199	" "	1	NENW	1883-09-10		A1
2200	" "	1	S½NW	1883-09-10		A1
2201	" "	12	N½NE	1883-09-10		A1
2202	" "	2	N½NW	1883-09-10		A1
2203	" "	2	NWNE	1883-09-10		A1
2204	" "	2	SENW	1883-09-10		A1
2212	" "	3	NENE	1883-09-10		A1
2213	" "	3	SWNE	1883-09-10		A1
2205	" "	24	NESE	1883-09-15		A1
2206	" "	24	S½SE	1883-09-15		A1
2207	" "	25	E½SW	1883-09-15		A1
2208	" "	25	N½SE	1883-09-15		A1
2209	" "	25	NE	1883-09-15		A1
2210	" "	25	SESE	1883-09-15		A1
2211	" "	26	NWNE	1883-09-15		A1
2214	" "	33	4	1883-09-15		A1
2215	" "	33	5	1883-09-15		A1
2216	" "	36	N½NE	1883-09-15		A1
2266	HANSON, James	36	SWSE	1905-11-13		A1 R2399
2181	HARRINGTON, Charles A	23	NENE	1872-11-01		A1 G103
2182	" "	36	SENE	1872-11-01		A1 G103
2271	HOXIE, John C	31	SESE	1875-12-30		A1

ID	Individual in Patent	Sec.	Sec. Part	Date Issued	Other Counties	For More Info . . .
2272	HOXIE, John C (Cont'd)	32	SWSW	1875-12-30		A1
2225	HYLAND, George	15	SWSE	1883-09-15		A1 G111
2226	" "	18	SESW	1883-09-15		A1 G111
2227	" "	19	3	1883-09-15		A1 G111
2229	" "	19	NWNE	1883-09-15		A1 G111
2230	" "	21	N½NE	1883-09-15		A1 G111
2231	" "	21	SESW	1883-09-15		A1 G111
2232	" "	21	SWNE	1883-09-15		A1 G111
2233	" "	21	SWSE	1883-09-15		A1 G111
2234	" "	21	W½NW	1883-09-15		A1 G111
2235	" "	21	W½SW	1883-09-15		A1 G111
2236	" "	22	NWNW	1883-09-15		A1 G111
2237	" "	22	NWSW	1883-09-15		A1 G111
2238	" "	22	S½NW	1883-09-15		A1 G111
2239	" "	27	SWNW	1883-09-15		A1 G111
2240	" "	28	NENE	1883-09-15		A1 G111
2241	" "	28	NENW	1883-09-15		A1 G111
2242	" "	28	SWNE	1883-09-15		A1 G111
2244	" "	29	NWSW	1883-09-15		A1 G111
2245	" "	29	SWSE	1883-09-15		A1 G111
2246	" "	30	S½SE	1883-09-15		A1 G111
2247	" "	30	SESW	1883-09-15		A1 G111
2248	" "	30	SWNE	1883-09-15		A1 G111
2249	" "	31	E½NE	1883-09-15		A1 G111
2250	" "	31	N½SE	1883-09-15		A1 G111
2253	" "	32	3	1883-09-15		A1 G111
2254	" "	32	NW	1883-09-15		A1 G111
2255	" "	32	NWSW	1883-09-15		A1 G111
2256	" "	33	S½SE	1883-09-15		A1 G111
2257	" "	33	S½SW	1883-09-15		A1 G111
2228	" "	19	4	1884-06-20		A1 G111
2243	" "	29	1	1884-06-20		A1 G111
2251	" "	31	NWNE	1884-06-20		A1 G111
2252	" "	32	2	1884-06-20		A1 G111
2225	HYLAND, John	15	SWSE	1883-09-15		A1 G111
2226	" "	18	SESW	1883-09-15		A1 G111
2227	" "	19	3	1883-09-15		A1 G111
2229	" "	19	NWNE	1883-09-15		A1 G111
2230	" "	21	N½NE	1883-09-15		A1 G111
2231	" "	21	SESW	1883-09-15		A1 G111
2232	" "	21	SWNE	1883-09-15		A1 G111
2233	" "	21	SWSE	1883-09-15		A1 G111
2234	" "	21	W½NW	1883-09-15		A1 G111
2235	" "	21	W½SW	1883-09-15		A1 G111
2236	" "	22	NWNW	1883-09-15		A1 G111
2237	" "	22	NWSW	1883-09-15		A1 G111
2238	" "	22	S½NW	1883-09-15		A1 G111
2239	" "	27	SWNW	1883-09-15		A1 G111
2240	" "	28	NENE	1883-09-15		A1 G111
2241	" "	28	NENW	1883-09-15		A1 G111
2242	" "	28	SWNE	1883-09-15		A1 G111
2244	" "	29	NWSW	1883-09-15		A1 G111
2245	" "	29	SWSE	1883-09-15		A1 G111
2246	" "	30	S½SE	1883-09-15		A1 G111
2247	" "	30	SESW	1883-09-15		A1 G111
2248	" "	30	SWNE	1883-09-15		A1 G111
2249	" "	31	E½NE	1883-09-15		A1 G111
2250	" "	31	N½SE	1883-09-15		A1 G111
2253	" "	32	3	1883-09-15		A1 G111
2254	" "	32	NW	1883-09-15		A1 G111
2255	" "	32	NWSW	1883-09-15		A1 G111
2256	" "	33	S½SE	1883-09-15		A1 G111
2257	" "	33	S½SW	1883-09-15		A1 G111
2228	" "	19	4	1884-06-20		A1 G111
2243	" "	29	1	1884-06-20		A1 G111
2251	" "	31	NWNE	1884-06-20		A1 G111
2252	" "	32	2	1884-06-20		A1 G111
2179	JACKSON, Andrew B	6	2	1872-07-01		A1 G115
2177	" "	6	6	1872-07-01		A1 G113
2178	" "	6	7	1872-07-01		A1 G113
2180	" "	9	N½SE	1872-07-01		A1 G115
2177	JACKSON, E G	6	6	1872-07-01		A1 G113
2178	" "	6	7	1872-07-01		A1 G113

ID	Individual in Patent	Sec.	Sec. Part	Date Issued	Other Counties	For More Info . . .
2345	LAIRD, William H	19	E½NE	1884-06-20		A1 G127
2348	" "	20	N½NW	1884-06-20		A1 G127
2349	" "	20	S½NE	1884-06-20		A1 G127
2350	" "	20	SENW	1884-06-20		A1 G127
2351	" "	21	NESW	1884-06-20		A1 G127
2352	" "	21	SENE	1884-06-20		A1 G127
2353	" "	22	E½SW	1884-06-20		A1 G127
2354	" "	22	NENW	1884-06-20		A1 G127
2355	" "	22	NWNE	1884-06-20		A1 G127
2356	" "	22	SE	1884-06-20		A1 G127
2357	" "	23	E½SE	1884-06-20		A1 G127
2358	" "	23	NWNE	1884-06-20		A1 G127
2359	" "	23	S½NE	1884-06-20		A1 G127
2360	" "	24	NWSE	1884-06-20		A1 G127
2361	" "	24	S½NW	1884-06-20		A1 G127
2362	" "	24	SW	1884-06-20		A1 G127
2363	" "	25	NW	1884-06-20		A1 G127
2364	" "	25	W½SW	1884-06-20		A1 G127
2365	" "	26	3	1884-06-20		A1 G127
2366	" "	26	4	1884-06-20		A1 G127
2367	" "	26	E½NE	1884-06-20		A1 G127
2368	" "	26	N½SE	1884-06-20		A1 G127
2369	" "	26	SESE	1884-06-20		A1 G127
2370	" "	26	SWSW	1884-06-20		A1 G127
2371	" "	27	1	1884-06-20		A1 G127
2372	" "	27	2	1884-06-20		A1 G127
2373	" "	27	E½SW	1884-06-20		A1 G127
2374	" "	27	SE	1884-06-20		A1 G127
2375	" "	27	W½NE	1884-06-20		A1 G127
2376	" "	28	N½SW	1884-06-20		A1 G127
2377	" "	28	NWNE	1884-06-20		A1 G127
2378	" "	28	SE	1884-06-20		A1 G127
2379	" "	28	SENE	1884-06-20		A1 G127
2380	" "	28	SENW	1884-06-20		A1 G127
2381	" "	29	NESW	1884-06-20		A1 G127
2382	" "	29	NWSE	1884-06-20		A1 G127
2385	" "	31	NESW	1884-06-20		A1 G127
2386	" "	32	SESE	1884-06-20		A1 G127
2387	" "	33	6	1884-06-20		A1 G127
2388	" "	33	7	1884-06-20		A1 G127
2389	" "	34	N½NE	1884-06-20		A1 G127
2390	" "	34	NESE	1884-06-20		A1 G127
2391	" "	34	SENE	1884-06-20		A1 G127
2392	" "	35	N½NW	1884-06-20		A1 G127
2393	" "	35	NENE	1884-06-20		A1 G127
2394	" "	35	NESW	1884-06-20		A1 G127 R2340
2395	" "	35	NWSE	1884-06-20		A1 G127
2396	" "	35	S½NE	1884-06-20		A1 G127
2397	" "	35	SENW	1884-06-20		A1 G127
2398	" "	36	NESW	1884-06-20		A1 G127
2399	" "	36	SWSE	1884-06-20		A1 G127 R2266
2346	" "	2	E½NE	1884-06-30		A1 G127
2347	" "	2	SESE	1884-06-30		A1 G127
2383	" "	3	NENW	1884-06-30		A1 G127
2384	" "	3	NWNE	1884-06-30		A1 G127
2400	" "	4	1	1884-06-30		A1 G127
2401	" "	4	2	1884-06-30		A1 G127
2402	" "	4	3	1884-06-30		A1 G127
2403	" "	4	4	1884-06-30		A1 G127
2404	" "	4	5	1884-06-30		A1 G127
2405	" "	4	W½SW	1884-06-30		A1 G127
2406	" "	5	1	1884-06-30		A1 G127
2407	" "	5	2	1884-06-30		A1 G127
2408	" "	5	3	1884-06-30		A1 G127
2409	" "	6	3	1884-06-30		A1 G127
2410	" "	6	5	1884-06-30		A1 G127
2411	" "	6	SESE	1884-06-30		A1 G127
2412	" "	6	SESW	1884-06-30		A1 G127
2413	" "	7	1	1884-06-30		A1 G127
2414	" "	7	2	1884-06-30		A1 G127
2415	" "	8	NWNE	1884-06-30		A1 G127
2416	" "	9	E½NW	1884-06-30		A1 G127
2174	LOVEJOY, Allen P	12	SWNE	1872-05-10		A1

ID	Individual in Patent	Sec.	Sec. Part	Date Issued	Other Counties	For More Info . . .
2175	LOVEJOY, Allen P (Cont'd)	2	SWNW	1872-05-10		A1
2176	" "	3	SENE	1872-05-10		A1
2282	MAYO, John W	17	SESW	1903-02-12		A3 G136
2345	NORTON, James L	19	E½NE	1884-06-20		A1 G127
2348	" "	20	N½NW	1884-06-20		A1 G127
2349	" "	20	S½NE	1884-06-20		A1 G127
2350	" "	20	SENW	1884-06-20		A1 G127
2351	" "	21	NESW	1884-06-20		A1 G127
2352	" "	21	SENE	1884-06-20		A1 G127
2353	" "	22	E½SW	1884-06-20		A1 G127
2354	" "	22	NENW	1884-06-20		A1 G127
2355	" "	22	NWNE	1884-06-20		A1 G127
2356	" "	22	SE	1884-06-20		A1 G127
2357	" "	23	E½SE	1884-06-20		A1 G127
2358	" "	23	NWNE	1884-06-20		A1 G127
2359	" "	23	S½NE	1884-06-20		A1 G127
2360	" "	24	NWSE	1884-06-20		A1 G127
2361	" "	24	S½NW	1884-06-20		A1 G127
2362	" "	24	SW	1884-06-20		A1 G127
2363	" "	25	NW	1884-06-20		A1 G127
2364	" "	25	W½SW	1884-06-20		A1 G127
2365	" "	26	3	1884-06-20		A1 G127
2366	" "	26	4	1884-06-20		A1 G127
2367	" "	26	E½NE	1884-06-20		A1 G127
2368	" "	26	N½SE	1884-06-20		A1 G127
2369	" "	26	SESE	1884-06-20		A1 G127
2370	" "	26	SWSW	1884-06-20		A1 G127
2371	" "	27	1	1884-06-20		A1 G127
2372	" "	27	2	1884-06-20		A1 G127
2373	" "	27	E½SW	1884-06-20		A1 G127
2374	" "	27	SE	1884-06-20		A1 G127
2375	" "	27	W½NE	1884-06-20		A1 G127
2376	" "	28	N½SW	1884-06-20		A1 G127
2377	" "	28	NWNE	1884-06-20		A1 G127
2378	" "	28	SE	1884-06-20		A1 G127
2379	" "	28	SENE	1884-06-20		A1 G127
2380	" "	28	SENW	1884-06-20		A1 G127
2381	" "	29	NESW	1884-06-20		A1 G127
2382	" "	29	NWSE	1884-06-20		A1 G127
2385	" "	31	NESW	1884-06-20		A1 G127
2386	" "	32	SESE	1884-06-20		A1 G127
2387	" "	33	6	1884-06-20		A1 G127
2388	" "	33	7	1884-06-20		A1 G127
2389	" "	34	N½NE	1884-06-20		A1 G127
2390	" "	34	NESE	1884-06-20		A1 G127
2391	" "	34	SENE	1884-06-20		A1 G127
2392	" "	35	N½NW	1884-06-20		A1 G127
2393	" "	35	NENE	1884-06-20		A1 G127
2394	" "	35	NESW	1884-06-20		A1 G127 R2340
2395	" "	35	NWSE	1884-06-20		A1 G127
2396	" "	35	S½NE	1884-06-20		A1 G127
2397	" "	35	SENW	1884-06-20		A1 G127
2398	" "	36	NESW	1884-06-20		A1 G127
2399	" "	36	SWSE	1884-06-20		A1 G127 R2266
2346	" "	2	E½NE	1884-06-30		A1 G127
2347	" "	2	SESE	1884-06-30		A1 G127
2383	" "	3	NENW	1884-06-30		A1 G127
2384	" "	3	NWNE	1884-06-30		A1 G127
2400	" "	4	1	1884-06-30		A1 G127
2401	" "	4	2	1884-06-30		A1 G127
2402	" "	4	3	1884-06-30		A1 G127
2403	" "	4	4	1884-06-30		A1 G127
2404	" "	4	5	1884-06-30		A1 G127
2405	" "	4	W½SW	1884-06-30		A1 G127
2406	" "	5	1	1884-06-30		A1 G127
2407	" "	5	2	1884-06-30		A1 G127
2408	" "	5	3	1884-06-30		A1 G127
2409	" "	6	3	1884-06-30		A1 G127
2410	" "	6	5	1884-06-30		A1 G127
2411	" "	6	SESE	1884-06-30		A1 G127
2412	" "	6	SESW	1884-06-30		A1 G127
2413	" "	7	1	1884-06-30		A1 G127
2414	" "	7	2	1884-06-30		A1 G127

ID	Individual in Patent	Sec.	Sec. Part	Date Issued	Other Counties	For More Info . . .
2415	NORTON, James L (Cont'd)	8	NWNE	1884-06-30		A1 G127
2416	"	"	9	E½NW	1884-06-30		A1 G127
2345	NORTON, Matthew G	19	E½NE	1884-06-20		A1 G127
2348	"	"	20	N½NW	1884-06-20		A1 G127
2349	"	"	20	S½NE	1884-06-20		A1 G127
2350	"	"	20	SENW	1884-06-20		A1 G127
2351	"	"	21	NESW	1884-06-20		A1 G127
2352	"	"	21	SENE	1884-06-20		A1 G127
2353	"	"	22	E½SW	1884-06-20		A1 G127
2354	"	"	22	NENW	1884-06-20		A1 G127
2355	"	"	22	NWNE	1884-06-20		A1 G127
2356	"	"	22	SE	1884-06-20		A1 G127
2357	"	"	23	E½SE	1884-06-20		A1 G127
2358	"	"	23	NWNE	1884-06-20		A1 G127
2359	"	"	23	S½NE	1884-06-20		A1 G127
2360	"	"	24	NWSE	1884-06-20		A1 G127
2361	"	"	24	S½NW	1884-06-20		A1 G127
2362	"	"	24	SW	1884-06-20		A1 G127
2363	"	"	25	NW	1884-06-20		A1 G127
2364	"	"	25	W½SW	1884-06-20		A1 G127
2365	"	"	26	3	1884-06-20		A1 G127
2366	"	"	26	4	1884-06-20		A1 G127
2367	"	"	26	E½NE	1884-06-20		A1 G127
2368	"	"	26	N½SE	1884-06-20		A1 G127
2369	"	"	26	SESE	1884-06-20		A1 G127
2370	"	"	26	SWSW	1884-06-20		A1 G127
2371	"	"	27	1	1884-06-20		A1 G127
2372	"	"	27	2	1884-06-20		A1 G127
2373	"	"	27	E½SW	1884-06-20		A1 G127
2374	"	"	27	SE	1884-06-20		A1 G127
2375	"	"	27	W½NE	1884-06-20		A1 G127
2376	"	"	28	N½SW	1884-06-20		A1 G127
2377	"	"	28	NWNE	1884-06-20		A1 G127
2378	"	"	28	SE	1884-06-20		A1 G127
2379	"	"	28	SENE	1884-06-20		A1 G127
2380	"	"	28	SENW	1884-06-20		A1 G127
2381	"	"	29	NESW	1884-06-20		A1 G127
2382	"	"	29	NWSE	1884-06-20		A1 G127
2385	"	"	31	NESW	1884-06-20		A1 G127
2386	"	"	32	SESE	1884-06-20		A1 G127
2387	"	"	33	6	1884-06-20		A1 G127
2388	"	"	33	7	1884-06-20		A1 G127
2389	"	"	34	N½NE	1884-06-20		A1 G127
2390	"	"	34	NESE	1884-06-20		A1 G127
2391	"	"	34	SENE	1884-06-20		A1 G127
2392	"	"	35	N½NW	1884-06-20		A1 G127
2393	"	"	35	NENE	1884-06-20		A1 G127
2394	"	"	35	NESW	1884-06-20		A1 G127 R2340
2395	"	"	35	NWSE	1884-06-20		A1 G127
2396	"	"	35	S½NE	1884-06-20		A1 G127
2397	"	"	35	SENW	1884-06-20		A1 G127
2398	"	"	36	NESW	1884-06-20		A1 G127
2399	"	"	36	SWSE	1884-06-20		A1 G127 R2266
2346	"	"	2	E½NE	1884-06-30		A1 G127
2347	"	"	2	SESE	1884-06-30		A1 G127
2383	"	"	3	NENW	1884-06-30		A1 G127
2384	"	"	3	NWNE	1884-06-30		A1 G127
2400	"	"	4	1	1884-06-30		A1 G127
2401	"	"	4	2	1884-06-30		A1 G127
2402	"	"	4	3	1884-06-30		A1 G127
2403	"	"	4	4	1884-06-30		A1 G127
2404	"	"	4	5	1884-06-30		A1 G127
2405	"	"	4	W½SW	1884-06-30		A1 G127
2406	"	"	5	1	1884-06-30		A1 G127
2407	"	"	5	2	1884-06-30		A1 G127
2408	"	"	5	3	1884-06-30		A1 G127
2409	"	"	6	3	1884-06-30		A1 G127
2410	"	"	6	5	1884-06-30		A1 G127
2411	"	"	6	SESE	1884-06-30		A1 G127
2412	"	"	6	SESW	1884-06-30		A1 G127
2413	"	"	7	1	1884-06-30		A1 G127
2414	"	"	7	2	1884-06-30		A1 G127
2415	"	"	8	NWNE	1884-06-30		A1 G127

ID	Individual in Patent	Sec.	Sec. Part	Date Issued	Other Counties	For More Info . . .
2416	NORTON, Matthew G (Cont'd)	9	E½NW	1884-06-30		A1 G127
2420	PATRICK, William S	10	E½NW	1872-11-01		A1
2282	PAULSON, Peter	17	SESW	1903-02-12		A3 G136
2313	PILLSBURY, Oliver P	10	W½SW	1884-06-30		A1
2314	" "	12	SESW	1884-06-30		A1
2315	" "	13	NWNW	1884-06-30		A1
2316	" "	17	SWSW	1884-06-30		A1
2317	" "	20	NWSW	1884-06-30		A1
2318	" "	7	N½SE	1884-06-30		A1
2319	" "	9	E½SW	1884-06-30		A1
2320	" "	9	NWNE	1884-06-30		A1
2321	" "	9	S½NE	1884-06-30		A1
2181	REEVE, Thomas T	23	NENE	1872-11-01		A1 G103
2182	" "	36	SENE	1872-11-01		A1 G103
2323	ROBISON, R D	10	NWNE	1872-07-01		A1
2324	" "	10	SESE	1872-07-01		A1
2325	" "	14	NENE	1872-07-01		A1
2326	" "	14	NWNW	1872-07-01		A1
2327	" "	21	NENW	1872-07-01		A1
2328	" "	9	SESE	1872-07-01		A1
2273	ROBSON, John	31	SWNE	1884-06-20		A1
2274	" "	32	E½SW	1884-06-20		A1
2275	" "	32	N½SE	1884-06-20		A1
2276	" "	33	2	1884-06-20		A1
2277	" "	35	SESE	1884-06-20		A1
2278	" "	35	SESW	1884-06-20		A1
2279	" "	35	SWNW	1884-06-20		A1
2280	" "	36	NESE	1884-06-20		A1
2281	" "	36	SWNW	1884-06-20		A1 R2259
2181	ROE, Gilbert W	23	NENE	1872-11-01		A1 G103
2182	" "	36	SENE	1872-11-01		A1 G103
2417	ROY, William	7	5	1898-04-06		A1
2418	" "	7	6	1898-04-06		A1
2419	" "	7	7	1898-04-06		A1
2333	SCOTT, Thomas B	33	3	1883-04-20		A1
2334	" "	33	NENE	1883-04-20		A1
2335	" "	34	NW	1883-04-20		A1
2336	" "	34	SESW	1883-04-20		A1
2337	" "	34	SWNE	1883-04-20		A1
2338	" "	34	W½SE	1883-04-20		A1
2339	" "	35	NESE	1883-04-20		A1
2340	" "	35	NESW	1883-04-20		A1 R2394
2341	" "	36	N½NW	1883-04-20		A1
2329	" "	11	NWNE	1883-05-15		A1
2330	" "	14	SENW	1883-05-15		A1
2331	" "	15	S½SW	1883-05-15		A1
2332	" "	23	NENW	1883-05-15		A1
2342	" "	36	SENW	1883-05-15		A1
2343	" "	36	SWNE	1883-05-15		A1
2191	SHEPARD, Claude E	14	NWSW	1902-03-17		A1
2197	SHEPARD, Eugene S	33	1	1902-02-07		A1
2265	SHERRY, Henry	35	SWSE	1883-09-10		A1
2258	SILVERTHORN, George	26	2	1889-05-09		A1
2259	" "	36	SWNW	1889-05-09		A1 R2281
2260	SLAUSON, George W	19	2	1875-02-20		A1
2261	" "	19	N½NW	1875-02-20		A1
2296	THOMPSON, Neil A	14	SWNE	1873-11-15		A1
2297	" "	14	SWNW	1873-11-15		A1
2298	" "	15	N½SE	1873-11-15		A1
2299	" "	15	NE	1873-11-15		A1
2300	" "	15	NESW	1873-11-15		A1
2301	" "	15	SESE	1873-11-15		A1
2302	" "	22	E½NE	1873-11-15		A1
2303	" "	22	SWNE	1873-11-15		A1
2304	" "	23	SENW	1873-11-15		A1
2305	" "	23	SW	1873-11-15		A1
2306	" "	23	W½NW	1873-11-15		A1
2307	" "	23	W½SE	1873-11-15		A1
2308	" "	26	1	1873-11-15		A1
2309	" "	3	NESE	1873-11-15		A1
2310	" "	34	1	1873-11-15		A1
2311	" "	34	SWSW	1873-11-15		A1
2312	" "	35	SWSW	1873-11-15		A1

ID	Individual in Patent	Sec.	Sec. Part	Date Issued	Other Counties	For More Info . . .
2217	WASHBURN, Ganem W	11	SWSE	1872-11-01		A1
2218	" "	14	NENW	1872-11-01		A1
2219	" "	14	NWNE	1872-11-01		A1
2220	" "	24	NWNW	1872-11-01		A1
2221	" "	5	W½SE	1872-11-01		A1
2222	" "	8	1	1872-11-01		A1
2223	" "	8	2	1872-11-01		A1
2224	" "	8	E½NW	1872-11-01		A1
2283	WATERMAN, Leslie J	20	SWNW	1884-06-30		A1 G168
2284	" "	27	W½SW	1884-06-30		A1 G168
2285	" "	28	1	1884-06-30		A1 G168
2286	" "	28	2	1884-06-30		A1 G168
2287	" "	29	NESE	1884-06-30		A1 G168
2288	" "	29	SESW	1884-06-30		A1 G168
2289	" "	30	1	1884-06-30		A1 G168
2290	" "	36	NWSW	1884-06-30		A1 G168
2291	" "	36	S½SW	1884-06-30		A1 G168
2292	" "	36	SESE	1884-06-30		A1 G168
2293	" "	6	SWSE	1884-06-30		A1 G168
2294	WATERMAN, Leslie W	1	NWNW	1884-06-30		A1 G169
2295	" "	26	NESW	1884-06-30		A1 G169
2344	WHEELIHAN, W P	15	SENW	1889-03-29		A1
2179	WILCOX, George G	6	2	1872-07-01		A1 G115
2180	" "	9	N½SE	1872-07-01		A1 G115
2294	WILEY, Charles L	1	NWNW	1884-06-30		A1 G169
2283	" "	20	SWNW	1884-06-30		A1 G168
2295	" "	26	NESW	1884-06-30		A1 G169
2284	" "	27	W½SW	1884-06-30		A1 G168
2285	" "	28	1	1884-06-30		A1 G168
2286	" "	28	2	1884-06-30		A1 G168
2287	" "	29	NESE	1884-06-30		A1 G168
2288	" "	29	SESW	1884-06-30		A1 G168
2289	" "	30	1	1884-06-30		A1 G168
2290	" "	36	NWSW	1884-06-30		A1 G168
2291	" "	36	S½SW	1884-06-30		A1 G168
2292	" "	36	SESE	1884-06-30		A1 G168
2293	" "	6	SWSE	1884-06-30		A1 G168

Patent Map

T42-N R8-E
4th PM - 1831 MN/WI

Map Group 13

Township Statistics

Parcels Mapped	:	247
Number of Patents	:	77
Number of Individuals	:	41
Patentees Identified	:	32
Number of Surnames	:	35
Multi-Patentee Parcels	:	127
Oldest Patent Date	:	5/10/1872
Most Recent Patent	:	11/13/1905
Block/Lot Parcels	:	43
Parcels Re - Issued	:	3
Parcels that Overlap	:	0
Cities and Towns	:	0
Cemeteries	:	0

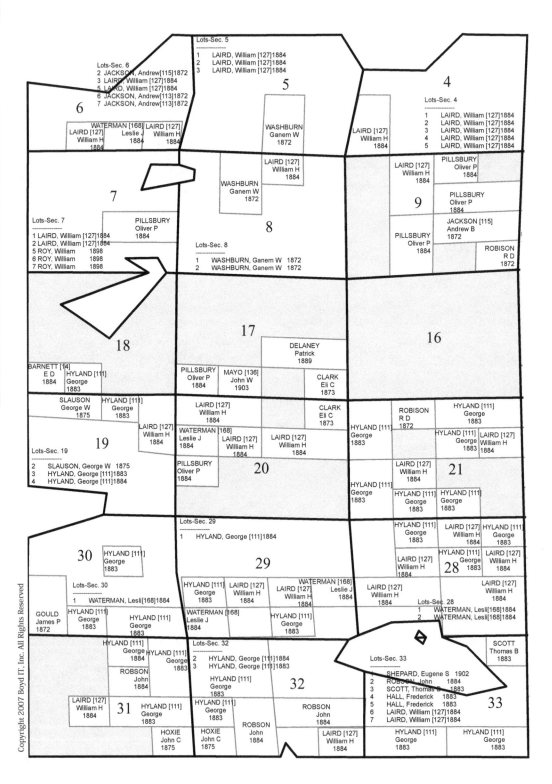

Section 3
GRISWOLD Harrison 1889
LAIRD [127] William H 1884
LAIRD [127] William H 1884
HALL Frederick 1883
HALL Frederick 1883
LOVEJOY Allen P 1872
THOMPSON Neil A 1873

Section 2
HALL Frederick 1883
HALL Frederick 1883
LAIRD [127] William H 1884
LOVEJOY Allen P 1872
HALL Frederick 1883
GRISWOLD Harrison 1889
LAIRD [127] William H 1884

Section 1
WATERMAN [169] Leslie W 1884
HALL Frederick 1883
HALL Frederick 1883
HALL Frederick 1883

Section 10
PATRICK William S 1872
ROBISON R D 1872
PILLSBURY Oliver P 1884
ROBISON R D 1872

Section 11
SCOTT Thomas B 1883
WASHBURN Ganem W 1872

Section 12
HALL Frederick 1883
LOVEJOY Allen P 1872
FARWELL Charles B 1883
PILLSBURY Oliver P 1884
FARWELL Charles B 1883

Section 15
WHEELIHAN W P 1889
THOMPSON Neil A 1873
THOMPSON Neil A 1873
THOMPSON Neil A 1873
SCOTT Thomas B 1883
HYLAND [111] George 1883
THOMPSON Neil A 1873

Section 14
ROBISON R D 1872
WASHBURN Ganem W 1872
WASHBURN Ganem W 1872
ROBISON R D 1872
THOMPSON Neil A 1873
SCOTT Thomas B 1883
THOMPSON Neil A 1873
SHEPARD Claude E 1902

Section 13
PILLSBURY Oliver P 1884
FARWELL Charles B 1883
FARWELL Charles B 1883
FARWELL Charles B 1883
FARWELL Charles B 1883

Section 22
HYLAND [111] George 1883
LAIRD [127] William H 1884
THOMPSON Neil A 1873
HYLAND [111] George 1883
THOMPSON Neil A 1873
HYLAND [111] George 1883
LAIRD [127] William H 1884
LAIRD [127] William H 1884

Section 23
SCOTT Thomas B 1883
HARRINGTON [103] Charles A 1872
LAIRD [127] William H 1884
THOMPSON Neil A 1873
THOMPSON Neil A 1873
LAIRD [127] William H 1884
LAIRD [127] William H 1884
THOMPSON Neil A 1873
THOMPSON Neil A 1873

Section 24
WASHBURN Ganem W 1872
FARWELL Charles B 1883
LAIRD [127] William H 1884
FARWELL Charles B 1883
LAIRD [127] William H 1884
HALL Frederick 1883
HALL Frederick 1883

Section 27
Lots-Sec. 27
1   LAIRD, William [127] 1884
2   LAIRD, William [127] 1884
HYLAND [111] George 1883
BARNETT [14] E D 1884
LAIRD [127] William H 1884
LAIRD [127] William H 1884
LAIRD [127] William H 1884
WATERMAN [168] Leslie J 1884

Section 26
Lots-Sec. 26
1 THOMPSON, Neil A   1873
2 SILVERTHORN, George 1889
3 LAIRD, William [127] 1884
4 LAIRD, William [127] 1884
HALL Frederick 1883
LAIRD [127] William H 1884
WATERMAN [169] Leslie W 1884
LAIRD [127] William H 1884
LAIRD [127] William H 1884
GOULD James P 1872
GOULD James P 1872
LAIRD [127] William H 1884

Section 25
LAIRD [127] William H 1884
HALL Frederick 1883
LAIRD [127] William H 1884
HALL Frederick 1883
CLARK Eli C 1873
HALL Frederick 1883

Section 34
Lots-Sec. 34
1   THOMPSON, Neil A   1873
SCOTT Thomas B 1883
SCOTT Thomas B 1883
LAIRD [127] William H 1884
SCOTT Thomas B 1883
LAIRD [127] William H 1884
THOMPSON Neil A 1873
SCOTT Thomas B 1883

Section 35
LAIRD [127] William H 1884
GOULD James P 1872
LAIRD [127] William H 1884
ROBSON John 1884
LAIRD [127] William H 1884
LAIRD [127] William H 1884
GRISWOLD Harrison 1889
LAIRD [127] William H 1884
SCOTT Thomas B 1883
LAIRD [127] William H 1884
THOMPSON Neil A 1873
ROBSON John 1884
SHERRY Henry 1883
ROBSON John 1884

Section 36
SCOTT Thomas B 1883
HALL Frederick 1883
SILVERTHORN George 1889
ROBSON John 1884
SCOTT Thomas B 1883
HARRINGTON [103] Charles A 1872
SCOTT Thomas B 1883
WATERMAN [168] Leslie J 1884
LAIRD [127] William H 1884
ROBSON John 1884
WATERMAN [168] Leslie J 1884
LAIRD [127] William H 1884 HANSON James 1905
WATERMAN [168] Leslie J 1884

Helpful Hints

1. This Map's INDEX can be found on the preceding pages.

2. Refer to Map "C" to see where this Township lies within Vilas County, Wisconsin.

3. Numbers within square brackets [ ] denote a multi-patentee land parcel (multi-owner). Refer to Appendix "C" for a full list of members in this group.

4. Areas that look to be crowded with Patentees usually indicate multiple sales of the same parcel (Re-issues) or Overlapping parcels. See this Township's Index for an explanation of these and other circumstances that might explain "odd" groupings of Patentees on this map.

Legend

— Patent Boundary

— Section Boundary

No Patents Found (or Outside County)

1., 2., 3., ...   Lot Numbers (when beside a name)

[ ]   Group Number (see Appendix "C")

Scale: Section = 1 mile X 1 mile (generally, with some exceptions)

Road Map

T42-N R8-E
4th PM - 1831 MN/WI

Map Group 13

Cities & Towns

None

Cemeteries

None

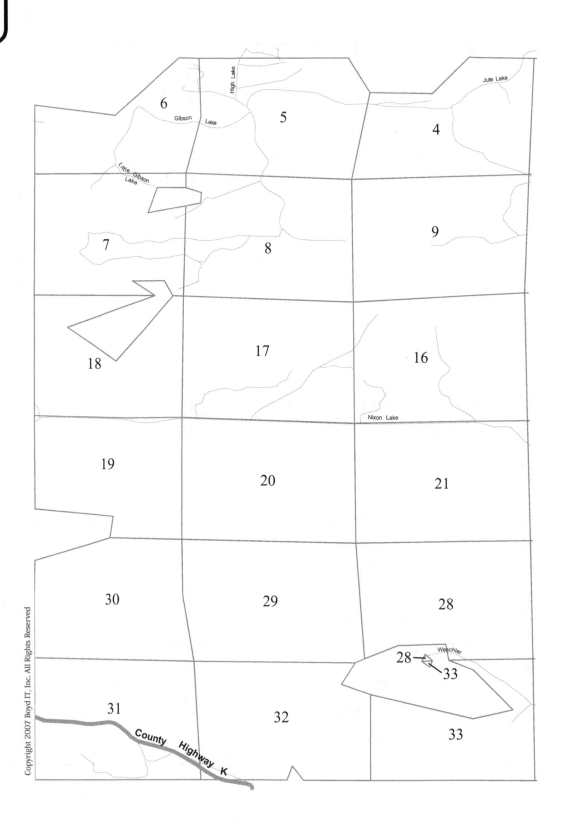

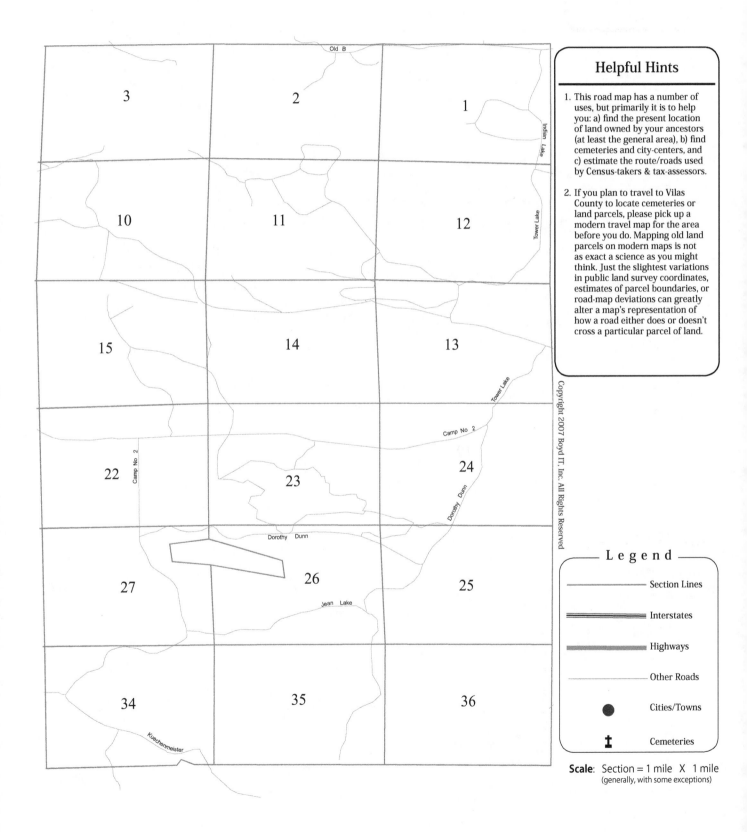

Helpful Hints

1. This road map has a number of uses, but primarily it is to help you: a) find the present location of land owned by your ancestors (at least the general area), b) find cemeteries and city-centers, and c) estimate the route/roads used by Census-takers & tax-assessors.

2. If you plan to travel to Vilas County to locate cemeteries or land parcels, please pick up a modern travel map for the area before you do. Mapping old land parcels on modern maps is not as exact a science as you might think. Just the slightest variations in public land survey coordinates, estimates of parcel boundaries, or road-map deviations can greatly alter a map's representation of how a road either does or doesn't cross a particular parcel of land.

Legend

— Section Lines

≡ Interstates

▬ Highways

— Other Roads

● Cities/Towns

⚰ Cemeteries

Scale: Section = 1 mile X 1 mile
(generally, with some exceptions)

Historical Map

T42-N   R8-E
4th PM - 1831 MN/WI

Map Group 13

Cities & Towns
None

Cemeteries
None

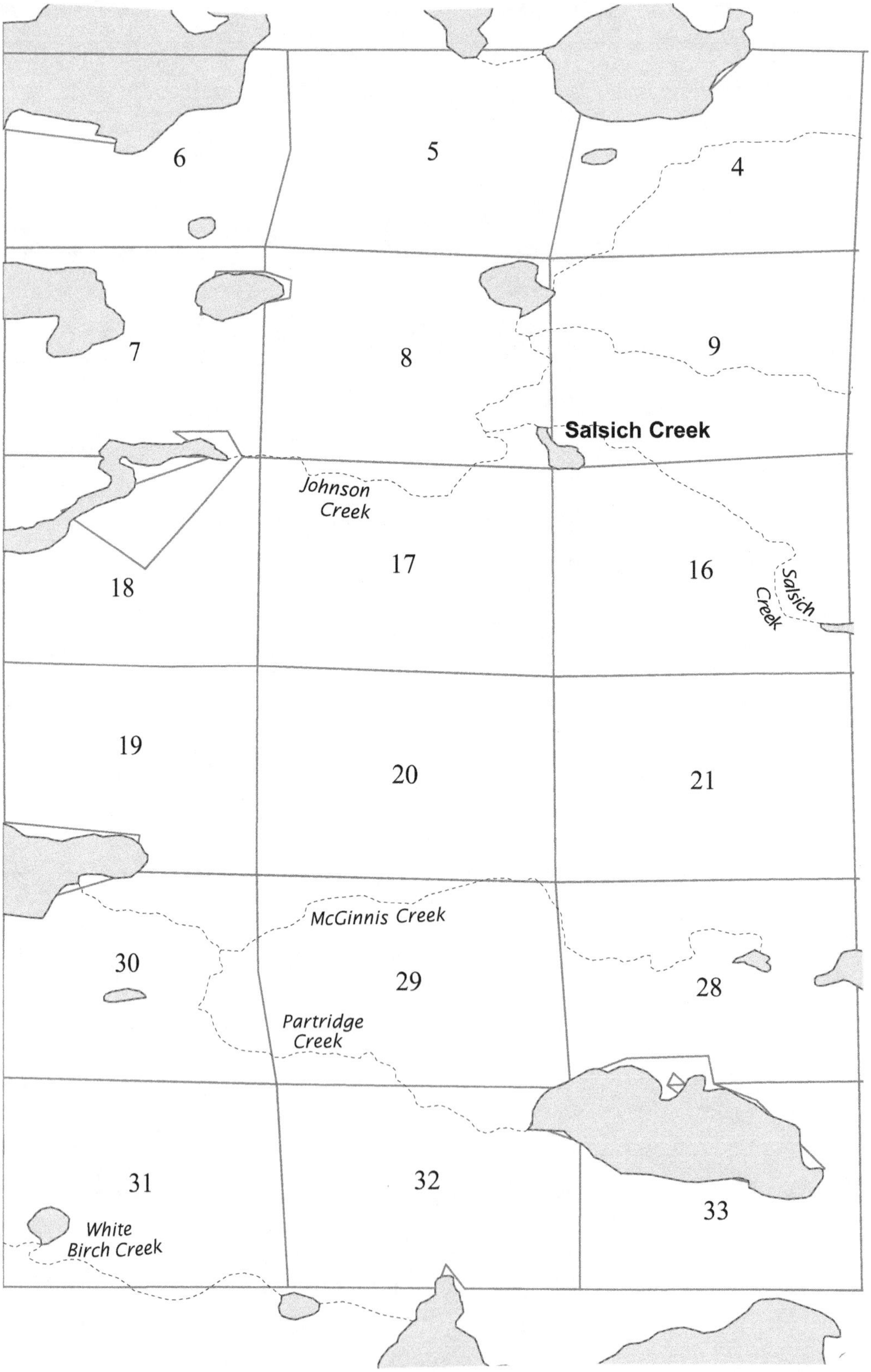

6

5

4

7

8

9

Salsich Creek

Johnson
Creek

18

17

16

Salsich
Creek

19

20

21

McGinnis Creek

30

29

28

Partridge
Creek

31

32

33

White
Birch Creek

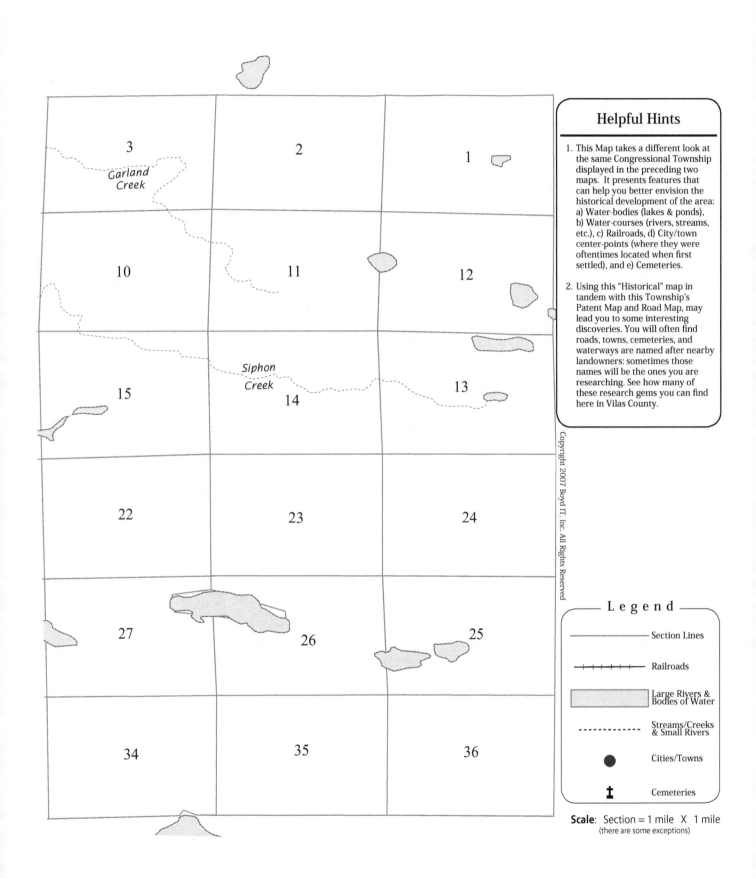

Helpful Hints

1. This Map takes a different look at the same Congressional Township displayed in the preceding two maps. It presents features that can help you better envision the historical development of the area: a) Water-bodies (lakes & ponds), b) Water-courses (rivers, streams, etc.), c) Railroads, d) City/town center-points (where they were oftentimes located when first settled), and e) Cemeteries.

2. Using this "Historical" map in tandem with this Township's Patent Map and Road Map, may lead you to some interesting discoveries. You will often find roads, towns, cemeteries, and waterways are named after nearby landowners: sometimes those names will be the ones you are researching. See how many of these research gems you can find here in Vilas County.

L e g e n d

————	Section Lines
+++++	Railroads
▬	Large Rivers & Bodies of Water
- - - - -	Streams/Creeks & Small Rivers
●	Cities/Towns
✝	Cemeteries

Scale: Section = 1 mile X 1 mile
(there are some exceptions)

Map Group 14: Index to Land Patents

Township 42-North Range 9-East (4th PM - 1831 MN/WI)

After you locate an individual in this Index, take note of the Section and Section Part then proceed to the Land Patent map on the pages immediately following. You should have no difficulty locating the corresponding parcel of land.

The "For More Info" Column will lead you to more information about the underlying Patents. See the *Legend* at right, and the "How to Use this Book" chapter, for more information.

```
                        LEGEND
            "For More Info . . . " column
A = Authority (Legislative Act, See Appendix "A")
B = Block or Lot (location in Section unknown)
C = Cancelled Patent
F = Fractional Section
G = Group  (Multi-Patentee Patent, see Appendix "C")
V = Overlaps another Parcel
R = Re-Issued (Parcel patented more than once)

(A & G items require you to look in the Appendixes referred
to above. All other Letter-designations followed by a number
require you to locate line-items in this index that possess
the ID number found after the letter).
```

ID	Individual in Patent	Sec.	Sec. Part	Date Issued	Other Counties	For More Info . . .
2634	ALLEN, William N	2	NENW	1888-07-10		A1 G6 F
2451	ARPIN, D J	17	NWSW	1889-05-09		A1
2478	BARNETT, E D	25	NWSW	1884-06-30		A1 G14
2478	BARNETT, Joel D	25	NWSW	1884-06-30		A1 G14
2593	BELANGER, Ovid	13	NESW	1902-12-30		A1
2594	" "	13	SENW	1902-12-30		A1
2595	" "	13	W½NE	1902-12-30		A1
2426	BREWER, Addison P	24	NESE	1888-07-10		A1
2427	" "	24	SWNE	1888-07-10		A1
2612	BROOKS, Virgil	1	SWSW	1886-07-30		A1
2613	" "	11	NWSE	1886-07-30		A1
2614	" "	12	S½SW	1886-07-30		A1
2615	" "	13	NENW	1886-07-30		A1
2616	" "	13	NWSE	1886-07-30		A1
2617	" "	2	SESE	1886-07-30		A1
2437	CHIDESTER, Buek	4	8	1909-02-15		A3 G42
2479	CLARK, Eli C	30	SENW	1873-05-01		A1
2480	" "	30	SESE	1873-05-01		A1
2481	" "	30	W½NE	1873-05-01		A1
2482	" "	33	SESE	1873-05-01		A1
2539	CLARK, James	20	SESW	1872-11-01		A1 G47
2540	" "	20	SWSE	1872-11-01		A1 G47
2541	" "	28	SENW	1872-11-01		A1 G47
2542	" "	28	SWSW	1872-11-01		A1 G47
2543	" "	29	N½NW	1872-11-01		A1 G47
2544	" "	29	NWNE	1872-11-01		A1 G47
2545	" "	30	N½SW	1872-11-01		A1 G47
2546	" "	30	NENW	1872-11-01		A1 G47
2547	" "	30	SWNW	1872-11-01		A1 G47
2548	" "	31	E½NE	1872-11-01		A1 G47
2549	" "	31	NESE	1872-11-01		A1 G47
2550	" "	31	NESW	1872-11-01		A1 G47
2551	" "	31	S½NW	1872-11-01		A1 G47
2552	" "	32	NENW	1872-11-01		A1 G47
2553	" "	32	SESE	1872-11-01		A1 G47
2555	CLARK, James G	30	E½NE	1873-05-01		A1 G46
2556	" "	31	NWSE	1873-05-01		A1 G46
2557	" "	31	SWNE	1873-05-01		A1 G46
2554	" "	25	S½SE	1878-08-20		A1 G45
2554	CLARK, John	25	S½SE	1878-08-20		A1 G45
2539	CLARK, John J	20	SESW	1872-11-01		A1 G47
2540	" "	20	SWSE	1872-11-01		A1 G47
2541	" "	28	SENW	1872-11-01		A1 G47
2542	" "	28	SWSW	1872-11-01		A1 G47
2543	" "	29	N½NW	1872-11-01		A1 G47
2544	" "	29	NWNE	1872-11-01		A1 G47

ID	Individual in Patent	Sec.	Sec. Part	Date Issued	Other Counties	For More Info . . .
2545	CLARK, John J (Cont'd)	30	N½SW	1872-11-01		A1 G47
2546	" "	30	NENW	1872-11-01		A1 G47
2547	" "	30	SWNW	1872-11-01		A1 G47
2548	" "	31	E½NE	1872-11-01		A1 G47
2549	" "	31	NESE	1872-11-01		A1 G47
2550	" "	31	NESW	1872-11-01		A1 G47
2551	" "	31	S½NW	1872-11-01		A1 G47
2552	" "	32	NENW	1872-11-01		A1 G47
2553	" "	32	SESE	1872-11-01		A1 G47
2428	CO, Alexander Stewart Lumber	14	SWSE	1886-07-30		A1
2429	" "	23	NWNE	1886-07-30		A1
2437	COLMAN, Niles A	4	8	1909-02-15		A3 G42
2529	COOK, Grant	11	NENE	1899-04-22		A3
2530	" "	11	W½NE	1899-04-22		A3
2600	DOYLE, Thomas M	17	SWSW	1884-06-20		A1
2601	" "	18	SESE	1884-06-20		A1
2602	" "	18	SESW	1884-06-20		A1
2603	" "	19	SWNE	1884-06-20		A1
2604	" "	20	NWNW	1884-06-20		A1
2605	" "	20	NWSW	1884-06-20		A1
2606	" "	20	SWNW	1884-06-20		A1
2607	" "	30	SWSE	1884-06-20		A1
2608	" "	32	SENW	1884-06-20		A1
2609	" "	32	SWNW	1884-06-20		A1
2610	" "	6	NESW	1884-06-20		A1
2611	" "	7	SENW	1884-06-20		A1
2531	DUNFIELD, Hiram	31	SWSE	1883-05-15		A1
2532	" "	32	SESW	1883-05-15		A1
2440	FARWELL, Charles B	17	1	1883-03-30		A1
2441	" "	17	2	1883-03-30		A1
2442	" "	17	NW	1883-03-30		A1
2443	" "	17	SWNE	1883-03-30		A1
2444	" "	18	N½	1883-03-30		A1
2445	" "	5		1883-03-30		A1
2446	" "	6	SE	1883-03-30		A1
2447	" "	7	NE	1883-03-30		A1
2448	" "	7	S½	1883-03-30		A1
2449	" "	8		1883-03-30		A1
2554	FORBES, D H	25	S½SE	1878-08-20		A1 G45
2539	FORBES, Daniel H	20	SESW	1872-11-01		A1 G47
2540	" "	20	SWSE	1872-11-01		A1 G47
2541	" "	28	SENW	1872-11-01		A1 G47
2542	" "	28	SWSW	1872-11-01		A1 G47
2543	" "	29	N½NW	1872-11-01		A1 G47
2544	" "	29	NWNE	1872-11-01		A1 G47
2545	" "	30	N½SW	1872-11-01		A1 G47
2546	" "	30	NENW	1872-11-01		A1 G47
2547	" "	30	SWNW	1872-11-01		A1 G47
2548	" "	31	E½NE	1872-11-01		A1 G47
2549	" "	31	NESE	1872-11-01		A1 G47
2550	" "	31	NESW	1872-11-01		A1 G47
2551	" "	31	S½NW	1872-11-01		A1 G47
2552	" "	32	NENW	1872-11-01		A1 G47
2553	" "	32	SESE	1872-11-01		A1 G47
2555	FORBES, John R	30	E½NE	1873-05-01		A1 G46
2556	" "	31	NWSE	1873-05-01		A1 G46
2557	" "	31	SWNE	1873-05-01		A1 G46
2477	FOSTER, David R	6	SESW	1903-05-19		A3
2488	GRISWOLD, Frank	12	SWNE	1905-02-10		A1
2489	HALL, Frederick	1	NWSE	1883-09-15		A1
2490	" "	1	S½SE	1883-09-15		A1
2491	" "	1	SWNW	1883-09-15		A1
2492	" "	11	SENE	1883-09-15		A1
2493	" "	12	NENW	1883-09-15		A1
2494	" "	12	NWNE	1883-09-15		A1
2495	" "	12	SESE	1883-09-15		A1
2496	" "	14	N½SE	1883-09-15		A1
2497	" "	18	N½SW	1883-09-15		A1
2498	" "	18	SWSW	1883-09-15		A1
2499	" "	19	E½NE	1883-09-15		A1
2500	" "	19	S½SE	1883-09-15		A1
2501	" "	19	W½	1883-09-15		A1
2502	" "	2	NE	1883-09-15		A1

ID	Individual in Patent	Sec.	Sec. Part	Date Issued	Other Counties	For More Info . . .
2503	HALL, Frederick (Cont'd)	2	NWNW	1883-09-15		A1
2504	" "	2	S½NW	1883-09-15		A1
2505	" "	2	SWSW	1883-09-15		A1
2506	" "	20	SWSW	1883-09-15		A1
2507	" "	30	NWNW	1883-09-15		A1
2508	" "	30	NWSE	1883-09-15		A1
2509	" "	30	S½SW	1883-09-15		A1
2510	" "	31	N½NW	1883-09-15		A1
2511	" "	31	NWNE	1883-09-15		A1
2512	" "	31	NWSW	1883-09-15		A1
2513	" "	6	SWNW	1883-09-15		A1
2514	" "	6	W½SW	1883-09-15		A1
2515	" "	7	SWNW	1883-09-15		A1
2598	HALL, Theadore	12	W½SE	1912-05-13		A3
2534	HAMILTON, Irenus K	33	NESW	1872-05-10		A1 G97
2535	" "	33	NWSE	1872-05-10		A1 G97
2536	" "	33	SENW	1872-05-10		A1 G97
2537	" "	33	SWNE	1872-05-10		A1 G97
2533	" "	22	SESW	1872-11-01		A1 G97
2538	" "	4	SWSE	1872-11-01		A1 G97 F
2534	HAMILTON, Woodman C	33	NESW	1872-05-10		A1 G97
2535	" "	33	NWSE	1872-05-10		A1 G97
2536	" "	33	SENW	1872-05-10		A1 G97
2537	" "	33	SWNE	1872-05-10		A1 G97
2533	" "	22	SESW	1872-11-01		A1 G97
2538	" "	4	SWSE	1872-11-01		A1 G97 F
2561	HARPER, John L	10	NENW	1874-08-01		A1 G98
2562	" "	11	SWSE	1874-08-01		A1 G98
2563	" "	3	3	1874-08-01		A1 G98
2564	" "	3	NENE	1874-08-01		A1 G98
2565	" "	3	SENE	1874-08-01		A1 G98
2566	" "	4	4	1874-08-01		A1 G98
2438	HARRINGTON, Charles A	1	NESW	1872-11-01		A1 G103
2439	" "	26	SENW	1872-11-01		A1 G103
2450	HASELTINE, Charles P	25	NWNW	1885-01-20		A1
2567	HOBART, John W	13	SESW	1900-06-11		A1
2568	" "	24	N½NW	1900-06-11		A1
2569	" "	24	SENW	1900-06-11		A1
2523	HYLAND, George	28	NENW	1883-09-15		A1 G111
2524	" "	29	NWSE	1883-09-15		A1 G111
2525	" "	29	SENW	1883-09-15		A1 G111
2526	" "	29	SWNE	1883-09-15		A1 G111
2527	" "	29	SWSW	1883-09-15		A1 G111
2523	HYLAND, John	28	NENW	1883-09-15		A1 G111
2524	" "	29	NWSE	1883-09-15		A1 G111
2525	" "	29	SENW	1883-09-15		A1 G111
2526	" "	29	SWNE	1883-09-15		A1 G111
2527	" "	29	SWSW	1883-09-15		A1 G111
2631	LAIRD, William H	19	N½SE	1884-06-20		A1 G127
2632	" "	36	SWNW	1884-06-20		A1 G127
2633	" "	7	NWNW	1884-06-30		A1 G127
2452	LIBBEY, D L	11	NESE	1889-05-31		A1
2453	" "	12	NWSW	1889-05-31		A1
2432	LOVEJOY, Allen P	1	NESE	1872-02-20		A1
2434	" "	12	NENE	1872-02-20		A1
2430	" "	1	E½NW	1872-05-10		A1
2431	" "	1	NE	1872-05-10		A1
2433	" "	1	NWNW	1872-05-10		A1
2435	" "	3	4	1872-05-10		A1
2436	" "	3	NESE	1872-05-10		A1
2483	MALCOLM, Elmer G	23	E½NE	1901-05-08		A1
2558	MCPARTLIN, John A	25	NESE	1897-05-12		A1
2559	" "	25	SWNW	1897-05-12		A1
2560	" "	26	SENE	1897-05-12		A1
2634	MERCER, John	2	NENW	1888-07-10		A1 G6 F
2631	NORTON, James L	19	N½SE	1884-06-20		A1 G127
2632	" "	36	SWNW	1884-06-20		A1 G127
2633	" "	7	NWNW	1884-06-30		A1 G127
2631	NORTON, Matthew G	19	N½SE	1884-06-20		A1 G127
2632	" "	36	SWNW	1884-06-20		A1 G127
2633	" "	7	NWNW	1884-06-30		A1 G127
2421	PATTEN, A W	20	NENE	1882-06-30		A1
2422	" "	23	SWSE	1882-06-30		A1

ID	Individual in Patent	Sec.	Sec. Part	Date Issued	Other Counties	For More Info . . .
2423	PATTEN, A W (Cont'd)	32	NESE	1882-06-30		A1
2424	" "	33	NWSW	1882-06-30		A1
2425	" "	35	NWNE	1882-06-30		A1
2590	PILLSBURY, Oliver P	12	NESE	1884-06-30		A1
2591	" "	12	SENE	1884-06-30		A1
2592	" "	2	NWSW	1884-06-30		A1
2467	PRESTON, David	10	NENE	1869-11-10		A1
2468	" "	15	2	1869-11-10		A1
2470	" "	22	1	1869-11-10		A1
2472	" "	3	2	1869-11-10		A1
2476	" "	4	1	1869-11-10		A1
2561	" "	10	NENW	1874-08-01		A1 G98
2562	" "	11	SWSE	1874-08-01		A1 G98
2563	" "	3	3	1874-08-01		A1 G98
2564	" "	3	NENE	1874-08-01		A1 G98
2565	" "	3	SENE	1874-08-01		A1 G98
2566	" "	4	4	1874-08-01		A1 G98
2469	" "	20	NESW	1883-09-15		A1
2471	" "	28	NWSW	1883-09-15		A1
2473	" "	31	SWSW	1883-09-15		A1
2474	" "	32	NESW	1883-09-15		A1
2475	" "	32	W½SE	1883-09-15		A1
2438	REEVE, Thomas T	1	NESW	1872-11-01		A1 G103
2439	" "	26	SENW	1872-11-01		A1 G103
2438	ROE, Gilbert W	1	NESW	1872-11-01		A1 G103
2439	" "	26	SENW	1872-11-01		A1 G103
2621	RUST, William A	12	NWNW	1872-02-20		A1
2622	" "	15	NWSW	1872-02-20		A1
2623	" "	22	N½SE	1872-05-10		A1
2624	" "	25	SESW	1872-05-10		A1
2625	" "	34	SENW	1872-05-10		A1
2626	" "	35	NENE	1872-05-10		A1
2627	" "	36	NESE	1872-05-10		A1
2628	" "	36	SWSE	1872-05-10		A1
2589	RYAN, Michael	1	SESW	1898-05-10		A1
2599	SCOTT, Thomas B	31	SESW	1883-05-15		A1
2528	SILVERTHORN, George	18	NWSE	1890-07-15		A1
2596	SIMPSON, Reuben B	13	W½SW	1896-08-04		A1
2597	" "	14	SESE	1896-08-04		A1
2485	STEVENSON, Francis W	6	NE	1883-09-10		A1
2486	" "	6	NWNW	1883-09-10		A1
2487	" "	6	SENW	1883-09-10		A1
2618	STUBBINGS, W H	17	E½SE	1889-06-28		A1
2619	" "	17	E½SW	1889-06-28		A1
2620	" "	17	SWSE	1889-06-28		A1
2630	THOMPSON, William E	33	SWSE	1900-06-11		A1
2629	" "	24	SESW	1902-01-25		A1
2484	TOWNSEND, Evan	12	NESW	1873-05-01		A1
2516	WASHBURN, Ganem W	23	NWSE	1872-11-01		A1
2517	" "	23	SWNE	1872-11-01		A1
2518	" "	26	NWSW	1872-11-01		A1
2519	" "	27	NWNE	1872-11-01		A1
2520	" "	29	SWSE	1872-11-01		A1
2521	" "	33	NWNW	1872-11-01		A1
2522	" "	33	S½SW	1872-11-01		A1
2571	WATERMAN, Leslie J	17	NWSE	1884-06-30		A1 G168
2572	" "	18	NESE	1884-06-30		A1 G168
2573	" "	18	SWSE	1884-06-30		A1 G168
2574	" "	19	NWNE	1884-06-30		A1 G168
2575	" "	20	NENW	1884-06-30		A1 G168
2576	" "	20	NWNE	1884-06-30		A1 G168
2577	" "	24	NESW	1884-06-30		A1 G168
2578	" "	24	NWSE	1884-06-30		A1 G168
2579	" "	25	NENW	1884-06-30		A1 G168
2580	" "	25	SWNE	1884-06-30		A1 G168
2581	" "	25	SWSW	1884-06-30		A1 G168
2582	" "	26	E½SW	1884-06-30		A1 G168
2583	" "	26	N½NE	1884-06-30		A1 G168
2584	" "	26	SWNE	1884-06-30		A1 G168
2585	" "	28	E½SW	1884-06-30		A1 G168
2586	" "	28	NESE	1884-06-30		A1 G168
2587	" "	28	S½SE	1884-06-30		A1 G168
2588	" "	7	NENW	1884-06-30		A1 G168

ID	Individual in Patent	Sec.	Sec. Part	Date Issued	Other Counties	For More Info . . .
2570	WATTERS, John	33	N½NE	1896-08-04		A1
2571	WILEY, Charles L	17	NWSE	1884-06-30		A1 G168
2572	" "	18	NESE	1884-06-30		A1 G168
2573	" "	18	SWSE	1884-06-30		A1 G168
2574	" "	19	NWNE	1884-06-30		A1 G168
2575	" "	20	NENW	1884-06-30		A1 G168
2576	" "	20	NWNE	1884-06-30		A1 G168
2577	" "	24	NESW	1884-06-30		A1 G168
2578	" "	24	NWSE	1884-06-30		A1 G168
2579	" "	25	NENW	1884-06-30		A1 G168
2580	" "	25	SWNE	1884-06-30		A1 G168
2581	" "	25	SWSW	1884-06-30		A1 G168
2582	" "	26	E½SW	1884-06-30		A1 G168
2583	" "	26	N½NE	1884-06-30		A1 G168
2584	" "	26	SWNE	1884-06-30		A1 G168
2585	" "	28	E½SW	1884-06-30		A1 G168
2586	" "	28	NESE	1884-06-30		A1 G168
2587	" "	28	S½SE	1884-06-30		A1 G168
2588	" "	7	NENW	1884-06-30		A1 G168
2635	WILSON, William	6	NENW	1884-06-30		A1
2457	WYLIE, Daniel B	1	NWSW	1883-09-15		A1 G172
2458	" "	13	E½NE	1883-09-15		A1 G172
2459	" "	13	NESE	1883-09-15		A1 G172
2460	" "	13	SESE	1883-09-15		A1 G172
2461	" "	13	SWSE	1883-09-15		A1 G172
2454	" "	2	E½SW	1883-09-15		A1
2455	" "	2	N½SE	1883-09-15		A1
2456	" "	2	SWSE	1883-09-15		A1
2462	" "	24	SESE	1883-09-15		A1 G172
2463	" "	24	SWSE	1883-09-15		A1 G172
2464	" "	25	NENE	1883-09-15		A1 G172
2465	" "	25	SENE	1883-09-15		A1 G172
2466	" "	36	SESE	1883-09-15		A1 G172
2457	WYLIE, Winfred	1	NWSW	1883-09-15		A1 G172
2458	" "	13	E½NE	1883-09-15		A1 G172
2459	" "	13	NESE	1883-09-15		A1 G172
2460	" "	13	SESE	1883-09-15		A1 G172
2461	" "	13	SWSE	1883-09-15		A1 G172
2462	" "	24	SESE	1883-09-15		A1 G172
2463	" "	24	SWSE	1883-09-15		A1 G172
2464	" "	25	NENE	1883-09-15		A1 G172
2465	" "	25	SENE	1883-09-15		A1 G172
2466	" "	36	SESE	1883-09-15		A1 G172

Patent Map

T42-N R9-E
4th PM - 1831 MN/WI

Map Group 14

Township Statistics

Parcels Mapped	:	215
Number of Patents	:	90
Number of Individuals	:	63
Patentees Identified	:	49
Number of Surnames	:	51
Multi-Patentee Parcels	:	72
Oldest Patent Date	:	11/10/1869
Most Recent Patent	:	5/13/1912
Block/Lot Parcels	:	10
Parcels Re - Issued	:	0
Parcels that Overlap	:	0
Cities and Towns	:	0
Cemeteries	:	0

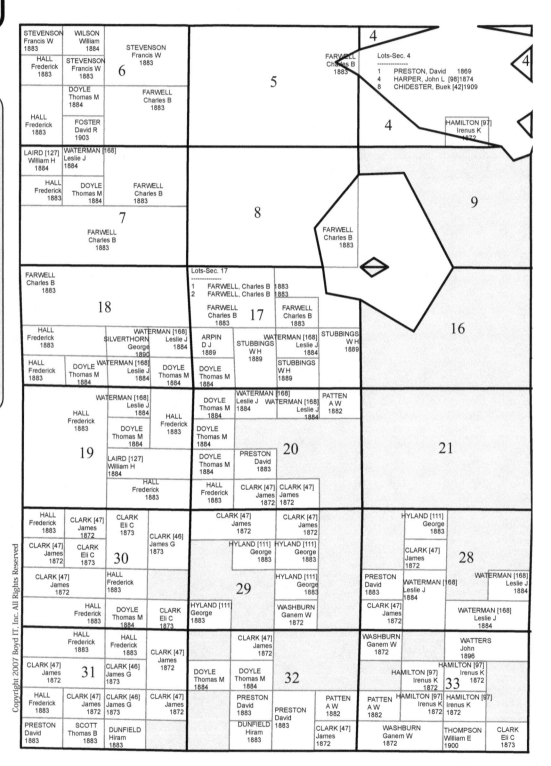

Helpful Hints

1. This Map's INDEX can be found on the preceding pages.

2. Refer to Map "C" to see where this Township lies within Vilas County, Wisconsin.

3. Numbers within square brackets [ ] denote a multi-patentee land parcel (multi-owner). Refer to Appendix "C" for a full list of members in this group.

4. Areas that look to be crowded with Patentees usually indicate multiple sales of the same parcel (Re-issues) or Overlapping parcels. See this Township's Index for an explanation of these and other circumstances that might explain "odd" groupings of Patentees on this map.

Map Parcels

Section 3

Lots-Sec. 3
----
2 PRESTON, David 1869
3 HARPER, John L [98]1874
4 LOVEJOY, Allen P 1872

HARPER [98] John L 1874
HALL Frederick 1883
ALLEN [6] William N 1888
HARPER [98] John L 1874
HALL Frederick 1883
LOVEJOY Allen P 1872
PILLSBURY Oliver P 1884
WYLIE Daniel B 1883
HALL Frederick 1883

Section 2

HALL Frederick 1883
WYLIE Daniel B 1883
WYLIE Daniel B 1883
BROOKS Virgil 1886

Section 1

LOVEJOY Allen P 1872
LOVEJOY Allen P 1872
LOVEJOY Allen P 1872
HALL Frederick 1883
WYLIE [172] Daniel B 1883
HARRINGTON [103] Charles A 1872
HALL Frederick 1883
LOVEJOY Allen P 1872
BROOKS Virgil 1886
RYAN Michael 1898
HALL Frederick 1883

Section 10

HARPER [98] John L 1874
PRESTON David 1869

Section 11

COOK Grant 1899
COOK Grant 1899
HALL Frederick 1883
BROOKS Virgil 1886
LIBBEY D L 1889
HARPER [98] John L 1874

Section 12

RUST William A 1872
HALL Frederick 1883
HALL Frederick 1883
GRISWOLD Frank 1905
PILLSBURY Oliver P 1884
LIBBEY D L 1889
TOWNSEND Evan 1873
HALL Theadore 1912
PILLSBURY Oliver P 1884
BROOKS Virgil 1886
HALL Frederick 1883

Section 15

Lots-Sec. 15
----
2 PRESTON, David 1869

RUST William A 1872

Section 14

HALL Frederick 1883
CO Alexander Stewart Lumber 1886
SIMPSON Reuben B 1896
CO Alexander Stewart Lumber 1886

Section 13

BROOKS Virgil 1886
BELANGER Ovid 1902
WYLIE [172] Daniel B 1883
BELANGER Ovid 1902
SIMPSON Reuben B 1896
BELANGER Ovid 1902
BROOKS Virgil 1886
WYLIE [172] Daniel B 1883
HOBART John W 1900
WYLIE [172] Daniel B 1883
WYLIE [172] Daniel B 1883

Section 22

Lots-Sec. 22
----
1 PRESTON, David 1869

RUST William A 1872
HAMILTON [97] Irenus K 1872

Section 23

MALCOLM Elmer G 1901
WASHBURN Ganem W 1872
WASHBURN Ganem W 1872
PATTEN A W 1882

Section 24

HOBART John W 1900
HOBART John W 1900
BREWER Addison P 1888
WATERMAN [168] Leslie J 1884
WATERMAN [168] Leslie J 1884
BREWER Addison P 1888
THOMPSON William E 1902
WYLIE [172] Daniel B 1883
WYLIE [172] Daniel B 1883

Section 27

WASHBURN Ganem W 1872

Section 26

WATERMAN [168] Leslie J 1884
HARRINGTON [103] Charles A 1872
WATERMAN [168] Leslie J 1884
MCPARTLIN John A 1897
WASHBURN Ganem W 1872
WATERMAN [168] Leslie J 1884

Section 25

HASELTINE Charles P 1885
WATERMAN [168] Leslie J 1884
WYLIE [172] Daniel B 1883
MCPARTLIN John A 1897
WATERMAN [168] Leslie J 1884
WYLIE [172] Daniel B 1883
BARNETT [14] E D 1884
MCPARTLIN John A 1897
WATERMAN [168] Leslie J 1884
RUST William A 1872
CLARK [45] James G 1878

Section 34

RUST William A 1872

Section 35

PATTEN A W 1882
RUST William A 1872
LAIRD [127] William H 1884

Section 36

RUST William A 1872
RUST William A 1872
WYLIE [172] Daniel B 1883

Legend

——— Patent Boundary

▬▬▬ Section Boundary

No Patents Found (or Outside County)

1., 2., 3., ... Lot Numbers (when beside a name)

[ ] Group Number (see Appendix "C")

Scale: Section = 1 mile X 1 mile (generally, with some exceptions)

Road Map

T42-N R9-E
4th PM - 1831 MN/WI

Map Group 14

Cities & Towns

None

Cemeteries

None

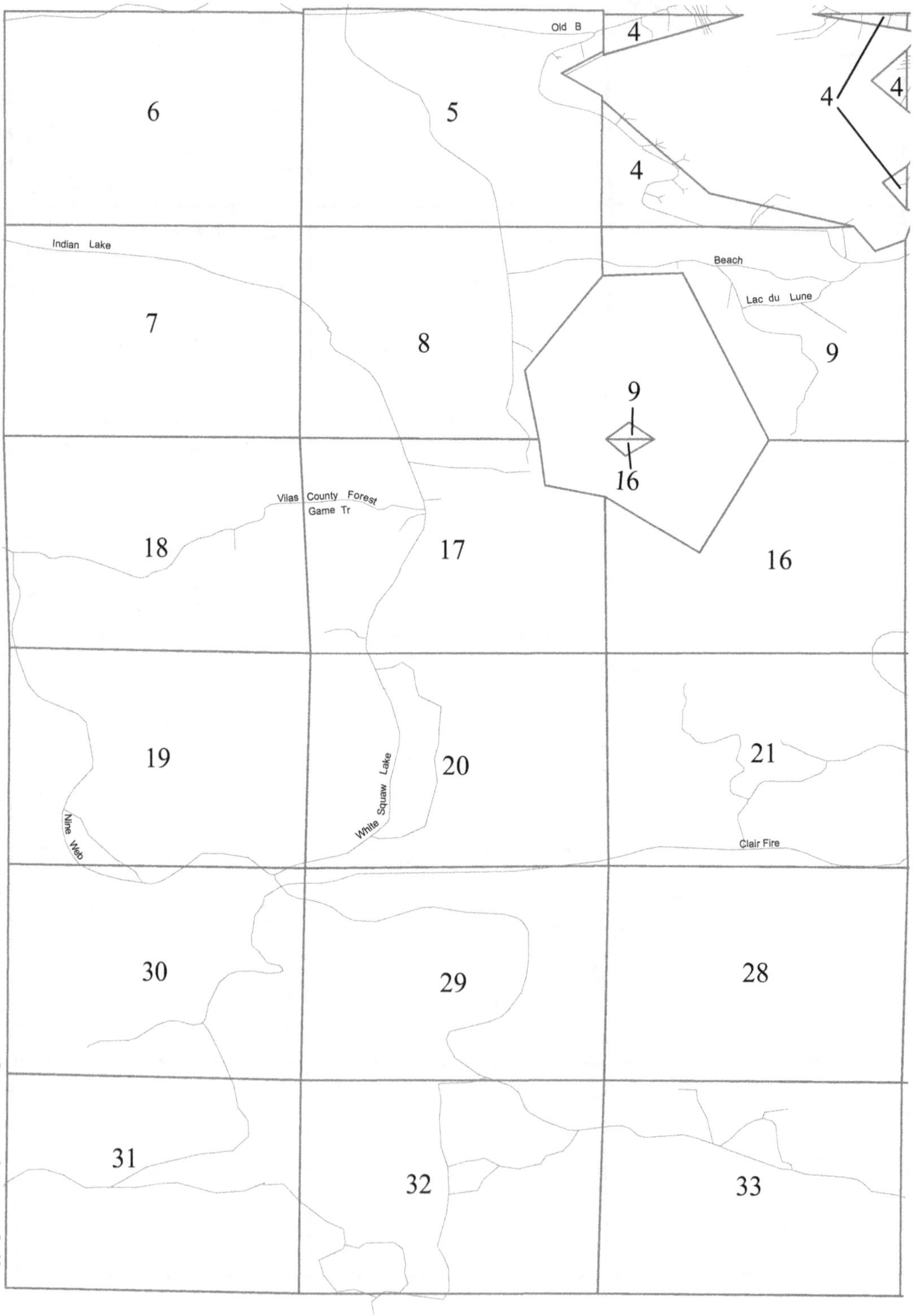

6	5	4
7	8	9
18	17	16
19	20	21
30	29	28
31	32	33

Old B

Beach

Lac du Lune

Indian Lake

Vilas County Forest
Game Tr

9

16

White Squaw Lake

Nine Web

Clair Fire

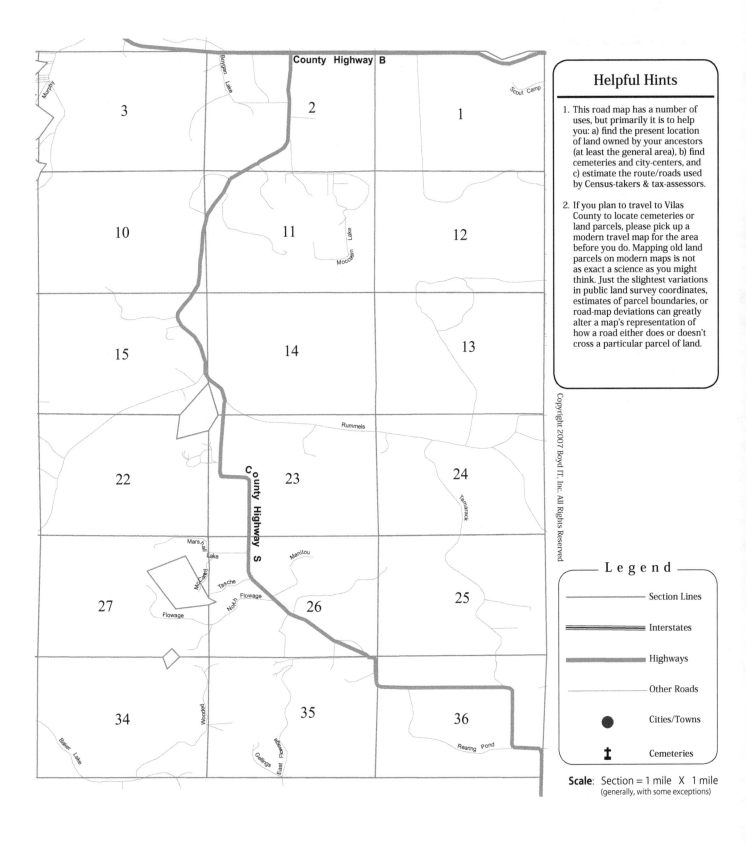

Helpful Hints

1. This road map has a number of uses, but primarily it is to help you: a) find the present location of land owned by your ancestors (at least the general area), b) find cemeteries and city-centers, and c) estimate the route/roads used by Census-takers & tax-assessors.

2. If you plan to travel to Vilas County to locate cemeteries or land parcels, please pick up a modern travel map for the area before you do. Mapping old land parcels on modern maps is not as exact a science as you might think. Just the slightest variations in public land survey coordinates, estimates of parcel boundaries, or road-map deviations can greatly alter a map's representation of how a road either does or doesn't cross a particular parcel of land.

Legend

———————	Section Lines
═══════	Interstates
━━━━━━━	Highways
———————	Other Roads
●	Cities/Towns
✝	Cemeteries

Scale: Section = 1 mile X 1 mile
(generally, with some exceptions)

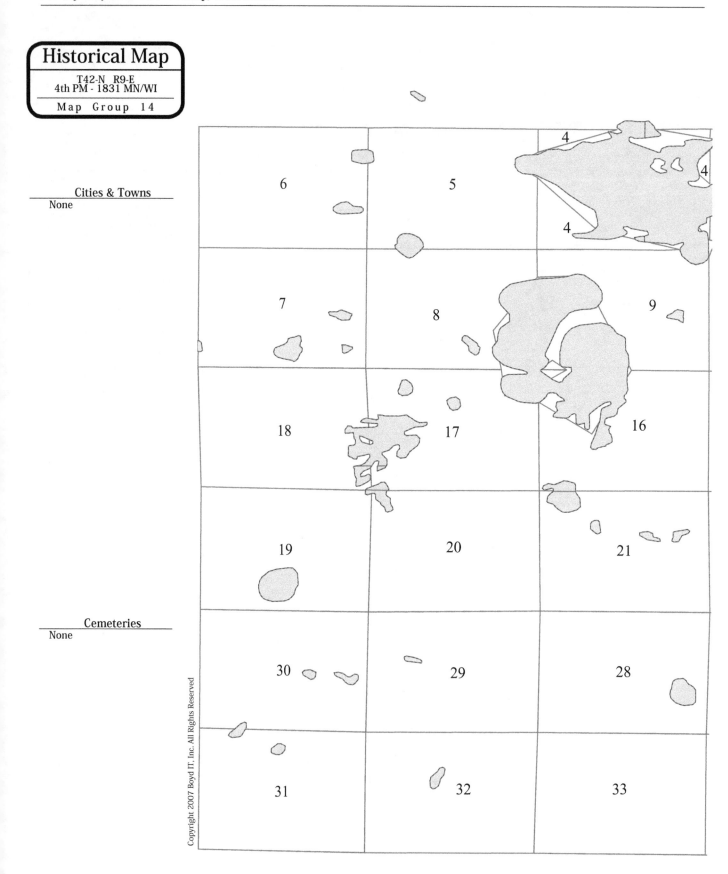

Historical Map

T42-N R9-E
4th PM - 1831 MN/WI

Map Group 14

Cities & Towns
None

Cemeteries
None

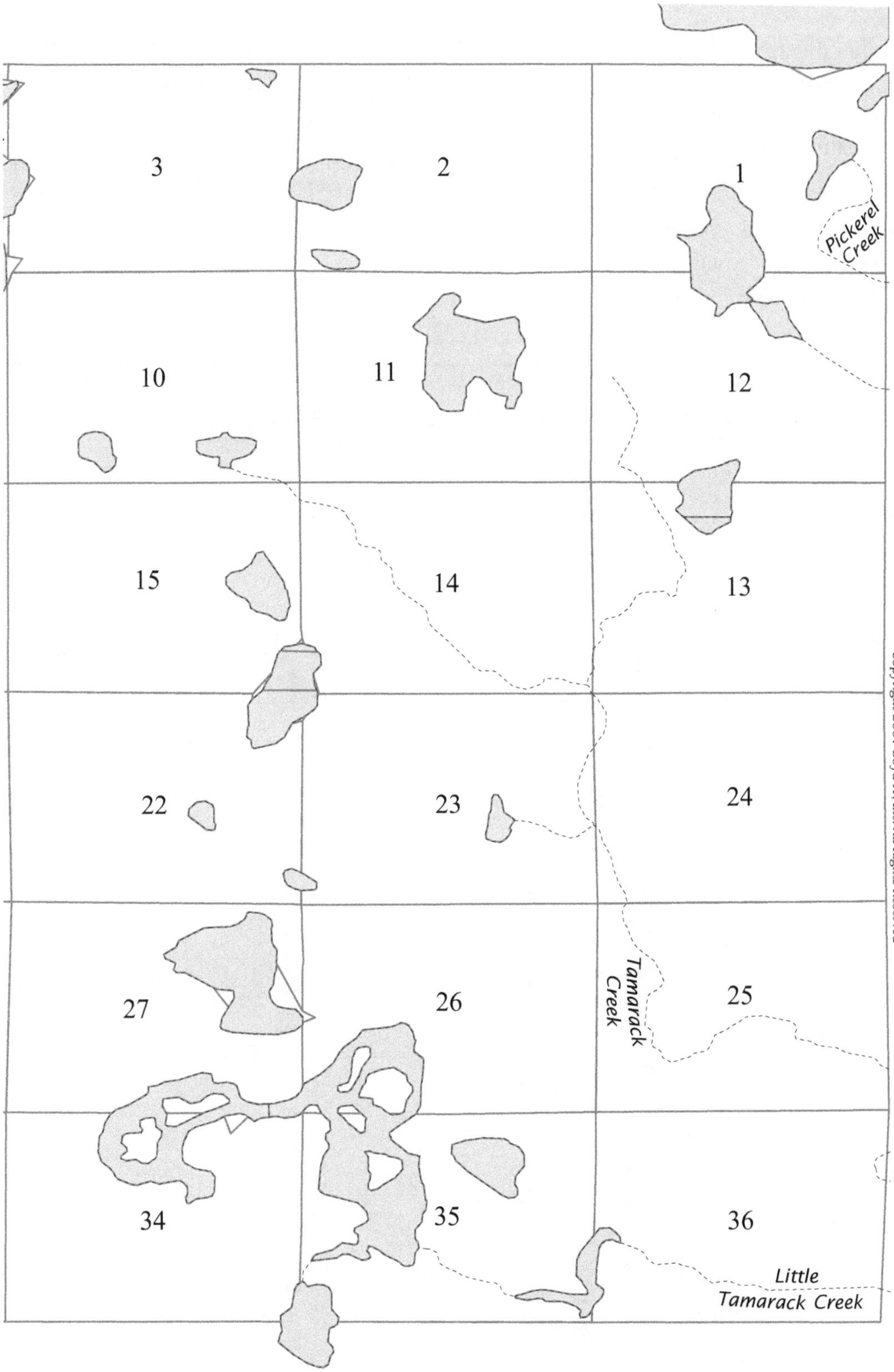
3
2
1
Pickerel Creek
10
11
12
15
14
13
22
23
24
27
26
Tamarack Creek
25
34
35
36
Little Tamarack Creek

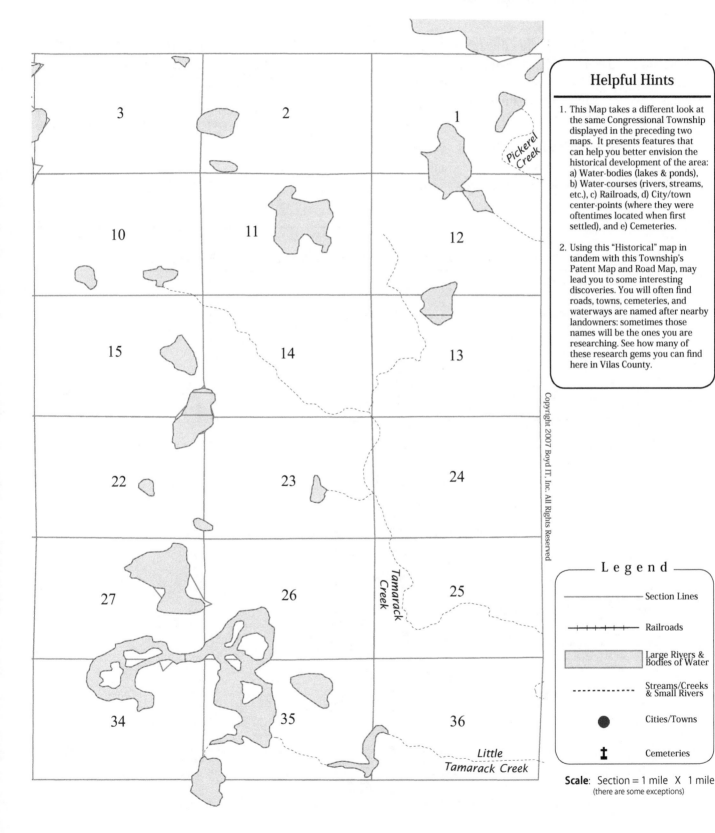

Helpful Hints

1. This Map takes a different look at the same Congressional Township displayed in the preceding two maps. It presents features that can help you better envision the historical development of the area: a) Water-bodies (lakes & ponds), b) Water-courses (rivers, streams, etc.), c) Railroads, d) City/town center-points (where they were oftentimes located when first settled), and e) Cemeteries.
2. Using this "Historical" map in tandem with this Township's Patent Map and Road Map, may lead you to some interesting discoveries. You will often find roads, towns, cemeteries, and waterways are named after nearby landowners: sometimes those names will be the ones you are researching. See how many of these research gems you can find here in Vilas County.

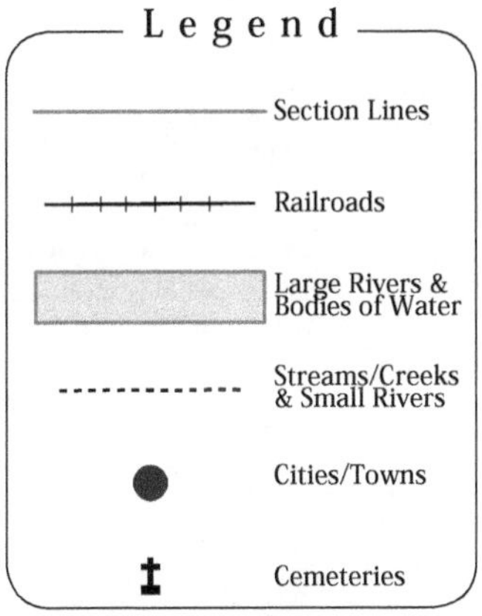
Legend
Section Lines
Railroads
Large Rivers & Bodies of Water
Streams/Creeks & Small Rivers
Cities/Towns
Cemeteries

Scale: Section = 1 mile X 1 mile
(there are some exceptions)

Map Group 15: Index to Land Patents

Township 42-North Range 10-East (4th PM - 1831 MN/WI)

After you locate an individual in this Index, take note of the Section and Section Part then proceed to the Land Patent map on the pages immediately following. You should have no difficulty locating the corresponding parcel of land.

The "For More Info" Column will lead you to more information about the underlying Patents. See the *Legend* at right, and the "How to Use this Book" chapter, for more information.

```
                        LEGEND
              "For More Info . . . " column
A = Authority (Legislative Act, See Appendix "A")
B = Block or Lot (location in Section unknown)
C = Cancelled Patent
F = Fractional Section
G = Group  (Multi-Patentee Patent, see Appendix "C")
V = Overlaps another Parcel
R = Re-Issued (Parcel patented more than once)

(A & G items require you to look in the Appendixes referred
to above. All other Letter-designations followed by a number
require you to locate line-items in this index that possess
the ID number found after the letter).
```

ID	Individual in Patent	Sec.	Sec. Part	Date Issued	Other Counties	For More Info . . .
2851	ALEXANDER, Walter	18	SWSW	1886-08-10		A1 F
2852	" "	19	SENW	1886-08-10		A1
2794	ANDERSON, Mary J	8	4	1885-01-15		A1
2684	BACKMAN, Charles O	19	NWSW	1904-01-11		A1 F
2740	BAIN, George A	13	NESE	1902-12-30		A3
2741	" "	13	SENE	1902-12-30		A3
2742	" "	13	W½SE	1902-12-30		A3
2673	BAKER, Cary	19	NENW	1901-05-08		A1
2674	" "	27	SENE	1903-12-31		A1
2820	BEACH, Orville	4	SWNE	1890-07-15		A1 G19
2821	" "	4	SWSE	1890-07-15		A1 G19
2791	BERG, Karl August	3	NWNE	1911-01-16		A3 F
2746	BLISH, George M	22	SENW	1903-04-20		A1
2766	BRESNAN, John	15	NWNW	1903-12-31		A1
2767	" "	15	SENW	1904-12-12		A1
2637	BROWN, A W	32	NENE	1885-05-20		A1 G30
2657	BROWN, Anderson W	20	S½SE	1883-04-20		A1 G32
2659	" "	28	NESW	1883-04-20		A1 G32
2660	" "	28	NWNW	1883-04-20		A1 G32
2661	" "	29	1	1883-04-20		A1 G32
2662	" "	29	7	1883-04-20		A1 G32
2663	" "	29	8	1883-04-20		A1 G32
2664	" "	29	NWNW	1883-04-20		A1 G32
2665	" "	30	2	1883-04-20		A1 G32
2667	" "	32	NWNE	1883-04-20		A1 G32
2668	" "	33	NWNE	1883-04-20		A1 G32
2669	" "	35	NWSE	1883-04-20		A1 G32
2670	" "	35	SENW	1883-04-20		A1 G32
2658	" "	28	NESE	1883-09-10		A1 G32
2666	" "	32	NESE	1883-09-10		A1 G32
2656	" "	35	NWNW	1885-01-15		A1 G31
2637	BROWN, E O	32	NENE	1885-05-20		A1 G30
2656	BROWN, Edward O	35	NWNW	1885-01-15		A1 G31
2637	BROWN, W E	32	NENE	1885-05-20		A1 G30
2657	BROWN, Webster E	20	S½SE	1883-04-20		A1 G32
2659	" "	28	NESW	1883-04-20		A1 G32
2660	" "	28	NWNW	1883-04-20		A1 G32
2661	" "	29	1	1883-04-20		A1 G32
2662	" "	29	7	1883-04-20		A1 G32
2663	" "	29	8	1883-04-20		A1 G32
2664	" "	29	NWNW	1883-04-20		A1 G32
2665	" "	30	2	1883-04-20		A1 G32
2667	" "	32	NWNE	1883-04-20		A1 G32
2668	" "	33	NWNE	1883-04-20		A1 G32
2669	" "	35	NWSE	1883-04-20		A1 G32
2670	" "	35	SENW	1883-04-20		A1 G32

ID	Individual in Patent	Sec.	Sec. Part	Date Issued	Other Counties	For More Info . . .
2658	BROWN, Webster E (Cont'd)	28	NESE	1883-09-10		A1 G32
2666	" "	32	NESE	1883-09-10		A1 G32
2656	" "	35	NWNW	1885-01-15		A1 G31
2768	BUCKSTAFF, John	3	NENW	1873-11-15		A1
2769	" "	3	NESW	1873-11-15		A1
2770	" "	3	NWSE	1873-11-15		A1
2771	" "	3	S½NE	1873-11-15		A1
2772	" "	20	SESW	1884-06-30		A1 G35
2773	" "	29	2	1884-06-30		A1 G35
2778	" "	29	E½SW	1884-06-30		A1 G35
2779	" "	29	NENW	1884-06-30		A1 G35
2774	" "	29	3	1885-11-25		A1 G35
2775	" "	29	4	1885-11-25		A1 G35
2776	" "	29	5	1885-11-25		A1 G35
2777	" "	29	6	1885-11-25		A1 G35
2780	" "	29	NWNE	1885-11-25		A1 G35
2781	" "	32	E½NW	1885-11-25		A1 G35
2772	CHASE, James	20	SESW	1884-06-30		A1 G35
2773	" "	29	2	1884-06-30		A1 G35
2778	" "	29	E½SW	1884-06-30		A1 G35
2779	" "	29	NENW	1884-06-30		A1 G35
2774	" "	29	3	1885-11-25		A1 G35
2775	" "	29	4	1885-11-25		A1 G35
2776	" "	29	5	1885-11-25		A1 G35
2777	" "	29	6	1885-11-25		A1 G35
2780	" "	29	NWNE	1885-11-25		A1 G35
2781	" "	32	E½NW	1885-11-25		A1 G35
2687	CO, Cutler And Savidge Lumber	5	1	1885-01-15		A1
2688	" "	5	2	1885-01-15		A1
2689	" "	5	N½SE	1885-01-15		A1
2690	" "	5	S½NE	1885-01-15		A1
2691	" "	8	2	1885-01-15		A1
2692	" "	8	3	1885-01-15		A1
2693	" "	8	5	1885-01-15		A1
2694	" "	8	S½NE	1885-01-15		A1
2695	" "	8	SESE	1885-01-15		A1
2696	" "	9	6	1885-01-15		A1
2854	COLE, William E	19	S½SE	1883-09-15		A1 G52
2855	" "	33	NENE	1883-09-15		A1 G52
2834	COMPANY, T B Scott Lumber	32	SWSE	1885-07-13		A1
2833	" "	32	NWSW	1885-09-10		A1
2848	DAWLEY, W H	20	SENW	1884-06-30		A1 G68
2847	" "	30	3	1884-06-30		A1 G69
2671	DISHAW, Angus	23	NWNW	1902-12-30		A3
2682	DUNBAR, Charles F	1	N½NW	1883-09-15		A1
2683	" "	1	NENE	1883-09-15		A1
2782	DUSSAULT, John	35	NESE	1916-08-14		A1
2848	EDWARDS, Nathaniel M	20	SENW	1884-06-30		A1 G68
2749	FITZGERALD, Henry	10	SESW	1898-12-12		A3
2750	" "	15	NENW	1898-12-12		A3
2751	" "	15	W½NE	1898-12-12		A3
2748	FREEMAN, H G	17	SESE	1888-07-10		A1
2764	GILLETT, Joel D	20	NWSW	1885-05-20		A1
2752	GOODWILL, Henry	22	W½SE	1901-05-08		A1
2753	" "	27	N½NE	1901-05-08		A1
2732	GUSE, Friedrich	3	S½SW	1900-06-11		A3
2733	" "	3	SWSE	1900-06-11		A3
2734	" "	4	SESE	1900-06-11		A3
2654	HAGSTROM, Amanda	25	S½NE	1917-02-07		A3
2655	" "	25	S½NW	1917-02-07		A3
2719	HALL, Frederick	17	E½NE	1883-09-15		A1
2720	" "	17	NESE	1883-09-15		A1
2721	" "	18	NWSW	1883-09-15		A1
2722	" "	4	NWSE	1883-09-15		A1
2723	" "	5	NENW	1883-09-15		A1
2724	" "	7	NWSW	1883-09-15		A1
2679	HARRINGTON, Charles A	6	SWSW	1872-11-01		A1 G103
2680	" "	7	SWNW	1872-11-01		A1 G103
2675	" "	1	NESW	1882-05-20		A1 G104
2676	" "	1	NWNE	1882-05-20		A1 G104
2677	" "	1	S½SW	1882-05-20		A1 G104
2678	" "	1	SWNW	1882-05-20		A1 G104
2716	HAYWARD, Enos F	27	S½SW	1909-09-02		A3

ID	Individual in Patent	Sec.	Sec. Part	Date Issued	Other Counties	For More Info . . .
2672	HEINEMANN, Benjamin	30	1	1889-05-31		A1
2795	HOBART, Mary J	15	NWSW	1900-06-11		A1
2754	HOWLETT, Henry	32	NESW	1904-12-12		A1
2755	" "	32	NWSE	1904-12-12		A1
2756	" "	32	S½SW	1904-12-12		A1
2760	HUGHES, James	30	N½SW	1898-02-18		A1
2830	JOHNSTON, Stevn	21	SESE	1905-03-30		A3
2831	" "	22	SWSW	1905-03-30		A3
2832	" "	28	N½NE	1905-03-30		A3
2713	KOHL, Emma	7	1	1884-06-30		A1 G124
2714	" "	7	2	1884-06-30		A1 G124
2715	" "	7	NESW	1884-06-30		A1 G124
2713	KOHL, H A	7	1	1884-06-30		A1 G124
2714	" "	7	2	1884-06-30		A1 G124
2715	" "	7	NESW	1884-06-30		A1 G124
2761	LANGILL, James	11	E½SW	1898-11-11		A1
2762	" "	20	SWSW	1898-11-11		A1
2763	" "	32	W½NW	1899-05-05		A1
2820	LIBBEY, L D	4	SWNE	1890-07-15		A1 G19
2821	" "	4	SWSE	1890-07-15		A1 G19
2638	LOVEJOY, Allen P	11	E½SE	1872-02-20		A1
2639	" "	11	NENW	1872-02-20		A1
2640	" "	11	SENE	1872-02-20		A1
2641	" "	17	SWNE	1872-02-20		A1
2642	" "	17	W½SE	1872-02-20		A1
2643	" "	19	SENE	1872-02-20		A1
2647	" "	6	N½SW	1872-02-20		A1
2649	" "	6	S½NE	1872-02-20		A1
2650	" "	6	S½NW	1872-02-20		A1
2651	" "	6	SESW	1872-02-20		A1
2652	" "	7	3	1872-02-20		A1
2653	" "	7	N½NW	1872-02-20		A1
2644	" "	2	NENW	1872-05-10		A1
2645	" "	2	NWNE	1872-05-10		A1
2646	" "	3	NENE	1872-05-10		A1
2648	" "	6	NWSE	1872-07-01		A1
2681	MATHER, Charles B	3	SESE	1901-12-12		A1
2718	MAYO, Fred	1	E½SE	1909-03-29		A1
2765	MEADE, Joel	11	W½SE	1873-06-10		A1 G142
2849	MILLER, W H	18	1	1889-05-09		A1
2850	" "	18	7	1889-05-09		A1
2796	MORAN, Michael	10	W½SW	1901-11-22		A1
2712	OSTERBERG, Edward	25	E½SE	1910-09-26		A3
2824	OTTO, Rudolph	4	NENW	1889-03-28		A1
2823	" "	3	SENW	1890-07-15		A1
2825	" "	4	NESW	1890-07-15		A1
2798	PILLSBURY, Oliver P	11	NENE	1884-06-30		A1
2799	" "	11	SENW	1884-06-30		A1
2800	" "	11	SWNE	1884-06-30		A1
2801	" "	15	SWNW	1884-06-30		A1
2802	" "	2	SWNW	1884-06-30		A1
2803	" "	21	N½SE	1884-06-30		A1
2804	" "	21	S½SW	1884-06-30		A1
2805	" "	21	SENE	1884-06-30		A1
2806	" "	21	SWSE	1884-06-30		A1
2807	" "	22	SWNW	1884-06-30		A1
2808	" "	27	S½NW	1884-06-30		A1
2809	" "	27	SWNE	1884-06-30		A1
2810	" "	29	NENE	1884-06-30		A1
2811	" "	3	NESE	1884-06-30		A1
2812	" "	3	NWSW	1884-06-30		A1
2813	" "	4	NENE	1884-06-30		A1
2814	" "	4	NESE	1884-06-30		A1
2815	" "	4	NWSW	1884-06-30		A1
2816	" "	4	S½SW	1884-06-30		A1
2817	" "	4	W½NW	1884-06-30		A1
2818	" "	5	SENW	1884-06-30		A1
2819	" "	9	NENW	1884-06-30		A1
2785	PROCTOR, John	15	W½SE	1896-08-04		A1
2679	REEVE, Thomas T	6	SWSW	1872-11-01		A1 G103
2680	" "	7	SWNW	1872-11-01		A1 G103
2725	RHINELANDER, Frederick W	11	W½NW	1884-06-30		A1
2726	" "	11	W½SW	1884-06-30		A1

ID	Individual in Patent	Sec.	Sec. Part	Date Issued	Other Counties	For More Info . . .
2727	RHINELANDER, Frederick W (Cont'd)	15	E½NE	1884-06-30		A1
2728	"	"	15	E½SE	1884-06-30		A1
2729	"	"	22	E½SW	1884-06-30		A1
2730	"	"	22	W½NE	1884-06-30		A1
2731	"	"	27	N½NW	1884-06-30		A1
2765	RIPLEY, Sylvanus	11	W½SE	1873-06-10		A1 G142
2679	ROE, Gilbert W	6	SWSW	1872-11-01		A1 G103
2680	"	"	7	SWNW	1872-11-01		A1 G103
2675	"	"	1	NESW	1882-05-20		A1 G104
2676	"	"	1	NWNE	1882-05-20		A1 G104
2677	"	"	1	S½SW	1882-05-20		A1 G104
2678	"	"	1	SWNW	1882-05-20		A1 G104
2747	"	"	1	NWSE	1883-06-07		A1
2797	RYAN, Michael	7	SWSW	1898-05-10		A1
2717	SANDERS, Frank D	22	NWSW	1903-04-20		A1
2793	SCHERIBEL, Louisa R	20	NESW	1908-09-17		A1
2786	SCOTT, John	9	2	1889-03-28		A1 R2787
2787	"	"	9	2	1889-03-28		A1 R2786
2788	"	"	9	SENE	1889-03-28		A1
2789	"	"	9	W½NE	1889-03-28		A1 R2790
2790	"	"	9	W½NE	1889-03-28		A1 R2789
2839	SCOTT, Thomas B	33	N½SW	1883-04-20		A1
2840	"	"	33	SENW	1883-04-20		A1
2841	"	"	33	SWNE	1883-04-20		A1
2842	"	"	33	SWSW	1883-04-20		A1
2835	"	"	13	NENE	1883-09-15		A1
2836	"	"	20	NESE	1883-09-15		A1
2837	"	"	21	NWSW	1883-09-15		A1
2838	"	"	27	NWSW	1883-09-15		A1
2843	"	"	9	3	1883-09-15		A1
2844	"	"	9	4	1883-09-15		A1
2845	"	"	9	5	1883-09-15		A1
2846	"	"	9	E½SE	1883-09-15		A1
2822	SHERIDAN, Peter	13	W½NW	1884-06-30		A1
2848	SHERMAN, F M	20	SENW	1884-06-30		A1 G68
2847	"	"	30	3	1884-06-30		A1 G69
2636	SMITH, A D	32	SENE	1890-07-15		A1
2757	STEINBERG, Henry	2	NWNW	1872-07-01		A1 G167
2757	STEINBERG, Herman	2	NWNW	1872-07-01		A1 G167
2758	STEINMETZ, Henry	32	SWNE	1917-02-07		A3
2743	STREETER, George B	20	NWSE	1889-04-04		A1
2744	"	"	29	SENW	1889-04-04		A1
2745	"	"	30	E½NW	1889-04-04		A1
2783	THAYER, John O	28	NWSE	1884-06-30		A1
2784	"	"	32	SESE	1884-06-30		A1
2826	THOMPSON, Samuel	13	E½NW	1892-02-23		A1
2827	"	13	NWNE	1892-02-23		A1
2759	TOLMAN, James B	25	SWSE	1872-11-01		A1
2792	WADE, L D	27	NESW	1889-04-04		A1
2828	WALTERS, Samuel	15	E½SW	1895-06-04		A1
2829	"	"	22	N½NW	1895-06-04		A1
2735	WASHBURN, Ganem W	17	1	1872-11-01		A1
2736	"	"	17	2	1872-11-01		A1
2737	"	"	20	NENW	1872-11-01		A1
2738	"	"	20	NWNE	1872-11-01		A1
2739	"	"	6	N½NW	1872-11-01		A1
2685	WIEGAND, Conrad	33	E½SE	1900-06-28		A3
2686	"	33	SENE	1900-06-28		A3
2854	WILLIAMS, Orin T	19	S½SE	1883-09-15		A1 G52
2855	"	"	33	NENE	1883-09-15		A1 G52
2853	WINTON, William C	19	NWNW	1886-03-01		A1 F
2698	WYLIE, Daniel B	1	S½NE	1883-09-15		A1 G172
2699	"	"	1	SENW	1883-09-15		A1 G172
2700	"	"	1	SWSE	1883-09-15		A1 G172
2701	"	"	19	SWSW	1883-09-15		A1 G172
2697	"	"	2	NENE	1883-09-15		A1
2702	"	"	3	W½NW	1883-09-15		A1 G172
2703	"	"	30	NWNW	1883-09-15		A1 G172
2704	"	"	30	SWNW	1883-09-15		A1 G172
2705	"	"	4	NWNE	1883-09-15		A1 G172
2706	"	"	4	SENE	1883-09-15		A1 G172
2707	"	"	5	W½NW	1883-09-15		A1 G172
2708	"	"	5	W½SW	1883-09-15		A1 G172

ID	Individual in Patent	Sec.	Sec. Part	Date Issued	Other Counties	For More Info . . .
2709	WYLIE, Daniel B (Cont'd)	6	N½NE	1883-09-15		A1 G172
2710	" "	6	NESE	1883-09-15		A1 G172
2711	" "	8	1	1883-09-15		A1 G172
2698	WYLIE, Winfred	1	S½NE	1883-09-15		A1 G172
2699	" "	1	SENW	1883-09-15		A1 G172
2700	" "	1	SWSE	1883-09-15		A1 G172
2701	" "	19	SWSW	1883-09-15		A1 G172
2702	" "	3	W½NW	1883-09-15		A1 G172
2703	" "	30	NWNW	1883-09-15		A1 G172
2704	" "	30	SWNW	1883-09-15		A1 G172
2705	" "	4	NWNE	1883-09-15		A1 G172
2706	" "	4	SENE	1883-09-15		A1 G172
2707	" "	5	W½NW	1883-09-15		A1 G172
2708	" "	5	W½SW	1883-09-15		A1 G172
2709	" "	6	N½NE	1883-09-15		A1 G172
2710	" "	6	NESE	1883-09-15		A1 G172
2711	" "	8	1	1883-09-15		A1 G172

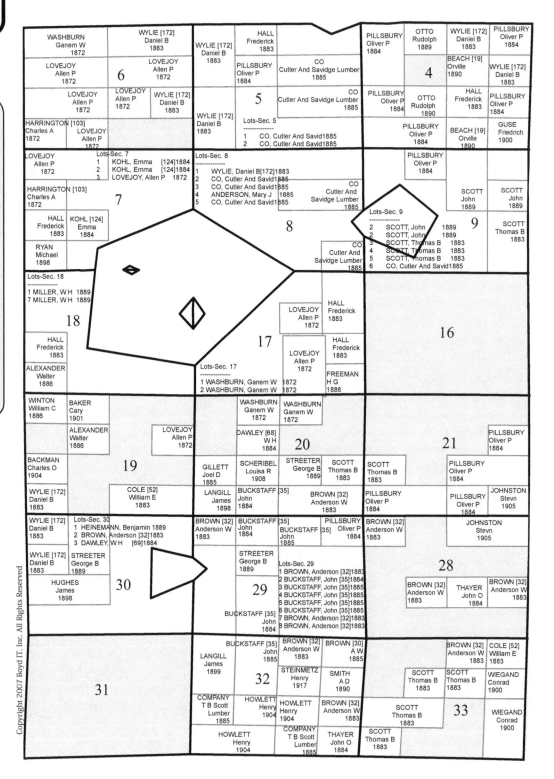

Patent Map

T42-N R10-E
4th PM - 1831 MN/WI

Map Group 15

Township Statistics

Parcels Mapped	:	220
Number of Patents	:	109
Number of Individuals	:	80
Patentees Identified	:	71
Number of Surnames	:	71
Multi-Patentee Parcels	:	57
Oldest Patent Date	:	2/20/1872
Most Recent Patent	:	2/7/1917
Block/Lot Parcels	:	31
Parcels Re - Issued	:	2
Parcels that Overlap	:	0
Cities and Towns	:	0
Cemeteries	:	1

WYLIE [172] Daniel B 1883	BUCKSTAFF John 1873	BERG Karl August 1911	LOVEJOY Allen P 1872	STEINBERG [167] Henry 1872	LOVEJOY Allen P 1872	LOVEJOY Allen P 1872	WYLIE Daniel B 1883	DUNBAR Charles F 1883	HARRINGTON [104] Charles A 1882	DUNBAR Charles F 1883

Section 3 — OTTO Rudolph 1890 · BUCKSTAFF John 1873 · PILLSBURY Oliver P 1884

Section 2

Section 1 — HARRINGTON [104] Charles A 1882 · WYLIE [172] Daniel B 1883 · WYLIE [172] Daniel B 1883 · HARRINGTON [104] Charles A 1882 · ROE Gilbert W 1883 · MAYO Fred 1909 · HARRINGTON [104] Charles A 1882 · WYLIE [172] Daniel B 1883

PILLSBURY Oliver P 1884 · BUCKSTAFF John 1873 · BUCKSTAFF John 1873 · PILLSBURY Oliver P 1884

GUSE Friedrich 1900 · GUSE Friedrich 1900 · MATHER Charles B 1901

Section 10 — MORAN Michael 1901 · FITZGERALD Henry 1898

Section 11 — RHINELANDER Frederick W 1884 · LOVEJOY Allen P 1872 · PILLSBURY Oliver P 1884 · PILLSBURY Oliver P 1884 · PILLSBURY Oliver P 1884 · LOVEJOY Allen P 1872 · LANGILL James 1898 · MEADE [142] Joel 1873 · LOVEJOY Allen P 1872 · RHINELANDER Frederick W 1884

Section 12

Section 15 — BRESNAN John 1903 · FITZGERALD Henry 1898 · RHINELANDER Frederick W 1884 · PILLSBURY Oliver P 1884 · BRESNAN John 1904 · FITZGERALD Henry 1898 · HOBART Mary J 1900 · WALTERS Samuel 1895 · PROCTOR John 1896 · RHINELANDER Frederick W 1884

Section 14

Section 13 — SHERIDAN Peter 1884 · THOMPSON Samuel 1892 · THOMPSON Samuel 1892 · SCOTT Thomas B 1883 · BAIN George A 1902 · BAIN George A 1902 · BAIN George A 1902

Section 22 — WALTERS Samuel 1895 · PILLSBURY Oliver P 1884 · BLISH George M 1903 · RHINELANDER Frederick W 1884 · SANDERS Frank D 1903 · GOODWILL Henry 1901 · JOHNSTON Stevn 1905 · RHINELANDER Frederick W 1884

Section 23 — DISHAW Angus 1902

Section 24

Section 27 — RHINELANDER Frederick W 1884 · GOODWILL Henry 1901 · PILLSBURY Oliver P 1884 · PILLSBURY Oliver P 1884 · BAKER Cary 1903 · SCOTT Thomas B 1883 · WADE L D 1889 · HAYWARD Enos F 1909

Section 26

Section 25 — HAGSTROM Amanda 1917 · HAGSTROM Amanda 1917 · OSTERBERG Edward 1910 · TOLMAN James B 1872

Section 34

Section 35 — BROWN [31] Anderson W 1885 · BROWN [32] Anderson W 1883 · BROWN [32] Anderson W 1883 · DUSSAULT John 1916

Section 36

Helpful Hints

1. This Map's INDEX can be found on the preceding pages.

2. Refer to Map "C" to see where this Township lies within Vilas County, Wisconsin.

3. Numbers within square brackets [ ] denote a multi-patentee land parcel (multi-owner). Refer to Appendix "C" for a full list of members in this group.

4. Areas that look to be crowded with Patentees usually indicate multiple sales of the same parcel (Re-issues) or Overlapping parcels. See this Township's Index for an explanation of these and other circumstances that might explain "odd" groupings of Patentees on this map.

Legend

———— Patent Boundary

▬▬▬▬ Section Boundary

No Patents Found (or Outside County)

1., 2., 3., ... Lot Numbers (when beside a name)

[ ] Group Number (see Appendix "C")

Scale: Section = 1 mile X 1 mile (generally, with some exceptions)

Road Map

T42-N R10-E
4th PM - 1831 MN/WI

Map Group 15

Cities & Towns
None

Cemeteries
Oak Hill Cemetery

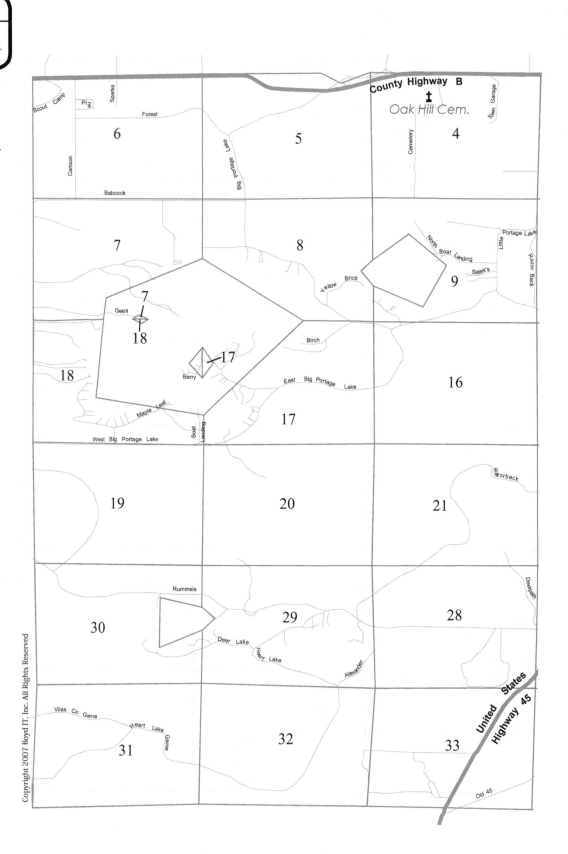

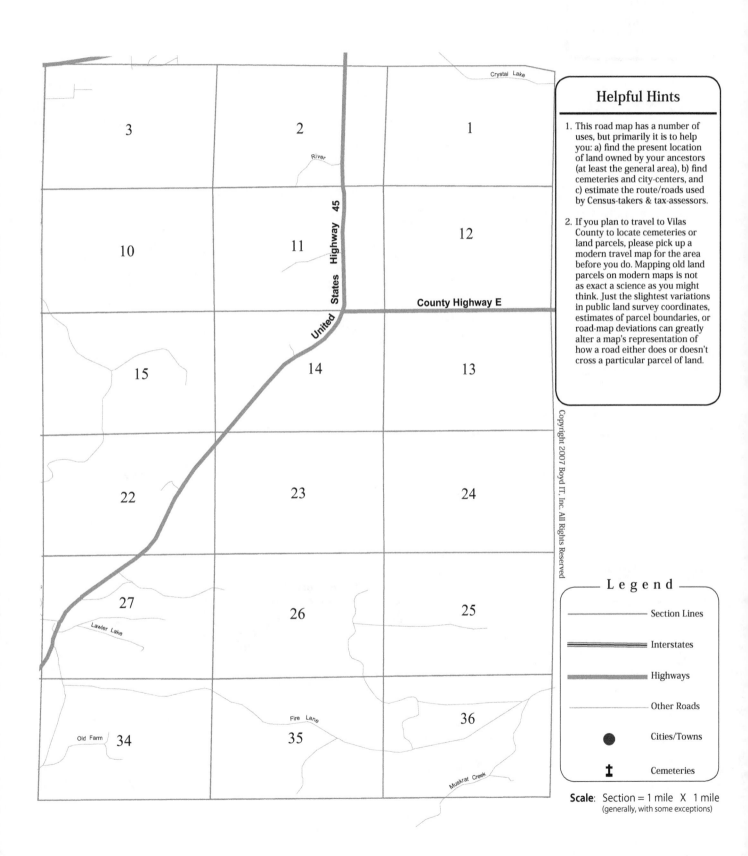

Helpful Hints

1. This road map has a number of uses, but primarily it is to help you: a) find the present location of land owned by your ancestors (at least the general area), b) find cemeteries and city-centers, and c) estimate the route/roads used by Census-takers & tax-assessors.

2. If you plan to travel to Vilas County to locate cemeteries or land parcels, please pick up a modern travel map for the area before you do. Mapping old land parcels on modern maps is not as exact a science as you might think. Just the slightest variations in public land survey coordinates, estimates of parcel boundaries, or road-map deviations can greatly alter a map's representation of how a road either does or doesn't cross a particular parcel of land.

L e g e n d

————	Section Lines
═══════	Interstates
▬▬▬▬	Highways
————	Other Roads
●	Cities/Towns
✝	Cemeteries

Scale: Section = 1 mile X 1 mile
(generally, with some exceptions)

Historical Map

T42-N R10-E
4th PM - 1831 MN/WI

Map Group 15

<u>Cities & Towns</u>
None

<u>Cemeteries</u>
Oak Hill Cemetery

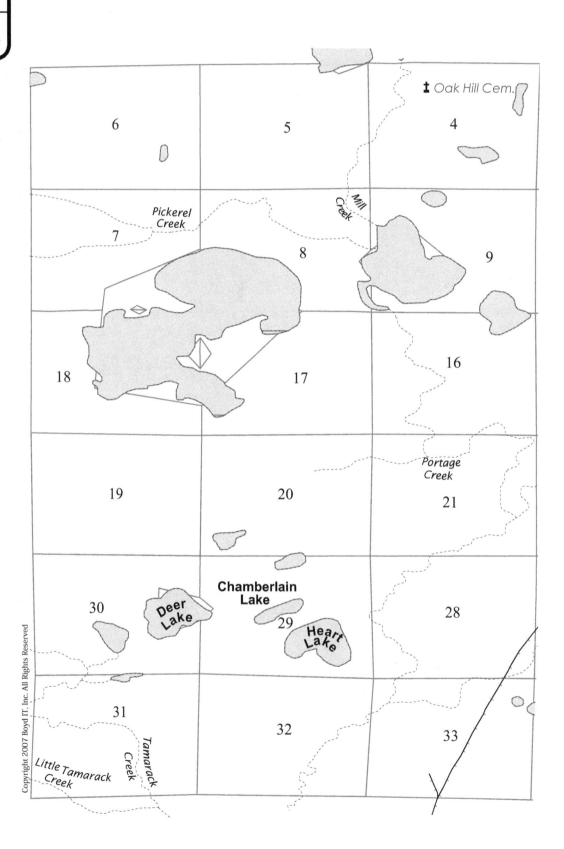

✝ *Oak Hill Cem.*

6	5	4
7	8	9
18	17	16
19	20	21
30	29	28
31	32	33

Pickerel Creek

Mill Creek

Portage Creek

Chamberlain Lake

Deer Lake

Heart Lake

Tamarack Creek

Little Tamarack Creek

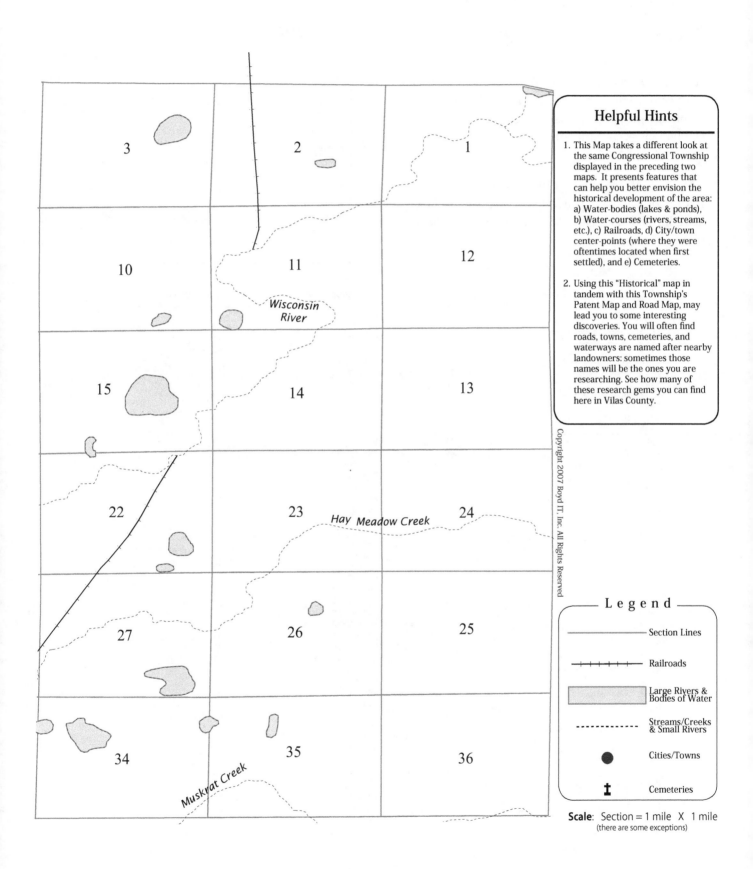

Helpful Hints

1. This Map takes a different look at the same Congressional Township displayed in the preceding two maps. It presents features that can help you better envision the historical development of the area: a) Water-bodies (lakes & ponds), b) Water-courses (rivers, streams, etc.), c) Railroads, d) City/town center-points (where they were oftentimes located when first settled), and e) Cemeteries.

2. Using this "Historical" map in tandem with this Township's Patent Map and Road Map, may lead you to some interesting discoveries. You will often find roads, towns, cemeteries, and waterways are named after nearby landowners: sometimes those names will be the ones you are researching. See how many of these research gems you can find here in Vilas County.

Legend

————	Section Lines
—+—+—+—	Railroads
� bar	Large Rivers & Bodies of Water
- - - - - - -	Streams/Creeks & Small Rivers
●	Cities/Towns
⚏	Cemeteries

Scale: Section = 1 mile X 1 mile
(there are some exceptions)

Map Group 16: Index to Land Patents

Township 42-North Range 11-East (4th PM - 1831 MN/WI)

After you locate an individual in this Index, take note of the Section and Section Part then proceed to the Land Patent map on the pages immediately following. You should have no difficulty locating the corresponding parcel of land.

The "For More Info" Column will lead you to more information about the underlying Patents. See the *Legend* at right, and the "How to Use this Book" chapter, for more information.

```
                        LEGEND
              "For More Info . . . " column
A = Authority (Legislative Act, See Appendix "A")
B = Block or Lot (location in Section unknown)
C = Cancelled Patent
F = Fractional Section
G = Group  (Multi-Patentee Patent, see Appendix "C")
V = Overlaps another Parcel
R = Re-Issued (Parcel patented more than once)

(A & G items require you to look in the Appendixes referred
to above. All other Letter-designations followed by a number
require you to locate line-items in this index that possess
the ID number found after the letter).
```

ID	Individual in Patent	Sec.	Sec. Part	Date Issued	Other Counties	For More Info . . .
2953	AYERS, Ranient	19	2	1872-11-01		A1 G11
2954	" "	21	SESW	1872-11-01		A1 G11
2955	" "	21	SWSE	1872-11-01		A1 G11
2956	" "	29	NENE	1872-11-01		A1 G11
2901	BALKE, George Burt	33	SWNW	1911-04-10		A1
2947	BERGSTROM, Olaf	36	S½NW	1906-03-28		A3
2948	" "	36	W½NE	1906-03-28		A3
2895	BLONG, George	29	E½SE	1910-07-14		A3
2896	" "	29	SENE	1910-07-14		A3
2897	BRADY, George	26	2	1884-06-30		A1
2898	" "	26	3	1884-06-30		A1
2899	" "	26	4	1884-06-30		A1
2900	" "	26	SWNE	1884-06-30		A1
2939	BRADY, L J	13	NWSW	1883-04-20		A1
2940	" "	13	S½SW	1883-04-20		A1
2944	BRADY, Luke	14	SE	1883-04-20		A1
2951	BRADY, Patrick H	23	W½NW	1884-06-30		A1
2952	" "	23	W½SW	1884-06-30		A1
2924	BURNS, James A	3	1	1919-11-07		A3
2902	CAMP, H H	14	SWNW	1888-07-28		A1
2903	" "	15	W½SE	1888-07-28		A1
2904	" "	23	2	1888-07-28		A1
2905	" "	23	3	1888-07-28		A1
2906	" "	23	4	1888-07-28		A1
2907	" "	23	SWNE	1888-07-28		A1
2908	" "	23	W½SE	1888-07-28		A1
2909	" "	26	1	1888-07-28		A1
2910	" "	26	E½NW	1888-07-28		A1
2911	" "	26	NESW	1888-07-28		A1
2912	" "	26	NWNE	1888-07-28		A1
2857	CASKEY, Albert	17	3	1898-12-12		A3
2925	CAVANEY, James	29	NESW	1884-06-30		A1
2926	" "	29	NWSE	1884-06-30		A1
2927	" "	29	SENW	1884-06-30		A1
2928	" "	29	SWNE	1884-06-30		A1
2984	COLE, William E	33	NENW	1883-09-10		A1 G52
2985	" "	33	NWNE	1883-09-10		A1 G52
2865	COMPANY, Badger Paper	19	SWSW	1890-07-15		A1
2986	COVEY, William L	24	5	1924-05-27		A1
2866	DONOHUE, C	7	NENW	1888-08-29		A1 G74
2867	" "	7	SWNW	1888-08-29		A1 G74
2923	DOW, Herman	7	SESW	1884-06-20		A1 G77
2934	DRAPER, John	14	1	1906-06-30		A3
2935	" "	14	2	1906-06-30		A3
2936	" "	15	3	1906-06-30		A3
2937	" "	15	4	1906-06-30		A3

ID	Individual in Patent	Sec.	Sec. Part	Date Issued	Other Counties	For More Info . . .
2874	DUNBAR, Charles F	13	NESW	1883-04-20		A1
2873	" "	13	N½SE	1883-05-15		A1
2875	" "	13	SWNE	1883-09-15		A1
2876	" "	24	NWNE	1883-09-15		A1
2877	" "	5	1	1883-09-15		A1
2953	EDWARDS, Henry	19	2	1872-11-01		A1 G11
2954	" "	21	SESW	1872-11-01		A1 G11
2955	" "	21	SWSE	1872-11-01		A1 G11
2956	" "	29	NENE	1872-11-01		A1 G11
2870	ERICKSON, Carl Victor	19	SESW	1918-03-05		A3
2953	FISH, E B	19	2	1872-11-01		A1 G11
2954	" "	21	SESW	1872-11-01		A1 G11
2955	" "	21	SWSE	1872-11-01		A1 G11
2956	" "	29	NENE	1872-11-01		A1 G11
2913	FRANK, Harry G	13	1	1906-08-10		A3
2914	" "	13	SENW	1906-08-10		A3
2915	" "	14	3	1906-08-10		A3
2916	" "	14	4	1906-08-10		A3
2923	GILKEY, George F	7	SESW	1884-06-20		A1 G77
2958	GOODRICH, Rudolph O	23	1	1884-06-30		A1
2959	" "	23	NWNE	1884-06-30		A1
2894	HALL, Frederick	7	NESW	1883-09-15		A1
2885	HALMINIAK, Edward	7	NWNW	1910-01-06		A1 F
2871	HARRINGTON, Charles A	7	NWSW	1882-05-20		A1 G104 F
2872	" "	7	SENW	1882-05-20		A1 G104
2919	HASTINGS, Henry	27	NW	1883-09-15		A1
2957	KEESLER, Richard	7	S½SE	1893-02-07		A1
2889	LAWLER, Finn	10	2	1899-06-22		A1
2890	" "	11	1	1899-06-22		A1
2858	LOVEJOY, Allen P	17	S½SW	1872-02-20		A1 F
2859	" "	21	N½SE	1872-02-20		A1
2863	" "	31	N½SW	1872-02-20		A1
2860	" "	21	NWSW	1872-05-10		A1
2861	" "	29	NENW	1872-05-10		A1
2862	" "	29	NWNE	1872-05-10		A1
2920	MACK, Henry J	35	2	1895-12-21		A1
2921	" "	35	N½SW	1895-12-21		A1
2922	" "	35	SENW	1895-12-21		A1
2879	MARKHAM, D	27	NE	1885-01-20		A1 G133
2880	" "	27	NESW	1885-01-20		A1 G133
2881	" "	33	E½NE	1885-01-20		A1 G133
2879	MARKHAM, Herbert L	27	NE	1885-01-20		A1 G133
2880	" "	27	NESW	1885-01-20		A1 G133
2881	" "	33	E½NE	1885-01-20		A1 G133
2933	MARKHAM, John D	33	SWNE	1885-01-20		A1
2866	MCCARTHY, C	7	NENW	1888-08-29		A1 G74
2867	" "	7	SWNW	1888-08-29		A1 G74
2929	MEADE, Joel	31	NESE	1873-06-10		A1 G142
2930	" "	31	SWSW	1873-06-10		A1 G142
2931	" "	5	SWSW	1873-06-10		A1 G142
2932	" "	7	SWSW	1873-06-10		A1 G142
2967	MILLER, W H	21	SESE	1888-07-28		A1
2968	" "	21	SWSW	1888-07-28		A1
2969	" "	24	1	1888-07-28		A1
2970	" "	24	2	1888-07-28		A1
2971	" "	24	3	1888-07-28		A1
2972	" "	24	E½NW	1888-07-28		A1
2973	" "	24	SWNE	1888-07-28		A1
2974	" "	24	W½SE	1888-07-28		A1
2975	" "	26	6	1888-07-28		A1
2976	" "	27	NWSW	1888-07-28		A1
2977	" "	33	NWNW	1888-07-28		A1
2978	" "	35	N½NW	1888-07-28		A1
2979	" "	35	SESE	1888-07-28		A1
2980	" "	35	SWNW	1888-07-28		A1
2981	" "	36	N½SW	1888-07-28		A1
2982	" "	36	SE	1888-07-28		A1
2983	" "	36	SESW	1888-07-28		A1
2945	NELSON, Nels	11	2	1906-12-17		A3
2946	" "	12	1	1906-12-17		A3
2868	OBERG, Carl J	29	SESW	1905-05-02		A3 G151
2869	" "	29	W½SW	1905-05-02		A3 G151
2868	OBERG, Sophia	29	SESW	1905-05-02		A3 G151

ID	Individual in Patent	Sec.	Sec. Part	Date Issued	Other Counties	For More Info . . .
2869	OBERG, Sophia (Cont'd)	29	W½SW	1905-05-02		A3 G151
2891	PALMS, Francis	17	4	1867-10-10		A1
2892	" "	17	5	1867-10-10		A1
2966	PAULUS, Valentine	33	W½SE	1888-07-28		A1
2864	PINTO, Arthur M	27	SE	1884-06-30		A1
2886	PRESTON, Edward L	7	NENE	1924-05-27		A3
2887	" "	7	NWSE	1924-05-27		A3
2888	" "	7	S½NE	1924-05-27		A3
2987	REAY, William	5	6	1893-10-30		A1
2917	RIBENACK, Henry C	35	SENE	1885-01-15		A1
2918	" "	36	SWSW	1885-01-15		A1
2929	RIPLEY, Sylvanus	31	NESE	1873-06-10		A1 G142
2930	" "	31	SWSW	1873-06-10		A1 G142
2931	" "	5	SWSW	1873-06-10		A1 G142
2932	" "	7	SWSW	1873-06-10		A1 G142
2871	ROE, Gilbert W	7	NWSW	1882-05-20		A1 G104 F
2872	" "	7	SENW	1882-05-20		A1 G104
2883	SARGENT, Daniel H	31	SESW	1904-11-30		A1
2884	" "	31	W½SE	1904-11-30		A1
2960	SCOTT, Thomas B	19	S½NE	1883-09-15		A1
2961	" "	29	W½NW	1883-09-15		A1
2962	" "	31	SESE	1883-09-15		A1
2963	" "	5	2	1883-09-15		A1
2964	" "	5	3	1883-09-15		A1
2965	" "	5	SESW	1883-09-15		A1
2949	SHADICK, Oliver	29	SWSE	1890-07-15		A1 G159
2950	" "	33	SENW	1890-07-15		A1 G159
2893	STEWART, Frank C	33	E½SW	1885-01-20		A1
2941	SWIMM, Louie E	35	1	1895-03-30		A1
2942	" "	35	N½SE	1895-03-30		A1
2943	" "	35	SWNE	1895-03-30		A1
2878	THOMAS, Clara	7	NESE	1901-05-08		A1
2949	WEBSTER, R L	29	SWSE	1890-07-15		A1 G159
2950	" "	33	SENW	1890-07-15		A1 G159
2984	WILLIAMS, Orin T	33	NENW	1883-09-10		A1 G52
2985	" "	33	NWNE	1883-09-10		A1 G52
2856	WIPPERMANN, Adolph G	33	E½SE	1888-07-28		A1
2938	WOOLWORTH, John O	13	SENE	1906-12-17		A1
2882	WYLIE, Daniel B	5	4	1883-09-15		A1 G172
2882	WYLIE, Winfred	5	4	1883-09-15		A1 G172

Patent Map

T42-N R11-E
4th PM - 1831 MN/WI

Map Group 16

Township Statistics

Parcels Mapped	:	132
Number of Patents	:	59
Number of Individuals	:	62
Patentees Identified	:	51
Number of Surnames	:	55
Multi-Patentee Parcels	:	23
Oldest Patent Date	:	10/10/1867
Most Recent Patent	:	5/27/1924
Block/Lot Parcels	:	36
Parcels Re - Issued	:	0
Parcels that Overlap	:	0
Cities and Towns	:	0
Cemeteries	:	0

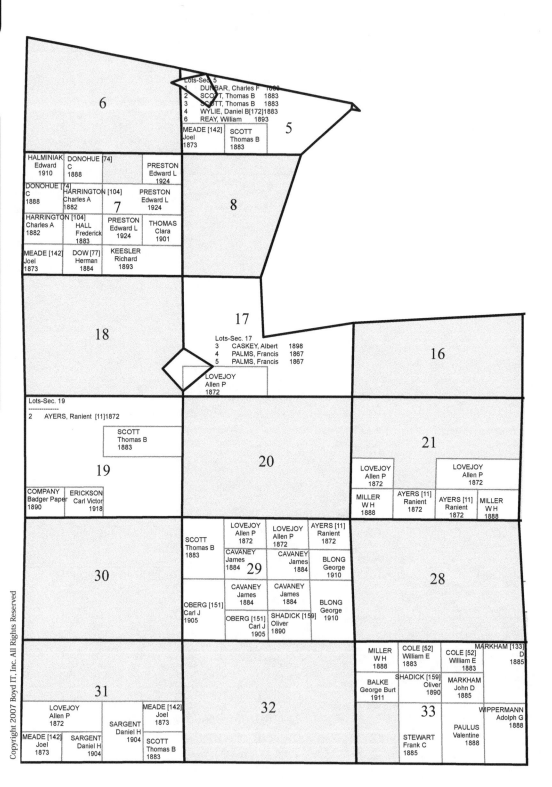

Lots-Sec. 5
1 DUNBAR, Charles F 1883
2 SCOTT, Thomas B 1883
3 SCOTT, Thomas B 1883
4 WYLIE, Daniel B[172] 1883
6 REAY, William 1893

6

5

MEADE [142]
Joel
1873

SCOTT
Thomas B
1883

HALMINIAK
Edward
1910

DONOHUE [74]
C
1888

PRESTON
Edward L
1924

DONOHUE [74]
C
1888

HARRINGTON [104]
Charles A
1882

7

PRESTON
Edward L
1924

8

HARRINGTON [104]
Charles A
1882

HALL
Frederick
1883

PRESTON
Edward L
1924

THOMAS
Clara
1901

MEADE [142]
Joel
1873

DOW [77]
Herman
1884

KEESLER
Richard
1893

17

Lots-Sec. 17
3 CASKEY, Albert 1898
4 PALMS, Francis 1867
5 PALMS, Francis 1867

16

18

LOVEJOY
Allen P
1872

Lots-Sec. 19
----
2 AYERS, Ranient [11]1872

SCOTT
Thomas B
1883

19

20

21

LOVEJOY
Allen P
1872

LOVEJOY
Allen P
1872

COMPANY
Badger Paper
1890

ERICKSON
Carl Victor
1918

MILLER
W H
1888

AYERS [11]
Ranient
1872

AYERS [11]
Ranient
1872

MILLER
W H
1888

30

SCOTT
Thomas B
1883

LOVEJOY
Allen P
1872

LOVEJOY
Allen P
1872

AYERS [11]
Ranient
1872

28

CAVANEY
James
1884

29

CAVANEY
James
1884

BLONG
George
1910

OBERG [151]
Carl J
1905

CAVANEY
James
1884

CAVANEY
James
1884

BLONG
George
1910

OBERG [151]
Carl J
1905

SHADICK [159]
Oliver
1890

31

LOVEJOY
Allen P
1872

SARGENT
Daniel H
1904

MEADE [142]
Joel
1873

32

MILLER
W H
1888

COLE [52]
William E
1883

COLE [52]
William E
1883

MARKHAM [133]
D
1885

BALKE
George Burt
1911

SHADICK [159]
Oliver
1890

MARKHAM
John D
1885

33

WIPPERMANN
Adolph G
1888

MEADE [142]
Joel
1873

SARGENT
Daniel H
1904

SCOTT
Thomas B
1883

STEWART
Frank C
1885

PAULUS
Valentine
1888

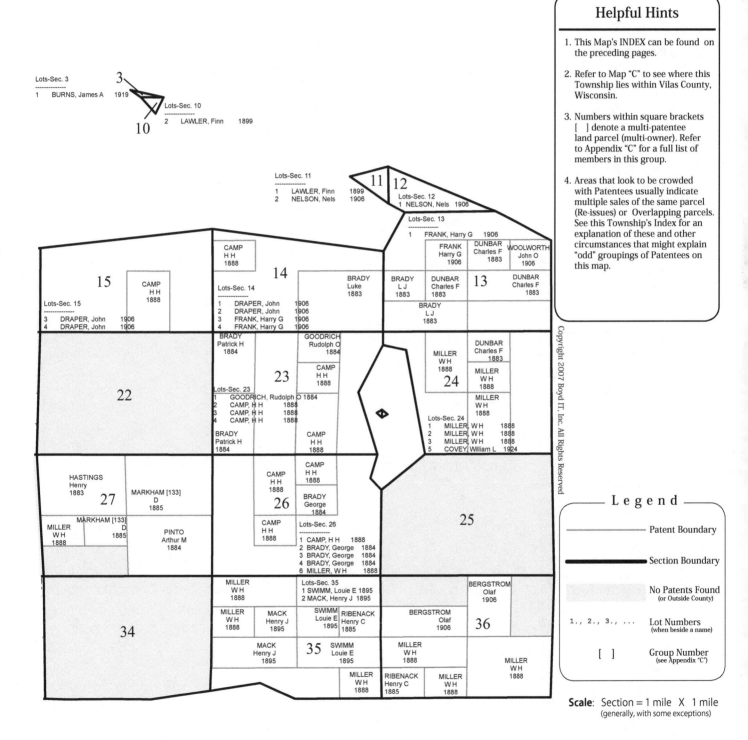

Helpful Hints

1. This Map's INDEX can be found on the preceding pages.

2. Refer to Map "C" to see where this Township lies within Vilas County, Wisconsin.

3. Numbers within square brackets [ ] denote a multi-patentee land parcel (multi-owner). Refer to Appendix "C" for a full list of members in this group.

4. Areas that look to be crowded with Patentees usually indicate multiple sales of the same parcel (Re-issues) or Overlapping parcels. See this Township's Index for an explanation of these and other circumstances that might explain "odd" groupings of Patentees on this map.

Lots-Sec. 3
----
1   BURNS, James A   1919

3

10

Lots-Sec. 10
----
2   LAWLER, Finn   1899

Lots-Sec. 11
----
1   LAWLER, Finn   1899
2   NELSON, Nels   1906

11 12

Lots-Sec. 12
----
1   NELSON, Nels   1906

Lots-Sec. 13
----
1   FRANK, Harry G   1906

CAMP
H H
1888

15

CAMP
H H
1888

14

FRANK
Harry G
1906

DUNBAR
Charles F
1883

WOOLWORTH
John O
1906

Lots-Sec. 15
----
3   DRAPER, John   1906
4   DRAPER, John   1906

Lots-Sec. 14
----
1   DRAPER, John   1906
2   DRAPER, John   1906
3   FRANK, Harry G   1906
4   FRANK, Harry G   1906

BRADY
Luke
1883

BRADY
L J
1883

DUNBAR
Charles F
1883

13

DUNBAR
Charles F
1883

BRADY
L J
1883

BRADY
Patrick H
1884

GOODRICH
Rudolph O
1884

DUNBAR
Charles F
1883

22

23

CAMP
H H
1888

MILLER
W H
1888

24

MILLER
W H
1888

Lots-Sec. 23
----
1   GOODRICH, Rudolph O 1884
2   CAMP, H H   1888
3   CAMP, H H   1888
4   CAMP, H H   1888

MILLER
W H
1888

Lots-Sec. 24
----
1   MILLER, W H   1888
2   MILLER, W H   1888
3   MILLER, W H   1888
5   COVEY, William L 1924

BRADY
Patrick H
1884

CAMP
H H
1888

CAMP
H H
1888

HASTINGS
Henry
1883

27

MARKHAM [133]
D
1885

CAMP
H H
1888

26

BRADY
George
1884

25

MILLER
W H
1888

MARKHAM [133]
D
1885

PINTO
Arthur M
1884

CAMP
H H
1888

Lots-Sec. 26
----
1   CAMP, H H   1888
2   BRADY, George 1884
3   BRADY, George 1884
4   BRADY, George 1884
6   MILLER, W H   1888

MILLER
W H
1888

MILLER
W H
1888

MACK
Henry J
1895

Lots-Sec. 35
1 SWIMM, Louie E 1895
2 MACK, Henry J 1895

BERGSTROM
Olaf
1906

34

SWIMM
Louie E
1895

RIBENACK
Henry C
1885

BERGSTROM
Olaf
1906

36

MACK
Henry J
1895

35

SWIMM
Louie E
1895

MILLER
W H
1888

MILLER
W H
1888

MILLER
W H
1888

RIBENACK
Henry C
1885

MILLER
W H
1888

Legend

———————— Patent Boundary

———————— Section Boundary

No Patents Found
(or Outside County)

1., 2., 3., ...   Lot Numbers
(when beside a name)

[   ]   Group Number
(see Appendix "C")

Scale: Section = 1 mile X 1 mile
(generally, with some exceptions)

Road Map

T42-N R11-E
4th PM - 1831 MN/WI

Map Group 16

Cities & Towns
None

Cemeteries
None

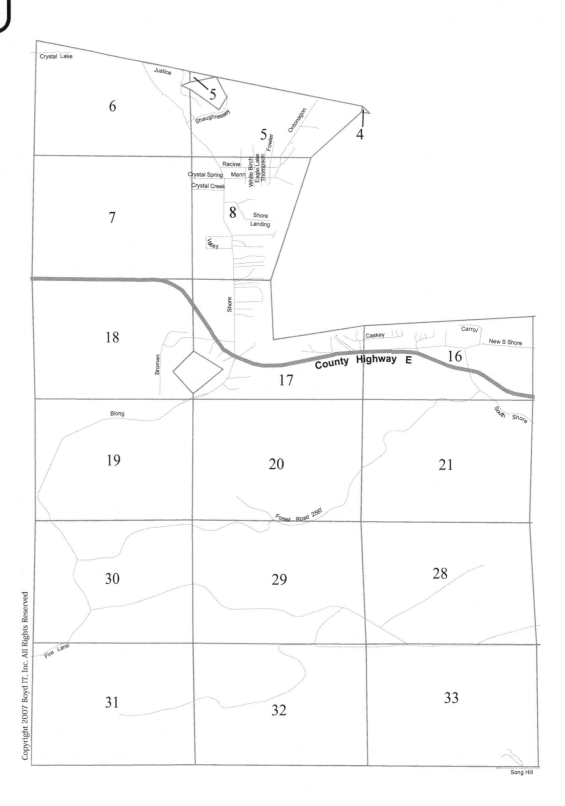

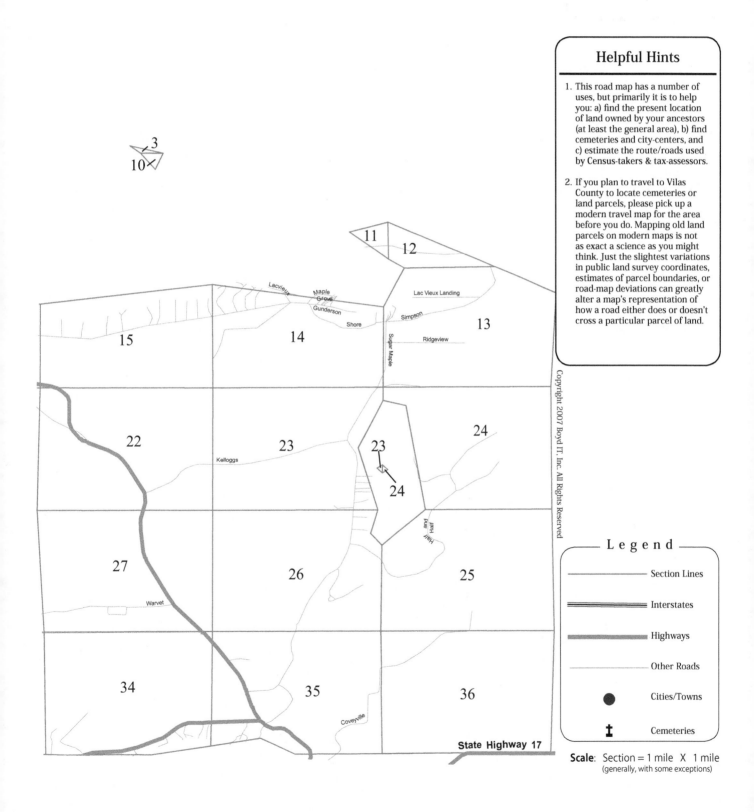

Helpful Hints

1. This road map has a number of uses, but primarily it is to help you: a) find the present location of land owned by your ancestors (at least the general area), b) find cemeteries and city-centers, and c) estimate the route/roads used by Census-takers & tax-assessors.

2. If you plan to travel to Vilas County to locate cemeteries or land parcels, please pick up a modern travel map for the area before you do. Mapping old land parcels on modern maps is not as exact a science as you might think. Just the slightest variations in public land survey coordinates, estimates of parcel boundaries, or road-map deviations can greatly alter a map's representation of how a road either does or doesn't cross a particular parcel of land.

Legend

———	Section Lines
≡≡≡	Interstates
━━━	Highways
———	Other Roads
●	Cities/Towns
⊥	Cemeteries

Scale: Section = 1 mile X 1 mile
(generally, with some exceptions)

11
12

Lacvieux
Maple Grove
Gunderson
Shore
Lac Vieux Landing
Simpson
Ridgeview
Sugar Maple

15
14
13

22
23
24
Kelloggs
23
24

27
26
25
Warvet
Half Pue

34
35
36
Coveyville
State Highway 17

211

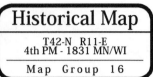

Historical Map

T42-N R11-E
4th PM - 1831 MN/WI

Map Group 16

Cities & Towns
None

Cemeteries
None

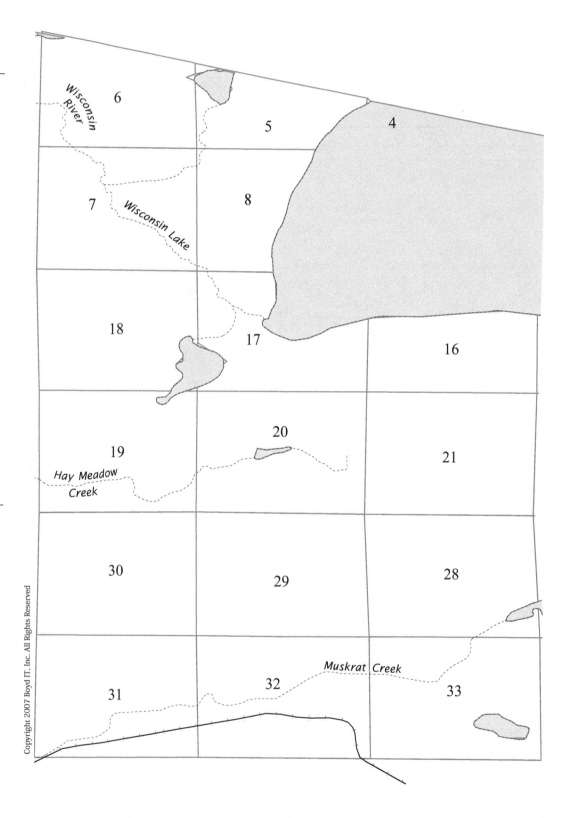

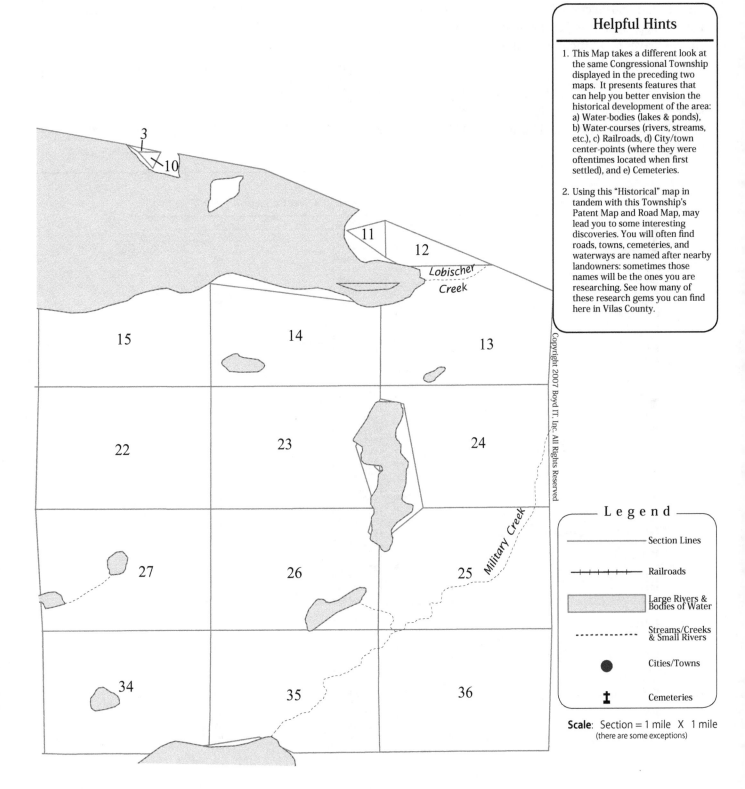

Helpful Hints

1. This Map takes a different look at the same Congressional Township displayed in the preceding two maps. It presents features that can help you better envision the historical development of the area: a) Water-bodies (lakes & ponds), b) Water-courses (rivers, streams, etc.), c) Railroads, d) City/town center-points (where they were oftentimes located when first settled), and e) Cemeteries.

2. Using this "Historical" map in tandem with this Township's Patent Map and Road Map, may lead you to some interesting discoveries. You will often find roads, towns, cemeteries, and waterways are named after nearby landowners: sometimes those names will be the ones you are researching. See how many of these research gems you can find here in Vilas County.

L e g e n d

————————	Section Lines
+++++++++	Railroads
▭	Large Rivers & Bodies of Water
- - - - - - - -	Streams/Creeks & Small Rivers
●	Cities/Towns
⭱	Cemeteries

Scale: Section = 1 mile X 1 mile
(there are some exceptions)

Map Group 17: Index to Land Patents

Township 42-North Range 12-East (4th PM - 1831 MN/WI)

After you locate an individual in this Index, take note of the Section and Section Part then proceed to the Land Patent map on the pages immediately following. You should have no difficulty locating the corresponding parcel of land.

The "For More Info" Column will lead you to more information about the underlying Patents. See the *Legend* at right, and the "How to Use this Book" chapter, for more information.

ID	Individual in Patent	Sec.	Sec. Part	Date Issued	Other Counties	For More Info . . .
2989	BALDWIN, George	19	SESE	1884-04-24		A1
2990	" "	20	2	1884-04-24		A1
2991	" "	20	S½SE	1884-04-24		A1
2992	" "	20	SW	1884-04-24		A1
2993	" "	27	1	1884-04-24		A1
2994	" "	27	2	1884-04-24		A1
2995	" "	27	3	1884-04-24		A1
2996	" "	27	NWSE	1884-04-24		A1
2997	" "	27	SW	1884-04-24		A1
2998	" "	27	SWNW	1884-04-24		A1
2999	" "	29	N½NE	1884-04-24		A1
3000	" "	29	NW	1884-04-24		A1
3001	" "	29	NWSW	1884-04-24		A1
3002	" "	29	SWNE	1884-04-24		A1
3003	" "	31		1884-04-24		A1
3004	" "	33	1	1884-04-24		A1
3005	" "	33	2	1884-04-24		A1
3006	" "	33	3	1884-04-24		A1
3007	" "	33	4	1884-04-24		A1
3008	BEYER, George	21	1	1889-03-20		A1
3009	" "	21	2	1889-03-20		A1
3010	" "	21	3	1889-03-20		A1
3011	" "	21	S½SW	1889-03-20		A1
3012	" "	22	1	1889-03-20		A1
3061	CYR, Lewis D	19	S½NW	1885-06-03		A1
3062	" "	19	W½SW	1885-06-03		A1
2988	FAY, George A	32	4	1884-04-24		A1
3017	HAGERMAN, James J	26	1	1882-06-30		A1
3018	" "	26	2	1882-06-30		A1
3019	" "	26	3	1882-06-30		A1
3020	" "	26	SWSW	1882-06-30		A1
3021	" "	27	S½SE	1882-06-30		A1
3024	" "	33	5	1882-06-30		A1
3025	" "	33	6	1882-06-30		A1
3026	" "	33	8	1882-06-30		A1
3027	" "	34	1	1882-06-30		A1
3028	" "	34	2	1882-06-30		A1
3029	" "	34	3	1882-06-30		A1
3030	" "	34	6	1882-06-30		A1
3031	" "	34	E½NW	1882-06-30		A1
3032	" "	34	NE	1882-06-30		A1
3033	" "	34	NWNW	1882-06-30		A1
3034	" "	35	1	1882-06-30		A1
3035	" "	35	3	1882-06-30		A1
3036	" "	35	4	1882-06-30		A1
3037	" "	35	5	1882-06-30		A1

ID	Individual in Patent	Sec.	Sec. Part	Date Issued	Other Counties	For More Info . . .
3038	HAGERMAN, James J (Cont'd)	35	6	1882-06-30		A1
3039	" "	35	NW	1882-06-30		A1
3040	" "	35	NWNE	1882-06-30		A1
3041	" "	36	1	1882-06-30		A1
3042	" "	36	2	1882-06-30		A1
3043	" "	36	3	1882-06-30		A1
3044	" "	36	4	1882-06-30		A1
3045	" "	36	5	1882-06-30		A1
3046	" "	36	6	1882-06-30		A1
3047	" "	36	E½SW	1882-06-30		A1
3048	" "	36	S½SE	1882-06-30		A1
3022	" "	28	E½NW	1885-12-19		A1
3023	" "	28	SW	1885-12-19		A1
3014	HAMILTON, I K	19	E½SW	1872-05-01		A1 G95
3015	" "	19	N½SE	1872-05-01		A1 G95
3016	" "	19	S½NE	1872-05-01		A1 G95
3014	HAMILTON, W C	19	E½SW	1872-05-01		A1 G95
3015	" "	19	N½SE	1872-05-01		A1 G95
3016	" "	19	S½NE	1872-05-01		A1 G95
3063	MATHEWS, Peter	29	SWSE	1884-12-30		A1
3064	" "	33	NWNW	1884-12-30		A1
3014	MERRYMAN, A C	19	E½SW	1872-05-01		A1 G95
3015	" "	19	N½SE	1872-05-01		A1 G95
3016	" "	19	S½NE	1872-05-01		A1 G95
3013	SANBORN, George F	17	1	1900-11-28		A1
3049	SEMER, John	19	N½NE	1884-04-24		A1
3050	" "	19	NENW	1884-04-24		A1
3051	" "	19	SWSE	1884-04-24		A1
3052	" "	20	1	1884-04-24		A1
3053	" "	20	3	1884-04-24		A1
3054	" "	20	4	1884-04-24		A1
3055	" "	20	5	1884-04-24		A1
3056	" "	20	W½NW	1884-04-24		A1
3057	" "	21	4	1884-04-24		A1
3058	" "	27	4	1884-04-24		A1
3059	" "	29	SESE	1884-04-24		A1
3060	" "	35	2	1884-04-24		A1

Patent Map

T42-N R12-E
4th PM - 1831 MN/WI

Map Group 17

Township Statistics

Parcels Mapped	:	77
Number of Patents	:	21
Number of Individuals	:	11
Patentees Identified	:	9
Number of Surnames	:	10
Multi-Patentee Parcels	:	3
Oldest Patent Date	:	5/1/1872
Most Recent Patent	:	11/28/1900
Block/Lot Parcels	:	42
Parcels Re - Issued	:	0
Parcels that Overlap	:	0
Cities and Towns	:	0
Cemeteries	:	0

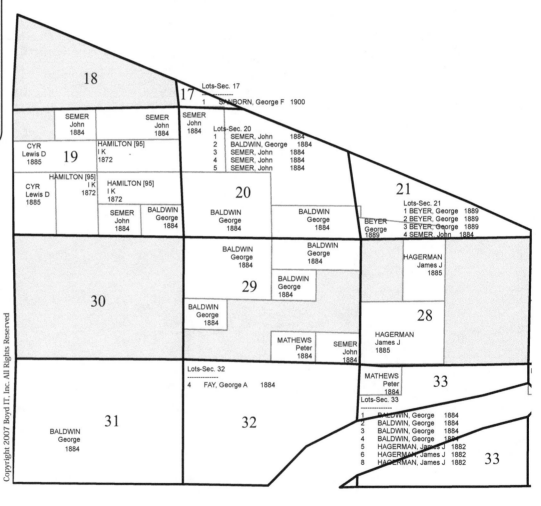

Helpful Hints

1. This Map's INDEX can be found on the preceding pages.

2. Refer to Map "C" to see where this Township lies within Vilas County, Wisconsin.

3. Numbers within square brackets [ ] denote a multi-patentee land parcel (multi-owner). Refer to Appendix "C" for a full list of members in this group.

4. Areas that look to be crowded with Patentees usually indicate multiple sales of the same parcel (Re-issues) or Overlapping parcels. See this Township's Index for an explanation of these and other circumstances that might explain "odd" groupings of Patentees on this map.

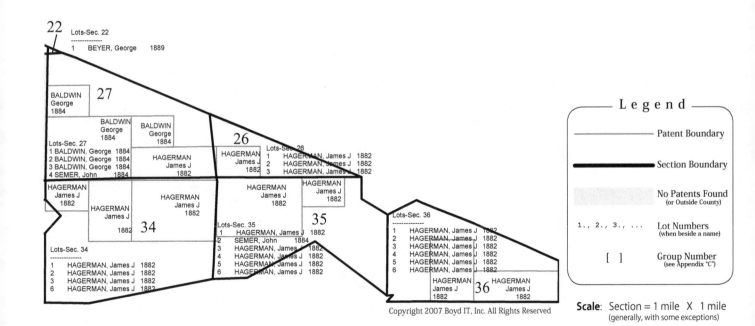

22

Lots-Sec. 22
----
1   BEYER, George   1889

27

BALDWIN
George
1884

BALDWIN
George
1884

BALDWIN
George
1884

26

Lots-Sec. 27
1 BALDWIN, George 1884
2 BALDWIN, George 1884
3 BALDWIN, George 1884
4 SEMER, John   1884

HAGERMAN
James J
1882

HAGERMAN
James J
1882

Lots-Sec. 26
1   HAGERMAN, James J 1882
2   HAGERMAN, James J 1882
3   HAGERMAN, James J 1882

HAGERMAN
James J
1882

HAGERMAN
James J
1882

HAGERMAN
James J
1882

HAGERMAN
James J
1882

34

35

Lots-Sec. 36
----
1   HAGERMAN, James J 1882
2   HAGERMAN, James J 1882
3   HAGERMAN, James J 1882
4   HAGERMAN, James J 1882
5   HAGERMAN, James J 1882
6   HAGERMAN, James J 1882

Lots-Sec. 34
----
1   HAGERMAN, James J 1882
2   HAGERMAN, James J 1882
3   HAGERMAN, James J 1882
6   HAGERMAN, James J 1882

Lots-Sec. 35
1   HAGERMAN, James J 1882
2   SEMER, John   1884
3   HAGERMAN, James J 1882
4   HAGERMAN, James J 1882
5   HAGERMAN, James J 1882
6   HAGERMAN, James J 1882

HAGERMAN
James J
1882

36

HAGERMAN
James J
1882

Legend

Patent Boundary

Section Boundary

No Patents Found
(or Outside County)

1., 2., 3., ...   Lot Numbers
(when beside a name)

[   ]   Group Number
(see Appendix "C")

Scale: Section = 1 mile X 1 mile
(generally, with some exceptions)

Road Map

T42-N R12-E
4th PM - 1831 MN/WI

Map Group 17

Cities & Towns

None

Cemeteries

None

Helpful Hints

1. This road map has a number of uses, but primarily it is to help you: a) find the present location of land owned by your ancestors (at least the general area), b) find cemeteries and city-centers, and c) estimate the route/roads used by Census-takers & tax-assessors.

2. If you plan to travel to Vilas County to locate cemeteries or land parcels, please pick up a modern travel map for the area before you do. Mapping old land parcels on modern maps is not as exact a science as you might think. Just the slightest variations in public land survey coordinates, estimates of parcel boundaries, or road-map deviations can greatly alter a map's representation of how a road either does or doesn't cross a particular parcel of land.

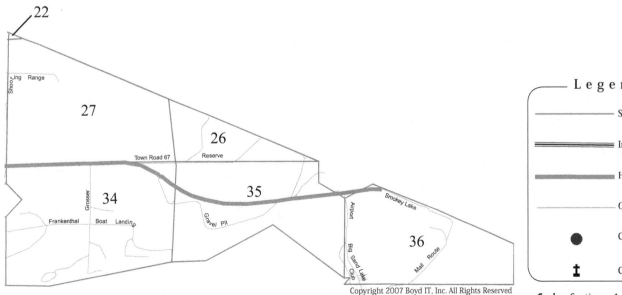

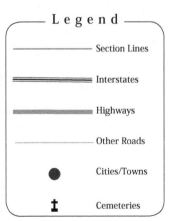

Scale: Section = 1 mile X 1 mile
(generally, with some exceptions)

Historical Map

T42-N R12-E
4th PM - 1831 MN/WI

Map Group 17

Cities & Towns
None

Cemeteries
None

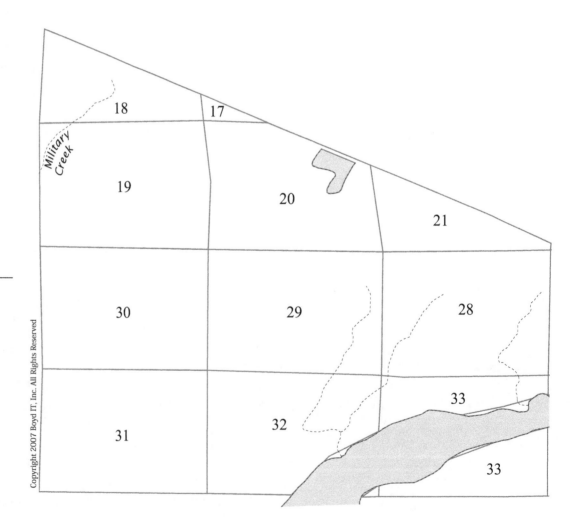

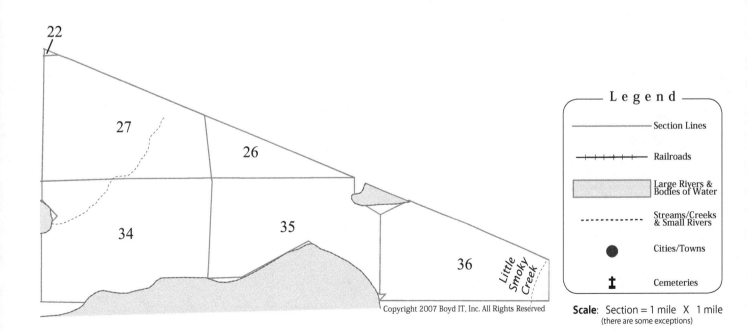

Copyright 2007 Boyd IT, Inc. All Rights Reserved

Legend

Section Lines

Railroads

Large Rivers & Bodies of Water

Streams/Creeks & Small Rivers

● Cities/Towns

✝ Cemeteries

Scale: Section = 1 mile X 1 mile
(there are some exceptions)

Map Group 18: Index to Land Patents

Township 41-North Range 5-East (4th PM - 1831 MN/WI)

After you locate an individual in this Index, take note of the Section and Section Part then proceed to the Land Patent map on the pages immediately following. You should have no difficulty locating the corresponding parcel of land.

The "For More Info" Column will lead you to more information about the underlying Patents. See the *Legend* at right, and the "How to Use this Book" chapter, for more information.

```
                        LEGEND
              "For More Info . . . " column
A = Authority (Legislative Act, See Appendix "A")
B = Block or Lot (location in Section unknown)
C = Cancelled Patent
F = Fractional Section
G = Group  (Multi-Patentee Patent, see Appendix "C")
V = Overlaps another Parcel
R = Re-Issued (Parcel patented more than once)

(A & G items require you to look in the Appendixes referred
to above. All other Letter-designations followed by a number
require you to locate line-items in this index that possess
the ID number found after the letter).
```

ID	Individual in Patent	Sec.	Sec. Part	Date Issued	Other Counties	For More Info . . .
None						

We have not located any Federal Land
Patent records within the
Bureau of Land Management's database for

**Township 41-N Range 5-E
(Map Group 18)**

in **Vilas County.**

Accordingly, we have no
"Patent Map" for this township.

Nonetheless, we have included our
Road and Historical Maps, which
begin on the following page.

Road Map

T41-N R5-E
4th PM - 1831 MN/WI

Map Group 18

Cities & Towns

None

Cemeteries

None

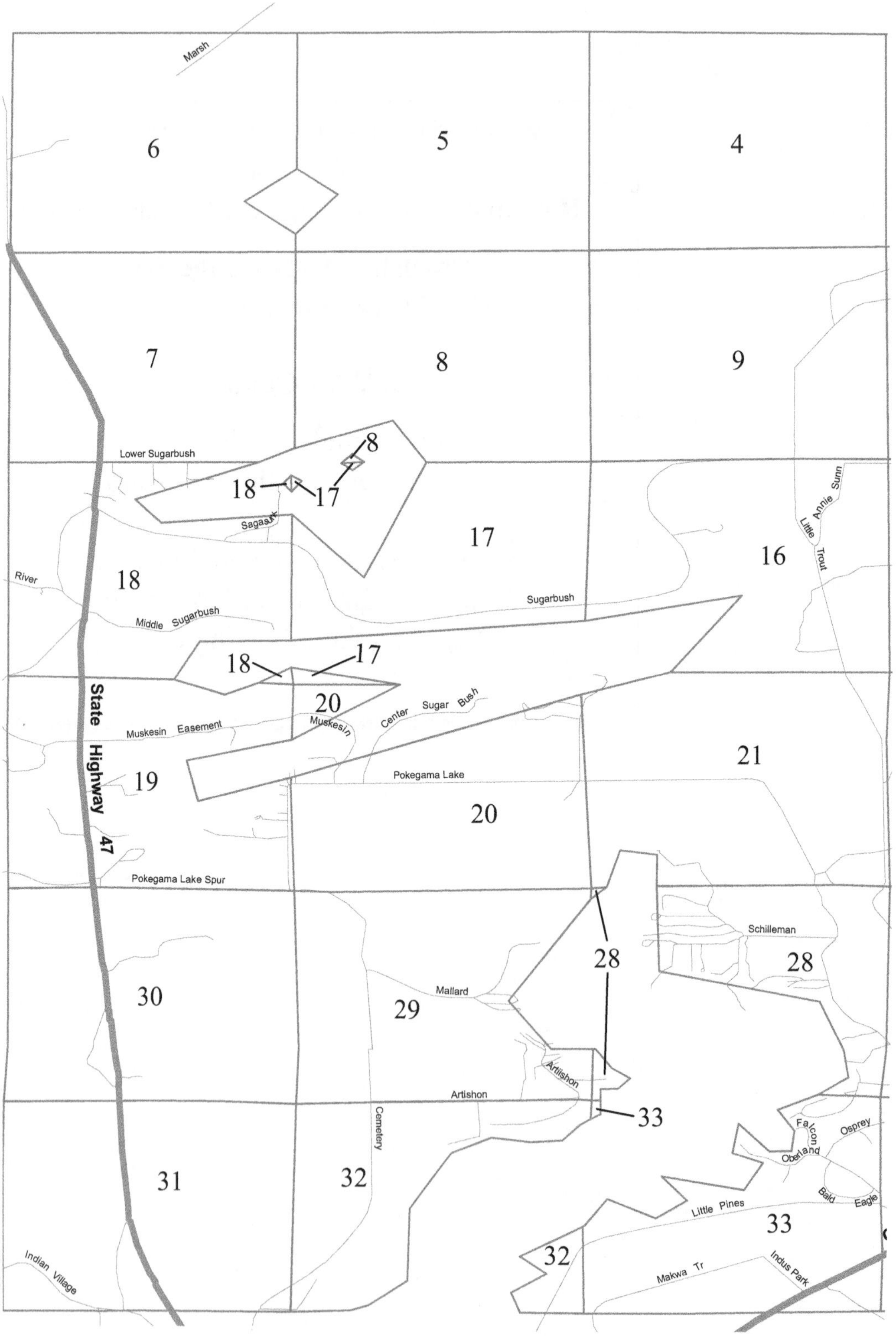

Marsh
6
5
4
7
8
9
Lower Sugarbush
8
18
17
Sagaash
17
16
Annie Sunn
Little Trout
River
18
Middle Sugarbush
Sugarbush
18
17
20
State Highway 47
Center Sugar Bush
Muskesin Easement
Muskesin
21
19
Pokegama Lake
20
Pokegama Lake Spur
Schilleman
28
28
30
Mallard
29
Artishon
Artishon
33
Cemetery
Falcon
Osprey
Oberland
31
32
Bald
Eagle
Little Pines
33
Indian Village
32
Makwa Tr
Indus Park

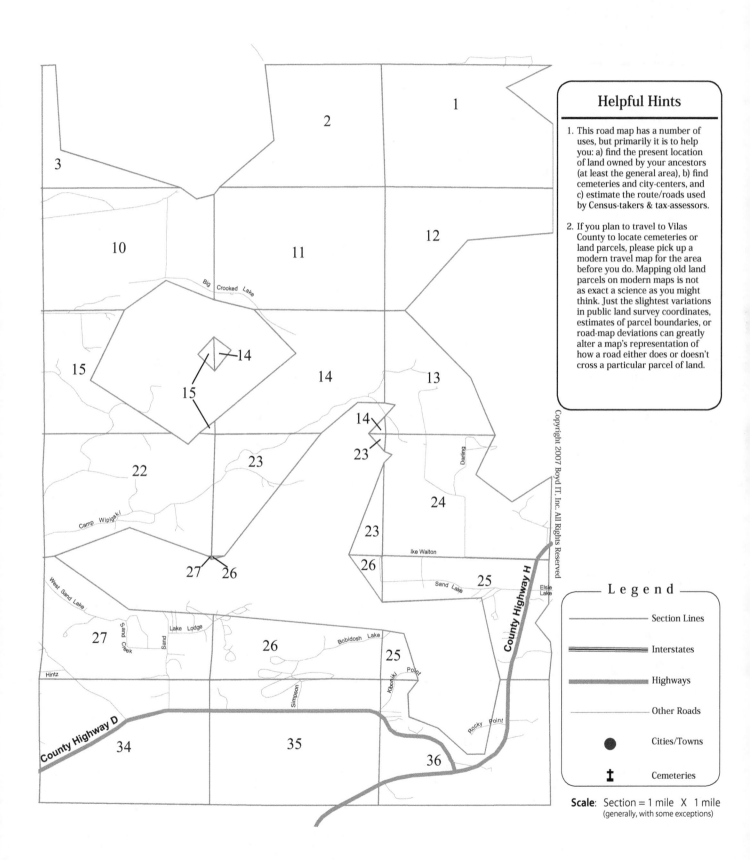

Copyright 2007 Boyd IT, Inc. All Rights Reserved

Helpful Hints

1. This road map has a number of uses, but primarily it is to help you: a) find the present location of land owned by your ancestors (at least the general area), b) find cemeteries and city-centers, and c) estimate the route/roads used by Census-takers & tax-assessors.

2. If you plan to travel to Vilas County to locate cemeteries or land parcels, please pick up a modern travel map for the area before you do. Mapping old land parcels on modern maps is not as exact a science as you might think. Just the slightest variations in public land survey coordinates, estimates of parcel boundaries, or road-map deviations can greatly alter a map's representation of how a road either does or doesn't cross a particular parcel of land.

L e g e n d

————————	Section Lines
════════	Interstates
━━━━━━	Highways
————	Other Roads
●	Cities/Towns
✝	Cemeteries

Scale: Section = 1 mile X 1 mile
(generally, with some exceptions)

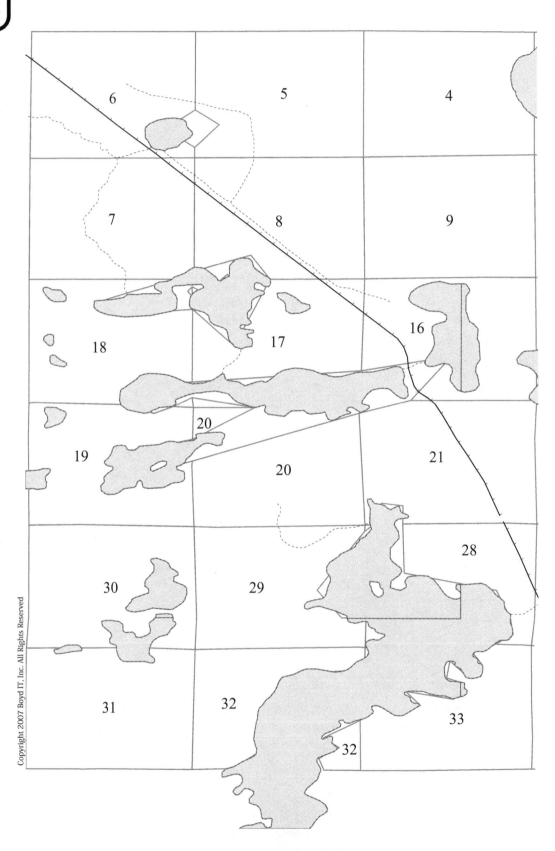

Historical Map

T41-N R5-E
4th PM - 1831 MN/WI

Map Group 18

Cities & Towns
None

Cemeteries
None

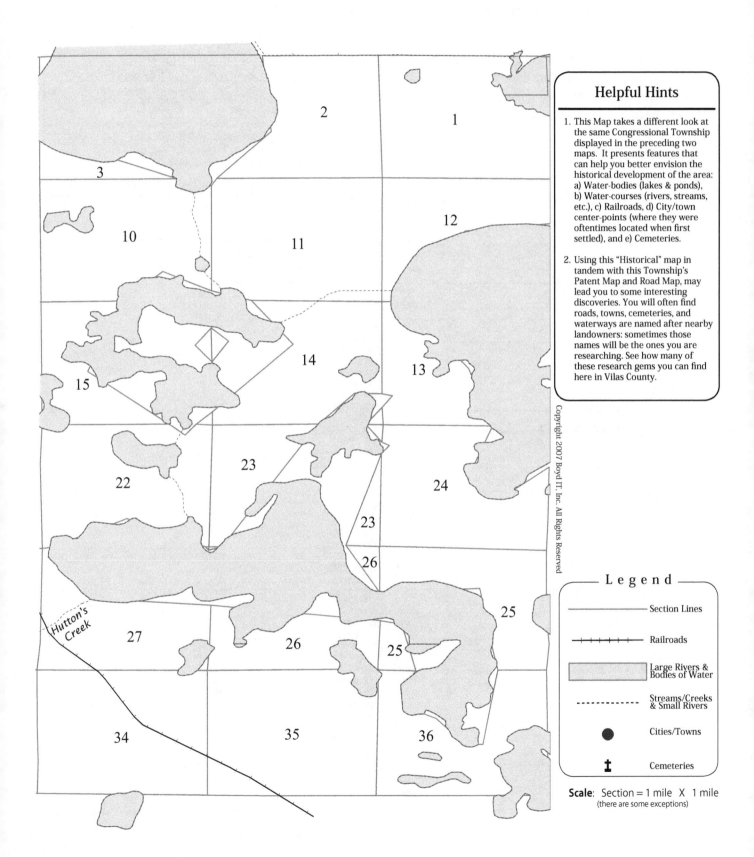

Helpful Hints

1. This Map takes a different look at the same Congressional Township displayed in the preceding two maps. It presents features that can help you better envision the historical development of the area: a) Water-bodies (lakes & ponds), b) Water-courses (rivers, streams, etc.), c) Railroads, d) City/town center-points (where they were oftentimes located when first settled), and e) Cemeteries.

2. Using this "Historical" map in tandem with this Township's Patent Map and Road Map, may lead you to some interesting discoveries. You will often find roads, towns, cemeteries, and waterways are named after nearby landowners: sometimes those names will be the ones you are researching. See how many of these research gems you can find here in Vilas County.

Legend

————————	Section Lines
+++++++++	Railroads
�	Large Rivers & Bodies of Water
- - - - - - -	Streams/Creeks & Small Rivers
●	Cities/Towns
✝	Cemeteries

Scale: Section = 1 mile X 1 mile
(there are some exceptions)

Map Group 19: Index to Land Patents

Township 41-North Range 6-East (4th PM - 1831 MN/WI)

After you locate an individual in this Index, take note of the Section and Section Part then proceed to the Land Patent map on the pages immediately following. You should have no difficulty locating the corresponding parcel of land.

The "For More Info" Column will lead you to more information about the underlying Patents. See the *Legend* at right, and the "How to Use this Book" chapter, for more information.

```
                        LEGEND
            "For More Info . . . " column
A = Authority (Legislative Act, See Appendix "A")
B = Block or Lot (location in Section unknown)
C = Cancelled Patent
F = Fractional Section
G = Group (Multi-Patentee Patent, see Appendix "C")
V = Overlaps another Parcel
R = Re-Issued (Parcel patented more than once)

(A & G items require you to look in the Appendixes referred
to above. All other Letter-designations followed by a number
require you to locate line-items in this index that possess
the ID number found after the letter).
```

ID	Individual in Patent	Sec.	Sec. Part	Date Issued	Other Counties	For More Info . . .
3071	BARROWS, Augustus R	25	NESE	1873-05-01		A1 G16
3072	" "	25	SENE	1873-05-01		A1 G16
3073	" "	35	2	1873-05-01		A1 G16
3074	" "	35	3	1873-05-01		A1 G16
3075	" "	35	N½SE	1873-05-01		A1 G16
3076	" "	35	S½NE	1873-05-01		A1 G16
3067	" "	4	6	1873-05-01		A1
3068	" "	9	1	1873-05-01		A1
3069	" "	9	2	1873-05-01		A1
3070	" "	9	3	1873-05-01		A1
3136	BLAISDELL, John C	13	2	1902-01-17		A3 R3131
3077	BOLLES, Charles	4	4	1873-11-15		A1
3216	BRADLEY, William H	14	3	1888-07-07		A1
3217	" "	23	NENE	1888-07-07		A1
3201	BRAZIL, Patrick	13	3	1898-01-12		A1 R3078
3142	BREWSTER, Loren D	23	2	1883-09-15		A1
3143	" "	23	NWSE	1883-09-15		A1
3144	" "	25	NWSE	1883-09-15		A1
3145	" "	25	SWNE	1883-09-15		A1
3146	" "	36	3	1883-09-15		A1
3147	" "	36	NENW	1883-09-15		A1
3148	" "	36	SWNW	1883-09-15		A1
3082	CARR, Edward	34	E½SW	1900-10-04		A1
3085	CLARK, Eli C	33	1	1873-05-01		A1
3086	" "	33	SWSE	1873-05-01		A1
3087	" "	9	W½NW	1873-05-01		A1
3141	COMPANY, Land Log And Lumber	23	NWNE	1885-12-10		A1
3227	COON, Willie A	10	1	1904-11-30		A1
3228	" "	10	SWSE	1904-11-30		A1
3135	COX, Jesse	33	SESW	1904-08-30		A3 G59
3078	CUTTER, Charles C	13	3	1888-07-07		A1 R3201
3079	" "	24	1	1888-07-07		A1 G63
3137	DALEY, John	10	NENE	1884-06-20		A1 G64
3138	" "	11	NWNW	1884-06-20		A1 G64
3204	DIAMOND, William	10	NWNE	1889-04-04		A1
3205	" "	10	SWSW	1889-04-04		A1
3206	" "	3	4	1889-04-04		A1
3207	" "	3	5	1889-04-04		A1
3208	" "	3	6	1889-04-04		A1
3209	" "	3	SESW	1889-04-04		A1
3210	" "	3	W½SE	1889-04-04		A1
3211	" "	4	2	1889-04-04		A1
3212	" "	4	3	1889-04-04		A1
3213	" "	4	5	1889-04-04		A1
3214	" "	4	S½NW	1889-04-04		A1
3215	" "	9	9	1889-04-04		A1

ID	Individual in Patent	Sec.	Sec. Part	Date Issued	Other Counties	For More Info . . .
3089	DOOLITTLE, Frances	15	SESE	1899-08-14		A1
3149	DOYLE, Mike F	11	3	1902-03-07		A3 G78
3125	DWIGHT, Jeremiah W	1	1	1872-11-01		A1 G79
3126	" "	1	2	1872-11-01		A1 G79
3127	" "	1	NENW	1872-11-01		A1 G79
3128	" "	1	SENE	1872-11-01		A1 G79
3129	" "	10	S½NE	1872-11-01		A1 G79
3130	" "	13	1	1872-11-01		A1 G79
3131	" "	13	2	1872-11-01		A1 G79 R3136
3132	" "	14	2	1872-11-01		A1 G79
3133	" "	14	E½NW	1872-11-01		A1 G79
3134	" "	14	NWNE	1872-11-01		A1 G79
3071	EARLY, Henry W	25	NESE	1873-05-01		A1 G16
3072	" "	25	SENE	1873-05-01		A1 G16
3073	" "	35	2	1873-05-01		A1 G16
3074	" "	35	3	1873-05-01		A1 G16
3075	" "	35	N½SE	1873-05-01		A1 G16
3076	" "	35	S½NE	1873-05-01		A1 G16
3071	FORSMAN, Robert M	25	NESE	1873-05-01		A1 G16
3072	" "	25	SENE	1873-05-01		A1 G16
3073	" "	35	2	1873-05-01		A1 G16
3074	" "	35	3	1873-05-01		A1 G16
3075	" "	35	N½SE	1873-05-01		A1 G16
3076	" "	35	S½NE	1873-05-01		A1 G16
3202	GLEASON, Patrick	35	NWNW	1898-06-17		A1
3065	HAIGHT, Augustus	4	1	1872-11-01		A1
3066	" "	4	NENW	1872-11-01		A1
3080	HILLIS, David R	26	SWSW	1901-05-08		A1
3081	" "	27	SESE	1901-05-08		A1
3102	HYLAND, George	1	S½SE	1883-09-15		A1 G111
3103	" "	1	SW	1883-09-15		A1 G111
3104	" "	1	SWNE	1883-09-15		A1 G111
3105	" "	12	1	1883-09-15		A1 G111 R3218
3106	" "	12	NWNE	1883-09-15		A1 G111
3107	" "	12	S½NE	1883-09-15		A1 G111
3102	HYLAND, John	1	S½SE	1883-09-15		A1 G111
3103	" "	1	SW	1883-09-15		A1 G111
3104	" "	1	SWNE	1883-09-15		A1 G111
3105	" "	12	1	1883-09-15		A1 G111 R3218
3106	" "	12	NWNE	1883-09-15		A1 G111
3107	" "	12	S½NE	1883-09-15		A1 G111
3137	INGRAHAM, James E	10	NENE	1884-06-20		A1 G64
3138	" "	11	NWNW	1884-06-20		A1 G64
3092	JOHNSON, Frederick S	12	2	1873-05-01		A1 G118
3093	" "	12	3	1873-05-01		A1 G118
3094	" "	12	NW	1873-05-01		A1 M118
3095	" "	12	NWSE	1873-05-01		A1 G118
3096	" "	2	6	1873-05-01		A1 G118
3097	" "	2	7	1873-05-01		A1 G118
3098	" "	2	S½SE	1873-05-01		A1 G118
3099	" "	2	W½SW	1873-05-01		A1 G118
3100	" "	3	3	1873-05-01		A3 G118
3101	" "	3	E½SE	1873-05-01		A1 G118
3092	JOHNSON, Thew	12	2	1873-05-01		A1 G118
3093	" "	12	3	1873-05-01		A1 G118
3094	" "	12	NW	1873-05-01		A1 G118
3095	" "	12	NWSE	1873-05-01		A1 G118
3096	" "	2	6	1873-05-01		A1 G118
3097	" "	2	7	1873-05-01		A1 G118
3098	" "	2	S½SE	1873-05-01		A1 G118
3099	" "	2	W½SW	1873-05-01		A1 G118
3100	" "	3	3	1873-05-01		A1 G118
3101	" "	3	E½SE	1873-05-01		A1 G118
3149	JONES, Adoniram J	11	3	1902-03-07		A3 G78
3071	LENTZ, George W	25	NESE	1873-05-01		A1 G16
3072	" "	25	SENE	1873-05-01		A1 G16
3073	" "	35	2	1873-05-01		A1 G16
3074	" "	35	3	1873-05-01		A1 G16
3075	" "	35	N½SE	1873-05-01		A1 G16
3076	" "	35	S½NE	1873-05-01		A1 G16
3123	LOUGHRIN, James H	21	N½NW	1893-07-19		A1
3124	" "	21	W½NE	1893-07-19		A1
3218	MCARTHUR, William	12	1	1903-10-01		A3 R3105

ID	Individual in Patent	Sec.	Sec. Part	Date Issued	Other Counties	For More Info . . .
3083	MCCALL, Edwin	15	NWSW	1892-05-16		A1
3084	" "	15	S½SW	1892-05-16		A1
3088	MCDONALD, Finley	23	SWNE	1888-07-18		A1
3125	MCGRAW, John	1	1	1872-11-01		A1 G79
3126	" "	1	2	1872-11-01		A1 G79
3127	" "	1	NENW	1872-11-01		A1 G79
3128	" "	1	SENE	1872-11-01		A1 G79
3129	" "	10	S½NE	1872-11-01		A1 G79
3130	" "	13	1	1872-11-01		A1 G79
3131	" "	13	2	1872-11-01		A1 G79 R3136
3132	" "	14	2	1872-11-01		A1 G79
3133	" "	14	E½NW	1872-11-01		A1 G79
3134	" "	14	NWNE	1872-11-01		A1 G79
3229	MILLER, Wilmot H	3	1	1889-03-28		A1
3230	" "	3	2	1889-03-28		A1
3231	" "	3	SENE	1889-03-28		A1
3139	NEWMAN, L M	25	SWSE	1883-04-20		A1
3140	" "	36	W½NE	1883-04-20		A1
3219	PATRICK, William S	11	4	1872-11-01		A1
3220	" "	11	5	1872-11-01		A1
3221	" "	11	6	1872-11-01		A1
3222	" "	11	E½SE	1872-11-01		A1
3223	" "	11	NENE	1872-11-01		A1
3224	" "	11	S½NE	1872-11-01		A1
3225	" "	14	1	1872-11-01		A1
3226	" "	23	E½NW	1872-11-01		A1
3120	PILLSBURY, H M	26	3	1889-05-31		A1
3079	PILLSBURY, Harry	24	1	1888-07-07		A1 G63
3150	PILLSBURY, Oliver P	11	NENW	1885-01-15		A1
3151	" "	11	NWNE	1885-01-15		A1
3152	" "	14	4	1885-01-15		A1
3153	" "	14	E½SW	1885-01-15		A1
3154	" "	14	SWSE	1885-01-15		A1
3155	" "	2	3	1885-01-15		A1
3156	" "	2	5	1885-01-15		A1
3157	" "	2	NWNW	1885-01-15		A1
3158	" "	2	SESW	1885-01-15		A1
3159	" "	2	SWNW	1885-01-15		A1
3160	" "	23	1	1885-01-15		A1
3161	" "	26	1	1885-01-15		A1
3162	" "	26	2	1885-01-15		A1
3163	" "	26	4	1885-01-15		A1
3164	" "	26	NW	1885-01-15		A1
3165	" "	26	NWSW	1885-01-15		A1
3166	" "	27	3	1885-01-15		A1
3167	" "	27	NESE	1885-01-15		A1
3168	" "	27	NWNW	1885-01-15		A1
3169	" "	27	NWSW	1885-01-15		A1
3170	" "	27	SENE	1885-01-15		A1
3171	" "	28	4	1885-01-15		A1
3172	" "	28	NESE	1885-01-15		A1
3173	" "	28	SESE	1885-01-15		A1
3174	" "	28	SWSE	1885-01-15		A1
3175	" "	3	7	1885-01-15		A1
3176	" "	33	N½NE	1885-01-15		A1
3177	" "	33	N½SE	1885-01-15		A1
3178	" "	33	N½SW	1885-01-15		A1
3179	" "	33	NENW	1885-01-15		A1
3180	" "	33	SENE	1885-01-15		A1
3181	" "	33	SENW	1885-01-15		A1
3182	" "	33	SWNE	1885-01-15		A1
3183	" "	33	SWNW	1885-01-15		A1
3184	" "	33	SWSW	1885-01-15		A1
3185	" "	34	1	1885-01-15		A1
3186	" "	34	2	1885-01-15		A1
3187	" "	34	3	1885-01-15		A1
3188	" "	34	NENE	1885-01-15		A1
3189	" "	34	NESE	1885-01-15		A1
3190	" "	34	NWNW	1885-01-15		A1
3191	" "	34	NWSE	1885-01-15		A1
3192	" "	34	SENW	1885-01-15		A1
3193	" "	34	SWNE	1885-01-15		A1
3194	" "	34	SWNW	1885-01-15		A1

ID	Individual in Patent	Sec.	Sec. Part	Date Issued	Other Counties	For More Info . . .
3195	PILLSBURY, Oliver P (Cont'd)	35	SENW	1885-01-15		A1
3196	" "	36	SENE	1885-01-15		A1
3197	" "	36	SENW	1885-01-15		A1
3198	" "	36	SW	1885-01-15		A1
3199	" "	4	8	1885-01-15		A1
3200	" "	9	SENE	1885-01-15		A1
3137	SAMPSON, Henry	10	NENE	1884-06-20		A1 G64
3138	" "	11	NWNW	1884-06-20		A1 G64
3092	SHAFFER, Isaac	12	2	1873-05-01		A1 G118
3093	" "	12	3	1873-05-01		A1 G118
3094	" "	12	NW	1873-05-01		A1 G118
3095	" "	12	NWSE	1873-05-01		A1 G118
3096	" "	2	6	1873-05-01		A1 G118
3097	" "	2	7	1873-05-01		A1 G118
3098	" "	2	S½SE	1873-05-01		A1 G118
3099	" "	2	W½SW	1873-05-01		A1 G118
3100	" "	3	3	1873-05-01		A1 G118
3101	" "	3	E½SE	1873-05-01		A1 G118
3108	SILVERTHORN, George	1	N½NE	1886-07-30		A1 F
3109	" "	1	N½SE	1886-07-30		A1
3110	" "	2	1	1886-07-30		A1
3111	" "	2	2	1886-07-30		A1
3112	" "	21	W½SE	1886-07-30		A1
3113	" "	27	2	1886-07-30		A1
3115	" "	27	SWNW	1886-07-30		A1
3117	" "	35	1	1886-07-30		A1
3118	" "	4	7	1886-07-30		A1
3119	" "	9	7	1886-07-30		A1
3116	" "	34	SWSE	1886-08-10		A1
3114	" "	27	4	1889-05-09		A1
3135	STEVENS, Earl	33	SESW	1904-08-30		A3 G59
3121	STOECKEL, Heinrich	28	3	1905-12-30		A3
3122	" "	33	NWNW	1905-12-30		A3
3090	WACHTER, Franz	21	NESW	1906-12-17		A3
3091	" "	21	SENW	1906-12-17		A3
3203	WALSH, Richard	28	5	1904-06-27		A1
3137	WITTER, Jere D	10	NENE	1884-06-20		A1 G64
3138	" "	11	NWNW	1884-06-20		A1 G64

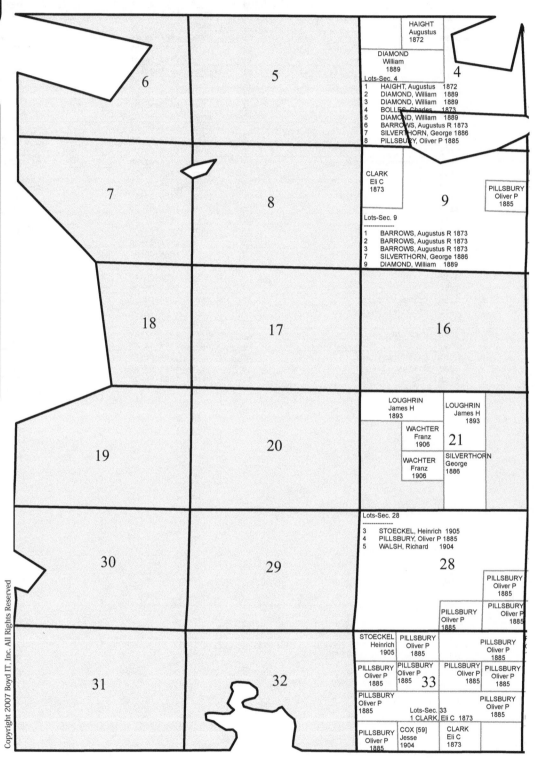

Patent Map

T41-N R6-E
4th PM - 1831 MN/WI

Map Group 19

Township Statistics

Parcels Mapped	:	167
Number of Patents	:	60
Number of Individuals	:	48
Patentees Identified	:	37
Number of Surnames	:	44
Multi-Patentee Parcels	:	37
Oldest Patent Date	:	11/1/1872
Most Recent Patent	:	12/17/1906
Block/Lot Parcels	:	67
Parcels Re - Issued	:	3
Parcels that Overlap	:	0
Cities and Towns	:	0
Cemeteries	:	0

6

5

HAIGHT
Augustus
1872

DIAMOND
William
1889

4

Lots-Sec. 4
------
1   HAIGHT, Augustus   1872
2   DIAMOND, William   1889
3   DIAMOND, William   1889
4   BOLLES, Charles   1873
5   DIAMOND, William   1889
6   BARROWS, Augustus R 1873
7   SILVERTHORN, George 1886
8   PILLSBURY, Oliver P 1885

7

8

CLARK
Eli C
1873

9

PILLSBURY
Oliver P
1885

Lots-Sec. 9
------
1   BARROWS, Augustus R 1873
2   BARROWS, Augustus R 1873
3   BARROWS, Augustus R 1873
7   SILVERTHORN, George 1886
9   DIAMOND, William   1889

18

17

16

19

20

LOUGHRIN
James H
1893

WACHTER
Franz
1906

WACHTER
Franz
1906

LOUGHRIN
James H
1893

21

SILVERTHORN
George
1886

30

29

Lots-Sec. 28
------
3   STOECKEL, Heinrich 1905
4   PILLSBURY, Oliver P 1885
5   WALSH, Richard   1904

28

PILLSBURY
Oliver P
1885

PILLSBURY
Oliver P
1885

PILLSBURY
Oliver P
1885

31

32

STOECKEL
Heinrich
1905

PILLSBURY
Oliver P
1885

PILLSBURY
Oliver P
1885

PILLSBURY
Oliver P
1885

PILLSBURY
Oliver P
1885

33

PILLSBURY
Oliver P
1885

PILLSBURY
Oliver P
1885

PILLSBURY
Oliver P
1885

Lots-Sec. 33
1 CLARK, Eli C 1873

PILLSBURY
Oliver P
1885

PILLSBURY
Oliver P
1885

COX [59]
Jesse
1904

CLARK
Eli C
1873

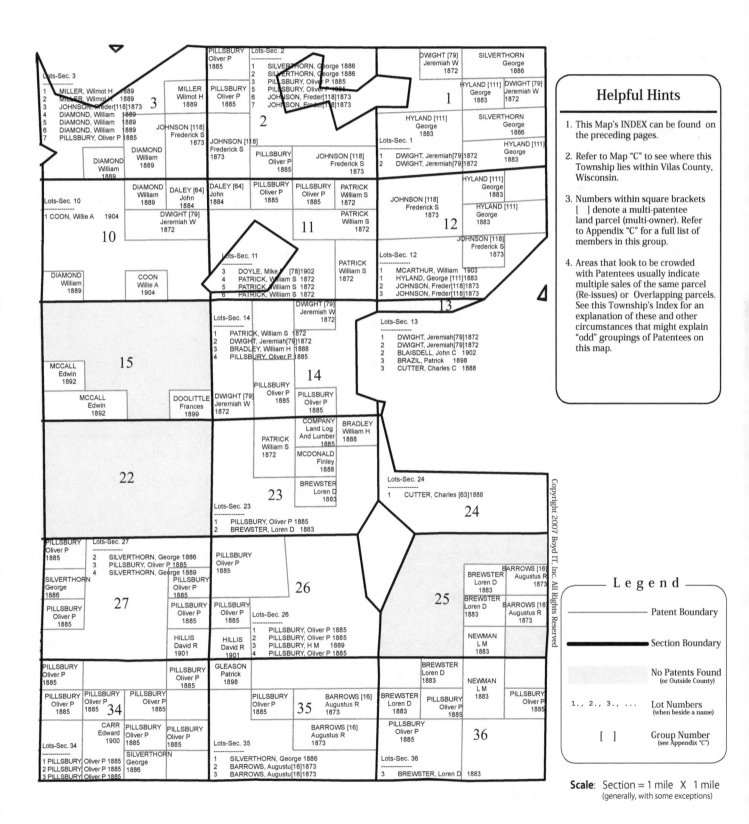

Helpful Hints

1. This Map's INDEX can be found on the preceding pages.

2. Refer to Map "C" to see where this Township lies within Vilas County, Wisconsin.

3. Numbers within square brackets [ ] denote a multi-patentee land parcel (multi-owner). Refer to Appendix "C" for a full list of members in this group.

4. Areas that look to be crowded with Patentees usually indicate multiple sales of the same parcel (Re-issues) or Overlapping parcels. See this Township's Index for an explanation of these and other circumstances that might explain "odd" groupings of Patentees on this map.

Copyright 2007 Boyd IT, Inc. All Rights Reserved

Legend

————— Patent Boundary

━━━━━ Section Boundary

　　　 No Patents Found
　　　 (or Outside County)

1., 2., 3., ...　Lot Numbers
　　　 (when beside a name)

[ ]　Group Number
　　　 (see Appendix "C")

Scale: Section = 1 mile X 1 mile
(generally, with some exceptions)

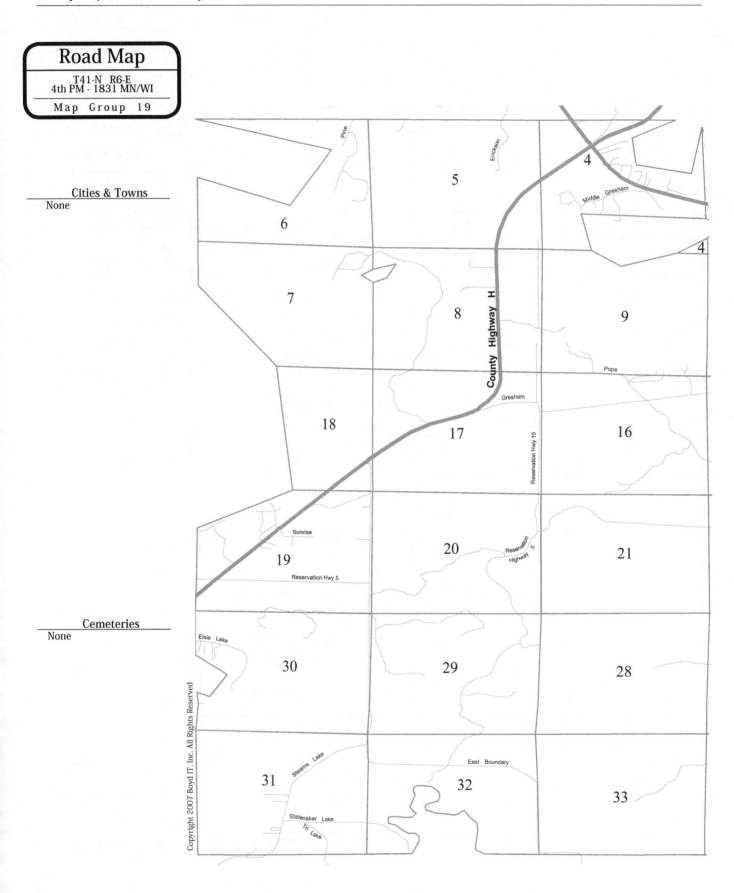

Road Map

T41-N R6-E
4th PM - 1831 MN/WI

Map Group 19

Cities & Towns
None

Cemeteries
None

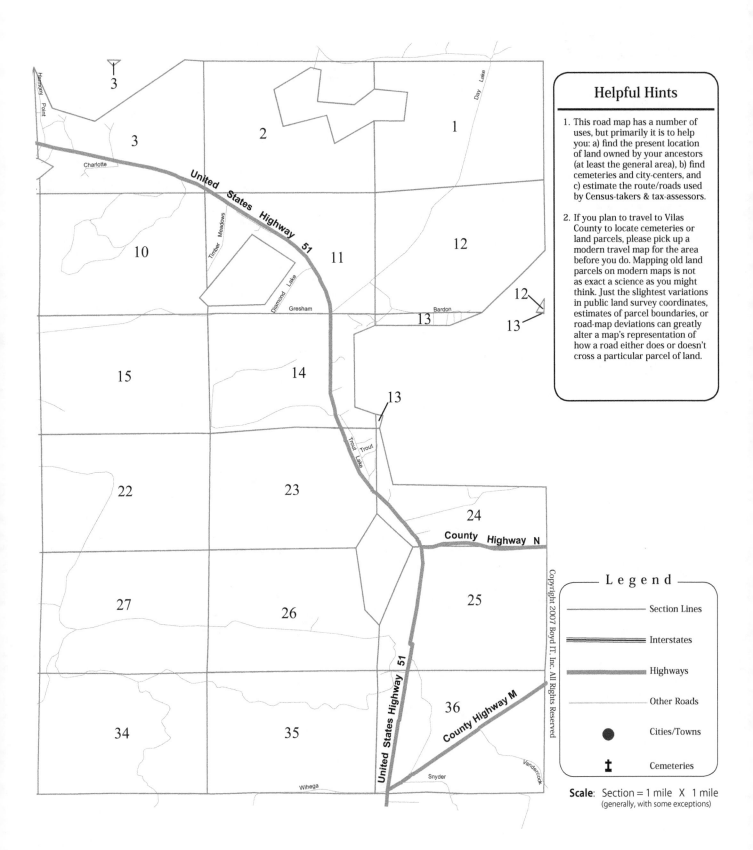

1. This road map has a number of uses, but primarily it is to help you: a) find the present location of land owned by your ancestors (at least the general area), b) find cemeteries and city-centers, and c) estimate the route/roads used by Census-takers & tax-assessors.

2. If you plan to travel to Vilas County to locate cemeteries or land parcels, please pick up a modern travel map for the area before you do. Mapping old land parcels on modern maps is not as exact a science as you might think. Just the slightest variations in public land survey coordinates, estimates of parcel boundaries, or road-map deviations can greatly alter a map's representation of how a road either does or doesn't cross a particular parcel of land.

Legend

———— Section Lines

━━━━ Interstates

━━━━ Highways

———— Other Roads

● Cities/Towns

† Cemeteries

Scale: Section = 1 mile X 1 mile
(generally, with some exceptions)

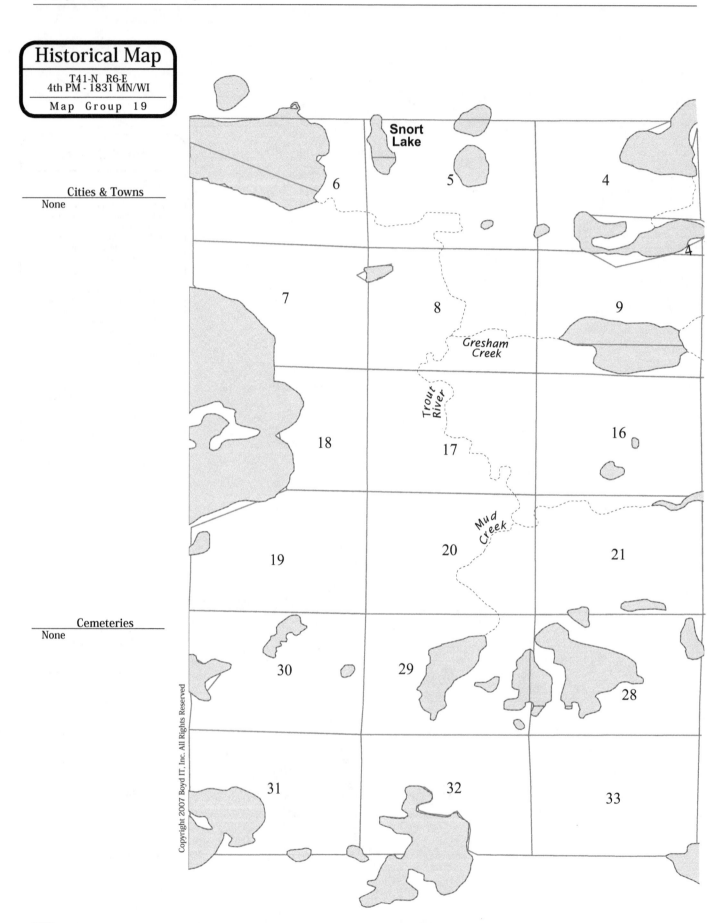

Historical Map

T41-N R6-E
4th PM - 1831 MN/WI

Map Group 19

Cities & Towns
None

Cemeteries
None

Snort
Lake

6

5

4

4

7

8

9

Gresham
Creek

Trout
River

18

17

16

19

20

Mud
Creek

21

30

29

28

31

32

33

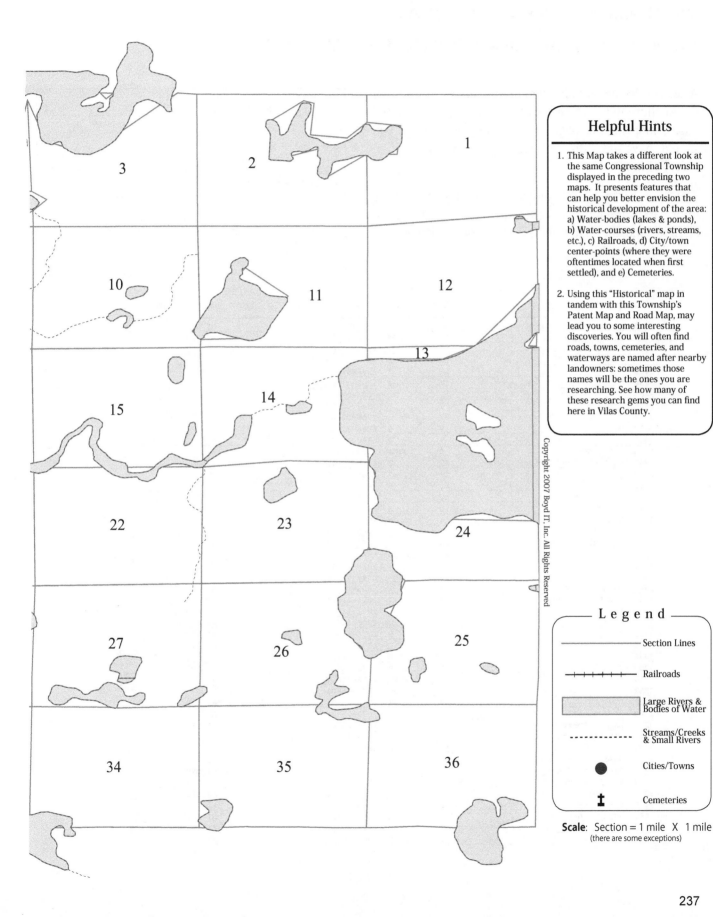

Helpful Hints

1. This Map takes a different look at the same Congressional Township displayed in the preceding two maps. It presents features that can help you better envision the historical development of the area: a) Water-bodies (lakes & ponds), b) Water-courses (rivers, streams, etc.), c) Railroads, d) City/town center-points (where they were oftentimes located when first settled), and e) Cemeteries.

2. Using this "Historical" map in tandem with this Township's Patent Map and Road Map, may lead you to some interesting discoveries. You will often find roads, towns, cemeteries, and waterways are named after nearby landowners: sometimes those names will be the ones you are researching. See how many of these research gems you can find here in Vilas County.

Legend

———————	Section Lines
┼┼┼┼┼┼┼	Railroads
▭	Large Rivers & Bodies of Water
- - - - - - -	Streams/Creeks & Small Rivers
●	Cities/Towns
⚱	Cemeteries

Scale: Section = 1 mile X 1 mile
(there are some exceptions)

Map Group 20: Index to Land Patents

Township 41-North Range 7-East (4th PM - 1831 MN/WI)

After you locate an individual in this Index, take note of the Section and Section Part then proceed to the Land Patent map on the pages immediately following. You should have no difficulty locating the corresponding parcel of land.

The "For More Info" Column will lead you to more information about the underlying Patents. See the *Legend* at right, and the "How to Use this Book" chapter, for more information.

```
                    LEGEND
          "For More Info . . . " column
A = Authority (Legislative Act, See Appendix "A")
B = Block or Lot (location in Section unknown)
C = Cancelled Patent
F = Fractional Section
G = Group  (Multi-Patentee Patent, see Appendix "C")
V = Overlaps another Parcel
R = Re-Issued (Parcel patented more than once)

(A & G items require you to look in the Appendixes referred
to above. All other Letter-designations followed by a number
require you to locate line-items in this index that possess
the ID number found after the letter).
```

ID	Individual in Patent	Sec.	Sec. Part	Date Issued	Other Counties	For More Info . . .
3243	BARROWS, Augustus R	30	SWNW	1873-05-01		A1 G16
3453	BLACKWELL, Samuel V	11	SENW	1906-06-16		A3 G24
3481	BRADLEY, William H	17	1	1888-07-07		A1
3482	" "	17	2	1888-07-07		A1
3483	" "	17	3	1888-07-07		A1
3484	" "	17	4	1888-07-07		A1
3485	" "	19	2	1888-07-07		A1
3486	" "	20	5	1888-07-07		A1
3487	" "	20	6	1888-07-07		A1
3488	" "	7	5	1888-07-07		A1
3489	" "	8	4	1888-07-07		A1
3255	CARR, Edward	9	SWNE	1900-10-04		A1
3348	COMPANY, Land Log And Lumber	22	2	1888-07-10		A1
3349	" "	22	7	1888-07-10		A1
3350	" "	22	8	1888-07-10		A1
3460	COOK, Thomas D	31	1	1889-05-09		A1 G57
3341	DALEY, John	19	3	1884-06-20		A1 G64
3342	DERN, John	15	NESW	1899-04-22		A3
3351	DOOLITTLE, Lettie	20	2	1900-10-04		A1
3233	DRINKER, Albert E	25	2	1883-09-15		A1
3234	" "	25	SESW	1883-09-15		A1
3235	" "	36	1	1883-09-15		A1
3236	" "	36	NENW	1883-09-15		A1
3343	DRINKER, John T	25	1	1883-09-15		A1
3331	DWIGHT, Jeremiah W	2	7	1872-11-01		A1 G79
3332	" "	2	8	1872-11-01		A1 G79
3334	" "	20	7	1872-11-01		A1 G79
3335	" "	20	9	1872-11-01		A1 G79
3336	" "	23	NWNW	1872-11-01		A1 G79
3338	" "	3	SESE	1872-11-01		A1 G79
3339	" "	33	SESE	1872-11-01		A1 G79
3330	" "	12	E½NE	1873-05-01		A1 G79
3333	" "	2	SWSW	1873-05-01		A1 G79
3337	" "	29	NWNW	1873-05-01		A1 G79
3340	" "	4	NENE	1873-05-01		A1 G79
3243	EARLY, Henry W	30	SWNW	1873-05-01		A1 G16
3243	FORSMAN, Robert M	30	SWNW	1873-05-01		A1 G16
3477	GILBERT, W R	19	1	1888-07-07		A1
3496	GRAYSON, William S	30	NWSW	1912-01-04		A3 G94
3324	HAMILTON, Irenus K	36	3	1873-05-01		A1 G97
3324	HAMILTON, Woodman C	36	3	1873-05-01		A1 G97
3329	HARTMAN, Jacob H	3	8	1905-08-26		A3 G105
3460	HYDE, Edwin	31	1	1889-05-09		A1 G57
3262	HYLAND, George	1	N½SE	1883-09-15		A1 G111
3263	" "	1	SESE	1883-09-15		A1 G111
3264	" "	1	SWSE	1883-09-15		A1 G111

ID	Individual in Patent	Sec.	Sec. Part	Date Issued	Other Counties	For More Info . . .
3265	HYLAND, George (Cont'd)	10	N½SE	1883-09-15		A1 G111
3266	" "	10	NENE	1883-09-15		A1 G111
3267	" "	10	NWNE	1883-09-15		A1 G111
3268	" "	10	S½NE	1883-09-15		A1 G111
3270	" "	10	SWSE	1883-09-15		A1 G111
3271	" "	10	W½	1883-09-15		A1 G111
3272	" "	11	NESE	1883-09-15		A1 G111
3273	" "	11	NWNW	1883-09-15		A1 G111
3275	" "	11	SWNE	1883-09-15		A1 G111
3278	" "	12	SESW	1883-09-15		A1 G111
3279	" "	12	W½SE	1883-09-15		A1 G111
3280	" "	13	6	1883-09-15		A1 G111
3281	" "	13	N½NW	1883-09-15		A1 G111
3282	" "	13	NWNE	1883-09-15		A1 G111
3283	" "	13	SENW	1883-09-15		A1 G111
3284	" "	14	NENE	1883-09-15		A1 G111
3285	" "	14	NWNW	1883-09-15		A1 G111
3286	" "	14	S½NE	1883-09-15		A1 G111
3287	" "	14	S½NW	1883-09-15		A1 G111
3288	" "	15	NENE	1883-09-15		A1 G111
3289	" "	15	NESE	1883-09-15		A1 G111
3291	" "	15	NWSW	1883-09-15		A1 G111
3292	" "	2	6	1883-09-15		A1 G111
3293	" "	22	1	1883-09-15		A1 G111
3294	" "	22	4	1883-09-15		A1 G111
3296	" "	25	NENW	1883-09-15		A1 G111
3297	" "	25	SWSW	1883-09-15		A1 G111
3298	" "	26	SESE	1883-09-15		A1 G111
3299	" "	27	3	1883-09-15		A1 G111
3300	" "	28	2	1883-09-15		A1 G111
3301	" "	28	3	1883-09-15		A1 G111
3302	" "	28	4	1883-09-15		A1 G111
3303	" "	28	5	1883-09-15		A1 G111
3304	" "	28	6	1883-09-15		A1 G111
3305	" "	3	3	1883-09-15		A1 G111
3306	" "	3	4	1883-09-15		A1 G111
3307	" "	3	SWSW	1883-09-15		A1 G111
3308	" "	34	NWSW	1883-09-15		A1 G111
3309	" "	4	S½SE	1883-09-15		A1 G111
3310	" "	5	1	1883-09-15		A1 G111
3311	" "	5	2	1883-09-15		A1 G111
3312	" "	5	3	1883-09-15		A1 G111
3313	" "	5	SENE	1883-09-15		A1 G111
3314	" "	6	1	1883-09-15		A1 G111
3315	" "	6	2	1883-09-15		A1 G111
3316	" "	6	3	1883-09-15		A1 G111
3317	" "	7	1	1883-09-15		A1 G111
3318	" "	8	NESE	1883-09-15		A1 G111
3319	" "	8	SENW	1883-09-15		A1 G111
3320	" "	9	1	1883-09-15		A1 G111
3321	" "	9	4	1883-09-15		A1 G111
3322	" "	9	NESE	1883-09-15		A1 G111
3323	" "	9	SENE	1883-09-15		A1 G111
3269	" "	10	SESE	1884-06-20		A1 G111
3274	" "	11	SESE	1884-06-20		A1 G111
3276	" "	11	SWNW	1884-06-20		A1 G111
3277	" "	11	SWSW	1884-06-20		A1 G111
3290	" "	15	NWNE	1884-06-20		A1 G111
3295	" "	22	5	1884-06-20		A1 G111
3262	HYLAND, John	1	N½SE	1883-09-15		A1 G111
3263	" "	1	SESE	1883-09-15		A1 G111
3264	" "	1	SWSE	1883-09-15		A1 G111
3265	" "	10	N½SE	1883-09-15		A1 G111
3266	" "	10	NENE	1883-09-15		A1 G111
3267	" "	10	NWNE	1883-09-15		A1 G111
3268	" "	10	S½NE	1883-09-15		A1 G111
3270	" "	10	SWSE	1883-09-15		A1 G111
3271	" "	10	W½	1883-09-15		A1 G111
3272	" "	11	NESE	1883-09-15		A1 G111
3273	" "	11	NWNW	1883-09-15		A1 G111
3275	" "	11	SWNE	1883-09-15		A1 G111
3278	" "	12	SESW	1883-09-15		A1 G111
3279	" "	12	W½SE	1883-09-15		A1 G111

ID	Individual in Patent	Sec.	Sec. Part	Date Issued	Other Counties	For More Info . . .
3280	HYLAND, John (Cont'd)	13	6	1883-09-15		A1 G111
3281	" "	13	N½NW	1883-09-15		A1 G111
3282	" "	13	NWNE	1883-09-15		A1 G111
3283	" "	13	SENW	1883-09-15		A1 G111
3284	" "	14	NENE	1883-09-15		A1 G111
3285	" "	14	NWNW	1883-09-15		A1 G111
3286	" "	14	S½NE	1883-09-15		A1 G111
3287	" "	14	S½NW	1883-09-15		A1 G111
3288	" "	15	NENE	1883-09-15		A1 G111
3289	" "	15	NESE	1883-09-15		A1 G111
3291	" "	15	NWSW	1883-09-15		A1 G111
3292	" "	2	6	1883-09-15		A1 G111
3293	" "	22	1	1883-09-15		A1 G111
3294	" "	22	4	1883-09-15		A1 G111
3296	" "	25	NENW	1883-09-15		A1 G111
3297	" "	25	SWSW	1883-09-15		A1 G111
3298	" "	26	SESE	1883-09-15		A1 G111
3299	" "	27	3	1883-09-15		A1 G111
3300	" "	28	2	1883-09-15		A1 G111
3301	" "	28	3	1883-09-15		A1 G111
3302	" "	28	4	1883-09-15		A1 G111
3303	" "	28	5	1883-09-15		A1 G111
3304	" "	28	6	1883-09-15		A1 G111
3305	" "	3	3	1883-09-15		A1 G111
3306	" "	3	4	1883-09-15		A1 G111
3307	" "	3	SWSW	1883-09-15		A1 G111
3308	" "	34	NWSW	1883-09-15		A1 G111
3309	" "	4	S½SE	1883-09-15		A1 G111
3310	" "	5	1	1883-09-15		A1 G111
3311	" "	5	2	1883-09-15		A1 G111
3312	" "	5	3	1883-09-15		A1 G111
3313	" "	5	SENE	1883-09-15		A1 G111
3314	" "	6	1	1883-09-15		A1 G111
3315	" "	6	2	1883-09-15		A1 G111
3316	" "	6	3	1883-09-15		A1 G111
3317	" "	7	1	1883-09-15		A1 G111
3318	" "	8	NESE	1883-09-15		A1 G111
3319	" "	8	SENW	1883-09-15		A1 G111
3320	" "	9	1	1883-09-15		A1 G111
3321	" "	9	4	1883-09-15		A1 G111
3322	" "	9	NESE	1883-09-15		A1 G111
3323	" "	9	SENE	1883-09-15		A1 G111
3269	" "	10	SESE	1884-06-20		A1 G111
3274	" "	11	SESE	1884-06-20		A1 G111
3276	" "	11	SWNW	1884-06-20		A1 G111
3277	" "	11	SWSW	1884-06-20		A1 G111
3290	" "	15	NWNE	1884-06-20		A1 G111
3295	" "	22	5	1884-06-20		A1 G111
3341	INGRAHAM, James E	19	3	1884-06-20		A1 G64
3496	JONES, Granville D	30	NWSW	1912-01-04		A3 G94
3490	KELLY, William P	25	NWSE	1873-11-15		A1
3491	" "	25	SWNE	1873-11-15		A1
3492	" "	36	2	1873-11-15		A1
3493	" "	36	4	1873-11-15		A1
3494	" "	36	8	1873-11-15		A1
3495	" "	36	SESE	1873-11-15		A1
3347	KENNAN, K K	21	1	1889-05-09		A1
3232	LAFONTAISIE, Adolphe	1	E½SW	1900-11-28		A3
3243	LENTZ, George W	30	SWNW	1873-05-01		A1 G16
3450	LEVINGSTON, Robert	2	4	1901-12-30		A3
3451	" "	2	5	1901-12-30		A3
3452	" "	3	2	1901-12-30		A3
3354	LOVELESS, Oliver A	17	7	1902-05-27		A3
3355	" "	17	SWNE	1902-05-27		A3
3329	MANSON, Herbert H	3	8	1905-08-26		A3 G105
3256	MATHEWS, F E	28	1	1889-03-28		A1
3257	MCDONALD, Finley	31	4	1888-07-18		A1
3258	" "	33	W½SE	1888-07-18		A1
3331	MCGRAW, John	2	7	1872-11-01		A1 G79
3332	" "	2	8	1872-11-01		A1 G79
3334	" "	20	7	1872-11-01		A1 G79
3335	" "	20	9	1872-11-01		A1 G79
3336	" "	23	NWNW	1872-11-01		A1 G79

ID	Individual in Patent	Sec.	Sec. Part	Date Issued	Other Counties	For More Info . . .
3338	MCGRAW, John (Cont'd)	3	SESE	1872-11-01		A1 G79
3339	" "	33	SESE	1872-11-01		A1 G79
3330	" "	12	E½NE	1873-05-01		A1 G79
3333	" "	2	SWSW	1873-05-01		A1 G79
3337	" "	29	NWNW	1873-05-01		A1 G79
3340	" "	4	NENE	1873-05-01		A1 G79
3253	MILES, E M	32	2	1890-07-15		A1
3254	" "	32	9	1890-07-15		A1
3455	MILLER, Thomas A	19	7	1911-01-19		A1
3461	MILLER, W L	24	SESE	1889-03-29		A1
3462	" "	25	NWNE	1889-03-29		A1
3463	" "	26	SESW	1889-03-29		A1
3464	" "	26	W½SW	1889-03-29		A1
3465	" "	27	SESE	1889-03-29		A1
3466	" "	33	E½NE	1889-03-29		A1
3467	" "	34	E½NE	1889-03-29		A1
3468	" "	34	E½SW	1889-03-29		A1
3469	" "	34	NENW	1889-03-29		A1
3470	" "	34	NESE	1889-03-29		A1
3471	" "	34	SWNE	1889-03-29		A1
3472	" "	34	SWNW	1889-03-29		A1
3473	" "	35	NWNW	1889-03-29		A1
3474	" "	35	S½NW	1889-03-29		A1
3475	" "	35	S½SE	1889-03-29		A1
3476	" "	35	SW	1889-03-29		A1
3478	MILLER, Walter L	1	SWSW	1889-03-29		A1
3479	" "	11	NENE	1889-03-29		A1
3480	" "	12	NENW	1889-03-29		A1
3498	MILLER, Wilmot H	11	N½SW	1889-03-28		A1
3499	" "	11	NENW	1889-03-28		A1
3500	" "	11	NWNE	1889-03-28		A1
3501	" "	11	SENE	1889-03-28		A1
3502	" "	11	W½SE	1889-03-28		A1
3503	" "	12	SENW	1889-03-28		A1
3504	" "	12	W½NW	1889-03-28		A1
3505	" "	12	W½SW	1889-03-28		A1
3506	" "	15	NWSE	1889-03-28		A1
3507	" "	25	NENE	1889-03-28		A1
3245	MILLERD, B F	2	SESW	1888-07-10		A1
3454	NIELSEN, Theodor	35	N½NE	1888-07-18		A1
3453	NOEL, Peter J	11	SENW	1906-06-16		A3 G24
3325	PARSONS, Isaac	28	8	1884-06-30		A1 G152
3326	" "	29	NESW	1884-06-30		A1 G152
3327	" "	30	NWNW	1884-06-30		A1 G152
3328	" "	33	SWNE	1884-06-30		A1 G152
3497	PATRICK, William S	29	3	1872-11-01		A1
3435	PETERS, Richard G	25	NESW	1883-09-15		A1
3436	" "	26	NESE	1883-09-15		A1
3437	" "	26	NWNW	1883-09-15		A1
3438	" "	28	11	1883-09-15		A1
3439	" "	28	SWSE	1883-09-15		A1
3440	" "	30	NWNE	1883-09-15		A1
3441	" "	33	1	1883-09-15		A1
3442	" "	33	2	1883-09-15		A1
3443	" "	33	4	1883-09-15		A1
3444	" "	33	NESE	1883-09-15		A1
3445	" "	33	NWNE	1883-09-15		A1
3446	" "	34	SESE	1883-09-15		A1
3447	" "	34	SWSW	1883-09-15		A1
3448	" "	35	NENW	1883-09-15		A1
3449	" "	36	NWNW	1883-09-15		A1
3356	PILLSBURY, Oliver P	1	SENE	1884-06-30		A1
3358	" "	12	NWNE	1884-06-30		A1
3376	" "	2	2	1884-06-30		A1
3377	" "	2	3	1884-06-30		A1
3425	" "	36	5	1884-06-30		A1
3426	" "	36	6	1884-06-30		A1
3427	" "	36	7	1884-06-30		A1
3428	" "	36	SWNW	1884-06-30		A1
3357	" "	11	SESW	1885-01-15		A1
3359	" "	13	4	1885-01-15		A1
3360	" "	13	SWNW	1885-01-15		A1
3361	" "	14	NENW	1885-01-15		A1

ID	Individual in Patent	Sec.	Sec. Part	Date Issued	Other Counties	For More Info . . .
3362	PILLSBURY, Oliver P (Cont'd)	14	NWNE	1885-01-15		A1
3363	" "	15	1	1885-01-15		A1
3364	" "	15	2	1885-01-15		A1
3365	" "	15	3	1885-01-15		A1
3366	" "	15	4	1885-01-15		A1
3367	" "	15	NENW	1885-01-15		A1
3368	" "	15	S½NE	1885-01-15		A1
3369	" "	15	S½NW	1885-01-15		A1
3370	" "	17	5	1885-01-15		A1
3371	" "	17	6	1885-01-15		A1
3372	" "	17	N½NE	1885-01-15		A1
3373	" "	19	4	1885-01-15		A1
3374	" "	19	6	1885-01-15		A1
3375	" "	19	SESE	1885-01-15		A1
3378	" "	20	1	1885-01-15		A1
3379	" "	20	8	1885-01-15		A1
3380	" "	21	5	1885-01-15		A1
3381	" "	22	6	1885-01-15		A1
3382	" "	23	N½SW	1885-01-15		A1
3383	" "	23	NWSE	1885-01-15		A1
3384	" "	23	SENE	1885-01-15		A1
3385	" "	23	SWNW	1885-01-15		A1
3386	" "	23	SWSW	1885-01-15		A1
3387	" "	24	1	1885-01-15		A1
3388	" "	24	NENW	1885-01-15		A1
3389	" "	25	NWSW	1885-01-15		A1
3390	" "	25	SENW	1885-01-15		A1
3391	" "	26	NENW	1885-01-15		A1
3392	" "	26	NESW	1885-01-15		A1
3393	" "	26	SENW	1885-01-15		A1
3394	" "	26	SWNW	1885-01-15		A1
3395	" "	26	W½SE	1885-01-15		A1
3396	" "	27	1	1885-01-15		A1
3397	" "	27	4	1885-01-15		A1
3398	" "	27	N½SE	1885-01-15		A1
3399	" "	27	S½NE	1885-01-15		A1
3400	" "	27	SENW	1885-01-15		A1
3401	" "	27	SWSE	1885-01-15		A1
3402	" "	28	7	1885-01-15		A1
3403	" "	29	SESE	1885-01-15		A1
3404	" "	29	W½SE	1885-01-15		A1
3406	" "	3	6	1885-01-15		A1
3407	" "	30	1	1885-01-15		A1
3408	" "	30	NESW	1885-01-15		A1
3409	" "	31	NESW	1885-01-15		A1
3410	" "	31	NWNW	1885-01-15		A1
3411	" "	31	NWSE	1885-01-15		A1
3412	" "	31	S½SE	1885-01-15		A1
3413	" "	31	S½SW	1885-01-15		A1
3414	" "	31	SWNW	1885-01-15		A1
3415	" "	32	1	1885-01-15		A1
3416	" "	32	4	1885-01-15		A1
3417	" "	32	5	1885-01-15		A1
3418	" "	32	NWNE	1885-01-15		A1
3419	" "	33	3	1885-01-15		A1
3420	" "	34	NWNE	1885-01-15		A1
3421	" "	34	NWNW	1885-01-15		A1
3422	" "	34	NWSE	1885-01-15		A1
3423	" "	34	SENW	1885-01-15		A1
3424	" "	34	SWSE	1885-01-15		A1
3430	" "	7	4	1885-01-15		A1
3431	" "	8	3	1885-01-15		A1
3432	" "	8	NWSE	1885-01-15		A1
3433	" "	8	S½SE	1885-01-15		A1
3434	" "	9	2	1885-01-15		A1
3405	" "	3	5	1885-01-20		A1
3429	" "	4	SENE	1885-01-20		A1
3341	SAMPSON, Henry	19	3	1884-06-20		A1 G64
3251	SCHRIBER, Charles	12	NESW	1889-03-29		A1
3252	" "	12	SWNE	1889-03-29		A1
3456	SCOTT, Thomas B	17	8	1883-09-15		A1
3457	" "	24	SESW	1883-09-15		A1
3458	" "	24	W½SE	1883-09-15		A1

ID	Individual in Patent	Sec.	Sec. Part	Date Issued	Other Counties	For More Info . . .
3459	SCOTT, Thomas B (Cont'd)	25	SENE	1883-09-15		A1
3344	SEVERANCE, Joseph	13	1	1903-11-10		A3 G158
3244	STARKS, B C	30	S½NE	1889-03-29		A1 G165
3259	STEVENSON, Francis W	4	N½SE	1883-09-15		A1
3260	" "	4	NW	1883-09-15		A1
3261	" "	4	W½NE	1883-09-15		A1
3244	STICKLES, C R	30	S½NE	1889-03-29		A1 G165
3352	THOMPSON, Neil A	12	E½SE	1873-11-15		A1
3353	" "	13	5	1873-11-15		A1
3325	TILLOTSON, Levi	28	8	1884-06-30		A1 G152
3326	" "	29	NESW	1884-06-30		A1 G152
3327	" "	30	NWNW	1884-06-30		A1 G152
3328	" "	33	SWNE	1884-06-30		A1 G152
3345	TOOLEY, Joseph	14	NESW	1895-03-30		A1
3346	" "	14	NWSE	1895-03-30		A1
3237	VINECORE, Alexander	23	NESE	1883-09-15		A1
3238	" "	23	S½SE	1883-09-15		A1
3239	" "	23	SESW	1883-09-15		A1
3240	" "	24	N½SW	1883-09-15		A1
3241	" "	25	SWNW	1883-09-15		A1
3242	" "	26	NE	1883-09-15		A1
3344	WELKER, George W	13	1	1903-11-10		A3 G158
3325	WELLS, Charles W	28	8	1884-06-30		A1 G152
3326	" "	29	NESW	1884-06-30		A1 G152
3327	" "	30	NWNW	1884-06-30		A1 G152
3328	" "	33	SWNE	1884-06-30		A1 G152
3246	WINTON, C J	30	SWSW	1889-05-09		A1 F
3247	" "	31	2	1889-05-09		A1
3248	" "	31	3	1889-05-09		A1
3249	" "	31	5	1889-05-09		A1
3250	" "	31	NWSW	1889-05-09		A1 F
3341	WITTER, Jere D	19	3	1884-06-20		A1 G64

Patent Map

T41-N R7-E
4th PM - 1831 MN/WI

Map Group 20

Township Statistics

Parcels Mapped	:	276
Number of Patents	:	95
Number of Individuals	:	61
Patentees Identified	:	44
Number of Surnames	:	55
Multi-Patentee Parcels	:	86
Oldest Patent Date	:	11/1/1872
Most Recent Patent	:	1/4/1912
Block/Lot Parcels	:	104
Parcels Re - Issued	:	0
Parcels that Overlap	:	0
Cities and Towns	:	0
Cemeteries	:	0

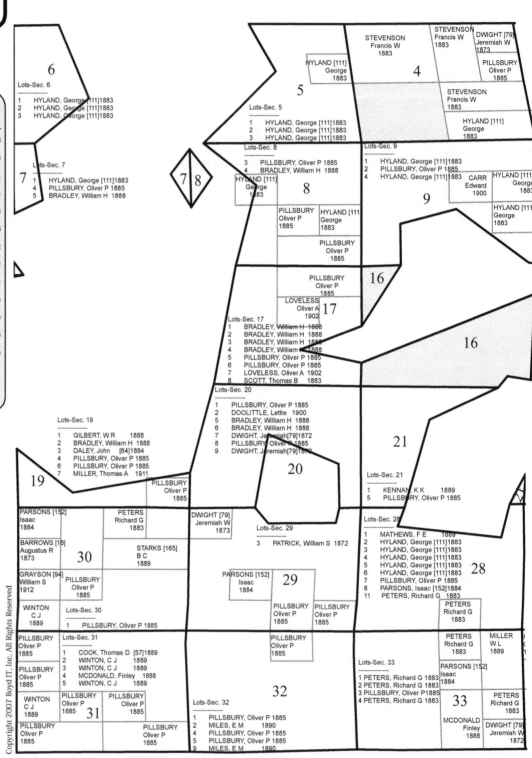

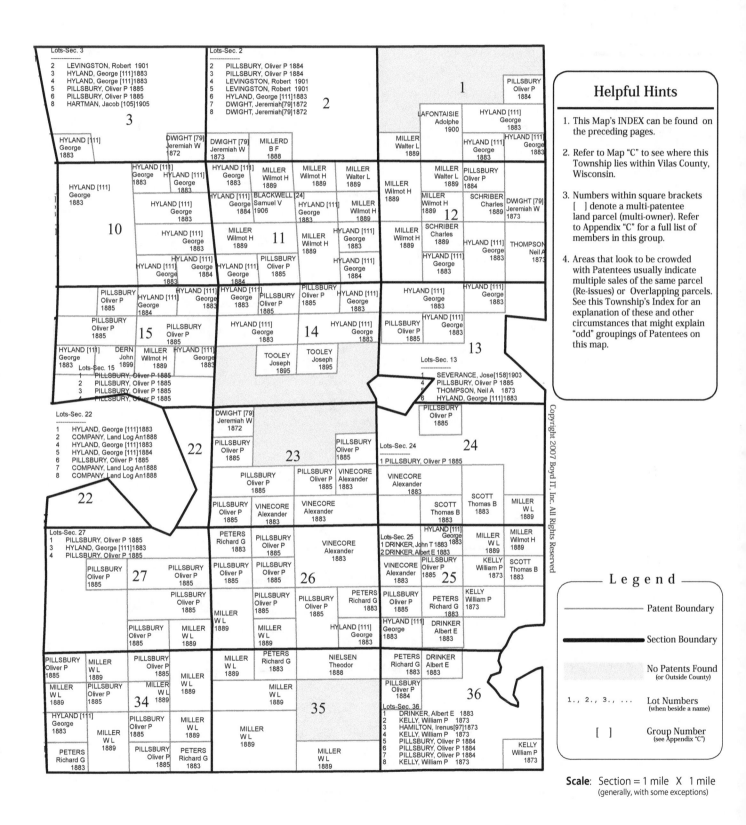

Lots-Sec. 3
2   LEVINGSTON, Robert 1901
3   HYLAND, George [111]1883
4   HYLAND, George [111]1883
5   PILLSBURY, Oliver P 1885
6   PILLSBURY, Oliver P 1885
8   HARTMAN, Jacob [105]1905

Lots-Sec. 2
2   PILLSBURY, Oliver P 1884
3   PILLSBURY, Oliver P 1884
4   LEVINGSTON, Robert 1901
5   LEVINGSTON, Robert 1901
6   HYLAND, George [111]1883
7   DWIGHT, Jeremiah[79]1872
8   DWIGHT, Jeremiah[79]1872

Lots-Sec. 15
1   PILLSBURY, Oliver P 1885
2   PILLSBURY, Oliver P 1885
3   PILLSBURY, Oliver P 1885
4   PILLSBURY, Oliver P 1885

Lots-Sec. 13
1   SEVERANCE, Jose[158]1903
4   PILLSBURY, Oliver P 1885
5   THOMPSON, Neil A 1873
6   HYLAND, George [111]1883

Lots-Sec. 22
1   HYLAND, George [111]1883
2   COMPANY, Land Log An1888
4   HYLAND, George [111]1883
5   HYLAND, George [111]1884
6   PILLSBURY, Oliver P 1885
7   COMPANY, Land Log An1888
8   COMPANY, Land Log An1888

Lots-Sec. 24
1 PILLSBURY, Oliver P 1885

Lots-Sec. 27
1   PILLSBURY, Oliver P 1885
3   HYLAND, George [111]1883
4   PILLSBURY, Oliver P 1885

Lots-Sec. 25
1 DRINKER, John T 1883
2 DRINKER, Albert E 1883

Lots-Sec. 36
1   DRINKER, Albert E 1883
2   KELLY, William P   1873
3   HAMILTON, Irenus[97]1873
4   KELLY, William P   1873
5   PILLSBURY, Oliver P 1884
6   PILLSBURY, Oliver P 1884
7   PILLSBURY, Oliver P 1884
8   KELLY, William P   1873

Helpful Hints

1. This Map's INDEX can be found on the preceding pages.

2. Refer to Map "C" to see where this Township lies within Vilas County, Wisconsin.

3. Numbers within square brackets [ ] denote a multi-patentee land parcel (multi-owner). Refer to Appendix "C" for a full list of members in this group.

4. Areas that look to be crowded with Patentees usually indicate multiple sales of the same parcel (Re-issues) or Overlapping parcels. See this Township's Index for an explanation of these and other circumstances that might explain "odd" groupings of Patentees on this map.

Legend

——— Patent Boundary

▬▬▬ Section Boundary

No Patents Found
(or Outside County)

1., 2., 3., ...   Lot Numbers
(when beside a name)

[ ]   Group Number
(see Appendix "C")

Scale: Section = 1 mile X 1 mile
(generally, with some exceptions)

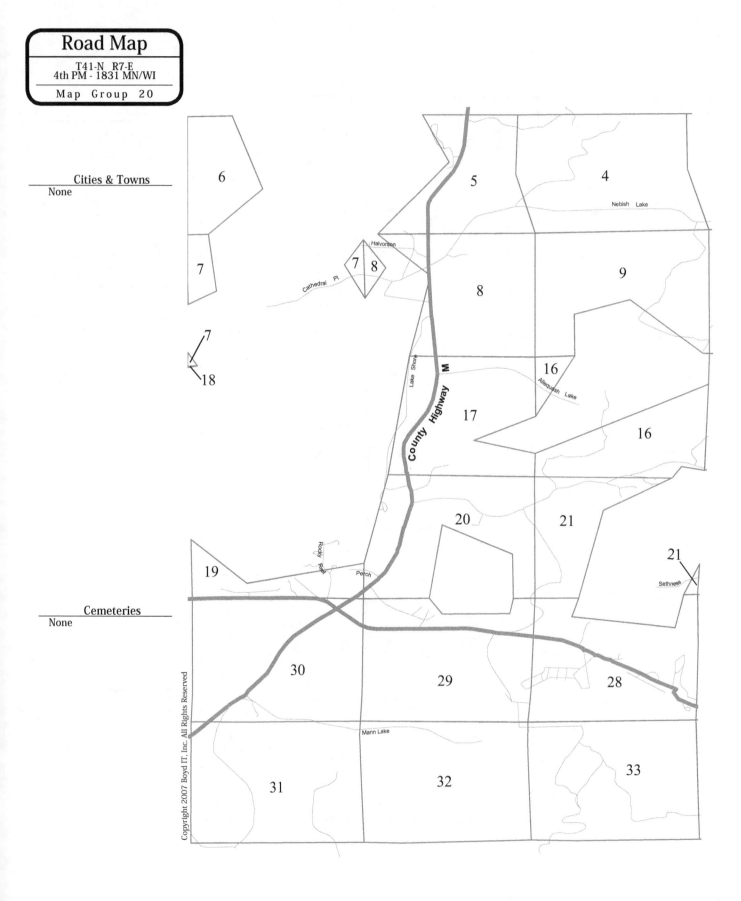

Road Map

T41-N R7-E
4th PM - 1831 MN/WI

Map Group 20

Cities & Towns

None

Cemeteries

None

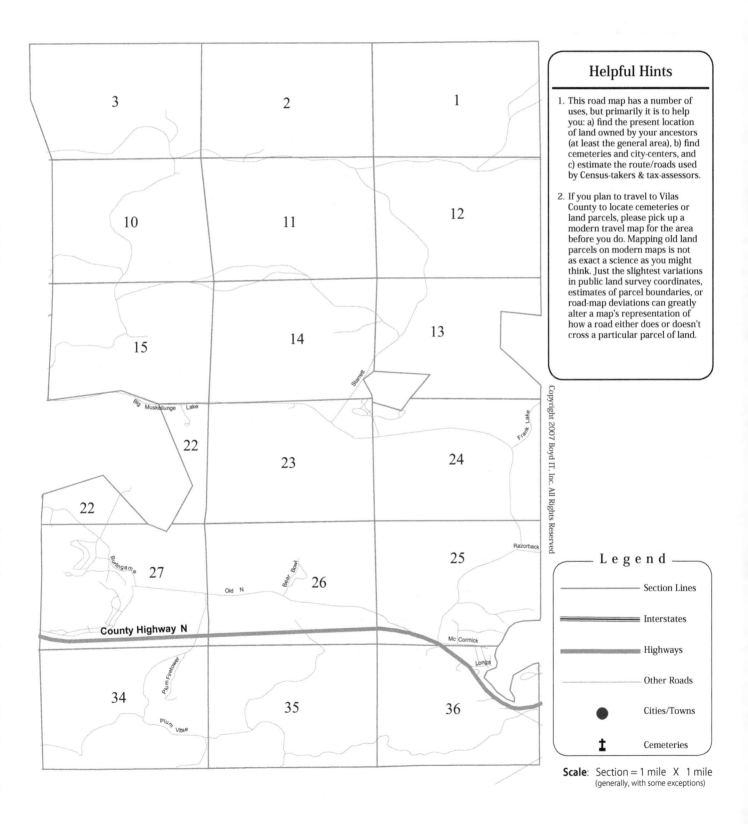

Helpful Hints

1. This road map has a number of uses, but primarily it is to help you: a) find the present location of land owned by your ancestors (at least the general area), b) find cemeteries and city-centers, and c) estimate the route/roads used by Census-takers & tax-assessors.

2. If you plan to travel to Vilas County to locate cemeteries or land parcels, please pick up a modern travel map for the area before you do. Mapping old land parcels on modern maps is not as exact a science as you might think. Just the slightest variations in public land survey coordinates, estimates of parcel boundaries, or road-map deviations can greatly alter a map's representation of how a road either does or doesn't cross a particular parcel of land.

Legend

———	Section Lines
≡≡≡	Interstates
▬▬▬	Highways
———	Other Roads
●	Cities/Towns
⸸	Cemeteries

Scale: Section = 1 mile X 1 mile
(generally, with some exceptions)

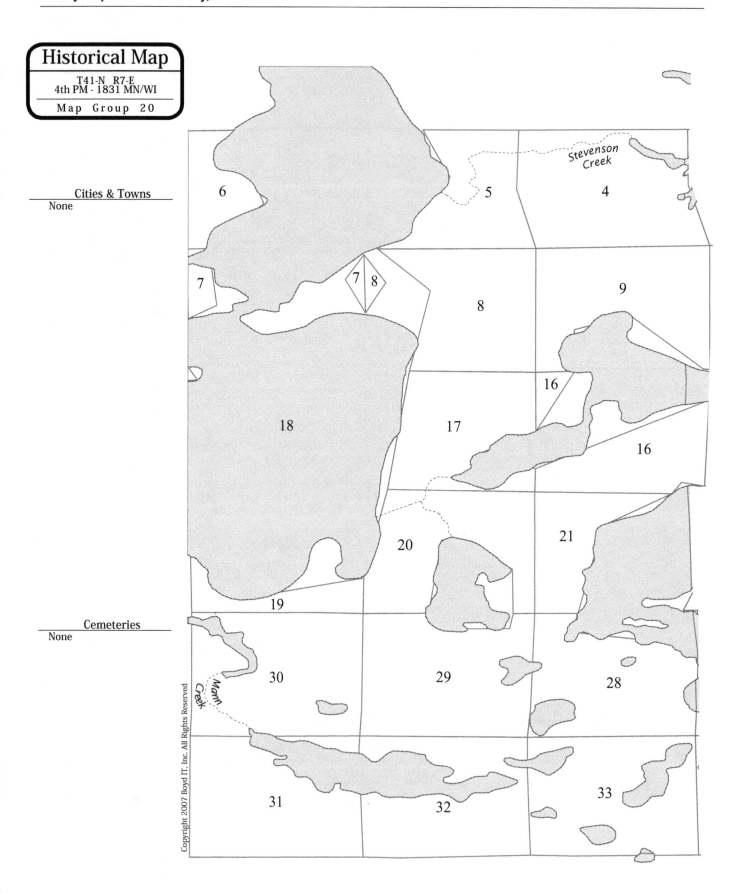

Historical Map

T41-N R7-E
4th PM - 1831 MN/WI

Map Group 20

Cities & Towns
None

Cemeteries
None

Stevenson Creek

Mann Creek

6

5

4

7

7 | 8

8

9

18

17

16

16

20

21

19

30

29

28

31

32

33

Helpful Hints

1. This Map takes a different look at the same Congressional Township displayed in the preceding two maps. It presents features that can help you better envision the historical development of the area: a) Water-bodies (lakes & ponds), b) Water-courses (rivers, streams, etc.), c) Railroads, d) City/town center-points (where they were oftentimes located when first settled), and e) Cemeteries.

2. Using this "Historical" map in tandem with this Township's Patent Map and Road Map, may lead you to some interesting discoveries. You will often find roads, towns, cemeteries, and waterways are named after nearby landowners: sometimes those names will be the ones you are researching. See how many of these research gems you can find here in Vilas County.

Legend

————————	Section Lines
+++++++++	Railroads
▭	Large Rivers & Bodies of Water
- - - - - - -	Streams/Creeks & Small Rivers
●	Cities/Towns
✝	Cemeteries

Scale: Section = 1 mile X 1 mile
(there are some exceptions)

Map Group 21: Index to Land Patents

Township 41-North Range 8-East (4th PM - 1831 MN/WI)

After you locate an individual in this Index, take note of the Section and Section Part then proceed to the Land Patent map on the pages immediately following. You should have no difficulty locating the corresponding parcel of land.

The "For More Info" Column will lead you to more information about the underlying Patents. See the *Legend* at right, and the "How to Use this Book" chapter, for more information.

```
                        LEGEND
            "For More Info . . . " column
A = Authority (Legislative Act, See Appendix "A")
B = Block or Lot (location in Section unknown)
C = Cancelled Patent
F = Fractional Section
G = Group  (Multi-Patentee Patent, see Appendix "C")
V = Overlaps another Parcel
R = Re-Issued (Parcel patented more than once)

(A & G items require you to look in the Appendixes referred
to above. All other Letter-designations followed by a number
require you to locate line-items in this index that possess
the ID number found after the letter).
```

ID	Individual in Patent	Sec.	Sec. Part	Date Issued	Other Counties	For More Info . . .
3573	ALLEN, Frank	36	S½NE	1884-06-30		A1 G5
3790	ALLEN, William N	13	NESE	1888-07-10		A1 G6
3791	" "	25	SWSE	1888-07-10		A1 G6
3792	" "	35	N½SE	1888-07-10		A1 G6
3780	AVERILL, William	12	1	1883-04-20		A1 G10
3781	" "	12	2	1883-04-20		A1 G10
3782	" "	12	3	1883-04-20		A1 G10
3783	" "	12	NWSE	1883-04-20		A1 G10
3784	" "	21	5	1883-04-20		A1 G10
3785	" "	21	6	1883-04-20		A1 G10
3786	" "	5	SESE	1883-04-20		A1 G10
3787	" "	8	NENE	1883-04-20		A1 G10
3788	" "	9	N½NW	1883-04-20		A1 G10
3606	BENNER, Isreal A	29	11	1906-04-14		A3 G21
3557	BIRD, Claire B	19	2	1897-01-12		A1
3789	BRADLEY, William H	19	NWSW	1884-06-20		A1
3564	BROWN, Edward D	10	6	1875-02-20		A1
3565	" "	10	SENE	1875-02-20		A1
3566	" "	11	SWNW	1875-02-20		A1
3567	" "	9	1	1875-02-20		A1
3633	CARPENTER, Lorenzo	21	7	1898-08-01		A1
3767	CHAPMAN, Thomas C	28	7	1905-03-30		A3 G41
3568	CLARK, Eli C	13	SWSW	1873-05-01		A1
3569	" "	24	NWNW	1873-05-01		A1
3570	" "	35	SWSE	1873-05-01		A1
3628	COMPANY, Land Log And Lumber	18	7	1886-08-10		A1
3629	" "	19	1	1886-08-10		A1
3630	" "	19	3	1886-08-10		A1
3631	" "	19	4	1886-08-10		A1
3632	" "	19	SWSW	1886-08-10		A1 F
3627	COOK, L J	30	SENE	1889-06-28		A1 G54
3780	DEREG, William	12	1	1883-04-20		A1 G10
3781	" "	12	2	1883-04-20		A1 G10
3782	" "	12	3	1883-04-20		A1 G10
3783	" "	12	NWSE	1883-04-20		A1 G10
3784	" "	21	5	1883-04-20		A1 G10
3785	" "	21	6	1883-04-20		A1 G10
3786	" "	5	SESE	1883-04-20		A1 G10
3787	" "	8	NENE	1883-04-20		A1 G10
3788	" "	9	N½NW	1883-04-20		A1 G10
3627	DICKINSON, George P	30	SENE	1889-06-28		A1 G54
3508	DRINKER, Albert E	31	NESE	1883-09-15		A1
3509	" "	31	S½SW	1883-09-15		A1
3510	" "	31	SENW	1883-09-15		A1
3511	" "	31	SWNE	1883-09-15		A1
3512	" "	31	W½SE	1883-09-15		A1

ID	Individual in Patent	Sec.	Sec. Part	Date Issued	Other Counties	For More Info . . .
3619	DRINKER, John T	31	1	1883-09-15		A1
3620	" "	31	4	1883-09-15		A1
3621	" "	31	NESE	1883-09-15		A1
3622	" "	32	1	1883-09-15		A1
3623	" "	32	NENW	1883-09-15		A1
3624	" "	32	NWNE	1883-09-15		A1
3625	" "	32	S½NW	1883-09-15		A1
3626	" "	32	SW	1883-09-15		A1
3608	DWIGHT, Jeremiah W	7	W½NW	1873-05-01		A1 G79
3571	EXTINE, Emerson	10	10	1896-01-15		A1
3527	FLYNN, Andrew	30	NENE	1900-06-11		A3
3609	GILLET, Joel D	35	NWNE	1884-06-30		A1
3610	" "	35	S½NE	1884-06-30		A1
3611	" "	36	E½NW	1884-06-30		A1
3612	" "	36	NESW	1884-06-30		A1
3613	" "	36	NWNE	1884-06-30		A1
3614	" "	36	W½SE	1884-06-30		A1
3606	GOODSPEED, Florence M	29	11	1906-04-14		A3 G21
3606	GOODSPEED, George S	29	11	1906-04-14		A3 G21
3604	HAMILTON, Irenus K	10	NWNE	1872-07-01		A1 G97
3605	"	3	8	1872-07-01		A1 G97
3604	HAMILTON, Woodman C	10	NWNE	1872-07-01		A1 G97
3605	" "	3	8	1872-07-01		A1 G97
3615	HOXIE, John C	5	3	1875-12-30		A1
3616	" "	6	NENW	1875-12-30		A1 F
3617	" "	6	NWNE	1875-12-30		A1 F
3574	HYLAND, George	17	N½NE	1883-09-15		A1 G111
3575	" "	17	NENW	1883-09-15		A1 G111
3576	" "	17	NWSE	1883-09-15		A1 G111
3577	" "	4	2	1883-09-15		A1 G111
3578	" "	4	3	1883-09-15		A1 G111
3579	" "	4	4	1883-09-15		A1 G111
3580	" "	5	1	1883-09-15		A1 G111
3581	" "	5	2	1883-09-15		A1 G111
3582	" "	5	5	1883-09-15		A1 G111
3583	" "	5	7	1883-09-15		A1 G111
3584	" "	5	8	1883-09-15		A1 G111
3585	" "	5	9	1883-09-15		A1 G111
3586	" "	5	SWSE	1883-09-15		A1 G111
3587	" "	6	SWSE	1883-09-15		A1 G111
3588	" "	7	NWNE	1883-09-15		A1 G111
3589	" "	7	SENE	1883-09-15		A1 G111
3590	" "	8	E½SE	1883-09-15		A1 G111
3591	" "	8	N½SW	1883-09-15		A1 G111
3592	" "	8	NW	1883-09-15		A1 G111
3593	" "	8	NWNE	1883-09-15		A1 G111
3594	" "	8	SENE	1883-09-15		A1 G111
3595	" "	9	NWSW	1883-09-15		A1 G111
3596	" "	9	SWSW	1883-09-15		A1 G111
3574	HYLAND, John	17	N½NE	1883-09-15		A1 G111
3575	" "	17	NENW	1883-09-15		A1 G111
3576	" "	17	NWSE	1883-09-15		A1 G111
3577	" "	4	2	1883-09-15		A1 G111
3578	" "	4	3	1883-09-15		A1 G111
3579	" "	4	4	1883-09-15		A1 G111
3580	" "	5	1	1883-09-15		A1 G111
3581	" "	5	2	1883-09-15		A1 G111
3582	" "	5	5	1883-09-15		A1 G111
3583	" "	5	7	1883-09-15		A1 G111
3584	" "	5	8	1883-09-15		A1 G111
3585	" "	5	9	1883-09-15		A1 G111
3586	" "	5	SWSE	1883-09-15		A1 G111
3587	" "	6	SWSE	1883-09-15		A1 G111
3588	" "	7	NWNE	1883-09-15		A1 G111
3589	" "	7	SENE	1883-09-15		A1 G111
3590	" "	8	E½SE	1883-09-15		A1 G111
3591	" "	8	N½SW	1883-09-15		A1 G111
3592	" "	8	NW	1883-09-15		A1 G111
3593	" "	8	NWNE	1883-09-15		A1 G111
3594	" "	8	SENE	1883-09-15		A1 G111
3595	" "	9	NWSW	1883-09-15		A1 G111
3596	" "	9	SWSW	1883-09-15		A1 G111
3779	LEE, Waterman Da	20	7	1906-09-14		A3 G131

ID	Individual in Patent	Sec.	Sec. Part	Date Issued	Other Counties	For More Info . . .
3513	LOVEJOY, Allen P	10	1	1872-05-10		A1
3514	" "	10	7	1872-05-10		A1
3515	" "	15	1	1872-05-10		A1
3516	" "	15	3	1872-05-10		A1
3517	" "	15	4	1872-05-10		A1
3518	" "	17	1	1872-05-10		A1
3519	" "	17	2	1872-05-10		A1
3520	" "	17	SW	1872-05-10		A1
3521	" "	18	9	1872-05-10		A1
3522	" "	18	NESE	1872-05-10		A1
3523	" "	20	1	1872-05-10		A1
3524	" "	21	4	1872-05-10		A1
3525	" "	34	N½NW	1872-05-10		A1
3526	" "	34	SWNW	1872-05-10		A1
3767	MCCROSSEN, James	28	7	1905-03-30		A3 G41
3607	MCCROSSEN, James W	20	6	1905-08-26		A3 G139
3779	" "	20	7	1906-09-14		A3 G131
3608	MCGRAW, John	7	W½NW	1873-05-01		A1 G79
3790	MERCER, John	13	NESE	1888-07-10		A1 G6
3791	" "	25	SWSE	1888-07-10		A1 G6
3792	" "	35	N½SE	1888-07-10		A1 G6
3558	MILES, D E	15	5	1889-05-31		A1 G144
3559	" "	22	1	1889-05-31		A1 G144
3560	MILES, E M	10	9	1890-07-15		A1
3561	" "	3	6	1890-07-15		A1
3562	" "	4	1	1890-07-15		A1
3563	" "	7	SWSE	1890-07-15		A1
3558	MILES, J O	15	5	1889-05-31		A1 G144
3559	" "	22	1	1889-05-31		A1 G144
3635	MILLARD, Miriam W	6	NENE	1873-05-01		A1 G146
3769	MILLER, W L	26	E½NW	1889-03-29		A1 C
3770	" "	26	NWNW	1889-03-29		A1 C
3771	" "	26	SWNE	1889-03-29		A1 C
3772	" "	27	SENE	1889-03-29		A1 C
3774	MILLER, Walter L	28	5	1889-03-29		A1
3775	" "	28	6	1889-03-29		A1
3776	" "	32	SWSE	1889-03-29		A1
3777	" "	33	NENW	1889-03-29		A1
3778	" "	33	NWNE	1889-03-29		A1
3795	MILLER, Wilmot H	32	SENE	1889-03-28		A1
3796	" "	33	NENE	1889-03-28		A1
3618	NELSON, John	22	SESE	1904-06-27		A1
3793	PATRICK, William S	23	NENE	1872-11-01		A1
3794	" "	35	W½NW	1872-11-01		A1
3729	PETERS, Richard G	24	N½SW	1883-09-15		A1
3730	" "	24	NENE	1883-09-15		A1
3731	" "	24	SWNE	1883-09-15		A1
3732	" "	28	3	1883-09-15		A1
3733	" "	29	10	1883-09-15		A1
3734	" "	31	2	1883-09-15		A1
3735	" "	31	SESE	1883-09-15		A1
3736	" "	32	NENE	1883-09-15		A1
3737	" "	33	W½NW	1883-09-15		A1
3738	" "	8	SWNE	1883-09-15		A1
3739	" "	8	SWSW	1883-09-15		A1
3660	PILLSBURY, Oliver P	1	1	1884-06-30		A1
3661	" "	1	2	1884-06-30		A1
3662	" "	1	N½NE	1884-06-30		A1 F
3663	" "	10	4	1884-06-30		A1
3664	" "	12	SESE	1884-06-30		A1
3665	" "	13	NENE	1884-06-30		A1
3666	" "	13	SESE	1884-06-30		A1
3668	" "	20	NWSW	1884-06-30		A1
3669	" "	24	NESE	1884-06-30		A1
3670	" "	24	S½SE	1884-06-30		A1
3671	" "	24	SESW	1884-06-30		A1
3672	" "	25	E½NE	1884-06-30		A1
3673	" "	25	E½SE	1884-06-30		A1
3674	" "	25	N½SW	1884-06-30		A1
3675	" "	25	NENW	1884-06-30		A1
3676	" "	25	S½NW	1884-06-30		A1
3677	" "	25	SESW	1884-06-30		A1
3678	" "	25	SWNE	1884-06-30		A1

ID	Individual in Patent	Sec.	Sec. Part	Date Issued	Other Counties	For More Info . . .
3680	PILLSBURY, Oliver P (Cont'd)	26	SWNW	1884-06-30		A1
3683	" "	29	NWNW	1884-06-30		A1
3684	" "	30	3	1884-06-30		A1
3685	" "	30	SWNE	1884-06-30		A1
3686	" "	32	SESE	1884-06-30		A1
3687	" "	33	NESW	1884-06-30		A1
3688	" "	33	NWSW	1884-06-30		A1
3689	" "	33	S½SW	1884-06-30		A1
3690	" "	33	SENW	1884-06-30		A1
3691	" "	33	SWSE	1884-06-30		A1
3692	" "	34	NWSW	1884-06-30		A1
3693	" "	36	NENE	1884-06-30		A1
3694	" "	36	NESE	1884-06-30		A1
3695	" "	36	NWSW	1884-06-30		A1
3696	" "	6	N½SW	1884-06-30		A1
3697	" "	6	NWSE	1884-06-30		A1
3698	" "	6	S½NE	1884-06-30		A1
3699	" "	6	SENW	1884-06-30		A1
3700	" "	6	SESW	1884-06-30		A1
3701	" "	7	E½NW	1884-06-30		A1
3702	" "	7	NESE	1884-06-30		A1
3703	" "	7	SESE	1884-06-30		A1
3704	" "	7	SWNE	1884-06-30		A1
3667	" "	17	SWNE	1885-01-15		A1
3705	" "	9	SENW	1885-01-15		A1
3706	" "	9	SESW	1885-01-15		A1
3707	" "	9	SWNW	1885-01-15		A1
3679	" "	26	E½SE	1885-01-20		A1
3681	" "	29	8	1885-01-20		A1
3682	" "	29	9	1885-01-20		A1
3607	QUAW, Samuel M	20	6	1905-08-26		A3 G139
3709	ROBISON, R D	10	8	1872-07-01		A1
3710	" "	11	S½	1872-07-01		A1
3711	" "	11	S½NE	1872-07-01		A1
3712	" "	12	SW	1872-07-01		A1
3713	" "	12	SWNW	1872-07-01		A1
3714	" "	13	N½SW	1872-07-01		A1
3715	" "	13	NW	1872-07-01		A1
3716	" "	14		1872-07-01		A1
3717	" "	15	6	1872-07-01		A1
3718	" "	17	NESE	1872-07-01		A1
3719	" "	17	SENE	1872-07-01		A1
3720	" "	21	3	1872-07-01		A1
3721	" "	21	NWNW	1872-07-01		A1
3722	" "	23	1	1872-07-01		A1
3723	" "	23	2	1872-07-01		A1
3724	" "	23	NWNE	1872-07-01		A1
3725	" "	23	SENW	1872-07-01		A1
3726	" "	26	W½SW	1872-07-01		A1
3727	" "	27	E½SE	1872-07-01		A1
3728	" "	34	E½	1872-07-01		A1
3550	SCHRIBER, Charles	32	N½SE	1889-03-29		A1
3551	" "	32	SWNE	1889-03-29		A1
3552	" "	33	NWSE	1889-03-29		A1
3553	" "	33	SWNE	1889-03-29		A1
3536	" "	1	3	1889-04-04		A1
3537	" "	1	4	1889-04-04		A1
3538	" "	13	SENE	1889-04-04		A1
3539	" "	13	W½NE	1889-04-04		A1
3540	" "	2	3	1889-04-04		A1
3541	" "	2	4	1889-04-04		A1
3542	" "	2	N½NE	1889-04-04		A1 F
3543	" "	20	5	1889-04-04		A1
3544	" "	24	NWSE	1889-04-04		A1
3545	" "	24	S½NW	1889-04-04		A1
3546	" "	24	SENE	1889-04-04		A1
3547	" "	29	1	1889-04-04		A1
3548	" "	29	2	1889-04-04		A1
3549	" "	29	3	1889-04-04		A1
3554	" "	36	SESE	1889-04-04		A1
3555	" "	36	SESW	1889-04-04		A1
3556	" "	9	NESW	1889-04-04		A1
3635	SCHWALM, Louis	6	NENE	1873-05-01		A1 G146

ID	Individual in Patent	Sec.	Sec. Part	Date Issued	Other Counties	For More Info . . .
3740	SCOTT, Thomas B	1	5	1883-04-20		A1
3741	" "	10	2	1883-04-20		A1
3742	" "	10	3	1883-04-20		A1
3743	" "	10	5	1883-04-20		A1
3744	" "	12	SWSE	1883-04-20		A1
3745	" "	13	SWSE	1883-04-20		A1
3761	" "	35	SESE	1883-04-20		A1
3762	" "	4	5	1883-04-20		A1
3763	" "	4	6	1883-04-20		A1
3764	" "	9	2	1883-04-20		A1
3765	" "	9	S½NE	1883-04-20		A1
3766	" "	9	SE	1883-04-20		A1
3746	" "	20	2	1883-09-15		A1
3747	" "	20	3	1883-09-15		A1
3748	" "	21	1	1883-09-15		A1
3749	" "	21	2	1883-09-15		A1
3750	" "	21	NENW	1883-09-15		A1
3751	" "	21	SWNE	1883-09-15		A1
3752	" "	22	NESE	1883-09-15		A1
3753	" "	22	S½SW	1883-09-15		A1
3754	" "	22	SWSE	1883-09-15		A1
3755	" "	27	3	1883-09-15		A1
3759	" "	33	NESE	1883-09-15		A1
3760	" "	33	SENE	1883-09-15		A1
3756	" "	3	3	1885-05-09		A1
3757	" "	3	5	1885-05-09		A1
3758	" "	3	7	1885-05-09		A1
3634	SHAPE, Michael P	36	SWNW	1905-07-18		A1
3572	SHEPARD, Eugene S	3	1	1902-02-07		A1
3598	SHERRY, Henry	13	NWSE	1883-09-10		A1
3599	" "	13	SESW	1883-09-10		A1
3600	" "	24	NENW	1883-09-10		A1
3601	" "	24	NWNE	1883-09-10		A1
3602	" "	5	10	1883-09-10		A1
3597	STARR, Harry	6	W½NW	1899-08-14		A3 F
3708	SULLIVAN, Patrick	29	7	1901-01-10		A3
3636	THOMPSON, Neil A	11	1	1873-11-15		A1
3637	" "	11	2	1873-11-15		A1
3638	" "	11	N½NE	1873-11-15		A1
3639	" "	11	SENW	1873-11-15		A1
3640	" "	18	1	1873-11-15		A1
3641	" "	18	2	1873-11-15		A1
3642	" "	18	3	1873-11-15		A1
3643	" "	18	4	1873-11-15		A1
3644	" "	2	1	1873-11-15		A1
3645	" "	2	2	1873-11-15		A1
3646	" "	2	5	1873-11-15		A1
3647	" "	2	6	1873-11-15		A1
3648	" "	2	SESE	1873-11-15		A1
3649	" "	21	8	1873-11-15		A1
3650	" "	21	9	1873-11-15		A1
3651	" "	22	2	1873-11-15		A1
3652	" "	22	3	1873-11-15		A1
3653	" "	22	4	1873-11-15		A1
3654	" "	23	S½	1873-11-15		A1
3655	" "	23	S½NE	1873-11-15		A1
3656	" "	26	N½NE	1873-11-15		A1
3657	" "	3	4	1873-11-15		A1
3658	" "	35	E½NW	1873-11-15		A1
3659	" "	7	W½SW	1873-11-15		A1
3603	WARNER, Herbert	28	2	1903-01-20		A1
3573	WASTE, Lee	36	S½NE	1884-06-30		A1 G5
3768	WELCH, Thomas	18	SWNE	1899-04-22		A3
3773	WHEELIHAN, W P	5	SWSW	1889-03-29		A1
3528	WINTON, C J	17	NWNW	1889-05-09		A1
3529	" "	18	N½NE	1889-05-09		A1
3530	" "	25	NWNE	1889-05-09		A1
3531	" "	25	NWSE	1889-05-09		A1
3532	" "	31	3	1889-05-09		A1
3533	" "	36	SWSW	1889-05-09		A1
3534	" "	7	E½SW	1889-05-09		A1
3535	" "	7	NWSE	1889-05-09		A1

Patent Map

T41-N R8-E
4th PM - 1831 MN/WI

Map Group 21

Township Statistics

Parcels Mapped	:	289
Number of Patents	:	88
Number of Individuals	:	60
Patentees Identified	:	47
Number of Surnames	:	50
Multi-Patentee Parcels	:	47
Oldest Patent Date	:	5/10/1872
Most Recent Patent	:	9/14/1906
Block/Lot Parcels	:	107
Parcels Re - Issued	:	0
Parcels that Overlap	:	0
Cities and Towns	:	2
Cemeteries	:	0

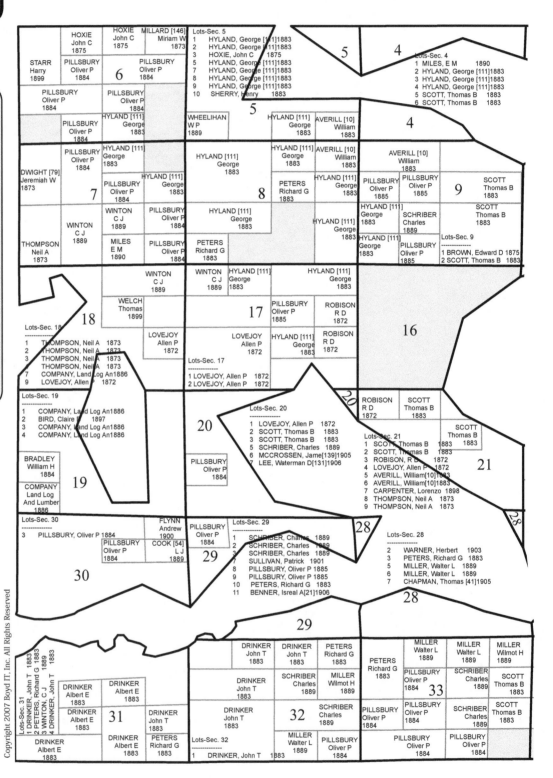

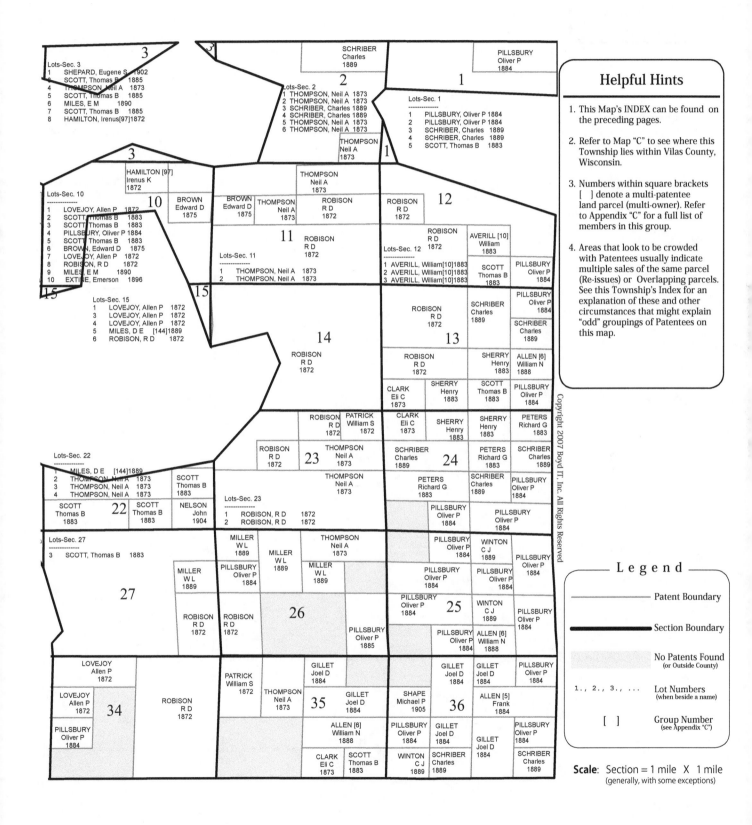

Helpful Hints

1. This Map's INDEX can be found on the preceding pages.

2. Refer to Map "C" to see where this Township lies within Vilas County, Wisconsin.

3. Numbers within square brackets [ ] denote a multi-patentee land parcel (multi-owner). Refer to Appendix "C" for a full list of members in this group.

4. Areas that look to be crowded with Patentees usually indicate multiple sales of the same parcel (Re-issues) or Overlapping parcels. See this Township's Index for an explanation of these and other circumstances that might explain "odd" groupings of Patentees on this map.

Legend

————	Patent Boundary
▬▬▬▬	Section Boundary
▓▓▓▓	No Patents Found (or Outside County)
1., 2., 3., ...	Lot Numbers (when beside a name)
[ ]	Group Number (see Appendix "C")

Scale: Section = 1 mile X 1 mile
(generally, with some exceptions)

257

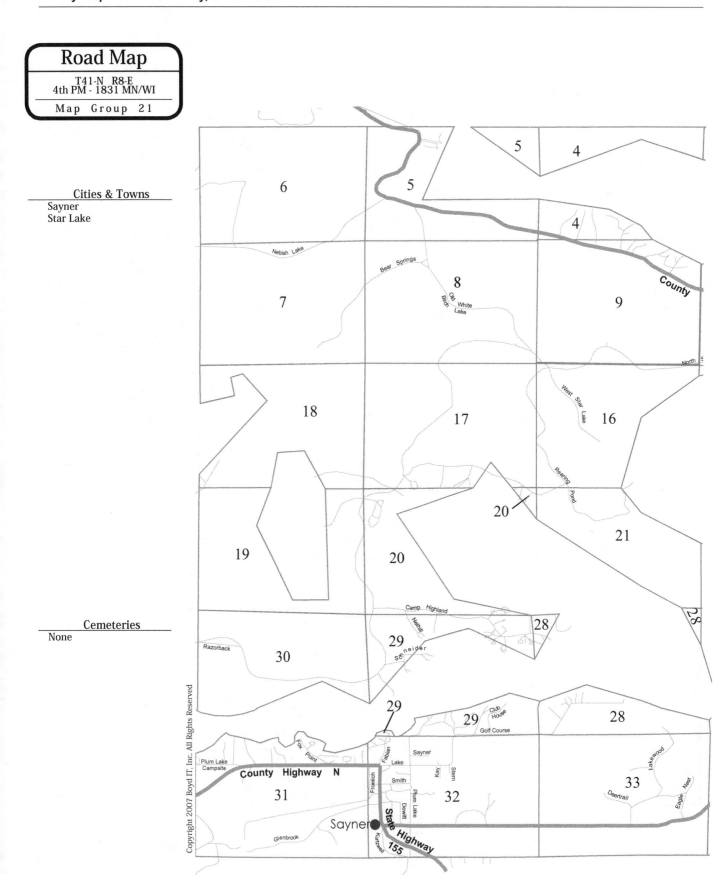

Road Map

T41-N R8-E
4th PM - 1831 MN/WI

Map Group 21

Cities & Towns

Sayner
Star Lake

Cemeteries

None

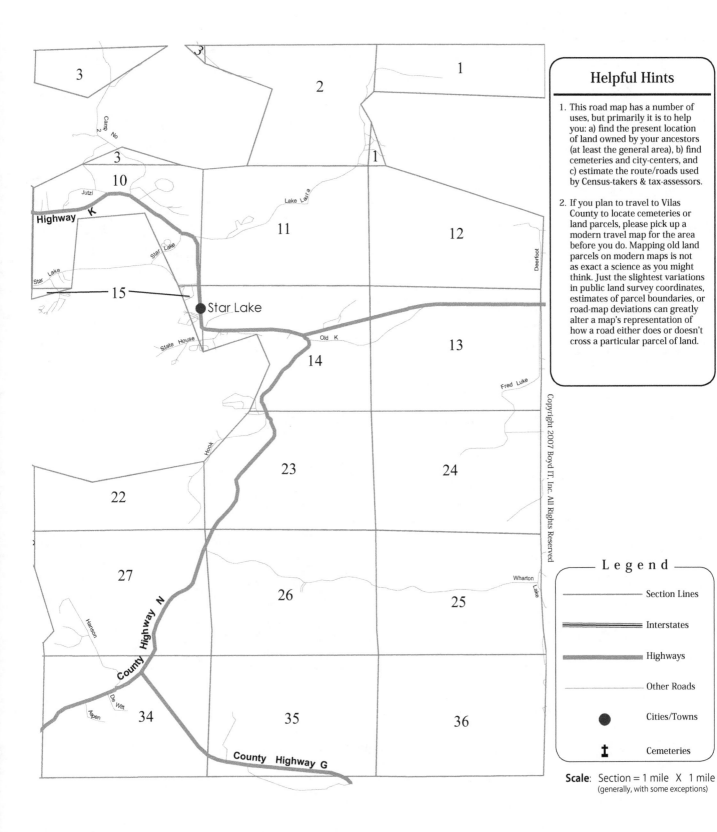

Helpful Hints

1. This road map has a number of uses, but primarily it is to help you: a) find the present location of land owned by your ancestors (at least the general area), b) find cemeteries and city-centers, and c) estimate the route/roads used by Census-takers & tax-assessors.

2. If you plan to travel to Vilas County to locate cemeteries or land parcels, please pick up a modern travel map for the area before you do. Mapping old land parcels on modern maps is not as exact a science as you might think. Just the slightest variations in public land survey coordinates, estimates of parcel boundaries, or road-map deviations can greatly alter a map's representation of how a road either does or doesn't cross a particular parcel of land.

Legend

————————	Section Lines
═══════════	Interstates
▬▬▬▬▬▬	Highways
————————	Other Roads
●	Cities/Towns
✝	Cemeteries

Scale: Section = 1 mile X 1 mile
(generally, with some exceptions)

Historical Map

T41-N R8-E
4th PM - 1831 MN/WI

Map Group 21

Cities & Towns

Sayner
Star Lake

Cemeteries

None

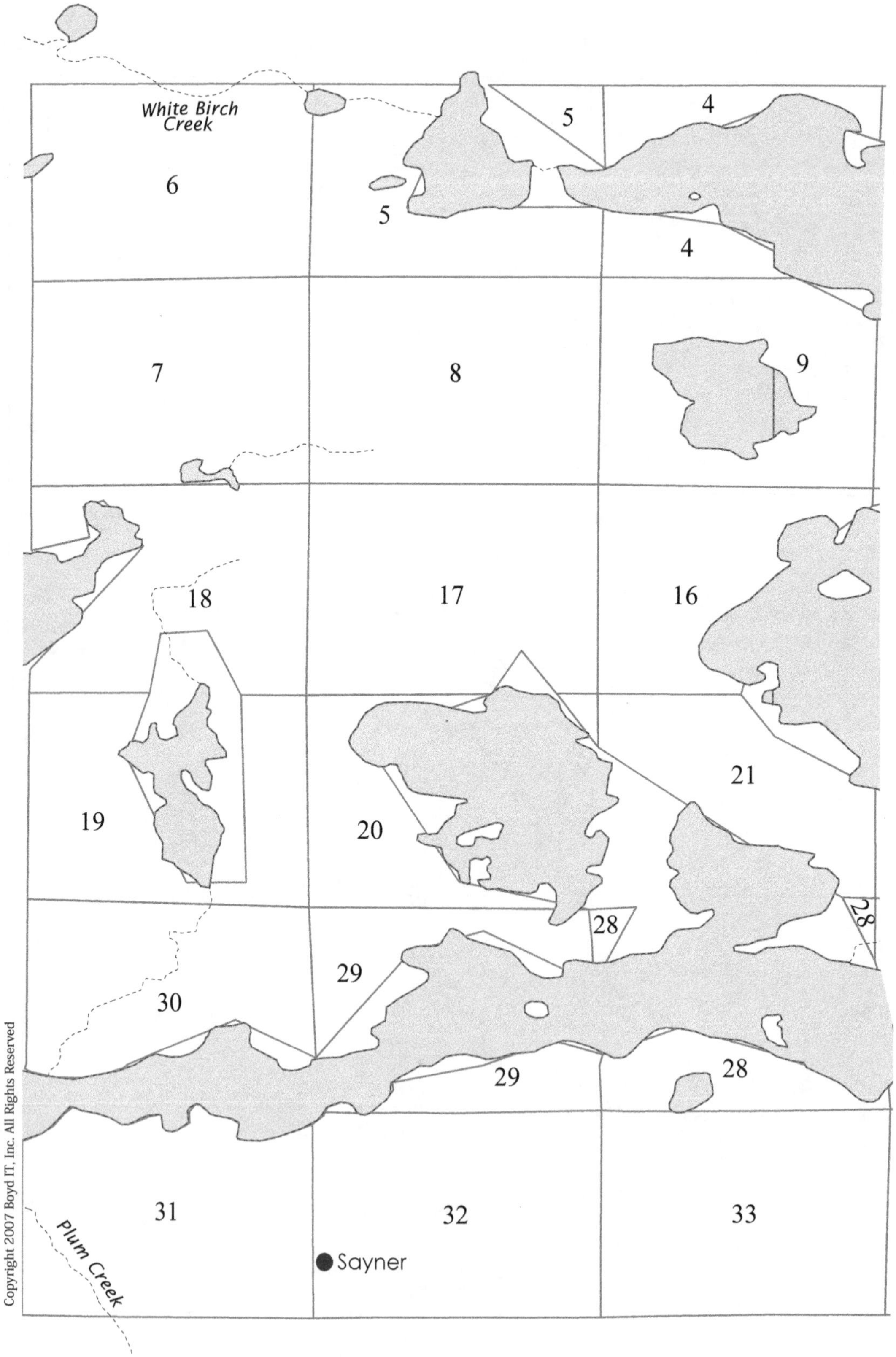
White Birch Creek
6
5
5
4
4
7
8
9
18
17
16
19
20
21
28
28
30
29
29
28
31
32
33
Sayner
Plum Creek
Copyright 2007 Boyd IT, Inc. All Rights Reserved

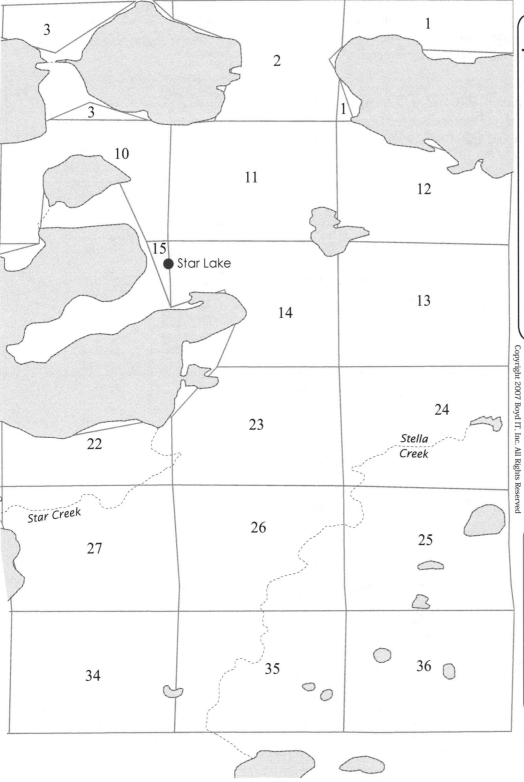

Helpful Hints

1. This Map takes a different look at the same Congressional Township displayed in the preceding two maps. It presents features that can help you better envision the historical development of the area: a) Water-bodies (lakes & ponds), b) Water-courses (rivers, streams, etc.), c) Railroads, d) City/town center-points (where they were oftentimes located when first settled), and e) Cemeteries.

2. Using this "Historical" map in tandem with this Township's Patent Map and Road Map, may lead you to some interesting discoveries. You will often find roads, towns, cemeteries, and waterways are named after nearby landowners: sometimes those names will be the ones you are researching. See how many of these research gems you can find here in Vilas County.

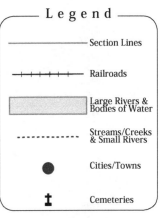

Legend

————	Section Lines
—+—+—+—	Railroads
▭	Large Rivers & Bodies of Water
- - - - - -	Streams/Creeks & Small Rivers
●	Cities/Towns
♱	Cemeteries

Scale: Section = 1 mile X 1 mile
(there are some exceptions)

Map Group 22: Index to Land Patents

Township 41-North Range 9-East (4th PM - 1831 MN/WI)

After you locate an individual in this Index, take note of the Section and Section Part then proceed to the Land Patent map on the pages immediately following. You should have no difficulty locating the corresponding parcel of land.

The "For More Info" Column will lead you to more information about the underlying Patents. See the *Legend* at right, and the "How to Use this Book" chapter, for more information.

```
                    LEGEND
           "For More Info . . . " column
A = Authority (Legislative Act, See Appendix "A")
B = Block or Lot (location in Section unknown)
C = Cancelled Patent
F = Fractional Section
G = Group  (Multi-Patentee Patent, see Appendix "C")
V = Overlaps another Parcel
R = Re-Issued (Parcel patented more than once)

(A & G items require you to look in the Appendixes referred
to above. All other Letter-designations followed by a number
require you to locate line-items in this index that possess
the ID number found after the letter).
```

ID	Individual in Patent	Sec.	Sec. Part	Date Issued	Other Counties	For More Info . . .
4044	ALLEN, William N	19	NWNE	1888-07-10		A1 G6
4045	" "	19	SWSW	1888-07-10		A1 G6 F
4046	" "	20	SWNE	1888-07-10		A1 G6
4047	" "	22	NWSW	1888-07-10		A1 G6
4048	" "	22	SWNW	1888-07-10		A1 G6
4049	" "	28	E½SE	1888-07-10		A1 G6
4050	" "	28	SESE	1888-07-10		A1 G6
4051	" "	30	NESW	1888-07-10		A1 G6
4052	" "	31	E½NE	1888-07-10		A1 G6
4053	" "	31	NESE	1888-07-10		A1 G6
4054	" "	31	NWSW	1888-07-10		A1 G6 F
4055	" "	32	NWSE	1888-07-10		A1 G6
4056	" "	7	W½SE	1888-07-10		A1 G6
3954	ANDERSON, Mary J	22	1	1883-09-15		A1
3955	" "	7	E½NE	1883-09-15		A1
3956	" "	8	N½NW	1883-09-15		A1
3957	" "	8	SWNW	1883-09-15		A1
3863	BARNETT, George A	17	NWNW	1902-03-07		A3 G15
3839	BEGLE, Charles A	35	SWSE	1885-06-12		A1 G20
3882	BROWN, Isaac	13	NWNW	1873-05-01		A1
3883	" "	2	SESW	1873-05-01		A1
3884	" "	2	SWSE	1873-05-01		A1
3885	" "	3	NWSW	1873-05-01		A1
3925	BUCKSTAFF, John	12	S½SW	1873-11-15		A1
3926	" "	13	SENW	1873-11-15		A1
3927	" "	17	NESE	1873-11-15		A1
3928	" "	17	SWNE	1873-11-15		A1
3929	" "	17	W½SE	1873-11-15		A1
3930	" "	26	3	1873-11-15		A1
3931	" "	26	NWSE	1873-11-15		A1
3932	" "	26	SENW	1873-11-15		A1
3933	" "	26	SWNE	1873-11-15		A1
3934	" "	27	SWNE	1873-11-15		A1
3935	" "	27	SWSE	1873-11-15		A1
3936	" "	28	NESW	1873-11-15		A1
3937	" "	28	NWSE	1873-11-15		A1
3938	" "	28	SENW	1873-11-15		A1
3939	" "	28	SWNE	1873-11-15		A1
3940	" "	29	SWNE	1873-11-15		A1
3941	" "	30	NWSE	1873-11-15		A1
3942	" "	8	NESW	1873-11-15		A1
3943	" "	8	NWSE	1873-11-15		A1
3944	" "	8	SENW	1873-11-15		A1
3945	" "	8	SWNE	1873-11-15		A1
3807	CHRISTENSEN, Abel	21	NWSE	1916-01-24		A3
3845	CLARK, Eli C	17	NENE	1873-05-01		A1

ID	Individual in Patent	Sec.	Sec. Part	Date Issued	Other Counties	For More Info . . .
3846	CLARK, Eli C (Cont'd)	19	SESE	1873-05-01		A1
3847	" "	20	SESW	1873-05-01		A1
3848	" "	20	SWSW	1873-05-01		A1
3849	" "	21	SWSW	1873-05-01		A1
3850	" "	27	NESW	1873-05-01		A1
3851	" "	27	NWSE	1873-05-01		A1
3852	" "	27	SENW	1873-05-01		A1
3853	" "	30	NENE	1873-05-01		A1
3854	" "	30	SENE	1873-05-01		A1
3855	" "	4	NESE	1873-05-01		A1
3856	" "	4	SENE	1873-05-01		A1
3905	CLARK, James	4	NWNW	1872-11-01		A1 G47
3906	" "	5	NENE	1872-11-01		A1 G47
3915	CLARK, James G	26	NENW	1873-05-01		A1 G46
3916	" "	35	NESW	1873-05-01		A1 G46
3917	" "	35	NWSE	1873-05-01		A1 G46
3907	" "	25	NENE	1878-08-20		A1 G45
3908	" "	25	NENW	1878-08-20		A1 G45
3909	" "	25	NWNW	1878-08-20		A1 G45
3910	" "	26	NENE	1878-08-20		A1 G45
3911	" "	26	NWNE	1878-08-20		A1 G45
3912	" "	26	SESE	1878-08-20		A1 G45
3913	" "	35	E½NE	1878-08-20		A1 G45
3914	" "	35	NWSW	1878-08-20		A1 G45
3907	CLARK, John	25	NENE	1878-08-20		A1 G45
3908	" "	25	NENW	1878-08-20		A1 G45
3909	" "	25	NWNW	1878-08-20		A1 G45
3910	" "	26	NENE	1878-08-20		A1 G45
3911	" "	26	NWNE	1878-08-20		A1 G45
3912	" "	26	SESE	1878-08-20		A1 G45
3913	" "	35	E½NE	1878-08-20		A1 G45
3914	" "	35	NWSW	1878-08-20		A1 G45
3905	CLARK, John J	4	NWNW	1872-11-01		A1 G47
3906	" "	5	NENE	1872-11-01		A1 G47
3844	COCHRAN, David	15	NWSW	1889-06-28		A1
3842	DAVISON, Crosier	13	3	1870-05-25		A1
3958	DEVLIN, Michael	25	SENW	1872-11-01		A1
3959	" "	25	SWNE	1872-11-01		A1 F
3960	" "	25	W½SW	1872-11-01		A1 F
3961	" "	26	E½SW	1872-11-01		A1 F
3962	" "	26	SWSE	1872-11-01		A1 F
3963	" "	35	NWNE	1872-11-01		A1
3964	" "	36	NENW	1872-11-01		A1 F
3965	" "	36	SENW	1872-11-01		A1
3966	" "	36	W½NE	1872-11-01		A1
4043	DICER, William	24	SWSE	1884-06-30		A1
4034	DOYLE, Thomas M	4	E½NW	1883-09-15		A1
4035	" "	4	NWSW	1883-09-15		A1
4036	" "	4	SESE	1883-09-15		A1
4037	" "	4	SWNE	1883-09-15		A1
4039	" "	9	NENE	1883-09-15		A1
4038	" "	6	3	1884-06-20		A1
3869	DUNFIELD, Hiram	17	SENE	1883-05-15		A1
3870	" "	5	S½NW	1883-05-15		A1
3871	" "	5	SWSW	1883-05-15		A1
3872	" "	6	N½NE	1883-05-15		A1
3873	" "	6	NENW	1883-05-15		A1
3874	" "	6	SESE	1883-05-15		A1
3875	" "	6	SWNE	1883-05-15		A1
3876	" "	6	W½SE	1883-05-15		A1
3877	" "	7	NWNE	1883-05-15		A1
3878	DUNFIELD, Hiram M	12	2	1886-07-30		A1
3879	" "	25	5	1886-07-30		A1
3880	" "	25	6	1886-07-30		A1
3881	" "	7	SWNE	1886-07-30		A1
3864	FITCH, George	30	NESE	1885-05-09		A1 G84
3907	FORBES, D H	25	NENE	1878-08-20		A1 G45
3908	" "	25	NENW	1878-08-20		A1 G45
3909	" "	25	NWNW	1878-08-20		A1 G45
3910	" "	26	NENE	1878-08-20		A1 G45
3911	" "	26	NWNE	1878-08-20		A1 G45
3912	" "	26	SESE	1878-08-20		A1 G45
3913	" "	35	E½NE	1878-08-20		A1 G45

ID	Individual in Patent	Sec.	Sec. Part	Date Issued	Other Counties	For More Info . . .
3914	FORBES, D H (Cont'd)	35	NWSW	1878-08-20		A1 G45
3905	FORBES, Daniel H	4	NWNW	1872-11-01		A1 G47
3906	" "	5	NENE	1872-11-01		A1 G47
3915	FORBES, John R	26	NENW	1873-05-01		A1 G46
3916	" "	35	NESW	1873-05-01		A1 G46
3917	" "	35	NWSE	1873-05-01		A1 G46
3839	GRIFFITH, Griffith J	35	SWSE	1885-06-12		A1 G20
3946	HARPER, John L	10	NENW	1874-08-01		A1 G98
3947	" "	10	SWNW	1874-08-01		A1 G98
3948	" "	3	SWSW	1874-08-01		A1 G98
3949	" "	33	2	1874-08-01		A1 G98
3950	" "	9	SENE	1874-08-01		A1 G98
3951	" "	9	SENW	1874-08-01		A1 G98
3840	HARRINGTON, Charles A	3	N½NE	1872-11-01		A1 G103
3841	" "	3	NENW	1872-11-01		A1 G103
3918	HOWLETT, James	19	N½SW	1898-12-01		A3 F
3919	" "	19	NWSE	1898-12-01		A3
3920	" "	19	SESW	1898-12-01		A3
3858	JONES, Evan J	20	NWSW	1875-02-20		A1 G119
3859	" "	20	S½NW	1875-02-20		A1 G119
3857	KOHL, Emma	6	NWNW	1884-06-30		A1 G124
3857	KOHL, H A	6	NWNW	1884-06-30		A1 G124
3989	LAMBORN, Paul H	19	NENW	1904-02-25		A1
3860	LAWLER, Finn	17	SENW	1900-06-11		A1
3921	LAWLER, James	21	N½NE	1912-04-01		A3
3922	" "	21	SENE	1912-04-01		A3
3808	LOVEJOY, Allen P	1	SE	1872-02-20		A1 F
3809	" "	1	SW	1872-02-20		A1 F
3810	" "	1	SWNE	1872-02-20		A1 F
3811	" "	10	N½NE	1872-02-20		A1
3814	" "	2	N½SE	1872-02-20		A1
3815	" "	2	NWNE	1872-02-20		A1
3825	" "	3	NWNW	1872-02-20		A1
3829	" "	4	NENE	1872-02-20		A1
3826	" "	32	S½SE	1872-05-10		A1
3828	" "	35	S½SW	1872-05-10		A1
3812	" "	17	SESE	1872-07-01		A1
3813	" "	17	SWSW	1872-07-01		A1
3816	" "	20	NENE	1872-07-01		A1
3817	" "	20	NWNW	1872-07-01		A1
3818	" "	22	5	1872-07-01		A1
3819	" "	26	1	1872-07-01		A1
3820	" "	26	SWNW	1872-07-01		A1
3821	" "	27	1	1872-07-01		A1
3822	" "	27	2	1872-07-01		A1
3823	" "	27	NENW	1872-07-01		A1
3824	" "	27	SENE	1872-07-01		A1
3827	" "	34	NENE	1872-07-01		A1
3862	LUCK, Fred	18	N½SW	1903-12-31		A1 F
3831	MARTEN, August	31	NWSE	1899-05-05		A3
3832	" "	31	SWNE	1899-05-05		A3
3830	MATHEWS, Arthur	31	SWSW	1899-08-14		A1
3833	MEIHACK, August	7	1	1899-05-05		A3
3834	" "	7	E½SW	1899-05-05		A3
3835	" "	7	SENW	1899-05-05		A3
4044	MERCER, John	19	NWNE	1888-07-10		A1 G6
4045	" "	19	SWSW	1888-07-10		A1 G6 F
4046	" "	20	SWNE	1888-07-10		A1 G6
4047	" "	22	NWSW	1888-07-10		A1 G6
4048	" "	22	SWNW	1888-07-10		A1 G6
4049	" "	28	E½SE	1888-07-10		A1 G6
4050	" "	28	SESW	1888-07-10		A1 G6
4051	" "	30	NESW	1888-07-10		A1 G6
4052	" "	31	E½NE	1888-07-10		A1 G6
4053	" "	31	NESE	1888-07-10		A1 G6
4054	" "	31	NWSW	1888-07-10		A1 G6 F
4055	" "	32	NWSE	1888-07-10		A1 G6
4056	" "	7	W½SE	1888-07-10		A1 G6
3864	MILLER, W H	30	NESE	1885-05-09		A1 G84
3988	MORRISON, Patrick	33	1	1913-07-18		A3
3865	MUCHLER, George	28	SWSE	1913-02-04		A3
3866	" "	33	NWNE	1913-02-04		A3
4057	PATRICK, William S	29	E½NE	1872-11-01		A1

ID	Individual in Patent	Sec.	Sec. Part	Date Issued	Other Counties	For More Info . . .
4058	PATRICK, William S (Cont'd)	29	E½SE	1872-11-01		A1
4059	" "	33	W½	1872-11-01		A1
3797	PATTEN, A W	10	SWSE	1882-06-30		A1
3798	" "	15	NWNE	1882-06-30		A1
3799	" "	24	2	1882-06-30		A1
3800	" "	24	NESW	1882-06-30		A1
3801	" "	35	SWNE	1882-06-30		A1
3802	" "	8	SENE	1882-06-30		A1
3803	" "	9	NESW	1882-06-30		A1
3804	" "	9	S½SW	1882-06-30		A1
3805	" "	9	SWNW	1882-06-30		A1
3806	" "	9	W½SE	1882-06-30		A1
3967	PILLSBURY, Oliver P	17	N½SW	1884-06-30		A1
3968	" "	17	NENW	1884-06-30		A1
3969	" "	18	E½SE	1884-06-30		A1
3970	" "	18	N½NE	1884-06-30		A1
3971	" "	18	SENE	1884-06-30		A1
3972	" "	18	SESW	1884-06-30		A1
3973	" "	18	SWSW	1884-06-30		A1
3974	" "	18	W½NW	1884-06-30		A1
3975	" "	19	NENE	1884-06-30		A1
3976	" "	19	NWNW	1884-06-30		A1
3977	" "	19	SWSE	1884-06-30		A1
3978	" "	20	NWSE	1884-06-30		A1
3979	" "	21	SWSE	1884-06-30		A1
3980	" "	28	NWNW	1884-06-30		A1
3981	" "	30	NW	1884-06-30		A1
3982	" "	30	NWSW	1884-06-30		A1
3983	" "	30	S½SW	1884-06-30		A1
3984	" "	31	E½SW	1884-06-30		A1
3985	" "	31	SESE	1884-06-30		A1
3986	" "	31	SWSE	1884-06-30		A1
3987	" "	7	W½SW	1884-06-30		A1
3923	PINKERTON, Jennie C	28	N½NE	1905-06-09		A1
3924	" "	28	SENE	1905-06-09		A1
3867	POPE, Herman	5	NENW	1901-05-08		A3
3868	"	5	NWNE	1901-05-08		A3
3946	PRESTON, David	10	NENW	1874-08-01		A1 G98
3947	" "	10	SWNW	1874-08-01		A1 G98
3948	" "	3	SWSW	1874-08-01		A1 G98
3949	" "	33	2	1874-08-01		A1 G98
3950	" "	9	SENE	1874-08-01		A1 G98
3951	" "	9	SENW	1874-08-01		A1 G98
3840	REEVE, Thomas T	3	N½NE	1872-11-01		A1 G103
3841	" "	3	NENW	1872-11-01		A1 G103
3990	RICHMOND, Pliny M	19	S½NE	1899-07-26		A3
3991	" "	19	S½NW	1899-07-26		A3
3840	ROE, Gilbert W	3	N½NE	1872-11-01		A1 G103
3841	" "	3	NENW	1872-11-01		A1 G103
4040	ROUNDS, W P	34	S½	1872-05-10		A1
3992	RUST, R E	10	SWSW	1885-01-15		A1
3993	" "	3	SESW	1885-01-15		A1
3994	" "	4	NWNE	1885-01-15		A1
3864	SACKETT, George B	30	NESE	1885-05-09		A1 G84
3995	SCOTT, Thomas B	10	NWNW	1883-04-20		A1
3996	" "	10	SENW	1883-04-20		A1
3997	" "	10	SWNE	1883-04-20		A1
3998	" "	11	3	1883-04-20		A1
4005	" "	17	SWNW	1883-04-20		A1
4006	" "	18	SWSE	1883-04-20		A1
4007	" "	19	NESE	1883-04-20		A1
4021	" "	6	1	1883-04-20		A1
3999	" "	15	E½NW	1883-05-15		A1
4000	" "	15	NESW	1883-05-15		A1
4001	" "	15	SENE	1883-05-15		A1
4002	" "	15	SESW	1883-05-15		A1
4003	" "	17	NWNE	1883-05-15		A1
4004	" "	17	SESW	1883-05-15		A1
4008	" "	20	NENW	1883-05-15		A1
4009	" "	20	NESW	1883-05-15		A1
4010	" "	20	NWNE	1883-05-15		A1
4011	" "	21	E½SE	1883-05-15		A1
4012	" "	21	SESW	1883-05-15		A1

ID	Individual in Patent	Sec.	Sec. Part	Date Issued	Other Counties	For More Info . . .
4013	SCOTT, Thomas B (Cont'd)	22	4	1883-05-15		A1
4014	" "	22	N½NW	1883-05-15		A1
4015	" "	28	NENW	1883-05-15		A1
4016	" "	36	NESW	1883-05-15		A1
4018	" "	5	NWSW	1883-05-15		A1
4022	" "	6	2	1883-05-15		A1
4023	" "	6	NESE	1883-05-15		A1
4024	" "	6	SENE	1883-05-15		A1
4025	" "	6	SENW	1883-05-15		A1
4026	" "	7	E½SE	1883-05-15		A1
4027	" "	8	NESE	1883-05-15		A1
4028	" "	8	NWNE	1883-05-15		A1
4030	" "	8	SESW	1883-05-15		A1
4031	" "	8	SWSE	1883-05-15		A1
4032	" "	8	W½SW	1883-05-15		A1
4033	" "	9	NWSW	1883-05-15		A1
4017	" "	5	NESW	1884-06-30		A1
4019	" "	5	SE	1884-06-30		A1
4029	" "	8	SESE	1885-05-09		A1
4020	" "	5	SESW	1886-08-10		A1
3863	SLATTERY, William C	17	NWNW	1902-03-07		A3 G15
3861	STEIN, Frank	7	2	1896-11-24		A1
3953	STROUP, John	30	W½NE	1900-06-11		A1
4041	TELLEFSON, William C	35	SESE	1901-05-08		A3
4042	" "	36	SWSW	1901-05-08		A3
3886	TOLMAN, James B	13	2	1872-11-01		A1
3887	" "	14	NWNW	1872-11-01		A1
3888	" "	14	S½NW	1872-11-01		A1
3889	" "	14	SW	1872-11-01		A1
3890	" "	14	SWSE	1872-11-01		A1
3891	" "	15	SE	1872-11-01		A1
3892	" "	15	SWNE	1872-11-01		A1
3893	" "	2	NENW	1872-11-01		A1
3894	" "	2	NWNW	1872-11-01		A1
3895	" "	22	NENE	1872-11-01		A1
3896	" "	22	NWNE	1872-11-01		A1
3897	" "	23		1872-11-01		A1
3898	" "	24	E½SE	1872-11-01		A1
3899	" "	24	NWSE	1872-11-01		A1
3900	" "	24	NWSW	1872-11-01		A1
3901	" "	24	S½SW	1872-11-01		A1
3902	" "	24	SENE	1872-11-01		A1
3903	" "	24	W½NE	1872-11-01		A1
3904	" "	24	W½NW	1872-11-01		A1
3858	TOWNSEND, Danville L	20	NWSW	1875-02-20		A1 G119
3859	" "	20	S½NW	1875-02-20		A1 G119
3858	WELLINGTON, Richard H	20	NWSW	1875-02-20		A1 G119
3859	" "	20	S½NW	1875-02-20		A1 G119
3952	WILD, John M	9	SESE	1904-09-08		A1
3843	WYLIE, Daniel B	1	NENE	1883-09-15		A1 G172
3843	WYLIE, Winfred	1	NENE	1883-09-15		A1 G172
3836	ZIEMKE, August	18	E½NW	1899-04-22		A3
3837	" "	18	NWSE	1899-04-22		A3
3838	" "	18	SWNE	1899-04-22		A3

Patent Map

T41-N R9-E
4th PM - 1831 MN/WI

Map Group 22

Township Statistics

Parcels Mapped	:	263
Number of Patents	:	95
Number of Individuals	:	66
Patentees Identified	:	50
Number of Surnames	:	56
Multi-Patentee Parcels	:	41
Oldest Patent Date	:	5/25/1870
Most Recent Patent	:	1/24/1916
Block/Lot Parcels	:	21
Parcels Re - Issued	:	0
Parcels that Overlap	:	0
Cities and Towns	:	0
Cemeteries	:	0

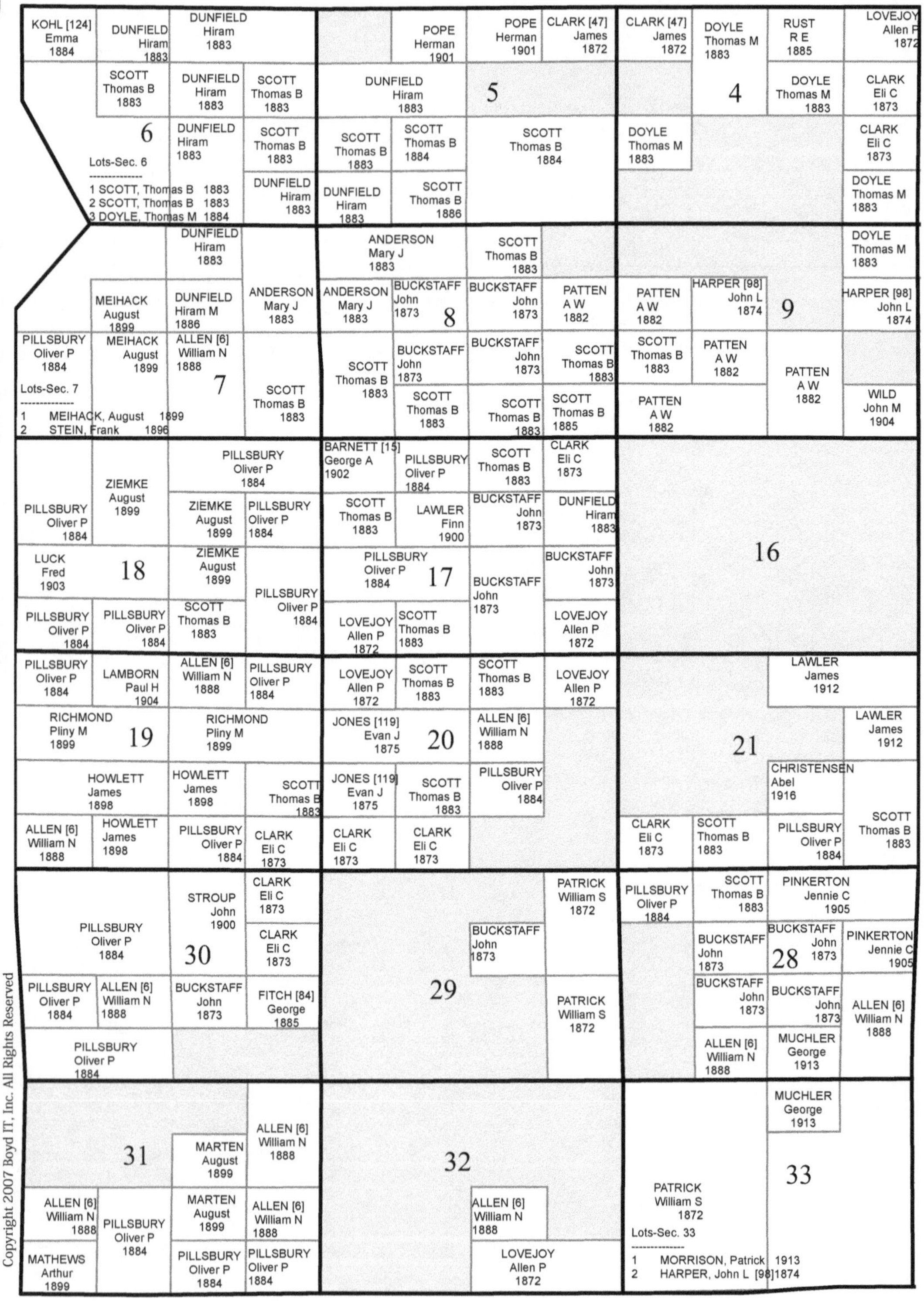

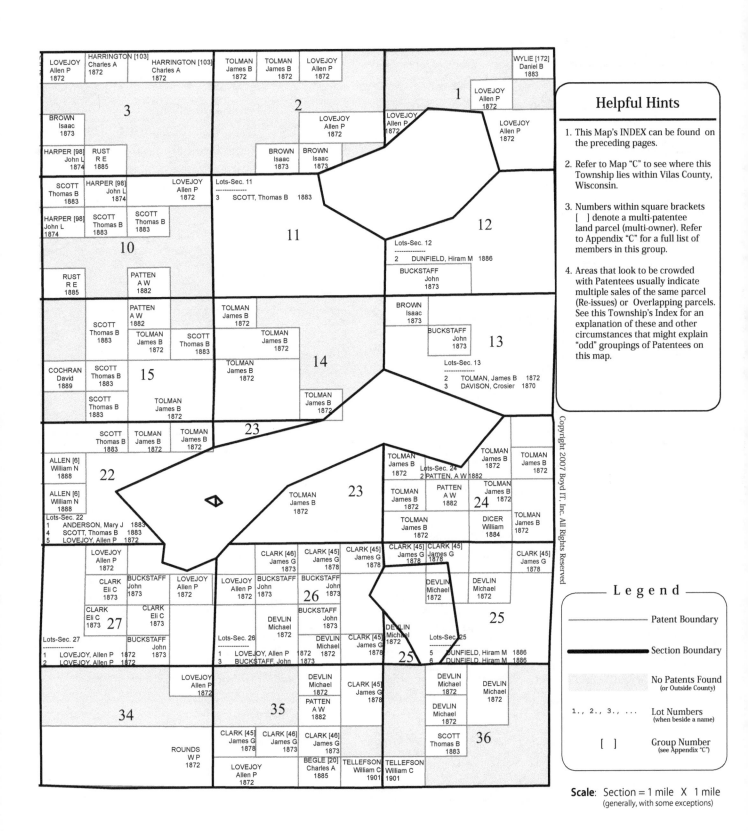

Helpful Hints

1. This Map's INDEX can be found on the preceding pages.

2. Refer to Map "C" to see where this Township lies within Vilas County, Wisconsin.

3. Numbers within square brackets [ ] denote a multi-patentee land parcel (multi-owner). Refer to Appendix "C" for a full list of members in this group.

4. Areas that look to be crowded with Patentees usually indicate multiple sales of the same parcel (Re-issues) or Overlapping parcels. See this Township's Index for an explanation of these and other circumstances that might explain "odd" groupings of Patentees on this map.

Copyright 2007 Boyd IT, Inc. All Rights Reserved

L e g e n d

———————— Patent Boundary

━━━━━━━━ Section Boundary

No Patents Found (or Outside County)

1., 2., 3., ...   Lot Numbers (when beside a name)

[ ]   Group Number (see Appendix "C")

Scale: Section = 1 mile X 1 mile (generally, with some exceptions)

Road Map

T41-N R9-E
4th PM - 1831 MN/WI

Map Group 22

Cities & Towns

None

Cemeteries

None

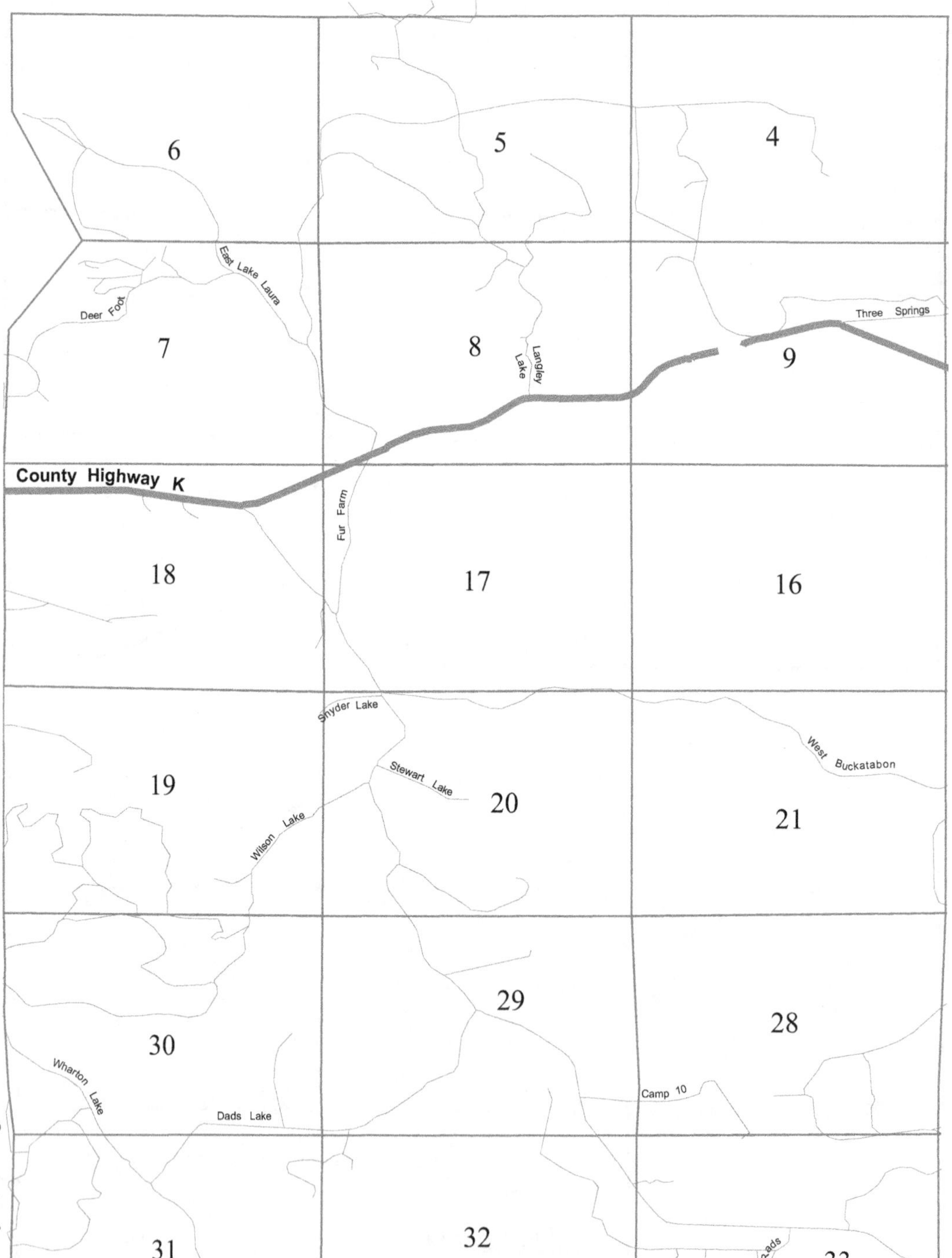

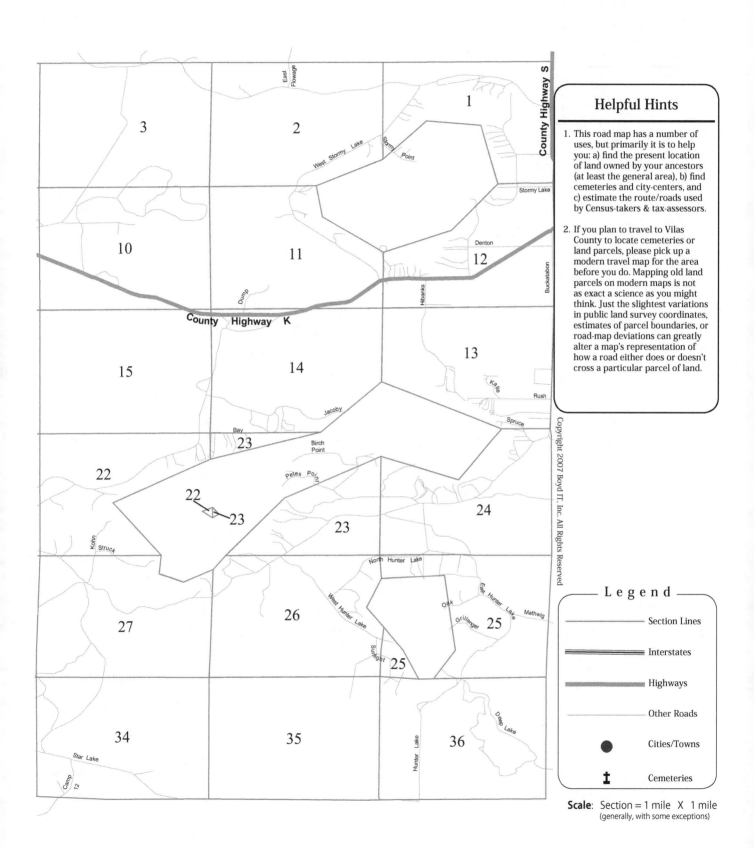

Helpful Hints

1. This road map has a number of uses, but primarily it is to help you: a) find the present location of land owned by your ancestors (at least the general area), b) find cemeteries and city-centers, and c) estimate the route/roads used by Census-takers & tax-assessors.

2. If you plan to travel to Vilas County to locate cemeteries or land parcels, please pick up a modern travel map for the area before you do. Mapping old land parcels on modern maps is not as exact a science as you might think. Just the slightest variations in public land survey coordinates, estimates of parcel boundaries, or road-map deviations can greatly alter a map's representation of how a road either does or doesn't cross a particular parcel of land.

Legend

———	Section Lines
≡≡≡	Interstates
▬▬▬	Highways
——	Other Roads
●	Cities/Towns
✝	Cemeteries

Scale: Section = 1 mile X 1 mile
(generally, with some exceptions)

Historical Map

T41-N R9-E
4th PM - 1831 MN/WI

Map Group 22

Cities & Towns
None

Cemeteries
None

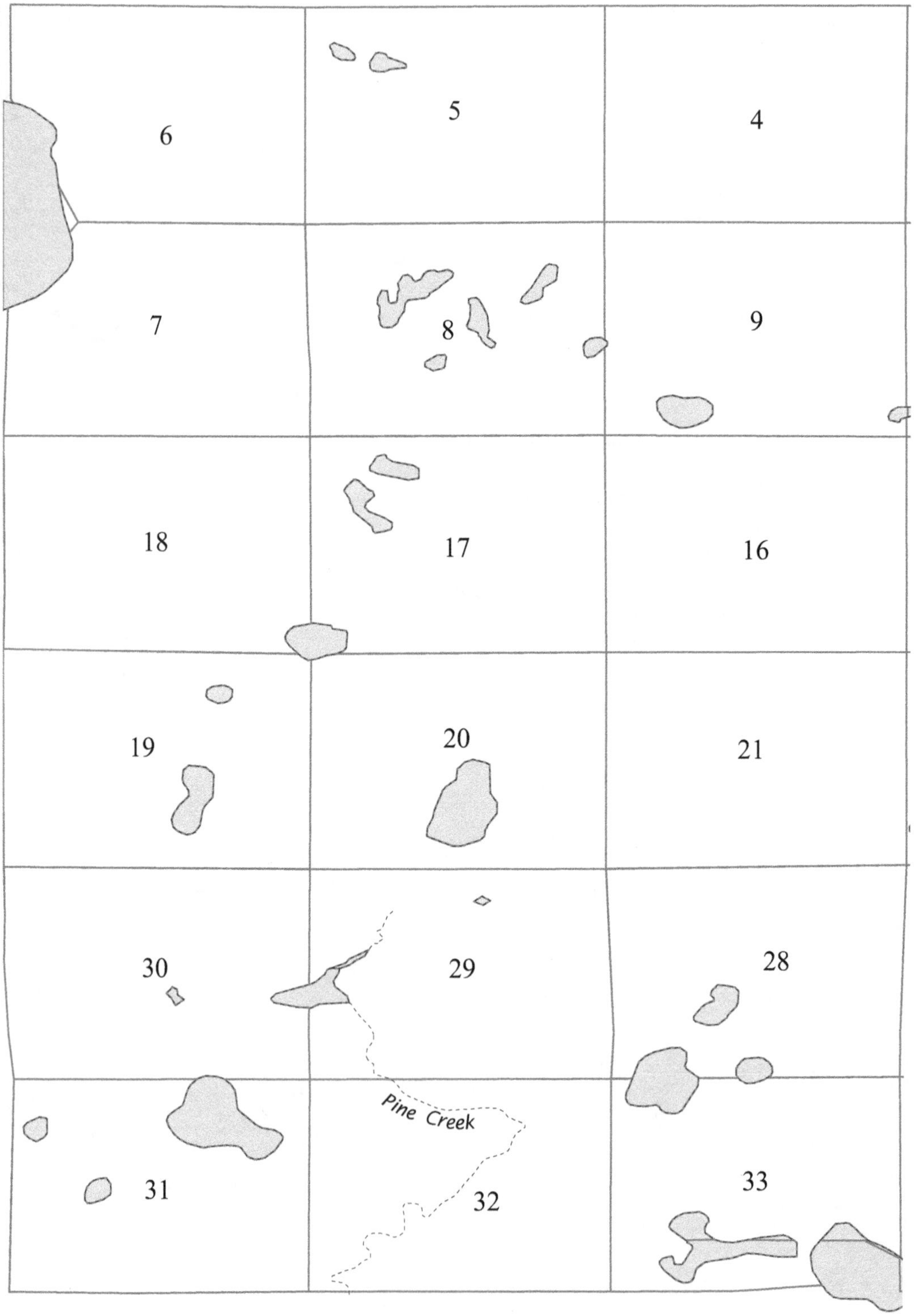

6	5	4
7	8	9
18	17	16
19	20	21
30	29	28
31	32	33

Pine Creek

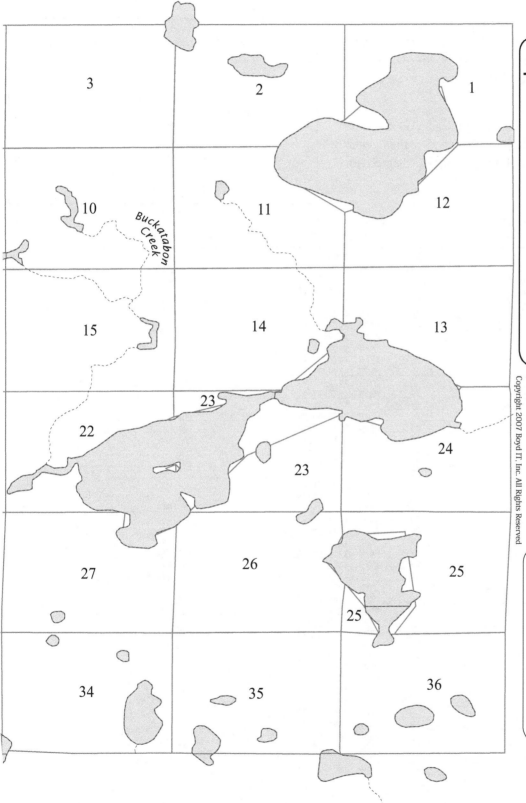

3

2

1

10

Buckatabon Creek

11

12

15

14

13

23

22

23

24

27

26

25

25

34

35

36

Helpful Hints

1. This Map takes a different look at the same Congressional Township displayed in the preceding two maps. It presents features that can help you better envision the historical development of the area: a) Water-bodies (lakes & ponds), b) Water-courses (rivers, streams, etc.), c) Railroads, d) City/town center-points (where they were oftentimes located when first settled), and e) Cemeteries.

2. Using this "Historical" map in tandem with this Township's Patent Map and Road Map, may lead you to some interesting discoveries. You will often find roads, towns, cemeteries, and waterways are named after nearby landowners: sometimes those names will be the ones you are researching. See how many of these research gems you can find here in Vilas County.

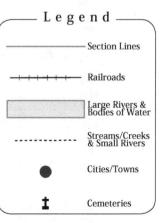

Legend

——————— Section Lines

—+—+—+— Railroads

▭ Large Rivers & Bodies of Water

---------- Streams/Creeks & Small Rivers

● Cities/Towns

⚱ Cemeteries

Scale: Section = 1 mile X 1 mile
(there are some exceptions)

Map Group 23: Index to Land Patents

Township 41-North Range 10-East (4th PM - 1831 MN/WI)

After you locate an individual in this Index, take note of the Section and Section Part then proceed to the Land Patent map on the pages immediately following. You should have no difficulty locating the corresponding parcel of land.

The "For More Info" Column will lead you to more information about the underlying Patents. See the *Legend* at right, and the "How to Use this Book" chapter, for more information.

```
                    LEGEND
        "For More Info . . . " column
A = Authority (Legislative Act, See Appendix "A")
B = Block or Lot (location in Section unknown)
C = Cancelled Patent
F = Fractional Section
G = Group  (Multi-Patentee Patent, see Appendix "C")
V = Overlaps another Parcel
R = Re-Issued (Parcel patented more than once)

(A & G items require you to look in the Appendixes referred
to above. All other Letter-designations followed by a number
require you to locate line-items in this index that possess
the ID number found after the letter).
```

ID	Individual in Patent	Sec.	Sec. Part	Date Issued	Other Counties	For More Info . . .
4155	ADAMS, William	23	7	1906-01-30		A3 G2
4077	BARTLETT, C R	5	NENE	1888-07-10		A1 G17 F
4076	BAUMANN, August F	32	NE	1892-05-16		A1
4155	BRASLEY, George	23	7	1906-01-30		A3 G2
4075	BROWN, Anderson W	2	SWNW	1883-04-20		A1 G32
4114	BROWN, Isaac	27	N½SW	1873-05-01		A1
4115	" "	27	SENW	1873-05-01		A1
4116	" "	27	SESW	1873-05-01		A1
4117	" "	31	E½SE	1873-05-01		A1
4118	" "	31	SENE	1873-05-01		A1
4119	" "	32	NESW	1873-05-01		A1
4120	" "	32	S½NW	1873-05-01		A1
4121	" "	32	W½SW	1873-05-01		A1
4123	" "	34	E½NW	1873-05-01		A1
4124	" "	34	N½SE	1873-05-01		A1
4125	" "	34	NESW	1873-05-01		A1
4126	" "	34	NWSW	1873-05-01		A1
4127	" "	34	SWNW	1873-05-01		A1
4122	" "	33	1	1873-11-15		A1
4075	BROWN, Webster E	2	SWNW	1883-04-20		A1 G32
4062	BUDDE, Albert F	30	NENW	1903-06-24		A1
4063	" "	30	NWNE	1903-06-24		A1
4131	CLARK, James G	20	N½SW	1873-05-01		A1 G46
4132	" "	20	S½SE	1873-05-01		A1 G46
4133	" "	20	SESW	1873-05-01		A1 G46
4134	" "	29	N½SW	1873-05-01		A1 G46
4135	" "	29	NENW	1873-05-01		A1 G46
4136	" "	29	NWNE	1873-05-01		A1 G46
4137	" "	29	SWNW	1873-05-01		A1 G46 R4158
4150	COMPANY, T B Scott Lumber	30	SWNE	1885-06-12		A1
4151	" "	6	NESE	1885-07-13		A1
4148	" "	18	SENW	1885-09-10		A1
4152	" "	7	SWSW	1885-09-10		A1 F
4149	" "	30	SENE	1885-12-10		A1
4143	COOK, Lyman J	34	SWSE	1885-01-15		A1 G55
4143	CURTIS, Charles H	34	SWSE	1885-01-15		A1 G55
4083	DAVISON, Crosier	18	NWNW	1870-05-25		A1
4084	" "	6	SWNW	1870-05-25		A1
4086	DENT, Edward H	29	SWNE	1899-08-14		A1
4156	DICER, William	19	S½SW	1884-06-30		A1 C R4157
4158	" "	29	SWNW	1884-06-30		A1 C R4137
4157	" "	19	S½SW	1885-06-12		A1 R4156
4153	DOYLE, Thomas M	17	SENE	1884-06-20		A1
4079	DUNBAR, Charles F	20	N½SE	1883-09-15		A1
4131	FORBES, John R	20	N½SW	1873-05-01		A1 G46
4132	" "	20	S½SE	1873-05-01		A1 G46

ID	Individual in Patent	Sec.	Sec. Part	Date Issued	Other Counties	For More Info . . .
4133	FORBES, John R (Cont'd)	20	SESW	1873-05-01		A1 G46
4134	" "	29	N½SW	1873-05-01		A1 G46
4135	" "	29	NENW	1873-05-01		A1 G46
4136	" "	29	NWNE	1873-05-01		A1 G46
4137	" "	29	SWNW	1873-05-01		A1 G46 R4158
4100	FREEMAN, H G	6	NWNW	1888-07-10		A1
4101	" "	6	SENW	1888-07-10		A1
4102	" "	6	SESE	1888-07-10		A1
4103	" "	7	SESE	1888-07-10		A1
4138	GILLETT, Joel D	4	SWNW	1883-03-30		A1
4105	HAMILTON, Irenus K	19	E½SE	1872-11-01		A1 G97
4106	" "	20	SWSW	1872-11-01		A1 G97
4107	" "	29	NWNW	1872-11-01		A1 G97
4108	" "	30	E½SW	1872-11-01		A1 G97
4109	" "	30	NENE	1872-11-01		A1 G97
4110	" "	30	SWSE	1872-11-01		A1 G97
4111	" "	30	SWSW	1872-11-01		A1 G97
4112	" "	5	SWSW	1872-11-01		A1 G97
4113	" "	8	S½NW	1872-11-01		A1 G97
4105	HAMILTON, Woodman C	19	E½SE	1872-11-01		A1 G97
4106	" "	20	SWSW	1872-11-01		A1 G97
4107	" "	29	NWNW	1872-11-01		A1 G97
4108	" "	30	E½SW	1872-11-01		A1 G97
4109	" "	30	NENE	1872-11-01		A1 G97
4110	" "	30	SWSE	1872-11-01		A1 G97
4111	" "	30	SWSW	1872-11-01		A1 G97
4112	" "	5	SWSW	1872-11-01		A1 G97
4113	" "	8	S½NW	1872-11-01		A1 G97
4078	HARRINGTON, Charles A	30	NESE	1872-11-01		A1 G103
4140	KAISER, John	3	N½SE	1904-03-01		A3
4141	" "	3	NESW	1904-03-01		A3
4142	" "	3	SENE	1904-03-01		A3
4128	LOOMIS, J B	5	NWSW	1889-05-31		A1
4070	LOVEJOY, Allen P	3	SWSW	1872-02-20		A1
4073	" "	4	NENW	1872-02-20		A1
4064	" "	28	N½	1872-05-10		A1
4065	" "	28	NWSW	1872-05-10		A1
4066	" "	29	E½NE	1872-05-10		A1
4067	" "	29	NESE	1872-05-10		A1
4068	" "	3	SESW	1872-05-10		A1
4069	" "	3	SWSE	1872-05-10		A1
4071	" "	31	W½SE	1872-05-10		A1
4072	" "	32	SESW	1872-05-10		A1
4074	" "	8	NENE	1872-07-01		A1
4159	LUETZER, William	6	SESW	1900-04-26		A3
4160	" "	6	SWSE	1900-04-26		A3
4161	" "	7	N½NW	1900-04-26		A3 F
4139	MEADE, Joel	2	W½SE	1873-06-10		A1 G142
4146	MORAN, Michael S	7	N½NE	1900-06-11		A1
4097	PALMS, Francis	9	SENE	1872-07-01		A1
4098	" "	9	SESW	1872-07-01		A1
4094	" "	14	W½NW	1872-11-01		A1
4095	" "	23	1	1872-11-01		A1
4096	" "	23	2	1872-11-01		A1
4091	" "	11	N½SE	1873-05-01		A1
4092	" "	14	NE	1873-05-01		A1
4093	" "	14	S½	1873-05-01		A1
4060	PATTEN, A W	19	N½SW	1882-06-30		A1 F
4061	" "	19	SWNW	1882-06-30		A1
4147	PILLSBURY, Oliver P	6	SWSW	1884-06-30		A1
4099	POLAR, H B	5	SENE	1873-05-01		A1
4082	REED, Charles P	29	NWSE	1909-05-24		A3
4078	REEVE, Thomas T	30	NESE	1872-11-01		A1 G103
4139	RIPLEY, Sylvanus	2	W½SE	1873-06-10		A1 G142
4078	ROE, Gilbert W	30	NESE	1872-11-01		A1 G103
4144	SANBORN, Marcus E	7	NESW	1902-03-17		A1
4145	" "	7	SENW	1902-03-17		A1
4077	SHAW, John	5	NENE	1888-07-10		A1 G17 F
4104	SHERRY, Henry	34	SESE	1884-06-20		A1
4162	SILVERTHORN, Willis V	4	NWNW	1900-06-11		A1
4087	STURDEVANT, Elijah C	7	NESE	1900-11-28		A1
4088	" "	7	SWNE	1900-11-28		A1
4089	" "	7	W½SE	1900-11-28		A1

ID	Individual in Patent	Sec.	Sec. Part	Date Issued	Other Counties	For More Info . . .
4154	TELLEFSON, W C	19	SENW	1900-07-30		A1
4129	TOLMAN, James B	19	W½NE	1872-11-01		A1
4130	" "	3	SESE	1872-11-01		A1
4090	TOWNSEND, Evan	19	NWSE	1873-05-01		A1
4080	WILEY, Charles L	6	NWSE	1883-09-15		A1
4081	" "	7	SENE	1883-09-15		A1
4085	WYLIE, Daniel B	6	NWSW	1883-09-15		A1 G172
4085	WYLIE, Winfred	6	NWSW	1883-09-15		A1 G172

Patent Map

T41-N R10-E
4th PM - 1831 MN/WI

Map Group 23

Township Statistics

Parcels Mapped	:	103
Number of Patents	:	52
Number of Individuals	:	48
Patentees Identified	:	38
Number of Surnames	:	44
Multi-Patentee Parcels	:	23
Oldest Patent Date	:	5/25/1870
Most Recent Patent	:	5/24/1909
Block/Lot Parcels	:	4
Parcels Re - Issued	:	2
Parcels that Overlap	:	0
Cities and Towns	:	1
Cemeteries	:	1

Map (Section 6):
FREEMAN H G 1888
DAVISON Crosier 1870
FREEMAN H G 1888
6
WYLIE [172] Daniel B 1883
WILEY Charles L 1883
COMPANY T B Scott Lumber 1885
LOOMIS J B 1889
PILLSBURY Oliver P 1884
LUETZER William 1900
LUETZER William 1900
FREEMAN H G 1888
HAMILTON [97] Irenus K 1872

Section 5:
BARTLETT [17] C R 1888
SILVERTHORN Willis V 1900
LOVEJOY Allen P 1872
POLAR H B 1873
GILLETT Joel D 1883
5

Section 4:
4

Section 7:
LUETZER William 1900
MORAN Michael S 1900
SANBORN Marcus E 1902
STURDEVANT Elijah C 1900
WILEY Charles L 1883
STURDEVANT Elijah C 1900
SANBORN Marcus E 1902
7
COMPANY T B Scott Lumber 1885
STURDEVANT Elijah C 1900
FREEMAN H G 1888

Section 8:
HAMILTON [97] Irenus K 1872
8

Section 9:
LOVEJOY Allen P 1872
9
PALMS Francis 1872
PALMS Francis 1872

Section 18:
DAVISON Crosier 1870
COMPANY T B Scott Lumber 1885
18

Section 17:
17
DOYLE Thomas M 1884

Section 16:
16

Section 19:
PATTEN A W 1882
TELLEFSON W C 1900
TOLMAN James B 1872
PATTEN A W 1882
TOWNSEND Evan 1873
19
DICER William 1885
DICER William 1884
HAMILTON [97] Irenus K 1872

Section 20:
20
CLARK [46] James G 1873
DUNBAR Charles F 1883
HAMILTON [97] Irenus K 1872
CLARK [46] James G 1873
CLARK [46] James G 1873

Section 21:
21

Section 30:
BUDDE Albert F 1903
BUDDE Albert F 1903
30
COMPANY T B Scott Lumber 1885
COMPANY T B Scott Lumber 1885
HAMILTON [97] Irenus K 1872
HARRINGTON [103] Charles A 1872
HAMILTON [97] Irenus K 1872
HAMILTON [97] Irenus K 1872

Section 29:
HAMILTON [97] Irenus K 1872
HAMILTON [97] Irenus K 1872
CLARK [46] James G 1873
CLARK [46] James G 1873
CLARK [46] James G 1873
DICER William 1884
29
DENT Edward H 1899
CLARK James G 1873
REED Charles P 1909
LOVEJOY Allen P 1872
LOVEJOY Allen P 1872

Section 28:
LOVEJOY Allen P 1872
LOVEJOY Allen P 1872
28

Section 31:
31

Section 32:
BROWN Isaac 1873
BROWN Isaac 1873
32
BROWN Isaac 1873
BROWN Isaac 1873
LOVEJOY Allen P 1872
BROWN Isaac 1873
LOVEJOY Allen P 1872
LOVEJOY Allen P 1872
BROWN Isaac 1873

Section 33:
Lots-Sec. 33
----
1   BROWN, Isaac   1873
BAUMANN August F 1892
33

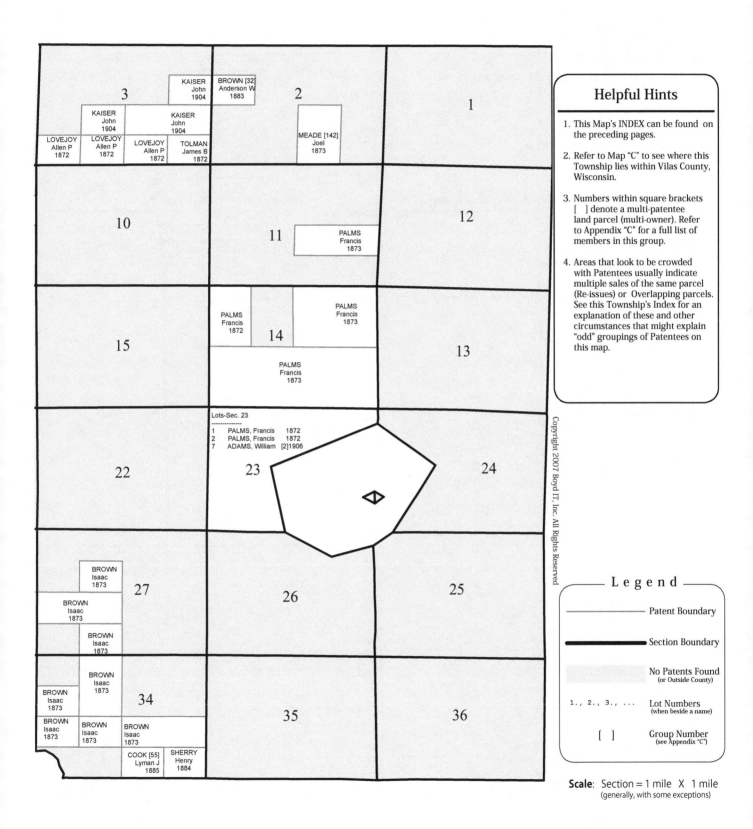

Helpful Hints

1. This Map's INDEX can be found on the preceding pages.

2. Refer to Map "C" to see where this Township lies within Vilas County, Wisconsin.

3. Numbers within square brackets [ ] denote a multi-patentee land parcel (multi-owner). Refer to Appendix "C" for a full list of members in this group.

4. Areas that look to be crowded with Patentees usually indicate multiple sales of the same parcel (Re-issues) or Overlapping parcels. See this Township's Index for an explanation of these and other circumstances that might explain "odd" groupings of Patentees on this map.

Legend

Patent Boundary

Section Boundary

No Patents Found
(or Outside County)

1., 2., 3., ... Lot Numbers
(when beside a name)

[ ] Group Number
(see Appendix "C")

Scale: Section = 1 mile X 1 mile
(generally, with some exceptions)

Road Map

T41-N R10-E
4th PM - 1831 MN/WI

Map Group 23

County Highway S

Cities & Towns
Conover

Cemeteries
Hildegard Cemetery

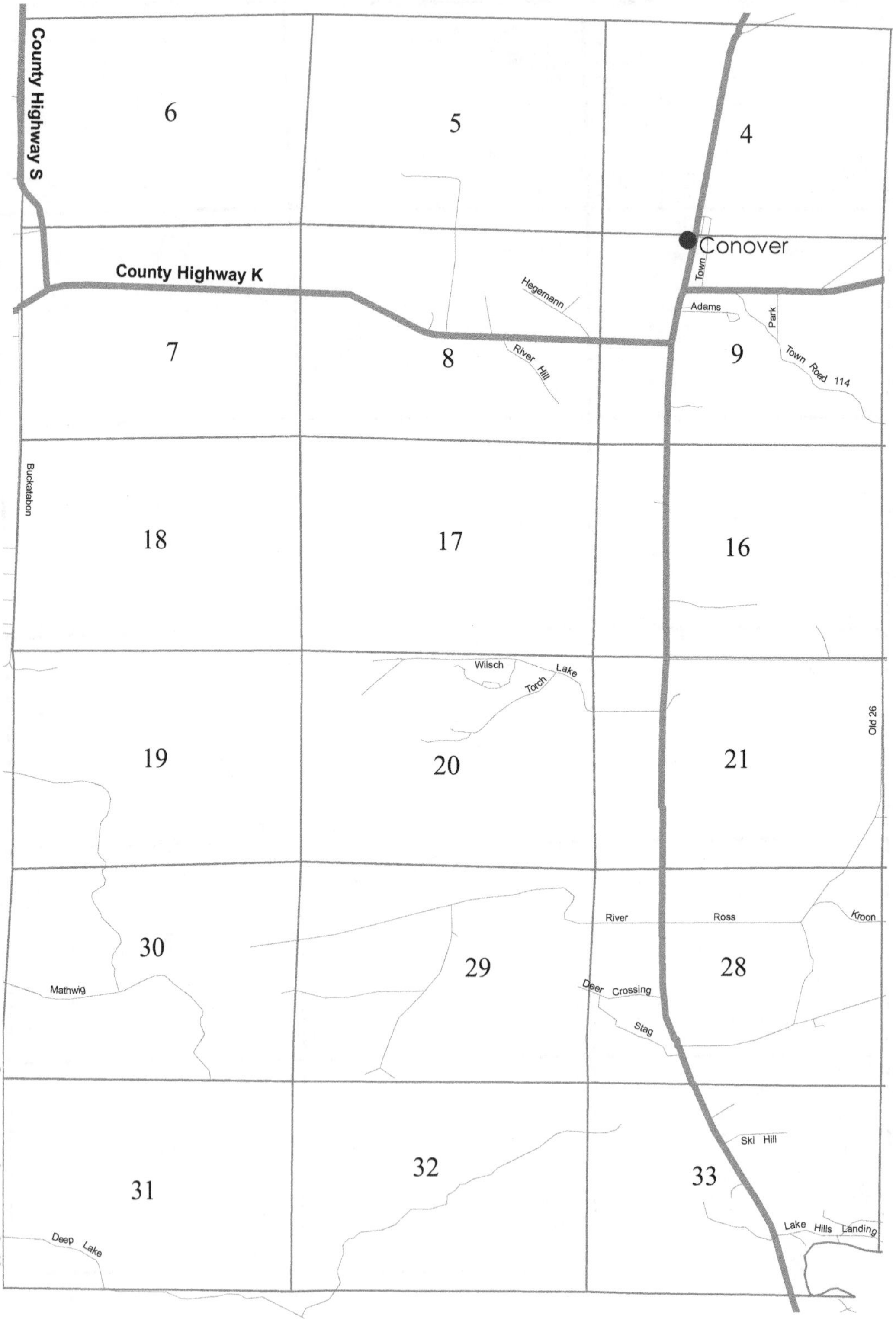

6

5

4

● Conover

County Highway K

Hegemann

Adams

Park

Town Road 114

7

8

River Hill

9

Buckatabon

18

17

16

Old 26

Wilsch Lake

Torch

19

20

21

River

Ross

Kroon

30

29

Deer Crossing

28

Mathwig

Stag

31

32

Ski Hill

33

Deep Lake

Lake Hills Landing

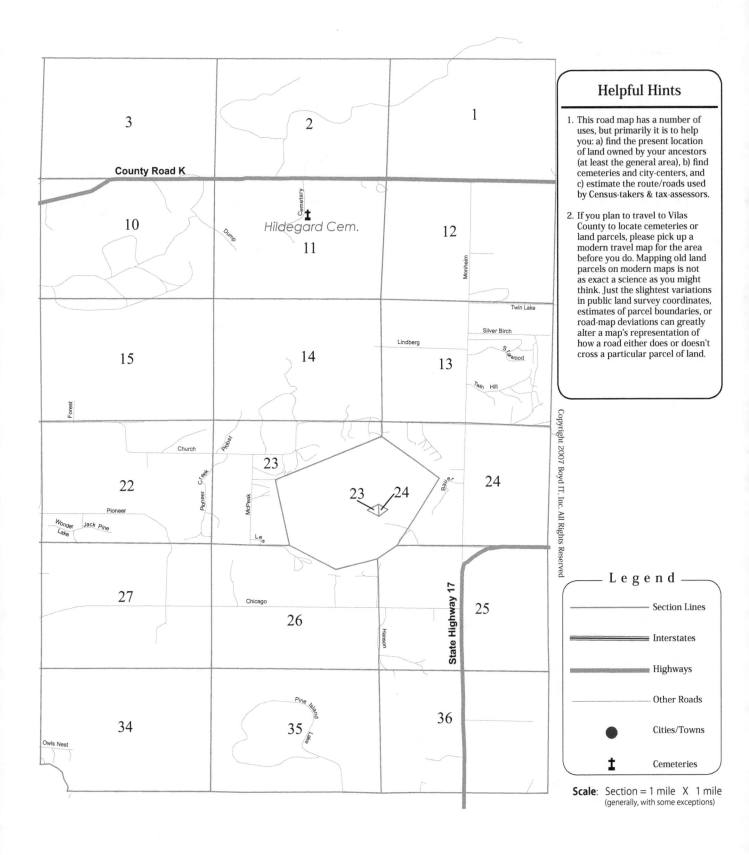

Helpful Hints

1. This road map has a number of uses, but primarily it is to help you: a) find the present location of land owned by your ancestors (at least the general area), b) find cemeteries and city-centers, and c) estimate the route/roads used by Census-takers & tax-assessors.

2. If you plan to travel to Vilas County to locate cemeteries or land parcels, please pick up a modern travel map for the area before you do. Mapping old land parcels on modern maps is not as exact a science as you might think. Just the slightest variations in public land survey coordinates, estimates of parcel boundaries, or road-map deviations can greatly alter a map's representation of how a road either does or doesn't cross a particular parcel of land.

Legend

— Section Lines

══ Interstates

━━ Highways

— Other Roads

● Cities/Towns

♱ Cemeteries

Scale: Section = 1 mile X 1 mile
(generally, with some exceptions)

Historical Map

T41-N R10-E
4th PM - 1831 MN/WI

Map Group 23

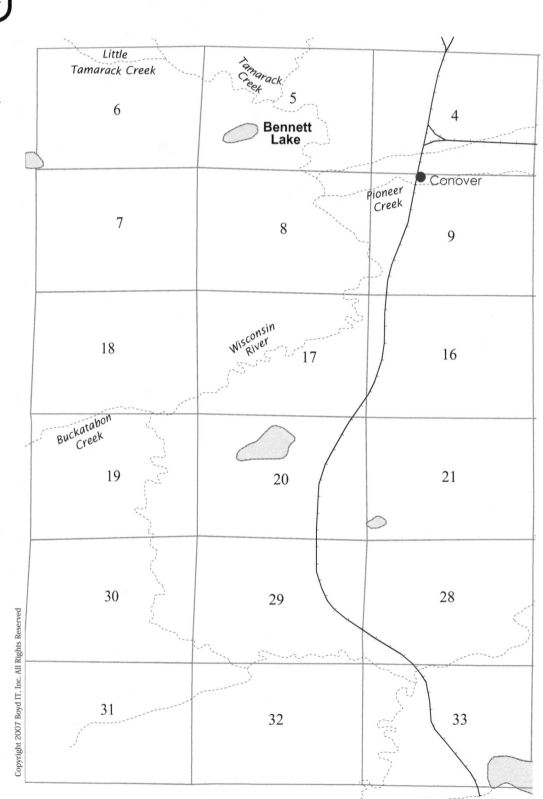

Cities & Towns
Conover

Cemeteries
Hildegard Cemetery

Little
Tamarack Creek

Tamarack
Creek

5

Bennett
Lake

4

6

Conover

Pioneer
Creek

7

8

9

Wisconsin
River

18

17

16

Buckatabon
Creek

19

20

21

30

29

28

31

32

33

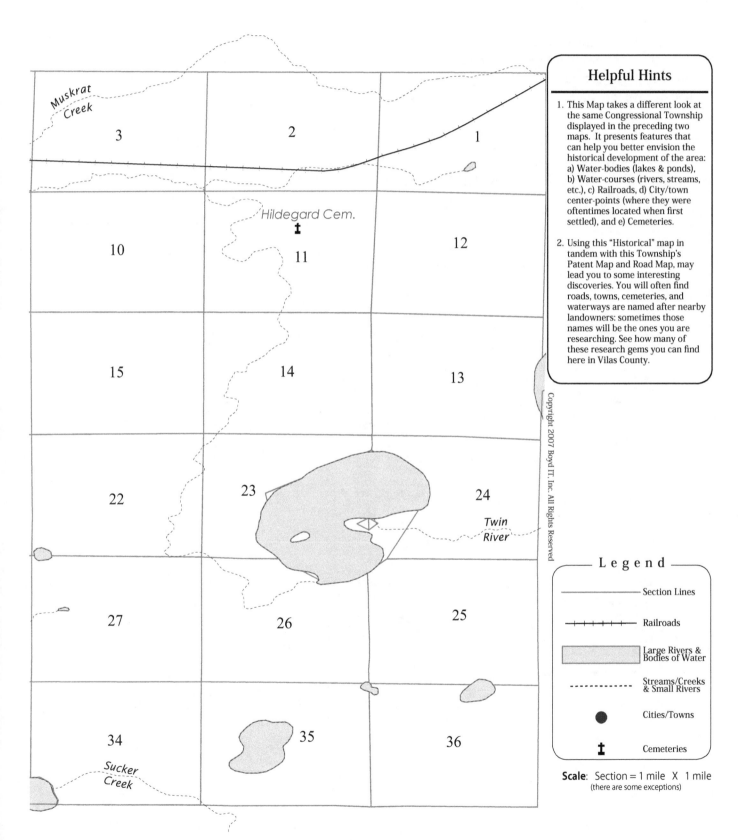

Helpful Hints

1. This Map takes a different look at the same Congressional Township displayed in the preceding two maps. It presents features that can help you better envision the historical development of the area: a) Water-bodies (lakes & ponds), b) Water-courses (rivers, streams, etc.), c) Railroads, d) City/town center-points (where they were oftentimes located when first settled), and e) Cemeteries.

2. Using this "Historical" map in tandem with this Township's Patent Map and Road Map, may lead you to some interesting discoveries. You will often find roads, towns, cemeteries, and waterways are named after nearby landowners: sometimes those names will be the ones you are researching. See how many of these research gems you can find here in Vilas County.

Muskrat Creek

3

2

1

Hildegard Cem.

10

11

12

15

14

13

22

23

24

Twin River

27

26

25

34

35

36

Sucker Creek

Legend

——————— Section Lines

—+—+—+—+—+— Railroads

Large Rivers & Bodies of Water

- - - - - - - - Streams/Creeks & Small Rivers

● Cities/Towns

☩ Cemeteries

Scale: Section = 1 mile X 1 mile
(there are some exceptions)

Map Group 24: Index to Land Patents

Township 41-North Range 11-East (4th PM - 1831 MN/WI)

After you locate an individual in this Index, take note of the Section and Section Part then proceed to the Land Patent map on the pages immediately following. You should have no difficulty locating the corresponding parcel of land.

The "For More Info" Column will lead you to more information about the underlying Patents. See the *Legend* at right, and the "How to Use this Book" chapter, for more information.

```
                    LEGEND
              "For More Info . . . " column
A = Authority (Legislative Act, See Appendix "A")
B = Block or Lot (location in Section unknown)
C = Cancelled Patent
F = Fractional Section
G = Group  (Multi-Patentee Patent, see Appendix "C")
V = Overlaps another Parcel
R = Re-Issued (Parcel patented more than once)

(A & G items require you to look in the Appendixes referred
to above. All other Letter-designations followed by a number
require you to locate line-items in this index that possess
the ID number found after the letter).
```

ID	Individual in Patent	Sec.	Sec. Part	Date Issued	Other Counties	For More Info . . .
4205	BEYER, George	13	SWSW	1883-09-15		A1
4206	" "	13	W½SE	1883-09-15		A1
4207	" "	23	NWSW	1883-09-15		A1
4208	" "	25	NENW	1883-09-15		A1
4209	" "	25	SESE	1883-09-15		A1
4225	BROWN, Isaac	29	NESW	1873-05-01		A1
4227	" "	33	S½NE	1873-05-01		A1
4228	" "	33	SE	1873-05-01		A1
4230	" "	9	2	1873-05-01		A1
4226	" "	33	NWNE	1873-11-15		A1
4229	" "	33	SWSW	1873-11-15		A1
4252	COLMAN, John	33	NENE	1889-05-31		A1
4213	COOPER, Grant	3	3	1905-11-08		A3 R4223
4214	" "	3	SESW	1905-11-08		A3 F
4251	DIAMOND, John A	19	NWSW	1904-10-22		A1
4171	DIXON, Alice	19	NESW	1884-06-30		A1
4172	" "	19	NWSE	1884-06-30		A1
4215	EVANS, Henry A	21	SWNE	1910-08-29		A1
4198	FOSTER, David	27	SENW	1889-05-09		A1 G87
4199	" "	33	NENW	1889-05-09		A1 G87
4231	GOULD, James	19	3	1872-11-01		A1
4232	" "	19	NESE	1872-11-01		A1
4233	" "	19	S½SE	1872-11-01		A1
4234	" "	19	S½SW	1872-11-01		A1
4235	" "	19	SENE	1872-11-01		A1
4236	" "	21	N½NW	1872-11-01		A1
4237	" "	7	3	1872-11-01		A1
4238	" "	7	4	1872-11-01		A1
4239	" "	7	NESW	1872-11-01		A1
4219	HAMILTON, Irenus K	11	NENW	1872-11-01		A1 G97 C R4220
4221	" "	11	W½NW	1872-11-01		A1 G97 C R4222
4223	" "	3	3	1872-11-01		A1 G97 C R4213
4220	" "	11	NENW	1905-11-27		A1 G97 R4219
4222	" "	11	W½NW	1905-11-27		A1 G97 R4221
4224	" "	3	4	1905-11-27		A1 G97
4219	HAMILTON, Woodman C	11	NENW	1872-11-01		A1 G97 C R4220
4221	" "	11	W½NW	1872-11-01		A1 G97 C R4222
4223	" "	3	3	1872-11-01		A1 G97 C R4213
4220	" "	11	NENW	1905-11-27		A1 G97 R4219
4222	" "	11	W½NW	1905-11-27		A1 G97 R4221
4224	" "	3	4	1905-11-27		A1 G97
4195	HARRINGTON, Charles A	25	SWNE	1882-02-10		A1 G104
4196	" "	25	W½SE	1882-02-10		A1 G104
4277	HOLLISTER, Seymour W	35	SENE	1883-09-15		A1 G108
4189	HOWES, Bertha	11	NE	1888-07-28		A1 G110
4190	" "	11	SENW	1888-07-28		A1 G110

ID	Individual in Patent	Sec.	Sec. Part	Date Issued	Other Counties	For More Info . . .
4191	HOWES, Bertha (Cont'd)	11	SW	1888-07-28		A1 G110
4192	" "	11	W½SE	1888-07-28		A1 G110
4193	" "	15	NE	1888-07-28		A1 G110
4194	" "	15	NESE	1888-07-28		A1 G110
4189	HOWES, Clara E	11	NE	1888-07-28		A1 G110
4190	" "	11	SENW	1888-07-28		A1 G110
4191	" "	11	SW	1888-07-28		A1 G110
4192	" "	11	W½SE	1888-07-28		A1 G110
4193	" "	15	NE	1888-07-28		A1 G110
4194	" "	15	NESE	1888-07-28		A1 G110
4189	HOWES, Emma A	11	NE	1888-07-28		A1 G110
4190	" "	11	SENW	1888-07-28		A1 G110
4191	" "	11	SW	1888-07-28		A1 G110
4192	" "	11	W½SE	1888-07-28		A1 G110
4193	" "	15	NE	1888-07-28		A1 G110
4194	" "	15	NESE	1888-07-28		A1 G110
4189	HOWES, Mary D	11	NE	1888-07-28		A1 G110
4190	" "	11	SENW	1888-07-28		A1 G110
4191	" "	11	SW	1888-07-28		A1 G110
4192	" "	11	W½SE	1888-07-28		A1 G110
4193	" "	15	NE	1888-07-28		A1 G110
4194	" "	15	NESE	1888-07-28		A1 G110
4263	KREITZER, Joseph	27	SE	1909-04-01		A3
4264	LAEV, Joseph	21	SESE	1885-01-20		A1
4266	" "	21	SWNW	1885-01-20		A1
4267	" "	23	SESW	1885-01-20		A1
4269	" "	25	NENE	1885-01-20		A1
4270	" "	27	NWNW	1885-01-20		A1
4272	" "	29	SWNE	1885-01-20		A1
4265	" "	21	SESW	1890-07-15		A1
4268	" "	23	W½SE	1890-07-15		A1
4271	" "	27	SWNW	1890-07-15		A1
4240	LANGILL, James	19	4	1895-03-30		A1
4243	" "	35	SESW	1900-06-11		A1
4244	" "	35	SWSE	1900-06-11		A1
4245	" "	35	SWSW	1904-02-25		A1
4241	" "	35	N½NW	1909-01-25		A3
4242	" "	35	NWNE	1909-01-25		A3
4278	LANGILL, Stewart	35	NESW	1905-05-02		A3
4279	" "	35	S½NW	1905-05-02		A3
4173	LOVEJOY, Allen P	11	SESE	1872-02-20		A1
4177	" "	23	E½NW	1872-02-20		A1
4178	" "	25	NWNE	1872-02-20		A1
4179	" "	25	S½NW	1872-02-20		A1
4185	" "	7	NWSW	1872-02-20		A1
4186	" "	7	S½SW	1872-02-20		A1
4174	" "	19	1	1872-05-10		A1
4175	" "	19	2	1872-05-10		A1
4176	" "	19	SWNW	1872-05-10		A1
4180	" "	29	NWSW	1872-05-10		A1
4181	" "	31	N½NE	1872-05-10		A1
4182	" "	31	NWSE	1872-05-10		A1
4183	" "	31	SWNE	1872-05-10		A1
4184	" "	31	W½	1872-05-10		A1
4216	MANUEL, Henry E	15	1	1903-10-01		A3
4217	" "	15	2	1903-10-01		A3
4218	" "	15	W½SW	1903-10-01		A3
4246	MEADE, Joel	29	S½SW	1873-06-10		A1 G142
4247	" "	31	1	1873-06-10		A1 G142
4248	" "	31	2	1873-06-10		A1 G142
4249	" "	31	NESE	1873-06-10		A1 G142
4250	" "	31	SENE	1873-06-10		A1 G142
4290	MILLER, W H	15	3	1888-07-28		A1
4291	" "	15	SENW	1888-07-28		A1 R4281
4292	" "	15	W½NW	1888-07-28		A1
4293	" "	25	NESE	1888-07-28		A1
4294	" "	25	SENE	1888-07-28		A1
4295	" "	5	N½NE	1888-07-28		A1 F
4253	MURRAY, John D	23	NESE	1913-12-02		A3
4168	NAGEL, Adolf	27	E½NE	1914-12-12		A1
4166	PATTEN, A W	29	W½SE	1884-06-20		A1
4167	" "	35	NWSW	1884-06-20		A1
4256	PHELPS, John	29	NESE	1883-09-15		A1 G154

ID	Individual in Patent	Sec.	Sec. Part	Date Issued	Other Counties	For More Info . . .
4257	PHELPS, John (Cont'd)	29	SENE	1883-09-15		A1 G154
4198	PHILLIPS, A N	27	SENW	1889-05-09		A1 G87
4199	" "	33	NENW	1889-05-09		A1 G87
4165	" "	27	NESW	1889-05-31		A1
4163	" "	21	NWSE	1889-06-28		A1
4164	" "	21	SWSE	1890-07-15		A1
4258	RADCLIFFE, John	35	N½SE	1906-03-16		A1
4259	" "	35	SESE	1906-03-16		A1
4246	RIPLEY, Sylvanus	29	S½SW	1873-06-10		A1 G142
4247	" "	31	1	1873-06-10		A1 G142
4248	" "	31	2	1873-06-10		A1 G142
4249	" "	31	NESE	1873-06-10		A1 G142
4250	" "	31	SENE	1873-06-10		A1 G142
4195	ROE, Gilbert W	25	SWNE	1882-02-10		A1 G104
4196	" "	25	W½SE	1882-02-10		A1 G104
4197	ROGERS, Charles W	33	SENW	1909-10-04		A3
4273	SALZMAN, Louis	5	1	1892-05-16		A1
4274	" "	5	S½NW	1892-05-16		A1
4210	SANBORN, George F	11	NESE	1903-11-11		A1
4280	SCOTT, Thomas B	15	4	1883-04-20		A1
4281	" "	15	SENW	1883-04-20		A1 R4291
4282	" "	21	NESW	1883-04-20		A1
4283	" "	21	SENW	1883-04-20		A1
4284	" "	21	W½SW	1883-04-20		A1
4285	" "	23	W½NW	1883-04-20		A1
4286	" "	27	NENW	1883-04-20		A1
4287	" "	27	W½NE	1883-04-20		A1
4288	" "	29	N½NE	1883-04-20		A1
4289	" "	29	NW	1883-04-20		A1
4256	" "	29	NESE	1883-09-15		A1 G154
4257	" "	29	SENE	1883-09-15		A1 G154
4298	SCOTT, William	13	W½NE	1883-09-15		A1
4169	STEVENS, Alfred H	13	N½SW	1904-03-01		A3
4170	" "	13	SESW	1904-03-01		A3
4275	STEWART, Robert	17	3	1897-08-30		A1 F
4276	" "	9	1	1897-08-30		A1
4188	TALMAGE, Bert B	23	SWSW	1910-01-13		A3
4187	" "	23	NESW	1916-12-02		A3
4200	WALSH, Frank	27	SESW	1908-08-13		A3
4201	" "	27	W½SW	1908-08-13		A3
4260	WALSH, John	5	2	1893-11-16		A1
4261	" "	5	3	1893-11-16		A1
4262	" "	5	4	1893-11-16		A1
4296	WALSH, William J	7	1	1893-09-28		A1
4297	" "	7	2	1893-09-28		A1
4211	WENTWORTH, George K	35	NENE	1895-02-19		A1 G171
4212	" "	35	SWNE	1895-06-04		A1 G171
4211	WENTWORTH, Justin	35	NENE	1895-02-19		A1 G171
4212	" "	35	SWNE	1895-06-04		A1 G171
4277	WESCOTT, Marion	35	SENE	1883-09-15		A1 G108
4277	WESCOTT, Sheldon P	35	SENE	1883-09-15		A1 G108
4202	WESTCOTT, Frank	21	N½NE	1891-11-16		A1
4203	" "	21	NESE	1891-11-16		A1
4204	" "	21	SENE	1891-11-16		A1
4254	WOOLWORTH, John O	3	1	1903-01-27		A3
4255	" "	3	2	1903-01-27		A3

Patent Map

T41-N R11-E
4th PM - 1831 MN/WI

Map Group 24

Township Statistics

Parcels Mapped	:	136
Number of Patents	:	61
Number of Individuals	:	50
Patentees Identified	:	41
Number of Surnames	:	40
Multi-Patentee Parcels	:	26
Oldest Patent Date	:	2/20/1872
Most Recent Patent	:	12/2/1916
Block/Lot Parcels	:	26
Parcels Re - Issued	:	4
Parcels that Overlap	:	0
Cities and Towns	:	1
Cemeteries	:	0

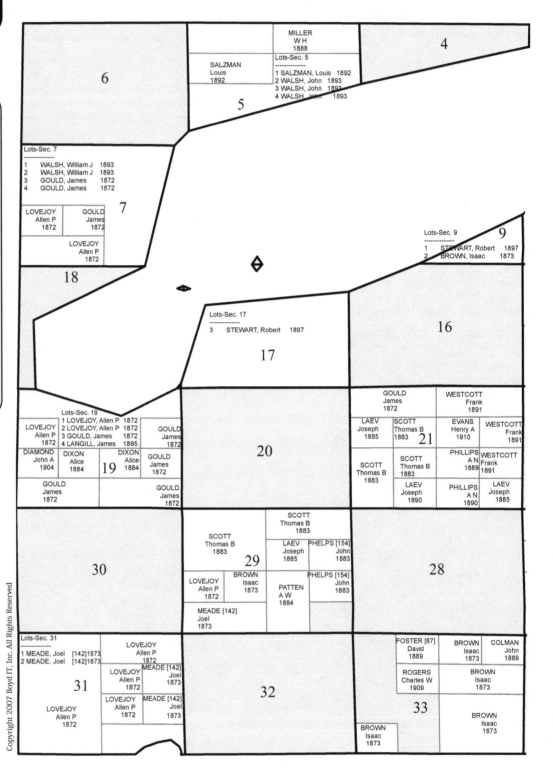

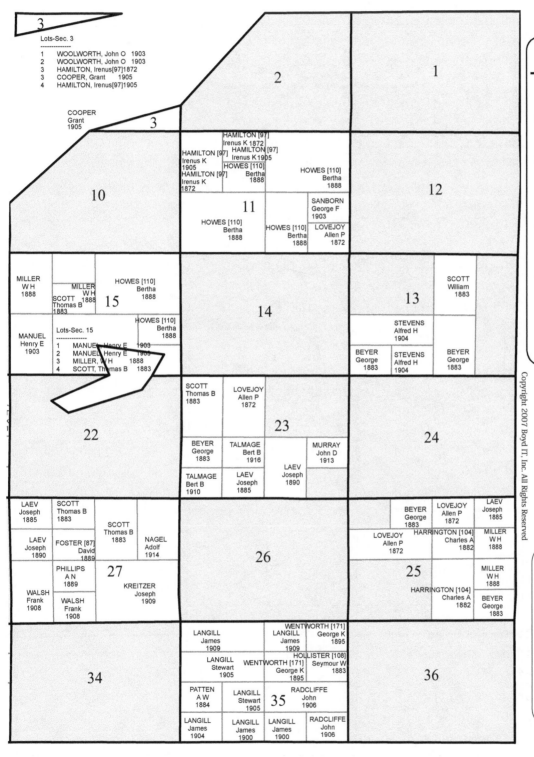

3

Lots-Sec. 3
----
1 WOOLWORTH, John O 1903
2 WOOLWORTH, John O 1903
3 HAMILTON, Irenus[97]1872
3 COOPER, Grant 1905
4 HAMILTON, Irenus[97]1905

COOPER
Grant
1905

3

2

1

HAMILTON [97]
Irenus K 1872
HAMILTON [97]
Irenus K 1905
HOWES [110]
Bertha
1888

HAMILTON [97]
Irenus K
1905
HAMILTON [97]
Irenus K
1872

HOWES [110]
Bertha
1888

11

HOWES [110]
Bertha
1888

HOWES [110]
Bertha
1888

SANBORN
George F
1903

LOVEJOY
Allen P
1872

12

10

MILLER
W H
1888

MILLER
W H
1888
SCOTT
Thomas B
1883

HOWES [110]
Bertha
1888

15

HOWES [110]
Bertha
1888

14

SCOTT
William
1883

13

STEVENS
Alfred H
1904

MANUEL
Henry E
1903

Lots-Sec. 15
----
1 MANUEL, Henry E 1903
2 MANUEL, Henry E 1905
3 MILLER, W H 1888
4 SCOTT, Thomas B 1883

BEYER
George
1883

STEVENS
Alfred H
1904

BEYER
George
1883

22

SCOTT
Thomas B
1883

LOVEJOY
Allen P
1872

23

BEYER
George
1883

TALMAGE
Bert B
1916

MURRAY
John D
1913

24

TALMAGE
Bert B
1910

LAEV
Joseph
1885

LAEV
Joseph
1890

LAEV
Joseph
1885

SCOTT
Thomas B
1883

SCOTT
Thomas B
1883

NAGEL
Adolf
1914

BEYER
George
1883

LOVEJOY
Allen P
1872

LAEV
Joseph
1885

LAEV
Joseph
1890

FOSTER [87]
David
1889

LOVEJOY
Allen P
1872

HARRINGTON [104]
Charles A
1882

MILLER
W H
1888

PHILLIPS
A N
1889

27

KREITZER
Joseph
1909

26

25

MILLER
W H
1888

WALSH
Frank
1908

WALSH
Frank
1908

HARRINGTON [104]
Charles A
1882

BEYER
George
1883

LANGILL
James
1909

WENTWORTH [171]
LANGILL
James
1909
George K
1895

34

LANGILL
Stewart
1905

WENTWORTH [171]
George K
1895

HOLLISTER [108]
Seymour W
1883

36

PATTEN
A W
1884

LANGILL
Stewart
1905

RADCLIFFE
John
1906

35

LANGILL
James
1904

LANGILL
James
1900

LANGILL
James
1900

RADCLIFFE
John
1906

Helpful Hints

1. This Map's INDEX can be found on the preceding pages.

2. Refer to Map "C" to see where this Township lies within Vilas County, Wisconsin.

3. Numbers within square brackets [ ] denote a multi-patentee land parcel (multi-owner). Refer to Appendix "C" for a full list of members in this group.

4. Areas that look to be crowded with Patentees usually indicate multiple sales of the same parcel (Re-issues) or Overlapping parcels. See this Township's Index for an explanation of these and other circumstances that might explain "odd" groupings of Patentees on this map.

Legend

_____ Patent Boundary

▬▬▬▬ Section Boundary

No Patents Found
(or Outside County)

1., 2., 3., ...   Lot Numbers
(when beside a name)

[ ]   Group Number
(see Appendix "C")

Scale: Section = 1 mile X 1 mile
(generally, with some exceptions)

Road Map

T41-N R11-E
4th PM - 1831 MN/WI

Map Group 24

<u>Cities & Towns</u>

Phelps

<u>Cemeteries</u>

None

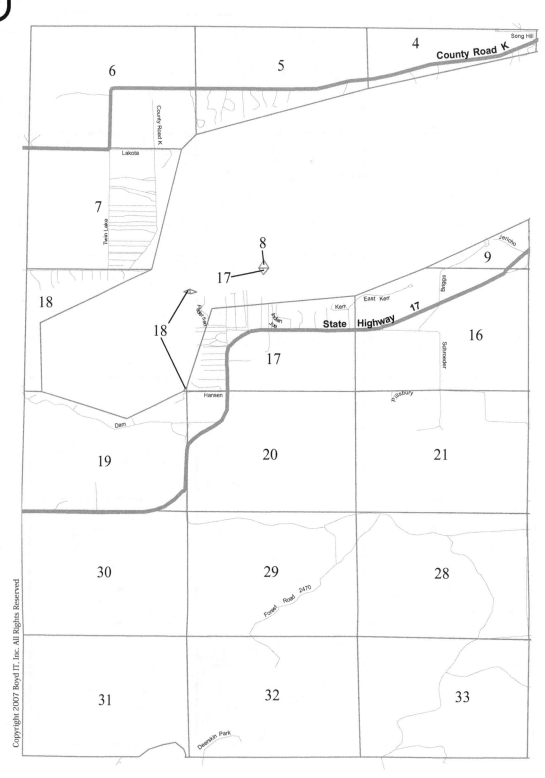

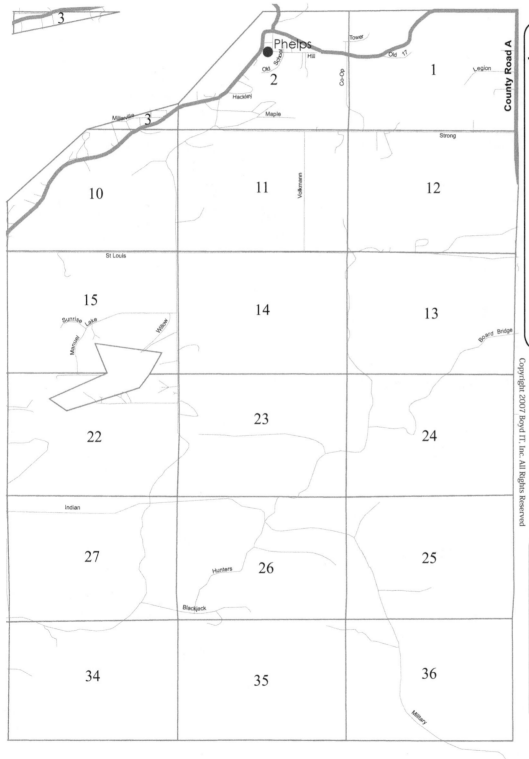

Phelps

Tower

Old 17

Legion

County Road A

1

Hill

Co-Op

2

Hackley

Maple

Strong

Millanille

3

10

11

Volkmann

12

St Louis

15

14

13

Sunrise Lake

Willow

Manuel

Board Bridge

22

23

24

Indian

27

Hunters

26

25

Blackjack

34

35

36

Military

Helpful Hints

1. This road map has a number of uses, but primarily it is to help you: a) find the present location of land owned by your ancestors (at least the general area), b) find cemeteries and city-centers, and c) estimate the route/roads used by Census-takers & tax-assessors.

2. If you plan to travel to Vilas County to locate cemeteries or land parcels, please pick up a modern travel map for the area before you do. Mapping old land parcels on modern maps is not as exact a science as you might think. Just the slightest variations in public land survey coordinates, estimates of parcel boundaries, or road-map deviations can greatly alter a map's representation of how a road either does or doesn't cross a particular parcel of land.

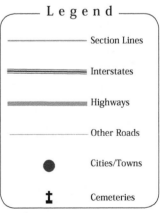

Legend

—————— Section Lines

══════ Interstates

━━━━━━ Highways

——————— Other Roads

● Cities/Towns

✝ Cemeteries

Scale: Section = 1 mile X 1 mile
(generally, with some exceptions)

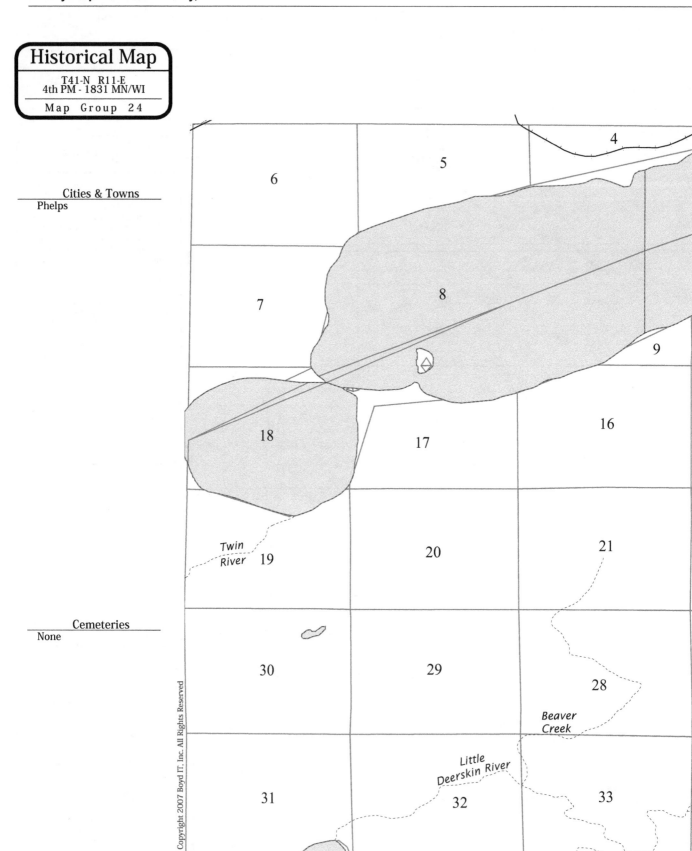

Historical Map

T41-N R11-E
4th PM - 1831 MN/WI

Map Group 24

Cities & Towns
Phelps

Cemeteries
None

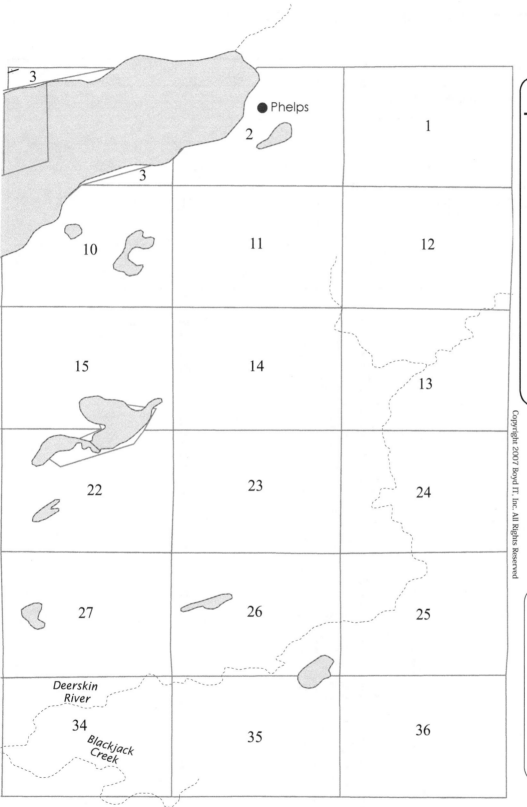

Phelps

3

3

1

2

10

11

12

15

14

13

22

23

24

27

26

25

Deerskin River

34

35

36

Blackjack Creek

Helpful Hints

1. This Map takes a different look at the same Congressional Township displayed in the preceding two maps. It presents features that can help you better envision the historical development of the area: a) Water-bodies (lakes & ponds), b) Water-courses (rivers, streams, etc.), c) Railroads, d) City/town center-points (where they were oftentimes located when first settled), and e) Cemeteries.

2. Using this "Historical" map in tandem with this Township's Patent Map and Road Map, may lead you to some interesting discoveries. You will often find roads, towns, cemeteries, and waterways are named after nearby landowners: sometimes those names will be the ones you are researching. See how many of these research gems you can find here in Vilas County.

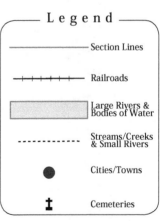

Legend

———————— Section Lines

+++++++ Railroads

Large Rivers & Bodies of Water

- - - - - Streams/Creeks & Small Rivers

● Cities/Towns

‡ Cemeteries

Scale: Section = 1 mile X 1 mile
(there are some exceptions)

Map Group 25: Index to Land Patents

Township 41-North Range 12-East (4th PM - 1831 MN/WI)

After you locate an individual in this Index, take note of the Section and Section Part then proceed to the Land Patent map on the pages immediately following. You should have no difficulty locating the corresponding parcel of land.

The "For More Info" Column will lead you to more information about the underlying Patents. See the *Legend* at right, and the "How to Use this Book" chapter, for more information.

```
                          LEGEND
              "For More Info . . . " column
A = Authority (Legislative Act, See Appendix "A")
B = Block or Lot (location in Section unknown)
C = Cancelled Patent
F = Fractional Section
G = Group  (Multi-Patentee Patent, see Appendix "C")
V = Overlaps another Parcel
R = Re-Issued (Parcel patented more than once)

(A & G items require you to look in the Appendixes referred
to above. All other Letter-designations followed by a number
require you to locate line-items in this index that possess
the ID number found after the letter).
```

ID	Individual in Patent	Sec.	Sec. Part	Date Issued	Other Counties	For More Info . . .
4363	BARNES, John	31	N½NE	1900-06-11		A1 C
4361	" "	31	1	1902-04-10		A1
4362	" "	31	2	1902-04-10		A1
4379	COLE, Timothy	13	N½SE	1884-12-30		A1
4380	" "	13	NE	1884-12-30		A1
4381	" "	13	SESE	1884-12-30		A1
4319	COLMAN, C F	31	NWNW	1902-05-12		A1
4321	COLMAN, Francis	23	E½NE	1904-12-29		A1
4322	" "	23	NESE	1904-12-29		A1
4368	DE GROOT, MARTIN	13	1	1895-03-30		A1
4369	" "	13	NESW	1895-03-30		A1
4370	" "	13	SENW	1895-03-30		A1
4323	FAY, George A	3	1	1884-04-24		A1
4324	" "	9	1	1884-04-24		A1
4374	GILKEY, Nathaniel C	23	NWSW	1884-04-24		A1 G91
4375	" "	23	W½NE	1884-04-24		A1 G91
4376	" "	23	E½NW	1885-06-03		A1 G92
4377	" "	23	NESW	1885-06-03		A1 G92
4378	" "	23	NWSE	1885-06-03		A1 G92
4329	HAGERMAN, James J	1	N½	1882-06-30		A1
4330	" "	1	N½SE	1882-06-30		A1
4331	" "	1	SW	1882-06-30		A1
4332	" "	11		1882-06-30		A1 F
4333	" "	15		1882-06-30		A1
4334	" "	17		1882-06-30		A1
4335	" "	19	E½	1882-06-30		A1
4336	" "	3	2	1882-06-30		A1
4337	" "	3	3	1882-06-30		A1
4338	" "	3	4	1882-06-30		A1
4339	" "	5	1	1882-06-30		A1
4340	" "	5	2	1882-06-30		A1
4341	" "	5	3	1882-06-30		A1
4342	" "	5	4	1882-06-30		A1
4343	" "	5	5	1882-06-30		A1
4344	" "	5	6	1882-06-30		A1
4345	" "	5	NWNW	1882-06-30		A1
4346	" "	7	1	1882-06-30		A1
4347	" "	7	2	1882-06-30		A1
4348	" "	7	4	1882-06-30		A1
4349	" "	7	5	1882-06-30		A1
4350	" "	7	NW	1882-06-30		A1
4351	" "	7	NWSW	1882-06-30		A1
4352	" "	7	S½SW	1882-06-30		A1
4353	" "	7	SWSE	1882-06-30		A1
4354	" "	9	2	1882-06-30		A1
4355	" "	9	3	1882-06-30		A1

ID	Individual in Patent	Sec.	Sec. Part	Date Issued	Other Counties	For More Info . . .
4356	HAGERMAN, James J (Cont'd)	9	4	1882-06-30		A1
4357	" "	9	5	1882-06-30		A1
4358	" "	9	S½SE	1882-06-30		A1
4359	" "	9	SW	1882-06-30		A1
4360	" "	9	W½NW	1882-06-30		A1
4328	HAMILTON, I K	1	S½SE	1872-05-01		A1 G95
4328	HAMILTON, W C	1	S½SE	1872-05-01		A1 G95
4371	HAYNNE, Martin	23	W½NW	1898-04-06		A1
4367	HIGGINS, Martha	19	S½SW	1904-03-26		A1
4374	JENNINGS, Ellis	23	NWSW	1884-04-24		A1 G91
4375	" "	23	W½NE	1884-04-24		A1 G91
4376	" "	23	E½NW	1885-06-03		A1 G92
4377	" "	23	NESW	1885-06-03		A1 G92
4378	" "	23	NWSE	1885-06-03		A1 G92
4364	LAEV, Joseph	19	E½NW	1884-12-30		A1
4365	" "	19	NESW	1884-12-30		A1
4366	" "	19	NWNW	1884-12-30		A1
4299	LOVEJOY, A P	19	NWSW	1871-12-15		A1
4306	LOVEJOY, Allen P	19	SWNW	1872-05-01		A1
4372	MCCULLOUGH, Morris M	13	NWSW	1906-04-26		A1
4373	" "	13	S½SW	1906-04-26		A1
4328	MERRYMAN, A C	1	S½SE	1872-05-01		A1 G95
4320	PULLING, David J	13	SWSE	1884-04-15		A1
4376	SARGENT, James	23	E½NW	1885-06-03		A1 G92
4377	" "	23	NESW	1885-06-03		A1 G92
4378	" "	23	NWSE	1885-06-03		A1 G92
4325	WAKEFIELD, George M	21	N½SE	1882-06-30		A1
4326	" "	21	NE	1882-06-30		A1
4327	" "	21	W½	1882-06-30		A1
4300	WALLICH, Adolph	33	2	1884-12-30		A1
4301	" "	33	3	1884-12-30		A1
4302	" "	33	4	1884-12-30		A1
4303	" "	33	5	1884-12-30		A1
4304	" "	33	NW	1884-12-30		A1
4305	" "	33	NWSW	1884-12-30		A1
4307	WILSON, Andrew	29	1	1882-06-30		A1
4308	" "	29	10	1882-06-30		A1
4309	" "	29	2	1882-06-30		A1
4310	" "	29	3	1882-06-30		A1
4311	" "	29	4	1882-06-30		A1
4312	" "	29	5	1882-06-30		A1
4313	" "	29	6	1882-06-30		A1
4314	" "	29	7	1882-06-30		A1
4315	" "	29	8	1882-06-30		A1
4316	" "	29	9	1882-06-30		A1
4317	" "	29	NENW	1882-06-30		A1
4318	" "	29	W½NW	1882-06-30		A1

Patent Map

T41-N R12-E
4th PM - 1831 MN/WI

Map Group 25

Township Statistics

Parcels Mapped	:	83
Number of Patents	:	28
Number of Individuals	:	23
Patentees Identified	:	20
Number of Surnames	:	20
Multi-Patentee Parcels	:	6
Oldest Patent Date	:	12/15/1871
Most Recent Patent	:	4/26/1906
Block/Lot Parcels	:	36
Parcels Re - Issued	:	0
Parcels that Overlap	:	0
Cities and Towns	:	0
Cemeteries	:	0

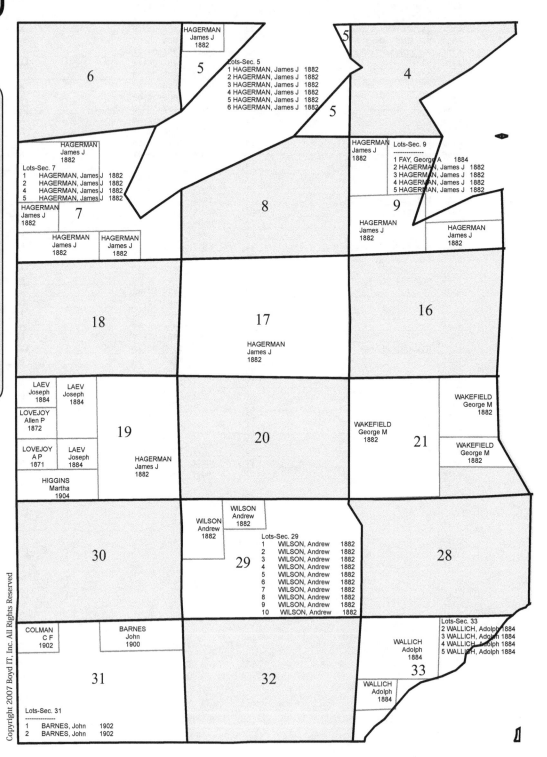

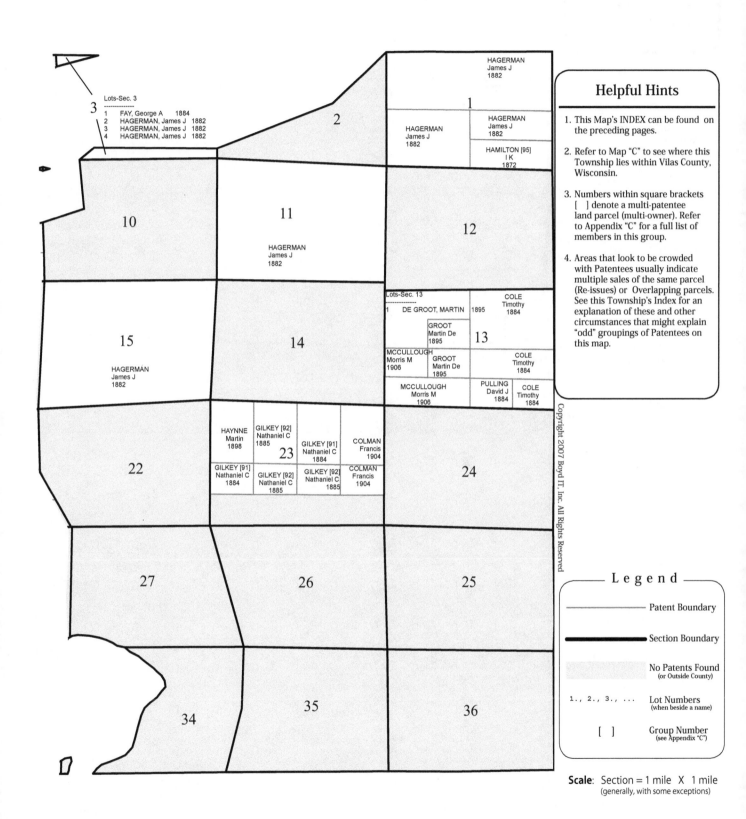

Lots-Sec. 3

3
1   FAY, George A   1884
2   HAGERMAN, James J   1882
3   HAGERMAN, James J   1882
4   HAGERMAN, James J   1882

HAGERMAN
James J
1882

1

HAGERMAN
James J
1882

HAGERMAN
James J
1882

HAMILTON [95]
I K
1872

2

10

11

HAGERMAN
James J
1882

12

15

14

HAGERMAN
James J
1882

Lots-Sec. 13
----
1   DE GROOT, MARTIN   1895

COLE
Timothy
1884

GROOT
Martin De
1895

13

MCCULLOUGH
Morris M
1906

GROOT
Martin De
1895

COLE
Timothy
1884

MCCULLOUGH
Morris M
1906

PULLING
David J
1884

COLE
Timothy
1884

22

HAYNNE
Martin
1898

GILKEY [92]
Nathaniel C
1885

23

GILKEY [91]
Nathaniel C
1884

COLMAN
Francis
1904

24

GILKEY [91]
Nathaniel C
1884

GILKEY [92]
Nathaniel C
1885

GILKEY [92]
Nathaniel C
1885

COLMAN
Francis
1904

27

26

25

34

35

36

Helpful Hints

1. This Map's INDEX can be found on the preceding pages.

2. Refer to Map "C" to see where this Township lies within Vilas County, Wisconsin.

3. Numbers within square brackets [ ] denote a multi-patentee land parcel (multi-owner). Refer to Appendix "C" for a full list of members in this group.

4. Areas that look to be crowded with Patentees usually indicate multiple sales of the same parcel (Re-issues) or Overlapping parcels. See this Township's Index for an explanation of these and other circumstances that might explain "odd" groupings of Patentees on this map.

Legend

————————— Patent Boundary

━━━━━━━━━ Section Boundary

▨▨▨ No Patents Found
(or Outside County)

1., 2., 3., ...   Lot Numbers
(when beside a name)

[ ]   Group Number
(see Appendix "C")

Scale: Section = 1 mile X 1 mile
(generally, with some exceptions)

Road Map

T41-N R12-E
4th PM - 1831 MN/WI

Map Group 25

Cities & Towns
None

Cemeteries
None

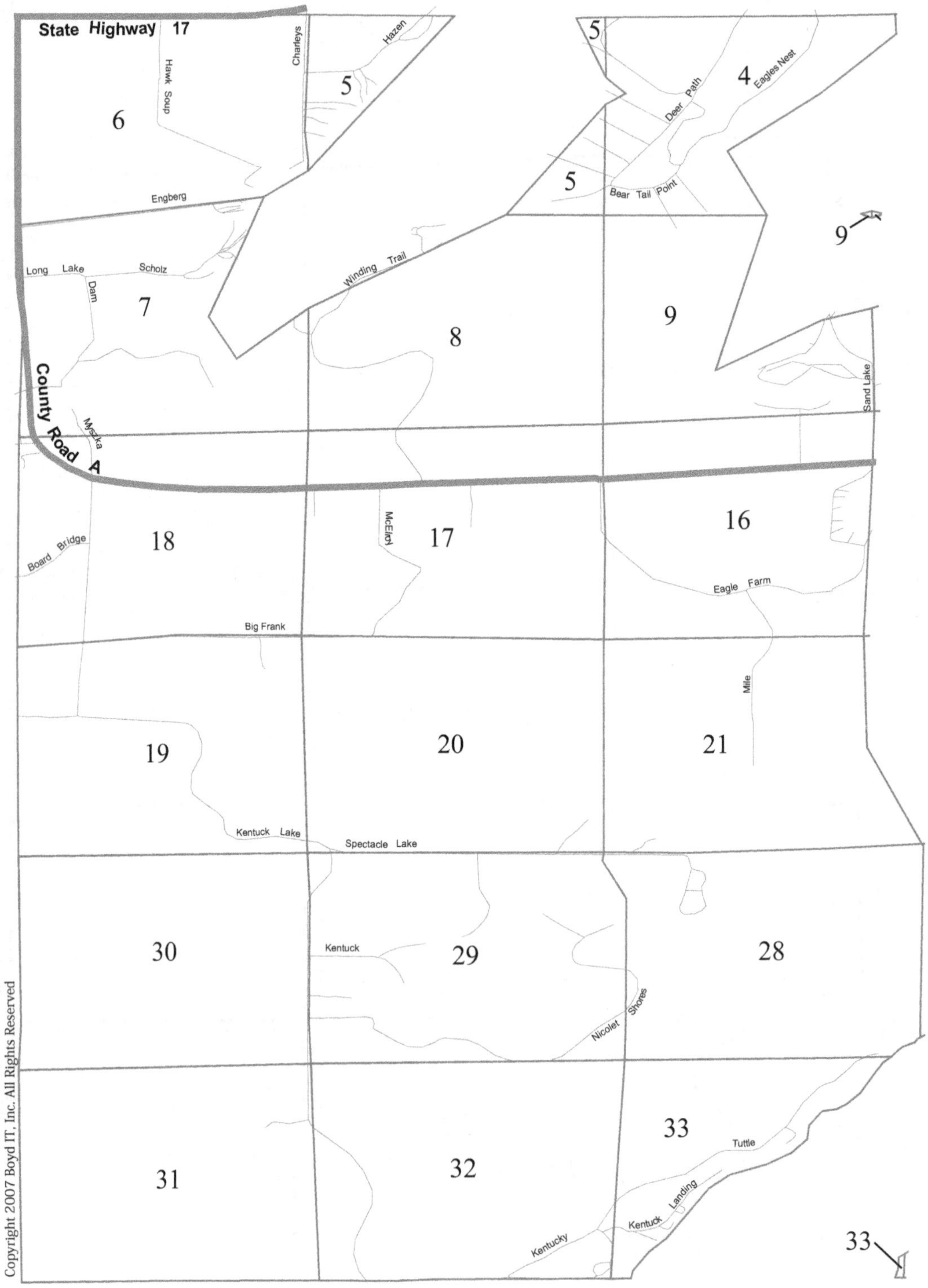

State Highway 17

Hazen

Charleys

Hawk Soup

6

5

5

4

Eagles Nest

Deer Path

Engberg

5

Bear Tail Point

9

Long Lake

Scholz

Dam

7

Winding Trail

8

9

Sand Lake

County Road A

Myszka

18

McElich

17

16

Board Bridge

Eagle Farm

Big Frank

Mile

19

20

21

Kentuck Lake

Spectacle Lake

30

Kentuck

29

28

Nicolet Shores

33

Tuttle

31

32

Kentuck Landing

Kentucky

33

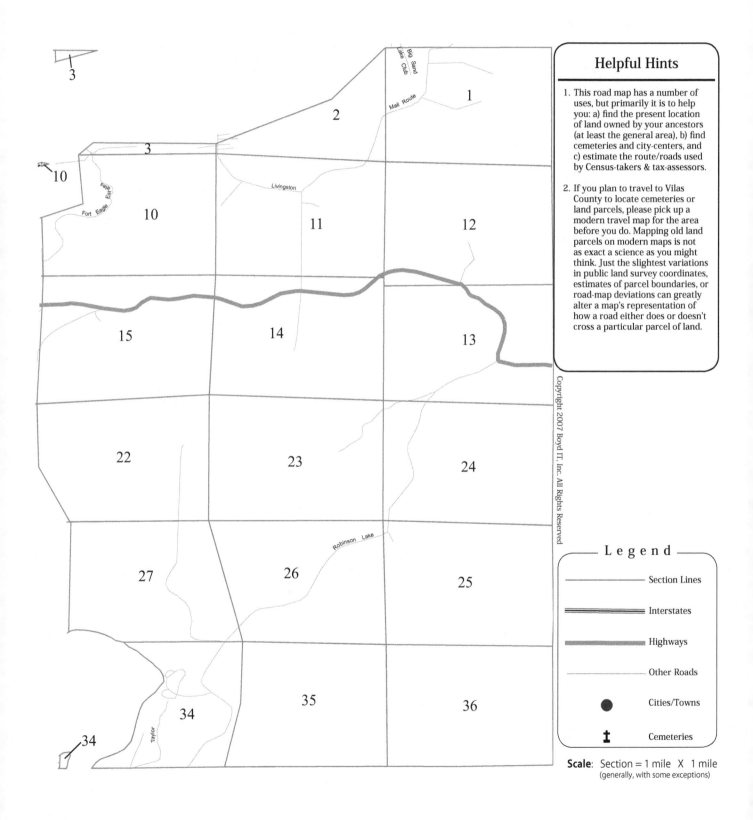

Helpful Hints

1. This road map has a number of uses, but primarily it is to help you: a) find the present location of land owned by your ancestors (at least the general area), b) find cemeteries and city-centers, and c) estimate the route/roads used by Census-takers & tax-assessors.

2. If you plan to travel to Vilas County to locate cemeteries or land parcels, please pick up a modern travel map for the area before you do. Mapping old land parcels on modern maps is not as exact a science as you might think. Just the slightest variations in public land survey coordinates, estimates of parcel boundaries, or road-map deviations can greatly alter a map's representation of how a road either does or doesn't cross a particular parcel of land.

Legend

———————	Section Lines
━━━━━━━	Interstates
▬▬▬▬▬▬▬	Highways
———————	Other Roads
●	Cities/Towns
✝	Cemeteries

Scale: Section = 1 mile X 1 mile
(generally, with some exceptions)

Historical Map

T41-N R12-E
4th PM - 1831 MN/WI

Map Group 25

Cities & Towns
None

Cemeteries
None

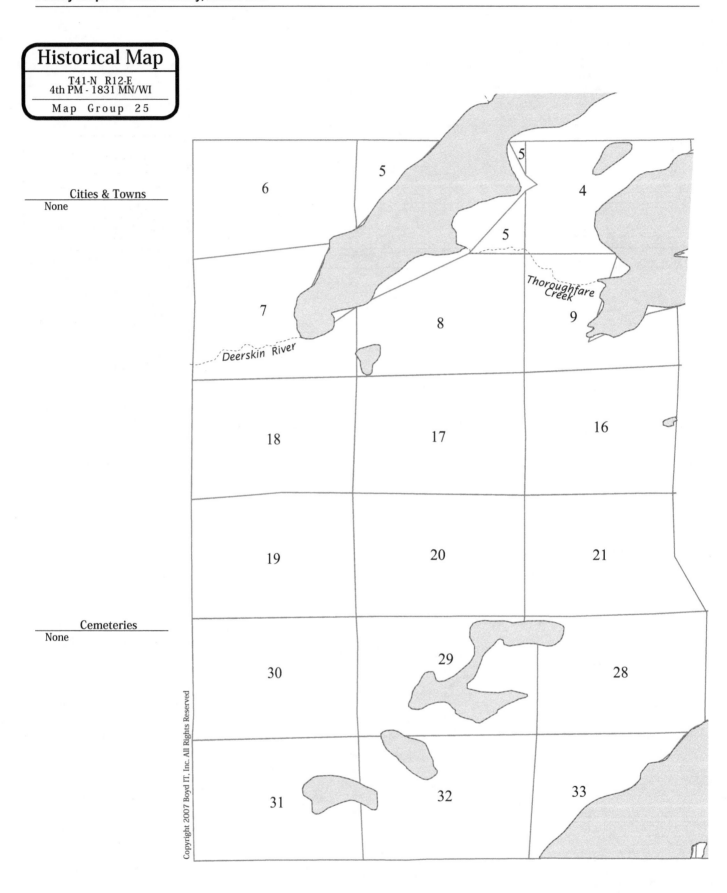

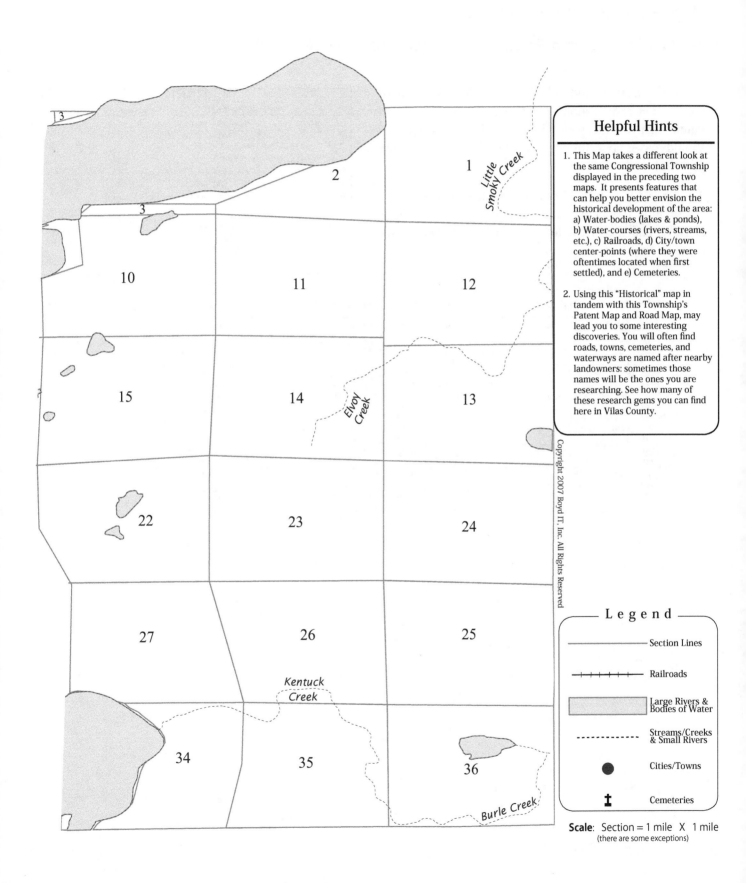

Helpful Hints

1. This Map takes a different look at the same Congressional Township displayed in the preceding two maps. It presents features that can help you better envision the historical development of the area: a) Water-bodies (lakes & ponds), b) Water-courses (rivers, streams, etc.), c) Railroads, d) City/town center-points (where they were oftentimes located when first settled), and e) Cemeteries.

2. Using this "Historical" map in tandem with this Township's Patent Map and Road Map, may lead you to some interesting discoveries. You will often find roads, towns, cemeteries, and waterways are named after nearby landowners: sometimes those names will be the ones you are researching. See how many of these research gems you can find here in Vilas County.

L e g e n d

———————	Section Lines
+++++++	Railroads
�	Large Rivers & Bodies of Water
- - - - - - -	Streams/Creeks & Small Rivers
●	Cities/Towns
⚐	Cemeteries

Scale: Section = 1 mile X 1 mile
(there are some exceptions)

Map Group 26: Index to Land Patents

Township 40-North Range 4-East (4th PM - 1831 MN/WI)

After you locate an individual in this Index, take note of the Section and Section Part then proceed to the Land Patent map on the pages immediately following. You should have no difficulty locating the corresponding parcel of land.

The "For More Info" Column will lead you to more information about the underlying Patents. See the *Legend* at right, and the "How to Use this Book" chapter, for more information.

LEGEND
"For More Info . . . " column
A = Authority (Legislative Act, See Appendix "A")
B = Block or Lot (location in Section unknown)
C = Cancelled Patent
F = Fractional Section
G = Group (Multi-Patentee Patent, see Appendix "C")
V = Overlaps another Parcel
R = Re-Issued (Parcel patented more than once)
(A & G items require you to look in the Appendixes referred to above. All other Letter-designations followed by a number require you to locate line-items in this index that possess the ID number found after the letter).

ID	Individual in Patent	Sec.	Sec. Part	Date Issued	Other Counties	For More Info . . .
4393	BRADLEY, William H	6	W½NE	1883-09-10		A1 F
4394	" "	8	NENW	1883-09-10		A1
4395	" "	8	SESE	1883-09-10		A1 F
4382	CLARK, Dewitt C	32	N½NE	1872-07-01		A1 G43
4386	MCGRAW, John	20	NWSE	1873-05-01		A1 G141
4387	" "	20	S½NE	1873-05-01		A1 G141
4388	PORTER, Luther C	6	3	1875-02-20		A1
4389	" "	8	NWNW	1875-02-20		A1
4383	PUTNAM, Henry C	30	N½SE	1873-05-01		A1 C
4384	SAGE, Henry W	20	N½NE	1872-11-01		A1
4385	" "	20	NESE	1872-11-01		A1
4386	" "	20	NWSE	1873-05-01		A1 G141
4387	" "	20	S½NE	1873-05-01		A1 G141
4382	SPAFFORD, E C	32	N½NE	1872-07-01		A1 G43
4392	WILCOX, Sextus N	32	N½NW	1871-04-25		A1
4390	" "	28	E½SE	1872-02-20		A1
4391	" "	28	SESW	1872-02-20		A1

Patent Map

T40-N R4-E
4th PM - 1831 MN/WI

Map Group 26

Township Statistics

Parcels Mapped	:	14
Number of Patents	:	9
Number of Individuals	:	8
Patentees Identified	:	7
Number of Surnames	:	8
Multi-Patentee Parcels	:	3
Oldest Patent Date	:	4/25/1871
Most Recent Patent	:	9/10/1883
Block/Lot Parcels	:	1
Parcels Re - Issued	:	0
Parcels that Overlap	:	0
Cities and Towns	:	0
Cemeteries	:	0

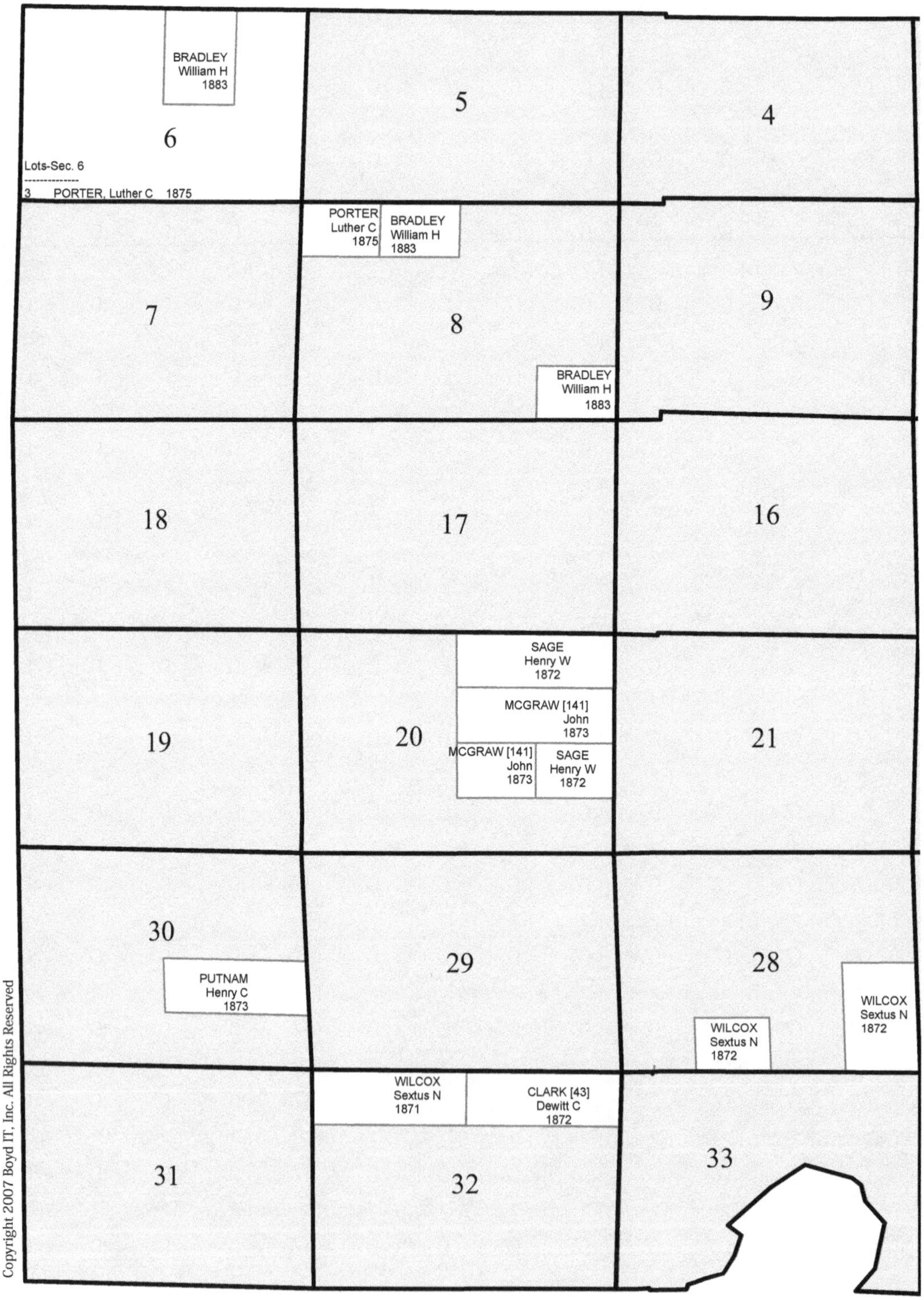

BRADLEY
William H
1883

6

5

4

Lots-Sec. 6
----
3   PORTER, Luther C   1875

PORTER
Luther C
1875

BRADLEY
William H
1883

7

8

9

BRADLEY
William H
1883

18

17

16

SAGE
Henry W
1872

MCGRAW [141]
John
1873

19

20

MCGRAW [141]
John
1873

SAGE
Henry W
1872

21

30

29

28

PUTNAM
Henry C
1873

WILCOX
Sextus N
1872

WILCOX
Sextus N
1872

WILCOX
Sextus N
1871

CLARK [43]
Dewitt C
1872

31

32

33

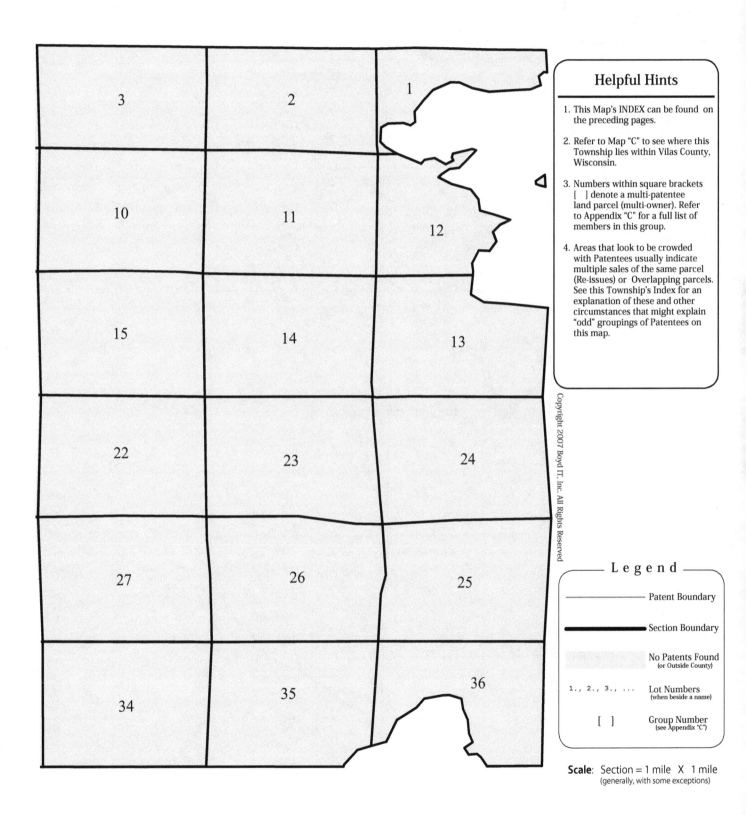

Helpful Hints

1. This Map's INDEX can be found on the preceding pages.

2. Refer to Map "C" to see where this Township lies within Vilas County, Wisconsin.

3. Numbers within square brackets [ ] denote a multi-patentee land parcel (multi-owner). Refer to Appendix "C" for a full list of members in this group.

4. Areas that look to be crowded with Patentees usually indicate multiple sales of the same parcel (Re-issues) or Overlapping parcels. See this Township's Index for an explanation of these and other circumstances that might explain "odd" groupings of Patentees on this map.

Legend

——————— Patent Boundary

━━━━━ Section Boundary

No Patents Found
(or Outside County)

1., 2., 3., ... Lot Numbers
(when beside a name)

[ ] Group Number
(see Appendix "C")

Scale: Section = 1 mile X 1 mile
(generally, with some exceptions)

Road Map

T40-N R4-E
4th PM - 1831 MN/WI

Map Group 26

Cities & Towns
None

Cemeteries
None

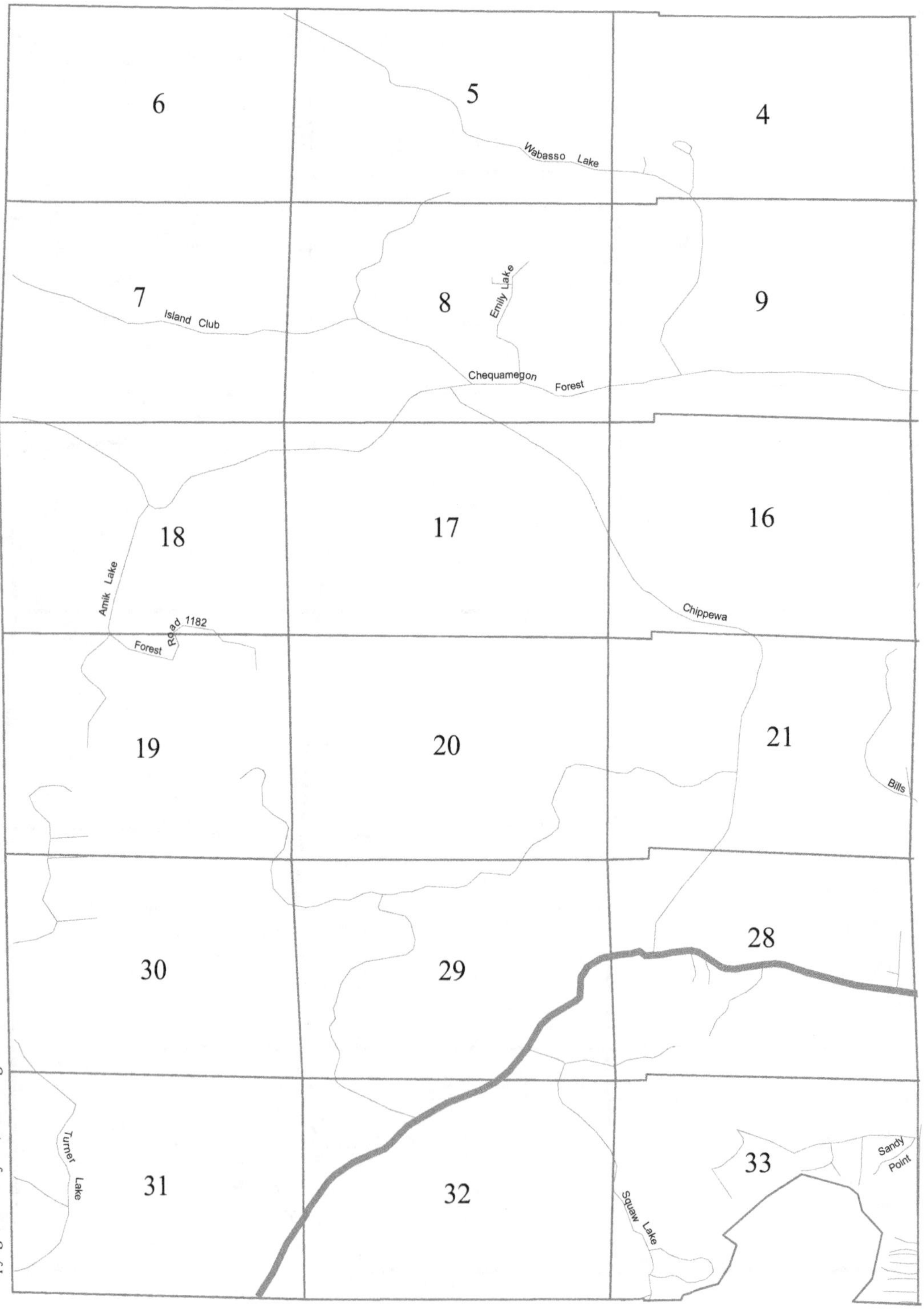

6	5	4
7	8	9
18	17	16
19	20	21
30	29	28
31	32	33

Wabasso Lake

Island Club

Emily Lake

Chequamegon Forest

Amik Lake

Forest Road 1182

Chippewa

Bills

Turner Lake

Squaw Lake

Sandy Point

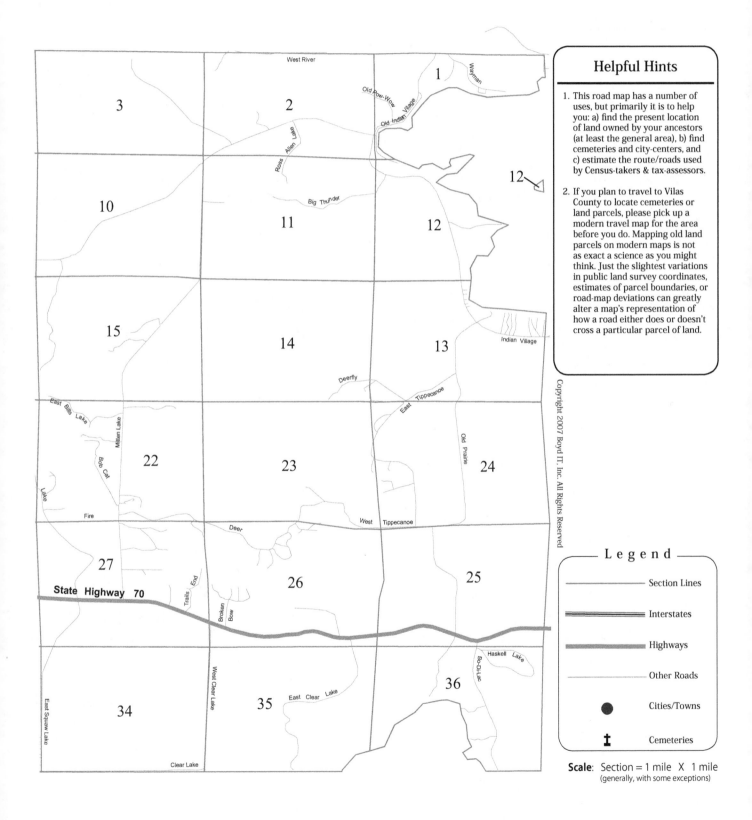

Helpful Hints

1. This road map has a number of uses, but primarily it is to help you: a) find the present location of land owned by your ancestors (at least the general area), b) find cemeteries and city-centers, and c) estimate the route/roads used by Census-takers & tax-assessors.

2. If you plan to travel to Vilas County to locate cemeteries or land parcels, please pick up a modern travel map for the area before you do. Mapping old land parcels on modern maps is not as exact a science as you might think. Just the slightest variations in public land survey coordinates, estimates of parcel boundaries, or road-map deviations can greatly alter a map's representation of how a road either does or doesn't cross a particular parcel of land.

Legend

———————	Section Lines
═══════	Interstates
━━━━━━	Highways
———————	Other Roads
●	Cities/Towns
✝	Cemeteries

Scale: Section = 1 mile X 1 mile
(generally, with some exceptions)

Historical Map

T40-N R4-E
4th PM - 1831 MN/WI

Map Group 26

Cities & Towns

None

Cemeteries

None

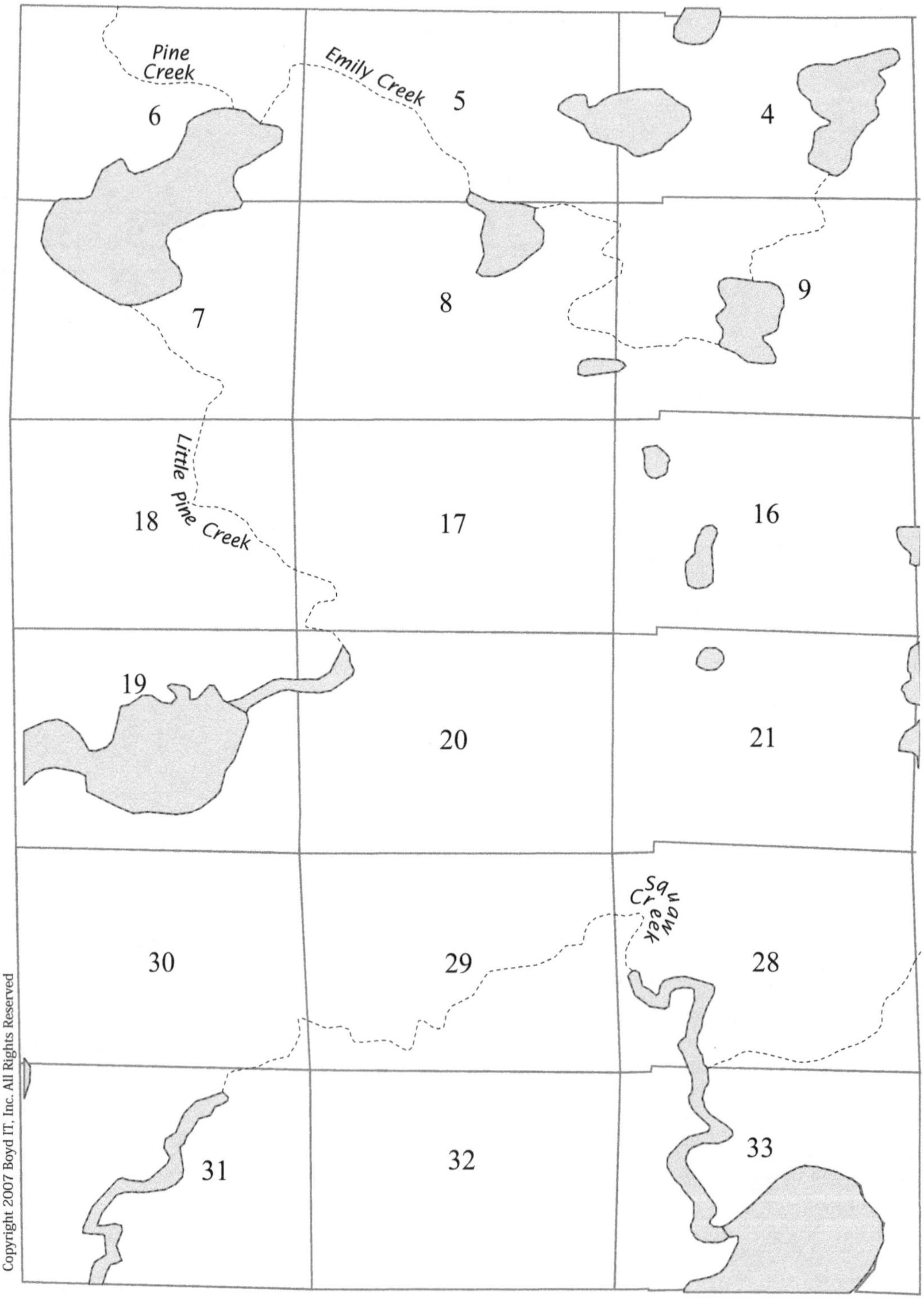

Pine Creek

Emily Creek

Little pine Creek

Squaw Creek

6

5

4

7

8

9

18

17

16

19

20

21

30

29

28

31

32

33

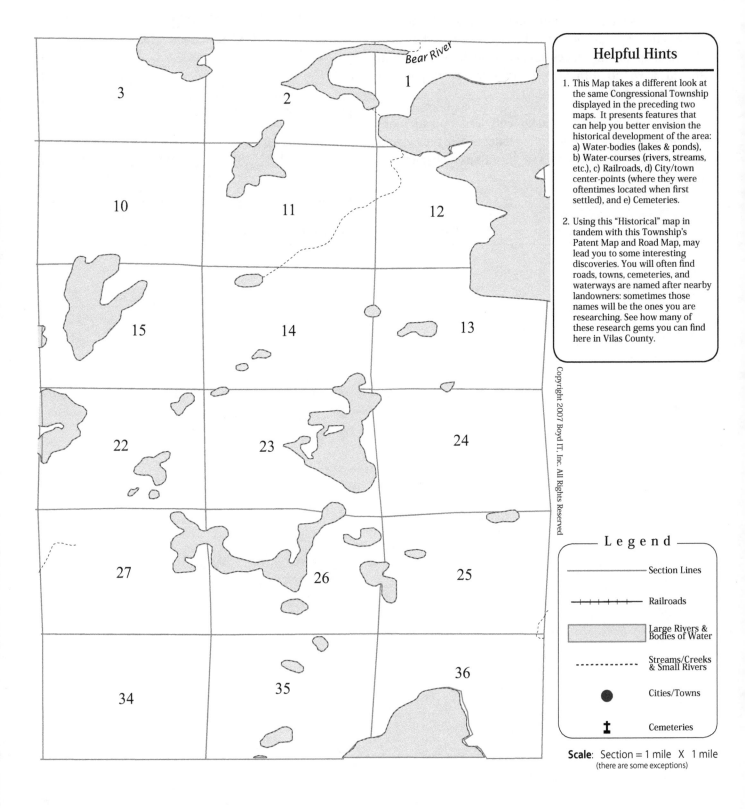

Bear River

3

2

1

10

11

12

15

14

13

22

23

24

27

26

25

34

35

36

Helpful Hints

1. This Map takes a different look at the same Congressional Township displayed in the preceding two maps. It presents features that can help you better envision the historical development of the area: a) Water-bodies (lakes & ponds), b) Water-courses (rivers, streams, etc.), c) Railroads, d) City/town center-points (where they were oftentimes located when first settled), and e) Cemeteries.

2. Using this "Historical" map in tandem with this Township's Patent Map and Road Map, may lead you to some interesting discoveries. You will often find roads, towns, cemeteries, and waterways are named after nearby landowners: sometimes those names will be the ones you are researching. See how many of these research gems you can find here in Vilas County.

Legend

———————	Section Lines
+++++++	Railroads
▭	Large Rivers & Bodies of Water
- - - - - - -	Streams/Creeks & Small Rivers
●	Cities/Towns
☨	Cemeteries

Scale: Section = 1 mile X 1 mile
(there are some exceptions)

Map Group 27: Index to Land Patents

Township 40-North Range 5-East (4th PM - 1831 MN/WI)

After you locate an individual in this Index, take note of the Section and Section Part then proceed to the Land Patent map on the pages immediately following. You should have no difficulty locating the corresponding parcel of land.

The "For More Info" Column will lead you to more information about the underlying Patents. See the *Legend* at right, and the "How to Use this Book" chapter, for more information.

```
                    LEGEND
              "For More Info . . . " column
A = Authority (Legislative Act, See Appendix "A")
B = Block or Lot (location in Section unknown)
C = Cancelled Patent
F = Fractional Section
G = Group  (Multi-Patentee Patent, see Appendix "C")
V = Overlaps another Parcel
R = Re-Issued (Parcel patented more than once)

(A & G items require you to look in the Appendixes referred
to above. All other Letter-designations followed by a number
require you to locate line-items in this index that possess
the ID number found after the letter).
```

ID	Individual in Patent	Sec.	Sec. Part	Date Issued	Other Counties	For More Info . . .
None

We have not located any Federal Land
Patent records within the
Bureau of Land Management's database for

**Township 40-N Range 5-E
(Map Group 27)**

in **Vilas County.**

Accordingly, we have no
"Patent Map" for this township.

Nonetheless, we have included our
Road and Historical Maps, which
begin on the following page.

Road Map

T40-N R5-E
4th PM - 1831 MN/WI

Map Group 27

Cities & Towns
Lac du Flambeau
Marlands

Cemeteries
None

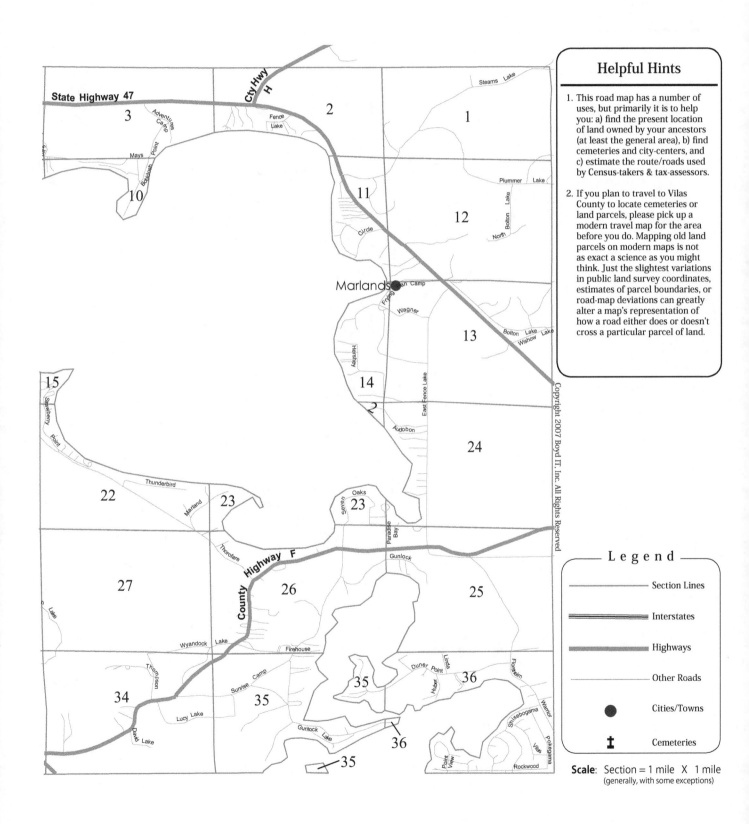

Helpful Hints

1. This road map has a number of uses, but primarily it is to help you: a) find the present location of land owned by your ancestors (at least the general area), b) find cemeteries and city-centers, and c) estimate the route/roads used by Census-takers & tax-assessors.

2. If you plan to travel to Vilas County to locate cemeteries or land parcels, please pick up a modern travel map for the area before you do. Mapping old land parcels on modern maps is not as exact a science as you might think. Just the slightest variations in public land survey coordinates, estimates of parcel boundaries, or road-map deviations can greatly alter a map's representation of how a road either does or doesn't cross a particular parcel of land.

Legend

Section Lines

Interstates

Highways

Other Roads

● Cities/Towns

† Cemeteries

Scale: Section = 1 mile X 1 mile
(generally, with some exceptions)

Historical Map

T40-N R5-E
4th PM - 1831 MN/WI

Map Group 27

Cities & Towns
Lac du Flambeau
Marlands

6

5

5

4

7

7

7

7

● Lac du
Flambeau

8

9

17

16

18

19

**Crawling
Stone Lake**

20

21

Cemeteries
None

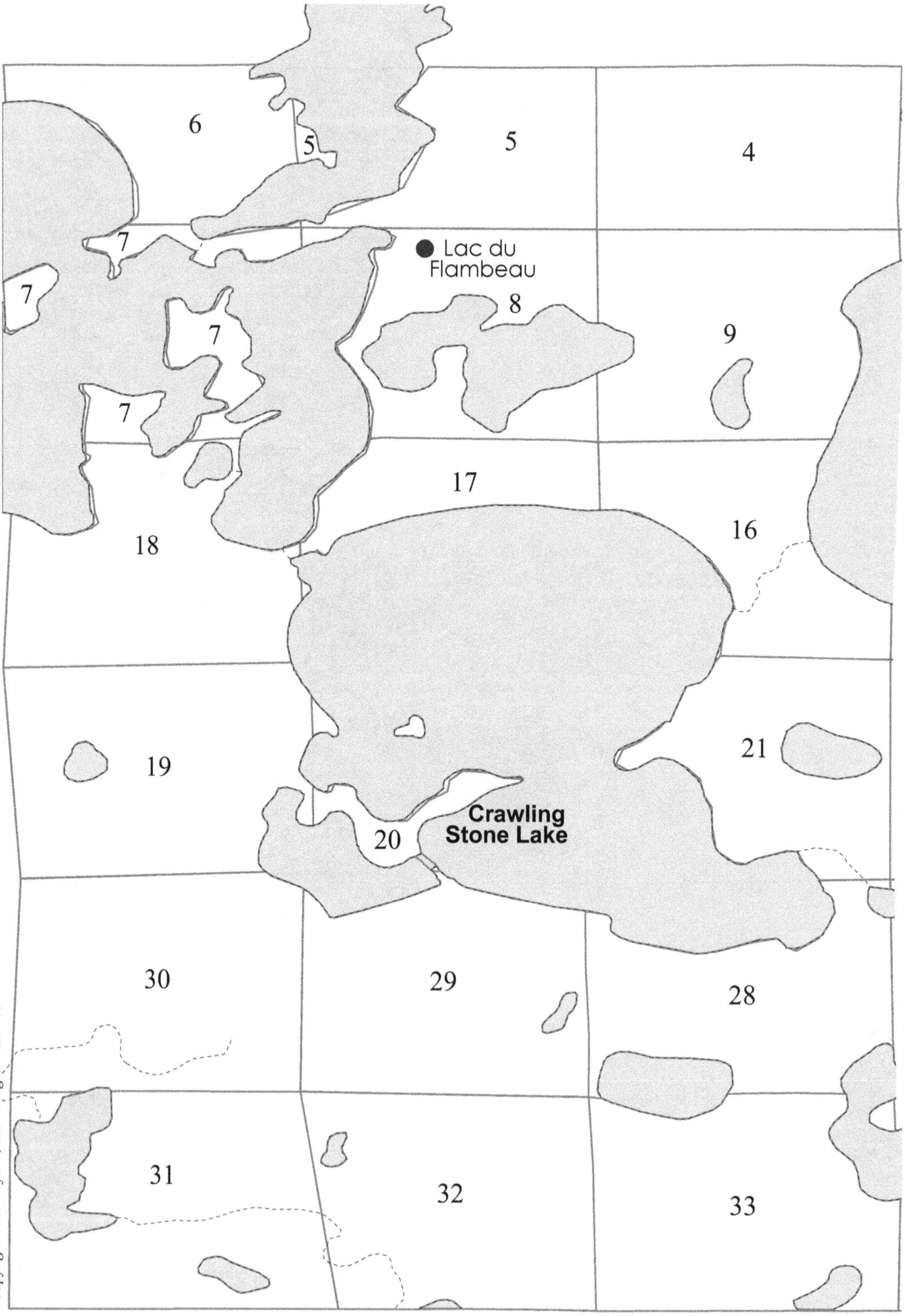

30

29

28

31

32

33

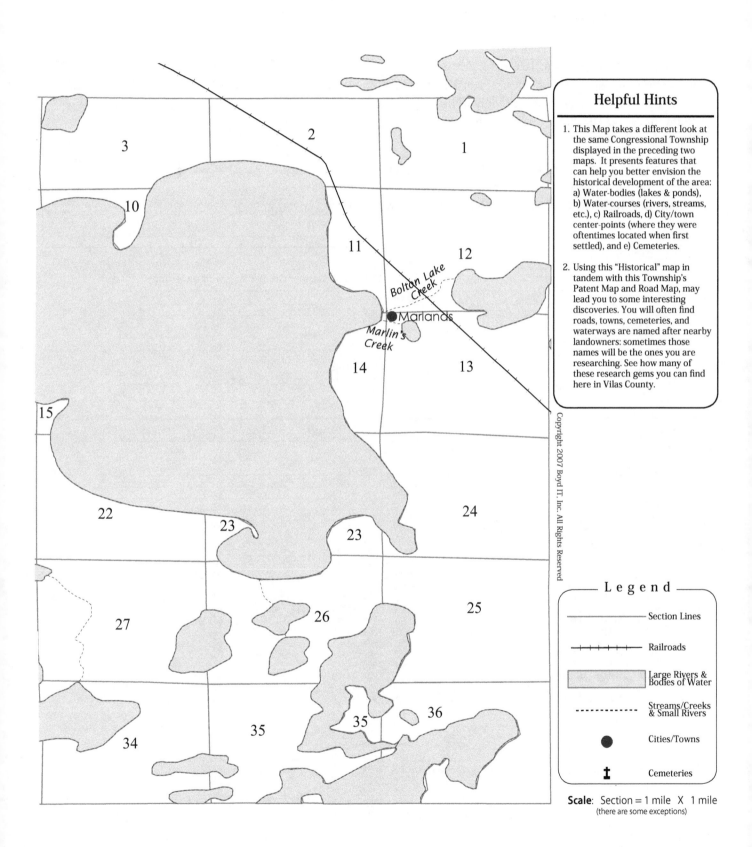

3

2

1

10

11

12

Bolton Lake Creek

● Marlands

Marlin's Creek

14

13

15

22

23

23

24

25

26

27

35

35

36

34

Helpful Hints

1. This Map takes a different look at the same Congressional Township displayed in the preceding two maps. It presents features that can help you better envision the historical development of the area: a) Water-bodies (lakes & ponds), b) Water-courses (rivers, streams, etc.), c) Railroads, d) City/town center-points (where they were oftentimes located when first settled), and e) Cemeteries.

2. Using this "Historical" map in tandem with this Township's Patent Map and Road Map, may lead you to some interesting discoveries. You will often find roads, towns, cemeteries, and waterways are named after nearby landowners: sometimes those names will be the ones you are researching. See how many of these research gems you can find here in Vilas County.

Legend

————————	Section Lines
┼┼┼┼┼┼┼┼	Railroads
�box	Large Rivers & Bodies of Water
- - - - - - -	Streams/Creeks & Small Rivers
●	Cities/Towns
☦	Cemeteries

Scale: Section = 1 mile X 1 mile
(there are some exceptions)

Map Group 28: Index to Land Patents

Township 40-North Range 6-East (4th PM - 1831 MN/WI)

After you locate an individual in this Index, take note of the Section and Section Part then proceed to the Land Patent map on the pages immediately following. You should have no difficulty locating the corresponding parcel of land.

The "For More Info" Column will lead you to more information about the underlying Patents. See the *Legend* at right, and the "How to Use this Book" chapter, for more information.

```
                          LEGEND
                "For More Info . . . " column
A = Authority (Legislative Act, See Appendix "A")
B = Block or Lot (location in Section unknown)
C = Cancelled Patent
F = Fractional Section
G = Group (Multi-Patentee Patent, see Appendix "C")
V = Overlaps another Parcel
R = Re-Issued (Parcel patented more than once)

(A & G items require you to look in the Appendixes referred
to above. All other Letter-designations followed by a number
require you to locate line-items in this index that possess
the ID number found after the letter).
```

ID	Individual in Patent	Sec.	Sec. Part	Date Issued	Other Counties	For More Info . . .
4479	ALLEN, Hiram S	1	SWSW	1873-05-01		A1
4480	" "	11	2	1873-05-01		A1
4481	" "	11	3	1873-05-01		A1
4482	" "	11	4	1873-05-01		A1
4483	" "	11	5	1873-05-01		A1
4484	" "	11	NWSE	1873-05-01		A1
4485	" "	12	1	1873-05-01		A1
4486	" "	12	2	1873-05-01		A1
4487	" "	12	3	1873-05-01		A1
4488	" "	12	E½SE	1873-05-01		A1
4489	" "	12	NWSE	1873-05-01		A1
4490	" "	13	1	1873-05-01		A1
4491	" "	13	2	1873-05-01		A1
4492	" "	14	1	1873-05-01		A1
4493	" "	14	2	1873-05-01		A1
4494	" "	2	1	1873-05-01		A1
4495	" "	2	2	1873-05-01		A1
4496	" "	2	E½NE	1873-05-01		A1 F
4497	" "	3	2	1873-05-01		A1
4498	" "	3	NESW	1873-05-01		A1
4456	BAYER, George	27	SENW	1900-06-11		A1
4457	" "	27	W½NW	1900-06-11		A1
4499	BEAUDIEN, J N	14	NESW	1898-03-21		A1
4453	BEAUME, Francis	33	N½SW	1892-05-16		A1
4454	" "	33	S½NW	1892-05-16		A1
4539	BELISLE, Moise	26	E½NW	1899-11-20		A1
4524	BELLIS, L R	10	7	1889-06-28		A1
4525	" "	15	2	1889-06-28		A1
4455	BETTIS, Frank L	21	NE	1899-05-05		A1
4461	BETTIS, George S	33	N½NW	1904-03-01		A3
4462	" "	33	W½NE	1904-03-01		A3
4426	BIRD, Claire B	24	NWSW	1900-06-11		A1
4504	BOILEAU, John	33	S½SW	1900-07-30		A1
4396	BOREMAN, Adline	23	5	1904-09-28		A3 G29 F
4397	" "	23	6	1904-09-28		A3 G29 F
4396	BOREMAN, Julius	23	5	1904-09-28		A3 G29 F
4397	" "	23	6	1904-09-28		A3 G29 F
4526	BREWSTER, Loren D	10	6	1883-09-15		A1
4527	" "	11	6	1883-09-15		A1
4528	" "	11	E½NE	1883-09-15		A1
4529	" "	11	NESE	1883-09-15		A1
4530	" "	12	NW	1883-09-15		A1
4531	" "	15	NENW	1883-09-15		A1
4532	" "	2	5	1883-09-15		A1
4533	" "	2	6	1883-09-15		A1
4534	" "	2	SESE	1883-09-15		A1

ID	Individual in Patent	Sec.	Sec. Part	Date Issued	Other Counties	For More Info . . .
4535	BREWSTER, Loren D (Cont'd)	22	NENE	1883-09-15		A1
4429	CARR, Edward	10	SENW	1900-10-04		A1
4422	CARRIVEAU, Charles	28	SWSW	1906-08-16		A3
4439	CLARK, Eli C	14	SWNE	1873-05-01		A1
4440	" "	15	SWNW	1873-05-01		A1
4441	" "	22	SENE	1873-05-01		A1
4442	" "	23	7	1873-05-01		A1
4443	" "	4	3	1873-05-01		A1
4444	" "	4	SESE	1873-05-01		A1
4445	" "	9	SESE	1873-05-01		A1
4467	CLARK, George W	34	3	1903-10-01		A3
4430	COLEMAN, Edward W	10	1	1873-05-01		A1 C
4431	" "	2	3	1873-05-01		A1 C
4432	" "	2	4	1873-05-01		A1 C
4433	" "	2	NW	1873-05-01		A1 C F
4434	" "	3	1	1873-05-01		A1 C
4435	" "	3	4	1873-05-01		A1 C
4436	" "	3	N½SE	1873-05-01		A1 C
4437	" "	3	SESE	1873-05-01		A1 C
4438	" "	3	W½NE	1873-05-01		A1 C F
4574	COOK, Thomas D	1	E½NE	1889-05-09		A1 G57 F
4588	CROSS, William W	21	SESW	1902-03-07		A3 G60
4538	DAVIDSON, Martin L	33	SE	1899-01-14		A3
4575	DESROSIERS, Thomas	23	3	1905-12-30		A3
4576	" "	23	4	1905-12-30		A3
4577	" "	23	SESE	1905-12-30		A3
4578	" "	23	SESW	1905-12-30		A3
4512	DEVOIN, John L	35	SWSE	1889-04-04		A1 G71
4513	" "	36	SESE	1889-04-04		A1 G71
4514	" "	36	SESW	1889-04-04		A1 G71
4588	DOYLE, Mike F	21	SESW	1902-03-07		A3 G60
4500	ELLIS, J S	35	1	1888-07-28		A1
4501	" "	35	5	1888-07-28		A1
4502	" "	35	NWNW	1888-07-28		A1
4503	" "	35	NWSE	1888-07-28		A1
4569	ENO, Peter	22	NESW	1900-06-11		A1
4570	FOELKNER, Philipp	28	E½SE	1905-06-30		A3
4505	GEBHART, John C	26	2	1889-05-09		A1
4506	" "	26	3	1889-05-09		A1
4567	GLEASON, Pat	12	NWNE	1899-02-06		A1
4568	" "	24	NESE	1899-02-06		A1
4458	HAIGHT, George E	34	1	1899-02-06		A3
4459	" "	34	2	1899-02-06		A3
4460	" "	34	NENE	1899-02-06		A3
4407	HEINEMANN, Benjamin	24	S½SE	1889-05-09		A1
4408	" "	25	N½NE	1889-05-09		A1
4409	" "	25	NENW	1889-05-09		A1
4410	" "	36	NENE	1889-05-09		A1
4411	" "	36	NESE	1889-05-09		A1
4579	HOLDSHIP, Thomas	28	E½SW	1897-11-01		A3
4580	" "	28	W½SE	1897-11-01		A3
4541	HOLWAY, O	15	SW	1890-07-15		A1
4542	" "	26	NWNW	1890-07-15		A1
4543	" "	27	NENE	1890-07-15		A1
4544	" "	27	NENW	1890-07-15		A1
4545	" "	27	SESE	1890-07-15		A1
4574	HYDE, Edwin	1	E½NE	1889-05-09		A1 G57 F
4413	IDE, Cassius H	21	1	1893-10-30		A1
4414	" "	21	3	1893-10-30		A1
4415	" "	22	1	1893-10-30		A1
4416	" "	22	2	1893-10-30		A1
4417	" "	28	1	1893-10-30		A1
4583	IRWIN, William P	13	NWSW	1872-02-20		A1 G112
4584	" "	23	1	1872-02-20		A1 G112
4585	" "	35	6	1872-02-20		A1 G112
4586	" "	35	7	1872-02-20		A1 G112
4587	" "	36	NWSE	1872-02-20		A1 G112
4412	JOHNSON, Carl A	22	W½NW	1898-04-06		A1
4396	LA CROSSE, ADLINE	23	5	1904-09-28		A3 G29 F
4397	" "	23	6	1904-09-28		A3 G29 F
4540	LAMOUREUX, Mose	36	SENE	1905-11-08		A3
4403	LOMBARD, Arnold B	21	2	1904-03-01		A3 F
4404	" "	28	2	1904-03-01		A3 F

ID	Individual in Patent	Sec.	Sec. Part	Date Issued	Other Counties	For More Info . . .
4405	LOMBARD, Arnold B (Cont'd)	28	3	1904-03-01		A3 F
4406	" "	28	4	1904-03-01		A3 F
4507	LONG, John H	34	4	1899-01-14		A3
4508	" "	34	N½SW	1899-01-14		A3
4509	" "	34	SWNW	1899-01-14		A3
4573	LONG, Simon	34	SWSW	1903-04-20		A1
4400	LOVEJOY, Allen P	1	E½SE	1872-07-01		A1
4401	" "	12	E½NE	1872-07-01		A1
4402	" "	12	SWNE	1872-07-01		A1
4449	MARKEE, Eugene	27	NESE	1893-07-19		A1
4450	" "	27	SENE	1893-07-19		A1
4451	" "	27	W½NE	1893-07-19		A1
4452	MATTKE, Ferdinand	27	SW	1904-03-01		A3
4418	MCBAIN, Catharine	9	NENW	1873-11-15		A1 G137
4419	" "	9	NWSW	1873-11-15		A1 G137
4420	" "	9	SWNW	1873-11-15		A1 G137
4421	" "	9	SWSE	1873-11-15		A1 G137
4516	MCILREE, Joseph A	25	SWNW	1903-04-20		A1
4476	MELANG, Herman	28	E½NW	1900-07-30		A1
4477	" "	28	NWSW	1900-07-30		A1
4478	" "	28	SWNW	1900-07-30		A1
4510	MERCER, John H	22	E½NW	1889-06-28		A1 G143
4511	" "	22	SESW	1889-06-28		A1 G143
4515	MONTGOMERY, John	21	NW	1893-08-14		A1
4448	NELSON, Elias	35	4	1889-04-04		A1 G150
4517	NEWMAN, L M	26	SW	1883-04-20		A1
4518	" "	26	SWNW	1883-04-20		A1
4519	" "	35	E½NW	1883-04-20		A1
4520	" "	35	W½NE	1883-04-20		A1
4521	" "	4	N½SW	1883-04-20		A1
4522	" "	4	NW	1883-04-20		A1 F
4523	" "	4	SWSW	1883-04-20		A1
4446	OBRAY, Eli	34	5	1897-06-11		A1
4447	" "	34	6	1897-06-11		A1
4427	PAQUETTE, Dennis	25	E½SE	1901-05-08		A3
4428	" "	25	S½NE	1901-05-08		A3
4581	PIERCE, William L	15	NWNW	1886-03-01		A1
4582	" "	15	SWNE	1886-03-01		A1
4468	PILLSBURY, H M	11	1	1890-07-15		A1
4469	" "	15	N½SE	1890-07-15		A1
4470	" "	15	SENE	1890-07-15		A1
4471	" "	15	SENW	1890-07-15		A1
4472	" "	15	SESE	1890-07-15		A1
4473	" "	4	2	1890-07-15		A1
4546	PILLSBURY, Oliver P	1	2	1885-01-15		A1
4547	" "	1	3	1885-01-15		A1
4548	" "	1	4	1885-01-15		A1
4549	" "	1	NWSW	1885-01-15		A1
4550	" "	11	NESW	1885-01-15		A1
4551	" "	11	SWSE	1885-01-15		A1
4552	" "	14	4	1885-01-15		A1
4553	" "	14	NWSW	1885-01-15		A1
4554	" "	14	S½NW	1885-01-15		A1
4555	" "	24	S½NW	1885-01-15		A1
4556	" "	25	NESW	1885-01-15		A1
4557	" "	25	NWSW	1885-01-15		A1
4558	" "	25	SENW	1885-01-15		A1
4559	" "	26	4	1885-01-15		A1
4560	" "	26	5	1885-01-15		A1
4561	" "	26	6	1885-01-15		A1
4562	" "	35	NENE	1885-01-15		A1
4563	" "	4	SESW	1885-01-15		A1
4564	" "	4	SWSE	1885-01-15		A1
4565	" "	9	NWNW	1885-01-15		A1
4583	REMMERT, Albert	13	NWSW	1872-02-20		A1 G112
4584	" "	23	1	1872-02-20		A1 G112
4585	" "	35	6	1872-02-20		A1 G112
4586	" "	35	7	1872-02-20		A1 G112
4587	" "	36	NWSE	1872-02-20		A1 G112
4423	RICHARDS, Charles S	21	N½SW	1901-02-20		A1
4424	" "	21	NWSE	1901-02-20		A1
4425	" "	21	SWSW	1901-02-20		A1
4399	RILEY, Albert M	1	1	1904-04-08		A1

ID	Individual in Patent	Sec.	Sec. Part	Date Issued	Other Counties	For More Info . . .
4583	RIPLEY, Emma	13	NWSW	1872-02-20		A1 G112
4584	" "	23	1	1872-02-20		A1 G112
4585	" "	35	6	1872-02-20		A1 G112
4586	" "	35	7	1872-02-20		A1 G112
4587	" "	36	NWSE	1872-02-20		A1 G112
4510	SHAW, W H	22	E½NW	1889-06-28		A1 G143
4511	" "	22	SESW	1889-06-28		A1 G143
4398	SHEW, Adrian	34	SENW	1903-10-01		A3
4536	SHEW, Lorenzo M	33	E½NE	1901-05-08		A3
4537	" "	34	N½NW	1901-05-08		A3
4463	SILVERTHORN, George	10	3	1888-07-10		A1
4464	" "	10	4	1888-07-10		A1
4465	" "	14	3	1888-07-10		A1
4466	" "	36	3	1888-07-10		A1
4571	SMITH, Sam A	27	W½SE	1898-12-12		A1
4572	" "	34	W½NE	1898-12-12		A1
4474	STOECKEL, Heinrich	15	SWSE	1898-04-06		A1
4475	" "	22	NWNE	1898-04-06		A1
4448	TRUSSEL, Peter	35	4	1889-04-04		A1 G150
4512	" "	35	SWSE	1889-04-04		A1 G71
4513	" "	36	SESE	1889-04-04		A1 G71
4514	" "	36	SESW	1889-04-04		A1 G71
4418	WEBSTER, Samuel H	9	NENW	1873-11-15		A1 G137
4419	" "	9	NWSW	1873-11-15		A1 G137
4420	" "	9	SWNW	1873-11-15		A1 G137
4421	" "	9	SWSE	1873-11-15		A1 G137
4566	WENNBERG, P A	36	SWSE	1889-05-09		A1
4512	WINSLOW, L	35	SWSE	1889-04-04		A1 G71
4513	" "	36	SESE	1889-04-04		A1 G71
4514	" "	36	SESW	1889-04-04		A1 G71

Patent Map

T40-N R6-E
4th PM - 1831 MN/WI

Map Group 28

Township Statistics

Parcels Mapped	:	193
Number of Patents	:	75
Number of Individuals	:	71
Patentees Identified	:	61
Number of Surnames	:	65
Multi-Patentee Parcels	:	19
Oldest Patent Date	:	2/20/1872
Most Recent Patent	:	8/16/1906
Block/Lot Parcels	:	68
Parcels Re - Issued	:	0
Parcels that Overlap	:	0
Cities and Towns	:	0
Cemeteries	:	0

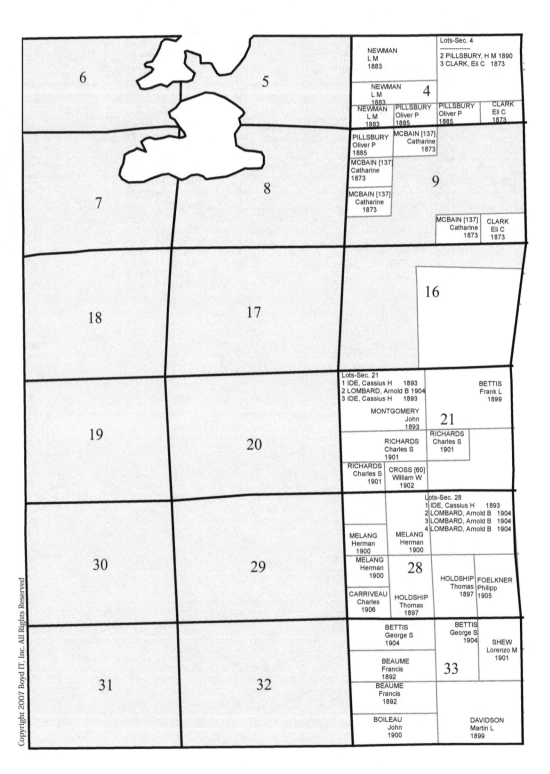

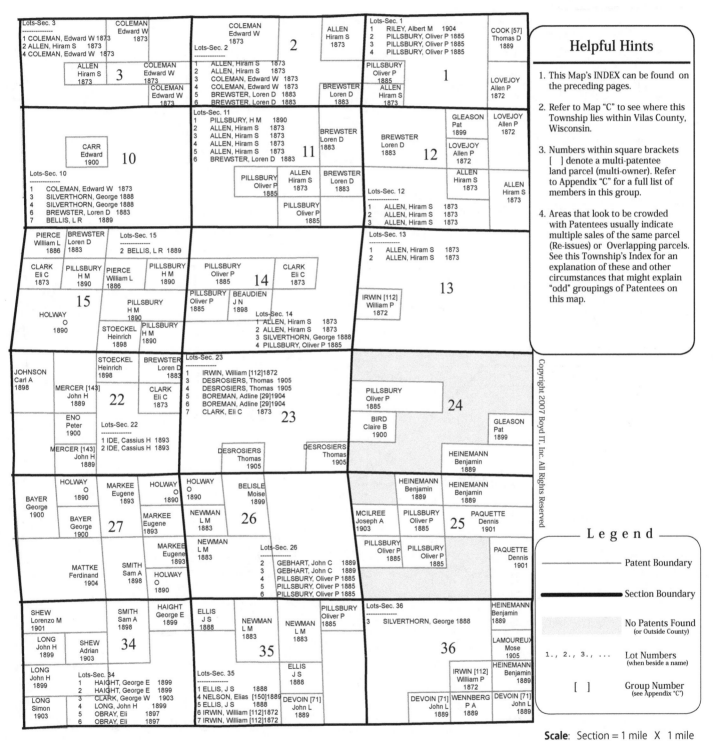

Helpful Hints

1. This Map's INDEX can be found on the preceding pages.

2. Refer to Map "C" to see where this Township lies within Vilas County, Wisconsin.

3. Numbers within square brackets [ ] denote a multi-patentee land parcel (multi-owner). Refer to Appendix "C" for a full list of members in this group.

4. Areas that look to be crowded with Patentees usually indicate multiple sales of the same parcel (Re-issues) or Overlapping parcels. See this Township's Index for an explanation of these and other circumstances that might explain "odd" groupings of Patentees on this map.

Legend

——————— Patent Boundary

━━━━━━━ Section Boundary

No Patents Found
(or Outside County)

1., 2., 3., ... Lot Numbers
(when beside a name)

[ ] Group Number
(see Appendix "C")

Scale: Section = 1 mile X 1 mile
(generally, with some exceptions)

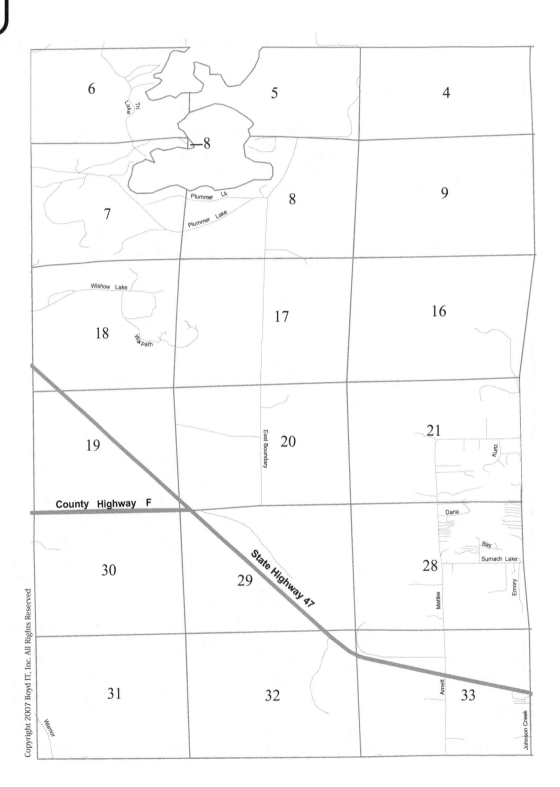

Road Map

T40-N R6-E
4th PM - 1831 MN/WI

Map Group 28

Cities & Towns

None

Cemeteries

None

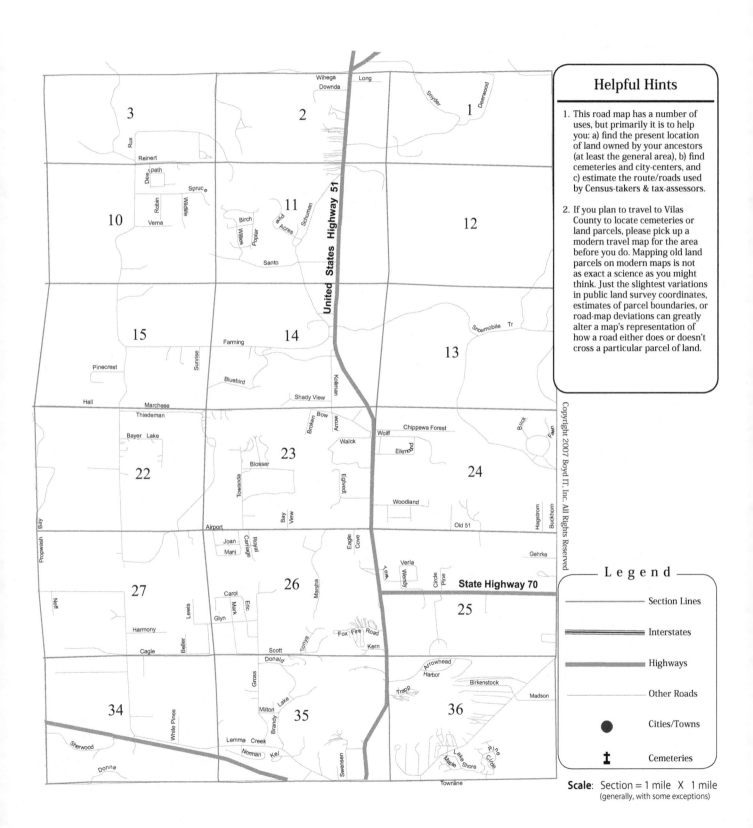

Helpful Hints

1. This road map has a number of uses, but primarily it is to help you: a) find the present location of land owned by your ancestors (at least the general area), b) find cemeteries and city-centers, and c) estimate the route/roads used by Census-takers & tax-assessors.

2. If you plan to travel to Vilas County to locate cemeteries or land parcels, please pick up a modern travel map for the area before you do. Mapping old land parcels on modern maps is not as exact a science as you might think. Just the slightest variations in public land survey coordinates, estimates of parcel boundaries, or road-map deviations can greatly alter a map's representation of how a road either does or doesn't cross a particular parcel of land.

Legend

———————	Section Lines
═══════	Interstates
━━━━━━━	Highways
———————	Other Roads
●	Cities/Towns
✝	Cemeteries

Scale: Section = 1 mile X 1 mile
(generally, with some exceptions)

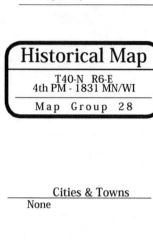

Historical Map

T40-N R6-E
4th PM - 1831 MN/WI

Map Group 28

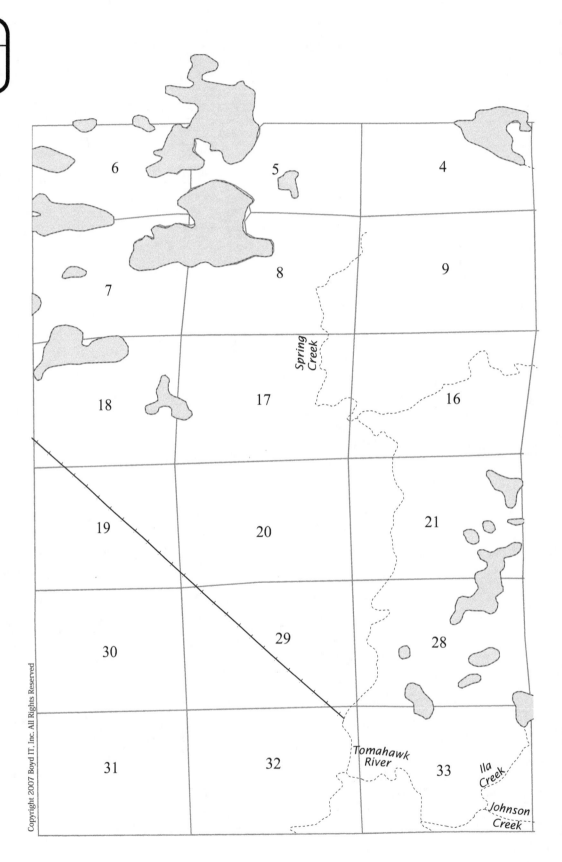

Cities & Towns
None

Cemeteries
None

6

5

4

7

8

9

18

17

Spring
Creek

16

19

20

21

30

29

28

31

32

Tomahawk
River

33

Ila
Creek

Johnson
Creek

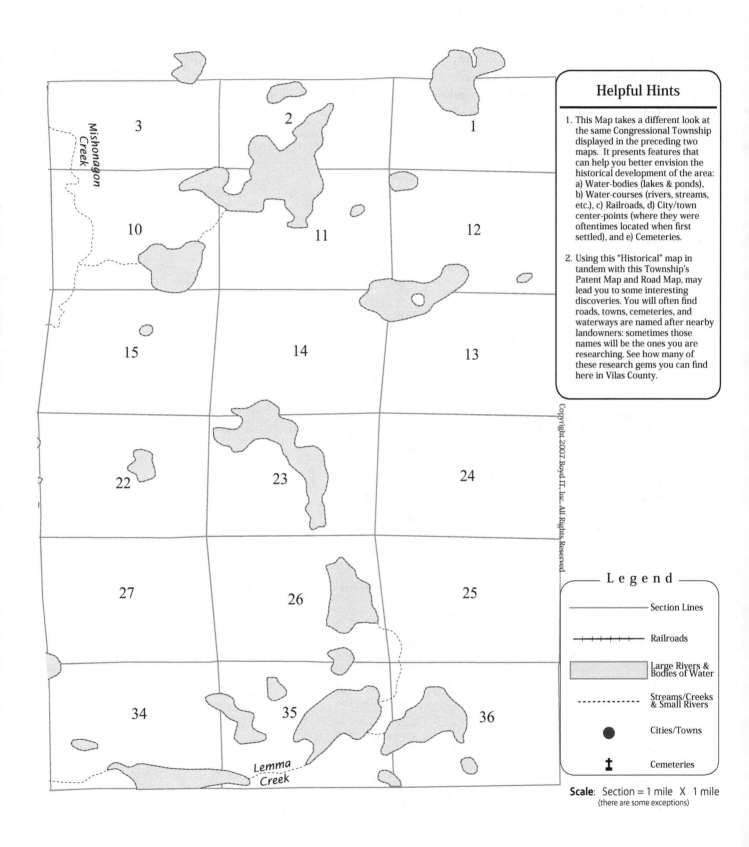

Helpful Hints

1. This Map takes a different look at the same Congressional Township displayed in the preceding two maps. It presents features that can help you better envision the historical development of the area: a) Water-bodies (lakes & ponds), b) Water-courses (rivers, streams, etc.), c) Railroads, d) City/town center-points (where they were oftentimes located when first settled), and e) Cemeteries.

2. Using this "Historical" map in tandem with this Township's Patent Map and Road Map, may lead you to some interesting discoveries. You will often find roads, towns, cemeteries, and waterways are named after nearby landowners: sometimes those names will be the ones you are researching. See how many of these research gems you can find here in Vilas County.

— L e g e n d —

⊢⊢⊢⊢⊢	Section Lines
┼┼┼┼┼	Railroads
▭	Large Rivers & Bodies of Water
- - - - -	Streams/Creeks & Small Rivers
●	Cities/Towns
✝	Cemeteries

Scale: Section = 1 mile X 1 mile
(there are some exceptions)

Map Group 29: Index to Land Patents

Township 40-North Range 7-East (4th PM - 1831 MN/WI)

After you locate an individual in this Index, take note of the Section and Section Part then proceed to the Land Patent map on the pages immediately following. You should have no difficulty locating the corresponding parcel of land.

The "For More Info" Column will lead you to more information about the underlying Patents. See the *Legend* at right, and the "How to Use this Book" chapter, for more information.

```
                              LEGEND
                "For More Info . . . " column
A = Authority (Legislative Act, See Appendix "A")
B = Block or Lot (location in Section unknown)
C = Cancelled Patent
F = Fractional Section
G = Group  (Multi-Patentee Patent, see Appendix "C")
V = Overlaps another Parcel
R = Re-Issued (Parcel patented more than once)

(A & G items require you to look in the Appendixes referred
to above. All other Letter-designations followed by a number
require you to locate line-items in this index that possess
the ID number found after the letter).
```

ID	Individual in Patent	Sec.	Sec. Part	Date Issued	Other Counties	For More Info . . .
4664	ALLEN, Hiram S	18	NENW	1873-05-01		A1
4665	" "	18	NWNE	1873-05-01		A1
4666	" "	6	NWSE	1873-05-01		A1
4667	" "	6	SESW	1873-05-01		A1
4668	" "	7	N½SW	1873-05-01		A1
4601	BARNES, Caleb A	36	E½NW	1911-01-23		A3
4602	" "	36	W½NE	1911-01-23		A3
4692	BOWEN, James	31	NENW	1895-03-30		A1
4792	BREHMER, Oscar	36	N½SE	1912-01-08		A1
4793	" "	36	NESW	1912-01-08		A1
4794	" "	36	SWSE	1912-01-08		A1
4646	BROWN, Edward D	24	W½NW	1875-02-20		A1
4812	BUCKINGHAM, Wait B	12	SWSE	1874-08-01		A1
4813	" "	13	NENW	1874-08-01		A1
4814	" "	13	NWNE	1874-08-01		A1
4815	" "	14	S½NE	1874-08-01		A1
4816	" "	29	2	1874-08-01		A1
4817	" "	29	3	1874-08-01		A1
4818	" "	29	SWSE	1874-08-01		A1
4819	" "	30	SWSE	1874-08-01		A1
4648	CARR, Edward J	10	SWNE	1899-12-21		A1
4693	CHOUSSE, James	25	E½NE	1894-08-14		A1
4694	" "	25	NESE	1894-08-14		A1
4654	CHRISTEN, Fritz C	29	SWSW	1904-02-25		A1
4709	COMPANY, Land Log And Lumber	18	3	1888-09-29		A1 F
4710	" "	18	SWSW	1888-09-29		A1 F
4711	" "	19	NWNW	1888-09-29		A1
4712	" "	21	1	1889-06-28		A1
4713	" "	21	2	1889-06-28		A1
4714	" "	21	NESW	1889-06-28		A1
4715	" "	21	SENW	1889-06-28		A1
4716	" "	21	W½NE	1889-06-28		A1
4717	" "	23	NESW	1889-06-28		A1
4718	" "	23	S½SW	1889-06-28		A1
4719	" "	26	NESE	1889-06-28		A1
4720	" "	26	SENE	1889-06-28		A1
4721	" "	30	W½SW	1889-06-28		A1 F
4722	" "	31	NWSW	1889-06-28		A1 F
4723	" "	31	S½SW	1889-06-28		A1 F
4724	" "	31	SENW	1889-06-28		A1
4725	" "	32	SWSW	1889-06-28		A1
4736	COMPANY, Menasha Wooden Ware	25	SESE	1884-06-20		A1
4735	" "	21	NWNW	1888-07-28		A1
4708	COOK, L J	4	E½SW	1889-04-04		A1 G53
4704	DAVIS, Joseph B	12	N½SE	1883-09-15		A1
4705	" "	12	NESW	1883-09-15		A1

ID	Individual in Patent	Sec.	Sec. Part	Date Issued	Other Counties	For More Info . . .
4706	DAVIS, Joseph B (Cont'd)	12	NWNE	1883-09-15		A1
4707	" "	12	S½NE	1883-09-15		A1
4708	DICKINSON, G P	4	E½SW	1889-04-04		A1 G53
4796	DRAVES, Rudolph	35	SENW	1897-01-08		A1
4600	EBY, C	2	NESE	1889-04-04		A1 G80
4643	EVANS, David J	6	SESE	1884-06-20		A1 G83
4644	" "	7	NENE	1884-06-20		A1 G83
4695	GALLAGHER, Jeremiah	24	E½SE	1894-04-27		A1
4696	" "	24	SWSE	1894-04-27		A1
4740	GELEFT, Nis J	1	NE	1900-10-04		A1 F
4741	" "	1	NWSE	1900-10-04		A1
4726	GORMAN, M	11	NENE	1884-06-30		A1 G93
4727	" "	12	N½NW	1884-06-30		A1 G93
4728	" "	12	SWNW	1884-06-30		A1 G93
4729	" "	13	NWSW	1884-06-30		A1 G93
4730	" "	14	NENW	1884-06-30		A1 G93
4731	" "	14	NWNE	1884-06-30		A1 G93
4732	" "	26	NENW	1884-06-30		A1 G93
4733	" "	26	NWNE	1884-06-30		A1 G93
4734	" "	26	SWSW	1884-06-30		A1 G93
4726	GORMAN, S	11	NENE	1884-06-30		A1 G93
4727	" "	12	N½NW	1884-06-30		A1 G93
4728	" "	12	SWNW	1884-06-30		A1 G93
4729	" "	13	NWSW	1884-06-30		A1 G93
4730	" "	14	NENW	1884-06-30		A1 G93
4731	" "	14	NWNE	1884-06-30		A1 G93
4732	" "	26	NENW	1884-06-30		A1 G93
4733	" "	26	NWNE	1884-06-30		A1 G93
4734	" "	26	SWSW	1884-06-30		A1 G93
4699	GUSTAFSON, John P	1	SWSW	1903-01-20		A1
4700	" "	2	SESE	1903-01-20		A1
4669	HAMILTON, Irenus H	13	SESE	1873-05-01		A1 G96
4670	" "	28	SENE	1873-05-01		A1 G96
4671	HAMILTON, Irenus K	1	E½SE	1873-05-01		A1 G97 C R4672
4673	" "	13	NESE	1873-05-01		A1 G97 C R4674
4675	" "	27	NWSW	1873-05-01		A1 G97 C R4676
4677	" "	27	SESE	1873-05-01		A1 G97 C R4678
4679	" "	27	SWNW	1873-05-01		A1 G97 C R4680
4682	" "	28	NWNW	1873-05-01		A1 G97 C R4683
4684	" "	28	SWNW	1873-05-01		A1 G97 C R4685
4686	" "	36	NENE	1873-05-01		A1 G97 C R4687
4688	" "	36	SESW	1873-05-01		A1 G97 C R4689
4690	" "	9	SESW	1873-05-01		A1 G97 C R4691
4672	" "	1	E½SE	1874-08-01		A1 G97 R4671
4674	" "	13	NESE	1874-08-01		A1 G97 R4673
4676	" "	27	NWSW	1874-08-01		A1 G97 R4675
4678	" "	27	SESE	1874-08-01		A1 G97 R4677
4680	" "	27	SWNW	1874-08-01		A1 G97 R4679
4681	" "	28	7	1874-08-01		A1 G97
4683	" "	28	NWNW	1874-08-01		A1 G97 R4682
4685	" "	28	SWNW	1874-08-01		A1 G97 R4684
4687	" "	36	NENE	1874-08-01		A1 G97 R4686
4689	" "	36	SESW	1874-08-01		A1 G97 R4688
4691	" "	9	SESW	1874-08-01		A1 G97 R4690
4671	HAMILTON, Woodman C	1	E½SE	1873-05-01		A1 G97 C R4672
4673	" "	13	NESE	1873-05-01		A1 G97 C R4674
4669	" "	13	SESE	1873-05-01		A1 G96
4675	" "	27	NWSW	1873-05-01		A1 G97 C R4676
4677	" "	27	SESE	1873-05-01		A1 G97 C R4678
4679	" "	27	SWNW	1873-05-01		A1 G97 C R4680
4682	" "	28	NWNW	1873-05-01		A1 G97 C R4683
4670	" "	28	SENE	1873-05-01		A1 G96
4684	" "	28	SWNW	1873-05-01		A1 G97 C R4685
4686	" "	36	NENE	1873-05-01		A1 G97 C R4687
4688	" "	36	SESW	1873-05-01		A1 G97 C R4689
4690	" "	9	SESW	1873-05-01		A1 G97 C R4691
4672	" "	1	E½SE	1874-08-01		A1 G97 R4671
4674	" "	13	NESE	1874-08-01		A1 G97 R4673
4676	" "	27	NWSW	1874-08-01		A1 G97 R4675
4678	" "	27	SESE	1874-08-01		A1 G97 R4677
4680	" "	27	SWNW	1874-08-01		A1 G97 R4679
4681	" "	28	7	1874-08-01		A1 G97
4683	" "	28	NWNW	1874-08-01		A1 G97 R4682

ID	Individual in Patent	Sec.	Sec. Part	Date Issued	Other Counties	For More Info . . .
4685	HAMILTON, Woodman C (Cont'd)	28	SWNW	1874-08-01		A1 G97 R4684
4687	" "	36	NENE	1874-08-01		A1 G97 R4686
4689	" "	36	SESW	1874-08-01		A1 G97 R4688
4691	" "	9	SESW	1874-08-01		A1 G97 R4690
4655	HAUPTMAN, George N	10	2	1882-09-30		A1
4656	" "	10	3	1882-09-30		A1
4657	" "	10	S½SW	1882-09-30		A1
4658	" "	17	5	1882-09-30		A1
4598	HEINEMANN, Benjamin	30	N½NW	1889-05-09		A1 F
4599	" "	31	NWNW	1889-05-09		A1 F
4647	HERMANSON, Edward	13	NENE	1898-01-12		A1
4649	HJELMSTAD, Elias J	13	S½NW	1897-01-08		A1
4832	IRWIN, William P	17	W½NE	1872-02-20		A1 G112
4833	" "	32	SESW	1872-02-20		A1 G112
4834	" "	32	SWSE	1872-02-20		A1 G112
4630	KAO, Charles	13	SWSE	1898-12-12		A3
4631	" "	24	E½NW	1898-12-12		A3
4632	" "	24	NWNE	1898-12-12		A3
4835	KELLY, William P	1	NWSW	1873-11-15		A1
4836	" "	1	W½NW	1873-11-15		A1
4837	" "	10	NESW	1873-11-15		A1
4838	" "	10	S½NW	1873-11-15		A1
4839	" "	13	SENE	1873-11-15		A1
4840	" "	2	E½NE	1873-11-15		A1
4603	KING, Charles G	13	E½SW	1871-04-01		A1 G122
4604	" "	13	SWSW	1871-04-01		A1 G122
4605	" "	14	S½NW	1871-04-01		A1 G122
4606	" "	14	SW	1871-04-01		A1 G122
4607	" "	15	E½	1871-04-01		A1 G122 F
4608	" "	15	N½SW	1871-04-01		A1 G122 F
4609	" "	20	N½	1871-04-01		A1 G122 F
4610	" "	20	SE	1871-04-01		A1 G122 F
4611	" "	21	E½NE	1871-04-01		A1 G122
4612	" "	21	E½SE	1871-04-01		A1 G122
4613	" "	21	SESW	1871-04-01		A1 G122
4614	" "	21	SWNW	1871-04-01		A1 G122
4615	" "	21	SWSE	1871-04-01		A1 G122
4616	" "	22		1871-04-01		A1 G122
4617	" "	23	NWSW	1871-04-01		A1 G122
4618	" "	23	W½NW	1871-04-01		A1 G122
4619	" "	24	NESW	1871-04-01		A1 G122
4620	" "	27	E½NW	1871-04-01		A1 G122
4621	" "	27	NWNW	1871-04-01		A1 G122
4622	" "	27	W½NE	1871-04-01		A1 G122 F
4623	" "	28	E½NW	1871-04-01		A1 G122 F
4624	" "	28	N½NE	1871-04-01		A1 G122
4625	" "	28	SWNE	1871-04-01		A1 G122
4626	" "	34	E½SE	1871-04-01		A1 G122
4627	" "	34	NWSE	1871-04-01		A1 G122
4628	" "	34	SENE	1871-04-01		A1 G122
4629	" "	35	SW	1871-04-01		A1 G122
4633	KNAPP, Charles	24	SWSW	1875-02-20		A1 G123
4634	" "	25	NWNW	1875-02-20		A1 G123
4633	KNAPP, Sheldon	24	SWSW	1875-02-20		A1 G123
4634	" "	25	NWNW	1875-02-20		A1 G123
4790	LILJEQVEST, Oran	25	N½SW	1904-02-25		A1
4791	" "	25	S½NW	1904-02-25		A1
4591	LOVEJOY, Allen P	30	NESW	1872-07-01		A1
4592	" "	30	SENW	1872-07-01		A1
4593	" "	6	W½SW	1872-07-01		A1
4594	" "	7	SWSW	1872-07-01		A1
4701	MCDONALD, John R	24	NWSW	1904-03-26		A1
4806	MILLER, Thomas A	1	E½NW	1894-08-14		A1 F
4807	" "	1	E½SW	1894-08-14		A1
4826	MILLER, Walter L	15	2	1889-03-28		A1
4820	" "	11	E½SE	1889-03-29		A1
4821	" "	11	NWSE	1889-03-29		A1
4822	" "	11	SENE	1889-03-29		A1
4823	" "	11	W½NE	1889-03-29		A1
4824	" "	12	NWSW	1889-03-29		A1
4825	" "	12	S½SW	1889-03-29		A1
4827	" "	15	3	1889-03-29		A1
4828	" "	2	W½NE	1889-04-04		A1 F

ID	Individual in Patent	Sec.	Sec. Part	Date Issued	Other Counties	For More Info . . .
4829	MILLER, Walter L (Cont'd)	3	NESW	1889-04-04		A1
4830	" "	3	NWSE	1889-04-04		A1
4831	" "	3	W½SW	1889-04-04		A1
4841	MILLER, Wilmot H	9	SENE	1889-03-28		A1
4697	MURRAY, John D	30	SWNW	1896-08-26		A1
4797	NIELSEN, Theodor	10	E½NE	1888-07-18		A1
4798	" "	11	1	1888-07-18		A1
4799	" "	11	NESW	1888-07-18		A1
4800	" "	11	NW	1888-07-18		A1
4801	" "	11	SWSE	1888-07-18		A1
4802	" "	14	NWNW	1888-07-18		A1
4803	" "	2	W½	1888-07-18		A1 F
4804	" "	2	W½SE	1888-07-18		A1
4805	" "	3	E½SE	1888-07-18		A1
4811	OCONNOR, Timothy	12	SENW	1899-06-22		A1
4645	PAQUETTE, Dennis	31	SWNW	1904-12-29		A1
4742	PILLSBURY, Oliver P	12	NENE	1885-01-15		A1
4743	" "	13	NWNW	1885-01-15		A1
4744	" "	14	NENE	1885-01-15		A1
4745	" "	15	1	1885-01-15		A1
4746	" "	15	SWSW	1885-01-15		A1
4747	" "	19	2	1885-01-15		A1
4748	" "	19	SWNW	1885-01-15		A1
4749	" "	19	W½SW	1885-01-15		A1
4750	" "	20	3	1885-01-15		A1
4751	" "	21	NENW	1885-01-15		A1
4752	" "	26	N½SW	1885-01-15		A1
4753	" "	26	NWNW	1885-01-15		A1
4754	" "	26	S½NW	1885-01-15		A1
4755	" "	26	SESW	1885-01-15		A1
4756	" "	26	SWNE	1885-01-15		A1
4757	" "	26	W½SE	1885-01-15		A1
4758	" "	27	1	1885-01-15		A1
4759	" "	27	4	1885-01-15		A1
4760	" "	27	N½SE	1885-01-15		A1
4761	" "	27	NESW	1885-01-15		A1
4762	" "	27	SENE	1885-01-15		A1
4763	" "	27	SWSE	1885-01-15		A1
4764	" "	29	1	1885-01-15		A1
4765	" "	3	E½NE	1885-01-15		A1 F
4766	" "	3	NW	1885-01-15		A1 F
4767	" "	3	SESW	1885-01-15		A1
4768	" "	3	SWSE	1885-01-15		A1
4769	" "	3	W½NE	1885-01-15		A1 F
4770	" "	33	3	1885-01-15		A1
4771	" "	33	4	1885-01-15		A1
4772	" "	33	6	1885-01-15		A1
4773	" "	33	7	1885-01-15		A1
4774	" "	33	NWSW	1885-01-15		A1
4775	" "	35	NENW	1885-01-15		A1
4776	" "	35	NWNW	1885-01-15		A1
4777	" "	35	SE	1885-01-15		A1
4778	" "	35	SENE	1885-01-15		A1
4779	" "	35	SWNE	1885-01-15		A1
4780	" "	4	E½NW	1885-01-15		A1 F
4781	" "	4	NWSE	1885-01-15		A1
4782	" "	4	SWSE	1885-01-15		A1
4783	" "	4	W½NE	1885-01-15		A1 F
4784	" "	6	NESW	1885-01-15		A1
4785	" "	6	NW	1885-01-15		A1 F
4786	" "	6	SWSE	1885-01-15		A1
4787	" "	7	NWNE	1885-01-15		A1
4788	" "	8	SENE	1885-01-15		A1
4789	" "	9	E½SE	1885-01-15		A1
4832	REMMERT, Albert	17	W½NE	1872-02-20		A1 G112
4833	" "	32	SESW	1872-02-20		A1 G112
4834	" "	32	SWSE	1872-02-20		A1 G112
4832	RIPLEY, Emma	17	W½NE	1872-02-20		A1 G112
4833	" "	32	SESW	1872-02-20		A1 G112
4834	" "	32	SWSE	1872-02-20		A1 G112
4650	RIPLEY, Emma A	28	3	1873-05-01		A1
4651	" "	28	NWSW	1873-05-01		A1
4652	" "	29	SESE	1873-05-01		A1

ID	Individual in Patent	Sec.	Sec. Part	Date Issued	Other Counties	For More Info . . .
4653	RIPLEY, Emma A (Cont'd)	32	SESE	1873-05-01		A1
4702	ROIT, John	25	NWSE	1894-08-14		A1
4703	" "	25	W½NE	1894-08-14		A1
4603	RUST, William A	13	E½SW	1871-04-01		A1 G122
4604	" "	13	SWSW	1871-04-01		A1 G122
4605	" "	14	S½NW	1871-04-01		A1 G122
4606	" "	14	SW	1871-04-01		A1 G122
4607	" "	15	E½	1871-04-01		A1 G122 F
4608	" "	15	N½SW	1871-04-01		A1 G122 F
4609	" "	20	N½	1871-04-01		A1 G122 F
4610	" "	20	SE	1871-04-01		A1 G122 F
4611	" "	21	E½NE	1871-04-01		A1 G122
4612	" "	21	E½SE	1871-04-01		A1 G122
4613	" "	21	SESW	1871-04-01		A1 G122
4614	" "	21	SWNW	1871-04-01		A1 G122
4615	" "	21	SWSE	1871-04-01		A1 G122
4616	" "	22		1871-04-01		A1 G122
4617	" "	23	NWSW	1871-04-01		A1 G122
4618	" "	23	W½NW	1871-04-01		A1 G122
4619	" "	24	NESW	1871-04-01		A1 G122
4620	" "	27	E½NW	1871-04-01		A1 G122
4621	" "	27	NWNW	1871-04-01		A1 G122
4622	" "	27	W½NE	1871-04-01		A1 G122 F
4623	" "	28	E½NW	1871-04-01		A1 G122 F
4624	" "	28	N½NE	1871-04-01		A1 G122
4625	" "	28	SWNE	1871-04-01		A1 G122
4626	" "	34	E½SE	1871-04-01		A1 G122
4627	" "	34	NWSE	1871-04-01		A1 G122
4628	" "	34	SENE	1871-04-01		A1 G122
4629	" "	35	SW	1871-04-01		A1 G122
4589	SCHAUDER, Adolph	24	SESW	1901-05-08		A1
4590	" "	25	NENW	1901-05-08		A1
4635	SCHRIBER, Charles	10	NWNW	1889-03-29		A1
4636	" "	23	E½NW	1889-03-29		A1
4637	" "	33	2	1889-03-29		A1
4638	" "	33	NESE	1889-03-29		A1
4639	" "	34	SWSE	1889-03-29		A1
4640	" "	35	NWNE	1889-03-29		A1
4641	" "	7	SWNE	1889-03-29		A1
4642	" "	9	N½NE	1889-03-29		A1
4808	SCOTT, Thomas B	26	SESE	1883-09-15		A1
4809	" "	36	W½SW	1883-09-15		A1
4810	" "	6	NESE	1883-09-15		A1
4737	SHEPARD, Mildred M	33	1	1889-06-28		A1
4662	SHERRY, Henry	21	NWSE	1885-05-09		A1
4663	" "	8	NESE	1886-07-30		A1
4795	SIEGEL, Ransferd C	24	NENE	1898-03-28		A3
4659	SILVERTHORN, George	28	2	1888-07-10		A1
4660	" "	30	SESW	1888-07-10		A1
4661	" "	31	SWSE	1888-07-10		A1
4698	STANDISH, John D	35	NENE	1882-09-30		A1
4595	STARKS, B C	31	N½SE	1889-03-29		A1 G166
4596	" "	31	SESE	1889-03-29		A1 G166
4597	" "	31	SWNE	1889-03-29		A1 G166
4595	STICKLES, C R	31	N½SE	1889-03-29		A1 G166
4596	" "	31	SESE	1889-03-29		A1 G166
4597	" "	31	SWNE	1889-03-29		A1 G166
4600	STUBBINGS, W H	2	NESE	1889-04-04		A1 G80
4595	TOBEY, E A	31	N½SE	1889-03-29		A1 G166
4596	" "	31	SESE	1889-03-29		A1 G166
4597	" "	31	SWNE	1889-03-29		A1 G166
4738	VENNER, Napoleon	17	1	1901-02-20		A1
4739	" "	8	1	1901-02-20		A1
4643	YAWKEY, William C	6	SESE	1884-06-20		A1 G83
4644	" "	7	NENE	1884-06-20		A1 G83

Patent Map

T40-N R7-E
4th PM - 1831 MN/WI

Map Group 29

Township Statistics

Parcels Mapped	:	253
Number of Patents	:	94
Number of Individuals	:	65
Patentees Identified	:	54
Number of Surnames	:	57
Multi-Patentee Parcels	:	71
Oldest Patent Date	:	4/1/1871
Most Recent Patent	:	1/8/1912
Block/Lot Parcels	:	28
Parcels Re - Issued	:	10
Parcels that Overlap	:	0
Cities and Towns	:	1
Cemeteries	:	0

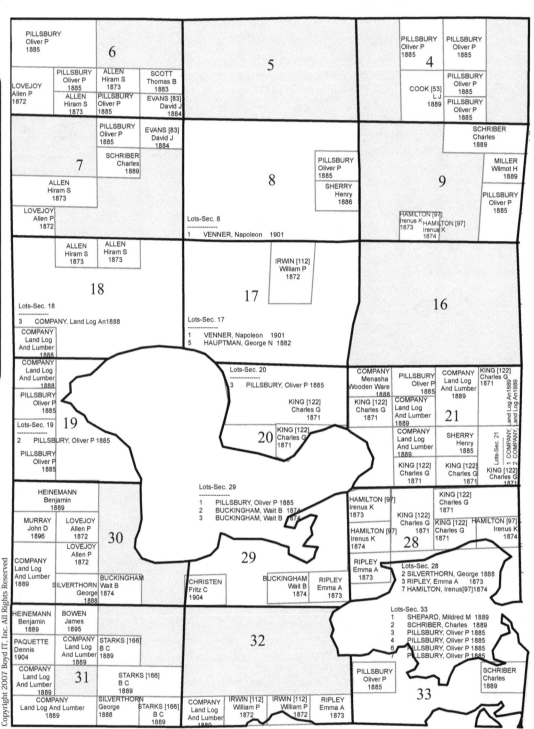

Helpful Hints

1. This Map's INDEX can be found on the preceding pages.

2. Refer to Map "C" to see where this Township lies within Vilas County, Wisconsin.

3. Numbers within square brackets [ ] denote a multi-patentee land parcel (multi-owner). Refer to Appendix "C" for a full list of members in this group.

4. Areas that look to be crowded with Patentees usually indicate multiple sales of the same parcel (Re-issues) or Overlapping parcels. See this Township's Index for an explanation of these and other circumstances that might explain "odd" groupings of Patentees on this map.

Section 3
PILLSBURY Oliver P 1885
PILLSBURY Oliver P 1885
PILLSBURY Oliver P 1885
3
MILLER Walter L 1889
MILLER Walter L 1889
NIELSEN Theodor 1888
MILLER Walter L 1889
PILLSBURY Oliver P 1885
PILLSBURY Oliver P 1885

Section 2
MILLER Walter L 1889
2
NIELSEN Theodor 1888
NIELSEN Theodor 1888
EBY [80] C 1889
GUSTAFSON John P 1903

Section 1
KELLY William P 1873
KELLY William P 1873
MILLER Thomas A 1894
GELEFT Nis J 1900
1
KELLY William P 1873
MILLER Thomas A 1894
GELEFT Nis J 1900
HAMILTON [97] Irenus K 1873
HAMILTON [97] Irenus K 1874
GUSTAFSON John P 1903

Section 10
SCHRIBER Charles 1889
NIELSEN Theodor 1888
KELLY William P 1873
CARR Edward J 1899
KELLY William P 1873
10
HAUPTMAN George N 1882
Lots-Sec. 10
2 HAUPTMAN, George N 1882
3 HAUPTMAN, George N 1882

Section 11
NIELSEN Theodor 1888
11
MILLER Walter L 1889
MILLER Walter L 1889
NIELSEN Theodor 1888
MILLER Walter L 1889
NIELSEN Theodor 1888
MILLER Walter L 1889
Lots-Sec. 11
----
1 NIELSEN, Theodor 1888

Section 12
GORMAN [93] M 1884
GORMAN [93] M 1884
DAVIS Joseph B 1883
PILLSBURY Oliver P 1885
GORMAN [93] M 1884
OCONNOR Timothy 1899
12
DAVIS Joseph B 1883
MILLER Walter L 1889
DAVIS Joseph B 1883
DAVIS Joseph B 1883
MILLER Walter L 1889
BUCKINGHAM Wait B 1874

Section 15
Lots-Sec. 15
----
1 PILLSBURY, Oliver P 1885
2 MILLER, Walter L 1889
3 MILLER, Walter L 1889
15
KING [122] Charles G 1871
KING [122] Charles G 1871
PILLSBURY Oliver P 1885

Section 14
NIELSEN Theodor 1888
GORMAN [93] M 1884
GORMAN [93] M 1884
PILLSBURY Oliver P 1885
KING [122] Charles G 1871
14
KING [122] Charles G 1871
BUCKINGHAM Wait B 1874

Section 13
PILLSBURY Oliver P 1885
BUCKINGHAM Wait B 1874
BUCKINGHAM Wait B 1874
HERMANSON Edward 1898
HJELMSTAD Elias J 1897
13
KELLY William P 1873
GORMAN [93] M 1884
KING [122] Charles G 1871
HAMILTON [97] Irenus K 1874
HAMILTON [97] Irenus K 1873
KING [122] Charles G 1871
KAO Charles 1898
HAMILTON [96] Irenus H

Section 22
22
KING [122] Charles G 1871

Section 23
KING [122] Charles G 1871
SCHRIBER Charles 1889
23
KING [122] Charles G 1871
COMPANY Land Log And Lumber 1889
COMPANY Land Log And Lumber 1889

Section 24
BROWN Edward D 1875
KAO Charles 1898
KAO Charles 1898
SIEGEL Ransferd C 1898
24
MCDONALD John R 1904
KING [122] Charles G 1871
GALLAGHER Jeremiah 1894
KNAPP [123] Charles 1875
SCHAUDER Adolph 1901
GALLAGHER Jeremiah 1894

Section 27
KING [122] Charles G 1871
Lots-Sec. 27
1 PILLSBURY, Oliver P 1885
4 PILLSBURY, Oliver P 1885
HAMILTON [97] Irenus K 1873
KING [122] Charles G 1871
KING [122] Charles G 1871
PILLSBURY Oliver P 1885
HAMILTON [97] Irenus K 1874
PILLSBURY Oliver P 1885
27
PILLSBURY Oliver P 1885
PILLSBURY Oliver P 1885
HAMILTON [97] Irenus K 1873
GORMAN [93] M 1884
PILLSBURY Oliver P 1885

Section 26
PILLSBURY Oliver P 1885
GORMAN [93] M 1884
GORMAN [93] M 1884
PILLSBURY Oliver P 1885
26
PILLSBURY Oliver P 1885
PILLSBURY Oliver P 1885

Section 25
KNAPP [123] Charles 1875
SCHAUDER Adolph 1901
COMPANY Land Log And Lumber 1889
LILJEQVEST Oran 1904
ROIT John 1894
CHOUSSE James 1894
25
COMPANY Land Log And Lumber 1889
LILJEQVEST Oran 1904
ROIT John 1894
CHOUSSE James 1894
SCOTT Thomas B 1883
COMPANY Menasha Wooden Ware 1884

Section 34
34
KING [122] Charles G 1871
KING [122] Charles G 1871
SCHRIBER Charles 1889

Section 35
PILLSBURY Oliver P 1885
PILLSBURY Oliver P 1885
SCHRIBER Charles 1889
STANDISH John D 1882
KING [122] Charles G 1871
DRAVES Rudolph 1897
PILLSBURY Oliver P 1885
PILLSBURY Oliver P 1885
35
KING [122] Charles G 1871
PILLSBURY Oliver P 1885

Section 36
BARNES Caleb A 1911
BARNES Caleb A 1911
HAMILTON [97] Irenus K 1874
36
SCOTT Thomas B 1883
BREHMER Oscar 1912
BREHMER Oscar 1912
HAMILTON [97] Irenus K 1873
BREHMER Oscar 1912

Legend
——— Patent Boundary
━━━ Section Boundary
No Patents Found (or Outside County)
1., 2., 3., ... Lot Numbers (when beside a name)
[ ] Group Number (see Appendix "C")

Scale: Section = 1 mile X 1 mile (generally, with some exceptions)

Copyright 2007 Boyd IT, Inc. All Rights Reserved

Road Map

T40-N R7-E
4th PM - 1831 MN/WI

Map Group 29

Cities & Towns
Arbor Vitae

Cemeteries
None

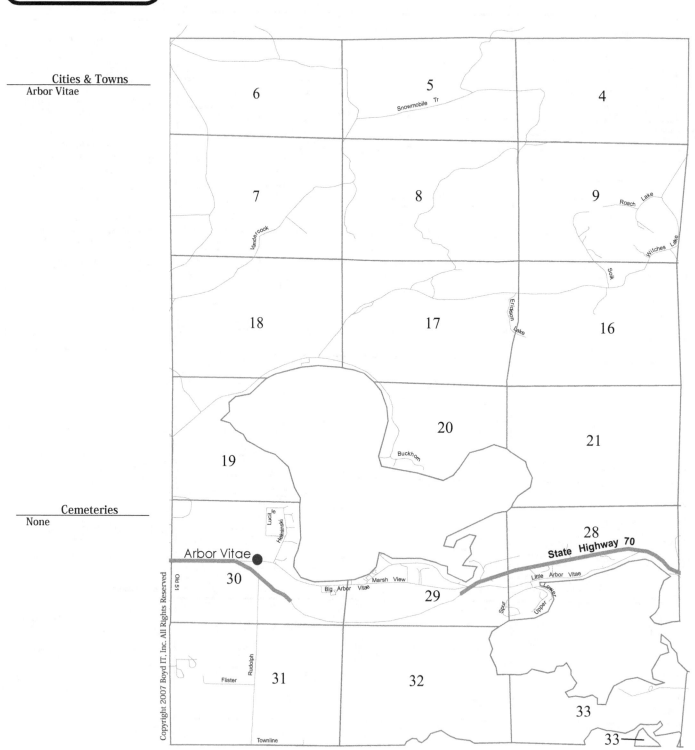

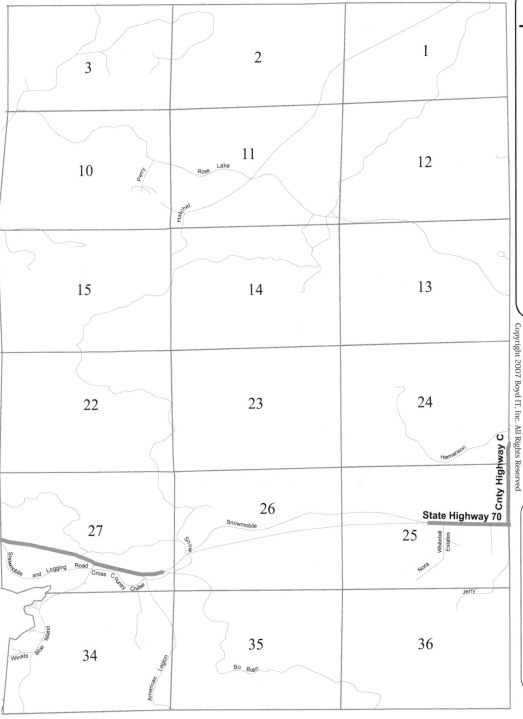

Helpful Hints

1. This road map has a number of uses, but primarily it is to help you: a) find the present location of land owned by your ancestors (at least the general area), b) find cemeteries and city-centers, and c) estimate the route/roads used by Census-takers & tax-assessors.

2. If you plan to travel to Vilas County to locate cemeteries or land parcels, please pick up a modern travel map for the area before you do. Mapping old land parcels on modern maps is not as exact a science as you might think. Just the slightest variations in public land survey coordinates, estimates of parcel boundaries, or road-map deviations can greatly alter a map's representation of how a road either does or doesn't cross a particular parcel of land.

Legend

————————	Section Lines
═══════════	Interstates
▬▬▬▬▬▬	Highways
————————	Other Roads
●	Cities/Towns
✝	Cemeteries

Scale: Section = 1 mile X 1 mile
(generally, with some exceptions)

Historical Map

T40-N R7-E
4th PM - 1831 MN/WI

Map Group 29

Cities & Towns
Arbor Vitae

Cemeteries
None

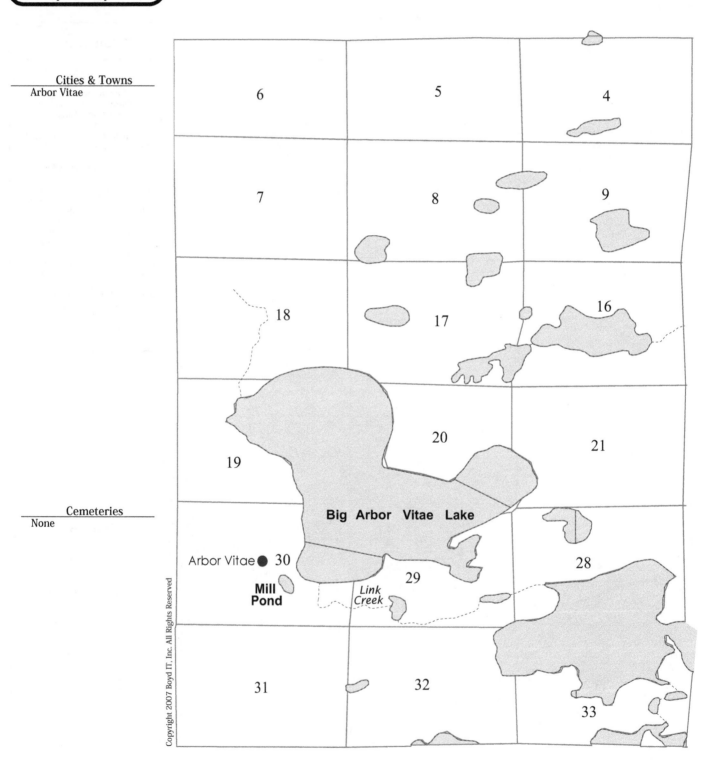

6   5   4

7   8   9

18   17   16

19   20   21

Big Arbor Vitae Lake

Arbor Vitae ● 30

Mill
Pond

29   28

Link
Creek

31   32   33

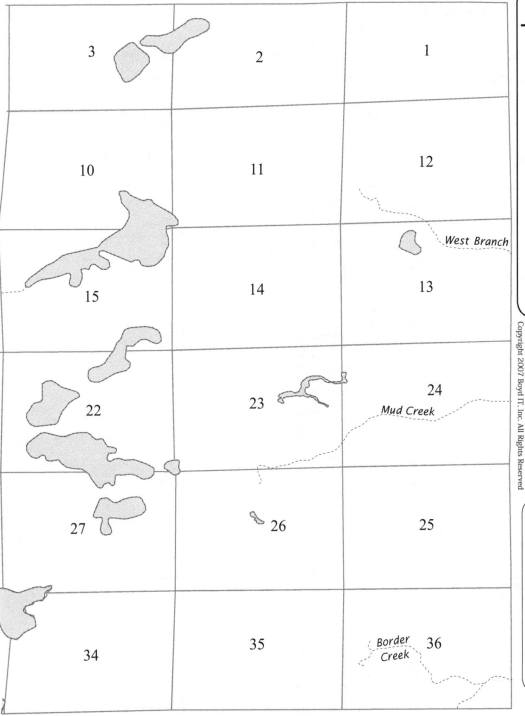

Helpful Hints

1. This Map takes a different look at the same Congressional Township displayed in the preceding two maps. It presents features that can help you better envision the historical development of the area: a) Water-bodies (lakes & ponds), b) Water-courses (rivers, streams, etc.), c) Railroads, d) City/town center-points (where they were oftentimes located when first settled), and e) Cemeteries.

2. Using this "Historical" map in tandem with this Township's Patent Map and Road Map, may lead you to some interesting discoveries. You will often find roads, towns, cemeteries, and waterways are named after nearby landowners: sometimes those names will be the ones you are researching. See how many of these research gems you can find here in Vilas County.

Legend

———————	Section Lines
+++++++	Railroads
▭	Large Rivers & Bodies of Water
- - - - - - -	Streams/Creeks & Small Rivers
●	Cities/Towns
✝	Cemeteries

Scale: Section = 1 mile X 1 mile
(there are some exceptions)

Map Group 30: Index to Land Patents

Township 40-North Range 8-East (4th PM - 1831 MN/WI)

After you locate an individual in this Index, take note of the Section and Section Part then proceed to the Land Patent map on the pages immediately following. You should have no difficulty locating the corresponding parcel of land.

The "For More Info" Column will lead you to more information about the underlying Patents. See the *Legend* at right, and the "How to Use this Book" chapter, for more information.

```
                    LEGEND
          "For More Info . . . " column
A = Authority (Legislative Act, See Appendix "A")
B = Block or Lot (location in Section unknown)
C = Cancelled Patent
F = Fractional Section
G = Group (Multi-Patentee Patent, see Appendix "C")
V = Overlaps another Parcel
R = Re-Issued (Parcel patented more than once)

(A & G items require you to look in the Appendixes referred
to above. All other Letter-designations followed by a number
require you to locate line-items in this index that possess
the ID number found after the letter).
```

ID	Individual in Patent	Sec.	Sec. Part	Date Issued	Other Counties	For More Info . . .
4917	ALLEN, Frank	12	NENE	1884-06-30		A1 G4
4918	" "	12	NENW	1884-06-30		A1 G4
4919	" "	12	NESE	1884-06-30		A1 G4
4920	" "	22	S½SE	1884-06-30		A1 G4
4921	" "	23	NWNE	1884-06-30		A1 G4
5061	ALLEN, Oscar	12	SESE	1895-06-04		A1
5013	ARPIN, John	17	NWSE	1884-06-30		A1
5014	" "	22	SESW	1884-06-30		A1
5015	" "	29	9	1884-06-30		A1
4856	BAKER, Cary	27	NESW	1900-06-11		A3
4857	" "	27	SENW	1900-06-11		A3
4858	" "	27	SWNE	1900-06-11		A3
5041	BANGS, N	27	NENE	1890-07-15		A1
4909	BENJAMIN, David M	19	4	1884-06-30		A1
4910	" "	30	3	1884-06-30		A1
4898	BIRD, Claire B	30	SWNW	1900-06-11		A1
4842	BROWN, A W	30	SESW	1888-07-18		A1 G30
4843	" "	31	SESW	1889-03-28		A1 G30
4842	BROWN, E O	30	SESW	1888-07-18		A1 G30
4843	" "	31	SESW	1889-03-28		A1 G30
4911	BROWN, Edward D	13	SWNE	1875-02-20		A1
4912	" "	29	2	1875-02-20		A1
4842	BROWN, W E	30	SESW	1888-07-18		A1 G30
4843	" "	31	SESW	1889-03-28		A1 G30
5073	BUCKINGHAM, Wait B	34	3	1875-02-20		A1 G34
5074	" "	34	4	1875-02-20		A1 G34
4922	CARLEY, Frank	34	7	1905-11-08		A3
4923	" "	34	8	1905-11-08		A3
4924	" "	34	SESE	1905-11-08		A3
4925	" "	35	SWSW	1905-11-08		A3
4969	CHOUSSE, James	30	NWSW	1894-08-14		A1
4914	CLARK, Eli C	2	E½NW	1873-05-01		A1 F
4915	" "	2	W½NE	1873-05-01		A1 F
5030	COMPANY, Land Log And Lumber	25	SESW	1885-05-20		A1
5035	COMPANY, Menasha Wooden Ware	28	1	1883-09-15		A1
5036	" "	28	2	1883-09-15		A1
5037	" "	28	3	1883-09-15		A1
5034	"	18	SWNW	1884-06-20		A1
4928	COON, Giles S	10	4	1900-07-30		A1
4929	" "	10	5	1900-07-30		A1
4930	" "	10	SWSE	1900-07-30		A1
4931	CORWITH, Henry	15	SWSW	1867-10-10		A1
4932	" "	23	1	1867-10-10		A1
4933	" "	23	2	1867-10-10		A1
4934	" "	23	SENE	1867-10-10		A1
4935	" "	24	2	1867-10-10		A1

ID	Individual in Patent	Sec.	Sec. Part	Date Issued	Other Counties	For More Info . . .
4936	CORWITH, Henry (Cont'd)	24	NESE	1867-10-10		A1
4937	" "	25	NESE	1867-10-10		A1
4938	" "	25	S½SE	1867-10-10		A1
4939	" "	26	3	1867-10-10		A1
4940	" "	26	4	1867-10-10		A1
4941	" "	27	SENE	1867-10-10		A1
4942	" "	28	NENE	1867-10-10		A1
4943	" "	30	2	1867-10-10		A1
4944	" "	32	SWSE	1867-10-10		A1
4947	" "	35	5	1867-10-10		A1
4948	" "	36	E½SE	1867-10-10		A1
4949	" "	36	NWNE	1867-10-10		A1
4945	" "	34	1	1873-05-01		A1
4946	" "	34	2	1873-05-01		A1
4963	COTTER, J N	10	2	1888-07-28		A1
4964	" "	11	1	1888-07-28		A1
4965	" "	11	SWNW	1888-07-28		A1
4966	" "	4	NESE	1888-07-28		A1
4967	" "	4	NESW	1888-07-28		A1
4968	" "	8	NESW	1888-07-28		A1
5020	DAVIS, Joseph B	5	E½NW	1883-09-15		A1 F
5021	" "	5	NESW	1883-09-15		A1
5022	" "	5	SE	1883-09-15		A1
5023	" "	6	NWSE	1883-09-15		A1
5024	" "	6	S½SE	1883-09-15		A1
5025	" "	6	W½NE	1883-09-15		A1 F
5026	" "	7	NENE	1883-09-15		A1
5027	" "	8	NENE	1883-09-15		A1
5028	" "	9	NWNW	1883-09-15		A1
4917	DAWLEY, Anna C	12	NENE	1884-06-30		A1 G4
4918	" "	12	NENW	1884-06-30		A1 G4
4919	" "	12	NESE	1884-06-30		A1 G4
4920	" "	22	S½SE	1884-06-30		A1 G4
4921	" "	23	NWNE	1884-06-30		A1 G4
5018	DAY, John F	27	NWNE	1890-07-15		A1
5016	ELIASON, John	10	NESE	1910-07-14		A3
5017	"	11	NWSW	1910-07-14		A3
4859	FELTON, Charles	6	E½NE	1899-05-05		A3 F
4860	" "	6	NESE	1899-05-05		A3 F
5038	FROEHLICH, Michael	9	3	1903-01-20		A1
5039	" "	9	NENW	1903-01-20		A1
5063	GAFFNEY, Patrick J	35	4	1905-11-13		A1
4977	GALLAGHER, Jeremiah	19	NWSW	1894-04-27		A1
5000	GILLET, Joel D	1	SESW	1884-06-30		A1
5001	" "	12	NWNE	1884-06-30		A1
5002	" "	12	NWSE	1884-06-30		A1
5003	" "	13	N½SE	1884-06-30		A1
5004	" "	13	SENE	1884-06-30		A1
5005	" "	13	SWSE	1884-06-30		A1
5006	" "	14	8	1884-06-30		A1
5007	" "	14	SESE	1884-06-30		A1
5008	" "	23	NENE	1884-06-30		A1
5009	" "	23	SWNE	1884-06-30		A1
5010	" "	35	9	1884-06-30		A1
5011	" "	9	SESW	1884-06-30		A1
5012	" "	9	SWNW	1884-06-30		A1
5064	GOERLING, Peter L	17	W½NW	1904-03-26		A1
4976	GOULD, James P	13	SESE	1873-05-01		A1
4917	GRAHAM, Daniel	12	NENE	1884-06-30		A1 G4
4918	" "	12	NENW	1884-06-30		A1 G4
4919	" "	12	NESE	1884-06-30		A1 G4
4920	" "	22	S½SE	1884-06-30		A1 G4
4921	" "	23	NWNE	1884-06-30		A1 G4
5031	GROUNDWATER, Mary J	5	SESW	1902-11-21		A3
5032	" "	8	E½NW	1902-11-21		A3
5033	" "	8	SWNW	1902-11-21		A3
4951	HAMILTON, Irenus K	18	N½NE	1873-05-01		A1 G97
4952	" "	30	1	1873-05-01		A1 G97
4953	" "	30	N½SE	1873-05-01		A1 G97
4954	" "	30	SWSW	1873-05-01		A1 G97
4955	" "	6	W½SW	1873-05-01		A1 G97
4956	" "	7	NENW	1873-05-01		A1 G97
4957	" "	7	NESE	1873-05-01		A1 G97

ID	Individual in Patent	Sec.	Sec. Part	Date Issued	Other Counties	For More Info . . .
4958	HAMILTON, Irenus K (Cont'd)	7	NESW	1873-05-01		A1 G97
4959	" "	7	SENW	1873-05-01		A1 G97
4960	" "	7	SWNE	1873-05-01		A1 G97
4961	" "	7	SWSW	1873-05-01		A1 G97
4962	" "	7	W½SE	1873-05-01		A1 G97
4951	HAMILTON, Woodman C	18	N½NE	1873-05-01		A1 G97
4952	" "	30	1	1873-05-01		A1 G97
4953	" "	30	N½SE	1873-05-01		A1 G97
4954	" "	30	SWSW	1873-05-01		A1 G97
4955	" "	6	W½SW	1873-05-01		A1 G97
4956	" "	7	NENW	1873-05-01		A1 G97
4957	" "	7	NESE	1873-05-01		A1 G97
4958	" "	7	NESW	1873-05-01		A1 G97
4959	" "	7	SENW	1873-05-01		A1 G97
4960	" "	7	SWNE	1873-05-01		A1 G97
4961	" "	7	SWSW	1873-05-01		A1 G97
4962	" "	7	W½SE	1873-05-01		A1 G97
4913	HOLLINDER, Edward	12	SENE	1895-06-04		A1
5045	HUNTER, Nelly E	9	5	1903-04-20		A1
5062	HUNTER, P S	9	1	1898-03-21		A1
5065	HUNTER, Philander S	10	3	1899-08-14		A1
5075	KELLY, William P	1	SWSW	1873-11-15		A1
5076	" "	2	N½SE	1873-11-15		A1
5077	" "	2	SESE	1873-11-15		A1
5078	" "	28	NWSE	1873-11-15		A1
5079	" "	4	SESE	1873-11-15		A1
5080	" "	6	E½SW	1873-11-15		A1
5081	" "	7	NWSW	1873-11-15		A1
5082	" "	9	4	1873-11-15		A1
4861	KING, Charles G	14	2	1871-04-01		A1 G122
4862	" "	14	3	1871-04-01		A1 G122
4863	" "	14	4	1871-04-01		A1 G122
4864	" "	14	5	1871-04-01		A1 G122
4865	" "	14	6	1871-04-01		A1 G122
4866	" "	14	NWNW	1871-04-01		A1 G122
4867	" "	15	E½SW	1871-04-01		A1 G122
4868	" "	15	S½NE	1871-04-01		A1 G122
4869	" "	15	SE	1871-04-01		A1 G122
4870	" "	17	1	1871-04-01		A1 G122
4871	" "	17	3	1871-04-01		A1 G122
4872	" "	17	4	1871-04-01		A1 G122
4873	" "	17	E½NE	1871-04-01		A1 G122
4874	" "	17	N½SW	1871-04-01		A1 G122
4875	" "	17	NESE	1871-04-01		A1 G122
4876	" "	22	N½NE	1871-04-01		A1 G122
4877	" "	22	NENW	1871-04-01		A1 G122
4878	" "	23	N½NW	1871-04-01		A1 G122
4879	" "	27	W½NW	1871-04-01		A1 G122
4880	" "	31	SENW	1871-04-01		A1 G122
4881	" "	31	SWNE	1871-04-01		A1 G122
4882	" "	31	W½SE	1871-04-01		A1 G122
4883	" "	7	SESE	1871-04-01		A1 G122
4884	KNAPP, Charles	28	SWSE	1875-02-20		A1 G123
4885	" "	32	E½SE	1875-02-20		A1 G123
4886	" "	32	SENE	1875-02-20		A1 G123
4887	" "	33	E½NW	1875-02-20		A1 G123
4888	" "	33	NESW	1875-02-20		A1 G123
4889	" "	33	SENE	1875-02-20		A1 G123
4890	" "	33	SWNW	1875-02-20		A1 G123
4891	" "	33	W½NE	1875-02-20		A1 G123
4892	" "	33	W½SW	1875-02-20		A1 G123
4884	KNAPP, Sheldon	28	SWSE	1875-02-20		A1 G123
4885	" "	32	E½SE	1875-02-20		A1 G123
4886	" "	32	SENE	1875-02-20		A1 G123
4887	" "	33	E½NW	1875-02-20		A1 G123
4888	" "	33	NESW	1875-02-20		A1 G123
4889	" "	33	SENE	1875-02-20		A1 G123
4890	" "	33	SWNW	1875-02-20		A1 G123
4891	" "	33	W½NE	1875-02-20		A1 G123
4892	" "	33	W½SW	1875-02-20		A1 G123
4950	LUHN, Herman	4	SWSE	1895-06-04		A1
4908	MCDONALD, Daniel	34	6	1889-03-29		A1
5069	MCGREGOR, Robert	30	NESW	1917-06-20		A3

ID	Individual in Patent	Sec.	Sec. Part	Date Issued	Other Counties	For More Info . . .
4916	MILLAR, Florence B	25	NESW	1908-08-13		A3 G145
4916	MOON, Florence B	25	NESW	1908-08-13		A3 G145
4916	MOON, George R	25	NESW	1908-08-13		A3 G145
4970	MOONEY, James	19	1	1888-07-28		A1
4971	"	19	2	1888-07-28		A1
4972	"	19	3	1888-07-28		A1
4973	"	28	4	1888-07-28		A1
4974	"	29	1	1888-07-28		A1
4975	"	30	4	1888-07-28		A1
4849	MORAN, Burnard N	18	E½SW	1904-03-26		A1
4850	"	18	SENW	1904-03-26		A1
4851	"	18	SWSE	1904-03-26		A1
5019	MUTTER, John G	19	5	1897-06-11		A1
4845	PAFF, Albert R	10	1	1889-05-31		A1
5083	PATRICK, William S	11	2	1872-11-01		A1
5084	"	11	E½NE	1872-11-01		A1
5085	"	11	SENW	1872-11-01		A1
5086	"	11	SWNE	1872-11-01		A1
5087	"	12	NWSW	1872-11-01		A1
5088	"	13	1	1872-11-01		A1
5089	"	13	NENW	1872-11-01		A1
5090	"	13	NWNE	1872-11-01		A1
5091	"	13	S½SW	1872-11-01		A1
5092	"	15	NWSW	1872-11-01		A1
5093	"	24	N½NW	1872-11-01		A1
5094	"	3	1	1872-11-01		A1
5095	"	3	2	1872-11-01		A1
5096	"	3	3	1872-11-01		A1
5097	"	3	4	1872-11-01		A1
5098	"	3	NE	1872-11-01		A1 F
5099	"	3	NESE	1872-11-01		A1
5100	"	3	NESW	1872-11-01		A1
5101	"	3	NW	1872-11-01		A1 F
5102	"	3	NWSE	1872-11-01		A1
5103	"	3	NWSW	1872-11-01		A1
5073	"	34	3	1875-02-20		A1 G34
5074	"	34	4	1875-02-20		A1 G34
5049	PILLSBURY, Oliver P	4	NWNW	1884-06-30		A1 F
5050	"	4	NWSE	1884-06-30		A1 F
5051	"	4	NWSW	1884-06-30		A1
5052	"	4	S½SW	1884-06-30		A1
5053	"	4	W½NE	1884-06-30		A1 F
5054	"	5	NE	1884-06-30		A1 F
5055	"	5	W½NW	1884-06-30		A1 F
5056	"	5	W½SW	1884-06-30		A1
5060	"	8	W½NE	1884-06-30		A1
5046	"	17	SENW	1885-01-15		A1
5047	"	21	5	1885-01-15		A1
5048	"	27	NENW	1885-01-15		A1
5057	"	6	E½NW	1885-01-15		A1 F
5058	"	7	NWNE	1885-01-15		A1
5059	"	7	SENE	1885-01-15		A1
5066	PURCELL, Phillip	19	NENW	1918-05-28		A3
4980	RUSSELL, Jesse M	1	SWSE	1884-06-30		A1
4983	"	11	NWNE	1884-06-30		A1
4984	"	11	SWSW	1884-06-30		A1
4986	"	15	NENW	1884-06-30		A1
4988	"	15	SWNW	1884-06-30		A1
4989	"	2	SESW	1884-06-30		A1
4990	"	2	SWSE	1884-06-30		A1
4991	"	23	SWSW	1884-06-30		A1
4992	"	25	4	1884-06-30		A1
4993	"	25	NWSW	1884-06-30		A1
4994	"	28	NESE	1884-06-30		A1
4995	"	35	NWSW	1884-06-30		A1
4996	"	36	NWSW	1884-06-30		A1
4997	"	36	S½SW	1884-06-30		A1
4998	"	36	SWNW	1884-06-30		A1
4999	"	36	SWSE	1884-06-30		A1
4978	"	1	N½SW	1885-01-20		A1
4979	"	1	NWSE	1885-01-20		A1
4981	"	10	6	1885-01-20		A1
4982	"	10	SESE	1885-01-20		A1

ID	Individual in Patent	Sec.	Sec. Part	Date Issued	Other Counties	For More Info . . .
4985	RUSSELL, Jesse M (Cont'd)	15	NENE	1885-01-20		A1
4987	" "	15	NWNW	1885-01-20		A1
4861	RUST, William A	14	2	1871-04-01		A1 G122
4862	" "	14	3	1871-04-01		A1 G122
4863	" "	14	4	1871-04-01		A1 G122
4864	" "	14	5	1871-04-01		A1 G122
4865	" "	14	6	1871-04-01		A1 G122
4866	" "	14	NWNW	1871-04-01		A1 G122
4867	" "	15	E½SW	1871-04-01		A1 G122
4868	" "	15	S½NE	1871-04-01		A1 G122
4869	" "	15	SE	1871-04-01		A1 G122
4870	" "	17	1	1871-04-01		A1 G122
4871	" "	17	3	1871-04-01		A1 G122
4872	" "	17	4	1871-04-01		A1 G122
4873	" "	17	E½NE	1871-04-01		A1 G122
4874	" "	17	N½SW	1871-04-01		A1 G122
4875	" "	17	NESE	1871-04-01		A1 G122
4876	" "	22	N½NE	1871-04-01		A1 G122
4877	" "	22	NENW	1871-04-01		A1 G122
4878	" "	23	N½NW	1871-04-01		A1 G122
4879	" "	27	W½NW	1871-04-01		A1 G122
4880	" "	31	SENW	1871-04-01		A1 G122
4881	" "	31	SWNE	1871-04-01		A1 G122
4882	" "	31	W½SE	1871-04-01		A1 G122
4883	" "	7	SESE	1871-04-01		A1 G122
5040	RYAN, Michael	31	NESW	1898-05-10		A1
4926	SAYNER, Frank	7	W½NW	1900-10-04		A1 F
4927	" "	8	NWNW	1904-02-25		A1
4893	SCHRIBER, Charles	1	E½NW	1889-03-29		A1 F
4894	" "	1	W½NE	1889-03-29		A1 F
4895	" "	12	SWNE	1889-03-29		A1
4896	" "	2	E½NE	1889-03-29		A1 F
4897	" "	2	N½SW	1889-03-29		A1
5070	SCOTT, Thomas B	11	NENW	1883-09-15		A1
5071	" "	2	1	1883-09-15		A1
5072	" "	9	2	1883-09-15		A1
5029	SEVERANCE, Joseph C	1	W½NW	1906-02-05		A1 F
5067	SIEGEL, Ransferd C	18	W½SW	1898-03-28		A3 F
5068	" "	19	NWNW	1898-03-28		A3 F
4848	SIEVWRIGHT, Archie	25	SWSW	1901-02-20		A1
4844	SMITH, Albert J	18	SWNE	1906-06-30		A1
5042	THOMPSON, Neil A	29	4	1873-11-15		A1
5043	" "	29	5	1873-11-15		A1
5044	" "	29	NWSW	1873-11-15		A1
4917	WASTE, Lee	12	NENE	1884-06-30		A1 G4
4918	" "	12	NENW	1884-06-30		A1 G4
4919	" "	12	NESE	1884-06-30		A1 G4
4920	" "	22	S½SE	1884-06-30		A1 G4
4921	" "	23	NWNE	1884-06-30		A1 G4
4852	WINTON, C J	13	NENE	1889-04-26		A1
4853	" "	14	SWSE	1889-04-26		A1
4854	" "	25	NWSE	1889-04-26		A1
4855	" "	31	SWSW	1889-04-26		A1 F
4846	WRIGHT, Anton	1	E½NE	1899-05-05		A3 F
4847	" "	1	E½SE	1899-05-05		A3
4899	WYLIE, Daniel B	28	5	1883-09-15		A1 G172
4900	" "	28	SESE	1883-09-15		A1 G172
4901	" "	28	SESW	1883-09-15		A1 G172
4902	" "	29	3	1883-09-15		A1 G172
4903	" "	29	6	1883-09-15		A1 G172
4904	" "	29	7	1883-09-15		A1 G172
4905	" "	29	S½SW	1883-09-15		A1 G172
4906	" "	32	NENE	1883-09-15		A1 G172
4907	" "	33	NWNW	1883-09-15		A1 G172
4899	WYLIE, Winfred	28	5	1883-09-15		A1 G172
4900	" "	28	SESE	1883-09-15		A1 G172
4901	" "	28	SESW	1883-09-15		A1 G172
4902	" "	29	3	1883-09-15		A1 G172
4903	" "	29	6	1883-09-15		A1 G172
4904	" "	29	7	1883-09-15		A1 G172
4905	" "	29	S½SW	1883-09-15		A1 G172
4906	" "	32	NENE	1883-09-15		A1 G172
4907	" "	33	NWNW	1883-09-15		A1 G172

Patent Map

T40-N R8-E
4th PM - 1831 MN/WI

Map Group 30

Township Statistics

Parcels Mapped	:	262
Number of Patents	:	102
Number of Individuals	:	72
Patentees Identified	:	61
Number of Surnames	:	61
Multi-Patentee Parcels	:	63
Oldest Patent Date	:	10/10/1867
Most Recent Patent	:	5/28/1918
Block/Lot Parcels	:	67
Parcels Re - Issued	:	0
Parcels that Overlap	:	0
Cities and Towns	:	1
Cemeteries	:	1

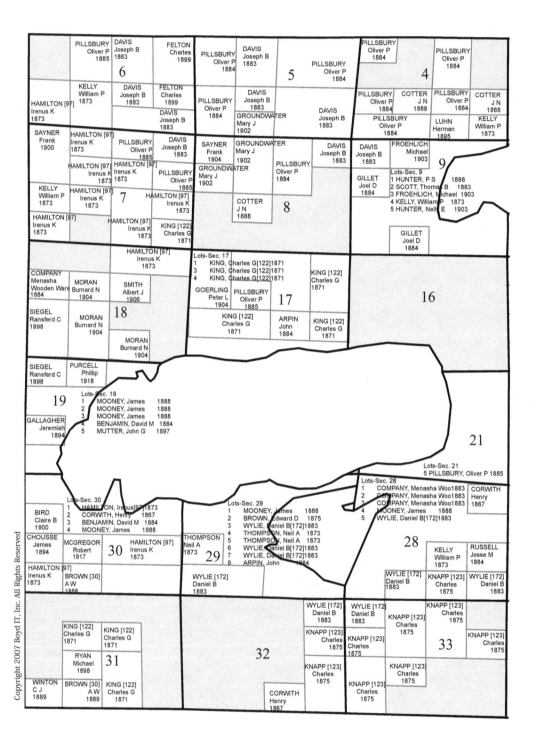

Copyright 2007 Boyd IT, Inc. All Rights Reserved

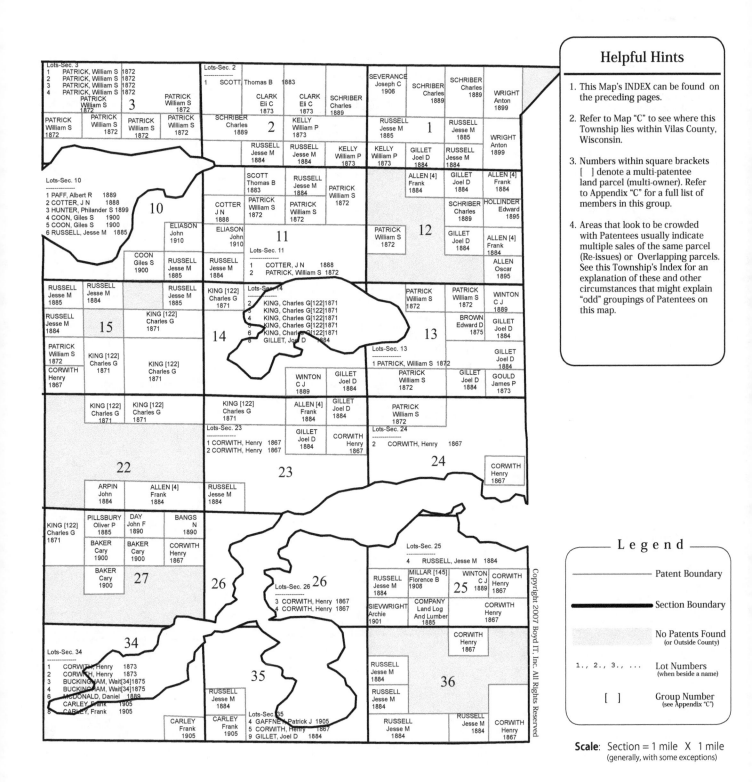

Copyright 2007 Boyd IT, Inc. All Rights Reserved

Helpful Hints

1. This Map's INDEX can be found on the preceding pages.

2. Refer to Map "C" to see where this Township lies within Vilas County, Wisconsin.

3. Numbers within square brackets [ ] denote a multi-patentee land parcel (multi-owner). Refer to Appendix "C" for a full list of members in this group.

4. Areas that look to be crowded with Patentees usually indicate multiple sales of the same parcel (Re-issues) or Overlapping parcels. See this Township's Index for an explanation of these and other circumstances that might explain "odd" groupings of Patentees on this map.

Legend

— Patent Boundary

— Section Boundary

No Patents Found
(or Outside County)

1., 2., 3., ... Lot Numbers
(when beside a name)

[ ] Group Number
(see Appendix "C")

Scale: Section = 1 mile X 1 mile
(generally, with some exceptions)

Road Map

T40-N R8-E
4th PM - 1831 MN/WI

Map Group 30

Cities & Towns
Saint Germain

Cemeteries
Saint Germain Cemetery

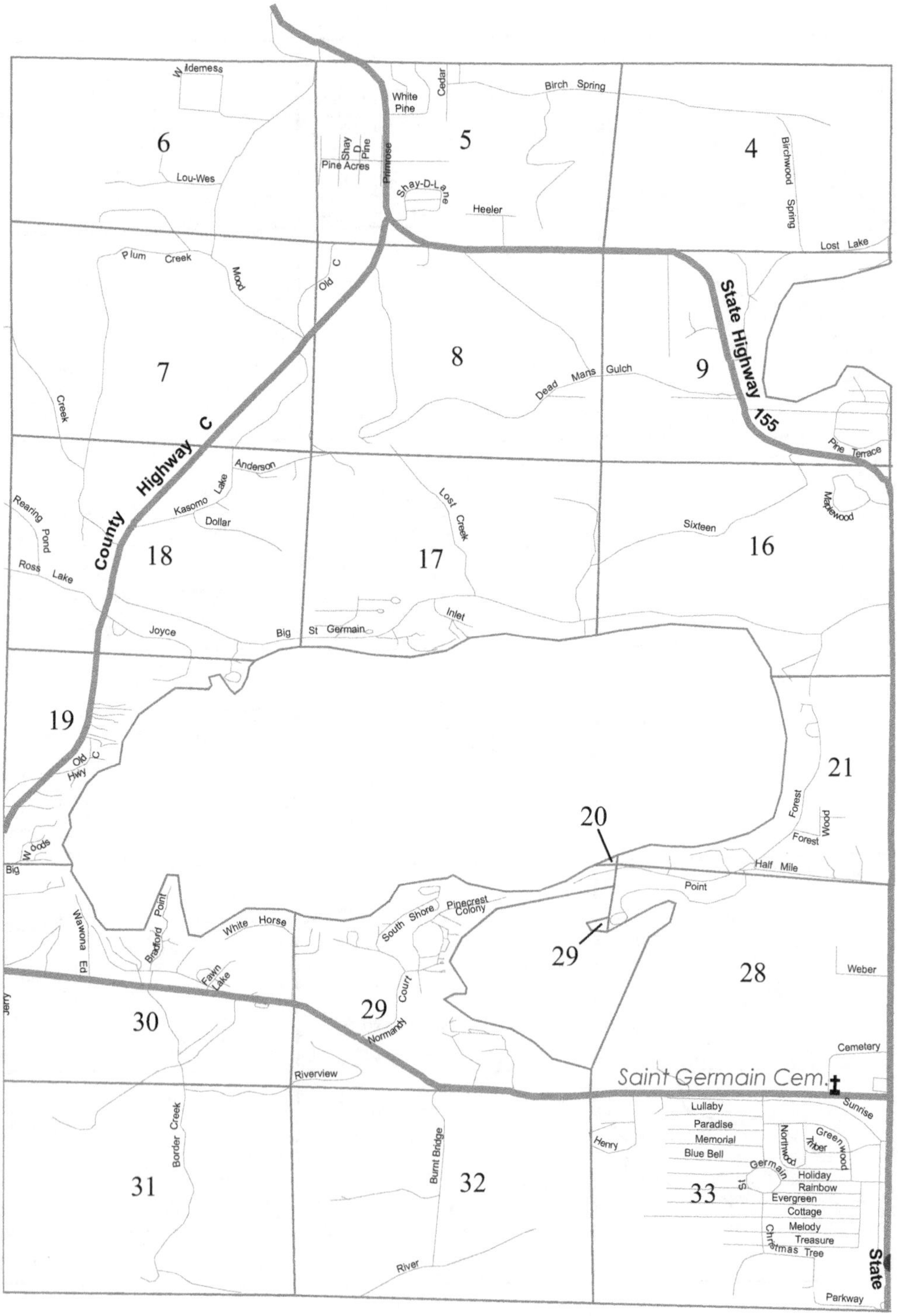

6

5

4

Wilderness

White Pine

Cedar

Birch Spring

Birchwood Spring

Lou-Wes

Shay D Pine

Pine Acres

Primrose

Shay-D-Lane

Heeler

Lost Lake

Plum   Creek

Mood

Old C

State Highway 155

7

8

9

Dead Mans Gulch

Pine Terrace

Creek

County Highway C

Anderson

Kasomo Lake

Dollar

Lost Creek

Sixteen

Maplewood

Rearing Pond

Ross Lake

18

17

16

Joyce

Big St Germain

Inlet

19

Old Hwy C

21

20

Forest

Forest Wood

Big

Woods

Wawona Rd

Bradford Point

White Horse

South Shore

Pinecrest Colony

Half Mile

Point

Weber

29

Jerry

Fawn Lake

Normandy Court

30

29

28

Riverview

Cemetery

Saint Germain Cem.

Lullaby

Sunrise

Border Creek

Burnt Bridge

Henry

Paradise

Memorial

Blue Bell

Normwood

Timber

Greenwood

Holiday

31

32

33

Germain St

Rainbow

Evergreen

Cottage

Melody

Christmas Tree

Treasure

River

State

Parkway

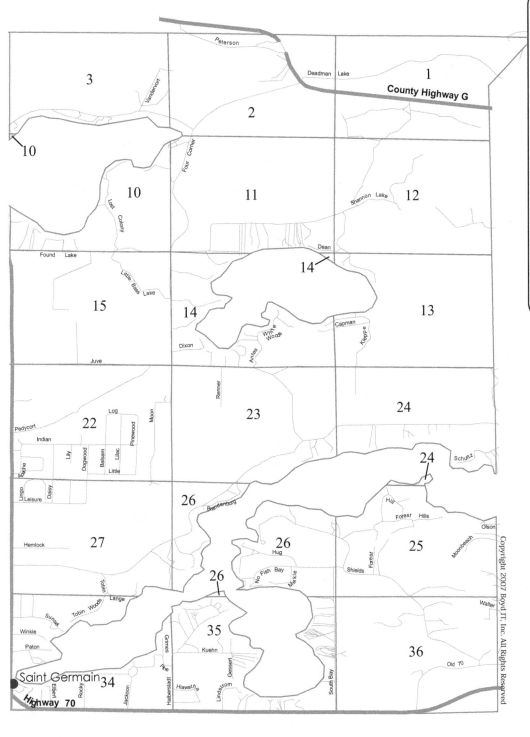

Copyright 2007 Boyd IT, Inc. All Rights Reserved

Helpful Hints

1. This road map has a number of uses, but primarily it is to help you: a) find the present location of land owned by your ancestors (at least the general area), b) find cemeteries and city-centers, and c) estimate the route/roads used by Census-takers & tax-assessors.

2. If you plan to travel to Vilas County to locate cemeteries or land parcels, please pick up a modern travel map for the area before you do. Mapping old land parcels on modern maps is not as exact a science as you might think. Just the slightest variations in public land survey coordinates, estimates of parcel boundaries, or road-map deviations can greatly alter a map's representation of how a road either does or doesn't cross a particular parcel of land.

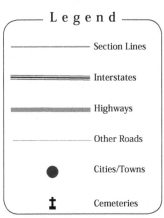

Legend

Section Lines

Interstates

Highways

Other Roads

Cities/Towns

Cemeteries

Scale: Section = 1 mile X 1 mile
(generally, with some exceptions)

Historical Map

T40-N R8-E
4th PM - 1831 MN/WI

Map Group 30

Cities & Towns
Saint Germain

Cemeteries
Saint Germain Cemetery

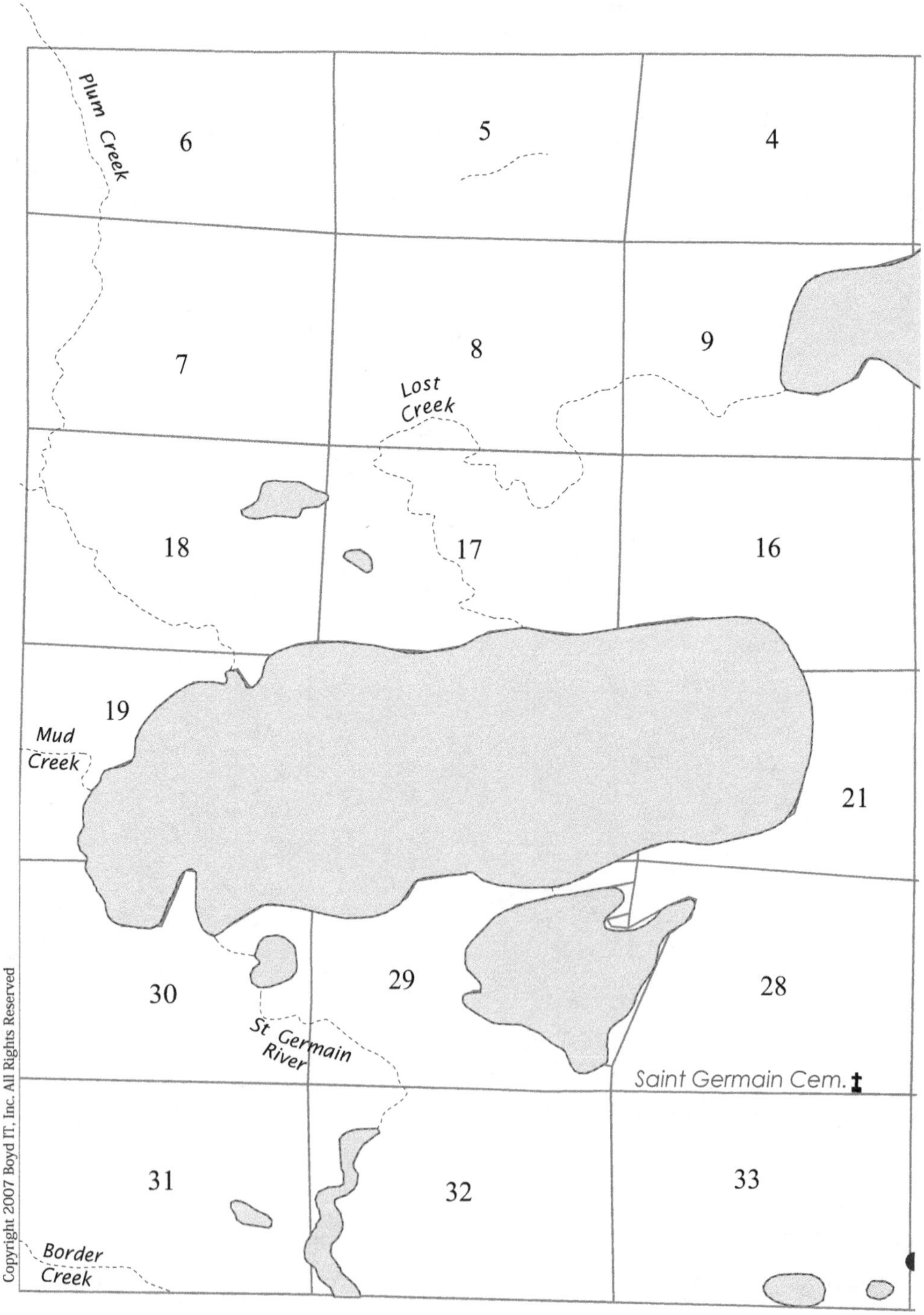

Plum Creek

6

5

4

7

8

9

Lost Creek

18

17

16

19

Mud Creek

21

30

29

28

St Germain River

Saint Germain Cem.

31

32

33

Border Creek

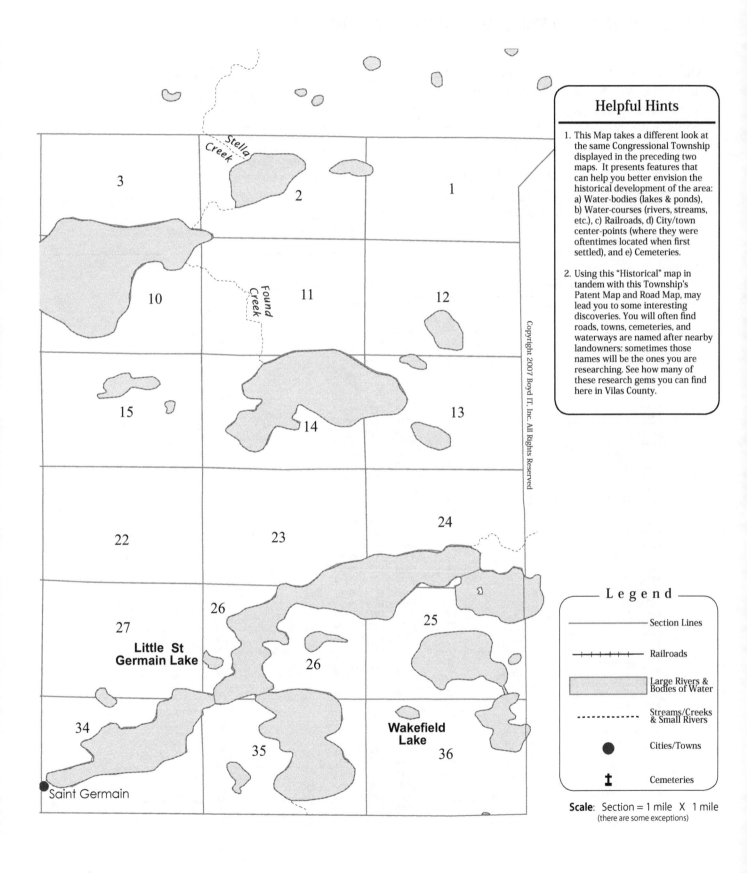

Helpful Hints

1. This Map takes a different look at the same Congressional Township displayed in the preceding two maps. It presents features that can help you better envision the historical development of the area: a) Water-bodies (lakes & ponds), b) Water-courses (rivers, streams, etc.), c) Railroads, d) City/town center-points (where they were oftentimes located when first settled), and e) Cemeteries.

2. Using this "Historical" map in tandem with this Township's Patent Map and Road Map, may lead you to some interesting discoveries. You will often find roads, towns, cemeteries, and waterways are named after nearby landowners: sometimes those names will be the ones you are researching. See how many of these research gems you can find here in Vilas County.

Stella Creek

Found Creek

3

2

1

10

11

12

15

14

13

22

23

24

26

27

25

Little St Germain Lake

26

34

35

Wakefield Lake

36

Saint Germain

Legend

———————— Section Lines

—+—+—+—+— Railroads

▭ Large Rivers & Bodies of Water

- - - - - - - Streams/Creeks & Small Rivers

● Cities/Towns

† Cemeteries

Scale: Section = 1 mile X 1 mile
(there are some exceptions)

Map Group 31: Index to Land Patents

Township 40-North Range 9-East (4th PM - 1831 MN/WI)

After you locate an individual in this Index, take note of the Section and Section Part then proceed to the Land Patent map on the pages immediately following. You should have no difficulty locating the corresponding parcel of land.

The "For More Info" Column will lead you to more information about the underlying Patents. See the *Legend* at right, and the "How to Use this Book" chapter, for more information.

```
                    LEGEND
            "For More Info . . . " column
A = Authority (Legislative Act, See Appendix "A")
B = Block or Lot (location in Section unknown)
C = Cancelled Patent
F = Fractional Section
G = Group  (Multi-Patentee Patent, see Appendix "C")
V = Overlaps another Parcel
R = Re-Issued (Parcel patented more than once)

(A & G items require you to look in the Appendixes referred
to above. All other Letter-designations followed by a number
require you to locate line-items in this index that possess
the ID number found after the letter).
```

ID	Individual in Patent	Sec.	Sec. Part	Date Issued	Other Counties	For More Info . . .
5264	ALEXANDER, Walter	13	SWSE	1890-07-15		A1
5265	" "	24	SENE	1890-07-15		A1
5129	ALLEN, Frank	18	1	1884-06-30		A1 G4
5130	" "	7	SWNE	1884-06-30		A1 G4
5240	ANDREWS, Orlin	27	N½SW	1873-06-10		A1 G7
5241	" "	27	SENW	1873-06-10		A1 G7
5242	" "	27	SWSE	1873-06-10		A1 G7
5243	" "	28	SESE	1873-06-10		A1 G7
5244	" "	33	9	1873-06-10		A1 G7
5245	" "	34	5	1873-06-10		A1 G7
5246	" "	34	NWSW	1873-06-10		A1 G7
5247	" "	35	7	1873-06-10		A1 G7
5248	" "	35	NENW	1873-06-10		A1 G7
5190	ANSON, Leonard	9	SESW	1889-05-09		A1 G8
5131	ARNDT, Fred	33	7	1897-12-01		A1
5132	" "	33	8	1897-12-01		A1
5113	BEGLE, Charles A	22	9	1885-06-12		A1
5123	BROWN, Edward D	32	5	1875-02-20		A1
5124	" "	32	6	1875-02-20		A1
5125	" "	32	7	1875-02-20		A1
5157	BROWN, Isaac	23	SENE	1873-05-01		A1
5158	" "	24	N½SW	1873-05-01		A1
5159	" "	24	S½NW	1873-05-01		A1
5161	" "	24	SWSW	1873-05-01		A1
5162	" "	24	W½SE	1873-05-01		A1
5163	" "	26	S½SW	1873-05-01		A1
5164	" "	27	NWSE	1873-05-01		A1
5165	" "	27	S½SW	1873-05-01		A1
5166	" "	27	SESE	1873-05-01		A1
5167	" "	27	SWNE	1873-05-01		A1
5168	" "	34	1	1873-05-01		A1
5169	" "	34	2	1873-05-01		A1
5170	" "	34	7	1873-05-01		A1
5171	" "	34	8	1873-05-01		A1
5172	" "	35	10	1873-05-01		A1
5173	" "	35	3	1873-05-01		A1
5174	" "	35	4	1873-05-01		A1
5175	" "	35	8	1873-05-01		A1
5176	" "	35	9	1873-05-01		A1
5177	" "	35	NWNW	1873-05-01		A1
5178	" "	35	SENW	1873-05-01		A1
5160	" "	24	SESE	1873-11-15		A1
5180	CAMPBELL, James	13	SENE	1907-04-11		A3
5104	CO, Alexander Stewart Lumber	3	SESW	1889-05-31		A1
5105	" "	3	SWNW	1889-05-31		A1
5191	COHN, Leopold	10	N½SE	1872-02-20		A1

ID	Individual in Patent	Sec.	Sec. Part	Date Issued	Other Counties	For More Info . . .
5192	COHN, Leopold (Cont'd)	10	SESE	1872-02-20		A1
5193	" "	10	SW	1872-02-20		A1
5194	" "	10	SWNE	1872-02-20		A1
5195	" "	10	W½NW	1872-02-20		A1
5196	" "	11	N½SW	1872-02-20		A1
5197	" "	11	SESW	1872-02-20		A1
5198	" "	15	E½NW	1872-02-20		A1
5199	" "	15	NWNW	1872-02-20		A1
5200	" "	15	SWNE	1872-02-20		A1
5201	" "	17	S½NW	1872-02-20		A1
5202	" "	17	S½SE	1872-02-20		A1
5203	" "	17	SW	1872-02-20		A1
5211	" "	19	S½SE	1872-02-20		A1 G51
5212	" "	20	NE	1872-02-20		A1 G51
5204	" "	20	NENW	1872-02-20		A1
5213	" "	20	SENW	1872-02-20		A1 G51
5214	" "	21	NW	1872-02-20		A1 G51
5215	" "	21	SWNE	1872-02-20		A1 G51
5216	" "	27	3	1872-02-20		A1 G51
5217	" "	27	4	1872-02-20		A1 G51
5218	" "	29	N½	1872-02-20		A1 G51
5219	" "	29	N½SW	1872-02-20		A1 G51
5220	" "	29	SESW	1872-02-20		A1 G51
5221	" "	30	N½SE	1872-02-20		A1 G51
5222	" "	30	NE	1872-02-20		A1 G51
5223	" "	30	SWSE	1872-02-20		A1 G51 F
5224	" "	31	SWSE	1872-02-20		A1 G51
5225	" "	33	3	1872-02-20		A1 G51
5226	" "	33	4	1872-02-20		A1 G51
5227	" "	33	5	1872-02-20		A1 G51
5228	" "	33	SESE	1872-02-20		A1 G51
5229	" "	34	SESE	1872-02-20		A1 G51
5230	" "	34	SWSW	1872-02-20		A1 G51
5205	" "	8	S½NE	1872-02-20		A1
5206	" "	9	E½NE	1872-02-20		A1
5207	" "	9	E½SE	1872-02-20		A1
5208	" "	9	NESW	1872-02-20		A1
5209	" "	9	NW	1872-02-20		A1
5210	" "	9	SWNE	1872-02-20		A1
5231	COHN, Leopold S	28	W½	1873-05-01		A1 G50
5232	" "	29	SE	1873-05-01		A1 G50
5189	COMPANY, Land Log And Lumber	18	SESW	1888-07-28		A1
5234	COOK, Lyman J	2	SENE	1885-06-12		A1 G56
5134	CORWITH, Henry	15	1	1867-10-10		A1
5135	" "	15	SWNW	1867-10-10		A1
5136	" "	19	W½NW	1867-10-10		A1
5137	" "	31	5	1867-10-10		A1
5179	COTTER, J N	34	NESW	1889-05-09		A1
5233	CURRAN, Lizzie S	32	9	1883-05-15		A1
5129	DAWLEY, Anna C	18	1	1884-06-30		A1 G4
5130	" "	7	SWNE	1884-06-30		A1 G4
5187	DAY, John F	18	NWSE	1890-07-15		A1
5234	DICKENSON, George P	2	SENE	1885-06-12		A1 G56
5114	DUNBAR, Charles F	1	2	1883-05-15		A1
5115	" "	1	NESW	1883-05-15		A1
5116	" "	1	W½SW	1883-05-15		A1
5117	" "	2	3	1883-05-15		A1
5118	" "	2	4	1883-05-15		A1
5119	" "	2	NENE	1883-05-15		A1
5120	" "	3	NENW	1883-05-15		A1
5121	" "	3	S½NE	1883-05-15		A1
5190	GILKEY, George F	9	SESW	1889-05-09		A1 G8
5186	GILLETT, Joel D	6	SWSE	1883-03-30		A1
5183	GOULD, James P	36	10	1872-07-01		A1
5184	" "	36	3	1872-07-01		A1
5185	" "	36	9	1872-07-01		A1
5182	" "	18	W½SW	1873-05-01		A1
5129	GRAHAM, Daniel	18	1	1884-06-30		A1 G4
5130	" "	7	SWNE	1884-06-30		A1 G4
5150	HAMILTON, Irenus K	11	1	1872-05-10		A1 G97
5151	" "	12	1	1872-05-10		A1 G97
5152	" "	12	2	1872-05-10		A1 G97
5153	" "	13	N½NW	1872-05-10		A1 G97

ID	Individual in Patent	Sec.	Sec. Part	Date Issued	Other Counties	For More Info . . .
5154	HAMILTON, Irenus K (Cont'd)	13	N½SE	1872-05-10		A1 G97
5155	"	9	NWSE	1872-05-10		A1 G97
5156	"	9	SWSW	1872-05-10		A1 G97
5150	HAMILTON, Woodman C	11	1	1872-05-10		A1 G97
5151	"	12	1	1872-05-10		A1 G97
5152	"	12	2	1872-05-10		A1 G97
5153	"	13	N½NW	1872-05-10		A1 G97
5154	"	13	N½SE	1872-05-10		A1 G97
5155	"	9	NWSE	1872-05-10		A1 G97
5156	"	9	SWSW	1872-05-10		A1 G97
5211	HEAZLIT, James F	19	S½SE	1872-02-20		A1 G51
5212	"	20	NE	1872-02-20		A1 G51
5213	"	20	SENW	1872-02-20		A1 G51
5214	"	21	NW	1872-02-20		A1 G51
5215	"	21	SWNE	1872-02-20		A1 G51
5216	"	27	3	1872-02-20		A1 G51
5217	"	27	4	1872-02-20		A1 G51
5218	"	29	N½	1872-02-20		A1 G51
5219	"	29	N½SW	1872-02-20		A1 G51
5220	"	29	SESW	1872-02-20		A1 G51
5221	"	30	N½SE	1872-02-20		A1 G51
5222	"	30	NE	1872-02-20		A1 G51
5223	"	30	SWSE	1872-02-20		A1 G51 F
5224	"	31	SWSE	1872-02-20		A1 G51
5225	"	33	3	1872-02-20		A1 G51
5226	"	33	4	1872-02-20		A1 G51
5227	"	33	5	1872-02-20		A1 G51
5228	"	33	SESE	1872-02-20		A1 G51
5229	"	34	SESE	1872-02-20		A1 G51
5230	"	34	SWSW	1872-02-20		A1 G51
5181	INGERSOLL, James H	32	10	1883-05-15		A1
5231	KARGER, Simon	28	W½	1873-05-01		A1 G50
5232	"	29	SE	1873-05-01		A1 G50
5126	KOHL, Emma	18	NESE	1884-06-30		A1 G124
5126	KOHL, H A	18	NESE	1884-06-30		A1 G124
5190	LANDERS, John	9	SESW	1889-05-09		A1 G8
5128	LAWLER, Finn	18	3	1900-07-30		A1
5106	LOVEJOY, Allen P	3	N½NE	1872-05-10		A1
5107	"	5	NENW	1872-05-10		A1
5240	MCCORD, Myron H	27	N½SW	1873-06-10		A1 G7
5241	"	27	SENW	1873-06-10		A1 G7
5242	"	27	SWSE	1873-06-10		A1 G7
5243	"	28	SESE	1873-06-10		A1 G7
5244	"	33	9	1873-06-10		A1 G7
5245	"	34	5	1873-06-10		A1 G7
5246	"	34	NWSW	1873-06-10		A1 G7
5247	"	35	7	1873-06-10		A1 G7
5248	"	35	NENW	1873-06-10		A1 G7
5236	"	32	11	1873-11-15		A1 G138
5237	"	34	6	1873-11-15		A1 G138
5238	"	36	1	1873-11-15		A1 G138
5263	MERRICK, Thomas	14	2	1885-06-12		A1
5298	MILLER, Wilmot H	32	8	1889-03-29		A1
5133	MURRAY, Gratton	25	NENE	1874-08-01		A1
5231	NAST, Daniel	28	W½	1873-05-01		A1 G50
5232	"	29	SE	1873-05-01		A1 G50
5108	OBERHOLTZER, Andrew J	13	SWNE	1905-07-13		A3
5270	PATRICK, William S	1	3	1872-11-01		A1
5271	"	10	SWSE	1872-11-01		A1
5272	"	11	2	1872-11-01		A1
5273	"	11	3	1872-11-01		A1
5274	"	12	4	1872-11-01		A1
5275	"	12	5	1872-11-01		A1
5276	"	14	1	1872-11-01		A1
5277	"	15	2	1872-11-01		A1
5278	"	18	SESE	1872-11-01		A1
5279	"	22	1	1872-11-01		A1
5280	"	22	8	1872-11-01		A1
5281	"	22	NENE	1872-11-01		A1
5282	"	23	N½NE	1872-11-01		A1 V5146
5283	"	24	NWNW	1872-11-01		A1
5284	"	26	1	1872-11-01		A1
5285	"	26	4	1872-11-01		A1

ID	Individual in Patent	Sec.	Sec. Part	Date Issued	Other Counties	For More Info . . .
5286	PATRICK, William S (Cont'd)	27	1	1872-11-01		A1
5287	" "	27	2	1872-11-01		A1
5288	" "	28	1	1872-11-01		A1
5289	" "	28	NESE	1872-11-01		A1
5290	" "	28	SWSE	1872-11-01		A1
5291	" "	31	N½NE	1872-11-01		A1
5292	" "	34	3	1872-11-01		A1
5293	" "	34	4	1872-11-01		A1
5294	" "	4	5	1872-11-01		A1
5295	" "	5	1	1872-11-01		A1
5296	" "	9	NWSW	1872-11-01		A1
5297	" "	9	SWSE	1872-11-01		A1
5249	PETERS, Richard G	17	N½NW	1883-09-15		A1
5250	" "	18	2	1883-09-15		A1
5251	" "	18	E½NE	1883-09-15		A1
5252	" "	6	S½NW	1883-09-15		A1
5253	" "	6	SW	1883-09-15		A1
5254	" "	7	S½	1883-09-15		A1
5255	" "	8	W½NW	1883-09-15		A1
5256	" "	8	W½SW	1883-09-15		A1
5239	PILLSBURY, Oliver P	8	SESW	1885-01-15		A1
5140	POLAR, Hiram B	33	2	1873-06-10		A1
5141	" "	33	NESE	1873-06-10		A1
5142	" "	34	SESW	1873-06-10		A1
5143	" "	35	5	1873-06-10		A1
5144	" "	36	5	1873-06-10		A1
5145	" "	36	8	1873-06-10		A1
5269	RACES, William	33	1	1914-10-24		A1
5236	ROCKWELL, A G	32	11	1873-11-15		A1 G138
5237	" "	34	6	1873-11-15		A1 G138
5238	" "	36	1	1873-11-15		A1 G138
5260	SCOTT, Thomas B	18	SWSE	1883-04-20		A1
5261	" "	27	SWNW	1883-04-20		A1
5262	" "	5	2	1883-04-20		A1
5257	" "	12	SWNE	1883-05-15		A1
5258	" "	14	E½NW	1883-05-15		A1
5259	" "	14	W½NE	1883-05-15		A1
5127	SHEPARD, Eugene S	35	NWNE	1874-08-01		A1
5138	SHERRY, Henry	18	4	1885-05-09		A1
5146	SMITH, Hiram	23	NENE	1882-02-10		A1 V5282
5147	" "	23	SWNE	1882-02-10		A1
5148	" "	24	NESE	1882-02-10		A1 G164
5149	" "	24	SWNE	1882-02-10		A1 G164
5139	STEINBERG, Henry	36	6	1872-07-01		A1 G167
5139	STEINBERG, Herman	36	6	1872-07-01		A1 G167
5268	TELLEFSON, William C	2	1	1906-04-14		A3
5122	TELLER, David A	17	N½SE	1873-06-10		A1
5148	VAN OSTRAND, D C	24	NESE	1882-02-10		A1 G164
5149	" "	24	SWNE	1882-02-10		A1 G164
5129	WASTE, Lee	18	1	1884-06-30		A1 G4
5130	" "	7	SWNE	1884-06-30		A1 G4
5235	WELCH, Mike	3	SENW	1910-01-24		A3
5266	WEST, William A	13	SESE	1907-02-25		A3
5267	" "	24	NENE	1907-02-25		A3
5109	WINTON, C J	6	N½NW	1889-05-09		A1 F
5110	" "	6	NWSE	1889-05-09		A1
5111	" "	6	W½NE	1889-05-09		A1 F
5112	" "	7	NW	1889-05-09		A1 F
5188	WOODLOCK, John	24	SESW	1883-03-30		A1

Patent Map

T40-N R9-E
4th PM - 1831 MN/WI

Map Group 31

Township Statistics

Parcels Mapped	:	195
Number of Patents	:	68
Number of Individuals	:	61
Patentees Identified	:	49
Number of Surnames	:	56
Multi-Patentee Parcels	:	49
Oldest Patent Date	:	10/10/1867
Most Recent Patent	:	10/24/1914
Block/Lot Parcels	:	71
Parcels Re - Issued	:	0
Parcels that Overlap	:	2
Cities and Towns	:	0
Cemeteries	:	0

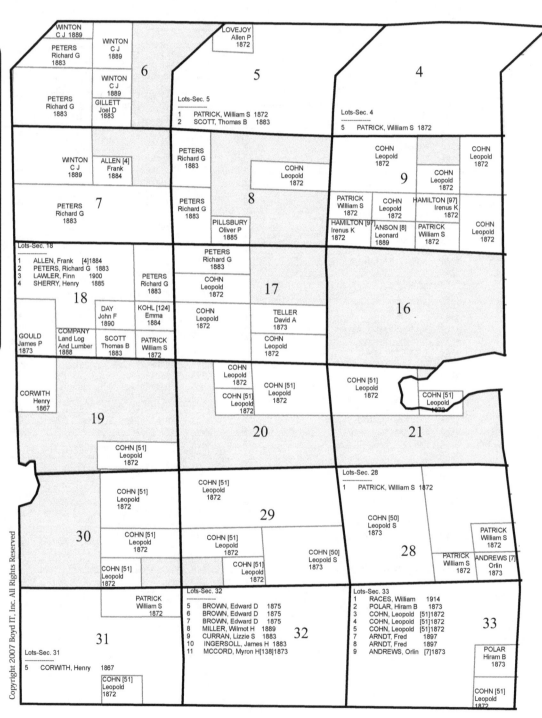

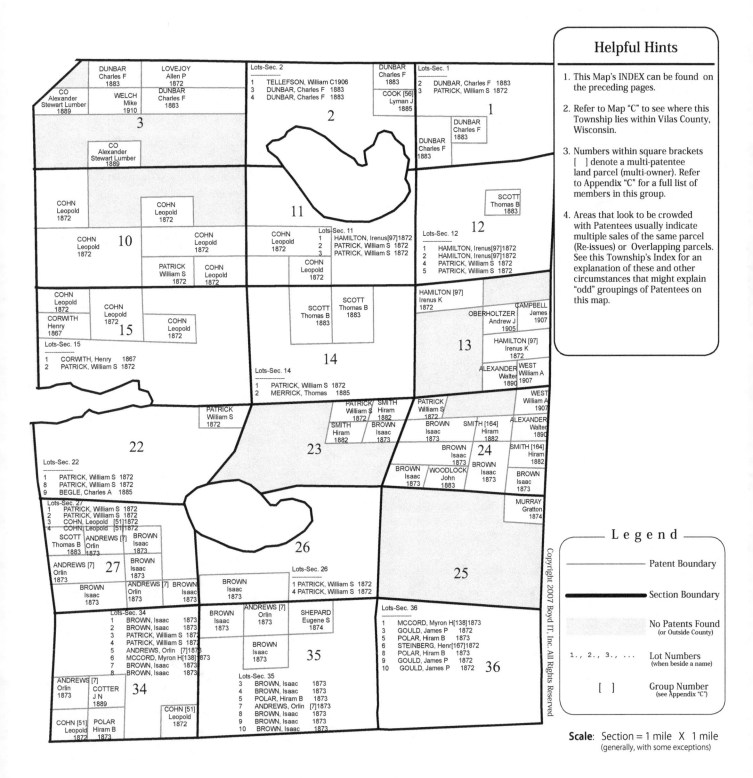

Helpful Hints

1. This Map's INDEX can be found on the preceding pages.

2. Refer to Map "C" to see where this Township lies within Vilas County, Wisconsin.

3. Numbers within square brackets [ ] denote a multi-patentee land parcel (multi-owner). Refer to Appendix "C" for a full list of members in this group.

4. Areas that look to be crowded with Patentees usually indicate multiple sales of the same parcel (Re-issues) or Overlapping parcels. See this Township's Index for an explanation of these and other circumstances that might explain "odd" groupings of Patentees on this map.

DUNBAR Charles F 1883
LOVEJOY Allen P 1872
CO Alexander Stewart Lumber 1889
WELCH Mike 1910
DUNBAR Charles F 1883

Lots-Sec. 2
1 TELLEFSON, William C 1906
3 DUNBAR, Charles F 1883
4 DUNBAR, Charles F 1883

DUNBAR Charles F 1883
COOK [56] Lyman J 1885

Lots-Sec. 1
2 DUNBAR, Charles F 1883
3 PATRICK, William S 1872

3

2

1

CO Alexander Stewart Lumber 1889

DUNBAR Charles F 1883

DUNBAR Charles F 1883

COHN Leopold 1872
COHN Leopold 1872

11

SCOTT Thomas B 1883

COHN Leopold 1872
10
COHN Leopold 1872

COHN Leopold 1872

Lots-Sec. 11
1 HAMILTON, Irenus [97]1872
2 PATRICK, William S 1872
3 PATRICK, William S 1872

Lots-Sec. 12
1 HAMILTON, Irenus [97]1872
2 HAMILTON, Irenus [97]1872
4 PATRICK, William S 1872
5 PATRICK, William S 1872

12

PATRICK William S 1872
COHN Leopold 1872

COHN Leopold 1872

HAMILTON [97] Irenus K 1872

CAMPBELL James 1907

COHN Leopold 1872
COHN Leopold 1872

SCOTT Thomas B 1883
SCOTT Thomas B 1883

OBERHOLTZER Andrew J 1905

CORWITH Henry 1867
15
COHN Leopold 1872

14

HAMILTON [97] Irenus K 1872

13

Lots-Sec. 15
1 CORWITH, Henry 1867
2 PATRICK, William S 1872

Lots-Sec. 14
1 PATRICK, William S 1872
2 MERRICK, Thomas 1885

ALEXANDER Walter 1890
WEST William A 1907

WEST William A 1907

PATRICK William S 1872
PATRICK William S 1872
SMITH Hiram 1882
PATRICK William S 1872

ALEXANDER Walter 1890

SMITH Hiram 1882
BROWN Isaac 1873
BROWN Isaac 1873
SMITH Hiram 1882

SMITH [164] Hiram 1882

22

23

BROWN Isaac 1873

24

BROWN Isaac 1873
BROWN Isaac 1873

Lots-Sec. 22
1 PATRICK, William S 1872
8 PATRICK, William S 1872
9 BEGLE, Charles A 1885

BROWN Isaac 1873
WOODLOCK John 1883
BROWN Isaac 1873

BROWN Isaac 1873

MURRAY Gratton 1874

Lots-Sec. 27
1 PATRICK, William S 1872
2 PATRICK, William S 1872
3 COHN, Leopold [51]1872
4 COHN, Leopold [51]1872

SCOTT Thomas B 1883
ANDREWS [7] Orlin 1873
BROWN Isaac 1873

26

ANDREWS [7] Orlin 1873
27
BROWN Isaac 1873

25

BROWN Isaac 1873
ANDREWS [7] Orlin 1873
BROWN Isaac 1873

BROWN Isaac 1873

Lots-Sec. 26
1 PATRICK, William S 1872
4 PATRICK, William S 1872

Lots-Sec. 34
1 BROWN, Isaac 1873
2 BROWN, Isaac 1873
3 PATRICK, William S 1872
4 PATRICK, William S 1872
5 ANDREWS, Orlin [7]1873
6 MCCORD, Myron H[138]1873
7 BROWN, Isaac 1873
8 BROWN, Isaac 1873

BROWN Isaac 1873
ANDREWS [7] Orlin 1873
SHEPARD Eugene S 1874

Lots-Sec. 36
1 MCCORD, Myron H[138]1873
3 GOULD, James P 1872
5 POLAR, Hiram B 1873
6 STEINBERG, Henr[167]1872
8 POLAR, Hiram B 1873
9 GOULD, James P 1872
10 GOULD, James P 1872

BROWN Isaac 1873

35

36

ANDREWS [7] Orlin 1873
COTTER J N 1889
34

Lots-Sec. 35
3 BROWN, Isaac 1873
4 BROWN, Isaac 1873
5 POLAR, Hiram B 1873
7 ANDREWS, Orlin [7]1873
8 BROWN, Isaac 1873
9 BROWN, Isaac 1873
10 BROWN, Isaac 1873

COHN [51] Leopold 1872

COHN [51] Leopold 1872
POLAR Hiram B 1873

Copyright 2007 Boyd IT, Inc. All Rights Reserved

Legend

———— Patent Boundary

■■■■ Section Boundary

No Patents Found (or Outside County)

1., 2., 3., ... Lot Numbers (when beside a name)

[ ] Group Number (see Appendix "C")

Scale: Section = 1 mile X 1 mile (generally, with some exceptions)

Road Map

T40-N R9-E
4th PM - 1831 MN/WI

Map Group 31

Cities & Towns
None

Cemeteries
None

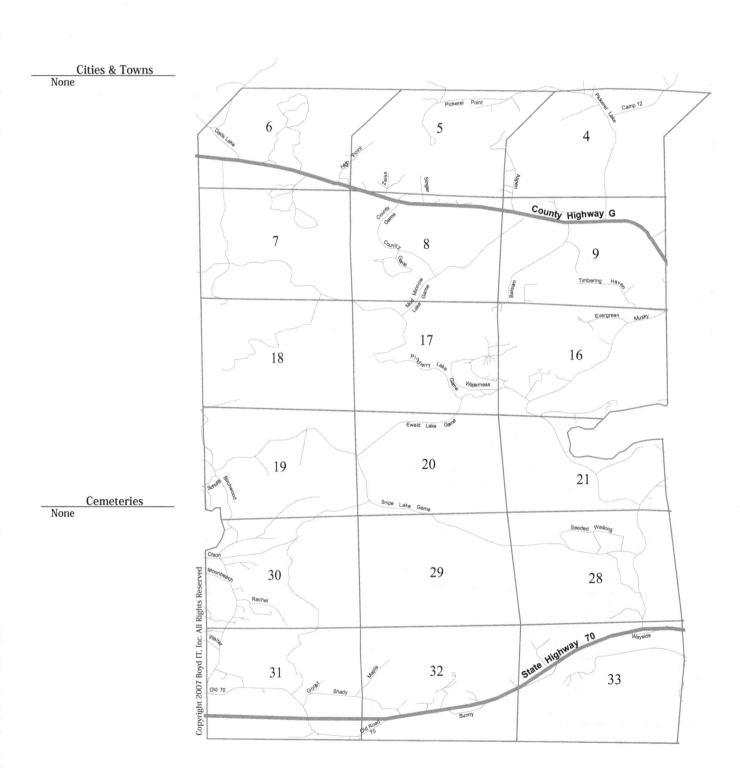

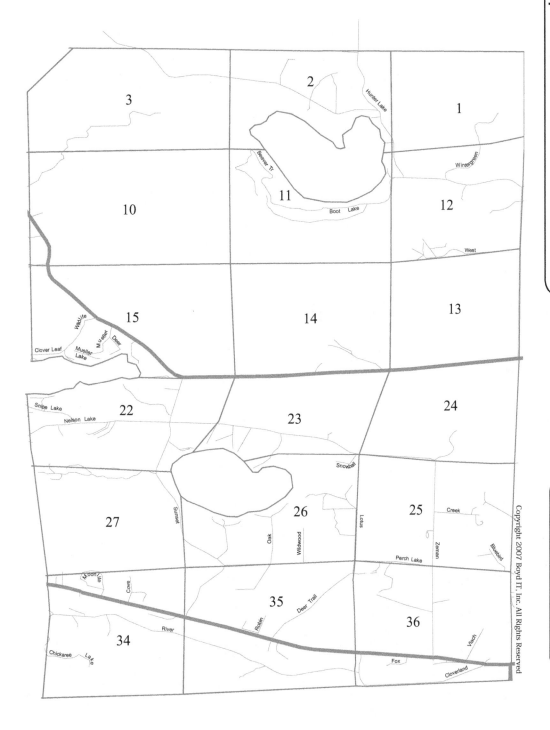

Helpful Hints

1. This road map has a number of uses, but primarily it is to help you: a) find the present location of land owned by your ancestors (at least the general area), b) find cemeteries and city-centers, and c) estimate the route/roads used by Census-takers & tax-assessors.

2. If you plan to travel to Vilas County to locate cemeteries or land parcels, please pick up a modern travel map for the area before you do. Mapping old land parcels on modern maps is not as exact a science as you might think. Just the slightest variations in public land survey coordinates, estimates of parcel boundaries, or road-map deviations can greatly alter a map's representation of how a road either does or doesn't cross a particular parcel of land.

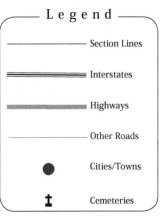

Legend

———	Section Lines
═══	Interstates
━━━	Highways
———	Other Roads
●	Cities/Towns
✝	Cemeteries

Scale: Section = 1 mile X 1 mile
(generally, with some exceptions)

Historical Map

T40-N R9-E
4th PM - 1831 MN/WI

Map Group 31

Cities & Towns
None

Cemeteries
None

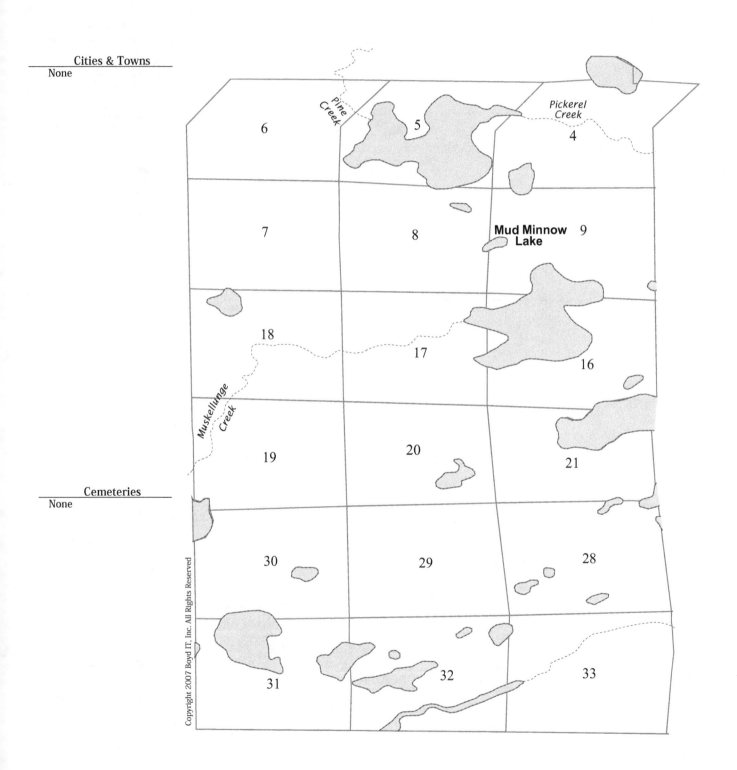

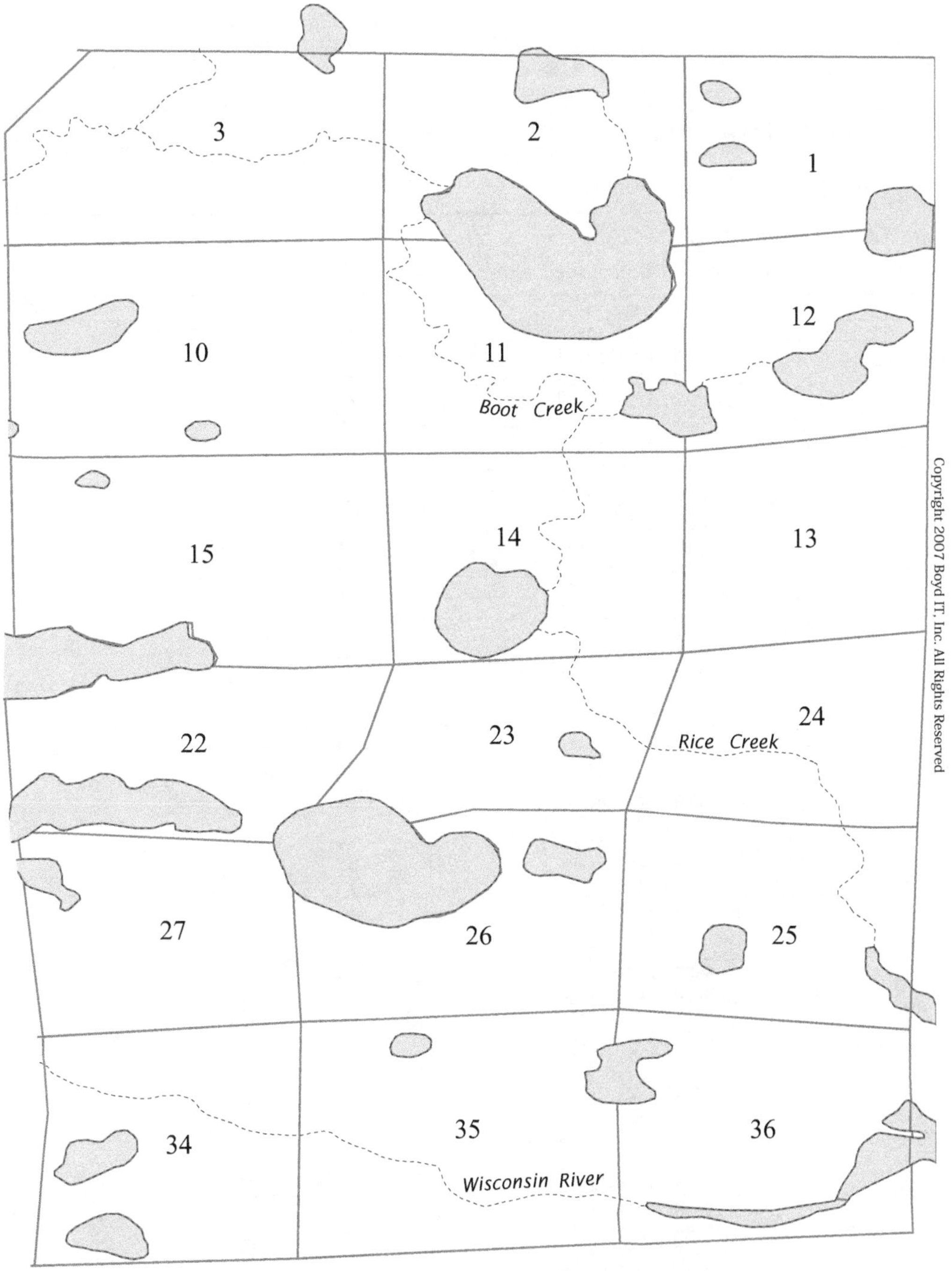
3
2
1
10
11
12
Boot Creek
15
14
13
22
23
24
Rice Creek
27
26
25
34
35
36
Wisconsin River
Copyright 2007 Boyd IT, Inc. All Rights Reserved

Helpful Hints

1. This Map takes a different look at the same Congressional Township displayed in the preceding two maps. It presents features that can help you better envision the historical development of the area: a) Water-bodies (lakes & ponds), b) Water-courses (rivers, streams, etc.), c) Railroads, d) City/town center-points (where they were oftentimes located when first settled), and e) Cemeteries.

2. Using this "Historical" map in tandem with this Township's Patent Map and Road Map, may lead you to some interesting discoveries. You will often find roads, towns, cemeteries, and waterways are named after nearby landowners: sometimes those names will be the ones you are researching. See how many of these research gems you can find here in Vilas County.

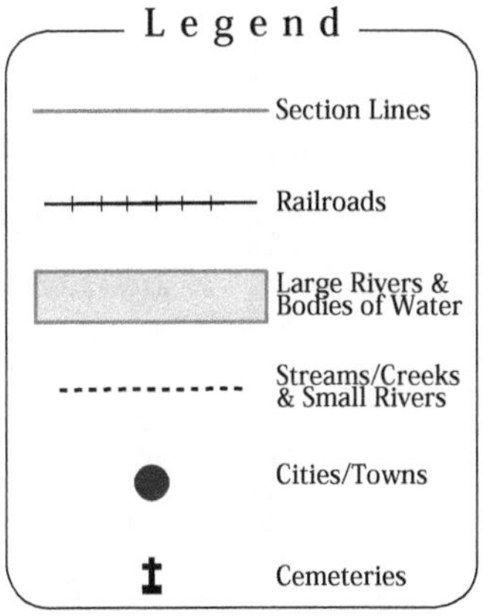
Legend
Section Lines
Railroads
Large Rivers & Bodies of Water
Streams/Creeks & Small Rivers
Cities/Towns
Cemeteries

Scale: Section = 1 mile X 1 mile
(there are some exceptions)

Map Group 32: Index to Land Patents

Township 40-North Range 10-East (4th PM - 1831 MN/WI)

After you locate an individual in this Index, take note of the Section and Section Part then proceed to the Land Patent map on the pages immediately following. You should have no difficulty locating the corresponding parcel of land.

The "For More Info" Column will lead you to more information about the underlying Patents. See the *Legend* at right, and the "How to Use this Book" chapter, for more information.

```
                        LEGEND
          "For More Info . . . " column
A = Authority (Legislative Act, See Appendix "A")
B = Block or Lot (location in Section unknown)
C = Cancelled Patent
F = Fractional Section
G = Group (Multi-Patentee Patent, see Appendix "C")
V = Overlaps another Parcel
R = Re-Issued (Parcel patented more than once)

(A & G items require you to look in the Appendixes referred
to above. All other Letter-designations followed by a number
require you to locate line-items in this index that possess
the ID number found after the letter).
```

ID	Individual in Patent	Sec.	Sec. Part	Date Issued	Other Counties	For More Info . . .
5520	ADAMS, William H	8	4	1900-10-04		A3
5521	" "	8	5	1900-10-04		A3
5522	" "	8	8	1900-10-04		A3
5498	AVERY, Orrin W	31	9	1896-08-12		A3
5505	BEMISS, Sarah	25	10	1901-10-23		A3
5506	" "	25	6	1901-10-23		A3
5507	" "	25	7	1901-10-23		A3
5508	" "	25	8	1901-10-23		A3
5330	BENSON, Elias H	21	1	1905-11-08		A3 G22
5311	BOWMAN, Charles	19	E½SW	1904-04-08		A3
5444	BRESNAN, John	9	NENE	1892-05-04		A1
5405	BROWN, Isaac	13	10	1873-05-01		A1
5406	" "	13	4	1873-05-01		A1
5407	" "	13	8	1873-05-01		A1
5408	" "	14	2	1873-05-01		A1
5409	" "	25	1	1873-05-01		A1
5411	" "	3	N½NE	1873-05-01		A1
5412	" "	3	NENW	1873-05-01		A1
5413	" "	30	4	1873-05-01		A1
5414	" "	30	5	1873-05-01		A1
5415	" "	30	W½SW	1873-05-01		A1
5416	" "	31	SESW	1873-05-01		A1
5417	" "	35	4	1873-05-01		A1
5418	" "	35	SENW	1873-05-01		A1
5419	" "	36	7	1873-05-01		A1
5420	" "	36	SWNW	1873-05-01		A1
5421	" "	5	SESW	1873-05-01		A1
5422	" "	8	2	1873-05-01		A1
5423	" "	8	SENW	1873-05-01		A1
5424	" "	9	1	1873-05-01		A1
5425	" "	9	5	1873-05-01		A1
5426	" "	9	W½NW	1873-05-01		A1
5410	" "	25	NWNW	1873-11-15		A1
5445	BUCKSTAFF, John	5	NWSE	1873-11-15		A1
5446	" "	5	NWSW	1873-11-15		A1
5447	" "	5	W½NW	1873-11-15		A1
5448	" "	8	NESW	1873-11-15		A1
5324	CARPENTER, Edward	14	4	1900-07-30		A1
5325	" "	22	6	1900-07-30		A1
5326	" "	23	4	1900-07-30		A1
5380	CARTER, George L	30	10	1904-12-29		A1
5381	" "	31	10	1904-12-29		A1
5382	" "	31	N½SE	1904-12-29		A1
5300	CO, Alexander Stewart Lumber	19	SENW	1890-07-15		A1
5327	CROKER, Edward	8	SESW	1893-08-28		A3
5328	" "	8	W½SW	1893-08-28		A3

ID	Individual in Patent	Sec.	Sec. Part	Date Issued	Other Counties	For More Info . . .
5397	CROKER, Hugh	17	NWSW	1896-08-12		A3
5398	" "	17	W½NW	1896-08-12		A3
5499	DECKERT, Otto	33	SESW	1901-10-23		A3
5483	DELEGLISE, Mary	21	S½SW	1885-01-15		A1
5484	" "	21	SWSE	1885-01-15		A1
5485	" "	27	SWNE	1885-01-15		A1
5519	DICKEY, William F	36	8	1892-05-04		A1
5456	DISHAW, Joseph	28	N½NW	1892-05-16		A1
5457	" "	28	SWNW	1892-05-16		A1
5458	" "	29	NENE	1892-05-16		A1
5369	DIXON, George A	21	W½NW	1901-11-22		A1
5509	DOCKERAY, Sarah	15	3	1897-06-07		A3 G73
5510	" "	15	E½NW	1897-06-07		A3 G73
5511	" "	15	SWNW	1897-06-07		A3 G73
5509	DOCKERAY, Wilson M	15	3	1897-06-07		A3 G73
5510	" "	15	E½NW	1897-06-07		A3 G73
5511	" "	15	SWNW	1897-06-07		A3 G73
5487	DORE, Mary Elizabeth	4	5	1923-10-18		A3 G75
5488	" "	5	5	1923-10-18		A3 G75
5500	DORE, Patrick	8	6	1921-08-15		A1
5487	" "	4	5	1923-10-18		A3 G75
5488	" "	5	5	1923-10-18		A3 G75
5449	DREGER, John	31	1	1903-05-19		A3 F
5450	" "	31	2	1903-05-19		A3 F
5391	DUNFIELD, Hiram	3	SENE	1886-08-10		A1
5385	ELLIOTT, George W	29	7	1924-12-11		A3 G81
5385	ELLIOTT, Mary Ellen	29	7	1924-12-11		A3 G81
5308	EWALD, Carl	32	N½SW	1902-03-07		A3
5309	" "	32	SESW	1902-03-07		A3
5491	FABIAN, Michael	8	NENE	1906-06-30		A3
5394	FOSTER, Horace R	21	E½NW	1888-10-11		A3
5395	" "	21	NESW	1888-10-11		A3
5396	" "	21	NWNE	1888-10-11		A3
5329	FRANK, Edward	29	8	1895-03-30		A1
5372	FULLER, George E	26	2	1904-01-27		A3
5373	" "	26	3	1904-01-27		A3
5374	" "	26	4	1904-01-27		A3
5375	" "	26	NESW	1904-01-27		A3
5376	" "	26	NWSE	1904-01-27		A3
5386	GILE, Gordon H	6	SESE	1883-05-15		A1
5516	GOODENOW, Wilber	25	SWSE	1903-05-19		A3
5517	" "	36	1	1903-05-19		A3 F
5518	" "	36	2	1903-05-19		A3 F
5438	GOULD, James P	31	5	1872-07-01		A1
5358	GROVER, Franklin B	18	N½NE	1884-06-30		A1
5359	" "	18	NESE	1884-06-30		A1
5360	" "	18	S½SE	1884-06-30		A1
5361	" "	18	SENE	1884-06-30		A1
5362	" "	18	SW	1884-06-30		A1 F
5363	" "	7	NWSE	1884-06-30		A1
5364	" "	7	S½SE	1884-06-30		A1
5399	HAMILTON, Irenus K	18	NENW	1872-05-10		A1 G97
5402	" "	6	NESE	1872-05-10		A1 G97
5403	" "	6	W½SE	1872-05-10		A1 G97
5404	" "	7	SW	1872-05-10		A1 G97
5401	" "	26	NESE	1872-07-01		A1 G97
5400	" "	18	NWNW	1872-11-01		A1 G97
5399	HAMILTON, Woodman C	18	NENW	1872-05-10		A1 G97
5402	" "	6	NESE	1872-05-10		A1 G97
5403	" "	6	W½SE	1872-05-10		A1 G97
5404	" "	7	SW	1872-05-10		A1 G97
5401	" "	26	NESE	1872-07-01		A1 G97
5400	" "	18	NWNW	1872-11-01		A1 G97
5481	HIRZEL, Mart	36	5	1906-04-14		A3 G106
5467	HOWE, Lyman	24	NESE	1867-10-10		A1 G109
5468	" "	24	SESW	1867-10-10		A1 G109
5469	" "	25	NENW	1867-10-10		A1 G109
5470	" "	25	SESW	1867-10-10		A1 G109
5471	" "	25	SWSW	1867-10-10		A1 G109
5472	" "	26	7	1867-10-10		A1 G109
5473	" "	26	8	1867-10-10		A1 G109
5474	" "	26	SWSW	1867-10-10		A1 G109
5475	" "	27	E½SW	1867-10-10		A1 G109

ID	Individual in Patent	Sec.	Sec. Part	Date Issued	Other Counties	For More Info . . .
5476	HOWE, Lyman (Cont'd)	33	NENE	1867-10-10		A1 G109
5477	" "	34	NENE	1867-10-10		A1 G109
5478	" "	35	N½NW	1867-10-10		A1 G109
5479	" "	35	SWNW	1867-10-10		A1 G109
5480	" "	36	NWNW	1867-10-10		A1 G109
5306	JACOBS, Benjamin F	29	1	1904-03-01		A3 G116 F
5427	JADISCHKE, Jacob	17	1	1901-10-23		A3
5428	" "	17	4	1901-10-23		A3
5429	" "	17	NENE	1901-10-23		A3
5319	JOHNSON, David D	28	8	1896-08-12		A3
5332	JONES, Evan J	21	2	1875-02-20		A1 G119
5333	" "	21	SWNE	1875-02-20		A1 G119
5334	" "	22	5	1875-02-20		A1 G119
5335	" "	22	7	1875-02-20		A1 G119
5336	" "	27	NENW	1875-02-20		A1 G119
5337	" "	27	NWNE	1875-02-20		A1 G119
5338	" "	28	2	1875-02-20		A1 G119
5339	" "	29	N½SE	1875-02-20		A1 G119
5340	" "	29	NWNE	1875-02-20		A1 G119
5341	" "	29	S½NE	1875-02-20		A1 G119
5492	KINNEY, Norman L	29	3	1900-10-04		A3
5493	" "	29	4	1900-10-04		A3
5494	" "	29	5	1900-10-04		A3
5495	" "	29	6	1900-10-04		A3
5496	" "	30	9	1900-10-04		A3
5497	" "	32	3	1900-10-04		A3
5523	KNOX, William H	21	3	1892-05-16		A1
5524	" "	21	4	1892-05-16		A1
5525	" "	21	5	1892-05-16		A1
5526	" "	21	NWSE	1892-05-16		A1
5365	KUENZLI, Fred A	25	2	1905-06-30		A3
5440	LAWLER, John A	32	SWSE	1893-10-30		A1
5503	LEWIS, Prince A	29	2	1905-11-08		A3
5504	" "	29	S½NW	1905-11-08		A3
5432	LOGG, James	25	3	1904-02-25		A1
5433	" "	25	4	1904-02-25		A1
5434	" "	26	1	1904-02-25		A1
5301	LOVEJOY, Allen P	5	2	1872-05-10		A1
5302	" "	5	NENW	1872-05-10		A1
5490	MAGEE, Maxwell	14	3	1902-12-30		A3 F
5331	MARCON, Emett	19	NE	1893-06-07		A3
5377	MAYO, George H	20	4	1904-09-28		A3 F
5378	" "	20	5	1904-09-28		A3 F
5379	" "	20	S½SE	1904-09-28		A3 F
5482	MAYO, Martha	21	NWSW	1903-12-31		A1
5486	MCDONALD, Mary E	15	NWNW	1882-06-30		A1
5481	MCKNIGHT, James	36	5	1906-04-14		A3 G106
5315	MCSHERRY, Charles	3	SWNE	1894-04-27		A1
5439	MEADE, Joel	1	NENW	1873-06-10		A1 G142
5310	MILLER, Charles A	25	5	1906-04-14		A3
5316	MILLER, Charley A	15	5	1897-11-22		A3
5317	" "	22	1	1897-11-22		A3
5318	" "	22	2	1897-11-22		A3
5366	MOREY, Fred	22	3	1903-04-20		A1
5367	" "	22	4	1903-04-20		A1
5368	" "	22	8	1903-04-20		A1
5435	MORGAN, James	32	N½SE	1900-06-11		A3
5436	" "	32	SESE	1900-06-11		A3
5437	" "	33	SWSW	1900-06-11		A3
5464	MORGAN, Louis W	23	5	1904-03-01		A3 F
5465	" "	23	6	1904-03-01		A3 F
5466	" "	24	3	1904-03-01		A3 F
5441	MORIN, John B	17	SWSW	1896-08-12		A3
5442	" "	20	SENW	1896-08-12		A3
5443	" "	20	W½NW	1896-08-12		A3
5299	PAFF, A R	28	1	1889-05-31		A1
5349	PALMS, Francis	11	1	1867-10-10		A1
5350	" "	11	2	1867-10-10		A1
5351	" "	13	12	1869-07-01		A1
5352	" "	13	7	1869-07-01		A1
5353	" "	15	1	1869-07-01		A1
5354	" "	15	2	1869-07-01		A1
5355	" "	27	4	1869-07-01		A1

ID	Individual in Patent	Sec.	Sec. Part	Date Issued	Other Counties	For More Info . . .
5527	PERCIVAL, William M	35	3	1892-05-04		A1
5312	PERRY, Charles L	28	3	1892-03-07		A3
5313	" "	28	4	1892-03-07		A3
5314	" "	28	SENW	1892-03-07		A3
5452	PETEY, John W	30	6	1905-03-30		A3
5453	" "	30	7	1905-03-30		A3
5454	" "	30	8	1905-03-30		A3
5455	" "	30	NESE	1905-03-30		A3
5383	PHELPS, George M	31	8	1882-05-20		A1
5320	PUNCHES, De Witt C	30	1	1901-05-08		A3
5321	" "	30	2	1901-05-08		A3
5322	" "	30	3	1901-05-08		A3
5323	" "	30	NENW	1901-05-08		A3
5370	PUNCHES, George B	20	7	1900-06-28		A3
5371	" "	20	8	1900-06-28		A3
5467	RABLIN, John	24	NESE	1867-10-10		A1 G109
5468	" "	24	SESW	1867-10-10		A1 G109
5469	" "	25	NENW	1867-10-10		A1 G109
5470	" "	25	SESW	1867-10-10		A1 G109
5471	" "	25	SWSW	1867-10-10		A1 G109
5472	" "	26	7	1867-10-10		A1 G109
5473	" "	26	8	1867-10-10		A1 G109
5474	" "	26	SWSW	1867-10-10		A1 G109
5475	" "	27	E½SW	1867-10-10		A1 G109
5476	" "	33	NENE	1867-10-10		A1 G109
5477	" "	34	NENE	1867-10-10		A1 G109
5478	" "	35	N½NW	1867-10-10		A1 G109
5479	" "	35	SWNW	1867-10-10		A1 G109
5480	" "	36	NWNW	1867-10-10		A1 G109
5489	RETTLER, Mathies	19	SWSW	1904-01-11		A1
5439	RIPLEY, Sylvanus	1	NENW	1873-06-10		A1 G142
5459	ROGERS, Judson B	14	NESW	1901-12-30		A3
5460	" "	14	NWSE	1901-12-30		A3
5461	" "	14	S½SE	1901-12-30		A3
5330	ROSENBERRY, Marvin B	21	1	1905-11-08		A3 G22
5385	SANBORN, George F	29	7	1924-12-11		A3 G81
5513	SCOTT, Thomas B	4	SESE	1883-04-20		A1
5514	" "	7	W½NE	1883-05-15		A1
5512	" "	3	SWSW	1883-09-15		A1
5306	SEVERANCE, Joseph C	29	1	1904-03-01		A3 G116 F
5385	SMITH, David A	29	7	1924-12-11		A3 G81
5393	SMITH, Hiram	30	W½NW	1882-02-10		A1 G164 F
5392	" "	5	SWSW	1882-02-10		A1
5303	SOMERS, Angus	19	N½NW	1903-03-17		A3 C F
5304	" "	19	NWSW	1903-03-17		A3 C F
5305	" "	19	SWNW	1903-03-17		A3 C F
5384	ST LOUIS, GEORGE	19	SE	1898-12-01		A3
5387	STEINBERG, Henry	31	6	1872-07-01		A1 G167
5388	" "	31	7	1872-07-01		A1 G167
5389	" "	31	S½SE	1872-07-01		A1 G167
5390	" "	32	SWSW	1872-07-01		A1 G167
5387	STEINBERG, Herman	31	6	1872-07-01		A1 G167
5388	" "	31	7	1872-07-01		A1 G167
5389	" "	31	S½SE	1872-07-01		A1 G167
5390	" "	32	SWSW	1872-07-01		A1 G167
5515	STONE, Timothy E	7	E½NE	1877-04-25		A1
5356	TAMBLING, Frank C	28	6	1890-04-22		A1
5357	" "	28	7	1890-04-22		A1
5462	THOMPSON, Leo C	27	1	0012-00-00		A3
5463	" "	27	2	0012-00-00		A3
5430	TOLMAN, James B	5	3	1872-11-01		A1
5431	" "	5	NESW	1872-11-01		A1
5332	TOWNSEND, Danville L	21	2	1875-02-20		A1 G119
5333	" "	21	SWNE	1875-02-20		A1 G119
5334	" "	22	5	1875-02-20		A1 G119
5335	" "	22	7	1875-02-20		A1 G119
5336	" "	27	NENW	1875-02-20		A1 G119
5337	" "	27	NWNE	1875-02-20		A1 G119
5338	" "	28	2	1875-02-20		A1 G119
5339	" "	29	N½SE	1875-02-20		A1 G119
5340	" "	29	NWNE	1875-02-20		A1 G119
5341	" "	29	S½NE	1875-02-20		A1 G119
5342	TOWNSEND, Evan	5	7	1873-05-01		A1

ID	Individual in Patent	Sec.	Sec. Part	Date Issued	Other Counties	For More Info . . .
5343	TOWNSEND, Evan (Cont'd)	5	SENW	1873-05-01		A1
5393	VAN OSTRAND, D C	30	W½NW	1882-02-10		A1 G164 F
5307	WALSH, Bridget A	15	4	1905-06-30		A3
5501	WALSH, Patrick	36	3	1893-09-28		A1
5502	" "	36	4	1893-09-28		A1
5332	WELLINGTON, Richard H	21	2	1875-02-20		A1 G119
5333	" "	21	SWNE	1875-02-20		A1 G119
5334	" "	22	5	1875-02-20		A1 G119
5335	" "	22	7	1875-02-20		A1 G119
5336	" "	27	NENW	1875-02-20		A1 G119
5337	" "	27	NWNE	1875-02-20		A1 G119
5338	" "	28	2	1875-02-20		A1 G119
5339	" "	29	N½SE	1875-02-20		A1 G119
5340	" "	29	NWNE	1875-02-20		A1 G119
5341	" "	29	S½NE	1875-02-20		A1 G119
5451	WISE, John H	20	6	1901-10-23		A3
5344	YOUNG, Florien S	14	5	1904-09-28		A3 F
5345	" "	23	1	1904-09-28		A3 F
5346	" "	23	2	1904-09-28		A3 F
5347	" "	23	3	1904-09-28		A3 F
5348	" "	24	4	1904-09-28		A3 F

Patent Map

T40-N R10-E
4th PM - 1831 MN/WI

Map Group 32

Township Statistics

Parcels Mapped	:	229
Number of Patents	:	106
Number of Individuals	:	98
Patentees Identified	:	85
Number of Surnames	:	85
Multi-Patentee Parcels	:	45
Oldest Patent Date	:	10/10/1867
Most Recent Patent	:	12/11/1924
Block/Lot Parcels	:	117
Parcels Re - Issued	:	0
Parcels that Overlap	:	0
Cities and Towns	:	1
Cemeteries	:	0

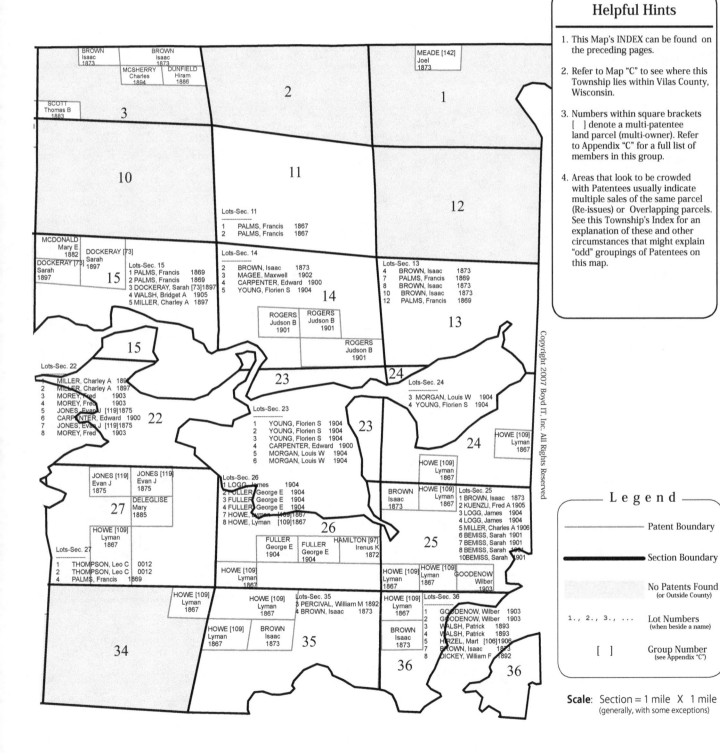

Helpful Hints

1. This Map's INDEX can be found on the preceding pages.

2. Refer to Map "C" to see where this Township lies within Vilas County, Wisconsin.

3. Numbers within square brackets [ ] denote a multi-patentee land parcel (multi-owner). Refer to Appendix "C" for a full list of members in this group.

4. Areas that look to be crowded with Patentees usually indicate multiple sales of the same parcel (Re-issues) or Overlapping parcels. See this Township's Index for an explanation of these and other circumstances that might explain "odd" groupings of Patentees on this map.

BROWN
Isaac
1873

BROWN
Isaac
1873

MCSHERRY
Charles
1894

DUNFIELD
Hiram
1886

MEADE [142]
Joel
1873

SCOTT
Thomas B
1883

3

2

1

10

11

12

Lots-Sec. 11
1   PALMS, Francis   1867
2   PALMS, Francis   1867

MCDONALD
Mary E
1882

DOCKERAY [73]
Sarah
1897

DOCKERAY [73]
Sarah
1897

15

Lots-Sec. 15
1 PALMS, Francis   1869
2 PALMS, Francis   1869
3 DOCKERAY, Sarah [73]1897
4 WALSH, Bridget A 1905
5 MILLER, Charley A 1897

Lots-Sec. 14
2   BROWN, Isaac   1873
3   MAGEE, Maxwell   1902
4   CARPENTER, Edward 1900
5   YOUNG, Florien S 1904

14

Lots-Sec. 13
4   BROWN, Isaac   1873
7   PALMS, Francis   1869
8   BROWN, Isaac   1873
10 BROWN, Isaac   1873
12 PALMS, Francis   1869

ROGERS
Judson B
1901

ROGERS
Judson B
1901

ROGERS
Judson B
1901

13

15

Lots-Sec. 22
1   MILLER, Charley A 189
2   MILLER, Charley A 1897
3   MOREY, Fred   1903
4   MOREY, Fred   1903
5   JONES, Evan J [119]1875
6   CARPENTER, Edward 1900
7   JONES, Evan J [119]1875
8   MOREY, Fred   1903

22

23

24

Lots-Sec. 24
3   MORGAN, Louis W   1904
4   YOUNG, Florien S 1904

Lots-Sec. 23
1   YOUNG, Florien S 1904
2   YOUNG, Florien S 1904
3   YOUNG, Florien S 1904
4   CARPENTER, Edward 1900
5   MORGAN, Louis W   1904
6   MORGAN, Louis W   1904

23

24

HOWE [109]
Lyman
1867

JONES [119]
Evan J
1875

JONES [119]
Evan J
1875

DELEGLISE
Mary
1885

27

HOWE [109]
Lyman
1867

Lots-Sec. 26
1 LOGG, James   1904
2 FULLER, George E 1904
3 FULLER, George E 1904
4 FULLER, George E 1904
7 HOWE, Lyman [109]1867
8 HOWE, Lyman [109]1867

26

HOWE [109]
Lyman
1867

BROWN
Isaac
1873

HOWE [109]
Lyman
1867

Lots-Sec. 25
1 BROWN, Isaac   1873
2 KUENZLI, Fred A 1905
3 LOGG, James   1904
4 LOGG, James   1904
5 MILLER, Charles A 1906
6 BEMISS, Sarah   1901
7 BEMISS, Sarah   1901
8 BEMISS, Sarah   1901
10 BEMISS, Sarah   1901

25

Lots-Sec. 27
1   THOMPSON, Leo C   0012
2   THOMPSON, Leo C   0012
4   PALMS, Francis   1869

FULLER
George E
1904

FULLER
George E
1904

HAMILTON [97]
Irenus K
1872

HOWE [109]
Lyman
1867

HOWE [109]
Lyman
1867

HOWE [109]
Lyman
1867

GOODENOW
Wilber
1903

HOWE [109]
Lyman
1867

HOWE [109]
Lyman
1867

Lots-Sec. 35
3 PERCIVAL, William M 1892
4 BROWN, Isaac   1873

HOWE [109]
Lyman
1867

Lots-Sec. 36
1   GOODENOW, Wilber   1903
2   GOODENOW, Wilber   1903
3   WALSH, Patrick   1893
4   WALSH, Patrick   1893
5   HIRZEL, Mart [106]1906
7   BROWN, Isaac   1873
8   DICKEY, William F 1892

34

HOWE [109]
Lyman
1867

BROWN
Isaac
1873

35

BROWN
Isaac
1873

36

36

Legend

———— Patent Boundary

▬▬▬▬ Section Boundary

No Patents Found
(or Outside County)

1., 2., 3., ...   Lot Numbers
(when beside a name)

[ ]   Group Number
(see Appendix "C")

Scale: Section = 1 mile X 1 mile
(generally, with some exceptions)

Road Map

T40-N R10-E
4th PM - 1831 MN/WI

Map Group 32

Cities & Towns
Eagle River

Cemeteries
None

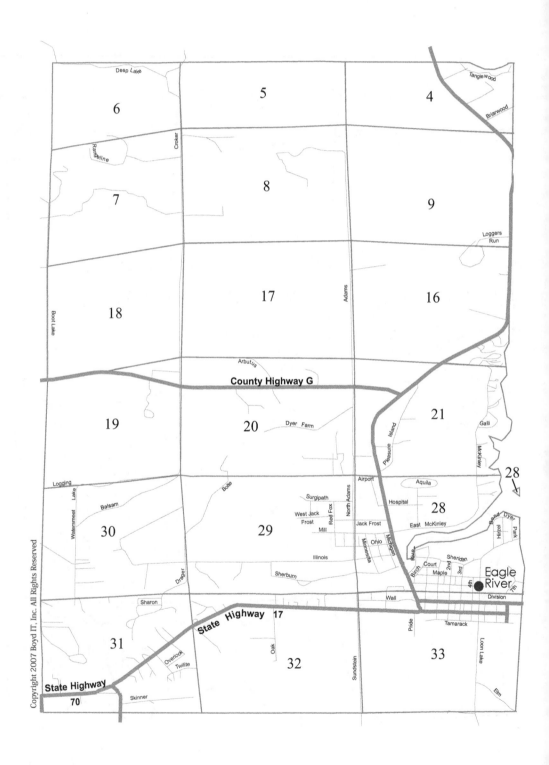

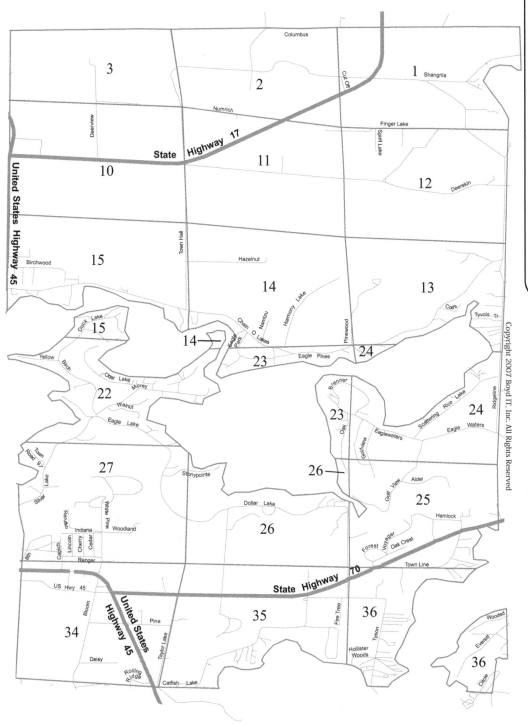

Helpful Hints

1. This road map has a number of uses, but primarily it is to help you: a) find the present location of land owned by your ancestors (at least the general area), b) find cemeteries and city-centers, and c) estimate the route/roads used by Census-takers & tax-assessors.

2. If you plan to travel to Vilas County to locate cemeteries or land parcels, please pick up a modern travel map for the area before you do. Mapping old land parcels on modern maps is not as exact a science as you might think. Just the slightest variations in public land survey coordinates, estimates of parcel boundaries, or road-map deviations can greatly alter a map's representation of how a road either does or doesn't cross a particular parcel of land.

Legend

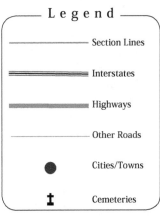

————	Section Lines
≡≡≡≡	Interstates
————	Highways
————	Other Roads
●	Cities/Towns
♰	Cemeteries

Scale: Section = 1 mile X 1 mile
(generally, with some exceptions)

Historical Map

T40-N R10-E
4th PM - 1831 MN/WI

Map Group 32

Cities & Towns

Eagle River

Cemeteries

None

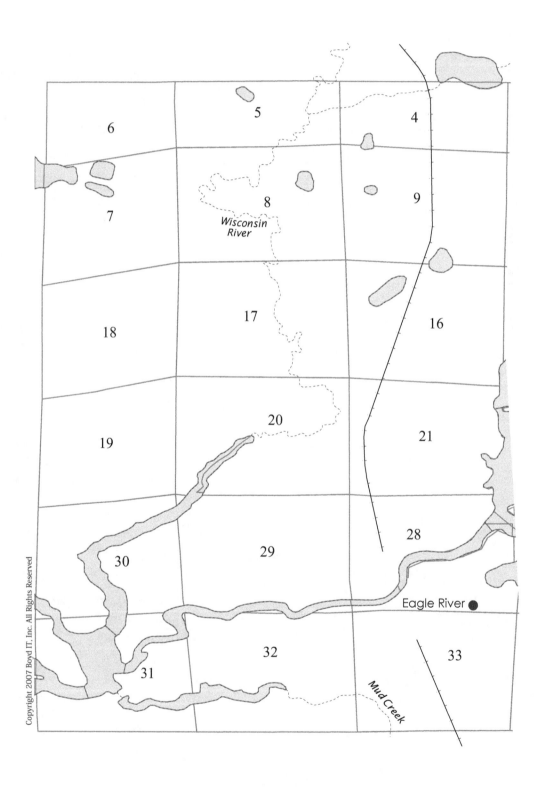

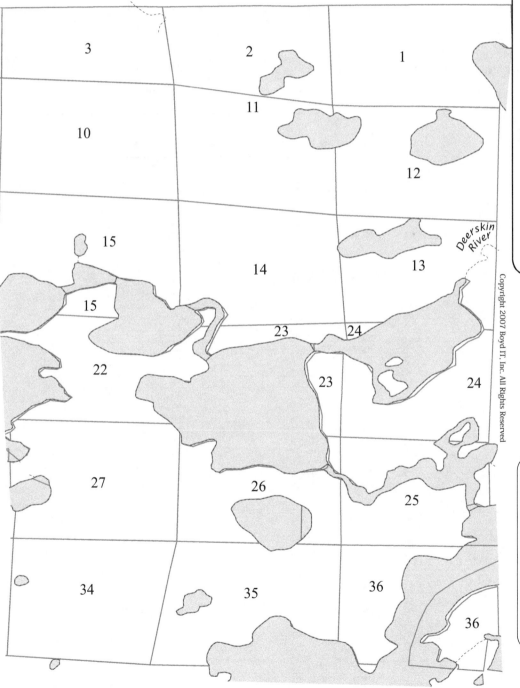

Helpful Hints

1. This Map takes a different look at the same Congressional Township displayed in the preceding two maps. It presents features that can help you better envision the historical development of the area: a) Water-bodies (lakes & ponds), b) Water-courses (rivers, streams, etc.), c) Railroads, d) City/town center-points (where they were oftentimes located when first settled), and e) Cemeteries.

2. Using this "Historical" map in tandem with this Township's Patent Map and Road Map, may lead you to some interesting discoveries. You will often find roads, towns, cemeteries, and waterways are named after nearby landowners: sometimes those names will be the ones you are researching. See how many of these research gems you can find here in Vilas County.

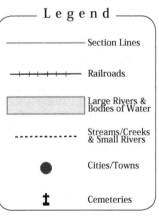

Legend

——————	Section Lines
++++++++	Railroads
� box	Large Rivers & Bodies of Water
- - - - - -	Streams/Creeks & Small Rivers
●	Cities/Towns
⊥	Cemeteries

Scale: Section = 1 mile X 1 mile
(there are some exceptions)

Map Group 33: Index to Land Patents

Township 40-North Range 11-East (4th PM - 1831 MN/WI)

After you locate an individual in this Index, take note of the Section and Section Part then proceed to the Land Patent map on the pages immediately following. You should have no difficulty locating the corresponding parcel of land.

The "For More Info" Column will lead you to more information about the underlying Patents. See the *Legend* at right, and the "How to Use this Book" chapter, for more information.

```
                    LEGEND
           "For More Info . . . " column
A = Authority (Legislative Act, See Appendix "A")
B = Block or Lot (location in Section unknown)
C = Cancelled Patent
F = Fractional Section
G = Group  (Multi-Patentee Patent, see Appendix "C")
V = Overlaps another Parcel
R = Re-Issued (Parcel patented more than once)

(A & G items require you to look in the Appendixes referred
to above. All other Letter-designations followed by a number
require you to locate line-items in this index that possess
the ID number found after the letter).
```

ID	Individual in Patent	Sec.	Sec. Part	Date Issued	Other Counties	For More Info . . .
5551	BERON, Francis	7	N½SW	1865-09-15		A1
5552	" "	7	NWSE	1865-09-15		A1
5553	" "	8	NESW	1865-09-15		A1
5560	BEYER, George	1	S½SE	1883-09-15		A1
5561	" "	1	SESW	1883-09-15		A1
5562	" "	11	SE	1883-09-15		A1
5563	" "	11	SENE	1883-09-15		A1
5564	" "	13	4	1883-09-15		A1
5565	" "	13	5	1883-09-15		A1
5566	" "	13	6	1883-09-15		A1
5567	" "	13	7	1883-09-15		A1
5579	BROWN, Isaac	21	NWSW	1873-05-01		A1
5580	" "	29	5	1873-05-01		A1
5581	" "	31	3	1873-05-01		A1
5582	" "	5	E½NW	1873-05-01		A1
5583	" "	5	NESW	1873-05-01		A1
5584	" "	5	W½NE	1873-05-01		A1
5585	" "	7	NENE	1873-05-01		A1
5535	BURNS, Daniel	30	1	1921-06-11		A1
5533	CASE, Charles	11	NENE	1910-02-11		A1
5534	CHASE, Charles	31	6	1903-10-01		A3
5586	CLEMENS, James T	31	1	1905-05-09		A3 G48
5593	CLEMENTS, John	31	10	1905-03-30		A3 G49
5572	COMPANY, Gerry Lumber	33	NWSE	1889-05-31		A1
5573	" "	33	SESE	1889-05-31		A1
5543	DASKAM, Edward	29	1	1889-05-09		A1
5541	" "	17	6	1890-07-15		A1
5542	" "	19	1	1890-07-15		A1
5544	DENT, Edward	7	NWNE	1912-07-08		A3
5595	DENTON, Louis	30	3	1894-04-27		A1
5596	" "	30	6	1894-04-27		A1
5597	" "	30	NESW	1894-04-27		A1
5603	FORSYTH, Peter N	15	E½NW	1909-02-04		A3
5574	GABRIELSON, Henry	30	4	1892-05-16		A1
5599	GILBERTSON, Meike	1	N½SE	1903-11-10		A3
5536	GRAHAM, Daniel	6	1	1897-10-25		A1
5537	" "	6	7	1897-10-25		A1
5575	HAMILTON, Irenus K	25	E½NW	1872-05-10		A1 G97
5576	" "	25	NE	1872-05-10		A1 G97
5577	" "	30	NENE	1872-07-01		A1 G97 R5578
5577	" "	30	NENE	1872-07-01		A1 G97 C R5578
5578	" "	30	NENE	1872-07-01		A1 G97 R5577
5578	" "	30	NENE	1872-07-01		A1 G97 C R5577
5575	HAMILTON, Woodman C	25	E½NW	1872-05-10		A1 G97
5576	" "	25	NE	1872-05-10		A1 G97
5577	" "	30	NENE	1872-07-01		A1 G97 R5578

ID	Individual in Patent	Sec.	Sec. Part	Date Issued	Other Counties	For More Info . . .
5577	HAMILTON, Woodman C (Cont'd)	30	NENE	1872-07-01		A1 G97 C R5578
5578	" "	30	NENE	1872-07-01		A1 G97 R5577
5578	" "	30	NENE	1872-07-01		A1 G97 C R5577
5593	HIRZEL, Mart	31	10	1905-03-30		A3 G49
5586	HIZEL, Mart	31	1	1905-05-09		A3 G48
5609	HOLLISTER, Seymour W	11	W½NE	1883-09-15		A1 G108
5598	HOWE, Lyman	19	N½SW	1867-10-10		A1 G109
5547	JONES, Evan J	19	3	1875-02-20		A1 G119
5548	" "	31	5	1875-02-20		A1 G119
5549	" "	31	8	1875-02-20		A1 G119
5550	" "	31	9	1875-02-20		A1 G119
5545	LACAU, Edward	29	8	1916-03-08		A3
5546	" "	29	9	1916-03-08		A3
5594	LAEV, Joseph	25	W½NW	1884-06-30		A1
5529	LOVEJOY, Allen P	13	1	1872-05-10		A1
5530	" "	13	2	1872-05-10		A1
5531	" "	13	3	1872-05-10		A1
5532	" "	13	NWNW	1872-05-10		A1
5528	MCCUAIG, Alexander	5	3	1913-01-10		A3
5587	MEADE, Joel	15	NWNW	1873-06-10		A1 G142
5588	" "	17	1	1873-06-10		A1 G142
5589	" "	17	2	1873-06-10		A1 G142
5590	" "	23	E½SE	1873-06-10		A1 G142
5591	" "	23	NWSE	1873-06-10		A1 G142
5592	" "	33	SWSE	1873-06-10		A1 G142
5554	PALMS, Francis	19	4	1867-10-10		A1
5557	" "	9	SENW	1867-10-10		A1
5555	" "	19	5	1869-07-01		A1
5556	" "	19	6	1869-07-01		A1
5608	PHELPS, Samantha C	29	6	1882-06-30		A1
5540	PULLING, David J	23	SWSW	1883-09-15		A1
5598	RABLIN, John	19	N½SW	1867-10-10		A1 G109
5587	RIPLEY, Sylvanus	15	NWNW	1873-06-10		A1 G142
5588	" "	17	1	1873-06-10		A1 G142
5589	" "	17	2	1873-06-10		A1 G142
5590	" "	23	E½SE	1873-06-10		A1 G142
5591	" "	23	NWSE	1873-06-10		A1 G142
5592	" "	33	SWSE	1873-06-10		A1 G142
5568	SANBORN, George F	1	NWNE	1903-11-11		A1
5604	SCHMIDT, Peter	1	E½NE	1895-02-19		A1 F
5605	" "	1	SWNE	1895-02-19		A1
5606	" "	15	SWNW	1895-02-19		A1
5607	" "	17	5	1895-02-19		A1
5610	SCOTT, Thomas B	21	N½SE	1883-09-15		A1
5611	" "	21	SESE	1883-09-15		A1
5538	SEWARD, David H	5	W½NW	1908-10-15		A3
5539	" "	5	W½SW	1908-10-15		A3
5569	STEINMETZ, George	21	NESW	1904-02-25		A1
5570	" "	21	S½SW	1904-02-25		A1
5571	" "	21	SWSE	1904-02-25		A1
5558	TAMBLING, Frank C	30	2	1892-05-04		A1
5559	" "	30	W½NW	1892-05-04		A1
5547	TOWNSEND, Danville L	19	3	1875-02-20		A1 G119
5548	" "	31	5	1875-02-20		A1 G119
5549	" "	31	8	1875-02-20		A1 G119
5550	" "	31	9	1875-02-20		A1 G119
5601	WALSH, Patrick	31	2	1893-09-28		A1
5602	" "	31	4	1893-09-28		A1
5600	WALSH, Patrick D	30	7	1906-06-08		A1
5547	WELLINGTON, Richard H	19	3	1875-02-20		A1 G119
5548	" "	31	5	1875-02-20		A1 G119
5549	" "	31	8	1875-02-20		A1 G119
5550	" "	31	9	1875-02-20		A1 G119
5609	WESCOTT, Marion	11	W½NE	1883-09-15		A1 G108
5609	WESCOTT, Sheldon P	11	W½NE	1883-09-15		A1 G108

Patent Map

T40-N R11-E
4th PM - 1831 MN/WI

Map Group 33

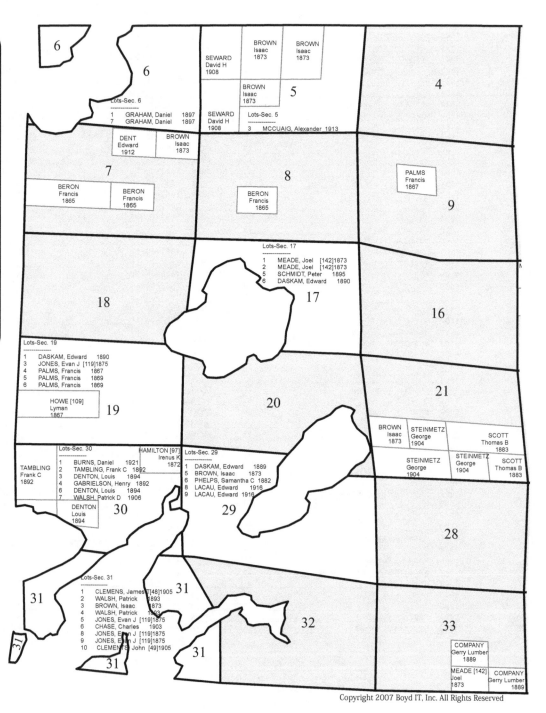

Township Statistics

Parcels Mapped	:	84
Number of Patents	:	48
Number of Individuals	:	45
Patentees Identified	:	36
Number of Surnames	:	42
Multi-Patentee Parcels	:	18
Oldest Patent Date	:	9/15/1865
Most Recent Patent	:	6/11/1921
Block/Lot Parcels	:	39
Parcels Re - Issued	:	1
Parcels that Overlap	:	0
Cities and Towns	:	0
Cemeteries	:	0

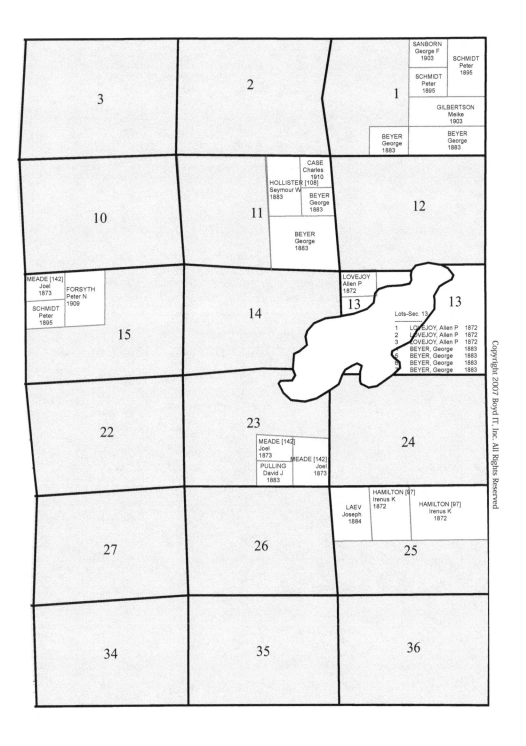

Helpful Hints

1. This Map's INDEX can be found on the preceding pages.

2. Refer to Map "C" to see where this Township lies within Vilas County, Wisconsin.

3. Numbers within square brackets [ ] denote a multi-patentee land parcel (multi-owner). Refer to Appendix "C" for a full list of members in this group.

4. Areas that look to be crowded with Patentees usually indicate multiple sales of the same parcel (Re-issues) or Overlapping parcels. See this Township's Index for an explanation of these and other circumstances that might explain "odd" groupings of Patentees on this map.

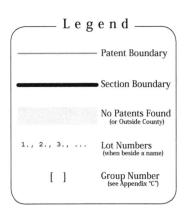

Legend

———— Patent Boundary

━━━━ Section Boundary

No Patents Found
(or Outside County)

1., 2., 3., ... Lot Numbers
(when beside a name)

[ ] Group Number
(see Appendix "C")

Scale: Section = 1 mile X 1 mile
(generally, with some exceptions)

Road Map

T40-N R11-E
4th PM - 1831 MN/WI

Map Group 33

Cities & Towns

None

Cemeteries

None

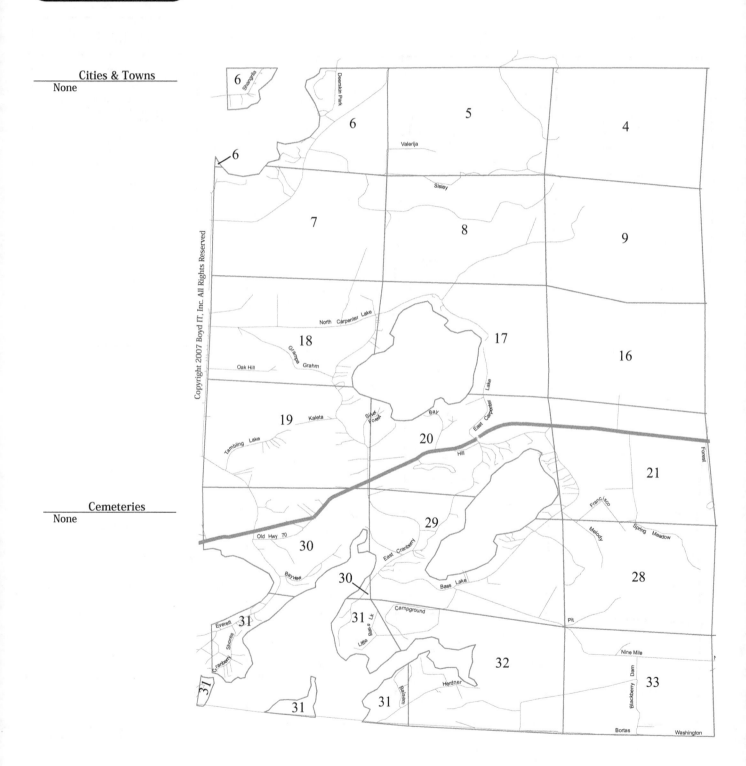

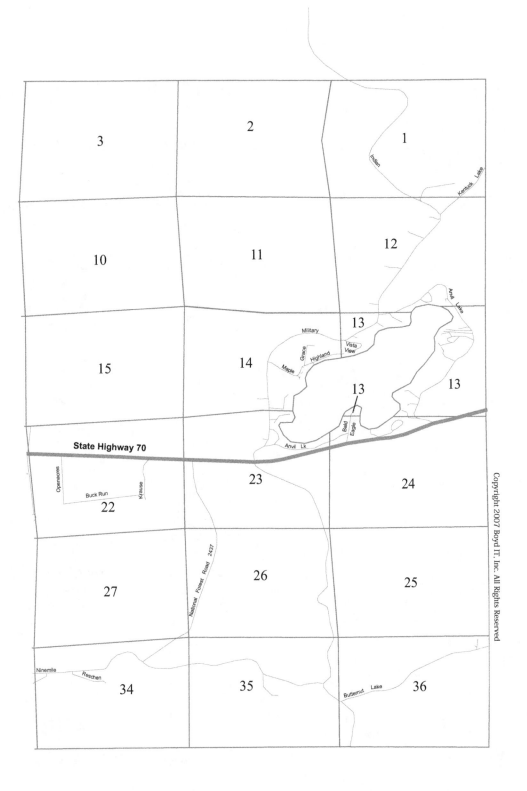

3

2

1

Indian

Kentuck Lake

10

11

12

Anvil Lake

13

Military

Grace

Highland

Vista View

Maple

15

14

13

13

Bald Eagle

Anvil Lk.

State Highway 70

Openacres

Buck Run

Krause

22

23

24

National Forest Road 2437

27

26

25

Ninemile

Reschen

34

35

Buttemut Lake

36

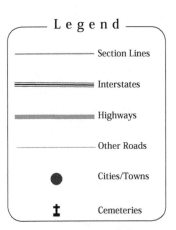

Scale: Section = 1 mile X 1 mile
(generally, with some exceptions)

Helpful Hints

1. This road map has a number of uses, but primarily it is to help you: a) find the present location of land owned by your ancestors (at least the general area), b) find cemeteries and city-centers, and c) estimate the route/roads used by Census-takers & tax-assessors.

2. If you plan to travel to Vilas County to locate cemeteries or land parcels, please pick up a modern travel map for the area before you do. Mapping old land parcels on modern maps is not as exact a science as you might think. Just the slightest variations in public land survey coordinates, estimates of parcel boundaries, or road-map deviations can greatly alter a map's representation of how a road either does or doesn't cross a particular parcel of land.

Historical Map

T40-N R11-E
4th PM - 1831 MN/WI

Map Group 33

Cities & Towns

None

Cemeteries

None

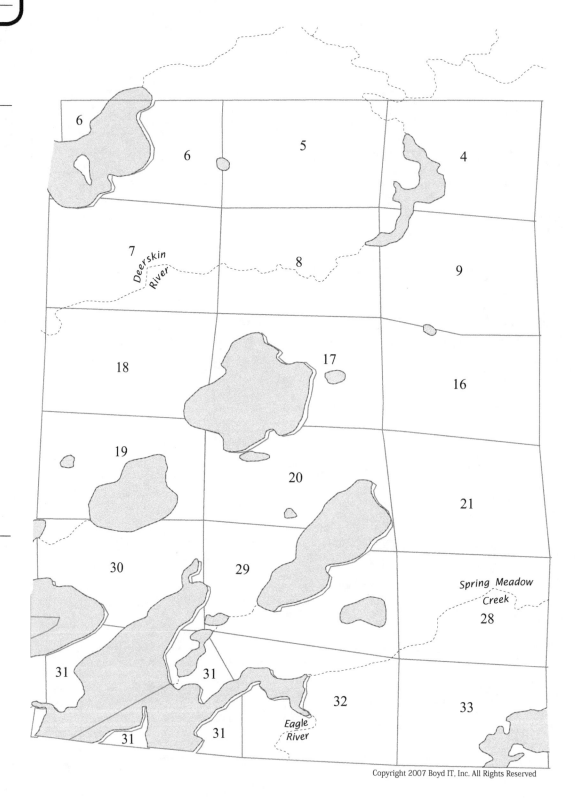

378

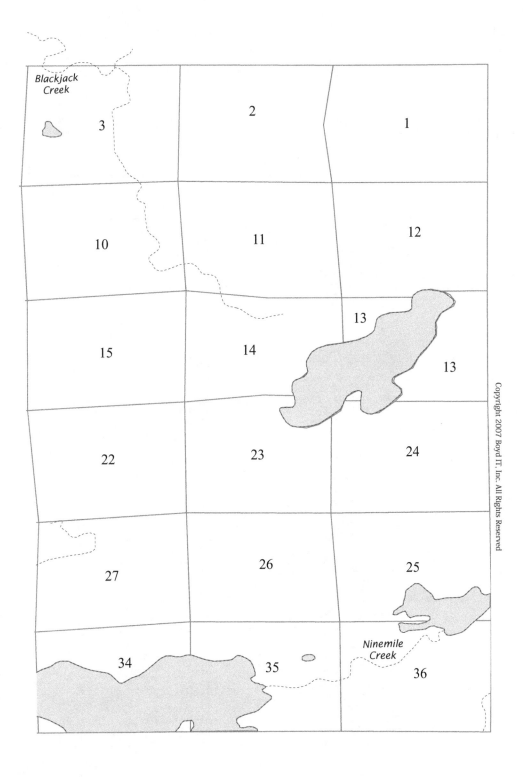

Blackjack
Creek

3

2

1

10

11

12

13

15

14

13

22

23

24

27

26

25

34

35

Ninemile
Creek

36

Helpful Hints

1. This Map takes a different look at the same Congressional Township displayed in the preceding two maps. It presents features that can help you better envision the historical development of the area: a) Water-bodies (lakes & ponds), b) Water-courses (rivers, streams, etc.), c) Railroads, d) City/town center-points (where they were oftentimes located when first settled), and e) Cemeteries.

2. Using this "Historical" map in tandem with this Township's Patent Map and Road Map, may lead you to some interesting discoveries. You will often find roads, towns, cemeteries, and waterways are named after nearby landowners: sometimes those names will be the ones you are researching. See how many of these research gems you can find here in Vilas County.

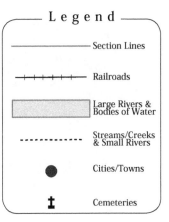

Legend

———	Section Lines
+-+-+-+-+-+-+	Railroads
▭	Large Rivers & Bodies of Water
- - - - - - -	Streams/Creeks & Small Rivers
●	Cities/Towns
✝	Cemeteries

Scale: Section = 1 mile X 1 mile
(there are some exceptions)

Map Group 34: Index to Land Patents

Township 39-North Range 10-East (4th PM - 1831 MN/WI)

After you locate an individual in this Index, take note of the Section and Section Part then proceed to the Land Patent map on the pages immediately following. You should have no difficulty locating the corresponding parcel of land.

The "For More Info" Column will lead you to more information about the underlying Patents. See the *Legend* at right, and the "How to Use this Book" chapter, for more information.

```
LEGEND
         "For More Info . . . " column
A = Authority (Legislative Act, See Appendix "A")
B = Block or Lot (location in Section unknown)
C = Cancelled Patent
F = Fractional Section
G = Group (Multi-Patentee Patent, see Appendix "C")
V = Overlaps another Parcel
R = Re-Issued (Parcel patented more than once)

(A & G items require you to look in the Appendixes referred
to above. All other Letter-designations followed by a number
require you to locate line-items in this index that possess
the ID number found after the letter).
```

ID	Individual in Patent	Sec.	Sec. Part	Date Issued	Other Counties	For More Info . . .
5695	BEYER, William	14	E½NE	1898-12-12		A3
5696	" "	14	N½SE	1898-12-12		A3
5653	BINGHAM, James M	3	NENE	1883-05-15		A1
5636	BIRGE, George Henry	15	NWNE	1913-01-10		A3
5644	BROWN, Isaac	10	5	1873-05-01		A1
5645	" "	11	N½NW	1873-05-01		A1
5646	" "	11	NESW	1873-05-01		A1
5647	" "	11	NWSE	1873-05-01		A1
5648	" "	2	3	1873-05-01		A1
5649	" "	2	4	1873-05-01		A1
5650	" "	2	5	1873-05-01		A1
5651	" "	2	SESE	1873-05-01		A1
5652	" "	3	NWNE	1873-11-15		A1
5699	CARTER, William L	2	6	1900-06-28		A3
5700	"	2	7	1900-06-28		A3
5637	COMPANY, Gerry Lumber	9	SENW	1889-05-31		A1
5658	CUNNINGHAM, Joseph E	2	8	1902-01-17		A3 G61
5659	" "	2	9	1902-01-17		A3 G61
5667	DECKERT, Otto	4	NENW	1901-10-23		A3
5612	DENTON, A A	11	SENW	1889-05-09		A1
5698	DICKEY, William F	1	6	1892-05-04		A1
5671	DOCKEREY, Sarah	10	2	1898-05-10		A3
5672	" "	10	SWNW	1898-05-10		A3
5674	DUTCHER, Thomas B	1	3	1903-06-08		A3 F
5675	" "	1	4	1903-06-08		A3 F
5676	" "	1	7	1903-06-08		A3 F
5627	ELDRIDGE, Eugene T	13	SWSE	1872-11-01		A1
5620	ERVIN, Charles S	1	1	1903-05-19		A3 F
5621	" "	1	2	1903-05-19		A3 F
5638	FELTON, Henry	15	NESW	1901-11-22		A1
5639	" "	15	NWSE	1901-11-22		A1
5668	FETT, Robert	13	1	1898-12-12		A3
5669	" "	13	2	1898-12-12		A3
5670	" "	13	3	1898-12-12		A3
5697	GILBERT, William C	9	N½SW	1886-07-30		A1
5643	HAMILTON, Irenus K	13	SESE	1872-07-01		A1 G97
5643	HAMILTON, Woodman C	13	SESE	1872-07-01		A1 G97
5662	HOWE, Lyman	3	NWNW	1867-10-10		A1 G109
5616	HUNTER, Allen J	1	5	1903-12-31		A1
5613	JOHNSON, Abe	18	6	1907-05-09		A3
5628	JONES, Evan J	4	3	1875-02-20		A1 G119
5629	" "	4	SENW	1875-02-20		A1 G119
5630	" "	5	S½NE	1875-02-20		A1 G119
5631	" "	9	NENW	1875-02-20		A1 G119
5632	" "	9	NWNE	1875-02-20		A1 G119
5663	KRAMER, Mathias	15	2	1899-05-05		A1

ID	Individual in Patent	Sec.	Sec. Part	Date Issued	Other Counties	For More Info . . .
5664	KRAMER, Mathias (Cont'd)	15	NWSW	1899-05-05		A1
5665	" "	15	S½SW	1899-05-05		A1
5618	MOOR, Charles	9	NENE	1904-03-01		A3
5619	"	9	SWNE	1904-03-01		A3
5658	NEVILLE, Wendell D	2	8	1902-01-17		A3 G61
5659	" "	2	9	1902-01-17		A3 G61
5617	NORWAY, Charles A	13	4	1885-05-09		A1
5633	PALMS, Francis	10	1	1867-10-10		A1
5634	" "	2	1	1867-10-10		A1
5635	" "	2	2	1867-10-10		A1
5657	PETERSON, John T	14	SWSE	1898-03-21		A1
5654	PHELPS, John	4	SWNW	1884-06-20		A1 G154
5655	" "	5	NENE	1884-06-20		A1 G154
5622	POOR, Chauncey P	4	2	1896-09-16		A3
5623	" "	4	E½SW	1896-09-16		A3
5624	" "	4	SWSE	1896-09-16		A3
5662	RABLIN, John	3	NWNW	1867-10-10		A1 G109
5685	RUST, William A	14	SESE	1872-05-10		A1
5686	" "	15	1	1872-05-10		A1
5687	" "	15	E½NW	1872-05-10		A1
5688	" "	15	NENE	1872-05-10		A1
5689	" "	15	SWSE	1872-05-10		A1
5690	" "	5	W½SW	1872-05-10		A1
5691	" "	7	N½SW	1872-05-10		A1
5692	" "	7	NWNW	1872-05-10		A1
5693	" "	7	SENW	1872-05-10		A1
5694	" "	9	S½SW	1872-05-10		A1
5666	SCHERIBEL, Mathieus	10	4	1897-06-11		A1
5677	SCOTT, Thomas B	4	NWNW	1883-03-30		A1
5680	" "	7	N½NE	1883-03-30		A1
5681	" "	7	NENW	1883-03-30		A1
5683	" "	8	NWNW	1883-03-30		A1
5678	" "	5	SESW	1883-05-15		A1
5679	" "	5	W½SE	1883-05-15		A1
5682	" "	8	NENW	1883-05-15		A1
5654	" "	4	SWNW	1884-06-20		A1 G154
5655	" "	5	NENE	1884-06-20		A1 G154
5641	SHERRY, Henry	3	S½NE	1882-09-30		A1
5640	" "	11	SWNW	1885-01-15		A1
5642	STEINBERG, Henry	6	NW	1872-07-01		A1 G167
5642	STEINBERG, Herman	6	NW	1872-07-01		A1 G167
5656	STORM, John	18	SESW	1910-09-15		A3
5684	STUBBINGS, W H	7	SWNW	1885-11-25		A1 F
5625	SULLIVAN, Daniel	1	8	1889-05-09		A1
5626	" "	11	NESE	1889-05-09		A1
5628	TOWNSEND, Danville L	4	3	1875-02-20		A1 G119
5629	" "	4	SENW	1875-02-20		A1 G119
5630	" "	5	S½NE	1875-02-20		A1 G119
5631	" "	9	NENW	1875-02-20		A1 G119
5632	" "	9	NWNE	1875-02-20		A1 G119
5628	WELLINGTON, Richard H	4	3	1875-02-20		A1 G119
5629	" "	4	SENW	1875-02-20		A1 G119
5630	" "	5	S½NE	1875-02-20		A1 G119
5631	" "	9	NENW	1875-02-20		A1 G119
5632	" "	9	NWNE	1875-02-20		A1 G119
5614	WILTERDING, Albert	10	S½SE	1892-05-16		A1
5615	" "	10	S½SW	1892-05-16		A1
5673	WISCONSIN, State Of	9	SWNW	1911-05-08		A4
5660	WOLFRAM, Lawrence	10	3	1902-01-25		A1
5661	" "	10	NESW	1902-01-25		A1

Patent Map

T39-N R10-E
4th PM - 1831 MN/WI

Map Group 34

Township Statistics

Parcels Mapped	:	89
Number of Patents	:	54
Number of Individuals	:	46
Patentees Identified	:	40
Number of Surnames	:	44
Multi-Patentee Parcels	:	12
Oldest Patent Date	:	10/10/1867
Most Recent Patent	:	1/10/1913
Block/Lot Parcels	:	31
Parcels Re - Issued	:	0
Parcels that Overlap	:	0
Cities and Towns	:	0
Cemeteries	:	0

Note: the area contained in this map amounts to far less than a full Township. Therefore, its contents are completely on this single page (instead of a "normal" 2-page spread).

Legend

——————— Patent Boundary

━━━━━━━ Section Boundary

 No Patents Found
(or Outside County)

1., 2., 3., ... Lot Numbers
(when beside a name)

[ ] Group Number
(see Appendix "C")

Scale: Section = 1 mile X 1 mile
(generally, with some exceptions)

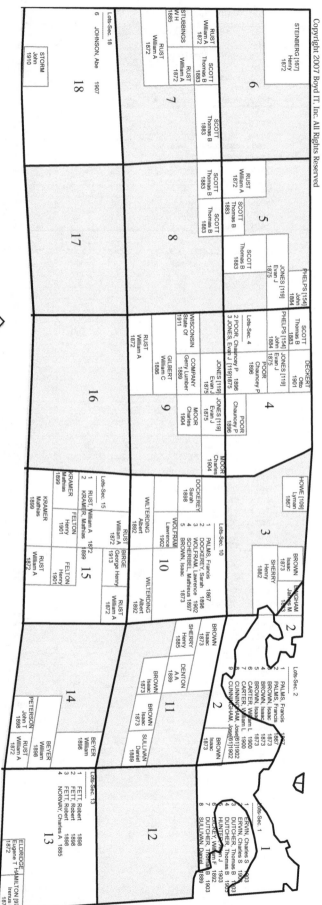

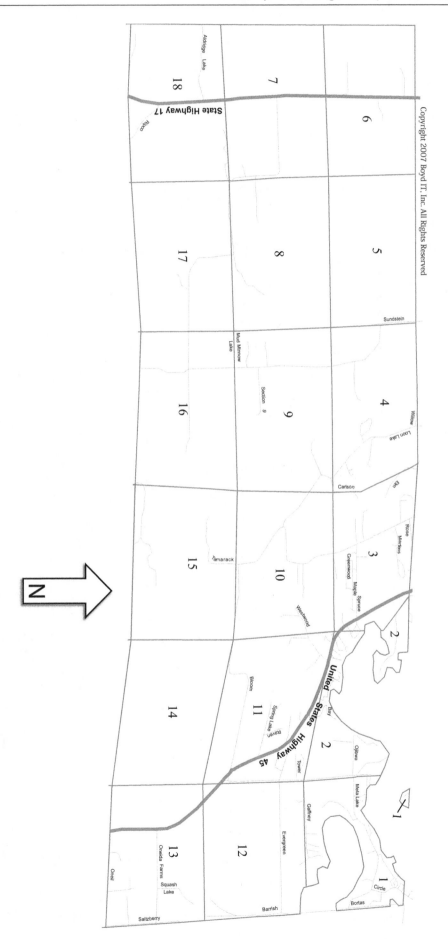

Road Map

T39-N R10-E
4th PM - 1831 MN/WI

Map Group 34

Note: the area contained in this map amounts to far less than a full Township. Therefore, its contents are completely on this single page (instead of a "normal" 2-page spread).

Cities & Towns
None

Cemeteries
None

Legend

Section Lines

Interstates

Highways

Other Roads

● Cities/Towns

✝ Cemeteries

Scale: Section = 1 mile X 1 mile
(generally, with some exceptions)

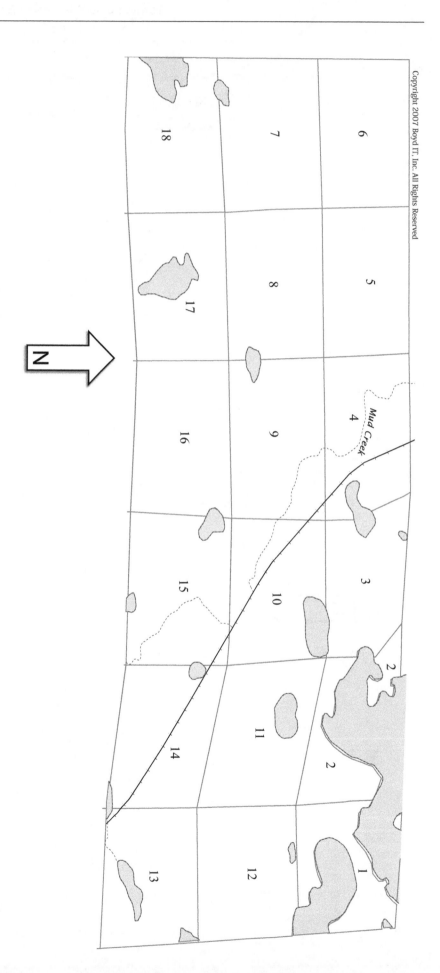

Historical Map

T39-N R10-E
4th PM - 1831 MN/WI

Map Group 34

Note: the area contained in this map amounts to far less than a full Township. Therefore, its contents are completely on this single page (instead of a "normal" 2-page spread).

Cities & Towns

None

Cemeteries

None

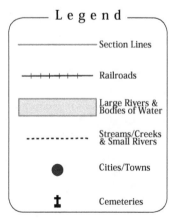

Legend

———— Section Lines

++++++++ Railroads

Large Rivers & Bodies of Water

- - - - - - Streams/Creeks & Small Rivers

● Cities/Towns

✝ Cemeteries

Scale: Section = 1 mile X 1 mile
(there are some exceptions)

Appendices

Appendix A - Acts of Congress Authorizing the Patents Contained in this Book

The following Acts of Congress are referred to throughout the Indexes in this book. The text of the Federal Statutes referred to below can usually be found on the web. For more information on such laws, check out the publishers's web-site at *www.arphax.com,* go to the "Research" page, and click on the "Land-Law" link.

Ref. No.	Date and Act of Congress	Number of Parcels of Land
1	April 24, 1820: Sale-Cash Entry (3 Stat. 566)	5221
2	March 17, 1842: Scrip or Nature of Scrip (5 Stat. 607)	18
3	May 20, 1862: Homestead EntryOriginal (12 Stat. 392)	454
4	September 4, 1841: Grant-Certain Land to State (5 Stat. 453)	7

Appendix B - Section Parts (Aliquot Parts)

The following represent the various abbreviations we have found thus far in describing the parts of a Public Land Section. Some of these are very obscure and rarely used, but we wanted to list them for just that reason. A full section is 1 square mile or 640 acres.

Section Part	Description	Acres
<none>	Full Acre (if no Section Part is listed, presumed a full Section)	640
<1-??>	A number represents a Lot Number and can be of various sizes	?
E½	East Half-Section	320
E½E½	East Half of East Half-Section	160
E½E½SE	East Half of East Half of Southeast Quarter-Section	40
E½N½	East Half of North Half-Section	160
E½NE	East Half of Northeast Quarter-Section	80
E½NENE	East Half of Northeast Quarter of Northeast Quarter-Section	20
E½NENW	East Half of Northeast Quarter of Northwest Quarter-Section	20
E½NESE	East Half of Northeast Quarter of Southeast Quarter-Section	20
E½NESW	East Half of Northeast Quarter of Southwest Quarter-Section	20
E½NW	East Half of Northwest Quarter-Section	80
E½NWNE	East Half of Northwest Quarter of Northeast Quarter-Section	20
E½NWNW	East Half of Northwest Quarter of Northwest Quarter-Section	20
E½NWSE	East Half of Northwest Quarter of Southeast Quarter-Section	20
E½NWSW	East Half of Northwest Quarter of Southwest Quarter-Section	20
E½S½	East Half of South Half-Section	160
E½SE	East Half of Southeast Quarter-Section	80
E½SENE	East Half of Southeast Quarter of Northeast Quarter-Section	20
E½SENW	East Half of Southeast Quarter of Northwest Quarter-Section	20
E½SESE	East Half of Southeast Quarter of Southeast Quarter-Section	20
E½SESW	East Half of Southeast Quarter of Southwest Quarter-Section	20
E½SW	East Half of Southwest Quarter-Section	80
E½SWNE	East Half of Southwest Quarter of Northeast Quarter-Section	20
E½SWNW	East Half of Southwest Quarter of Northwest Quarter-Section	20
E½SWSE	East Half of Southwest Quarter of Southeast Quarter-Section	20
E½SWSW	East Half of Southwest Quarter of Southwest Quarter-Section	20
E½W½	East Half of West Half-Section	160
N½	North Half-Section	320
N½E½NE	North Half of East Half of Northeast Quarter-Section	40
N½E½NW	North Half of East Half of Northwest Quarter-Section	40
N½E½SE	North Half of East Half of Southeast Quarter-Section	40
N½E½SW	North Half of East Half of Southwest Quarter-Section	40
N½N½	North Half of North Half-Section	160
N½NE	North Half of Northeast Quarter-Section	80
N½NENE	North Half of Northeast Quarter of Northeast Quarter-Section	20
N½NENW	North Half of Northeast Quarter of Northwest Quarter-Section	20
N½NESE	North Half of Northeast Quarter of Southeast Quarter-Section	20
N½NESW	North Half of Northeast Quarter of Southwest Quarter-Section	20
N½NW	North Half of Northwest Quarter-Section	80
N½NWNE	North Half of Northwest Quarter of Northeast Quarter-Section	20
N½NWNW	North Half of Northwest Quarter of Northwest Quarter-Section	20
N½NWSE	North Half of Northwest Quarter of Southeast Quarter-Section	20
N½NWSW	North Half of Northwest Quarter of Southwest Quarter-Section	20
N½S½	North Half of South Half-Section	160
N½SE	North Half of Southeast Quarter-Section	80
N½SENE	North Half of Southeast Quarter of Northeast Quarter-Section	20
N½SENW	North Half of Southeast Quarter of Northwest Quarter-Section	20
N½SESE	North Half of Southeast Quarter of Southeast Quarter-Section	20

Section Part	Description	Acres
N½SESW	North Half of Southeast Quarter of Southwest Quarter-Section	20
N½SESW	North Half of Southeast Quarter of Southwest Quarter-Section	20
N½SW	North Half of Southwest Quarter-Section	80
N½SWNE	North Half of Southwest Quarter of Northeast Quarter-Section	20
N½SWNW	North Half of Southwest Quarter of Northwest Quarter-Section	20
N½SWSE	North Half of Southwest Quarter of Southeast Quarter-Section	20
N½SWSE	North Half of Southwest Quarter of Southeast Quarter-Section	20
N½SWSW	North Half of Southwest Quarter of Southwest Quarter-Section	20
N½W½NW	North Half of West Half of Northwest Quarter-Section	40
N½W½SE	North Half of West Half of Southeast Quarter-Section	40
N½W½SW	North Half of West Half of Southwest Quarter-Section	40
NE	Northeast Quarter-Section	160
NEN½	Northeast Quarter of North Half-Section	80
NENE	Northeast Quarter of Northeast Quarter-Section	40
NENENE	Northeast Quarter of Northeast Quarter of Northeast Quarter	10
NENENW	Northeast Quarter of Northeast Quarter of Northwest Quarter	10
NENESE	Northeast Quarter of Northeast Quarter of Southeast Quarter	10
NENESW	Northeast Quarter of Northeast Quarter of Southwest Quarter	10
NENW	Northeast Quarter of Northwest Quarter-Section	40
NENWNE	Northeast Quarter of Northwest Quarter of Northeast Quarter	10
NENWNW	Northeast Quarter of Northwest Quarter of Northwest Quarter	10
NENWSE	Northeast Quarter of Northwest Quarter of Southeast Quarter	10
NENWSW	Northeast Quarter of Northwest Quarter of Southwest Quarter	10
NESE	Northeast Quarter of Southeast Quarter-Section	40
NESENE	Northeast Quarter of Southeast Quarter of Northeast Quarter	10
NESENW	Northeast Quarter of Southeast Quarter of Northwest Quarter	10
NESESE	Northeast Quarter of Southeast Quarter of Southeast Quarter	10
NESESW	Northeast Quarter of Southeast Quarter of Southwest Quarter	10
NESW	Northeast Quarter of Southwest Quarter-Section	40
NESWNE	Northeast Quarter of Southwest Quarter of Northeast Quarter	10
NESWNW	Northeast Quarter of Southwest Quarter of Northwest Quarter	10
NESWSE	Northeast Quarter of Southwest Quarter of Southeast Quarter	10
NESWSW	Northeast Quarter of Southwest Quarter of Southwest Quarter	10
NW	Northwest Quarter-Section	160
NWE½	Northwest Quarter of Eastern Half-Section	80
NWN½	Northwest Quarter of North Half-Section	80
NWNE	Northwest Quarter of Northeast Quarter-Section	40
NWNENE	Northwest Quarter of Northeast Quarter of Northeast Quarter	10
NWNENW	Northwest Quarter of Northeast Quarter of Northwest Quarter	10
NWNESE	Northwest Quarter of Northeast Quarter of Southeast Quarter	10
NWNESW	Northwest Quarter of Northeast Quarter of Southwest Quarter	10
NWNW	Northwest Quarter of Northwest Quarter-Section	40
NWNWNE	Northwest Quarter of Northwest Quarter of Northeast Quarter	10
NWNWNW	Northwest Quarter of Northwest Quarter of Northwest Quarter	10
NWNWSE	Northwest Quarter of Northwest Quarter of Southeast Quarter	10
NWNWSW	Northwest Quarter of Northwest Quarter of Southwest Quarter	10
NWSE	Northwest Quarter of Southeast Quarter-Section	40
NWSENE	Northwest Quarter of Southeast Quarter of Northeast Quarter	10
NWSENW	Northwest Quarter of Southeast Quarter of Northwest Quarter	10
NWSESE	Northwest Quarter of Southeast Quarter of Southeast Quarter	10
NWSESW	Northwest Quarter of Southeast Quarter of Southwest Quarter	10
NWSW	Northwest Quarter of Southwest Quarter-Section	40
NWSWNE	Northwest Quarter of Southwest Quarter of Northeast Quarter	10
NWSWNW	Northwest Quarter of Southwest Quarter of Northwest Quarter	10
NWSWSE	Northwest Quarter of Southwest Quarter of Southeast Quarter	10
NWSWSW	Northwest Quarter of Southwest Quarter of Southwest Quarter	10
S½	South Half-Section	320
S½E½NE	South Half of East Half of Northeast Quarter-Section	40
S½E½NW	South Half of East Half of Northwest Quarter-Section	40
S½E½SE	South Half of East Half of Southeast Quarter-Section	40

Section Part	Description	Acres
S½E½SW	South Half of East Half of Southwest Quarter-Section	40
S½N½	South Half of North Half-Section	160
S½NE	South Half of Northeast Quarter-Section	80
S½NENE	South Half of Northeast Quarter of Northeast Quarter-Section	20
S½NENW	South Half of Northeast Quarter of Northwest Quarter-Section	20
S½NESE	South Half of Northeast Quarter of Southeast Quarter-Section	20
S½NESW	South Half of Northeast Quarter of Southwest Quarter-Section	20
S½NW	South Half of Northwest Quarter-Section	80
S½NWNE	South Half of Northwest Quarter of Northeast Quarter-Section	20
S½NWNW	South Half of Northwest Quarter of Northwest Quarter-Section	20
S½NWSE	South Half of Northwest Quarter of Southeast Quarter-Section	20
S½NWSW	South Half of Northwest Quarter of Southwest Quarter-Section	20
S½S½	South Half of South Half-Section	160
S½SE	South Half of Southeast Quarter-Section	80
S½SENE	South Half of Southeast Quarter of Northeast Quarter-Section	20
S½SENW	South Half of Southeast Quarter of Northwest Quarter-Section	20
S½SESE	South Half of Southeast Quarter of Southeast Quarter-Section	20
S½SESW	South Half of Southeast Quarter of Southwest Quarter-Section	20
S½SESW	South Half of Southeast Quarter of Southwest Quarter-Section	20
S½SW	South Half of Southwest Quarter-Section	80
S½SWNE	South Half of Southwest Quarter of Northeast Quarter-Section	20
S½SWNW	South Half of Southwest Quarter of Northwest Quarter-Section	20
S½SWSE	South Half of Southwest Quarter of Southeast Quarter-Section	20
S½SWSE	South Half of Southwest Quarter of Southeast Quarter-Section	20
S½SWSW	South Half of Southwest Quarter of Southwest Quarter-Section	20
S½W½NE	South Half of West Half of Northeast Quarter-Section	40
S½W½NW	South Half of West Half of Northwest Quarter-Section	40
S½W½SE	South Half of West Half of Southeast Quarter-Section	40
S½W½SW	South Half of West Half of Southwest Quarter-Section	40
SE	Southeast Quarter Section	160
SEN½	Southeast Quarter of North Half-Section	80
SENE	Southeast Quarter of Northeast Quarter-Section	40
SENENE	Southeast Quarter of Northeast Quarter of Northeast Quarter	10
SENENW	Southeast Quarter of Northeast Quarter of Northwest Quarter	10
SENESE	Southeast Quarter of Northeast Quarter of Southeast Quarter	10
SENESW	Southeast Quarter of Northeast Quarter of Southwest Quarter	10
SENW	Southeast Quarter of Northwest Quarter-Section	40
SENWNE	Southeast Quarter of Northwest Quarter of Northeast Quarter	10
SENWNW	Southeast Quarter of Northwest Quarter of Northwest Quarter	10
SENWSE	Souteast Quarter of Northwest Quarter of Southeast Quarter	10
SENWSW	Southeast Quarter of Northwest Quarter of Southwest Quarter	10
SESE	Southeast Quarter of Southeast Quarter-Section	40
SESENE	SoutheastQuarter of Southeast Quarter of Northeast Quarter	10
SESENW	Southeast Quarter of Southeast Quarter of Northwest Quarter	10
SESESE	Southeast Quarter of Southeast Quarter of Southeast Quarter	10
SESESW	Southeast Quarter of Southeast Quarter of Southwest Quarter	10
SESW	Southeast Quarter of Southwest Quarter-Section	40
SESWNE	Southeast Quarter of Southwest Quarter of Northeast Quarter	10
SESWNW	Southeast Quarter of Southwest Quarter of Northwest Quarter	10
SESWSE	Southeast Quarter of Southwest Quarter of Southeast Quarter	10
SESWSW	Southeast Quarter of Southwest Quarter of Southwest Quarter	10
SW	Southwest Quarter-Section	160
SWNE	Southwest Quarter of Northeast Quarter-Section	40
SWNENE	Southwest Quarter of Northeast Quarter of Northeast Quarter	10
SWNENW	Southwest Quarter of Northeast Quarter of Northwest Quarter	10
SWNESE	Southwest Quarter of Northeast Quarter of Southeast Quarter	10
SWNESW	Southwest Quarter of Northeast Quarter of Southwest Quarter	10
SWNW	Southwest Quarter of Northwest Quarter-Section	40
SWNWNE	Southwest Quarter of Northwest Quarter of Northeast Quarter	10
SWNWNW	Southwest Quarter of Northwest Quarter of Northwest Quarter	10

Section Part	Description	Acres
SWNWSE	Southwest Quarter of Northwest Quarter of Southeast Quarter	10
SWNWSW	Southwest Quarter of Northwest Quarter of Southwest Quarter	10
SWSE	Southwest Quarter of Southeast Quarter-Section	40
SWSENE	Southwest Quarter of Southeast Quarter of Northeast Quarter	10
SWSENW	Southwest Quarter of Southeast Quarter of Northwest Quarter	10
SWSESE	Southwest Quarter of Southeast Quarter of Southeast Quarter	10
SWSESW	Southwest Quarter of Southeast Quarter of Southwest Quarter	10
SWSW	Southwest Quarter of Southwest Quarter-Section	40
SWSWNE	Southwest Quarter of Southwest Quarter of Northeast Quarter	10
SWSWNW	Southwest Quarter of Southwest Quarter of Northwest Quarter	10
SWSWSE	Southwest Quarter of Southwest Quarter of Southeast Quarter	10
SWSWSW	Southwest Quarter of Southwest Quarter of Southwest Quarter	10
W½	West Half-Section	320
W½E½	West Half of East Half-Section	160
W½N½	West Half of North Half-Section (same as NW)	160
W½NE	West Half of Northeast Quarter	80
W½NENE	West Half of Northeast Quarter of Northeast Quarter-Section	20
W½NENW	West Half of Northeast Quarter of Northwest Quarter-Section	20
W½NESE	West Half of Northeast Quarter of Southeast Quarter-Section	20
W½NESW	West Half of Northeast Quarter of Southwest Quarter-Section	20
W½NW	West Half of Northwest Quarter-Section	80
W½NWNE	West Half of Northwest Quarter of Northeast Quarter-Section	20
W½NWNW	West Half of Northwest Quarter of Northwest Quarter-Section	20
W½NWSE	West Half of Northwest Quarter of Southeast Quarter-Section	20
W½NWSW	West Half of Northwest Quarter of Southwest Quarter-Section	20
W½S½	West Half of South Half-Section	160
W½SE	West Half of Southeast Quarter-Section	80
W½SENE	West Half of Southeast Quarter of Northeast Quarter-Section	20
W½SENW	West Half of Southeast Quarter of Northwest Quarter-Section	20
W½SESE	West Half of Southeast Quarter of Southeast Quarter-Section	20
W½SESW	West Half of Southeast Quarter of Southwest Quarter-Section	20
W½SW	West Half of Southwest Quarter-Section	80
W½SWNE	West Half of Southwest Quarter of Northeast Quarter-Section	20
W½SWNW	West Half of Southwest Quarter of Northwest Quarter-Section	20
W½SWSE	West Half of Southwest Quarter of Southeast Quarter-Section	20
W½SWSW	West Half of Southwest Quarter of Southwest Quarter-Section	20
W½W½	West Half of West Half-Section	160